MW00911516

PUBLIC ADMINISTRATION

SECOND EDITION

Jeffrey D. Straussman

The Maxwell School of Citizenship and Public Affairs
Syracuse University

Longman
New York & London

Public Administration, Second Edition

Copyright © 1990 by Longman.
All rights reserved.
No part of this publication may be reproduced,
stored in a retrieval system, or transmitted
in any form or by any means, electronic, mechanical,
photocopying, recording, or otherwise,
without the prior permission of the publisher.

Longman, 95 Church Street, White Plains, N.Y. 10601

Associated companies:
Longman Group Ltd., London
Longman Cheshire Pty., Melbourne
Longman Paul Pty., Auckland
Copp Clark Pitman, Toronto

In the memory of my parents,
Max and Ella Straussman

Senior editor: David J. Estrin
Production editor: Camilla T.K. Palmer
Cover design: Susan J. Moore
Text art: K & S Graphics
Production supervisor: Priscilla Taguer

Library of Congress Cataloging in Publication Data
Straussman, Jeffrey D., 1945–
    Public administration / Jeffrey D. Straussman. —2nd ed.
        p.   cm.
    Includes bibliographical references.
    ISBN 0-8013-0179-3
    1. Public administration.   I. Title.
JF1351.S863 1990
350'.000973—dc20   89-36782
                                                   CIP

ABCDEFGHIJ-HA-99 98 97 96 95 94 93 92 91 90

Contents

Preface

"Why mess with a good thing?" I applied this basic principle to the revision of the first edition of *Public Administration*. Naturally, there were places in need of change. The budgeting chapter needed updating. Gone is the material on budget reforms; in its place there is a more extensive description of the congressional budget process. The personnel chapter now includes more material on contemporary personnel topics such as comparable worth. Tables and figures throughout the text have similarly been updated. Additional illustrative material, exercises, and cases have been added to this edition: a jail overcrowding case appears at the end of Chapter 12, "Law, the Courts, and Public Administration," and an evaluation exercise on public assistance "workfare" in four states, drawn from a General Accounting Office study, ends Chapter 13, "Evaluation."

Reviewers for Longman, Inc., recommended two major changes that have been encorporated in this revision. Chapter 1 now includes a historical overview of the study and practice of public administration. Nevertheless, like the first edition, this historical development is linked to evolution of "big" government in the United States. A new chapter, "Congressional–Agency Relations" (Chapter 3) is intended to fill a gap that appeared in the first edition of *Public Administration*. This new chapter covers essential topics such as the constitutional bases of legislative–agency relations and mechanisms of legislative oversight. But it does more. It challenges the reader to consider the debate among political scientists concerning legislative versus agency "dominance" in the relationship.

These changes are modest, and in my opinion, they strengthen the text. A key feature of the first edition, the informal writing style—along with what I call the funny side of public administration, is alive and well in this revision. Not everyone has the same sense of humor, however. Looking over the first edition I had to agree (although reluctantly) that a few quips could be interpreted as "bureaucrat bashing." I eliminated them. But to my faithful followers, fear not! Scowelly Selfish and Iggy "the Blade" McNasty are back. Moses still sets the tone for Chapter 5, "Public Management." Also, you can, once again, try your analytical hand with Project CRAP. The extended case studies are included in this revision. So is the International City Management Association's ethics questionnaire.

I appreciate the confidence Irving Rockwood of Rockwood Associates showed in the text. The same goes for David Estrin at Longman. My students in the Master of Public Administration program at Syracuse University have provided me with the joy of teaching for more than ten years. They give concrete meaning to the idea that government service is a noble profession. So does my wife, Jeannie, who is always a source of support—not to mention funny anecdotes, a few that made it into this book. Deborah, my daughter, is important too, partly because she keeps me on my toes. Finally, this revision is dedicated to the memory of my parents, Max and Ella Straussman. They would have been proud that the book adorning their coffee table is now in a second edition. The old one was getting worn out.

Preface to First Edition

"It was the best of times. It was the worst of times." No, I am not referring to those famous lines from Charles Dickens' *A Tale of Two Cities*. I am talking about public administration in the 1980s. The worst of times is easy; fiscal stress, managing with less, reductions in force, cutback management—these words have become virtually synonomous with the study and practice of public administration in the 1980s. The best of times is a little harder. But paradoxically, the very changes we have had in organizational life—many of them painful—provide challenges and opportunities for the public administrator of tomorrow. Consider just two. First, no longer can the public administrator neatly separate the private and public sectors, for they have become increasingly intertwined. Understanding the ramifications of this fact is indispensable for effective public management in the 1980s. Second, at one time it was simple to design and implement local government services. After all, how many ways *are* there to pick up the garbage? Now it is not so simple. With the growing interdependence of the public and private sectors, the complexity of our intergovernmental system, and the legal foundations of public administration surrounding the activities of the public manager, what was once simple is simple no more.

I wrote this book to capture some of the changes that have come to public administration. Retrenchment is sprinkled throughout the text, as are the linkages between the private and public sectors. The legal foundations of public administration, treated in Chapter 11, are now extremely important. In particular, I believe that students must become familiar with the growing liabilities of public administrators and with the important role judges have come to play in the administration of the public's business. But the book does not merely highlight the changes in public administration. On the contrary, much of the text is devoted to traditional topics—organizational theory, personnel, budgeting, program evaluation, to name a few. Yet even those core subjects include newer developments in the profession. For instance, collective bargaining is so pervasive that it deserves an entire chapter. Similarly, information processing and communication are tied to decision making—a sequence that seems to make sense to me. The blending of core topics with new themes is what public administration is all about.

Can public administration be presented in a way that seems "real" to students? Tone and style help a lot. I have tried the soft touch, the "lighter" approach. I hope you like it. There are other features in this book in addition to writing style. Retrenchment is a theme in three case studies: "Vacancy Review in Tight Belt County," "A Kick in the Seat of Higher Learning," and "Regional Health Planning: A Response to Declining Resources." Implementation is treated in a separate chapter, which ends with a long case, "The Siting of a Public Housing Project." Even the titles of these cases hint that state and local governments are treated more extensively in this book than in many other texts. Similarily, intergovernmental management is a major theme in Chapters 5, 6, 10, and 11.

Sometimes I have invented situations to get the point across: collective bargaining in the city of Kvetch, the budget process in Dullsville, and the personnel escapades of Sally Slick, I also believe there is nothing magical about "teaching aids." You know already that I have included some extended case studies, Chapter 6 ends with a case that can be used as a simulation exercise. To test the student's understanding of the fundamentals of evaluation, I have concluded Chapter 12 with an exercise called "Project CRAP." Ethics remains too removed from reality unless one *must* make decisions that have ethical components. That's how I end Chapter 13. I tried to make the book good reading by inserting items along the way that instruct and sometimes amuse. (Why, for example, would the FBI chase a bull semen thief across Canada?) Finally, if some of the chapters encourage the student to read more, I have provided a list of additional reading at the end of each chapter. For the student who wants to dig deeper into a topic (or is given a term assignment from his or her instructor), I have included a bibliography, arranged by chapter, at the end of the book.

Several people must be acknowledged for their assistance along the way. The people at Holt—Marie Schappert, Herman Makler, and Barbara Heinssen—have been very helpful. I have received valuable comments from Robert Gilmour, University of Connecticut; Kervin Mulcahy, Louisiana State University; Fred Springer, University of Missouri, St. Louis; Robert Sahr, Oregon State University; and Robert Whelan, University of New Orleans. My colleague Barry Bozeman helped me out in two ways: He chuckled in the right places, and he actually wrote "Project CRAP" and "A Kick in the Seat of Higher Learning"—and graciously "donated" them to the book. Daan Braveman and James Carroll, Jr., helped to clarify many of the subtle issues that comprise the topics in Chapter 11. Three former students deserve special mention for their contributions. Each prepared a case under my supervision. Jane Massey wrote "Vacancy Review in Tight Belt County," Michael Mullane prepared "Regional Health Planning: A Response to Declining Resources," and Katherine Potter did "The Sitting of a Public Housing Project." Corinne Hunter did a superb job typing the manuscript and only once said that she was "sick of it." My wife Jeannie, and my daughter, Deborah, won't have to hear about it anymore. I appreciate their support.

CHAPTER 1

The Rise of the Administrative State

Sir Thomas Hobbes, seventeenth-century British political philosopher, is most famous for his observation that, in the "state of nature, life is solitary, poor, nasty, brutish, and short." Hobbes was making a comment on human nature. He was neither the first nor the last to do so. Ever since Adam took a bite of the infamous apple, philosophers and theologians have debated the essence of man. Are we, at bottom, thoughtful to one another, kind, even charitable? Or are we naturally downright devious, nasty, vengeful, and even harmful? The answer depends on your perspective on human nature. The first perspective is obviously optimistic, upbeat, perhaps tinged with a hint of idealism. The second? No one would accuse the second perspective of being flattering! Since Adam's first bite, this second image of self-centered and selfish man has had no lack of philosophical advocates.

Hobbes was one of them. So was James Madison, one of the Founding Fathers, the fourth president of the United States, and a coauthor of *The Federalist Papers*. James Madison observed that if men were angels, government would be unnecessary. But alas, we are not so "heavenly" in our thoughts and our behavior! Based on this reference to human nature, Hobbes and Madison would be in the same philosophical company.

The antedote to man's baser instincts, according to Hobbes and Madison, was government. Hobbes envisioned a sovereign who would control the state of nature. Madison, together with his fellow Founding Fathers, constructed a constitutional experiment that recently celebrated its bicentennial birthday! Hobbes's image of government surely did not envision the huge, complex government that we have today. Nor did the Founders. What caused the transformation?

1

"MINIMAL" GOVERNMENT

Let's return to the state of nature. *If* we assume that, left untethered, man's natural inclination to do ill will ultimately triumph, the purpose of government is straightforward: design mechanisms that will deter individuals from harming others and, for those who are not deterred, establish procedures for punishing wrongdoers. Government, in this formulation, is essentially restricted to regulatory and policing functions. That is, government establishes *rules* of behavior (regulation) and enforces them through the legitimate use of force—the police function. The rules may govern economic exchanges; they may be designed to protect the physically weak from the physically strong. The police function, in turn, may extend to protection from outside invasion so that the justification for a defense establishment is the same as a justification for a domestic police force.

Notice, once we have established even this elementary form of government—a government that is designed to protect ourselves from one another and from external threats—we have given up something. I am no longer "free" to do whatever I want. I can't go around hitting people with impunity. I am not free to take someone else's property and use it without his or her permission. Rather, there are rules that I must now obey. Hobbes recognized this simple, yet extremely important, restriction on liberty. To be protected from the baser qualities of the state of nature, human beings surrendered some liberty to the sovereign in exchange for protection. This essential feature of government as a restriction on some aspects of individual liberty is so straightforward that we take it for granted. But it establishes the *necessary* justification for government intervention in our lives. But how far reaching should the intervention be?

Essential Government Activities

Some government activities are included in the Constitution of the United States. The national government, for instance, is given the power to raise and collect taxes, to raise an army, and to regulate interstate commerce. Notice, many government activities that we take for granted—police, fire protection, public education, and public recreation—are not included. Why not? One obvious answer is that they are mainly local government activities, and the Constitution identifies the powers and responsibilities of the branches of the national government. Also, some government services did not exist in 1789. Perhaps more fundamentally, the government activities mentioned reflect a *limited* government—a government that provides services and performs functions that are not easily provided through voluntary exchanges.

What must government provide? Let's consider a range of government services. Is it absolutely necessary for government to provide education? If you say yes, history would not be on your side. Compulsory public education is quite recent—perhaps less than two hundred years old. It is certainly technically possible to provide education for only those who can afford it. It may not be nice, it may not be fair, but it is surely possible to do it. How about libraries? Must government provide books? This one is even easier. Couldn't we leave books to the marketplace? If you want to read, buy or rent a book, pure and simple!

Fire protection, that's a good one for government, right? Not necessarily. Benjamin Franklin started a private fire department in Philadelphia. If you paid your fire insurance premium the company would put out a fire in your house. If you didn't pay, it was your tough luck. Sounds like something that couldn't happen these days, right? Wrong! Every few years some unlucky soul finds out that the volunteer fire department in the village refuses to put out a fire because the individual continually has refused solicitations of financial support.

Actually, only a few government activities are truly indispensible for civilized society—in a Hobbesian sense. The most basic one is national defense. Suppose a society asked individuals to contribute voluntarily to pay for national defense. What would happen? If each individual acted as a selfish individual, concerned only with his or her self-interest, no one would contribute to the fund even if each person agreed that national defense was extremely important. This would happen for two basic reasons. First, once national defense is provided to the society as a whole, it would be impossible to prevent a single individual in the society from getting the benefits of the protection. You couldn't tell your adversaries to harm only that selfish person and leave the rest of the members of the society alone. Second, national defense is not easily "exhausted" by the members of the society. The protection given to society member A does not diminish the amount of protection available for member B. The first condition is known as *nonrivalry;* the second is known as *joint consumption.* Economists call goods and services that have these two properties *public goods.* When you think carefully about the goods and services provided by government, you will be hard pressed to come up with many illustrations of public goods. Indeed, if contemporary government were restricted solely to providing public goods, government would be quite small.

What do public goods have to do with Hobbes, Madison, and the Constitution? Hobbes's notion of the sovereign was a ruling authority who would provide protection to the ruled. In the lexicon of modern economics, Hobbes's sovereign was the purveyor of "pure public goods." The sovereign's responsibilities did not extend to government "goods and services" that are supposed to enhance individual well being. Hobbes did not envisage a program for the homeless. But did Madison and the other Founding Fathers?

Minimal Government versus Limited Government

Minimal government refers to a society in which only the most basic government services needed—public safety, national defense, and perhaps, a small number of regulatory functions—are provided by government. Milton Friedman, a Nobel Prize winner in economics, provided a succinct statement of the role of a minimal government: "to provide a means whereby we can modify the rules, to mediate differences among us on the meaning of the rules, and to enforce compliance with the rules on the part of those few who would otherwise not play the game."[1] What game did Friedman have in mind? Essentially, the game was an economic one— voluntary exchanges in the marketplace between individuals and firms, left alone as long as the rules governing play are not violated. Minimal government, then, was a government born out of economic necessity, a government that would stand on the sidelines and let the economic realm dominate the relations among individuals.

The Founders were not quite so "econocentric." Limited government did not mean the same thing as minimal government. Rather, the concept referred to the amount of political authority granted the national government, the political authority reserved for the states, and the liberty enjoyed by the individual—perhaps expressed as freedom *from* government. The Founders debated these concepts and resolved them, at least initially, through the ratification of the Constitution and the adoption of the first ten amendments. Indeed, Thomas Jefferson's argument for a Bill of Rights was premised on the need for protection of the individual against unnecessary and unwarranted government encroachment. But unlike minimal government, limited government has no "natural" restrictions on the size of government or the legitimate spheres of government activity.

THE LAISSEZ-FAIRE THAT NEVER WAS

Government in the United States was once small by certain conventional standards. In 1800, for example, the federal government employed about 3,000 people; by 1980 this number had increased to approximately 2.8 million. The budget of the federal government in 1789 was less than $1 million. The federal budget for the 1988 fiscal year topped $1 trillion.

But small government did not mean passive government. A superficial image of government in the United States is that until roughly 1900, indeed up to the New Deal period (1933 to 1945), government's role in social and economic life was limited. The phrase *laissez-faire* (meaning to "leave alone") was used to portray the appropriate role of government in the economic affairs of the country. The phrase was simply inaccurate because the federal government has always had an important role in the economy.[2] The Constitution of United States included three key responsibilities for the new national government. First, it granted the right to coin and print money. Under the Articles of Confederation each colony established its own legal tender, which naturally made it cumbersome to transact economic activities across the boundaries of the colonies. By establishing one common currency (and prohibiting the states from coining and printing their own money), the new national government immediately took an active role in regulating and stabilizing economic activity in the new nation.

Regulation was extended to a second major activity, the right to regulate interstate commerce. Now conflicts between the states would be resolved by the federal government. Third, the Constitution gave the government the power to protect "life, liberty, and property." In addition to having the obvious protection against personal harm, individuals were protected from unwarranted intrusion into their personal affairs. This constitutional protection was interpreted to include a right against unlawful interference in one's "estate" or, more simply, one's property. It is in this sense that we may speak of *limited* government (rather than the more restricted economic concept of minimal government).

As early as 1789 the government took an active role in the economic affairs of the nation. Throughout the nineteenth century this role expanded greatly. The government bought and sold land, thereby encouraging westward expansion. Second, the government regulated labor through the enactment of immigration policy. Between 1815 and 1914, 35 million people came to the United States from Europe alone. Third, the government also protected the country's young industries from fierce foreign competition by establishing tariffs on foreign-produced goods. By the latter part of the nineteenth century the government had initiated a program of economic regulation. In 1890 the Sherman Antitrust Act was passed—an act designed to preserve competition in an age when some companies were rapidly becoming industrial giants. Meanwhile, some state legislatures passed laws regulating child labor, health, and safety in the workplace. (Many of these laws did not survive Supreme Court challenges.) The laissez-faire era, an era that never really existed, was over. Government intervention in the economy had become part of the political landscape.

BUILDING THE ADMINISTRATIVE STATE

Federalist Period

The Constitution of the United States says extremely little about the administrative structure of government other than the presidential authority to appoint department heads who must be confirmed by the Senate. Yet despite the lack of detailed constitutional specifications concerning administration, the rudiments of an administrative system were firmly established during the Federalist era. Historian Leonard White listed the following administrative achievements of the Federalists:

1. Creation of the chief executive and the administrative powers that went along with the formation of the presidency
2. Development of executive–legislative relations with respect to administrative detail
3. Delegation from president to his subordinates
4. Beginnings of administrative federalism—the linkages between states and the federal agencies
5. Relationships among officials based on law and precedents
6. Creation of a budgetary process
7. Use of moral and ethical guidelines in administrative practices[3]

Alexander Hamilton, as the first secretary of the Treasury, was particularly important in establishing these principles of administration that would set the stage for future generations. He was an advocate of strong central government, particularly with respect to executive powers in finance and international affairs—a position that put him at odds with Thomas Jefferson.

From Jackson to Grant

Whereas the history of the United States from the administration of President Jackson through the administration of President Grant is highlighted by the causes and consequences of the Civil War, little is remembered about the advances in public administration during this period. Perhaps most notable is the creation of the so-called spoils system under President Jackson. Government service under the Federalists was largely an aristocratic and upper-middle-class avocation. Popular democracy, expressed as direct representation of the "common people" through the election or appointment from their ranks, was not part of the early administrative landscape. Jacksonian democracy changed the social-class base of public administration; political parties and the rewards for partisan service replaced the previous era of government service based on social position. At the risk of overstatement, the Jacksonian "spoils system" did not sharply differentiate on the basis of aptitude or merit as a guide to political and administrative appointment, particularly at the local level. Although the common history textbook image of the Jacksonian spoils system is largely negative (and somewhat misleading since presidents both before and after him made appointments on the basis of partisanship), the principle of selecting government employees based on their "representativeness" has contemporary relevance for both the theory and practice of public administration.[4] Does it matter, for example, that civil servants reflect the race, ethnicity, and gender of the populations that they serve?

The Civil War was not an administrative interlude. On the contrary, raising and supporting a military force provided the nation with the experience of building a strong administrative machinery. Similarly, the occupation of the South after the war provided some administrative novelties including the enforcement of the newly established rights created by the Thirteenth, Fourteenth, and Fifteenth Amendments.

One important by-product of this period, especially associated with the Grant presidency, was widespread public corruption of the sort not unknown today. In the words of Alice and Donald Stone, "The corruption and patronage of the administration of President Ulysses S. Grant are probably the base line from which reform movements struggled toward higher standards of governance."[5] Municipal corruption in the large cities controlled by political party machines that saw their origins in the pre–Civil War period took the form of payoffs for municipal contracts. Meanwhile, government jobs were frequently filled by individuals of dubious distinction. Reform was in the air!

From Cleveland to Wilson

Several milestones of public administration were initiated during this period of American political history. The first administrative achievement was the Pendleton Act of 1883 passed during the administration of Grover Cleveland. The act created the rudiments of a civil service system for the national government. The major features included:

Creation of a Civil Service Commission charged with overseeing personnel practices in executive branch agencies

Development of the "merit" system of hiring civil servants in which knowledge, expertise, and impartiality determine the bases for personnel decisions

Beginning of a classification system for government jobs

One never knows how much a single act contributes to political reform. Neverthe-less, the assassination of President Garfield by a disgruntled campaign worker who did not receive a government position he felt was due him for his labors must have contributed to the impetus for administrative reform. Meanwhile, state and local governments also initiated reforms to weed out political corruption and make public administration more efficient and professional. The tenor of the times is captured by George Washington Plunkitt, the boss of Tammany Hall, the Dem-ocratic party machine that controlled New York City politics for almost a hundred years. Bemoaning the onslaught of civil service reform around the turn of the century as a "curse" on his beloved Tammany machine, Plunkitt recounted the story of Flaherty, a redheaded, blue-eyed Irishman from his district, found dead after the battle of San Juan Hill, clothed in a Spanish uniform. How did this sad tale unfold? Plunkitt tells us that poor Flaherty worked hard for the party in the local elections of 1897 and expected to be rewarded with a job for the city. In-stead, he had to take a civil service examination. Listen to Plunkitt recount the fate of Flaherty:

> He didn't know what these examinations were, so he went, all lighthearted, to the Civil Service Board. He read the questions about the mummies, the bird on the iron, and all the other fool questions—and he left that office an enemy of the country that he loved so well. The mummies and the bird blasted his patriotism. He went to Cuba, and died fightin' his country.[6]

Extreme? Of course, it is! But even Plunkitt's hyperbole gives you an indication of the intensity surrounding the changes that were taking place in public adminis-tration almost a hundred years ago.

The late nineteenth century also witnessed the creation of the independent regulatory commission with the birth of the Interstate Commerce Commission (ICC) in 1887. The commission was granted, by law, independence from both the president and Congress and charged with the responsibility of eliminating the collusion among the railroads in their rates. In other words, the ICC was supposed to foster competition by scrutinizing the marketplace for unfair business prac-tices. The notion of creating an independent commission was important for the evolution of public administration for it presumed that such independence would enhance nonpartisan, objective decisions.

By the turn of the century Progressive reformers at the state and local levels of government tried to weed out the corruption of the political party machines by neutralizing the machines' sources of political power. They did not try this be-cause of high-minded moral principles. On the contrary, the Progressives wanted to reduce the political power of the ethnic party machines that received much of their political support from immigrants who became American citizens. One method used to achieve this objective was through government reforms such as the city manager–city council form of government initiated in 1906. The logic of the city manager–city council form of government was simple: By replacing the partisan-strong mayor with a professional, nonpartisan city manager, local gov-ernment decisions would be based on expertise and an assessment of what is best for the entire community. Politics would become less important. Reformers were fond of saying that there was neither a Republican nor a Democratic way to clean the streets, thereby emphasizing the image that professional management would find the most efficient way to accomplish the task, unfettered by subjective political concerns. (Plunkitt would have responded that, although there may not be a Democratic versus a Republican way to clean the streets, there *are* Democratic and Republican street cleaners!) Other municipal reforms in the early part of the twentieth century—such as the at-large election—were all aimed at the same objective: reducing the political influence of the ethnic-based political party machines in cities like St. Louis, Boston, Pittsburgh, and New York.

Intellectual Rationale of the Administrative State

Another event happened in 1887, hardly noticed at the time. A newly minted Ph.D. from Johns Hopkins University by the name of Woodrow Wilson published an essay entitled "The Study of Administration."[7] It would become an intellectual driving force in the profession *and* academic discipline of public administration—and its significance continually debated.[8]

The young scholar was obviously a product of his times. He observed that the administrative class in Western Europe, particularly France and Germany, was professional unlike the amateurism so prevalent in the United States. What made it so professional? Wilson assumed that administrators were capable of implementing government policy in a "businesslike" manner. The notion of businesslike government, notoriously imprecise, then and now, probably meant that government needed to establish methods of administration that were grounded on principles that would withstand the tests of real application. Wilson believed that businesslike government would be "efficient" government. Once again, although the concept of efficiency may mean many different things, Wilson assumed that a science of administration would uncover principles and methods to guide administrative practice. Routine government tasks, for example, should be provided in the least costly manner—a concept of efficiency that dominated the practice of public administration from Grover Cleveland to Franklin Roosevelt.[9]

Wilson's enduring and most controversial observation is on the dichotomy between politics and administration. In Wilson's words, "The field of administration is a field of business. It is removed from the hurry and strife of politics. . . . Administrative questions are not political questions. . . . The broad plans of government action are not administrative; the detailed execution of such plans is administrative."[10] Wilson believed that a sharp demarcation of authority in constitutional democracies was required between those who are elected to formulate policies and the civil servants who have the responsibility for implementing the policies. For Wilson, administration was essentially the execution of public law—legislation enacted by popularly elected representatives. In Wilson's view, once the separation between politics and administration was understood, the next task would be to build a cadre of professional administrators—along the lines of the European administrative class—who were properly educated in the "science" of administration.

Woodrow Wilson was a reformer. Like other reformers of his day, he railed at the rank amateurism of public administration, a legacy of the Jacksonian era, and, more important, the public corruption that was so prevalent during the rise of industrialism. A minor academic industry has been created among public administration scholars concerning the literal interpretation of the politics/administration dichotomy and the importance of Wilson's essay to administrative theory.[11] Although it would be foolish to claim that the essay had direct influence shortly after it was written, it nevertheless reflects themes that remained ongoing well into the New Deal period of President Franklin Delano Roosevelt. They include the efforts to make government more "efficient" and to initiate the study of public administration to develop professional administrators.

Reform as a Reflection of Political Conflict

Ideas rarely surface in a political vacuum. In the last quarter of the nineteenth century and the first two decades of the twentieth century, administrative reform, particularly civil service reform, reflected a political struggle.[12] The emerging political elites who wanted the national government to protect the interests of the modernizing forces in a rapidly changing industrial America saw civil service reform as one way to rid government of the "rabble" and replace it with competent government employees. The illustration of George Washington Plunkitt above highlights that the rabble did not give up without a fight. Reform during this period was one by-product of a growing government presence in American life.

BIG GOVERNMENT BECOMES ROUTINE

The New Deal (1932–1945) is often described as a radical departure in the role of government in the United States. The New Deal expanded the government's intervention in the economy as a way to counteract the Depression brought on by the stock market crash of 1929. This was done through employment and public works programs designed to stimulate employment through government spending. In addition, the New Deal established the basis for many social welfare programs under the Social Security Act of 1935. Besides providing for social security, the act also included provisions for unemployment compensation and aid to families with dependent children. Now the government provides social welfare cash and "in-kind" benefits (such as food stamps and medical care benefits through Medicare and Medicaid) to millions of people.

How big is "big government"? Table 1.1 provides some illustrations:

There are several ways to gauge the size of government. One way is to examine the growth in government spending. Table 1.1 points out the obvious: total government expenditures from all levels of government in the United States went from $10.3 billion in 1929 to $1.5 trillion in 1986. But this tremendous increase in government spending is deceptive. First, the increase does not separate the upward trend that is caused by inflation from the *real* increases in spending. Second,

TABLE 1.1 Government Expenditures (All Levels of Government),
           Selected Years

Year	Total ($Billions)	%GNP
1929	10.3	9.9
1938	16.8	19.7
1944	103.1	48.8
1961	150.1	28.1
1971	346.8	31.5
1981	1,006.9	33.0
1986	1,487.1	35.1

Source: Tax Foundation, *Facts and Figures on Government Finance*, 1988–1989 (Baltimore: The Johns Hopkins Press, 1988), p. 34.

it is more useful to evaluate the size of government as a relationship to the production of goods and services in the economy. How much of the gross national product (GNP)—a measure of total economic production—is produced by government? The second column shows the trend. Although the percentage increased dramatically during World War II, note how it has grown only modestly since the 1960s.

The United States is not unique. The size of government, as measured by the government share of national output, measured comparatively as gross domestic product (GDP), has grown during the past twenty years for many industrialized countries as indicated by the information in Table 1.2.

Why has government grown so dramatically? Social scientists have suggested several alternative explanations. Here are four of them:

Wagner's Law

All discussions of the causes of big government begin with Wagner's law—a principle established by the German economist Adolph Wagner, who wrote in the last quarter of the nineteenth century. Wagner observed the rapid industrialization of Western Europe and the accompanying expansion of government. He reasoned that as real income increased, a shift from private consumption to public consumption took place. To put it another way, a minimal government, one with few goods and services, was incompatible with an industrialized society. Interestingly, one preeminent government expenditure in Germany under Bismarck was the first social security system in Europe. Although Wagner's law makes a great deal of sense, it has not been proven unequivocally through empirical observation.[13]

Displacement Effect

How much taxation will taxpayers tolerate? Two British economists, Alan Peacock and Jack Wiseman, argued that, at any given time, there was a maximum amount of taxation that the citizenry would accept. Public spending was limited

TABLE 1.2 General Government Total Expenditure as a Percentage of Gross Domestic Product, Selected Countries and Selected Years

Country	1965	1975	1980	1984
Australia	25.2	32.2	32.8	37.4
Belgium	32.3	44.5	51.0	55.4
Canada	29.1	40.0	40.4	46.8
France	38.4	43.5	46.4	52.7
Japan	18.8	27.3	32.1	33.1
United Kingdom	36.1	46.3	45.1	47.8
United States	27.4	34.6	33.9	37.2

Source: Organization for Economic Co-Operation and Development, *The Control and Management of Government Expenditure* (Paris, 1987), p. 18.

to that maximum level. When a crisis such as war occurs, however, the citizenry will accept a higher level of taxation. Once the crisis is over, the level of taxation does not return to the precrisis level. Peacock and Wiseman explained the growth of British government in the twentieth century along these lines.

Electoral-Spending Cycle

How do politicians get elected? Conventional wisdom has it that the chances of being *reelected* are enhanced by providing voters with tangible economic benefits. There are variations on this theme. One explanation is that the president will try to manipulate the economy, partly through government spending, in advance of an election.[14] An alternative thesis is that since the self-interest of legislators is in getting reelected, they will develop legislative rules that will facilitate their efforts to "bring home the bacon." This results in many questionable government programs; moreover, the size of government is expanded.[15]

Bureaucratic Behavior

"Work expands so as to fill the time available for its completion."[16] So starts one of the most well-known books on bureaucracy. Parkinson's "law" was intended to be funny. But a good deal of academic research has occurred that tries to show that the size of government can be attributed to actions by bureaucrats. The central feature of this perspective is that bureaucrats are portrayed as individuals who have individual self-interests. For example, they want prestige, influence, career advancement, and any number of perquisites.

To achieve their wants, bureaucrats must achieve certain objectives that will further their self-interest. An expanded agency under a bureaucrat's command, for instance, may be viewed as a sign of administrative effectiveness. Bureaucrats do not have to feather their nests alone. They get help from legislatures and interest groups who, in turn, see advantages to bureaucratic expansion. The result? Government grows because of the strategic position of the bureaucrat.[17]

Most of the theories of government growth have some truth to them; nevertheless, lack of adequate data and the inability to explain pursuasively the consequences of government growth make the issue one that will be with us for some time. Besides, policy-makers who would like to return to an earlier period of smaller government will keep the intellectual flame burning as an antidote to bigness.

FROM BIG GOVERNMENT
TO COMPLEX GOVERNMENT

There is little doubt that government today is large by almost any credible measure. But the concept of bigness does not express fully that character of government today. Big government has a one-dimensional ring to it—like describing the height and weight of a football player without portraying the athlete's speed, agility, or strength. Government today is not only big, it is complex. Complex government pertains to the activities of government in the economic and social spheres of the nation that were not even imagined not very many years ago. Sometimes complex government is subtle; sometimes it is indirect—but it is pervasive. To capture the context of complex government, consider the following cases.

Japanese Automobiles

Everywhere you look you see Japanese automobiles—Hondas, Nissans, Toyotas, Mazdas, and Subarus. The American car-buying public likes them. But Detroit doesn't like them. Japanese imports have created nothing but headaches for domestic automakers. Now there is a simple solution to the problem; it is called competition. Detroit has responded by trying to compete with the Japanese auto companies in the U.S. market by changing the product line, by offering various buyer incentives like low-cost financing and extensive "buyer protection plans," and, naturally, through prices. But it hasn't been easy.

The U.S. companies searched for help. In 1980 and 1981 they turned to the federal government, figuring that the probusiness Reagan administration would certainly understand their plight. They wanted Washington to restrict Japanese imports (through tariffs and quotas). Some members of the administration, however, were "free traders," opposed to trade barriers between countries. Besides, some of the policy-makers thought that Detroit would be better off in the long run if the companies "toughed it out" with Japan in the competitive marketplace.

Politics soon intruded. The stiff competition adversely affected the profits of the American companies, unemployment was high among auto workers, and some states (like Ohio and Michigan) that depended on the auto industry were facing financial difficulties. The Reagan administration decided to adopt a middle course by getting the Japanese "voluntarily" to restrict their imports. Meanwhile, if you were in the market for a Japanese car then, you would have wondered why the dealers were not always able to sell you what you wanted even though demand for Japanese cars was so strong. Government was the "invisible hand" influencing the market.

Whatever Happened to Private Colleges?

It is hard to find a truly "private" college. To be *truly* private a college would require the complete absence of government involvement, which is very rare. Consider the three basic ingredients of government involvement in so-called private colleges.

Student loans.   States and the federal government have provided loans (usually below the prevailing interest rate) for students eligible for the loan programs (based on family income) so that these students can finance their college education. These loans indirectly provide colleges with much needed funds *and* they bolster student enrollment—both extremely important to private colleges that depend on tuition for a large part of their finances.

Federal government grants.   Colleges and universities receive funds from the federal government in the form of grants, many of which are for faculty research or curriculum development. The money is used partially to support salaries and other expenses. Colleges and universities have come to depend on these funds, and they even plan that some percentage of their total costs will be so financed.

Regulation.   Once private colleges and universities accept funds from the federal government, they agree to implement a multitude of regulations about what they can, must, or must not do. Here are just a few:

> Colleges and universities must make their facilities accessible to the handicapped.
> They must "affirmatively act" to hire women and minorities to their faculties.
> They must not engage in research involving human subjects unless they follow government guidelines and restrictions concerning such research.

The point is simple. Private colleges are not very far removed from the reaches of government, and once they accept funds from the federal government (most do), they are no longer completely autonomous. Think about your own college or university. Can you identify direct, and indirect, government presence?

Guaranteed Loans for Chrysler

Let's go back to automobiles. As America entered the 1980s, our love affair with the automobile began to sour. Cheap gasoline seemed to be gone. The American car buyer's taste in automobiles quickly changed. Big gas guzzlers became less and less popular as they became more and more expensive to drive. As pointed out above, imports were ready, willing, and able to enter the U.S. auto market. The big three—General Motors, Ford, and Chrysler—were in trouble. Chrysler seemed about ready to go under. Enter the federal government and Lee Iaccoca!

The federal government did not take over the Chrysler Corporation and run the Dodge and Plymouth factories. The government did not provide technical assistance, nor did it hand out any money. What it did was more subtle. To prevent a total collapse, Chrysler needed money, and it needed it fast if it were to stay in business. Naturally, investors were reluctant to lend money to a large company that was in serious danger of going bankrupt. The financial stakes were high; the risk was great. Investors wanted the risk reduced. The federal government, after delicate negotiations with Chrysler's head, Lee Iaccoca—and prospective creditors—agreed to *guarantee* the company's loans. That is, the federal government would pay off the loans if the company defaulted. Financial risk was therefore reduced, and creditors came forward with the necessary funds.

Why did the government get involved in something that surely went far beyond any "minimalist" conception of government? After all, shouldn't the problems have been left to the marketplace? It is not that simple. The automobile industry is important to the U.S. economy. A failure on the magnitude of Chrysler Corporation would ripple through the economy. The government does not want that to happen. Also, the government wants U.S. auto companies to compete effectively with foreign companies so that the nation's trade balance is not constantly jeopardized. In short, the government is an active partner in the so-called private sector of the nation's economy. Meanwhile, complex government is also subtle government. After all, many people who bought a Chrysler car after the loan guarantee took effect probably didn't realize that the government's intervention allowed them to buy the car of their choice.

A Government-Supported Big Mac

What is a good symbol of the American economic ideology of "free enterprise"? Think of the Big Mac—the famous hamburger you can purchase at any McDonald's franchise. Suppose you wanted to get into the Big Mac business. Like many franchise arrangements you would have to buy a franchise from the McDonald's Corporation. The corporation, as anyone who has eaten in a McDonald's knows, retains a great deal of control over the franchises—price, quality of food, type of food served, method of preparation, customer relations, and so on. The corporation gives individual franchise owners technical assistance, and, in general, the franchises have a high rate of financial success.

So far, no government—aside from scores of government regulations concerning wages and working conditions, taxes, food inspection, and many more! Can a local government purchase a franchise store? No, but local governments have indirectly encouraged the construction of franchises in their jurisdictions. This has been accomplished through the use of tax-exempt industrial development bonds as a way to reduce the cost of financing new construction. Here is generally how it works:

1. The city wants to stimulate economic development by encouraging new businesses in the downtown area.
2. The city either directly or indirectly, through a nonprofit development corporation, sells tax-exempt bonds for new business development.

3. Investors buy the bonds because their tax-exempt status is desirable.
4. The city, or development agency, lends money to new businesses willing to locate in the downtown area (the cost of these loans is usually lower than the market cost).
5. Presto, a new McDonald's appears, facilitated by the sale of tax-exempt bonds (and the subsequent subsidy to a McDonald's franchise owner) for economic development.

The next time you bite into a Big Mac, you may be encouraging the economic revitalization of an aging city.

These four cases illustrate the complexity of modern government. Sometimes complex government can be subtle as in the example of a government subsidized Big Mac. The Chrysler episode was certainly front page news when it happened, although probably it has been forgotten by most people. The private college description depicts a situation that is routine. Nevertheless, one point remains: complex government is a fact of modern life that is here to stay. We are not likely to be successful at scaling back government to a smaller and simpler era.

THE PROFESSION OF PUBLIC ADMINISTRATION

Complexity usually generates the need for specialized expertise. This is no less true for government than it is for other situations. Yet the profession of public administration is young by the standards of other professions such as medicine or law.

The need for a profession of public administration was recognized by Woodrow Wilson in his famous essay "The Study of Administration." Wilson thought that the United States could learn much about administrative practices in Europe—especially France and Germany—without copying their form of government. In his words, "When we study the administrative systems of France and Germany, knowing that we are not in search of political principles, we need not care a peppercorn for the constitutional or political reasons which Frenchmen or Germans give for their practices when explaining them to us."[18] Indeed, Wilson believed that the challenge would be to develop public administrative competence that is highly professional and, at the same time, responsive and responsible to the citizenry. One hundred years later, Wilson's portrait of professional public administration in a democracy still rings true.

Wilson was before his time. No formal steps were taken until well into the twentieth century to develop professional training for government service. Nevertheless, the impetus was created by the reform efforts from the 1880s to 1930—particularly in the big cities. Professional municipal management was associated with the efforts to instill "efficiency" in city government operations. This was done by developing nonpartisan electoral systems, creating strong executives (such as the city manager), and separating politics from administration, in part, through the development of the civil service.[19] The practice of public administration in the first three decades of the twentieth century was largely responsible for making government service an "honorable" profession and demonstrating that ideas can be put into action. At the local level of government this was accomplished through municipal research bureaus in some cities, and the creation of professional organizations such as the International City Management Association, the Municipal Finance Officers Association, and the American Municipal Association. In 1939, the American Society for Public Administration (ASPA)—a national educational and professional organization with the objective of improving management in government—was founded. The ASPA now has more than 19,000 members working at all levels of government, educational institutions, nonprofit organizations, and proprietary organizations.

The profession has come a long way from those early years when the impetus was to rid government of corruption and bring a minimum standard of competence to bear on public administration. Beginning in the 1920s, formal higher education in public administration was established at Syracuse University; University of Southern California; Columbia University; University of California, Berkeley; Stanford University; and a few others.[20] Although no single undergraduate or graduate degree is required for entrance into public service (unlike medicine and law), the graduate master of public administration (MPA) degree is now offered by more than one hundred fifty universities in the United States. It is increasingly common to find public managers at all levels of government with an advanced degree in public administration or public policy.

So what do aspiring managers learn? They learn certain skills such as budgeting and financial management, personnel practices, program evaluation, computing, and statistical and economic analysis. These are some of the tools that you will find in most public administration programs. But public administration is more than a series of skills. It includes knowledge of history, politics, economics, sociology, and philosophy. The managers of tomorrow need to learn about the historical context and political environment within which skills are applied. They must learn about how individuals behave in groups and in organizations. Finally, they must learn how to evaluate the ethical dimensions of both their own behavior and the behavior of others. The rest of this book will describe some of the essential skills that aspiring public administrators will need to know. But it will do more. It will put those skills in a historical, political, and ethical context to prepare the administrators of tomorrow with the foundations that will be needed for effective public management.

SUMMARY

Government, according to one philosophical tradition, is a necessary consequence of humans' baser instincts. This point of view, associated with the seventeenth-century British philosopher, Sir Thomas Hobbes, was also held by James Madison, one of the nation's Founding Fathers and the fourth president of the United States. While the case for government is relatively straightforward, the amount of government involvement in economic and social life is not. Throughout U.S. history there has been a continuing debate about the legitimate scope of government activity. The principle of *limited government,* which refers to restrictions on the exercise of political authority, provides individuals with freedom from government. But limited government does not mean minimal government. On the contrary, much of the nineteenth century witnessed the building of the *administrative state.* The twentieth century, in contrast, experienced the growth of *big government,* and the transformation of big government into *complex government.* This complexity is illustrated by three broad themes in contemporary public administration:

1. There is no neat separation between the public and private sectors. Government action is often very important in decisions that many appear, at first, to be private sector decisions. The private sector, in turn, is very much a part of the public sector.
2. Government intervention in the economy started with the birth of the nation and has never ceased.
3. Government activity is cyclical. The relative amounts of activity have been stimulated by changing public perceptions about the worth of government. Changing public perceptions, in turn, help public officials shape policies and programs in light of these perceptions. Public administrators must manage these changes. As we will see throughout the following chapters, a rapidly changing public sector provides innumerable challenges, and frustrations, for the public administrator of today—and it won't get any easier tomorrow.

NOTES

1. Milton Friedman, *Capitalism and Freedom* (Chicago: University of Chicago Press, 1962), p. 25.
2. Jonathan R. T. Hughes, *The Governmental Habit* (New York: Basic Books, 1977).
3. White's list of the contributions of the Federalists to the development of the administrative state are found in Paul P. Van Riper, "The American Administrative State: Wilson and the Founders," in *A Centennial History of the American Administrative State,* ed. Ralph Clark Chandler (New York: Free Press, 1987), pp. 11–12.
4. Samuel Krislov, *Representative Bureaucracy* (Englewood Cliffs, N.J.: Prentice-Hall, 1974).
5. Alice B. Stone and Donald C. Stone, "Early Development of Education in Public Administration," in *American Public Administration: Past, Present, Future,* ed. Frederick C. Mosher (University: University of Alabama Press, 1975), pp. 11–12.
6. William L. Riordon, *Plunkitt of Tammany Hall* (New York: E. P. Dutton, 1963), p. 15.
7. Woodrow Wilson, "The Study of Public Administration," reprinted in *Classics of Public Administration,* ed. Jay M. Shafritz and Albert C. Hyde (Oak Park, Ill.: Moore Publishing, 1978), pp. 3–17.
8. See Van Riper, "The American Administrative State," and the various essays in *Politics and Administration,* ed. Jack Rabin and James S. Bowman (New York: Marcel Dekker, 1984).

9. Louis Gawthrop, "Toward an Ethical Convergence of Democratic Theory and Administrative Politics," in *A Centennial History of the American Administrative State*, p. 196.
10. Wilson, "The Study of Public Administration," pp. 10–11.
11. See the essays in *Politics and Administration*.
12. An excellent analysis of this period is found in Stephen Skowronek, *Building a New American State* (New York: Cambridge University Press, 1982).
13. An excellent in-depth review of several theories of government growth is Patrick D. Larkey, Chandler Stolp, and Mark Winer, "Theorizing about the Growth of Government: A Research Assessment," *Journal of Public Policy* 1 (May 1981): 157–220.
14. See, for example, Edward R. Tufte, *Political Control of the Economy* (Princeton, N.J.: Princeton University Press, 1978).
15. See Larkey, Stolp, and Winer, "Theorizing," pp. 180–187, for a review of voter-spending explanations of government growth.
16. C. Northcote Parkinson, *Parkinson's Law* (New York: Ballantine, 1957).
17. The classic statement along these lines is William A. Niskanen, Jr., *Bureaucracy and Representative Government* (Chicago, Ill.: Aldine, 1971).
18. Wilson, "The Study of Public Administration," p. 16.
19. See Martin J. Schiesl, *The Politics of Efficiency* (Berkeley: University of California Press, 1977).
20. Stone and Stone, "Early Development of Education," pp. 30–33.

FOR FURTHER READING

Hughes, Jonathan R. T. *The Governmental Habit*. New York: Basic Books, 1977.
    An excellent study of U.S. economic history, showing that government has intervened in economic life ever since the colonial period.

Kelman, Steven. *Making Public Policy: A Hopeful View of American Government*. New York: Basic Books, 1987.
    Kelman finds much to commend about government—not a small achievement in a period when "bureaucrat bashing" was so prevalent.

Knott, Jack H., and Gary Miller. *Reforming Bureaucracy: The Politics of Institutional Choice*. Englewood Cliffs, N.J.: Prentice-Hall, 1987.
    The authors show how "rules of the game" that government bureaucracies operate under have a great deal to do with governmental performance.

Riordan, William L. *Plunkitt of Tammany Hall*. New York: E. P. Dutton, 1963.
    It is always fun to read George Washington Plunkitt's portrait of political life around the turn of the century—especially his complaints about the reformers.

Waldo, Dwight. *The Administrative State*. New York: Ronald Press, 1948.
    A classic work that evaluates the intellectual history of public administration in the context of American political theory.

CHAPTER 2

Public Agencies: The Coming and Going of Organizations

People are born; they grow; eventually they die. We call this a "life cycle." Organizations have life cycles also.[1] They are born, they grow, they wither, and, yes, some even die. During the life cycle of a person we notice changes, most obviously physical changes. But we also frequently comment on other changes as well. "Isn't Auntie Bertha becoming increasingly crotchety in her old age?" may be a typical observation. Or "Grandpa Zeke is mellow these days. He must be at peace with himself." Obviously, these are comments about observed changes in the emotional traits of people during their life cycle.

Organizations also change. Sometimes they "look" different. They may become larger—or smaller. Their functions may change over time. Organizations are occasionally described as conservative, resistant, or even rigid. They can also be described as open or innovative. Some are adaptive.

People die in different ways. Some die unexpectedly. When we say that a person died prematurely we usually mean that the person died at a relatively young age. Some people resist death; they don't want to die even though all "objective" signs would indicate that they should have done so. Some people welcome death. It comes at the "right" time—a capstone to a full life that because of terminal illness or advanced age cannot continue.

Organizational rigor mortis is similarly multifaceted. Sometimes death is painfully slow for organizations, especially when they are "nickel and dimed" out of existence. Occasionally, organizations suffer institutional heart attacks when their central mission is abolished. But like many people who are so afflicted, many organizations fight back. Some make it; some perish. Some organizations have the ability to become reincarnated. Their names change; their personnel change; even some of their functions change. Yet a close look at the former self of reincarnated organizations will reveal an extension of the life cycle even after institutional rigor mortis has set in.

In this chapter we will learn about the life cycle of organizations—why they come into existence, how and why they grow, the various ways they maintain themselves from internal and external pressures, and how some of them die and still others are reborn. The life cycle of organizations is one approach to learning about organizations. In particular, its usefulness is highlighting the simple point that organizations do not just "spring up" from nowhere. There are reasons for their creation; there are reasons why they do not remain static; there are reasons why some whither away. But many of the *core* government organizations that we either take for granted or come into contact with on a regular basis—tax-collection agencies, police departments, prisons, fire departments, transportation agencies—do not really fit the life-cycle imagery. They all had to be created at one point, however, and they also experience change. But don't expect prisons, police, fire departments, and tax-collection departments to experience organizational euthansia in the near future—not unless you think that crime will cease to exist and all people will pay their taxes "voluntarily."

BIRTH

Public organizations are not conceived through miracles. There is always a reason why an organization is born, but like reasons offered for having children, some are sounder than others.

Market Failure

Suppose you lived in a big city without a police department. You heard rumors about crime. In fact, the rumors included comments that crime was "growing and reaching epidemic proportions." What could you do? You could arm yourself, put locks on your windows and doors, and transform yourself from a ninety-nine-pound weakling into a very strong and fearsome person. But if there was any truth to the rumors, all of these alternatives would probably not improve your safety.

You could try to convince others about the need to "do something." Suppose you are successful; that is, you convince others to join together to provide protection against crime. You may arrange a "neighborhood watch" program. Perhaps you and your neighbors initiate a street patrol and assign times when different people are responsible for coverage of specified areas.

Here is where your problems may start. Suppose you have an uncooperative neighbor—Scowelly Selfish, who won't have anything to do with anybody. Now the obvious thing to do is to "cut him out" of the benefits. But what are the benefits? They are public safety, which, one hopes, is reflected in less crime. Think about this for a moment. How, exactly, would you prevent Selfish from receiving some of the benefits of your community efforts to control crime?

Although I am sure that you can conjure up some ingenious ways to teach Scowelly a lesson—and convince him to be a team player—like it or not, you and your neighbors are really in a bind. You will not be able effectively to deny Selfish all of the benefits of public safety without adversely affecting its level for the entire community. After all, could you really stop a suspicious person and have the following conversation?

NEIGHBORHOOD PERSON: Hey you, where are you going?

SUSPICIOUS PERSON: Oh, I was just checking out the neighborhood.

NEIGHBORHOOD PERSON: Are you planning to burglarize a house around here?

SUSPICIOUS PERSON: Well, I was giving it some thought.

NEIGHBORHOOD PERSON: In that case, try the third one on the left. It belongs to Scowelly Selfish.

In this example, two aspects about public safety soon become apparent. First, when you decide to provide public safety in the area, providing it even to Scowelly Selfish does not really diminish what is provided to everyone else. Second, it is not feasible to deny Selfish the benefits of public safety. Economists label goods and services that have these properties public goods.[2] Examples of public goods are national defense, public safety, and, perhaps the best example of all, the lighthouse that provides a warning to all boats that pass close enough to see it.

Other central functions of government are less dramatic than national defense, though no less important for a nation's perseverance. Indeed, if you read the Constitution of the United States carefully you will learn about other central functions of government that required the birth of public organization. In Chapter 1, I mentioned that under the Articles of Confederation the colonies printed their own money. To stabilize economic conditions in the new nation, the Constitution said that only the national government could coin and print money. This, in turn, gave rise to the Bureau of the Mint. Today we take this central mission of government for granted, but it is only one illustration of an organization that is indispensable in modern society.

Expansion of Government Activity

Organizations are born when government grows, and government grows when it takes on additional responsibilities. The previous section identified two basic responsibilities of government—national defense and the coining and printing of money. We have come far from these limited functions of government. Government produces hundreds of goods and services, and it regulates all sorts of economic and social activities. When it does, organizations are born.

The historian Gabriel Kolko provided an interesting illustration of the birth of public organization when he explained the origins of meat-packing legislation in the latter part of the nineteenth century.[3] In 1881 an inspection organization was created in the U.S. Treasury Department to certify cattle export. In 1884 the Bureau of Animal Industry was established in the Department of Agriculture to insure that diseased cattle were not sent abroad. Why were these organizations established? Who wanted them? Kolko's explanation is intriguing.

It seems that in the 1880s most European countries banned the importation of meat from the United States because of diseased pork and beef that had reached

European shores. This decision to boycott American meat was a devastating blow to U.S. meat-packers because it dramatically cut into their markets. In Kolko's words, "These packers learned very early in the history of the industry that it was not to their profit to poison their customers, especially in a competitive market in which the consumer could go elsewhere."[4] But packers were not able to police themselves. They needed, indeed required, the help of the federal government to establish regulatory agencies that would force packers to improve the quality of their meat and thereby become more competitive in the international market. Kolko's analysis of this period of American history is interesting because he showed, contrary to the conventional view, that not only did packers not resist the regulations, they actively lobbied for federal laws that would establish regulatory mechanisms (certification in particular) for the meat-packing industry.

This illustration is only a single episode in the history of government intervention in the economy. Government organizations have been created to regulate many different types of economic activities. A brief list of federal regulatory agencies and their dates of creation includes Interstate Commerce Commission (1887), Antitrust Division of the U.S. Department of Justice (1890), Federal Trade Commission (1914), Food and Drug Administration (1931), National Labor Relations Board (1935), Federal Aviation Administration (1958), Environmental Protection Agency (1970), Occupational Safety and Health Administration (1972), and the Nuclear Regulatory Commission (1973).

Expansion of government activities has gone beyond regulation. In fact, some of the students reading these words may be in colleges and universities that were founded because of the federal government's expansion into a new activity during the Civil War. In 1862 Congress passed the Morrill Act, which provided states with federal funds to establish "land-grant" institutions of higher education. Since then scores of colleges and universities were started through the land-grant program—institutions that, at first, were supposed to provide technical assistance in agriculture. Naturally, as land-grant colleges grew, they also diversified. Michigan State University, an early land-grant institution, is one of the largest universities in the country; it offers a full range of undergraduate and graduate programs from architecture to zoology. Yet even after more than a hundred years, its first central mission—technical assistance in agriculture—remains a major program in the university.

These two illustrations—the regulation of meat-packers and the birth of land-grant colleges—have something in common. Both represent the intervention of government in the economic affairs of the country. By the turn of the century it became clear that government was at least a junior partner in the nation's growing industrial society. As the economy grew, so did the federal and state governments.

During the entire history of the twentieth century, organized economic groups learned that they could profit by having an "ear" in Washington. The best way to do so was to have a federal agency responsible for overseeing the economic activities of the group in question. Farmers, a perennially beleaguered class, learned this basic political principle.

First, farmers do not comprise a single interest group. Rather, their concerns differ, depending on what they grow or what they raise. Farmers may even be in conflict with one another. If the cost of feed grains goes up, it would naturally benefit the growers of the feed. But increases in the price of feed would hurt, say, poultry and dairy farmers because feed is a major expense for them. So we have interests that are in conflict with one another. Nevertheless, ongoing concerns of farmers since the late nineteenth century have been the cost of money, the prices of agricultural products, and government programs that have some impact on farm income. These problems have encouraged the birth of several government organizations, all part of the U.S. Department of Agriculture.[5]

Research and education.   We already learned about agriculture research and education programs that were begun by state land-grant colleges. When research provides some usable (applied) results—such as a new type of pest control—the information is made available by the government-sponsored Extension Service. Basic and applied research is also conducted by both the Agricultural Research Service and the Cooperative State Research Service. (The latter includes Agricultural Experiment Stations, which are both federal and state controlled.)

Credit programs.   Farmers, like everyone else, need money. But since the nineteenth century, they have complained that they are especially vulnerable to the booms and busts of the economic cycle. With the passage of the Federal Farm Loan Act in 1916, farmers have successfully pressured the federal government for financial assistance. They can now turn to the Farm Credit Administration, Farmers Home Administration, and the Rural Electrification Administration, depending on the specific help that is needed.

Price-support programs.   Would you like to get paid not to do something? Some farmers enjoy this unique situation. They get paid not to produce as much of a commodity as they can. The basic principle is to maintain the purchasing power of farmers in the face of economic fluctuations. From the 1930s to the present, price supports have remained central to the interests of various types of growers, and they have been a major feature of national agricultural policy debates during the past fifty years. Although specific supports vary from commodity to commodity, price supports have one of two possible features: Either the government provides money to farmers directly, or the government limits the actual production of the commodity (such as wheat) and thereby helps to raise its price in the marketplace. Agencies in the Department of Agriculture that deal with price supports are the Agricultural Stabilization and Conservation Service, Commodity Credit Corporation, Federal Crop Insurance Corporation, and Foreign Agricultural Service. By 1993 federal government spending by the Commodity Credit Corporation for various agricultural product subsidies and loans is expected to reach approximately $12 billion.

Research and education, credit, and price supports represent only three broad areas that have been very important to farmers for a long time. Throughout the years a complex administrative apparatus has grown up to deal with the varied and diverse interests of farmers. A series of ''iron triangles'' has been installed to insure that these interests are given proper attention. Theodore Lowi, a well-respected political scientist, has portrayed these agricultural iron triangles in some detail.[6] The Extension Service in the U.S. Department of Agriculture, for instance, has consistently received backing from various congressional supporters, who have served for many years on the agriculture committees, and from interest groups, who have lobbied on its behalf. These groups have included the Association of Land-Grant Colleges, the Farm Bureau Federation, and the National Association of County Agricultural Agents. It is important to realize that this is merely one illustration of an iron triangle. Agriculture is filled with many more. Is there a reason to be concerned about this development? Lowi thinks so:

> As in geometry and engineering, so in politics the triangle seems to be the most stable type of structure. There is an immense capacity in each agriculture system, once created, to maintain itself and to resist any type of representation except its own. These self-governing agriculture systems have such institutional legitimacy that they have become practically insulated from the three central sources of democratic political responsibility: (1) Within the Executive Branch they are autonomous. Secretaries of agriculture have tried and failed to consolidate or even to coordinate related programs. (2) Within Congress, they are sufficiently powerful within their own domain to be able to exercise an effective veto or to create stalemate. (3) Agriculture activities and agencies are almost totally removed from the view of the general public. Upon becoming the exclusive province of those who are most directly interested in them, programs are first split off from general elective political responsibility. (Rarely has there been more than one urban member on the House Committee on Agriculture, sometimes not even one.) After specialization there is total submersion.[7]

What is the overall lesson here? Once born, a government organization may receive much political nourishment. Critics of these cozy iron triangles would add, too much nourishment.

Organizational Birth as a Response to Crisis

Crises breed organizations. The best example is the governmental response to the Great Depression that occurred during the tenure of President Franklin D. Roosevelt. Roosevelt's New Deal promised a better tomorrow. But it took more than promises, hopes, and dreams. The Depression of the 1930s, and the New Deal's reaction to it, spurred the growth of many government organizations.

In 1929 the unemployment rate was 3.2 percent. In 1933 it was 24.9 percent. Between 1929 and 1933 the gross national product of the United States declined by 30.4 percent. Personal consumption during the same four-year period dropped by 19.2 percent. Economic disaster stimulated government action. In 1933 President Roosevelt, with the authorization of Congress, established the Civilian Conservation Corps (CCC), which soon employed a quarter of a million people in various jobs in the national forests. Next, the Public Works Administration (PWA) was created to provide a stimulus to the construction industry by funding various public projects. In 1935 the Works Projects Administration (WPA) was created to put the unemployed who could work back to work on federal programs.

The unemployed included artists, musicians, librarians, and construction workers, to name a few.

More government organizations were founded. The Tennessee Valley Authority (TVA) was created to provide low-cost energy to the Tennessee Valley. In 1935 the Social Security Act was passed, creating several new government agencies to deal with income maintenance and social services. This act alone would, during the next fifty years, provide the legislative support for mammoth growth in federal programs and organizations that provide assistance to the poor, handicapped, and aged.

The New Deal agencies marked a dramatic departure in the scope of government. No longer would government be a junior partner in the economic affairs of the nation. Crisis forced government action, and organizations were born. When the crisis ended, many of the New Deal agencies self-destructed; others, like the Social Security Administration, prospered and grew.[8]

War also stimulates the birth of organizations. To start, soldiers must be drafted, recruited, and trained. They must be transported to the battle areas. They must be fed, clothed, and cared for when wounded (or killed in action). Naturally, weapons must be manufactured. All of these activities require organizations.

War, however, particularly a large-scale one such as World War II, affects much more than simply military operations. War has a dramatic impact on the whole society and the economy in particular. During World War II a government organization was born to deal with some of the economic dislocations of American involvement: the Office of Price Administration (OPA).

Temporary shortages of civilian goods and services often occur when production is directed toward the war effort. When shortages are felt, the prices for goods and services in scarce supply tend to rise. Then inflation results, as does black marketeering. Since all these side-effects of war are usually considered undesirable, the OPA was established to control them.

The director of the OPA during World War II was a young economist, John Kenneth Galbraith. (Galbraith is world famous for his books on the economics of industrial society and American capitalism. He was also a celebrated spokesperson for the liberal wing of the Democratic party during the 1950s, 1960s, and 1970s and served as ambassador to India during the Kennedy administration.) Galbraith was put in charge of an organization that soon had approximately two thousand employees. In his memoirs he described the birth of the office:

> What does one do when one is put in charge of all prices in the United States? On my first Sunday in office I went to the Blaine Mansion and sat down by myself with the Census classification of American industry. From this I derived the subdivisions of my office—nonferrous metals, fuel; steel and iron and steel products; textiles, leather and apparel; and so forth. It seemed almost too simple.
>
> Then I invented a title for those who would be in charge of the various industry groupings, one that would last through the war. They would be called Price Executives. The title was to give an air of authority to a few individuals who made decisions granting or denying millions of dollars while being paid themselves $6500 a year before taxes.
>
> After so dividing up the economy, I put by each division the name of a plausible head. Most were economists of my acquaintance; the rest were civil servants from

peacetime agencies. In the next days I telephoned or telegraphed these nominees asking them to come to Washington. War tension was now high. Everyone I asked came.[9]

Organizational Birth as a Response to Perceived Crisis

Crises can be real. No one would deny that the Depression produced crises. Nor would anyone really doubt that war creates crises. But sometimes events happen that produce the appearance of a crisis. Policy-makers and the general public may react as if a genuine crisis is happening. With hindsight, the so-called crisis may really have been only a perception, perhaps an overreaction to a specific event. But the organizational effect may be the same.

In 1957 the Soviet Union launched a manned spaceship named Sputnik. Americans were shocked and outraged. It seemed as if the Soviets were beating us in the "space race." They would have a man on the moon before us. After the initial shock, President Eisenhower took steps to improve the ability of the United States to compete with the Soviets. Federal intervention in education was designed specifically to improve the technological, mathematical, and scientific literacy of American schoolchildren. But most important, in 1958 Congress passed the National Aeronautics and Space Act, which established the National Aeronautic and Space Administration: NASA was born.

Like a baby with an insatiable appetite NASA grew rapidly. Within two years it absorbed some research groups from the military. It expanded in physical size by acquiring new land and building new facilities, but it wanted most of all to solidify its organizational presence. It needed a big mission. President Kennedy, on May 25, 1961, gave NASA what it wanted. He announced that by the end of the 1960s the United States would successfully land a man on the moon. This was described as a national commitment, and NASA's grand mission received the requisite budgetary support to carry it out. The budget increased from $1.8 billion to $5.2 billion, and personnel climbed from 60,000 to 420,000.[10]

As it turned out, the fear of U.S. technological backwardness was ill founded. There was no real crisis. The United States was not losing the space race to the Soviets. Not only did we catch up, but we also outdistanced the Soviets and reached the objective and target date set by President Kennedy. But the perception of crisis was a necessary condition, and perhaps a sufficient one as well, for the birth of NASA.

Eventually, criticisms of NASA surfaced. Many had to do with the costliness of the program and questionable procurement practices. The spaceship *Challenger* disaster in 1986 (in which all members of the crew were killed in a midair explosion) undermined the agency's credibility with some members of Congress and the public. Yet after two trying years of organizational rebuilding following a probe of the *Challenger* tragedy, NASA regained some of its lost lustre.

Organizational Birth as a Response to Perceived "War on Poverty"

Fighting and winning a war when you know who the enemy is can be difficult. When the enemy is a concept, it can be next to impossible. Such is the saga of the famous "war on poverty." Although historians of the 1960s' "war" may debate just how many battles were won, few would deny that at least several organizations were hatched.

"The war on poverty" was the catchy phrase given to President Lyndon Johnson's efforts to alleviate poverty in the United States in the 1960s. It was a major focus of his Great Society administration.

The war on poverty took place on many fronts. In the area of education, programs for "disadvantaged" children were initiated. These various programs (the most famous was the federally funded Head Start) were based on the assumption that poor children start school with a decided disadvantage because their family and neighborhood environments do not prepare them adequately. Employment programs, most notably the Job Corps, were begun to provide job training and federally subsidized jobs to the "hard core" unemployed. These programs were based on the assumption that once the hard core unemployed adopted positive work habits and received some skills, they would be able to find (and hold) employment in the private sector with no federal subsidy. For the nonworking poor who were not employable, there were also new programs. The elderly received additional health benefits through Medicare. (Medicaid was also initiated during the Johnson administration.) Expanded social services funded by the federal government were provided to public assistance recipients through county welfare departments.

There is still considerable disagreement about the overall impact of the Great Society programs. Defenders of the original idea claim that the war turned out to be little more than a skirmish when one considers the amount of money that was actually spent (particularly when compared to defense spending). This argument is buttressed by the additional reference to the growing U.S. involvement in the war in Vietnam. As the Johnson administration became increasingly embroiled in the Vietnam quagmire, attention to the domestic war on poverty waned. Critics charged that the government was "throwing money at problems." The problems were immense, intractable for the most part, and spending large sums would not necessarily solve problems of poverty unless and until the underlying causes and the effective ways to deal with them were discovered.

One result of the war on poverty is clear. New government organizations were born. Births occurred not merely in Washington, D.C., but also all over the country as state and local governments forged organizational links with the Great Society. In Washington the Office of Economic Opportunity (OEO) was created to coordinate several antipoverty programs that were administered at the local level.[11] The range of OEO activities—the different facets of poverty-related programs—was broad. Among the more well-known OEO programs were Head Start, Job Corps, legal services, migrant programs, Neighborhood Youth Corps, Upward Bound, and Vista. Judged by the budget of the OEO, the war on poverty received modest support. At its height in 1969, spending for OEO programs reached $1.9 billion. The budget actually minimizes OEO's influence, however. As a new organization it did more than coordinate the intergovernmental aspects of the Great Society's antipoverty programs; it was also the organization focal point for antipoverty activities throughout the federal government. More important, the OEO organized a large grass-roots constituency at the local level in every state. Modest in size and although an organization infant, it was an important part of the war on poverty. As we will learn later, the OEO, a healthy infant, barely made it to organizational adolescence.

We have seen that there are different reasons for organizational births. Once born, organizations try to survive—and even to prosper. How organizations maintain themselves is an intriguing puzzle and the subject of the next section.

BUREAUCRATIC POLITICS OF ORGANIZATIONAL GROWTH

You have heard the expression "He who hesitates is lost." Well, organizations don't stand still either. They try to grow and prosper. What are some of the factors that nurture bureaucratic growth?

Statutory Birthright

You will have noticed that some of the organizations already mentioned were created by legislative action. Congress passed a law, designed to achieve a policy objective, which included the establishment of a government organization that would carry out the intent of the legislation. Not all public organizations are created by statute, however; some are brought into existence by executive order; that is, the president establishes the agency without legislative action. Perhaps the most significant difference between the two types of organizational births is that the former, by virtue of its statutory status, has much more security. Herbert Kaufman, a close observer of organizational births for many years, noted that "statutory underpinning is both sought and granted by those who want to confer a measure of security on their favorite administrative agencies, and why agencies buttressed by legislation can be expected to be more resistant to potentially lethal forces than their less fortunate counterparts."[12] Kaufman added that the original sponsors of the legislation, and thus the government organization, may be in Congress quite some time to protect the agency from hostile forces.[13] Indeed, each year the newspapers (and more specialized news journals such as *National Journal* and *Congressional Quarterly*) will name a program or organization that was on the budgetary chopping block—only to be rescued at the last minute by a congressional savior. Sometimes an organization that was destined for the bureaucratic dust bin ended up enjoying an organizational revival, as the following case of the Bureau of Alcohol, Tobacco and Firearms shows:

A Bureau That Battled Bootleggers Is Tough Target for Budget-Cutters

Wayne King

WASHINGTON, Jan. 29—Mounted in a prominent spot in the offices of one of Washington's major law-enforcement agencies is a blown-up formal photo of a man in his 30's, neatly dressed, hair parted in the middle.
    It is a picture of Eliot Ness, and, given his exploits as the head of an

anti-bootlegger strike force in the Prohibition era of Al Capone and other mob chieftains, he is a rather bland-looking fellow.

Ness was made famous in a later era by the television show that bore the name "The Untouchables."

What most people probably do not recall is just who the Untouchables actually were—or, as a trivia question might put it, which Federal agency did Eliot Ness actually work for?

NOT TRIVIAL TO AGENTS

Trivia, yes, but not trivial to the 1,600 largely unsung agents of the Bureau of Alcohol, Tobacco and Firearms, which is the agency where Ness's picture hangs, along with a photograph of his original credentials, identifying him as an agent of the Treasury Department's Bureau of Prohibition.

The Bureau of Prohibition is the bureaucratic ancestor of the agency that is now the Bureau of Alcohol, Tobacco and Firearms, usually referred to as the A.T.F.—or by pro-gun critics like the three-million-member National Rifle Association as "the dreaded gun police," to use one of the more polite epithets.

Faced with extinction six years ago because of opposition by the firearms lobby and Reagan Adminstration efforts to whittle down the Federal bureaucracy, the bureau not only survived but has returned to maximum full-agent strength. One reason sometimes offered in conversation is that the N.R.A. let up a bit, figuring that another agency—say, the Secret Service—might be even more intractable if given the bureau's mission.

NOT GETTING OVERCONFIDENT

At any rate, the bureau is within a few hundred employees of equaling the total work force of 4,100 it had in its heydey in the late 1970's, before the axmen started chopping.

Perhaps more importantly, while the agency is still far from a household name, the high-profile cases it handles these days—from abortion-clinic bombings to crime sprees by heavily armed neo-Nazi terrorists—have put the cumbersome name of the Bureau of Alcohol, Tobacco and Firearms before the public, even if a lot of people still seem think it is part of the F.B.I.

Moreover, while history has taught him to remain cautious, the bureau director, Stephen E. Higgins, who was deputy director during the purge a few years ago, feels a bit more secure.

"No one wants to be overconfident," he said. "Things beyond your control can affect your destiny.

"But I know we're doing about right when we get a little bit of criticism from both the people who would be called anti-gun, and from those who would be called pro-gun. When we're somewhere in the middle of those groups, we know we're probably doing what we're paid to do, which is enforce the existing laws, without going out and telling people there ought to be more or different laws."

TRACKING SALES OF GUNS

At the same time, the bureau is a bit more cautious in politically sensitive areas. It no longer brings criminal prosecutions against gun dealers for sloppy record-keeping—the kind that makes it tough to trace a gun used in a crime—but instead levies administrative penalties, including revoking licenses.

The bureau also tries to demonstrate the need for accurate, thorough recording of gun sales. With them, the bureau can act with remarkable speed. The revolver John W. Hinckley Jr. used to shoot President Reagan in 1981 was traced to a Dallas pawn shop within 16 minutes of the time the serial number was turned over to an A.T.F. agent.

Nor do bureau agents monitor the thousands of gun shows held around the country each year, as they once did.

Law-enforcement officials say the shows usually involve an enormous amount of trafficking in weapons among ostensible collectors, often with scant regard to record-keeping or proper identification of purchasers.

"If we wanted to, we could go to a gun show and arrest people coming out and just line 'em up," said Mr. Higgins. "They may never get convicted—certainly some of them would—but we don't think that's what the firearms laws are there for. That's like catching somebody jay-walking."

Such indulgence turns aside some of the "dreaded gun police" imagery that advocates of unfettered gun transactions try to pin on the bureau, but Mr. Higgins also said it was a matter of necessity. There are simply so many violations of gun laws that the bureau has to go after the big ones.

LONG LIST OF NAMES

"We use our statutes against crimes of violence," he said. "That's what society is really concerned with."

The agency has been known by various names over its history, usually dictated by its function. Ushered in by the Eighteenth Amendment in 1919, it was known first as the Prohibition Unit, later expanding into the Bureau of Prohibition and then changing to the Alcohol Tax Unit with the end of Prohibition in 1933.

It was renamed the Alcohol and Tobacco Tax Division with the added duties of enforcing tobacco taxes in 1951. Later, it became the Alcohol, Tobacco and Firearms Division and separated from the Internal Revenue Service, of which it had been a part. Finally, in 1972, it obtained full bureau status in the Treasury Department as the Bureau of Alcohol, Tobacco and Firearms.

Even that weighty title is a bit misleading. Today, unlike the heydey of Eliot Ness, the bureau spends less than five percent of its agent hours on alcohol and tobacco matters. Long gone is the agent of old, smashing barrels of moonshine with an ax, or tossing dynamite into barrels of mash, rocking the Southern hills with the sound of thunder and lacing the breeze with the smell of fermenting corn.

$10 BILLION IN TAXES

Today's agent is more likely to be involved with machineguns than souring mash, with truckloads of explosives rather than untaxed cigarets.

Although the bureau will collect more than $10 billion in taxes this year, mostly from whiskey and cigarets, the cutting edge of its enforcement involves drugs, guns, explosives, and the people who sell and use them.

The agency is not concerned with drugs, per se, but as Mr. Higgins notes, crime and drugs usually go together. Tracing one leads to the other.

Last year, the bureau was asked by authorities in Jamaica for help in tracing eight handguns found in the possession of a Jamaican man who appeared to have acquired the firearms in the United States. Bureau agents traced the weapons to other Jamaicans living in the United States, some illegally, and found that they had also purchased a number of other weapons.

'JAMAICAN POSSES' FOUND

Eventually, the investigation led to the discovery of an enormous national network of "Jamaican posses," criminal groups heavily involved in drug traffic. Investigators believe as many as 3,000 affiliated members were responsible for some 600 homicides over two and a half years. Agents recently arrested 150 suspects in a single day, and the investigation is continuing.

Similarly, it was a trace of weapon left at the scene of a $3.6 million armored-car robbery in Ukiah, Calif., that led to the arrest and prosecution of the neo-Nazi cult known as The Order. That group is believed by lawmen to have been responsible for armed robberies, murder, counterfeiting, arson and a host of other crimes in trying to foment a great race war that it hopes will topple the Government.

Bureau agents have also been chief investigators in bombings or arsons at 65 abortion clinics over the past five years, the most recent last month in Alabama. Forty-one cases are listed as solved, with 33 arrests and 22 convictions so far. Twenty-four cases are still under investigation.

□   *"A Bureau That Battled Bootleggers Is Tough Target for Budget Cutters," by Wayne King, February 1, 1988. Copyright © 1988 by The New York Times Company. Reprinted by permission.*

Sometimes the item saved from the budgetary executioner lacks high drama but may appeal to one's funny bone. In the 1983 budget, $500,000 for the start-up of a chimpanzee colony at New Mexico State University was saved from the blow of the budgetary axe. Could it be that Senator Pete V. Domenici, Republican from New Mexico and, at the time, chairman of the Senate Budget Committee, had an interest in monkeys?[14]

Cultivating Legislative Support

Maybe Senator Domenici curried favor with other chimpanzee lovers in Congress. More likely, it was the fact that a half a million dollars for New Mexico State University was "small change" in a budget that approached $800 billion in Fiscal Year (FY)1983. The Bureau of Alcohol, Tobacco and Firearms case shows us how government agencies can cultivate legislative support to survive and, indeed, to prosper.

What did the bureau do? The agency gained congressional support because of some high-profile cases. What member of Congress is going to be against an agency that is in the crime-fighting business? It also helps to be an agency that generates revenue for a deficit-plagued federal government. Being relatively small doesn't hurt either when budget-cutting fever runs high.

Growth through Assertiveness

Managers of public organizations have adopted the maxim "it never hurts to ask." It never hurts to ask for more funds to perform the agency's mission. Asking for more has been not only an operational rule of thumb for public managers but also an indispensable tool for managers "on the way up."

It seems in the Alice-in-Wonderland of bureaucratic politics, one goes backward if one stands still. Success, bureaucratic style, comes about from expansion, from organizational growth. One is doing better if one's organization gets bigger.

Getting bigger means taking on more personnel and organizational responsibilities, but most important, it means budget expansion. "Thin might be in" if you are referring to the manager's waistline, but if it is the budget you are talking about, organizational obesity is sheer heaven. How a manager goes about getting a bigger budget is a topic for a later chapter. Let us simply say here that asking for a larger budget, and showing the appropriate legislators that it is in their interest to give it to you, will often yield results. When it comes to organizational growth, being assertive pays off. Assertive organizations reap budgetary dividends.[15]

Finding a Niche

Sometimes public organizations need not resort to saber rattling. Consider the U.S. Postal Service. It has few friends and is constantly under fire from Congress, the public, and even the executive branch. The Postal Service has had a full range of difficulties—labor problems, funding problems, deficits, and antiquated procedures. It has been charged with being an inefficient monopoly. For years some critics have claimed that there is no justification for its privileged monopoly protection. Private alternatives would, it is claimed, deliver the mail more effectively for less money. Indeed, the Postal Service now finds itself in intense competition in both the overnight express delivery market and the parcel delivery market.

As a government corporation the Postal Service is supposed to operate like a business. If James Miller III, President Reagan's second director of the Office of Management of Budget and a free-market zealot, had his way, the Postal Service would have lost all of its budgetary protection and would have been forced to compete even more fully in the marketplace. But so far it has withstood a full frontal assault on its existence—with the help of members of Congress. Closing a post office, for example, is almost as difficult as closing a military installation. It means loss of jobs and, perhaps more importantly, symbolically expresses a dying community. In rural areas it could also mean a reduction in service. How has the Postal Service withstood the on-again–off-again pounding from free-market critics? With the help of well-placed members of Congress and an organized work force, it has found a niche, one that gives it a substantial lease on life.

Sometimes it pays to be inconspicuous. During the making of the 1982 federal budget, President Reagan's motto might have been "When in doubt, cut." Few agencies aside from the mammoth Department of Defense were spared the axe. One that was so spared was the U.S. Patent Office; indeed, it received an increase of 4.8 percent. Somehow the administration's budget cutters agreed with the Patent Office's claim that it needed additional funds to reduce the backlog of patent applications from America's inventors. Why is it so important to cut the backlog? As a patent office bureaucrat pointed out, "You can't have people out there spending time and money only to discover America all over again."[16] Translation: The Patent Office has an obligation to let the would-be Thomas Edisons of the country down gently—in a reasonable period of time. Evidently, the Patent Office found its niche even during fiscally perilous times.

BUREAUCRATIC POLITICS OF ORGANIZATIONAL MAINTENANCE

Not all organizations grow. Some languish; others wilt. Some regenerate; others degenerate. But public organizations have an uncanny ability to survive, if not prosper. What are the survival instincts of public organizations?

Three Sources of Organizational Conservatism

Organizations survive because they are conservative. They try to protect their current position, and they resist changes that may endanger their existence. Here are some of the sources of innate organizational conservatism:

Finite resources.   Even if a public organization's managers are budgetary wizards, resources are still finite. When the pie ceases to grow, when it even begins to shrink, organizations will adopt strategies to protect themselves from budgetary cuts. Organizational survival takes precedence over everything else, and preservation breeds caution—which, in turn, makes organizations conservative.

Size.   The organizational life cycle has a paradox. Much effort is put into those factors that will stimulate the growth of an organization. The young organization takes risks, it reaches out to its environment, and it adopts an assertive posture, especially when it comes to budgetary expansion. But once big organizations conserve, they get rigid. Anthony Downs argued that first, as organizations grow, it becomes necessary to impose external controls on them (often from monitoring agencies) in the form of rules and regulations. Meanwhile, the organizations try to circumvent the controls. Second, as organizations get bigger they become more specialized; therefore, it takes longer to make decisions because top management must coordinate the various specializations. Third, with increasing size, the distance between first-level managers and top management is lengthened, thereby making it more time-consuming to make decisions. Add all of this up, according to Downs, and you get an organization that becomes more and more rigid as it becomes larger and older.[17]

Statutory inertia.   Organizational conservatism is aided by the inertia inherent in the legislation that brought the organization into existence in the first place. Organizations, to put it another way, are not like old soldiers. They do not fade away. Congress must do something to put them to rest. Congress must stop funding the organization, or it must change the initial legislation that established the organization in the first place. If Congress does neither, organizations can have a long life—even when top management has prepared the organization for its eternal bureaucratic resting place.

The Appalachian Regional Commission is a case in point. The Reagan administration slated the commission for extinction. Albert P. Smith, Jr., the chairman of the commission, had accepted this fate. He even found another job—as publisher of six newspapers in Kentucky. But he just couldn't give up his $59,000-a-year job as commission chairman, even though his bureaucratic life was supposed to be terminal, because Congress was not prepared to sign the organizational death certificate. As Mr. Smith put it, "We had more bipartisan support than they [the administration] reckoned."[18] Meanwhile, the commission received a $150 million appropriation and an administrative guarantee of only a brief time to live. It is still alive.

Organizational Maintenance: The Logic of Politics

You can't always trust political ideology. A hallmark of the Reagan administration's approach to energy was to allow the marketplace to work more freely, unfettered by government interference. To achieve this objective the administration proposed changes in the tax laws that would stimulate corporate investment and the dismantling of government agencies that stood in the way of the market. One such agency was the Synthetic Fuels Corporation (often called Synfuels for short).

Synfuels, a public corporation, was created under the Carter administration. Reagan officials made it clear, even during the transition period between the two administrations, that they did not agree with the Synfuels concept. They simply did not believe that the federal government could really do much to produce synthetic fuels. Yet when they had the chance to abolish the agency, they failed to seize the opportunity. Since Synfuels was in its organizational infancy, this failure was not caused by any grudging acceptance of the corporation's effectiveness. Nor did the organization curry favor with influential members of Congress; interest groups were not demanding the organization's protection; and President Reagan did not make a philosophical about-face.

John A. Hill, deputy administrator of the Federal Energy Administration in the Ford administration offered an intriguing and simple explanation. Remember the period under discussion. President Reagan's chief budget cutter at the time, David Stockman, director of the Office of Management and Budget, was putting together massive budget cuts for the 1982 budget. As Hill put it, ''The only answer to this question [why Synfuels was not eliminated] that I can find is that Mr. Stockman may have decided that he could not fight every battle at once and that the corporation was the least harmful of the budgetary evils since it threatened no near-term outlays.''[19] As Hill readily conceded, even this explanation may be incorrect. But it does show that elementary political logic can take precedence over other explanations for why an organization survives in the face of all odds.

The Peace Corps—Yes, It Is Still Around!

The Peace Corps was founded in the early days of the New Frontier when thousands of young people answered President Kennedy's call, "Ask not what your country can do for you but what you can do for your country." By 1966, 15,500 volunteers enlisted to bring American know-how—or at least youthful enthusiasm—to developing countries around the world. Recruiters appeared on college and university campuses. Applicants who were selected took intensive language courses as preparation for assignments in Africa, Asia and Latin America. Some volunteers brought engineering and agricultural skills with them. Many taught English as a second language.

By 1976 the Corps withered. Several problems developed. Dissatisfaction with the Vietnam War brought the number of volunteers down to 6,000. President Nixon, no fan of the agency, merged it with a domestic volunteer effort and the new agency became Action. In addition, many developing countries did not find the volunteers all that helpful and wanted people with more specialized training. It looked like the agency would be "nickeled and dimed" out of existence.

In an unanticipated development, the Peace Corps was having a renaissance by the late 1980s. Under the vigorous leadership of Loret Miller Ruppe the Corps has been rejuvenated with the help of some friends in Congress. In particular, she initiated recruiting efforts to attract skilled individuals such as recent dental school graduates and farmers who are willing to serve for shorter periods than two years. Older volunteers are recruited; financial and educational incentives are being used to attract volunteers. While the Corps has not returned to the glory days of the New Frontier, it is certainly making a comeback.

□ Source: David Rampe, "Yes, the Peace Corps Is Alive and Full of Vigor," The New York Times, June 16, 1988, p. B9.

Organizational Maintenance through Planned Shrinkage

Some organizations hang on by getting smaller. Planned shrinkage is one way to respond to external threats to one's existence. By getting smaller, organizations may be able to accommodate a policy of retrenchment while solidifying a more modest organizational mission.

Anne Gorsuch Burford was head of the Environmental Protection Agency (EPA) during part of President Reagan's first term. Filled with antibureaucratic fervor, Burford was not merely a compliant soldier in the fight to "cut government back to size"; she relished the opportunity to lead the charge. In her view, a smaller EPA was a better EPA.

Why? As a probusiness, antigovernment zealot, Burford believed that less government interference would serve everyone's interests. She implemented her deregulation objective by reducing the number of personnel in the agency and the size of EPA's budget. With fewer people and less money, the agency would have to do less. As far as Burford and the administration were concerned, doing less was just what they wanted from EPA.

Burford found out that her zeal in shrinking the organization would contribute to her own political demise. During the unfolding of the 1982 budget she received a considerable amount of "bad press." The environmental interest groups mounted an attack on Burford and her efforts to castrate the agency. Their criticisms were partly successful. Congress restored some of the funds that were slashed by the Reagan administration's budgetary axe. For Fiscal Year (FY) 1983 Burford toned down her criticisms of the environmentalists and moderated her budget-cutting fervor. Environmental groups were relieved that her crusade was slowed down.[20] But unfortunately for Burford her accommodation came too late. With mounting criticism of EPA and charges of failure to enforce the law, she resigned in spring 1983 as EPA director. In an effort to restore the agency's tarnished image, President Reagan appointed William Ruckelshaus, EPA's first director, to head the battle-fatigued organization.

ORGANIZATIONAL DEATH

Organizations do expire. But they die in different ways. The causes of organizational death are the subject of the rest of this chapter.

Death through Success

In his classic book *The Politics of the Budgetary Process,* Aaron Wildavsky cautioned, "avoid too good results."[21] This advice is offered to the naive bureaucrat who, proud of the organization's performance, is prepared to claim total success in the achievement of a mission. The bureaucrat may be committing organizational suicide. Put yourself in the position of a fiscally tight-fisted legislator who hears that an organization has successfully fulfilled its mission; it has "solved" a complex public policy problem. What would you do? Surely there is no point in continuing the organization, for if it is 100 percent successful, there is little left to do.

Managers of public organizations have, by and large, heeded Wildavsky's advice. They may claim progress, at least satisfactory performance—but there is always room for some improvement, for the need to improve provides a lease on organizational life.

Death through success is rare in government. One reason is that since it is difficult to measure organizational effectiveness in the public sector, there are really no unambiguous indicators that can be used to determine success. Organizational success, like beauty, is in the eye of the beholder, and success is relative. One may judge organizational success in terms of other organizations, opportunities forgone, the cost of success, and the length of time it took to become successful. But perhaps most important, death through success is rare in government because organizations have adopted the famous "March of Dimes" strategy toward extended life. When a cure for polio was found, the March of Dimes did not disappear. It took on other functions, other causes, other responsibilities. Similarly, the U.S. cavalry is not extinct even though battles are no longer fought on horseback. Also, as we learned earlier, NASA did not close its doors right after an astronaut walked on the surface of the moon.

Death through Obsolescence

Sometimes problems are not solved by organizations; they just fade away. Problems may often have a fixed life span. When their time has come, when life is "supposed" to be over, the organizations that were created to manage the problems are put to rest.

This type of death is common to organizations that were created in response to a major external event or series of events—events that caused major societal dislocations, for example, war and depression. Recall that the OPA was established to deal with war-induced inflation during World War II. When the war was over, the agency was dismantled. The same situation applied to the "alphabet soup" agencies that were created by President Roosevelt during the New Deal. The purpose of the various agencies was to get the country out of the severe Depression. By the end of the 1930s the economic picture had brightened, and during World War II (1941–1945) unemployment disappeared. So did the agencies.

Were these organizations successful? Historians still debate the extent of success that can be attributed to the New Deal agencies. In the case of the OPA, even its director, hardly an unbiased observer, concedes in his memoirs that one cannot claim total success.[22] Success, it turns out, is not the source of some organizations' demise. It is more simple than that. They are just not needed anymore, and a quiet death comes to them.

Death through Reorganization

Not everyone believes in reincarnation, except when it comes to organizations.

Government organizations often seem to expire, from some superficial evidence. In Washington, D.C., telephone numbers change so frequently that government telephone directories are obsolete almost as soon as they are printed. Top political executives come and go. Most telling, the names of government agencies—offices, divisions, bureaus—are constantly being transformed. In all of this one would surely stumble over some corpses.

Kaufman, in *Are Government Organizations Immortal?*, commented that between 1923 and 1973, there were twenty-seven organizational deaths in the federal government. But once many of these deaths are analyzed carefully, their cause becomes obvious. Kaufman noted, for example, that the War Frauds Section in the Department of Justice was created after World War I to bring legal action against individuals who had committed fraud against the U.S. government during the war. It was later absorbed by the Claims Division and eventually expired. A second illustration is even more instructive. The Treasury Department had an agency called the Supervising Architect. It was taken over by the Public Buildings Branch, itself part of the Department's Procurement Division. During the New Deal it was absorbed by the Public Buildings Administration, which was part of the Federal Works Agency. The original agency, Supervising Architect, would not rest comfortably there either. It later became part of the Public Buildings Service in the General Services Administration. Eventually, it lost all traces of its original organizational identity when it was subsumed by the Division of Design and Construction.[23]

These geneological expositions highlight an important type of organizational death. Many organizations actually are transformed through reorganization. Sometimes the transformation can be subtle (and minor), offering an extended lease on organizational life. That is, reorganization can be like a "rebirth." But it can also be like reincarnation—where the new organization is only tangentially connected to the old.

Death through Changes in Policy

Sometimes it doesn't matter whether or not an organization is successful. Its very existence bespeaks of programs and policies that are anathema to the new ascendants to political office. When this happens organizational death is on the horizon.

Let's return to the Office of Economic Opportunity, the focal point of President Johnson's war on poverty. As noted, there has been (and continues to be) much debate about the effectiveness of the war and the organizations that did battle. President Nixon did not want to continue it. Indeed, he tried, through his ill-fated "family assistance plan," to redirect (and limit) the federal government's policies toward the poor, but his efforts ran up against many political stumbling blocks.[24] Nevertheless, one casualty of the changes in social welfare policy was the OEO.

A similar situation occurred during the administration of Jimmy Carter. President Carter accepted the idea, prevalent in the late 1970s, that many government regulations were counterproductive and costly. Many critics of government regulation argued, for example, that they often restricted competition and drove up costs, which were passed on to consumers in the form of higher prices. Deregulation would stimulate competition and drive down prices.

Deregulation was first applied to the airlines industry. The government organization the Civil Aeronautics Board (CAB) began to shrink. It loosened control over the industry and allowed the market to prevail. Initially, new companies entered the marketplace and fierce competition developed over popular routes such as New York City to Los Angeles, Washington, D.C., to Chicago, and Chicago to New York. Airlines mergers increased, however, thereby shrinking competition; ticket prices began to rise, and passengers complained. Meanwhile, the CAB underwent a slow, planned death.

Policy shifts often signal the end of an organization's life. But many a death certificate has had to be rewritten as the official date of expiration becomes delayed—and delayed again. President Reagan included the dismantling of the Departments of Education and Energy in his campaign platform in 1980. During his administration his policy stance never changed: Education was the province of state and local governments; the federal role should be diminished; and the Department of Education should be dismantled. In energy the president claimed that the federal government played no useful role. He argued that on the contrary, it interfered with the marketplace. But putting cabinet-level departments out of business is, at best, a long, protracted political struggle.

Death through Failure

The popular image of bureaucracy is not pretty![25] Bureaucrats are said to be bunglers; bureaucracies are inefficient and ineffective. Bureaucratic "horror stories" sometimes fill the lull at dinner parties. If it is so easy find fault with bureaucracies, why do they last so long? Some don't.

In 1976 Colorado was the first state to pass a "sunset" law, which required state agencies to justify their bureaucratic existence (by showing that they were effective and needed) or face sudden legislative death. Many states followed Colorado's lead. On July 1, 1977, Colorado held the first public execution. Three state agencies were put to death: the state Athletic Commission (a budget of $5,750), the Board of Registration for Sanitarians (a budget of $375), and the Board of Shorthand Reporters (a budget of $685). The total saving for the state was $6,810; it cost $212,000 to review the agencies under the sunset law and write their death certificates.[26]

The bureaucratic stakes can get bigger. In 1968 Congress passed the Omnibus Crime Control and Safe Streets Act. As part of the act Congress established the Law Enforcement Assistance Administration (LEAA), housed in the Department of Justice. Its mission was to give out money, and the amount of money it dispensed in the form of grants to state and local governments was not exactly trivial. In fiscal year 1973 it reached $850 million.

The LEAA funds were supposed to aid state and local governments in "fighting crime." Eight years after the passage of the act, observers were highly critical of the agency and concluded that it made no dent on the incidence of crime in the United States. Congressional criticism mounted, but the LEAA hung on and continued to receive funding. After all, there were a great many local police departments (and state police as well) that appreciated the federal funds and wanted the flow of money to continue. Eventually, the LEAA well ran dry. Its bureaucratic existence could no longer be defended, and it succumbed. The autopsy report read, "death caused by bureaucratic failure."[27]

SUMMARY

Our organizational life cycle has run its course. We saw how organizations are born, how they grow, how they wither, and even how they die. But the analogy has its limits. Human beings are really not like old soldiers; they do die. The only real doubt is how and when, not if or whether. With organizations, death is not inevitable, and cases of organizational rigor mortis, if not rare, are not plentiful. Death by success and death by failure are not very common. Rather, organizations have an inordinate ability to stay alive. One simple reason was mentioned at the beginning of this chapter: many organizations provide the core functions of government. These organizations—the organizations that provide public safety and form the criminal justice system, general government agencies such as tax collection—are highly resilient. They are not likely to experience the sharp cyclical swings evidenced in the organizational life cycle. But since public organizations are so resilient, public organization watchers have tried to understand them better. By understanding organizations, it may be possible to improve their performance.

NOTES

1. The concept of organizational life cycle is described at length in John Kimberly et al., *The Organizational Life Cycle* (San Francisco: Jossey-Bass, 1980).
2. The theory of public goods is found in John G. Head, *Public Goods and Public Welfare* (Durham, N.C.: Duke University Press, 1974).
3. Gabriel Kolko, *The Triumph of Conservatism* (New York: Free Press, 1963), pp. 98–108.
4. Ibid., p. 99.
5. This section is based on James E. Anderson, David W. Brady, and Charles Bullock III, *Public Policy and Politics in America* (North Scituate, Mass.: Duxbury Press, 1978), pp. 354–58.
6. Theodore J. Lowi, *The End of Liberalism* (New York: W. W. Norton, 1979).
7. Ibid., p. 75.
8. For a review of this period see Rowland Egger, "The Period of Crisis: 1933 to 1945," *American Public Administration: Past, Present, Future*, ed. Frederick C. Mosher (University: University of Alabama Press, 1975), pp. 49–96.
9. John Kenneth Galbraith, *A Life in Our Times: Memoirs* (Boston: Houghton Mifflin, 1981), pp. 134–135.
10. Paul R. Schulman, "Nonincremental Policy Making: Notes Toward an Alternative Paradigm," *American Political Science Review* 69 (December 1969): 1354–1370.
11. For a solid review of welfare policy that covers the Great Society programs, see Gilbert Y. Steiner, *The State of Welfare* (Washington, D.C.: Brookings Institution, 1971).
12. Herbert Kaufman, *Are Government Organizations Immortal?* (Washington, D.C.: Brookings Institution, 1976), p. 4.
13. Ibid., p. 5.
14. Martin Tolchin, "Where the Budget Cutters Didn't Want to Cut," *New York Times*, October 3, 1982, p. 8F.

15. Lance T. LeLoup and William B. Moreland, "Agency Strategies and Executive Review: The Hidden Politics of Budgeting," *Public Administration Review* 38 (May/June 1978): 232–239.
16. "Briefing," *New York Times,* October 7, 1981, p. 24A.
17. Anthony Downs, *Inside Bureaucracy* (Boston: Little, Brown, 1967), pp. 158–161.
18. Ben A. Franklin, "Bureaucrat Finds Job Hard to Quit," *New York Times,* August 29, 1982, p. 2A.
19. John A. Hill, "Why Didn't Reagan Simply Kill Synfuels?" *New York Times,* May 31, 1981, p. 2F.
20. Philip Shabercoff, "Environmental Chief Claims a Budget Victory," *New York Times,* October 3, 1982, p. 35.
21. Aaron Wildvasky, *The Politics of the Budgetary Process,* 4th ed. (Boston: Little, Brown, 1984), p. 93.
22. Galbraith, *A Life in Our Times,* pp. 170–175.
23. Kaufman, *Are Government Organizations Immortal?* pp. 58–59.
24. Daniel P. Moynihan, *The Politics of a Guaranteed Income* (New York: Random House, 1973).
25. For a defense of bureaucracy, see Charles F. Goodsell, *The Case For Bureaucracy,* 2nd ed. (Chatham, N.J.: Chantham House Publishers, 1985).
26. "With New Law, Colorado Spends $212,000 to Abolish 3 Agencies," *New York Times,* April 23, 1978, p. 46.
27. Robert Behn, "The False Dawn of The Sunset Laws," *The Public Interest,* no. 49 (Fall 1977): 112–113.

FOR FURTHER READING

Burcherding, Thomas E., ed. *Budgets and Bureaucrats: Theory of Government Growth.* Durham, N.C.: Duke University Press, 1977.
    A collection of essays that use economic reasoning and analysis to explain why government seems to grow.
Downs, Anthony. *Inside Bureaucracy.* Boston: Little, Brown, 1967.
    A modern classic of why and how bureaus and bureaucrats maintain themselves against external threats.
Kaufman, Herbert. *Are Government Organizations Immortal?* Washington, D.C.: Brookings Institution, 1976.
    A long-term public organization watcher tries to explain why so few government agencies actually die.
Kimberly, John, et al. *The Organizational Life Cycle.* San Francisco: Jossey-Bass, 1980.
    Private, nonprofit, and public organizations are all discussed in a series of essays that use the life-cycle concept to explain their coming and going.
United States Government Manual. Washington, D.C.: U.S. Government Printing Office, latest year available.
    A basic sourcebook for organization watchers of the federal government.

CHAPTER 3

Congressional–Agency Relations

The year 1987 provided some high drama for the Congress of the United States. A joint congressional committee investigated the so-called Iran-Contra Affair. This affair was a complicated series of covert actions that involved attempts to dupe the leadership of Iran through an "arms-for-hostages" deal. At the same time, profits from the arrangement were used to finance the Contra insurgents who are in a protracted military conflict with the military forces of Nicaragua. When the story broke, some members of Congress were livid. In their view, the covert activities violated congressional intent, probably violated the law, and demonstrated a total disregard for congressional oversight. In fact, some lawyers thought that the arms-for-hostages idea may have violated at least two statutes: the Intelligence Authorization Act, that was in existence from December 1985 to September 1986, and the Anti-Deficiency Act, which usually prohibits agency spending that was not approved by Congress.[1]

The key administration witnesses were unrepentant. Marine Lieutenant Colonel Oliver North, an assistant to Admiral John Poindexter, director of the National Security Council and a major architect of the Iran-Contra Affair, thought that it was, in his words, "a neat idea." He blamed Congress for vacillating in its commitment to the Contras and said that the administration had to develop strategies independent of the Congress. Admiral Poindexter, when questioned by the committee, said that it was important to establish "plausible deniability" when implementing the covert plan. Like his subordinate, Lieutenant Colonel North, Admiral Poindexter barely concealed his contempt for Congress during the hearings.

Not all executive branch–congressional interactions are so testy. On the contrary, many are routine. Members of Congress are constantly inquiring on behalf of a constituent about the status of an administrative decision. Here is a hypothetical illustration:

Congressman Jonah P. Jones
U. S. House of Representatives
Congress of the United States
Washington, DC 20515

Dear Congressman Jones:

I have been trying without success to find out why my disability check is no longer coming to me. The Social Security Administration says that I am no longer entitled to it. My doctor tells me that I am too sick to work. Could you do something about it?

Yours truly,

James Q. Constituent

This kind of letter from a constituent sets in motion the action known as legislative "casework." Away from the glare of television lights, casework provides few opportunities for the sort of high drama experienced during the Iran–Contra hearings of 1987. But it is one of the classic forms of congressional–agency relations. What creates this contiuum of activity? It is the tension between *administrative discretion* and *accountability*. This tension is reflected in the various occasions for contact between the legislature and executive branch agencies.

CONSTITUTIONAL BASES FOR CONGRESSIONAL–AGENCY RELATIONS

Article I of the Constitution of the United States enumerates the legislative powers of the Congress. Some, like the power to raise and spend money, are indispensable to the operation of government. But Article I does not specify precisely what government programs are to be established. Rather, Congress is granted the power to "provide for the common defence . . . general Welfare . . . (of) the United States." To do this the Constitution grants Congress power "To make all Laws which shall be necessary and proper for carrying into execution the foregoing Powers, and all other Powers vested by this Constitution in the Government of the United States, or in any Department or Officer thereof." The responsibility to *execute* congressional action resides with the executive branch as spelled out in Article II. This so-called separation of powers was never precise. Indeed, it is more accurate to describe the constitutional framework as a *sharing* of powers among the branches. But although sharing may be more descriptively accurate than separation, the relationship between the legislative and executive branches has not always been smooth.

Statutory Birthrights

Executive-branch agencies receive their initiation into the rough and tumble administrative world first through the passing of a statute. Yet the impetus for the creation of a federal government agency may begin with the president. Remember, the Constitution gives the president the power to appoint department heads as he sees fit; nevertheless, it is up to Congress to pass a statute creating the agency *and* providing the funds to keep it alive.

Congress may create an agency by establishing an administrative unit within an existing executive department. When a major new policy initiative is begun, and the president or Congress wants to emphasize the initiative, a new agency with an appointed administrator may be established. A good example is the creation of the National Aeronautics and Space Administration (NASA). NASA was established after the Soviet Union's launch of Sputnik in 1957. President Eisenhower, with the legislative support of the Congress, launched the space program, in part, through the creation of NASA. When agencies are supposed to be independent and nonpartisan, Congress has used the commission form of organization. The various regulatory agencies such as the National Labor Relations Board, the Federal Trade Commission, and the Interstate Commerce Commission were given quasi-judicial powers through their respective statutory birthrights.[2]

A statutory birthright comes with the power to implement legislative intent. Often, the intent of Congress is by no means clear. After all, since legislation may be the product of protracted conflicts and negotiations among congressional committees, interest groups, and individual members, the legislative language may be imprecise. Congress therefore *delegates* to the executive branch agencies the right to devine legislative intent from the statute. The scope of delegation, either narrow or broad, when not clearly specified in the law itself, may become the subject of future judicial interpretation.

Why wouldn't Congress specify precisely its intentions in statute? Let's consider an agency like the Environmental Protection Agency (EPA) as an illustration. The mission of the EPA, in a nutshell, is to enforce regulations concerning the environment. The practical problem, however, is that the state of our knowledge is rarely equal to the regulatory needs at the moment. One way to deal with this situation is to grant the agency a significant amount of administrative latitude to initiate new regulations, and retire existing ones that are no longer needed, as conditions change.

Executive appointments. Congressional–executive relations does not stop once the executive branch agency is created. A top manager must be appointed. The Constitution gives the president the power to appoint "Ministers and Consuls . . . and all other Officers of the United States." Article II, Section 2, of the Constitution requires that these appointments have the "Advice and Consent of the Senate." Senate confirmation is usually, but by no means always, routine. Sometimes a member of the Senate can hold up confirmation hearings and, in effect, "kill" a presidential nomination. Senator Jesse Helms of North Carolina, a staunch anti-Communist, frequently showed his displeasure with the thrust of foreign policy by bottling up nominations in committee.

The first weeks of President Bush's young administration in 1989 were filled with high drama concerning his nomination of former Texas Senator John Tower for the post of secretary of defense. A tough minded conservative Republican who was considered very knowledgeable about defense policy, Tower's nomination initially was considered a wise choice. But it quickly ran into serious trouble. Democrats were concerned about his close ties with defense contractors and felt that this could create conflicts of interest. Alone, this controversy would not have prevented his confirmation. But when information included in the Federal Bureau of Investigation (FBI) report was leaked to the press all "political hell" broke loose. According to the report, Senator Tower was said to have a drinking problem. In addition, allegations about marital infidelity surfaced. Republicans cried foul and said that these were smear tactics. Senator Sam Nunn of Georgia, seen by many as a scholarly gentleman of moderately conservative leanings, spearheaded the attacks in his position as chairman of the Senate Armed Services Committee. In March 1989 Senator Tower's nomination went down to defeat in the Senate where the Democrats held a majority.

Presidents naturally try to promote their policies through executive appointments. They may select individuals with a specific ideological cast to effect change in the executive agencies. Political "headhunters" search for young, intelligent people who can pass the various "litmus tests" on issues such as school prayer, abortion, the proper role of the federal government in regulating the economy, and social welfare. Here is one such profile from the previous administration.

'The Last Job a Normal Person Would Want'
Robert Pear

When Nabers Cabaniss was an undergraduate at Princeton University in the late 1970's, most students were political liberals. But already the conservative flame was beginning to flicker within her.

She was a strong believer in "minimal government" because she felt that "government's sole role was the protection of individual life and liberty." She majored in biology "out of a reverence for life," she says, and she originally intended to become a physician.

But instead, after working as a Senate aide for five years and after studying Christian theology for a year at Regent College in Vancouver, British Columbia, Miss Cabaniss became head of the Government's family planning program in Washington this summer. As such, she is on the front lines of a fierce battle over abortion as President Reagan tries to cut off Federal funds for family planning clinics that counsel poor women about abortion.

Miss Cabaniss, 30 years old, is also in charge of the Government's adolescent family life program, which was established in 1981 with the goals of reducing the number of teen-age pregnancies and discouraging adolescent sexual activity. Together, the two programs have a budget of $156.5 million and employ 35 people at the Federal level.

"I have strong pro-life convictions," Miss Cabaniss said in an interview in her modest but airy Government office.

"That is the motivating factor in the work I do. I can't imagine I would want to be in this spot if I didn't have those convictions. It's the last job a normal, sane person would want to inflict on himself or herself."

"Everything we deal with here is a prescription for controversy," she added.

Miss Cabaniss (pronounced CAB-uh-niss) is an example of the ardent young conservatives who have found a home in the Reagan Administration. Like New Deal alumni who populated later Democratic administrations, the young conservatives see themselves as having gained the professional experience and political credentials to run the Government and to perpetuate the Reagan brand of conservatism for years to come.

Miss Cabaniss's college roommate, Liza Schlafly Forshaw, now a lawyer, recalled that "the late 70's were still fairly radical times on American campuses," but that Miss Cabaniss was "always a person of conservative and traditional attitudes."

NO DRUGS, SEX, ALIENATION

Mrs. Forshaw, the daughter of Phyllis Schlafly, the conservative crusader who first became widely known for her opposition to the proposed equal rights amendment, said in an interview: "Nabers never touched drugs. She never engaged in premarital sex. She seldom drank, and when she did it was very abstemiously. She never experienced the kind of alienation from her parents that so many college students do."

Miss Cabaniss was recommended for her current job by leaders of the anti-abortion movement, including Senator Jesse Helms of North Carolina and Representative Henry J. Hyde of Illinois, both Republicans.

Her title at the Department of Health and Human Services is deputy assistant secretary for population affairs. The sensitivity of the job is obvious from the fact that her two predecessors left in a swirl of controversy.

One, Jo Ann Gasper, was dismissed in July by Dr. Otis R. Bowen, the Secretary of Health and Human Services, after she disobeyed his instructions to renew two grants for the training of nurses at clinics run by Planned Parenthood groups.

Another predecessor, Marjory E. Mecklenburg, resigned in February 1985 amid allegations by a Congressional aide that she had misused official travel funds. Investigators found no evidence of criminal wrongdoing.

A SOUTHERN ACCENT

Miss Cabaniss was born in Birmingham, Ala., and she still has more than a trace of a Southern accent. She grew up in northern Virginia. Her father, an Army colonel, retired when she was 12 years old. She says she remembers her family as being "politically aware and conservatively oriented."

A significant change in her views occurred in 1980 or 1981.

"In my earlier days, I opposed abortion, but I thought the wrongness in abortion was the infliction of pain upon innocent life," she recalled. "But if pain is the issue, you could justify euthanasia or even infanticide as long as you anesthetize the child.

"I could not go along with the logical consequences of my own beliefs when I framed the argument that way," she said. "As soon as society starts deciding what life is meaningful and judging by arbitrary standards such as pain, we put ourselves into a morally reprehensible position. So I rejected the pain argument, the idea that you could justify the destruction of human life as long as no pain is involved."

From 1982 to 1984 Miss Cabaniss worked on family issues for Senator Jeremiah Denton, a conservative Alabama Republican who designed the adolescent family life program. In 1985 she took a job at the Department of Health and Human Services as director of the program, which remains one of her responsibilities.

The program, derided by critics as an effort to promote chastity, is having some success, according to Miss Cabaniss, who insists that "abstinence is the only 100 percent effective method of family planning."

More than one million adolescents become pregnant each year, she said, and about half of all American teenagers have had sexual intercourse. But, she said, Government surveys suggest that the proportion of adolescent girls who are sexually active "is going down in the black community and has leveled off in the white community."

Thus, she asserted, even before people became alarmed about the AIDS epidemic, teen-agers were becoming more conservative in their sexual behavior.

The philosophy of the family life program is remarkably similar to the message of Nancy Reagan's campaign against drug abuse: "Just say no." A Government booklet urges teen-agers not to "give in" to their sexual feelings. "Saying 'no' can be the best way to say, 'I love you,'" the brochure advises.

In April, Judge Charles R. Richey of the Federal District Court here ruled that a key part of the program was unconstitutional because it violated the requirement for separation of church and state. Under the program, he said, Federal money has been used to finance sex education projects "directed by members of religious orders," as part of religious curriculums, in classrooms "adorned with religious symbols."

He issued an order forbidding the Government to distribute any more funds to religious organizations. But last month Chief Justice William H. Rehnquist suspended the order pending an appeal by the Reagan Administration.

THE GRANTS CONTINUE

As a result, Miss Cabaniss said, "we continue to give grants to religious organizations, as well as to other private and public groups."

Janet Benshoof, a lawyer for the American Civil Liberties Union who filed the lawsuit challenging the program, said that in disbursing funds to religious organizations, Miss Cabaniss had "carried out Senator Denton's intention to a tee."

"It's an ideological program, and she's an ideological person," Ms. Benshoof said.

Said Miss Cabaniss: "I won't dispute the notion of being ideological if that means having strong convictions."

□ *Source: "Profile: Nabers Cabaniss," by Robert Pear, September 16, 1987. Copyright © 1987 by the New York Times Company. Reprinted by permission.*

So-called New Right political appointees could be found throughout the federal government in the 1980s. But were they effective? Not completely! Many found their experiences frustrating; ideas worked out in conservative university political clubs are not easily put into practice in behemoth executive branch agencies. Not the least of their problems was the staying power of higher civil servants, always skeptical of political appointees who have a well-defined ''agenda'' that they want to implement.

Civil Service

The civil service, as a check on executive discretion, naturally predates the Reagan years. Indeed, the Pendleton Act of 1883 is generally viewed as the beginning of the modern civil service in the United States. Like other legislation, Congress may exercise influence on the executive branch by initiating or making changes in the federal civil service. Congress, through statutory controls, for example, can affect compensation, exemptions to the merit principle, classification of civil service positions, retirement benefits and the conditions for removal from a government job. The overall impact of the statutes has been to narrow an administration's discretion with respect to policies and procedures governing the federal government workforce. A similar pattern exists in most state governments as well.

OCCASIONS FOR CONTACT BETWEEN EXECUTIVE AGENCIES AND CONGRESS

Managers in the executive branch have frequent contact with Congress. Some of the contact is formal and is required by law. Much of the interaction has developed over many years and, even when not expressly required by law, is nevertheless expected if relations are to remain cordial. The skillful executive quickly learns the whys and ways of executive–legislative relations.

Hearings and Investigations

Turn on C-Span and you will sometimes tune in to a congressional hearing. You may even see a person from an executive-branch agency testifying before the committee. Often, to the uninitiated, the subject is arcane; the discussion may sound positively boring. You may wonder where the action is!

Sometimes what you see is all that there is to see. Congressional hearings may be perfunctory, when members routinely perform their "oversight" function inquiring about selected agency activities. Business-as-usual activities, after all, do not make headlines, they do not provide a member of Congress with much political mileage. Although agencies recognize these facts, they also understand that mundane oversight hearings cannot be taken totally for granted. For one thing, members of Congress can fall back on formal methods of control: appointment powers, the budget, and perferred legislation by the agency and the administration. In addition, what was initially a hearing may evolve into a more formal investigation, followed, in some instances, by litigation in the federal courts. This is precisely what happened in the "Irangate" episode that began this chapter.

Authorizations and Appropriations

The budget process in Washington, D.C., is an annual ritual. Agencies prepare budgets; they are reviewed by the Office of Management and Budget. Each year the president submits his budget, usually in early February, to the Congress. The process provides several opportunities for agency-congressional contacts. When agencies propose new programs or extensions of existing programs that are about to lapse, these proposals must be authorized by a standing committee in the House of Representatives and the Senate. The procedure often calls for congressional hearings where agency officials justify their programs before the committees. Once authorized, an agency must receive *appropriations* before funds can actually be spent by the agency. Both authorizations and appropriations give legislators the opportunity to scrutinize agency activities. Scrutiny does not stop at the appropriations stage. When Congress grants funds to an agency, it usually stipulates when and how the funds may be used. Rules governing the timing of spending and the ability to move funds from one part of the budget to another are methods to control agency activities. Why would Congress specify precisely, or loosely, what it will tolerate when an agency spends its budget? It depends on the agency's "track record" with Congress and the agency's current credibility. Consider the example of the Department of Defense (DOD):

According to Louis Fisher, the DOD's track record in the 1960s did not instill a great deal of congressional confidence in the agency. In particular, the DOD moved funds around in the department's budget, without adequate prior congressional approval, and thereby financed the extension of the Vietnam War into Cambodia in the early 1970s.[3] Eventually, the concealment of this activity from Congress moved some members of the House of Representatives to include the secret bombing of Cambodia as one of the proposed articles of impeachment of Present Nixon. The House Judiciary Committee, however, voted 26–12 not to include this article with the others that became the bases of the formal article of impeachment of the president.[4] Since that time, the DOD's ability to transfer funds without prior congressional approval has been circumscribed.[5]

Casework

Your social security check did not arrive. What can you do? Your son was arrested while traveling in Europe, and he is in an Italian jail. The Department of Veterans Affairs just informed you that you are no longer eligible for education benefits and you quit your job expecting to return to college on a full-time basis. Your mother's great aunt Coleen wants to emigrate from her native Ireland to the United States. What can you do in each of these situations? Write your elected representatives; sometimes it can be funny as I found out several years ago.

Several years ago I was in the U.S. Army Reserves. While on active duty at Fort Monmouth, New Jersey, I learned that it was possible to request an early discharge from active duty if the reason was that you planned to return to the university. It seemed like a loophole in an obscure army regulation to me and not designed for reservists, but I inquired and started the paperwork at the fort. In the meantime I decided to write to my congressman, the late Benjamin Rosenthal. I said that I wanted to go back to graduate school but I didn't think that my request for an early discharge from active duty would be approved. Well, it was. The problem was that the commanding general at the fort received an inquiry from the Department of the Army about the status of my request. Evidently, my letter to Congressman Rosenthal led to this inquiry and the congressman had to be answered. One day I received a call from an irate sergeant. "Straussman, get your butt over here right away. We got a 'congressional' on you." (That is what they called the inquiry.) The sergeant was given the task of drafting the reply, and he couldn't find out who approved my request, when it was approved, and why it was approved. He calmed down once I gave him the particulars and he was able to verify my story. Two days after I was discharged from active duty I received a letter from Congressman Rosenthal telling me that he was pleased to inform me that my request for an early discharge from active duty was granted by the army.

Mediation between executive branch agencies and constituents is known as *casework*. Representatives do not usually do the work themselves. Rather, legislative aides do the footwork—deciphering the nature of the request and its plausibility, contacting the appropriate executive-branch agency requesting information and clarification, and drafting a response to the constituent.

Casework has become a more and more time consuming feature of the legislator's job. Why? The political scientist Morris Fiorina provides an interesting interpretation. As everyone knows, the size and scope of federal government have expanded greatly since 1932. As Fiorina pointed out—and as my own anecdote above confirms—constituents have contact, and eventually problems, with federal bureaucracies. Who can the beleaguered constituent turn to? The elected representative, naturally. Also, since the government agencies know that the elected representatives have resources, particularly control over budgets, they are likely to be responsive to legislative requests. The responsiveness will increase as the legislator gains seniority in Congress. Notice, the demand of casework can now work to the incumbent's advantage since the legislator can point to the service provided to constituents while in office. The bureaucracy, by responding to the changed importance of legislative casework, is now a silent partner in the power of incumbency and the corresponding decline of marginal congressional districts.[6]

Drafting Legislation

A simplistic view of the federal government would presume that laws are drafted by members of Congress. Sometimes they are; frequently, they are not. Statutes can be technical and require expertise not ordinarily found in Congress—not even among the highly trained congressional staffs. Where are the specialists? They are in the executive branch agencies.

Why would unelected civil servants draft legislation that is later introduced by elected representatives? One answer is that legislative drafting is a way to pursue agency objectives. That is, framing a future statute furthers the agency's collective image of "good" public policy.

INTERPRETING AGENCY–LEGISLATIVE RELATIONS: THE SELF-INTEREST PRINCIPLE

What actually motivates the relations between bureaucrats and legislators? One analytic tool to explain the interactions, drawn from economic theory, is that both bureaucrats and legislators are motivated by their own self-interest. In an interesting application of this perspective, R. Douglas Arnold in *Congress and the Bureaucracy* showed that bureaucrats are presumably motivated by budgetary security for their agency, budgetary growth for their agency, and a sense of public service. Moreover, bureaucrats have a hierarchy of goals that have the rank order just listed. Legislators want to serve their constituencies, and they want to produce an acceptable voting record. Both goals are designed to fulfill an even higher goal—the goal of reelection.[7] Arnold then showed the interplay between the goals of bureaucrats and the goals of legislators (members of the U.S. House of Representatives) through the geographical allocation of selected federal government programs. What did he find? In his words:

> Committees play a dominant role in the politics of geographic allocation. Ordinarily, bureaucrats choose to allocate disproportionate shares of benefits to members of those committees that have jurisdiction over their programs. But these extra shares do not come automatically. They accrue to members who have performed important services, who control resources that bureaucrats desire, or who threaten in some way the achievement of bureaucrats' goals.[8]

But just who dominates the relationship?

DOES CONGRESS "DOMINATE" THE BUREAUCRACY?

There is some scholarly debate about the real influence that Congress has over executive-branch agencies. The debate has a curious history. In 1971 an important book by William A. Niskanen, Jr. (who worked in the U.S. Office of Management and Budget and was also a member of President Reagan's Council of Economic Advisors), entitled *Bureaucracy and Representative Government*, was published. Niskanen argued that government agencies enjoyed a "monopoly" of supply. That is, they could determine, largely unfettered, the amount of a government service that they wanted to produce and put the legislature in a difficult position in that the legislature, having no alternatives, would have to "buy" what the government agency was willing to offer. Niskanen claimed that the result of this monopoly position was a bloated public sector. In a nutshell, Congress was spending more of the public's money than was necessary.[9]

Niskanen's thesis certainly had appeal for those who believed that government spending was excessive. More generally, his book stimulated further studies under the rubric of "public choice" that tried to show why bureaucrats behave as they do. Eventually, a necessary corrective appeared in the scholarly literature. Beginning with the same assumption as Niskanen's—namely, that members of Congress, like bureaucrats, try to maximize their self-interest—this "congressional dominance" school shows that members of Congress will take positive steps to enhance their chances of reelection. How does controlling the bureaucracy help? Quite simply, if members of Congress, through the committee structure, believe that oversight will aid their primary motive, they will use their considerable resources, especially budgets and personnel powers, to force the agencies to "toe the line." Bureaucrats are well aware of these resources and thereby comply with congressional demands.

On closer inspection, the argument that Congress "controls" the bureaucracy is problematical at best. For one thing, the meaning of control is fuzzy. Do bureaucrats always jump when *any* member of Congress says jump? This seems implausible. Next, are bureaucracies constantly "on call," awaiting constant instructions from their legislative superiors? What about the resources at the disposal of Congress? The budget, perhaps the single best control mechanism, is not always an effective weapon in the Congress's arsenal. Some programs are "uncontrollable"; that is, Congress has little real choice over appropriations. Moreover, the very fact that budget decisions are made in several parts of the Congress reduces the effectiveness of the budget as a control mechanism for any single part of Congress. Similar restrictions apply to Congress's control over appointments. Whereas the Senate has confirmation responsibilities, the power of appointment is mainly presidential. Indeed, when Congress turns down a presidential appointment, it is usually front page news.[10]

So does Congress dominate the bureaucracy? The question simplifies a very complicated and fluid process—one that has been evolving for two hundred years. There are ample illustrations of bureaucracy run amuck to question the presumption of the all-powerful legislature. Yet there have similarly been enough testimonies from agency officials who have been chastened by their encounters with congressional committees.

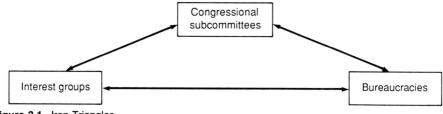

Figure 3.1. Iron Triangles

THE MISSING LINK: INTEREST GROUPS

Sometimes government agencies and parts of a legislative body have overlapping interests. When this happens, cooperative strategies may be employed, sometimes at the expense of the elected chief executive—like the president.

Iron Triangles

The best illustration of this principle of cooperative strategies is the infamous "iron triangles" as depicted in Figure 3.1. The image is simple. Contrary to a very elementary notion of American government that takes the separation of powers among the three branches very literally, the iron triangle concept shows that government decisions are often the product of a complex interplay among special interest groups in society that stand to benefit from a government decision, a part of a government bureaucracy that wants to see a particular decision pursued, and a legislative subcommittee or committee that also has some stake in the outcome. The principle of the iron triangle is that the *joint* action of the three can often overwhelm opposition that is not as organized or has a smaller stake in the outcome.

Illustrations of iron triangles can be found everywhere. Specialized farming interests have their friends in Congress and the U.S. Department of Agriculture. The results include price supports and subsidies. The elderly, through their lobbying group, the American Association of Retired Persons, the venerable octogenarian Congressman from Florida, Claude Pepper (who died in 1989), and sympathetic officials in the Social Security Administration, have promoted health and welfare benefits. College students and university officials have advanced their special interests—student loans and government funding of university research—before congressional committees and with high-level personnel in the Department of Education and the National Science Foundation.

What happens when the political thrust of the administration runs counter to the interests of the iron triangle? Consider the illustration of the "Choyce Cuts":

Adrian Choyce was director of research at the Advanced Agricultural Technology Development and Demonstration Bureau (AATDDB) in the U.S. Department of Commerce. The bureau finances agricultural research that yields technological improvements, particularly for smaller farmers who are not part of what has come to be called "agribusiness."

Although the AATDDB thrived under President Carter, the "cut govern-ment back to size" approach of the incoming Reagan administration spelled trouble for the small bureau. The assistant secretary in charge of the bureau, echoing the administration's ideological stance, said that, if the AATDDB really provides a useful service, it will be picked up by the private sector. Sharp budget cuts were in order and Choyce knew it.

Preparing the 1982 budget was not fun. Choyce and his staff worked out detailed budget cuts based on their best professional criteria. This meant that 15 percent of the work force would be eliminated. The cuts were "leaked" to supporters of the AATDDB—universities with strong agricultural programs, laboratory directors, and the Independent Farms of America organization. These agency "friends" spoke to influential members of Congress, a process some AATDDB members dubbed "co-vert politics." When the political dust cleared, the AATDDB received a 50 percent restoration in the administration's budget cut. Choyce did not rejoice because he knew that the budgetary battle would have to be fought again the next year.

□ *Source: "Budget Beef at AATDDB: The Choyce Cuts" (Kennedy School of Gov-ernment Case Program, 1983).*

Was the iron triangle effective? It depends how you look at it. From the administration's perspective the budget was reduced, and therefore, the objective of shrinking the government activity was working. From the vantage point of the agency and the interest groups, their efforts to mitigate the political fallout was also successful. They preserved some of their programs.

The concept of the iron triangle is not flawless. A literal acceptance of the idea would have you believe that all significant government activity is organized around iron triangles and, in particular, that interest groups have a dominant im-pact on government policy. This image, summarized in the well-known phrase "What is good for General Motors is good for the country" is flawed. Here is a list of criticisms of the idea:

1. Some groups are not effectively organized. They are underrepresented by not having powerful interest groups to advocate on their behalf. This pertains to the poor in particular.
2. Legislators are often confronted with pressures from different sides of the same issue. It is not always obvious that they will support one side against another.
3. A government agency may take a position on an issue that conflicts with an interest group because it has the best information on the subject.
4. Although a well-organized group may be a prerequisite for political influ-ence, the interest group may not always have a well-articulated position on a given policy issue.

5. The degree of political influence of an interest group may be related to the number of groups in the policy arena. This would represent the amount of competition that exists. More competition is likely to diminish the power of an iron triangle.

It makes much more sense to develop an analytical scheme from which to classify different patterns of interest group–bureaucracy–legislative relations. In some situations, for example, an interest group may have a *monopoly of supply* of something desired by an executive-branch agency. In this case the agency may restrict other groups from trying to influence policy. John Chubb, in his *Interest Groups and the Bureaucracy*, said that the Office of Oil and Gas in the U.S. Department of Interior supports the interests of the oil companies through the National Petroleum Council.[11] If there is weak legislative scrutiny of the association, or even aquiescence, the pattern that will emerge will be the stereotypical iron triangle. A more common variation, however, is a *competitive* situation—one in which interest groups in competition with one another vie for influence with both the bureaucracy and the legislature. The classic struggle between organized labor and associations representing business certainly compete to influence the decisions of the National Labor Relations Board and the U.S. Department of Labor. A perennial struggle that many readers of this book may have been affected by has been the minimum-wage laws. Organized labor has always been in favor of higher minimum-wage laws. Associations representing small businesses have opposed increases in the minimum wage. At the opposite pole from the monopolistic arrangement is a situation in which a government agency identifies with groups that would bear the costs of an interest group. In this situation the agency does not form a political association with the dominant interest group; rather, it forges a link between the *cost-bearing* groups and sympathetic segments of the legislature. Chubb described the gradual shift in the efforts to regulate the supply of energy that came about in the aftermath of the 1973 oil embargo. He suggested that this represents this third type of interest group–agency–legislature arrangement.[12]

Organizations and Public Policy

How can we predict when a particular constellation of organizational interests will influence government policy? A provocative scheme was presented by James Q. Wilson several years ago in his *Political Organizations*. Using the costs and benefits of government programs as a way to describe patterns of influence and opposition, Wilson identified four political arrangements that depend on whether the costs and benefits are concentrated narrowly or distributed widely.[13]

Distributed benefits and distributed costs.   Some government programs reach millions of people. These same programs are financed by a large number of people. The best example is social security payments to the elderly. Everyone who earns income and pays taxes also contributes to the Social Security Trust Fund. This is the budgetary mechanism that finances social security. Although criticisms of

both programs surface regularly, they have been largely ineffective. It looks un-
seemly to criticize programs designed to help the elderly. Even when debates
over government spending get intense, advocates of budget cutting invariably
mention that they are not including social security among the government programs that deserve severe pruning. Meanwhile, interest groups such as the Association of Retired Persons are successful in their efforts to protect the program
whereas business organizations who represent groups that will pay costs that exceed their members' benefits will most likely be ineffective.

Concentrated benefits and distributed costs.   Programs that are financed out of general revenue but benefit a targeted group fall under this category. Obviously, the
incentive to organize if you are on the beneficiary side of the equation is great.
Conversely, since costs are widely distributed, it is hard to organize opposition
to programs that fall into this category. Perhaps the best illustrations of this situation are veterans groups and their support of veterans' benefits. Can you sketch
the iron triangle of this illustration?

"Art Imitates Life on the Hill"

Martha Graham, founder of the world famous Martha Graham Dance
Company, needed more money for her company. One source of funding
was the National Endowment for the Arts (NEA), a federal government
agency that receives an annual appropriation from Congress. The NEA
provides money to arts organizations through competitive grant programs. Organizations submit proposals for funding to the NEA; they are
reviewed in an "objective" manner. Some are funded, more are not.

It seems that Graham thought that it would be more effective to go
directly to Congress and bypass the NEA. She found a friend in Senator
DeConcini, Democrat from Arizona. Senator DeConcini tried to put a
special $7 million line item in the 1989 budget for Graham's dance com-
pany because he believed that it was important to protect a "precious
national resource." Officials at the NEA were not pleased. Nor were the
directors of other professional dance companies who were incensed
about the special treatment and unorthodox approach to arts funding
taken by both Graham's company and the senator from Arizona. As one
critic put it, "I would have been thrilled if Senator DeConcini pushed for
increased funding for the NEA." But she was aghast at the idea that $7
million could go to one dance company while all of the other companies
would have to compete for $8 million—the amount that was being appro-
priated in the 1989 budget. It seems that art *can* imitate life when it comes
to interest group politics!

Distributed benefits and concentrated costs.   Who bears the cost of Medicare, the government health program designed to insure that the elderly have minimum health insurance coverage? Social security recipients pay a fee for the insurance; wage earners who pay social security taxes also finance Medicare. So far our costs seem dispersed. But doctors who accept patients who are eligible for Medicare benefits might claim that they also bear costs—the cost of government "red tape," a host of regulations, and payments that are below "market" rates. If you accept these complaints, you acknowledge that some of the costs of the program are concentrated while the benefits are widely distributed. In this situation interest groups representing the doctors will try to influence the legislature to enact statutes that reduce their burdens. Similarly, they will try to influence the Social Security Administration to minimize any adverse regulatory activities contemplated by the agency.

Concentrated benefits and concentrated costs.   Sometimes the benefits to one group come at the expense of another. One example offered by Wilson is the struggle between organized labor and business over control of the National Labor Relations Board. The struggle is ongoing; the product of the struggle at any given time is reflected in the political composition of the board's members. The composition, in turn, reflects the political partisanship of presidential appointments. Although there is no resolution to the struggle, it is largely contained by an unwritten rule—a tradition of professionalism and the avoidance of extremes should govern appointments and the administrative process of the agency. This moderates the influence of interest groups and avoids sharp, unanticipated swings in regulatory policy.[14]

PUTTING THE PIECES TOGETHER: THE CASE OF TAX REFORM

We could now put the pieces of the political mosaic together. Let's see how the components relate to one another in the context of a major change in public policy: the Tax Reform Act of 1986.[15]

Major Issues

No one really likes to pay taxes. Nevertheless, the federal tax system depends, to a large extent, on voluntary tax compliance. That means that most taxpayers file their tax returns by April 15 of each year. They record their earnings and compute their tax liability. Some individuals make mistakes and others are not exactly scrupulously honest. The Internal Revenue Service (IRS) in the U.S. Department of the Treasury has the responsibility for managing the tax system in the United States. This includes monitoring taxpayer compliance and collecting taxes that are owed but not paid.

By the late 1970s the tax system in the United States was in trouble. The list of criticisms included the following:

1. The tax system had become very complicated. Tax *simplification* was needed.
2. The tax system was *inequitable*. Some people did not pay their "fair share" whereas others were unduly burdened.
3. The tax system was *inefficient*. A large number of people were operating in the "underground economy," making unreported income and thereby not declaring some or all of their income.
4. The tax system was *distorting economic decisions*. Some tax laws encouraged economic choices that advantaged specific individuals while hurting the overall economy. Although it seemed that the time for tax reform had come, translating the broad policy objective into specific proposals would not be easy. The vast array of tax advantages for various groups and organizations that had been developed over many years could not be dismantled without serious opposition.

Why Tax Reform Is Difficult

The last sentence in the above list gives it away. When special interests want something, but do not want their benefit to be visible, tax benefits are often more desirable than direct government spending programs. Only the interested and tax specialists know the arcane intricacies of the tax laws. Yet a deduction, exemption, credit, or exclusion can save a company, an industry, or an individual a great deal of money when it is time to file a tax return. Nor are tax benefits only for the rich. The vast majority of the middle class in the United States enjoy tax benefits. Every homeowner, for example, can deduct mortgage interest payments and local property taxes as expenses that reduce federal income tax liability. Charitable deductions help to finance nonprofit organizations such as educational and religious institutions. The depreciation of capital investments helps the small farmer who buys a tractor and the multimillion dollar corporation. The buildup of deductions, exemptions, credits, and exclusions since the passage of the Sixteenth Amendment in 1913 that established the income tax reduced the base of the tax, narrowing taxable income. By the 1980s there were so many tax-shelter schemes that were designed to provide individuals with opportunities to reduce their tax liability that support for change was percolating in Congress and in the administration. Meanwhile, tax rates had climbed substantially to offset the decline in the income tax base. Naturally, this added to the dissatisfaction with the tax system.

By the early 1980s criticism of the federal tax system mounted. Strange things began to happen! Members of Congress from both political parties initiated legislation designed to overhaul some of the inequities and inefficiencies in the federal tax structure. Among the most influential advocates of reform were Senator Bradley, Democrat from New Jersey, and Congressman Gephardt, Democrat from Missouri, who introduced their version of tax reform. On the Republican side Senator Roth of Delaware and Congressman Kemp of Buffalo, New York, introduced their ideas. Meanwhile, the administration, through the Department of the Treasury, presented its version. These versions varied in the particulars; nevertheless, the three major tax-reform initiatives had a few basic objectives in common. They all wanted to reduce the tax rates while eliminating some of the so-called tax loopholes. They all wanted a fairer tax system—and a simpler one. But going from a broad objective to a major shift in policy would not be easy. For many organized interests the stakes were high. Also, for many members of Congress tax reform meant taking away one of the major ways that they could reward interest groups that supported them. It also meant reducing their ability to provide benefits to industry located in their legislative districts.

Getting the Idea Off the Ground

Tax reform received an initial boost from the new senator from New Jersey, former professional basketball star and Princeton University Rhodes Scholar Bill Bradley. Bradley and Congressman Gephardt introduced their "fair tax" legislative proposal in 1982. The heart of the proposal was a "swap"—eliminating and reducing tax loopholes for lowered tax rates. The idea tried to capture the major criticisms of the existing tax system and correct them. It looked as though it was going nowhere fast. Walter Mondale, the Democratic candidate for president in 1984, was lukewarm to the idea. With the federal deficit looming large as a major political issue, Mondale said that, if elected, he would *raise* taxes—an honest, though politically fatal, statement.

After the 1984 election the idea of tax reform resurfaced both in Congress and in the administration. Political executives in the Department of Treasury, under the direction of Secretary of Treasury Donald Regan, began putting together a tax-reform proposal. It was not easy. Inside the department there were differences of opinion about specific changes in the tax code. But the operating rationale for reform was simple: The tax system should not distort individual and corporate economic decisions because of complicated loopholes that work to the advantage of some but ultimately harm the economy. This meant that most tax breaks should be eliminated—an idea that would certainly bring out the tax lobbyists in Washington.

What became known as Treasury I—the administration's proposals—had to do political battle in Congress with other reform proposals. In the broad sense the various proposals shared the common objectives outlined above. But critics, particularly lobbyists, do not focus on the broad outlines; they go right to the specifics, the various provisions that will affect one or more of their cherished tax-code protections. The next phase of tax reform, between 1984 and 1986, was a series of political accommodations to create the needed legislative support for passage of a tax-reform bill. Here is one of many encounters in the words of Jeffrey Birnbaum and Alan Murray, two *Wall Street Journal* reporters who followed the tax-reform efforts carefully and chronicled them in *Showdown at Gucci Gulch:*

> Practical politics was a new and shocking change for the veterans of Treasury I. The transformation was typified by an encounter between Pearlman [a senior official at Treasury] and a group of angry war veterans. The veterans were deeply disturbed about the Treasury I proposal to tax veterans' disability payments, which for years had enjoyed tax-free status. . . . Pearlman, still ensconced in the theoretical tower of Treasury I, started the meeting by asking the triple amputee [the leader of the group] in Socratic fashion, "Why should veterans disability payments be treated differently than any other income?" The meeting went downhill from there.[16]

During 1985 many features of tax reform withered on the political vine. In a nutshell, the year was a constant struggle between the advocates of reform and groups that stood to lose by a particular change in the tax code. Each time a "giveback" was contemplated civil servants in the Treasury Department and congressional staffers had to estimate the impact on lost revenues.

Enter the Democrats

By late spring 1985 the Democrats joined the momentum for tax reform, led by Dan Rostenkowski, chairman of the House Ways and Means Committee. The Democrats were put in an awkward position by Treasury I. They could not be against tax reform, so what Rostenkowski had to do was make reform palatable to a lukewarm committee and a Democrat-controlled House of Representatives. This was a formidable task since some who stood to lose were traditional Democratic party supporters. The Ways and Means bill, for example, included the elimination of the deductibility of state and local taxes when itemizing deductions on the federal income tax return. This hurt so-called high-tax states like New York, and Mario Cuomo, the democratic governor, pressured hard for the repeal of this provision. Tax reform was in real trouble over this issue. Eventually, the idea was scrapped; the lost revenue from keeping the deduction would be replaced with tax rates that were higher than the Treasury proposal.

So it went throughout the fall of 1985 and spring and summer of 1986. Every important change in the code meant billions in revenues for the federal government. Every important change meant that one or more interest groups would be unhappy, thereby putting pressure on the legislative drafters to alter the proposed bill. The reader who wants the blow-by-blow details should consult *Showdown at Gucci Gulch*. As the authors of *Showdown* described, there were many times during the reform's two-year period when it looked as though political stalemates would kill the proposal. In the end, The Tax Reform Act was signed into law by President Reagan on October 22, 1986. The act, all seventeen hundred-plus pages of it, was not exactly what the ex–New York Knicks guard, Princeton graduate, and Rhodes Scholar-turned-senator initially had in mind. Nor was it the pristine Treasury I proposal that was developed in the federal agency. Lobbyists would find it more difficult to deduct their "three martini" lunch as a business expense while consoling one another over their legislative defeat. Meanwhile, many taxpayers couldn't see the advantages of "simplification" when they struggled over the new forms, and changes in the old ones, while trying to get their 1987 tax return in before the April 15, 1988, deadline.

SUMMARY

Both the constitutional principles of the separation of powers *and* checks and balances show that executive branch agencies do not operate in a political vacuum. In fact, *shared powers* between the executive and legislative branches provide the grist for interaction between the two branches. This interaction occurs along several dimensions: (a) when agencies are created by statutory "birthrights"; (b) when high-level political appointments in the executive branch are made; (c) when civil service procedures are initiated or changed by statute.

Executive-branch agencies are continually scrutinized by the legislative branch. Occasions for contact occur along several dimensions. The budget process, for example, gives legislative committees both in Washington, D.C., and in the fifty state capitals the opportunity to examine executive agencies and raise questions that go beyond the spending of the public's money. On a less visible level, legislative "casework"—essentially responding to inquiries from constituents—brings agencies and legislators together. Sometimes the inquiry can be routine. A constituent may complain to his or her representative in Washington that a social security check did not arrive. Perhaps a relative is having immigration problems. There are countless possibilities. As government has become larger and more complex, legislative casework has consumed more and more of the legislator's time. Nevertheless, responsiveness is one political ticket to reelection.

What motivates executive–legislative interactions? The last sentence of the previous paragraph provides a clue. Political scientists during the past twenty years have investigated the "self-interest" principle as the key to explaining legislative and agency behavior. Reduced to the key assumptions, legislators want to get reelected, and executive officials want to "feather their own nest." This may seem crass; however, the pursuit of self-interest can lead to benefical results—not merely for the legislators and executives but for the citizenry as well. Naturally, this view is not shared by all observors of legislative–executive politics. Its narrow perspective about what motivates public servants provides little room for an interpretation that includes the concept of the "public interest."

An alternative conceptual framework concerns the importance of interest groups in the political equation. Organized labor, business associations, retired persons, farmers, even college students, try to influence the conduct of public policy and advance their specific cause. Not all interest groups are equally effective. The chapter includes a perspective, borrowed from the political scientist James Q. Wilson, to explain when an interest group will and will not be successful in influencing policy. The approach shows why retired persons can influence social security, why some farm groups can convince members of Congress to maintain certain agricultural price supports, and why we now have a Department of Veterans' Affairs rather than the old Veterans' Administration.

The chapter ends with a case study of the Tax Reform Act of 1986—one of the more significant pieces of legislation from the past decade. The pieces are put together showing how important players in the executive branch, Congress, and interest groups did political battle over a cantankerous political issue—tax reform. The fact that the end product was a lot different from the initial perspective of the prime movers is testimony to the complexity of legislative–executive relations in the United States.

NOTES

1. Stuart Taylor, Jr., "Iran, Arms, and Nicaragua: Complex Legal Issues Raised," *New York Times*, November 26, 1986, p. A11.
2. Joseph P. Harris, *Congressional Control of Administration* (Garden City, N.Y.: Doubleday, 1964), pp. 34–35.
3. Louis Fisher, *Presidential Spending Power* (Princeton, N.J.: Princeton University Press, 1975).
4. Ibid., pp. 120–121.
5. See Bernard Pitsvada, "Flexibility in Federal Budget Execution," *Public Budgeting and Finance* 3 (Summer 1983): 83–101.
6. Morris P. Fiorina, "The Case of the Vanishing Marginals: The Bureaucracy Did It," *American Political Science Review* 71 (March 1977): 177–181.
7. R. Douglas Arnold, *Congress and the Bureaucracy* (New Haven: Yale University Press, 1979), pp. 20–28.
8. Ibid., p.207.
9. William Niskanen, Jr., *Bureaucracy and Representative Government* (Chicago: Aldine, 1971).
10. For a criticism of the congressional dominance thesis, see Terry Moe, "An Assessment of the Positive Theory of 'Congressional Dominance,'" *Legislative Studies Quarterly* 12 (November 1987): 475–520.
11. John E. Chubb, *Interest Groups and the Bureaucracy* (Stanford, Calif.: Stanford University Press, 1983), pp. 25–26.
12. Ibid., pp. 126–180.
13. The next section is taken from James Q. Wilson, *Political Organizations* (New York: Basic Books, 1973), pp. 332–340.
14. For an extended analysis of the National Labor Relations Board see Terry Moe, "Interests, Institutions, and Positive Theory: The Politics of the NLRB," *Studies in American Political Development*, ed. S. Skowronek (New Haven: Yale University Press, 1987).
15. The following description of tax reform relies heavily on the excellent analysis of the act by Jeffrey H. Birnbaum and Alan S. Murray, *Showdown at Gucci Gulch* (New York: Vintage Books, 1987).
16. Ibid., pp. 79–80.

FOR FURTHER READING

Arnold, R. Douglas. *Congress and the Bureaucracy*. New Haven: Yale University Press, 1979.

    Originally a doctoral dissertation, this study explores the thesis that many federal government programs take on a geographical distribution that mirrors political influence in Congress.

Cain, Bruce, John Ferejohn, and Morris Fiorina, *The Personal Vote: Constituency Service and Electoral Independence*. Cambridge, Mass.: Harvard University Press, 1987.

    Three of the finest political scientists who study legislatures provide a comparative study of constituency casework in the United States and Great Britain.

Fiorina, Morris. *Congress, Keystone of the Washington Establishment*. New Haven: Yale University Press, 1977.

    This very readable little book presents the case for a "self-interest" perspective on legislative politics.

Ogul, Morris. *Congress Oversees the Bureaucracy: Studies in Legislative Oversight*. Pittsburgh: University of Pittsburgh Press, 1976.

    Still one of the best studies of the oversight function of Congress.

Ripley, Randall B., and Grace Franklin. *Congress, The Bureaucracy, and Public Policy*, 4th ed. Chicago: Dorsey Press, 1987.

    Very good coverage of legislative–executive relations across policy areas including regulation, foreign and defense policy, and redistributive policies.

CHAPTER 4

Organization Theory

Most of the readers of this book are probably attending a college or university. Think about how you might describe it to a creature from another planet. You might start by describing the *parts* of the college: the library, athletic field, gymnasium, dormitories, buildings that have different academic departments, computer center, and student center. If you described your college in this way, you would be focusing on the *formal structure*—in fact, only the physical attributes of the formal structure.

If the creature from another planet arrives during registration, you might select a different way to describe your college. You might say, "A college is a place where a bunch of incompetents seem to get a lot of pleasure from harassing me. I have to wait in lines; I can't get the courses I want, at the times I want them, and with the professors I prefer. There is so much red tape here, you just wouldn't believe it." If you described your college in this fashion, you would be focusing on the *pathological* (or dysfunctional) aspects of its "normal" operating procedures.

There is a third explanation. You could say, "It goes like this. I pay money to take courses. In these courses I am supposed to learn things. People, called professors, try to insure that we *do* learn the things we are supposed to learn. To see if we did learn anything, the professors give us tests. If we pass the tests, we pass the course, and after we pass a certain number of courses, we get a piece of paper that says that we completed the courses. The paper is called a degree. Now there are other things that go on at my college besides learning. We play ball and do other types of athletics, and most of all, we party." This description is obviously different from the first two. It stresses some of the major *functions,* or objectives, of college.

The creature from another planet may still be puzzled. So you tell it that college is learning to live with other people. College is learning to take responsibility; it is about following directions. College is also about frustration; it is about accomplishing things. In other words, college is about *human relations*—people interacting with people.

You may even offer one further explanation if the creature isn't satisfied. People in a college receive and send information. The information can be about the queen of England, Isaac Newton's laws, lasers, computer programs, and the law of tort liability. Sometimes the information is about which professors to avoid, and some people need information about other people to decide whether to promote them or fire them. Colleges, like all organizations, use the gathering and processing of information for the purpose of *making decisions*.

Which of these explanations is correct? The answer is, *all* of them. Each explanation contains some truth about what a college is. We can think of the explanations as different kinds of road maps. They "guide" us to an understanding of the thing (in this case the understanding of college) we want to learn about. Road maps depict the crucial landmarks to help us find our way. Similarly, intellectual road maps, constructs, or theories help us understand what we are learning about. Just as there are theories to explain the origins of the universe and the evolution of *homo sapiens,* so, too, are there theories of organizations.

THE CONCEPT OF BUREAUCRACY

You have probably heard the phrase "it seems awfully bureaucratic," or sometimes people are described as acting in a bureaucratic way. The word *bureaucratic* is often used pejoratively. It means "inflexible," "unbending," "beholden to strict rules with no regard for individuals."

To understand how we have come to use this word to paint a negative image of behavior, we should go back to its original meaning. The concept of bureaucracy was described by the German sociologist Max Weber in the early years of this century. Weber identified the following as attributes of bureaucratic organizations:[1]

They are characterized by rules and regulations.
People in bureaucracies are given regular activities that become official responsibilities of their position.
Authority is given to people by virtue of their position in the organization.
People in bureaucratic organizations get their positions because of their specialized knowledge, experience, or competence.
Bureaucracies are organized in *hierarchical* fashion so that it is clear who supervises whom.

Weber assumed that bureaucracies would be efficient organizations. As a way of getting work done, bureaucracies were superior to other methods of organizing people to perform tasks:

> Precision, speed, unambiguity, knowledge of the files, continuity, discretion, unity, strict subordination, reduction of friction and of material and personal costs—these things are raised to the optimum point in the strictly bureaucratic administration.[2]

To the reader who may have waited on line at a state office to register an automobile, take a civil service examination, get a dog license, or pay a traffic violation, Weber's image of a smooth-operating bureaucratic machine may be at odds with a more frustrating reality.

Was Weber wrong? Not really. Weber was contrasting the legal–rational administrative apparatus he observed—which was relatively efficient—with the premodern feudal structures that were found in Europe before the beginning of the industrial age. By trying to present an "ideal type," he focused on what he believed were the essential features of bureaucracies of the late nineteenth and early twentieth centuries. Naturally, he observed these features and tried to capture the essence of bureaucratic organization, which, he thought, was a distinguishing aspect of industrial society. Weber most likely realized that many bureaucracies departed in practice from his ideal type. Besides, he did not study organizations in the same way that we do today. He did not interview managers or ask workers to fill out questionnaires or collect quantitative data on organizations and subject them to statistical analysis—and organizations have changed since Weber's day.

Let's think about a modern institution that should be bureaucratic, much in the way Weber described bureaucracy, and see just how it might depart from his description. The army is a good illustration. What can be more bureaucratic than the army?

First, let's consider the army in light of Weber's image of bureaucracy—the essential features. Does the army have rules and regulations? There is no shortage in this department. The army has rules about almost everything, from the length of your moustache to "fraternizing" between the sexes. Regular activities and official responsibilities? The army assigns people to specific tasks with corresponding duties, whether it is cook, machine gunner, computer operator, or chaplain. How about the principle of authority? Here also, people in the military have authority because of their formal positions, such as post commander, drill sergeant, or platoon leader. Finally, is the army hierarchical? You bet. Sergeants are higher than corporals, lieutenants are higher than sergeants, captains are higher than lieutenants, majors are higher than captains, all the way up to a five-star general. Surely Weber would identify the army as the kind of bureaucratic organization he had in mind.

If we think about the army a little more, however, some of the bureaucratic features become less solidified. Consider the principle of hierarchy once again. Does official rank always tell you who is in charge and who is subordinate? Not always. The commander of a typical basic training company is sometimes a lieutenant, who may have been in the army for a year or less. The drill sergeants in charge of the company and the individual platoons are the people who *really* run the basic training company because they have the experience and knowledge the lieutenant lacks. If we go by *formal* lines of authority, the sergeants are naturally subordinate to the lieutenant. But if we consider how decisions are made, especially the frequency of delegated authority to the sergeants, the hierarchy breaks down.

Why does hierarchy break down? The reason is that formal hierarchy may sometimes stifle the performance of the organization. To get around this, people in bureaucracies develop "informal organization," the various associations and relationships that develop over time. Naturally, these informal associations do not appear on any organization chart, but they can be central to the performance of the organization. Often they provide people with the opportunity to get around red tape. Surely you have heard something like the following: "Well, that's not the way it is supposed to be done." This is an *informal organization.*[3]

"SCIENTIFIC" MANAGEMENT

Let's go back to the description of the college at the beginning of the chapter. Notice that in each description some amount of *discretion* is exercised. In two places it is the beneficiary of the college's "product"—you—who exercises discretion. You choose among alternative majors, courses, and activities. Some of the employees exercise discretion as well. The instructors do so when they select the material and information they want to impart to the students, and naturally, they do so when they determine your performance by giving you a grade for the course. Also, discretion may have been the cause of foul-ups on registration day.

Bureaucracies try to manage discretion. Weber thought that by establishing rules and procedures, and by defining strict hierarchical lines of authority, discretion would be circumscribed. But we know that the drill sergeant is given a great deal of discretion. In other words, rules and regulations may not, by themselves, manage discretion because of the many information organizations that crop up to circumvent them.

If rules and regulations do not necessarily limit discretion, perhaps restricting the actual activities of employees—restraining their movements—would be more successful. This approach, begun in the first quarter of this century, was known as *scientific management.* An engineer by the name of Frederick W. Taylor advanced the thesis that the essence of any task could be broken down to a very few steps. Taylor thought that by studying jobs carefully, wasted movements could be eliminated. The "one best way" of performing a given task would be discovered; once discovered, the one best way could be taught to workers. The result would be a more efficient organization. Here is how Taylor described the procedure of scientific management.

First. Find, say, 10 or 15 different men . . . who are especially skillful in doing the particular work to be analyzed.

Second. Study the exact series of elementary operations or motions which each of these men uses in doing the work which is being investigated, as well as the implements each man uses.

Third. Study with a stop-watch the time required to make each of these elementary movements and then select the quickest way of doing each element of the work.

Fourth. Eliminate all false movements, slow movements, and useless movements.

Fifth. After doing away with all unnecessary movements, collect into one series the quickest and best movements as well as the best implements.[4]

Sounds funny? You don't believe that Taylor's scientific management ideas went anywhere beyond the pages of his book? Let's go back to the army and basic training.

One of the "skills" I learned as a recruit in basic training was how to use a bayonet fixed to the end of a rifle. Now you can't just jab away at your opponent; there is one way to do it. A drill sergeant would yell, "Assume the position." At that point, the recruits jumped forward one step, their feet apart about shoulder width. (They have to growl at this time, presumably because a menacing roar would scare the enemy.) The recruit held the rifle with two hands, bayonet pointing up at a forty-five-degree angle. Next, the recruit lunged toward the enemy (which is a dummy rather than a real person) and thrust the bayonet in the enemy's abdomen once, pulled it out, and stepped back, all the time yelling, "Kill!"

This represents an effort to reduce the number of unnecessary movements by the soldier. Why? The fewer the movements, the less chance there is for a mistake, and the fewer the movements, the more likely it is that the *basic* movements will be effective. (*One* good, hard thrust to the abdomen is presumably more effective than three weak blows that are not aimed at a vulnerable part of the body.)

Notice how the element of discretion is removed from the soldier. By making the procedure a routine, the soldier does not have to think very much, there is less chance of error, the result is predictable, and the outcome should be standardized. At least this is the theory behind scientific management. But if we replace the dummies with real enemy soldiers, the application of the principles of scientific management to bayonet fighting would receive a real test.

THE "PRINCIPLES" SCHOOL

Some theorists have tried to identify the core functions of public management, reasoning that if the principles of administration can be uncovered, they can be learned by aspiring managers and then put into practice. That is, if the principles of administration common to all public organizations were taught, the performance of the public sector would improve.

The principles school developed during the 1930s, when the government expanded dramatically under the first and second New Deals. It was believed that administrative management lagged behind the expansion of government activity. If the essential ingredients of management could be discovered, public managers would be equipped to assist the economic recovery and, later, win the war.

An intellectual leader of the principles school was Luther Gulick, an academic and a participant of the Committee on Administrative Management—a committee set up by President Franklin Roosevelt to propose changes in government administration. Gulick was part of the public administration tradition, begun in the late nineteenth century with Woodrow Wilson, that wanted to *reform* administrative practices by establishing general rules of thumb to guide public managers. Like Frederick Taylor, Gulick believed that certain features of organizations, once discovered, could provide administrators with the means to manage effectively. He assumed, like Max Weber before him, that organizations were *hierarchical*, that is, that some people supervise the work of others. One of the questions Gulick asked is, how many people should a supervisor manage? His answer, that it all depends on the *span of control*, became a hallmark of the principles of administration school.

> Where the work is of a routine, repetitive, measurable and homogeneous character, one man can perhaps direct several score workers. . . . Where the work is diversified, qualitative, and particularly when the workers are scattered, one man can supervise only a few.[5]

Notice how Gulick identified a few basic rules of thumb to determine the span of control. They include:

The limitations placed on a manager in terms of the ability to absorb information
The number of subordinates that must report to the manager
The complexity (or simplicity) of tasks
The clarity (or fuzziness) of the tasks that must be performed

Let's use these rules of thumb to evaluate the span of control in different types of administrative settings. Is the span of control of a manager who supervises a typing pool in a government agency greater or smaller than that of an administrator who supervises caseworkers in a government welfare office? Which type of job is more routinized? The typists in the typing pool perform tasks that are much more routinized than the caseworkers. Which job is more complex? The caseworkers, who have to deal with a series of "people problems," have a more complex job. This does not mean that the job is harder. Rather, it means that the job is more difficult to define, requires more subjective judgments, and is, therefore, more ambiguous. Actually, the job of typist may be more strenuous and more demanding, but if there are no additional tasks, it is evident that the manager of the typing pool can supervise more subordinates. To put it another way, the administrator has a wider span of control than the supervisor of caseworkers. Now try to apply the principle of the span of control to the following administrative environments:

A university president
A colonel in the army
A cardinal in the Catholic church
An administrator in a municipal hospital

We can now turn to another principle of administration. Have you ever heard someone complain about having to answer to two bosses? Generally, people complain about this situation because they feel that they are often given conflicting directions. Sometimes subordinates are unsure about which boss is really in a position to affect their careers.

Gulick claimed that *unity of command* is an essential ingredient of effective management. People should know whom they are responsible to in large organizations. According to Gulick, this principle allows managers to coordinate the various activities under supervision. Without unity of command there could not be adequate coordination, and without coordination the efficiency and effectiveness of the organization would suffer.[6]

You have been warned about not mixing apples and oranges. Gulick believed that organizations shouldn't mix apples and oranges either. This principle of administration concerns the *homogeneity of work.* In other words, government organizations should not combine dissimilar activities in single agencies. In Gulick's words, "No one would think of combining water supply and public education, or tax administration and public recreation."[7] Why not? He thought that when nonhomogeneous activities are combined, the efficiency and effectiveness of the organization suffer.

Gulick's last principle is perhaps his most famous. He tried to characterize the essential ingredients of management, the basic tasks that *any* manager would have to undertake. He called the work of a chief executive, the top manager in an organization, POSDCORB:[8]

Planning—developing the general outline of what the organization will do and establishing broad objectives

Organizing—setting the structure of authority and the division of work in the organization

Staffing—hiring, training, motivating, and terminating personnel

Directing—giving orders, leading, and making decisions

Coordinating—bringing the various components of the organization, especially the work units, together so that objectives can be achieved

Reporting—preparing adequate and accurate documentation of activities in the organization and keeping subordinates and superiors informed

Budgeting—planning, allocating, and accounting for financial resources

The acronym *POSDCORB* became the hallmark of the principles school of administration. Indeed, the essential features of management, or "what every manager needs to know," are contained in POSDCORB. It has additional appeal: By identifying the essential ingredients of administration, it creates a "generic" brand of management. It does not matter if you're secretary of the army, president of the University of Alabama, the pope, or the head of General Motors. Management is management. The particulars may be different, but every manager must do POSDCORB.

This concept has enjoyed considerable intellectual respect among administrators. For many, it is a handy way to depict the core elements of management, and learning it is necessary (if not sufficient) for administrative success.

Critique of the Principles School

In 1946 POSDCORB, and the principles school in general, received sharp criticism from Herbert Simon, now a professor at Carnegie-Mellon University and a Nobel Prize winner in economics. Simon argued that the common assumptions of the principles school of administrative theory were nothing more than *proverbs*. Here is the heart of Simon's critique.

> Most of the propositions that make up the body of administrative theory today share, unfortunately, proverbs. For almost every principle one can find an equally plausible and acceptable contradictory principle. Although the two principles pair will lead to exactly opposite organizational recommendations, there is nothing in the theory to indicate which is the proper one to apply.[9]

Simon then dissected the famous principles of administration to show that they can be reduced to nothing more than proverbs. Here, for example, is how he interpreted the famous principle of the span of control, which states that administrative efficiency is improved when the subordinates who must report to the manager are kept to a modest number. This principle is straightforward and is a widely held assumption. But Simon described a different principle of administrative efficiency that is incompatible with the span of control. Specifically, too many organizational levels breed inefficiency; therefore, it is unwise to have information go through too many levels before a decision is made.[10] *Think about these two principles carefully. Now create a situation in which the two cannot logically exist at the same time.*

Although Simon's critique was devastating, the "principles" approach has had remarkable staying power. Why? One reason is that they seem plausible, striking of basic common sense. Also, they can be applied in real settings unlike other, more abstract concepts and theories. Moreover, practicing managers are not especially concerned with the scientific status of an idea like POSDCORB. So although Simon's intellectual broadside against POSDCORB and the other principles is widely shared among most scholars of organizations and management, these principles occasionally reappear in recommendations for structural reform of organizations. Some ideas do not die easily.

TENETS OF HUMAN RELATIONS

About the same time that Taylor was developing his scientific management and Gulick was identifying his principles of administration, an alternative approach to organization theory was being developed. This approach can be characterized as the "human relations" school, and as its name implies, it focuses on people in organizations.

Whereas the Weberian image of bureaucracy depicts authority as a central feature of formal position, human relations portrays *leadership* as a major ingredient of organizational life. Notice the sharp contrast immediately. Authority is *ascribed* in the classic image of bureaucracy. A general assumes authority by virtue of the rank. But a general may or may not exercise leadership. Leadership requires certain human qualities that do not automatically come with the bureaucratic turf. Leadership is acquired; it is learned; and it requires discretion.

A second tenet of the human relations school is the concept of *motivation*. The contrast with scientific management could not be sharper—the workers, according to Taylor and his followers, will perform well if tasks are simple. Motivation, though they would not have used the term, is enhanced when the workers do not have to make decisions (and thereby risk the chance of making mistakes). Following the theory of Abraham Maslow, the human relations school believes that human beings have a *hierarchy of needs.* After the lower levels of need (which are physiological, followed by security), humans require inducements to stimulate their creative behavior. At the highest need level—Maslow called it *self-actualization*—individuals seek stimulation and fulfillment from their work.[11]

If organizations are to provide an atmosphere for personal growth, obviously a good deal of individual discretion is required. Individuals are not free to achieve self-actualization if they are not given freedom of choice and action. One of the basic signs of effective leadership, then, is to provide the environment and incentives, some would say motivation, for individuals to maximize their potential.

Why *should* managers be at all concerned with the psychological needs of employees? Interestingly, the rationale is similar to the one found in scientific management. Recall that Taylor's principle objective was to increase the productivity of workers. Similarly, the proponents of a human relations approach also wanted to improve productivity. It all started with the famous Hawthorne study.

Hawthorne was a plant in Cicero, Illinois, owned by Western Electric. In the late 1920s researchers conducted experiments with lighting to see if changing the environment in which employees worked would affect their productivity. The researchers selected two groups of workers: an experimental group and a control group. By increasing their lighting, the productivity of the workers in the test group improved. But so did the productivity of the control group. (Their lighting was *not* altered in any way.) No matter what the researchers did, they could find no substantial differences between the two groups of workers.

A few years after the experiments it became obvious that there was no difference in performance because both groups acted differently during the experiments; they both assumed that they were special. The control group was segregated from the rest of the workers, so they thought that they were supposed to be different. Somehow, this segregation stimulated their productivity. This phenomenon was later called the *Hawthorne effect.* It refers to the bias that may be introduced when an environment is altered for experimental purposes.[12]

The Hawthorne experiments tell us more about what *not* to do when conducting research in organizations that about the social psychology of employees' behavior. Yet since the Hawthorne studies in the late 1920s, there have been numerous efforts to study the relationship among leadership, morale, and productivity. One large body of research has investigated the proposition that employees' satisfaction affects their performance. If workers are happy with their jobs, if they are sufficiently motivated, the result will be high levels of productivity. Unfortunately, the most that can be said for this proposition is that at best, the research provides only very weak confirmation of the linkage.[13]

Why are studies so equivocal? The main reason is that the causes of organizational performance are more complex than the two-factor link between employees' satisfaction and productivity. Some things that influence performance, for example, have nothing to do with employees. They include the technologies used in the production of the organization's products, organizational structure, and leadership traits. In addition, the result of motivation is not only productivity; it is also employees' satisfaction. Satisfaction is a *result* of the workers' successful efforts. Finally, both satisfaction and productivity are part of a "feedback loop." That is, they become part of the inputs that stimulate organizational performance all over again.[14]

Two researchers, Edward Lawler and Lyman Porter, posed an interesting hypothesis. After reviewing all of the studies that failed to prove that satisfaction produces good performance, they suggested that the previous researchers had it backwards. Maybe productivity produces satisfaction *if* the employees are rewarded in some way for their performance. Their research confirmed this hypothesis. Thus maybe Maslow's higher need—self-actualization—really does make sense in an organizational setting.[15]

Leadership and Performance

Perhaps a crucial factor in the performance of employees is the role of managers, in particular, their *leadership qualities*. Several researchers in the human relations school have tried to find out which approaches to managerial leadership are more effective than others. Is it better to be a "tough guy"—hierarchical in outlook and authoritarian? Or an "essay mark," "soft"—a manager who considers the wishes of subordinates and is willing to share power and responsibility?

Rensis Likert, a well-known researcher at the University of Michigan, developed what he called "four systems" of leadership:

System 1—exploitive, authoritative
System 2—benevolent, authoritative
System 3—consultative
System 4—participative, group

Likert argued that research he conducted at the University of Michigan proves that system 4 of leadership and management would be effective in achieving organizational objectives and, in particular, in improving productivity. He claimed that most management and leadership values held in the United States are "Weberian," resembling his system 1. The implication of his research is that our concepts of leadership and management should change.[16]

You have heard the phrase "It's not black or white, but several shades of gray." Organization theory is like this too. Likert's efforts to depict systems of leadership doesn't allow for enough gray. Surely, there must be some authoritarian leaders who are successful. Think about General Patton, for instance. Also, there must be a few leaders who share power, adopt a consultative management style, and fail miserably. How can we account for such cases?

Fiedler's theory, known as *situational contingency*, tries to explain the conditions that allow one type of leader to be more effective than another. As the name of the theory implies, the situation that exists in an organization will be favorable or unfavorable to a particular type of leadership approach.[17] Suppose the group of subordinates is favorably disposed toward the manager. What leadership style is most effective? Should the manager cultivate interpersonal relationships to improve performance? Why? The employees already *like* the leader. Fiedler's situational contingency theory says that in this type of situation the manager should direct the group toward *tasks*—getting the job done. Now suppose the subordinates dislike the manager. Should the manager spend time cultivating interpersonal relationships? No, because it won't help anyway; therefore, the leader will, as in the first situation, focus on tasks.

Suppose that tasks are not well defined *and* the subordinates are not exactly crazy about the manager. What should be done? Fiedler's situational contingency theory says that in such a situation "stroking" the subordinates wouldn't work, nor would a Likert-type system 4 approach work. Clear, strong direction is needed. In other words, Fiedler's theory answers the question "What leadership style is most effective?" with the response "It all depends."

Putting Human Relations Theory to Work

"That may sound good in *theory,* but it would never work here." Theories are supposed to integrate information, particularly assumptions about interrelationships among seemingly disparate phenomena, so that we better understand why things are as they. Theories organize; theories enlighten; theories focus inquiry. But ultimately, theories should lead to the discovery of useful, or *applied,* practices.

The human relations school of organization theory has been put into practice. Following are some selected applied managerial approaches and techniques related to some of its assumptions. Above all, the various techniques and approaches are premised on the following ideas:

People in organizations perform best when they are given some discretion.
Organizations should be "open systems" rather than "closed systems."
Management and leadership should be closer to Likert's system 4 (as opposed to the system 1 side of the continuum).
People in organizations seek higher values than simply survival.
Consultation in organizations stimulates a good work environment, which, in turn, affects performance.

We will look at three managerial techniques that have tried to put human relations theory into practice.

Organization Development

Organization development (OD), an approach to managing organizational change, is based on the belief that problems that hamper organizational performance can be identified, diagnosed, and corrected by direct intervention in the organization. It proceeds with the following steps:[18]

A problem is identified.
Information is gathered on the problem.

Managers meet to analyze the information.

Desired changes in behavior are identified and specific "interventions" in the organization are selected that will bring about the desired changes.

A "change agent," often someone outside the organization, advises members of the organization as they go about putting the intervention into practice.

Collaborative efforts by members of the organizations try to insure that the *new* procedures continue to work effectively.

Training in the new procedures takes place and is ongoing. As you can already tell, OD tends to adopt a group decision-making approach. Managers do not bark orders. On the contrary, they often take part in *team building*, whereby several members of the organization will work together to diagnose and resolve specific problems.

Although OD tries to encourage cooperative behavior in an organization, it does not always avoid conflict. In fact, sometimes a third party, usually an OD consultant, will try to foment interpersonal conflict if the consultant believes that it will help the team discover its problems and find solutions for them. How would you construct an OD approach to the following common problem now happening on so many college and university campuses in the United States?

Keuka College Needs Help

Keuka College is a small liberal arts college for women located in rural Keuka Park, New York. Founded in 1890, Keuka College aspired to teach students pursuing a vocation in liberal arts education. Historically, Keuka mainly produced teachers, nurses, and Christian education workers, but in the 1970s it expanded its offerings to include social work, business management, medical technology, and special education.

The expansion did not seem to help. Whereas enrollment at Keuka College jumped from 447 in 1960–1961 to 857 in 1970–1971, by 1981–1982 the number of students had dropped to 524. Like most other small colleges, Keuka was heavily dependent on tuition, fees and charges for room and board for its revenue. In 1960–1961, 73 percent of Keuka's current fund income came from these sources. During the 1970s the college was forced to dip into its endowment fund to cover budget deficits. By 1981–1982 the endowment balance had to be used to cover a budget deficit of $370,638.

In 1981 the president of Keuka College, Dr. Elizabeth Woods Shaw, outlined a plan to deal with the college's mounting financial problems. First, the college would try to increase enrollment by establishing programs to attract the nontraditional student—people outside the usual eighteen- to twenty-one-year-old group. Second, a five-year fund-raising campaign was initiated. Said President Shaw, "Everything is riding on corporate support—we have not done that before." Third, the college planned to expand revenues by renting campus facilities for conferences. Unfortunately, college officials quickly learned that corporations were not attracted to Keuka's spartan conditions.

In the fall of 1983, projected enrollment was off by twenty-five students. Given the heavy reliance on tuition, fees, and room and board as the main sources of income, Keuka College was in real trouble. Although the president had a formal plan for Keuka's financial future, there was a hope that, in her words, "a rich, eccentric millionaire" would secure the college.

□ *This case is abridged from Christine E. Murray, "Resource Acquisition in a Period of Scarcity: The Case of Keuka College" (Unpublished paper, May 1983).*

Management by Objectives

"Well it wasn't *my* idea!" If something goes wrong and the blame starts drifting your way, you can always fall back on this excuse. Whose idea was it? "It was the boss's idea, and he hasn't been near this place for ten years. He's lost touch with what it is like being in the trenches."

Some causes of organizational malfunctions relate to organizational objectives. Sometimes the objectives are not clear, sometimes they are not realistic, sometimes they are not communicated clearly, and sometimes they are simply not accepted by subordinates in the organization. Management by objectives (MBO) tries to alleviate these problems.

There are three major components in MBO. First, managers *and* subordinates agree on *goals* that the subordinates should try to achieve. Second, both parties develop an *action plan* that will enable the subordinates to reach the goals. Third, both parties agree on the criteria that will be used to *measure* and *evaluate progress* toward the realization of the goals. Peter Drucker, a world-famous management theorist and advocate of MBO in business and government, summarized the basic thrust of MBO as follows:

Usually MBO says to the individual manager, here are the goals of this institution. What efforts do you have to make to further them? The right question is, what do you, given our mission, think the goals should be, the priorities should be, the strategies should be? What, by way of contribution to these goals, priorities, and strategies, should this institution hold you and your department accountable for over the next year or two? What goals, priorities, and strategies do you and your department aim for, separate and distinct from those of the institution? What will you have to contribute and what results will you have to produce to attain these goals? Where do you see major opportunities of contribution and performance for this institution and for your component? Where do you see major problems?[19]

Putting MBO into practice in government has required a great deal of time and patience. Managers must have a leadership style that allows them to delegate authority downward. But MBO also requires managers to hold subordinates accountable if results have not been obtained, if performance is below the agreed-upon level. More generally, some pervasive problems in the public sector have hindered the implementation of MBO. *Lindblom?*

Government programs often have ill-defined objectives. In addition, programs have multiple objectives; therefore, it is necessary to establish priorities among the various objectives of a government program.

To evaluate performance it is necessary to identify *measures* of results; otherwise there is no way to tell whether objectives are, or are not, being achieved.

Management must be willing to accept what Peter Drucker has called "informed dissent."[20] Managers must be willing to accept, even encourage, disagreement as a way to reach realistic objectives that are obtainable in a reasonable time. This requires a management style that is not exactly widespread in government.

For MBO to have an impact, it must ultimately be used to reallocate resources—which means that information from MBO must be integrated into budgeting. Since budgeting takes place on an annual cycle, it has been difficult for MBO to penetrate the routines of government budgeting.

The MBO plan has been tried in many state and local governments and in the federal government during the Nixon and Ford administrations. In most instances, the basic problems, just listed, were not resolved. One evaluation of federal MBO was that it "evaporated."[21] Basically, the sheer complexity of government reduced MBO's impact. Was MBO always a failure? Although we can give federal MBO advocates a B-minus for effort, it really didn't create any managerial miracles.

Flexitime

Most of you have had the experience of waking up and saying to yourself, "I could sure use another hour of sleep. I'm going to be useless today." But you have to be at work by nine o'clock so there is no sense in procrastinating.

Why shouldn't you be able to come in an hour later and make up the time at the end of the day by working until, say, six? As long as the work gets done there shouldn't be any problem. Many companies in the private sector and some governments agree. They have initiated a program called *flexitime* (F-T).

As a technique, F-T is simple. It allows employees to alter the hours they work. Some employers allow workers to change their hours of work between, say, the twelve-hour period of 7 A.M. to 7 P.M. any time they wish without notice. One day a person may arrive at 8 and leave at 4. Another day the worker may arrive at 9 and leave at 5. Some employers may allow workers to "bank" hours and then take "comp" time. A worker may work from 7 A.M. to 6 P.M. on one day, for example, thus allowing that person to bank three hours. Some employers, however, may require advance notice and approval of changes in hours. Here, a worker may work from 8 A.M. to 4 P.M. If the worker wishes to shift to a 7 A.M.

to 3 P.M. schedule, the worker's supervisor may have to review and approve the change.

Although F-T is very simple in principle, it is premised on central human relations values. Most obvious, F-T is supposed to give employees more personal discretion. But discretion, by itself, is not the major motivating factor. Rather, it is assumed that workers will be more motivated, more satisfied with their jobs, and, consequently, will improve their productivity.

Why is this so? Think about a simple scenario. You stayed up late the night before. Perhaps you had just "one too many." You say to yourself, "I'll never get up at 6:00 tomorrow morning and make it in by 7:00." Six o'clock rolls around and you're fast asleep. You wake up at 7:30. What is your first thought? "I guess I'll have to forget about work today." You use up a vacation day or a sick day. With F-T your decision can be different. You may get to work at 9:00 that day and stay until 5:00. Indeed, studies of F-T show that is *has* cut down on absenteeism, lateness, and sick leave. More generally, the studies show that both employees and their supervisors tend to like it.[22] It represents a specific application of OD values that is easy to implement, is fairly inexpensive, and appears to produce benefits that outweigh its costs.

DECISION MAKING

Herbert Simon, the critic of the "proverbs of administration," has advanced our understanding of organizations in other important ways. His greatest contribution to public administration is his insight into how individuals *make decisions* in bureaucratic organizations.[23] We can say that if Weber described the anatomy of the organization, Simon described its physiology.

Simon began by saying that individuals in organizations try to be "rational." What does it mean "to be rational" or "to act rationally"? We might say, for example, that a rational decision is one in which the "best" choice is selected from a range of alternatives. How do you know that the choice is the best one? Naturally, this depends on your objectives. Consider a routine consumer decision. What is usually considered the best decision when you buy something? A "best" choice may be the cheapest price paid for something from a group of items of identical quality. If there is no difference in quality among the alternatives, we would say that the rational decision is to choose the cheapest alternative.

If you are choosing among three packages of chopped meat in a supermarket, it may not be too difficult to act rationally. But making decisions in organizations is a little harder. Here are some of the complicating factors:[24]

> All available alternatives may not be known to the individual who wants to make a rational decision.
> The means–ends chain is frequently obscure. That is, the individual does not have sufficient knowledge about what will happen if each alternative is actually selected.
> Since means and ends are not adequately understood, the person cannot really *rank* the alternatives.

These three limitations means that actual choices depart from the strict canons of rationality. Here is Simon's most famous contribution to organization theory: When an individual in an organization must make a decision, the person makes a *selected search* of the alternatives available. Notice that the alternatives are limited to those that the person has some knowledge about or perhaps feels comfortable with. Some alternatives are consciously, or unconsciously, ignored. Next, the individual chooses the *first satisfactory* alternative, which Simon calls "satisficing." Satisficing administrative behavior has sometimes also been called "bounded rationality" because only a limited range of alternatives is considered. But it is still rational. If you read carefully you would have learned that under Simon's notion of decision making the individual doesn't select *any* alternative; that is, *unsatisfactory* options are discarded. Yet it is possible to select an option that is satisfactory to the decision maker but is not the "best." Why would this happen?

Satisficing as a description of how decisions are made has become firmly ingrained in organization theory because, quite simply, it seems to be in accord with the way things really are. People in organizations are inherently conservative, which means that they are reluctant to make broad changes that depart dramatically from present methods. Sometimes we are impatient with this type of innate conservatism. But the concepts of bounded rationality and satisficing behavior help us appreciate the causes of modest change that is so characteristic of bureaucracies. It would be unrealistic to expect individuals to spend their time searching for *all* of the alternatives each and every time they must make decisions. If they did try, they would spend all of their time searching and virtually no time doing. Also, even if they tried, they would be unsuccessful.

PATHOLOGIES OF PUBLIC BUREAUCRACY

"Work expands so as to fill the time available for its completion."[25] With this sentence begins one of the funniest books in public administration. C. Northcote Parkinson, a British civil servant in Singapore in the 1950s, developed a series of "laws" of administrative behavior. His laws were intended to poke fun at administration, but they soon became synonymous with bungling bureaucrats who could do nothing right. In short, bureaucracy was pathological.

Parkinson was kidding, but several other more recent observers of administrative behavior are not. There is an image of public organizations, one influenced by economic analyses of bureaucratic behavior, that portrays government as *inherently* inefficient. On what bases can such a conclusion rest?

First, bureaucracies are said to be *inherently* inefficient because, it is charged, many government services are "pure" public goods. That is, once they are provided to some people, they must be provided to everyone. Also, it is impractical and sometimes even impossible to prevent people from enjoying the benefits of public goods. The best example of a pure public good is national defense. It seems silly to say, "I don't want national defense so don't make me pay for it and you don't have to protect me."

The problem with public goods is that it is difficult to measure and to evaluate them. Think about national defense again. How do we know when we have a satisfactory level of national defense? We can say that we have reached a satisfactory level when the nation is secure from attack. But surely such an assessment is bound to be difficult to make. It is elusive and is likely to produce differences of opinion among otherwise reasonable people. Can we evaluate the quality or effectiveness of national defense? Naturally, if the country loses a war one can conclude that national defense could stand some improvement. But if there are no battles to fight, there are no "tests" of performance.

This last feature of government services is especially problematical. Since many government activities are not subjected to marketlike tests—they do not face competition—bureaucrats may have no real incentive to be efficient.

Since bureaucrats do not spend time worrying about a "bottom line" (like profits), they worry about other things. According to the proponents of this image of administration, they try to pursue their own self-interests by focusing on the following organizational characteristics:[26]

> *Budget expansion*—bureaucrats want to increase their budgets whenever possible because they believe that power, prestige, and other perquisites of government service are associated with big budgets.
>
> *Personnel*—bureaucrats also want to increase the size of personnel under them. Like budgets, personnel growth is a sign of success. Also, the number of subordinates supervised is frequently an indication of whether an individual is ripe for promotion. Moreover, it is supposedly always better to have a "bloated" staff rather than a "lean" one when it comes time to make cuts.
>
> *Technological advances*—bureaucrats often want the latest gadgets, or technological fads, to be "on top of things." Sometimes new technology is not always efficiently used in public agencies, but bureaucrats don't want to be left behind in the technological race.
>
> *Information control*—you have certainly heard the argument that "knowledge is power." In public bureaucracies, information is often a key to influence—which means that bureaucrats will spend a great deal of time and energy acquiring information and sharing it sparingly as they see fit. Information control affects bureaucratic power; it may not always serve the public interest.

Critics of bureaucracy claim that "maximizing" these properties of public organizations reflects rational self-interested behavior on the part of government employees. But the problem is that by pursuing their self-interest, bureaucrats do not necessarily improve the performance of government. Why not? The problem lies in the way government activity is organized and in the difficulties involved in carefully monitoring the "output" of government activities that are not sold in the marketplace.

Pathologies of bureaucracy can be eliminated only by altering the characteristics of government that give rise to them in the first place. The reforms are really simple in theory and are based on a few simple assumptions. First, since bureaucrats try to pursue their self-interest, why not reward (or punish) bureaucrats for doing things that would benefit (or harm) the public interest? Allowing bureaucrats to keep some budgetary savings—as a bonus—would fit this idea. Second, instead of having only one government agency providing a service, why not have two or more agencies *competing* for clients? This would make government agencies act like private firms. Third, why not allow private firms to compete with government agencies to provide services? The idea is that government agencies would either become more efficient or the government would turn over the service to the private firms entirely. Fourth, contract with private firms to provide services. This option assumes that the private sector will be more efficient than the public sector. Fifth, charging for government services will allow government agencies to adopt marketlike features and thereby become more efficient.[27]

Like most theories, the pathologies of bureaucracy school has has some grain of truth in it. Perhaps most important, during the 1980s it influenced some public policy discussions, particularly among conservatives who share a distrust of government, hold a negative image of bureaucracy, and believe that the things government does either can be done better and cheaper by the private sector or should not be done at all. Unfortunately, it is a short distance from constructive critiques of the public sector to "bureaucrat bashing."

DEFENDING BUREAUCRACY

Bureaucrat bashing is the easy way to avoid thinking about the complexities of modern public administration. A well-worn criticism of government, for example, is that it is hopelessly inefficient. The remedy? Simple. Government should be more "businesslike" and efficient. On careful reflection, however, we can see that the well-worn idea—operate government like a business—obscures fundamental differences between choices faced by business and choices faced by government agencies.

Consider the following illustration: a government agency has the responsibility of constructing a new office building. Now suppose this was a business decision in the private sector and the builder was largely unaffected by government. The builder would try to keep the construction costs as low as possible while satisfying the costumer. Isn't it the same for government? Not exactly. Let's assume that the government agency decides that it will contract with a private builder to build the office building. Surely there can't be any difference now between the business and government. Right? Wrong! First, the government may have to pay union wages (even if nonunion workers are available) because the Davis-Bacon Act mandates that governments must pay the prevailing union wage rate. Notice that the government manager is more constrained than the manager in the private sector. Yet a simple comparison of cost would show that the government manager was "inefficient." Let's continue the example. Second, the government manager may be required to provide some of the work to minority construction firms even if the firms do not have the lowest bids. Why? A public policy goal of stimulating economic activity and employment among minorities is relevant in this situation and thereby is attached to the specific construction decision. Notice once again that cost is not the only consideration in the decision. Finally, just before the construction crew begins work a public interest environmental group goes to court and asks that the construction should be postponed until a satisfactory environmental impact statement is prepared showing that the building will have no adverse impact on the bird sanctuary a half mile away. Does this seem unreasonable? Only if you want to totally discount the environmental objectives that have been enacted by Congress.[28]

The illustration should highlight an important theme: efficiency is only one value that public administrators must consider when they make decisions. Values such as fairness, equality, representation, and responsiveness mean that public managers must operate in an environment of multiple, and often competing, objectives. Unfortunately, when values in society are in flux, it is easy to search for scapegoats. Bureaucrats are easy targets.

SUMMARY

Organization theory can be thought of as a series of intellectual road maps that guide us toward different parts of organizations. Max Weber, the intellectual founder of the concept of bureaucracy, focused our attention on the *formal structure* of organizations. Frederick Taylor and, later, Luther Gulick shifted our attention from structure to *performance*. Their major objective was to describe the essential features or, as Gulick called them, "principles" of administration that could be learned by aspiring managers and then put to use in real organizations. Unfortunately, there is little scientific basis for these principles. Herbert Simon called them "proverbs" (rather than principles) that offer inconsistent and sometimes contradictory advice.

Because organizations are made up of people, it is not surprising that a great deal of organization theory concerns *people in organizations*. One strain—human relations—has tried to discover what motivates people and what leadership styles are conducive to improving morale and increasing performance. Many human relations theories (and studies) are certainly equivocal. Still, this strain of organization theory has been put into practice as management by objectives, organizational development, and even flexitime reforms in public bureaucracies.

The important work of Herbert Simon also has emphasized people in organization. Drawing from cognitive psychology, Simon showed that when people make decisions in organizations, their mode of behavior departs from the "pure rationality" of individual decision making. Rather than comparing all possible choices, people in organizations select the first satisfactory alternative. In his words, they *satisfice* Simon's deceptively simple explanation that has become a classic feature of organization theory.

Like all human beings, bureaucrats pursue their self-interests. The problem, say the adherents of the "pathological" school of bureaucracy, is that the pursuit of self-interest—which is certainly rational from an individual point of view—leads to inefficiency and a bloated public sector. The implication of this approach to organization theory is that since you can't change the motivations underlying individual behavior, the only way to improve the performance of the public sector is to change the structure of organizations. Sometimes road maps will bring you back to the place from which you started, if you are not careful.

NOTES

1. The classic piece by Max Weber is "Bureaucracy," from *Max Weber Essays in Sociology*, ed. H. H. Gerth and C. Wright Mills (New York: Oxford University Press, 1971), pp. 196–244.
2. Ibid., p. 214.
3. Chester I. Barnard, *The Functions of The Executive* (Cambridge, Mass.: Harvard University Press, 1960), pp. 114–123.
4. Frederick Winslow Taylor, *The Principles of Scientific Management* (New York: W. W. Norton, 1967), pp. 117–118.
5. Luther Gulick, "Notes on the Theory of Organization," in *Classics of Organization Theory*, ed. Jay M. Shafritz and Philip H. Whitbeck (Oak Park, Ill.: Moore Publishing Co., 1978), p. 56.
6. Ibid., p. 57.
7. Ibid.
8. Ibid.
9. Herbert A. Simon, "The Proverbs of Administration," in *Classics of Organization Theory*, ed. Jay M. Shafritz and Philip A. Whitbeck (Oak Park, Ill.: Moore Publishing Co., 1978), pp. 69–84.
10. Ibid., p. 70.
11. For a summary of Abraham Maslow's theory, see William B. Eddy, *Public Organization Behavior and Development* (Cambridge, Mass.: Winthrop Publishers, 1981), pp. 44–46.
12. The Hawthorne experiments are described in Charles Perrow, *Complex Organizations*, 2d ed. (Glenview, Ill.: Scott, Foresman, 1979), pp. 90–96.
13. Victor Vroom, *Work and Motivation* (New York: Wiley, 1964).
14. Stephen J. Carroll and Henry L. Tosi, *Organizational Behavior* (Chicago: St. Clair Press, 1977), p. 129.
15. See Edward E. Lawler III and Lyman W. Porter, "The Effect of Performance on Job Satisfaction," *Industrial Relations* 7 (October 1967): 20–28.
16. Rensis Likert, *The Human Organization* (New York: McGraw-Hill, 1961).
17. Fred E. Fiedler, *A Theory of Leadership Effectiveness* (New York: McGraw-Hill, 1967).
18. See Eddy, *Public Organization*, pp. 184–185.
19. Peter Drucker, "What Results Should You Expect? A Users' Guide to MBO," *Public Administration Review* 36 (January/February 1976): 18.
20. Ibid., p. 17.
21. Richard Rose, "Implementation and Evaporation: The Record of MBO," *Public Administration Review* 36 (January/February 1977): 64–71.
22. Robert T. Golembiewski and Carl W. Proehl, Jr., "Public Sector Applications of Flexible Workhours: A Review of Available Experience," *Public Administration Review* 40 (January/February 1980): 72–85.
23. Herbert Simon, *Administrative Behavior*, 3d ed. (New York: Free Press, 1976).

24. Simon's major contribution is described as "Neo-Weberian" by Perrow, *Complex Organizations*, pp. 141–142.
25. C. Northcote Parkinson, *Parkinson's Law* (New York: Ballantine, 1975), p. 15.
26. See, for example, William A. Niskanen, Jr., *Bureaucracy and Representative Government* (Chicago: Aldine, 1971).
27. Ibid., pp. 195–218.
28. H. Brinton Milward and Hal G. Rainey, "Don't Blame the Bureaucracy!" *Journal of Public Policy* 3 (May 1983): 149–168.

FOR FURTHER READING

Goodsell, Charles T. *The Case for Bureaucracy,* 2d ed. Chatham, N.J.: Chatham House Publishers, 1985.
>   A spirited response to the criticisms of bureaucrats and bureaucracy that reached a feverish pitch in the mid-1980s.

Hall, Richard H. *Organizations: Structure and Process,* 3d ed. Englewood Cliffs, N.J.: Prentice-Hall, 1982.
>   A text that summarizes much of the empirical work that has contributed to the subject of organization theory.

Harmon, Michael M., and Richard T. Mayer. *Organization Theory for Public Administration.* Boston: Little, Brown, 1986.
>   One of the few organization theory texts written with an explicitly public administration perspective.

McGregor, Douglas. *The Human Side of Enterprise.* New York: McGraw-Hill, 1960.
>   Perhaps the best-known work of a leading exponent of the human relations approach to management.

March, James G., and Herbert A. Simon. *Organizations.* New York: Wiley, 1958.
>   Still the leading text for the "administrative science" school of organization theory.

Perrow, Charles. *Complex Organizations.* 3rd ed. New York: Random House, 1986.
>   A very readable overview of the major approaches to organization theory by a well-known sociologist.

Shafritz, Jay M., and Philip H. Whitbeck. *Classics of Organization Theory.* Oak Park, Ill.,: Moore Publishing Co., 1978.
>   A collection of classic articles and excerpts from many of the most prominent contributors to organization theory.

CHAPTER 5

Public Management

Who was one of the first managers? If you are thinking of Henry Ford, Abraham Lincoln, maybe Alexander Hamilton, you are not even close. Give up? It was Moses. Think about it. He had a real demanding boss and a mission to accomplish. His resources to accomplish the mission were limited, and his leadership was frequently tested by his followers. Moses couldn't merely tell the Israelites, "Follow me and I'll lead you out of the land of Egypt." It was more complicated than that. His followers were a bit dubious, to say the least. ("Where did you really get those tablets, Mo?" "Burning bush?" "What else are you going to tell us, Mo?") Moses's boss wanted results. Poor Moses—he felt pressure from both sides. Managers always do.

WHO IS A MANAGER?

The one thing Moses lacked was a job title. After all, if you read the Old Testament you will not come up with a description that tells us Moses's "official position" among the Israelites. Nor did the Israelites have an organization chart with Moses at the top. So how do we know he was a manager? More seriously, how do we know when anyone is a manager?

You cannot judge a manager by his or her appearance. Perhaps at one time managers were the men who wore ties, but nowadays appearance would be a poor guide. There are, however, three ways to identify a manager.

Formal Positions in Organizations

Consider an organization shaped as in Figure 5.1. Where would you place the manager? Well, at the top (the apex), of course. But suppose we changed the shape of the organization to look like the illustration at the right. Now where

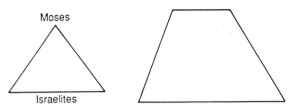

Figure 5.1.

would you place the manager? Again, the managers—there are more than one now—are at the top. But in this second case we assume that since there are fewer managers than underlings, simple geometry tells us that they must be at the top of the organization. So far, so good.

Now let's consider a more complicated organization that looks something like Figure 5.2. Where are the managers? Does each box have a manager? Is the box in the middle (1) the only one with managers? Can box 2 include managers? Consider one more form of organization, as shown in Figure 5.3. Notice that there is no obvious evidence of hierarchy here. Where should the managers be? Does each box have a manager?

We could continue to draw organizational boxes depicting increasingly complicated organizational arrangements. The more complicated our boxes become, the more difficult it is to determine the obvious location of managers. The lesson is simple. Formal positions in organizations do not always signify where managers are or who they are. Only in simple, hierarchical organizations will managers always be at the top. But even in large, hierarchical organizations there will be levels of managers well below the apex. How, then, do we identify these lower-level managers?

Management as a Job Title

Sometimes it is easy to know who the manager is by looking at a person's job title. If a person has the title "general manager," we would probably assume that this person is, indeed, a manager. Sometimes governments identify certain civil

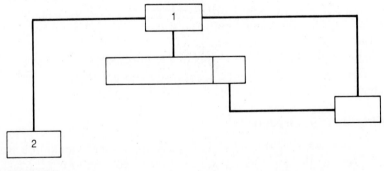

Figure 5.2.

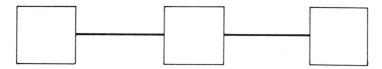

Figure 5.3.

service grades as "management." If a person is a grade 16 we can say that this person is a manager.

Simple, right? Wrong! Consider two simple (and common) exceptions. Suppose a person has the job title "management analyst." Is this person a manager? Probably not, since most analyst positions are not managerial. Rather, such a person may evaluate managerial problems. A second exception is also very common. A person may have a state government position of, say, psychiatric social worker II, grade 19. There may be no reason to assume by job title or grade level that such a person is a manager. Yet that person may be in charge of a program, have a staff of seven people, and have responsibilities that we might consider "managerial." To know, then, who is a manager, we should look at what the person does.

The Basic Task of Management

Management is the use of organizational resources to achieve programmatic objectives. This is deceptively simple as a description of management. Let's work backward. Organizations try to do things—achieve objectives. Police departments try to reduce crime; sanitation departments clean the streets; public hospitals try to make sick people healthier. To reach these ultimate objectives, organizations must achieve some intermediate "output." Police departments make arrests of people suspected of committing crimes; sanitation departments pick up garbage; public hospitals do medical tests, dispense medicine, and perform operations. A basic task of management is to determine how best to use the resources of the organization so that the activities of its members achieve the intended results. When police patrol the streets of a city, for example, it is assumed that this activity will both deter crime and apprehend people suspected of committing crimes. These activities should, in turn, lead to an improvement in public safety. Similarly, when sanitation workers pick up trash along their routes, it is expected that this trash pickup will produce a cleaner city. The task of management, then, is to harness organizational resources to reach some objective.

THE RESOURCES OF MANAGEMENT

Managers need resources to achieve their tasks, but organizational resources are both limited and scarce.

Organizational Structure

We saw earlier that organizations come in different sizes and shapes. Organizational structure can be an important managerial resource. Managerial decisions are facilitated or hindered, based on the ease of delegation of authority. When a manager wants to grant subordinates the authority to make decisions, the structure of the organization is important. Consider a simple example, such as the military. Delegation is simple (in theory at least) because superiors and subordinates are easily identified. Moreover, subunit managers are easily determined. A platoon leader is a lieutenant, a company commander is a captain, a battalion commander is a colonel. Sometimes organizational structures are easily broken down into subunits to perform specific tasks. When this can be done, the opportunities for delegation are enhanced.

One indication that organizational structure is an important resource is that managers often reorganize, and they do so because they think that a change in organizational structure would improve their ability to achieve their objectives. Perhaps they want more people reporting to them directly, or perhaps they want fewer people reporting to them. The number of staff units might be increased or decreased. Subunits might be reorganized according to the basic mission of the organization; they might reflect specializations. Although there is no magical type of reorganization, it is one way managers will attempt to get their objectives across to subordinates.

People

People are resources; they can also be liabilities. One of the tasks of management is to strengthen the resource potential of personnel and reduce the negative qualities of existing personnel. Managers can do so by hiring desirable people and firing personnel who are a burden to the organization.

Both hiring and firing are not so straightforward in practice. In the public sector hiring decisions are constrained by several factors: availability of labor, competition with the private sector for labor, ability of government to pay, civil service procedures that pertain to hiring, and collective-bargaining agreements with public unions.

Firing personnel in government can be even more difficult. Civil service procedures often spell out the legitimate reasons for firing. Poor performance is difficult to document. Moreover, civil service systems usually have several procedural safeguards designed to protect employees from indiscriminate firing. As a result, terminating an employee for just cause can be a lengthy and difficult process. Sometimes a manager will simply get rid of an undesirable employee by transferring the person or, occasionally, even "kicking the person upstairs" with a promotion (though both options are often plagued by legal and budgetary constraints).

Technologies and Information

Organizational technologies are "hard" and "soft." Hard technologies include various machinery available to help the manager and personnel perform their tasks. Most important in a typical government agency is the use of computers to store, retrieve, and analyze information appropriate to the agency's mission. Consider a simple illustration—a county social services department. It is increasingly common to put all information concerning clients (*case records* is the term often used) in a form that can be stored in the computer and easily retrieved. Much work that was once recorded on paper—case records, mail, memoranda—is stored in computer software packages such as word processors, data-base management programs, and spreadsheets. Personnel routinely record, retrieve, and analyze the information with either on-line terminals (connected to a mainframe computer) or micros. Computers speed the flow of information for the manager; therefore, advances in hard technologies help managers perform their tasks.

Managers also apply "soft" technologies, such as the application of human relations techniques to personnel in the organization so that people will perform more efficiently and effectively. Soft technologies often involve interpersonal communications that are aimed at improving the ability of people to process information. Since information is a valuable managerial resource, soft technologies are an important way to enhance the manager's ability to perform his or her tasks.

Finance

Managers need money, which they usually get in the form of a budget. This budget is a part of yet a larger budget—generally a department—that is provided by a legislative body, typically for one year. The budget gives the manager funds necessary to achieve his or her tasks. As such, money is a very important resource.

Like all resources, a budget has certain limitations. First, it is not a bottomless pit. On the contrary, it is a relatively fixed sum of money. Moreover, there are frequently restrictions pertaining to how the money can be spent, when it may be spent, and for what it can be spent. Constraints on the budget, then, require judicious use of the agency's funds. The budget is a major managerial resource, a tremendous headache, and a challenge.

IS PUBLIC MANAGEMENT DIFFERENT?

Training for managerial careers in the private sector typically takes place in the business schools of universities. Some of these schools have national reputations, and their top graduates are eagerly sought by the "Fortune 500" corporations. Among them are the Harvard Business School, the Wharton School at the University of Pennsylvania, Stanford University's Business School, and the University of Chicago's School of Business. Graduates from these schools receive master of business administration (MBA) degrees.

Training for public management has taken a similar, though distinct, route. Students study for a master of public administration (MPA) degree and usually find employment at some level of government. Well-known schools include the Maxwell School at Syracuse University, the Kennedy School at Harvard University, the School of Public and Environmental Affairs at Indiana University, and the public administration school at the University of Southern California. Although MPAs and MBAs follow different career paths in general, some MBAs enter government service. (It is less common for MPAs to find employment in the private sector.)

A few of the differences in training have been slowly breaking down. First, the resources necessary to manage in both sectors are similar. Second, in the broad sense, the tasks of management are similar. Third, the differences between the private sector and the public sector have been diminishing. Some graduate schools of management have responded to these trends by teaching a "generic" brand of management based on the view that there are more similarities than differences in management in the two sectors. Students are brought together from some generic courses and separated for classes that truly pertain to only one sector. Generic schools of management can be found at Yale University, Northwestern University, and the University of California, Irvine. (There is some question, however, about the real success of generic programs. The public sector side of the curriculum at Yale University, for example, has all but disappeared.)

Let's not overstate the similarities. Borrowing a phrase from Wally Sayre, Graham Allison, a past dean of the Kennedy School of Government at Harvard University, observed, "public and private management are alike in all unimportant respects."[1] Some of the common reasons given for this view are the following:

1.   There is no equivalent to the bottom line in government organization. Private companies, it is argued, want above all to make profits. Profits are what keep private organizations (literally) in business. Consequently, all activities of management ultimately must be designed to enhance the profitability of the firm. Otherwise, there will eventually be no need for management. In contrast, public organizations have elusive goals, usually multiple and hard to measure. Public managers cannot be judged against a single, widely accepted standard.

2.   Managers in the public sector have a short time horizon. Politics, especially electoral politics, guides decisions in public organizations—which means that the time frame of public managers is short. They have little incentive to look too far into the future. Business managers, in contrast, must plan ahead. They have to be aware of market developments, for example, if they expect to remain competitive.[2]

3.   Managers in the public sector are faced with competing pressures. In the business world, making more money is better than making less money. If being efficient leads to making more money, so much the better. Public organizations are not so straightforward. Although being more efficient is usually a worthwhile endeavor, it is rarely sufficient in itself. Many public organizations, for example, try to improve equity for specific groups even though it may occasionally lead to less efficiency.

4.   Public organizations are more visible to the public than private organizations. Try getting into a meeting of the board of directors of the Ford Motor Company. You won't get through the door! Government organizations are generally more accessible because of "open-meeting" or "sunshine" laws, which allow the public to attend. Besides, since some offi-

cials are elected directly by the public, they may feel obliged to permit access to government meetings. Moreover, public managers are constantly under the watchful eyes of the news media.

Legislative and Judicial Oversight

You can't do anything as a public manager without some external constraints from the legislature or the courts. Each time the manager goes before the legislature to ask for money—and that usually happens every year—elected legislators are able to inquire about the organization and the manager's performance. Clients of the organization, citizens who feel that they are being harmed by it, may complain to their elected representatives. Representatives, in turn, demand an explanation from the public organization. Legislators call this "constituency service." Public managers call it a "pain in the neck."

Judges also scrutinize the activities of a public organization if a plaintiff brings suit against it. Prisoners, for example, have initiated suits against state prison commissioners for overcrowding, lack of certain facilities (such as a library), lack of adequate medical care, and breach of visitation rights. Some mental health patients have sued for the "right to treatment." In those cases in which the court has agreed with the plaintiff's charges and ruled against the government agency, judges have required some type of corrective action.[3] Often public managers must inform the court about progress (or lack of progress) concerning the implementation of the judicial decree.

Few people would deny that differences between public and private management exist. But are they really so profound as implied by these four common reasons? First, private managers worry about more areas than just the bottom line. They worry about stable organizational growth, financial stability, employees' job satisfaction, reputation, competitive advantage, and innovation. Like public organizations, private firms (and therefore private sector managers) have multiple objectives. Naturally, private sector managers worry about profits, but they worry about a great deal more. Bottom-line management may not be possible in governmental organizations; it is incomplete management in private firms.

Second, although politics does tend to instill a short time horizon for top public managers, this point is less true of managers who are not political appointees. Indeed, career civil servants who rise to the highest managerial levels just below political appointees have long time horizons and institutional memories. Middle-level managers in government organizations, for example, often forecast spending and services in two-, three-, and five-year projections. In this respect, they employ strategic planning as one ingredient of their managerial style.

Third, private sector managers, like their public sector counterparts, also face competing pressures. At one time it was said that "the business of business is business." But private sector managers are also concerned with corporate image, community service, and social responsibility. Maybe these other pressures are not so important for every manager in the private sector, but they are important for some. Thus we cannot say that all public managers face pressures from several sides, whereas private managers only worry about profits. Of course, profits are not exactly trivial either.

Fourth, at one time it may have been true that private firms made all their decisions behind closed doors. This is less true today. When companies compete for government contracts, some of their actions are scrutinized by the media and the public. Moreover, private managers are often faced with lawsuits and charges levied against companies by consumer advocate groups, allowing the public to peek past partially opened corporate doors.

Fifth, private managers, like their public manager counterparts, often must appear before legislative committees to explain and justify the actions of their companies. This frequently happens when companies receive large government contracts. More generally, companies must comply with many legal constraints that place their managers before legislators and before the courts.

We can say, then, that although public and private management are different, the differences are often a matter of degree.[4] One way to appreciate both the similarities and differences is to look at the job of a private manager and a public manager: Doug Costle, the director of the Environmental Protection Agency in the Carter administration, and Roy Chapin, former chairman and chief executive officer of the American Motors Company.

An Operational Perspective

How Are the Jobs and Responsibilities of Doug Costle, Director of the EPA, and Roy Chapin, CEO of American Motors, Similar and Different?

If organizations could be separated neatly into two homogeneous piles, one public and one private, the task of identifying similarities and differences between managers of these enterprises would be relatively easy. In fact, as Dunlop has pointed out, "the real world of management is composed of distributions, rather than single undifferentiated forms, and there is an increasing variety of hybrids." Thus for each major attribute of organizations, specific entities can be located on a spectrum. On most dimensions, organizations classified as "predominantly public" and those "predominantly private" overlap. Private business organizations vary enormously among themselves in size, in management structure and philosophy, and in the constraints under which they operate. For example, forms of ownership and types of managerial control may be somewhat unrelated. Compare a family-held enterprise, for instance, with a public utility and a decentralized conglomerate, a Bechtel with ATT and Textron. Similarly, there are vast differences in management of governmental organizations. Compare the Government Printing Office or TVA or the Police Department of a small town with the Department of Energy or the Department of Health and Human Services. These distributions and varieties should encourage penetrating comparisons within both business and governmental organizations, as well as contrasts and comparisons across these broad categories, a point to which we shall return in considering directions for research.

Without a major research effort, it may nonetheless be worthwhile to examine the jobs and responsibilities of two specific managers, neither polar extremes, but one clearly public, the other private. For this purpose, and primarily because of the availability of cases that describe the problems and opportunities each confronted, consider Doug Costle, Administrator of EPA, and Roy Chapin, CEO of American Motors.

Doug Costle, Administrator of EPA, January 1977: The mission of EPA is prescribed by laws creating the agency and authorizing its major programs. That mission is "to control and abate pollution in the areas of air, water, solid wastes, noise, radiation, and toxic substances. EPA's mandate is to mount an integrated, coordinated attack on environmental pollution in cooperation with state and local government."

EPA's organizational structure follows from its legislative mandates to control particular pollutants in specific environments: air and water, solid wastes, noise, radiation, pesticides and chemicals. As the new Administrator, Costle inherited the Ford Administration's proposed budget for EPA of $802 million for fiscal year 1978 with a ceiling of 9,698 agency positions.

The setting into which Costle stepped is difficult to summarize briefly. As Costle characterized it:

> "Outside there is a confusion on the part of the public in terms of what this agency is all about: what it is doing, where it is going."
>
> "The most serious constraint on EPA is the inherent complexity in the state of our knowledge, which is constantly changing."
>
> "Too often, acting under extreme deadlines mandated by Congress, EPA has announced regulations, only to find out that they knew very little about the problem. The central problem is the inherent complexity of the job that the agency has been asked to do and the fact that what it is asked to do changes from day to day."
>
> "There are very difficult internal management issues not amenable to a quick solution: the skills mix problem within the agency; a research program with laboratory facilities scattered all over the country and cemented in place, largely by political alliances on the Hill that would frustrate efforts to pull together a coherent research program."
>
> "In terms of EPA's original mandate in the bulk pollutants we may be hitting the asymptotic part of the curve in terms of incremental cleanup costs. You have clearly conflicting national goals: Energy and environment, for example."

Costle judged his six major tasks at the outset to be:

> assembling a top management team (six assistant administrators and some 25 office heads);

addressing EPA's legislative agenda (EPA's basic legislative charter—the Clean Air Act and the Clean Water Act—were being rewritten as he took office; the pesticides program was up for reauthorization also in 1977);

establishing EPA's role in the Carter Administration (aware that the Administration would face hard tradeoffs between the environment and energy, energy regulations and the economy, EPA regulations of toxic substances and the regulations of FDA, CSPS, and OSHA, Costle identified the need to build relations with the other key players and to enhance EPA's standing);

building ties to constituent groups (both because of their role in legislating the agency's mandate and in successful implementation of EPA's programs);

making specific policy decisions (for example, whether to grant or deny a permit for the Seabrook Nuclear Generating Plant cooling system. Or how the Toxic Substance Control Act, enacted in October 1976, would be implemented: this act gave EPA new responsibilities for regulating the manufacture, distribution, and use of chemical substances so as to prevent unreasonable risks to health and the environment. Whether EPA would require chemical manufacturers to provide some minimum information on various substances, or require much stricter reporting requirements for the 1,000 chemical substances already known to be hazardous, or require companies to report all chemicals, and on what timetable, had to be decided and the regulations issued);

rationalizing the internal organization of the agency (EPA's extreme decentralization to the regions and its limited technical expertise).

No easy job.

Roy Chapin and American Motors, January 1977: In January 1967, in an atmosphere of crisis, Roy Chapin was appointed Chairman and Chief Executive Officer of American Motors (and William Luneburg, President and Chief Operating Officer). In the four previous years, AMC unit sales had fallen 37 percent and market share from over six percent to under three percent. Dollar volume in 1967 was off 42 percent from the all-time high of 1963 and earnings showed a new loss of $76 million on sales of $656 million. Columnists began writing obituaries for AMC. Newsweek characterized AMC as a "a flabby dispirited company, a product solid enough but styled with about as much flair as corrective shoes, and a public image that melted down to one unshakable label: loser." Said Chapin: "We were driving with one foot on the accelerator and one foot on the brake. We didn't know where the hell we were."

Chapin announced to his stockholders at the outset that "we plan to direct ourselves most specifically to those areas of the market where we can be fully effective. We are not going to attempt to be all things to all people, but to concentrate on those areas of consumer needs we can meet better than anyone else." As he recalled: "There were problems early in 1967 which demanded immediate attention, and which accounted for much of our time for several months. Nevertheless, we began planning beyond them, establishing objectives, programs and timetables through 1972. Whatever happened in the short run, we had to prove ourselves in the marketplace in the long run."

Chapin's immediate problems were five:

The company was virtually out of cash and an immediate supplemental bank loan of $20 million was essential.

Car inventories—company owned and dealer owned—had reached unprecedented levels. The solution to this glut took five months and could be accomplished only by a series of plant shutdowns in January 1967.

Sales of the Rambler American series had stagnated and inventories were accumulating; a dramatic merchandising move was concocted and implemented in February, dropping the price tag on the American to a position midway between the VW and competitive smaller U.S. compacts, by both cutting the price to dealers and trimming dealer discounts from 21 percent to 17 percent.

Administrative and commercial expenses were judged too high and thus a vigorous cost reduction program was initiated that trimmed $15 million during the first year. Manufacturing and purchasing costs were also trimmed significantly to approach the most effective levels in the industry.

The company's public image had deteriorated: the press was pessimistic and much of the financial community had written it off. To counteract this, numerous formal and informal meetings were held with bankers, investment firms, government officials, and the press.

As Chapin recalls, "with the immediate fires put out, we could put in place the pieces of a corporate growth plan—a definition of a way of life in the auto industry for American Motors. We felt that our reason for being, which would enable us not just to survive but to grow, lay in bringing a different approach to the auto market—in picking our spots and then being innovative and aggressive." The new corporate growth plan included a dramatic change in the approach to the market to establish a "youthful image" for the company (by bringing out new sporty models like the Javelin and by entering the racing field), "changing the product line from one end to the other" by 1972, acquiring Kaiser Jeep (selling the company's non-transportation assets and concentrating on specialized transportation, including Jeep, a company that had lost money in each of the preceding five years, but that Chapin believed could be turned around by substantial cost reductions and economies of scale in manufacturing, purchasing, and administration).

Chapin succeeded: for the year ending September 30, 1971, AMC earned $10.2 million on sales of $1.2 billion.

Strategy. Both Chapin and Costle had to establish objectives and priorities and to devise operational plans. In business, "corporate strategy is the pattern of major objectives, purposes, or goals and essential policies and plans for achieving these goals, stated in such a way as to define what business the company is in or is to be in and the kind of company it is or is to be." In reshaping the strategy of AMC and concentrating on particular segments of the transportation market, Chapin had to consult his Board and had to arrange financing. But the control was substantially his.

How much choice did Costle have at EPA as to the "business it is or is to be in" or the kind of agency "it is or is to be"? These major strategic choices emerged from the legislative process which mandated whether he should be in the business of controlling pesticides or toxic substances and if so on what timetable, and occasionally, even what level of particulate per million units he was required to control. The relative role of the President, other members of the Administration (including White House staff, Congressional relations, and other agency heads), the EPA Administrator, Congressional committee chairmen, and external groups in establishing the broad strategy of the agency constitutes an interesting question.

Managing internal components. For both Costle and Chapin, staffing was key. As Donald Rumsfeld has observed, "the single, most important task of the chief executive is to select the right people. I've seen terrible organization charts in both government and business that were made to work well by good people. I've seen beautifully charted organizations that didn't work very well because they had the wrong people."

The leeway of the two executives in organizing and staffing were considerably different, however. Chapin closed down plants, moved key managers, hired and fired, virtually at will. As Michael Blumenthal has written about Treasury, "If you wish to make substantive changes, policy changes, and the Department's employees don't like what you're doing, they have ways of frustrating you or stopping you that do not exist in private industry. The main method they have is Congress. If I say I want to shut down a particular unit or transfer the function of one area to another, there are ways of going to Congress and in fact using friends in the Congress to block the move. They can also use the press to try to stop you. If I at Bendix wished to transfer a division from Ann Arbor to Detroit because I figured out that we could save money that way, as long as I could do it decently and carefully, it's of no lasting interest to the press. The press can't stop me. They may write about it in the local paper, but that's about it."

For Costle, the basic structure of the agency was set by law. The labs, their location, and most of their personnel were fixed. Though he could recruit his key subordinates, again restrictions like the conflict of interest law and the prospect of a Senate confirmation fight led him to drop his first choice for the Assistant Administrator for Research and Development, since he had worked for a major chemical company. While Costle could resort to changes in the process for developing policy or regulations in order to circumvent key office directors whose views he did not share, for example, Eric Stork, the Deputy Assistant Administrator in charge of Mobile Source Air Program, such maneuvers took considerable time, provoked extensive infighting, and delayed significantly the development of Costle's program.

In the direction of personnel and management of the personnel system, Chapin exercised considerable authority. While the United Auto Workers limited his authority over workers, at the management level he assigned people and reassigned responsibility consistent with his general plan. While others may have felt that his decisions to close down particular plants or to drop a particular product were mistaken, they complied. As George Shultz has observed: "One of the first lessons I learned in moving from government to business is that in business you must be very careful when you tell someone who is working for you to do something because the probability is high that he or she will do it."

Costle faced a civil service system designed to prevent spoils as much as to promote productivity. The Civil Service Commission exercised much of the responsibility for the personnel function in his agency. Civil service rules severely restricted his discretion, took long periods to exhaust, and often required complex maneuvering in a specific case to achieve any results. Equal opportunity rules and their administration provided yet another network of procedural and substantive inhibitions. In retrospect, Costle found the civil service system a much larger constraint on his actions and demand on his time than he had anticipated.

In controlling performance, Chapin was able to use measures like profit and market share, to decompose those objectives to sub-objectives for lower levels of the organization and to measure the performance of managers of particular models, areas, divisions. Cost accounting rules permitted him to compare plants within AMC and to compare AMC's purchases, production, and even administration with the best practice in the industry.

Managing external constituencies. As Chief Executive Officer, Chapin had to deal only with the Board. For Costle, within the executive branch but beyond his agency lay many actors critical to the achievement of his agency's objectives: the President and the White House, Energy, Interior, the Council on Environmental Quality, OMB. Actions each could take, either independently or after a process of consultation in which they disagreed with him, could frustrate his agency's achievement of its assigned mission. Consequently, he spent considerable time building his agency's reputation and capital for interagency disputes.

Dealing with independent external organizations was a necessary and even larger part of Costle's job. Since his agency's mission, strategy, authorizations, and appropriations emerged from the process of legislations, attention to Congressional committees, and Congressmen, and Congressmen's staff, and people who affect Congressmen and Congressional staffers rose to the top of Costle's agenda. In the first year, top level EPA officials appeared over 140 times before some 60 different committees and subcommittees.

Chapin's ability to achieve AMC's objectives could also be affected by independent external organizations: competitors, government (the Clean Air Act that was passed in 1970), consumer groups (recall Ralph Nader), and even suppliers of oil. More than most private managers, Chapin had to deal with the press in attempting to change the image of AMC. Such occasions were primarily at Chapin's initiative, and around events that Chapin's public affairs office orchestrated, for example, the announcement of a new racing car. Chapin also managed a marketing effort to persuade consumers that their tastes could best be satisfied by AMC products.

Costle's work was suffused by the press, in the daily working of the organization, in the perception by key publics of the agency and thus the agency's influence with relevant parties, and even in the setting of the agenda of issues to which the agency had to respond.

For Chapin, the bottom line was profit, market share and the long-term competitive position of AMC. For Costle, what are the equivalent performance measures? Blumenthal answers by exaggerating the difference between appearance and reality: "At Bendix, it was the reality of the situation that in the end determined whether we succeeded or not. In the crudest sense, this meant the bottom line. You can dress up profits only for so long; if you're not successful, it's going to be clear. In government there is no bottom line, and that is why you can be successful if you appear to be successful—though, of course, appearance is not the only ingredient of success." Rumsfeld says: "In business, you're pretty much judged by results. I don't think the American people judge government officials this way. . . . In government, too often you're measured by how much you seem to care, how hard you seem to try—things that do not necessarily improve the human condition. . . . It's a lot easier for a President to get into something and end up with a few days of good public reaction than it is to follow through, to pursue policies to a point where they have a beneficial effect on human lives." As George Shultz says: "In government and politics, recognition and therefore incentives go to those who formulate policy and maneuver legislative compromise. By sharp contrast, the kudos and incentives in business go to the persons who can get something done. It is execution that counts. Who can get the plant built, who can bring home the sales contract, who can carry out the financing, and so on."

This casual comparison of one public and one private manager suggests what could be done—if the issue of comparisons were pursued systematically, horizontally across organizations and at various levels within organizations. While much can be learned by examining the chief executive officers of organizations, still more promising should be comparisons among the much larger numbers of middle managers. If one compared, for example, a Regional Administrator of EPA and an AMC division chief, or two Comptrollers, or equivalent plant managers, some functions would appear more similar, and other differences would stand out. The major barrier to such comparisons is the lack of cases describing problems and practices of middle-level managers. This should be a high priority in further research.

The differences noted in this comparison, for example, in the personnel area, have already changed with the Civil Service Reform Act of 1978 and the creation of the Senior Executive Service. Significant changes have also occurred in the automobile industry: under current circumstances, the CEO of Chrysler may seem much more like the Administrator of EPA. More precise comparison of different levels of management in both organizations, for example, accounting procedures used by Chapin to cut costs significantly as compared to equivalent procedures for judging the costs of EPA mandated pollution control devices, would be instructive.

□ *Source: From Graham I. Allison, Jr.,* Public and Private Management: Are They Fundamentally Alike in All Unimportant Respects? *Section 4, pp. 33–37. Paper prepared for the Public Management Research Conference, Brookings Institution, Washington, D.C., November 1979. Reprinted with permission.*

Are there different types of public managers? You bet. Theodore Marmor has sketched out four ideal types of public managers based on the relationship between a manager's commitment to program goals and the managerial skills held by the individual. Here is a summary of the four types:

Administrative Survivors—These managers have low commitment to the programmatic goals of their agencies and low management skills. They "hang in" and "hang on," but they are certainly not leaders.

Generalist Managers—Historically associated with "high flyers" in the French and British civil service, products of the best universities and professional schools, these managers have solid skills but are not necessarily strongly committed to programmatic goals. The reason, quite simply, is that these higher civil servants rotate across policy areas and agencies and develop no firm career attachment to any one in particular.

Program Zealots—Brought on board to make a programmatic splash, usually by shaking up the programmatic direction of the agency, these managers are often unsuccessful because their programmatic zeal is not backed up by managerial competence.

Program Loyalists—Armed with a strong commitment to program goals and a gift for effective management, these administrators tend to be the ones who spend the better part of a career in an agency working on policy initiatives and overseeing their implementation.[5]

DECIDING WHEN TO MANAGE

Did you ever have a job where you had something to do but couldn't make any progress because someone was always telling you, or showing you, how to do it? How often have you heard the expression "There are too many chiefs and not enough Indians"? Or did you ever see kids quarrel over the game "Follow the Leader" because everyone wanted to be the leader? These situations are part of a basic problem faced by all aspiring managers—deciding when to manage.

No Solution, No Problem

There was a time during the 1960s when policy-makers had faith that government could solve many social and economic problems affecting American society. A standing joke at the time was that a social scientist, eager to be involved in the prevailing optimism, would claim, "Who has a problem? I have a solution." Nowadays, the optimism is tempered by an appreciation of the difficulties of designing and carrying out effective programs. If there are no solutions, there are no problems. Naturally, this is overstated, but it contains more than a grain of truth when deciding when to manage.

We said earlier that management involves the use of organizational resources to achieve objectives. A head of a public sanitation department must determine how best to deploy personnel and equipment to pick up the trash. But picking up the trash is not the ultimate objective. The purpose of the operation is to clean the streets. Notice that in this illustration, clean streets is the objective the manager wants to reach. Picking up trash is an intermediate objective. The manager is reasonably confident that if the sanitation workers pick up the trash, the streets are likely to be clean. Part of the job of management is choosing the most efficient ways to use the resources of the sanitation department to achieve the objective of clean streets.

Many government programs resemble sanitation. Principals know they want to "produce" educated children; police commissioners want to improve public safety; and fire commissioners want to do the same by preventing and putting out fires. In each case there is some knowledge about the tasks that should be performed to reach an ultimate objective. Teachers must teach; police personnel must patrol streets to deter and catch criminals; firefighters have to inspect buildings to prevent fires and squelch fires in the shortest time possible to save lives and property.

Sometimes managers do not know whether the performance of tasks will actually lead to the objectives desired. Consider a very controversial issue of public policy—prison administration and reform. What is the objective of a typical prison warden? Many would say that the warden is supposed to use resources in such a way that when prisoners finish serving their terms, they can return to society and lead productive lives. In other words, prisons are supposed to rehabilitate prisoners. Success is not widespread because wardens still do not have adequate knowledge about what kinds of prison activities are most likely to be successful at rehabilitating convicts. So if there is no real solution to prison rehabilitation, is there a managerial problem?

Yes. Prisoners have to be fed, clothed, supervised, disciplined, and eventually discharged. State (or federal) laws regarding how prisons should be run must be enforced. Personnel must be hired, fired, motivated, and reprimanded. Also important, the warden must decide how to allocate the budget. Thus managerial decisions are constantly being made concerning the operations of the prison.

Operations are ongoing; they are also filled with problems. Four prison guards quit unexpectedly, and the warden is suddenly short of staff. A truckload of food did not arrive. Utility rate increases forced overspending for natural gas and electricity, and the warden is afraid that he may run out of funds before the end of the fiscal year. These are all managerial problems, but they all focus on running the prison. They are not part of the larger topic—the link between prison activities and the rehabilitative objective, a much more difficult problem. But since we have already said that it is a problem with no solution, it allows the manager to focus on operations.[6]

Routinized Decisions

Have you ever been on an airplane when the pilot suddenly walked past you on his way to the lavatory? "Gosh, who is flying the plane?" may have been your reaction. Most of us now realize that the captain put the plane on "automatic pilot" (though a real person, the copilot, is still in the cockpit). During this time the decisions about flying the plane were routinized; they were programmed; or to put it another way, they were controlled. While the plane was on automatic pilot the captain did not have to make choices or decisions. The automatic pilot made them.

Many activities in government organizations are similarly programmed. Consider a simple one like payroll. Typically, wages for personnel are "stored" in a computer file; a computer program calculates the weekly or biweekly payroll check, which typically includes gross pay, tax deductions, and special deductions like employee pension contributions, medical insurance charges, union dues, and voluntary payroll deductions for charity or savings. Decisions that have to be made are generally clerical. They may include listing the actual hours worked, recording vacation periods for individual employees, or recording sick leave. We can say that there are no managerial decisions here.

But what about a salary increase caused by a promotion? Isn't this an example of a managerial decision? Not really. When the manager decided to promote the employee, we can say that the personnel decision was indeed an exercise of managerial discretion. After the promotion was made, however, the subsequent salary and benefit provisions were routine. As we will see in a later chapter, most

civil service positions have accompanying salary and wage schedules that minimize the manager's discretion. Therefore, we can say that the decision is programmed.

When Control Should Be Avoided

Would you want your plane to be on automatic pilot when it is going through an
unanticipated storm? Probably not. Decisions will probably have to be made that
require judgment because the storm will provide surprises. These surprises, by
definition, cannot be programmed. When decisions cannot be programmed they
are not under control, and thus there is a need for management.[7]

Let's return to the promotion. In the discussion of managerial resources, we
said that personnel is very important. So when it comes time to make a decision
on promotion, the manager will want to consider the alternatives carefully. What
criteria will be used?

The manager will consider the major contenders for the promotion, perhaps
evaluating each person's performance in his or her current position. But this will
not make the choice a programmed one. After all, performance in one job may
not necessarily mean doing well in another. So the manager must make a judgment about each person's potential, a decision clearly based on insufficient information. Notice that whatever the manager does to reduce the uncertainty in this
situation will not alter a fundamental fact: The manager will not be able to control
the future. The essence of management—judgment, risk, and a complicated situation—dominate the decision.[8]

DECIDING HOW TO MANAGE

"Poor Ike, he will say do this, do that and nothing will happen." President Truman was speaking about General Eisenhower, World War II hero, who was about
to become the thirty-fourth president of the United States. President Truman was
making a simple point. Managing the federal government would be a lot more
difficult than managing an army, a fact President Eisenhower never denied.

Is there one best way to manage? Not really. Hugh Heclo recounted the reflections of two former high-level managers appointed by President Nixon. One
was a "tough guy"—a person who wanted to let the career civil service staff
know that he had an agenda that he was prepared to push in the agency. But the
tough guy conceded that "it is not really effective trying to browbeat people and
win every little battle."[9] So being a tough guy may not necessarily be effective.

Not every manager adopts this approach. A second appointee reflected on
his experiences in the federal government by suggesting that a "softer" approach
was ultimatively ineffective. The second political appointee lamented, "I made
the decisions but they [bureaucratic subordinates] just continued to argue. The
delays went on until I left office."[10] So being "Mr. Nice Guy" is not necessarily
a better way of managing.

Was one managerial style more effective than the other? A high-level career
civil servant who watched both of these presidential appointees in action noted

that both approaches failed because neither political appointee realized that the management task was to identify a small number of important issues, identify key supporters and opponents, and then use the organization's resources to influence change. In his words, "An appointee has got to make other people feel a part of the credit line."[11]

In other words, "tough guy" and "nice guy" managerial styles can both fail because they misinterpret the amount of influence managers have in public organizations. Managers must first decide when it is appropriate to manage, but they must also use their limited resources to convince subordinates that something should happen, that something should be done. Heclo, a keen observer of the federal bureaucracy, has called this the attempt to produce "conditionally cooperative behavior."[12] Subordinates have the capacity to follow initiatives from managers. But since people in organizations have their own nests to feather, they must be brought together to perform tasks—the essence of management. This is accomplished through leadership, the delegation of authority and responsibility, motivation, and the judicious application of incentives.

Leadership

Leadership is hard to define. Consider, first, what leadership is not.

> Leadership is not simply the army lieutenant who tells his men to "follow him" as he charges up the hill.
> Leadership is not the person who claims to be "in charge" by virtue of an official job title.
> Leadership is not automatically conferred on individuals in organizations simply because they have inherited formal positions of authority.
> Leadership is not easily distinguished from the organizational characteristics that it finds itself part of. It is not always transferable from one kind of organization to another (recall President Truman's comment about General Eisenhower).

It is easier to say what leadership is not than what it is. Nevertheless, some themes about leadership seem to be repeated over and over. Leaders in organizations, for example, take a prominent role in defining organizational goals. A new secretary of defense may be instrumental in shifting the Department of Defense's strategic objectives from one dominant point of view to a different one. In the 1950s the strategic position of the United States was one of "massive retaliation," which meant that in the event of a Soviet nuclear provocation, the United States would come out with the (nuclear) "guns blazing." During the Kennedy and Johnson administrations, the Defense Department reappraised the nuclear capabilities of both the Soviet Union and the United States. The secretary of defense at the time, Robert McNamara, was instrumental in bringing about a change in strategic policy. He argued that the U.S. military should be more prepared to fight conventional wars since, given the standoff in nuclear weapons between the two superpowers, such wars were more rather than less likely. He also led military planners in a reassessment of nuclear options that, perhaps ghoulishly, developed into a strategy for "limited" nuclear war.

This example highlights one basic aspect of leadership: Leaders are instrumental in clarifying and altering organizational objectives. What happens when leadership seems to be missing? Consider the personal reflections of Joseph A. Califano, Jr., a member of President Johnson's White House staff and President Carter's embattled secretary of health, education and welfare. Commenting on his impression of President Carter's lack of leadership, Califano wrote, "His [President Carter's] administration lacked cohesion."[13] In particular, White House staff and heads of the executive branch departments were sniping at one another. Relations with the Democratic party leadership in the House of Representatives was strained. The president, in Califano's opinion, seemed unable to recognize problems of confidence in his administration.

How can we appraise leadership? How can we tell the difference between effective and ineffective leadership? At one time President Eisenhower was not rated highly by historians who were critical of his leadership. More recently, his stature as an effective president and leader has risen. Our impression of a leader's performance changes with time. We notice subtle developments that may be hidden during the middle of the battle and can sometimes appreciate leadership qualities that were previously masked. President Eisenhower, for example, is said to have used his cabinet members effectively. He also delegated authority well. These leadership traits became more noticeable with the passage of time. They also became more appreciated by historians who reassessed their criteria for effective presidential leadership in light of the presidents who followed Eisenhower.

So what is effective leadership? Let's go back to Moses. Measuring performance, Moses got the job done. There is no doubt about it. He was told to lead his followers out of the land of Egypt and he certainly did that. In fact, Moses was so successful that Israelites did not return (peacefully) to Egypt until after the Camp David peace agreement President Carter helped negotiate between President Sadat of Egypt and Prime Minister Menachem Begin of Israel in 1978!

But there is another way to evaluate Moses's performance. If we adopt a literal interpretation of the Old Testament for the moment, we learn that it took Moses forty years to reach this objective. That's a long time. What was Moses's problem? Did his followers question his authority? Did they displace his goals with their own individual objectives and thereby make it more difficult for him to achieve his assigned task?

We know that the answers to these questions are affirmative. It wasn't clear sailing for Moses. It never is for managers. But the point to be learned from this illustration is that managers can only control a limited number of the factors that will contribute to the success or failure of an organization's mission. If we measure the effectiveness of a manager by the effectiveness of the organization, we may (1) damn the manager for failures caused by factors completely beyond his or her control or (2) praise the manager for success that was caused largely by events he or she had nothing to do with.

Cooperative behavior.   An axiom of elementary economics theory is that individuals pursue their own self-interest. If we accept this axiom, we also accept the idea that people in public organizations act in the same way. That is, people look out for themselves.

If everyone in an organization looks out for himself or herself, how can a manager generate cooperative behavior? People want to feel important and needed. They want to feel that they are making a contribution, that they are having some influence. Cooperative behavior, then, is more likely to develop if the manager is able to harness individual self-interest to the achievement of organizational tasks. In other words, appeals to serve the "public interest," the "common good," or even the organizational mission are unlikely to be effective unless they are accompanied with benefits for individual members.

Delegation.   Managing can also include the art of letting someone else decide. In a classic television commercial for a breakfast cereal, three kids were sitting around a table with the cereal box prominently displayed. The two older kids were reluctant to try it and agreed they would "let Mikey try it first." Mikey started to eat the cereal, smiled, and kept eating. "He likes it," said one of the older kids, and the two started eating away. Mikey didn't realize it, but a decision was delegated to him. By smiling, he influenced the behavior of the other two kids.

When should managers delegate? They should do so when they can trust subordinates to made the same kinds of decisions they would make themselves. This means that subordinates must be loyal. Consider the following description by a former assistant secretary in a federal department:

> People you yourself hire are going to be more supportive than anyone else. They can be career guys, but they should be your guys and have primary loyalty to you. Roberts, for example, is an excellent career man. I expected little but gave him some things to do, and he performed wonderfully after plodding along in (the bureau) for eight years. I got him a promotion from a GS 14 to a 15 and took him with me to a different agency and made him a project director. Now he's an office head. That's the kind of person you have to attract and hold with you.[14]

Notice that there is a mutual exchange here. The civil servant, Roberts, got two things: a promotion and responsibility, both of which were important to him. The assistant secretary got a loyal subordinate in return—someone he could trust and delegate decisions to. So delegation requires loyalty as a prerequisite.

Managers should also delegate when the scope of activities is too broad to oversee. Although there is no magic formula, a common public administration doctrine that applies is the span of control (see Chapter 4). This concept refers to the number of subordinates who should report to the manager. Think about this for a moment. How many people should report to the president of a large state university? How many people should report to the hospital administrator? Who should report to the general in charge of an army?

The answer really depends on the amount of interaction that occurs among the units responsible to the manager. In the case of the hospital, there is a great deal of interaction among nursing, surgery, occupational therapy, and the like. In the case of the university, there is less interaction. How often, for example, does the music department have to do something with the physics department? The more interaction there is among units in an organization, the more likely there is a need for coordination. When coordination is a central task for managers, they should keep the number of people who report directly to them low. Delegation of tasks that require coordination, then, is not frequent. Conversely, when there is little need for coordination, managers can have a larger number of subordinates reporting to them; consequently, delegation can be used more extensively.

Motivation

How did Moses get the Israelites to follow him out of the land of Egypt? First, he had some help from Pharaoh, who made life very unpleasant for them. But although the miserable existence in Egypt may have been a necessary condition to encourage the exodus, it was not sufficient. Moses had to motivate the Israelites to leave. He did so by providing a good example, claiming he had information "from above" that leaving Egypt was a good idea. He also had to convince the Israelites that they would eventually be better off in the long run if they left Egypt.In other words, he had to promise them some future benefit if they agreed to follow him.

Moses learned that managing is not simply giving orders. In the contemporary world of modern management much ink has been spilled, and many experiments tried, over just what motivates employees. We learned in Chapter 3 that there is a rich tradition in industrial and social psychology concerning the need for motivation in organizations. We also learned about the various techniques— consultation, management by objectives, organizational development—that are supposed to help.

In a study of bureau chiefs in the federal government, Herbert Kaufman of the Brookings Institution found that the bureau chiefs he interviewed spend about 10 to 20 percent of their time motivating employees.[15] According to Kaufman, bureau chiefs thought that subordinates had to be motivated because some of the very characteristics of government employment would eventually reduce their effectiveness. Government bureaucrats with high salaries, for example, could not look forward to large increases once they reached the top of their salary schedule. Sometimes bureaucrats feel "stuck" in their jobs. The manager cannot easily fire civil servants, so this threat is not available as a way to stimulate them through negative sanctions. Also, the bureaucrat is often the target of much criticism and abuse.[16]

Public managers counter these inherent problems of bureaucracy by motivating subordinates through esprit de corps—a sense of organizational cohesiveness. Cohesiveness is fostered through standard means—newsletters, promotions from within, intramural sporting events, and so on. But most important, managers must show individuals that their personal objectives are best achieved if they behave in such a way as to promote the interests of the organization.

Does this approach work? Studies of organizations have shown that their members have innate survival instincts. Indeed, when a major reform designed to reduce hierarchy and encourage participation in the U.S. Department of State was initiated, subordinates in the organization saw these reforms as threatening. They pushed for more rules and hierarchy—not less—as a strategy to maintain the organization in a way most conducive to their interests.[17] Subordinates in this illustration had esprit de corps, a commitment to the organization that was strong, perhaps too strong.

Motivating employees is necessary but not sufficient if managers want to bring subordinates together to perform organizational tasks. One crucial managerial tool is left: the judicious application of incentives.

Incentives

Managers cannot manage through moral suasion alone. Asking employees to do this or that "for the good of the agency" or "for the good of the public" is not a sufficient way to obtain results. Nor will motivational pep talks or pats on the back do it either. Although we all like to be loved, or at least appreciated, we also like some concrete benefits for our labors. Managers must employ incentives to encourage improved performance from employees. As the following case illustrates, money is a popular stimulus.

> "Catch a Mugger, Make a Buck." Several years ago the city of Orange, California, tried an experiment in which police officers would get a bonus at the end of the year if there was a reduction in four "repressible" crimes: rape, robberies, burglaries, and auto thefts. The objective of the bonus plan was to reward police personnel with extra cash if the rate for these crimes fell below the rate for an agreed-on base period. The police department focused on the prevention of burglaries because this crime made up 80 percent of the four repressible crimes included in the incentive plan.
>
> Did the bonus plan work? Well, yes and no. The crime rate did fall; nevertheless, Orange did not renew the incentive plan once it ended, as stipulated in an agreement between the city and the association representing policy personnel. The scheme was not continued because (1) the crime rate was low, and it did not seem that it could be reduced much further; (2) the work load had been increased; therefore, police officers wanted the city to hire additional personnel; (3) there was some criticism of the bonus plan from outside the city; some law-enforcement agencies thought it was inappropriate to provide money incentives to get police to fight crime. So the concept really did not become very popular.[18]

There are other ways to provide incentives. Money isn't everything, as this example points out:

> What is a "Fair" Day's Work? Several years ago Flint, Michigan, had some labor problems with its sanitation workers. The workers wanted more money, but the city's administrators wanted to reduce overtime costs. The city and the union representing the sanitation workers entered into a "productivity bargain" in which a bonus pool of money was established from the savings accrued from reductions in overtime pay. These reductions were a result of increases in workers' productivity. So far this is like the previous case. Money motivates workers. But besides money, the arrangement in Flint included a rearrangement of the

work routes into what was called a "task" system. Workers were allowed to go home after six hours if their assigned route was satisfactorily completed. Workers liked this system because it gave them more leisure time. City administrators liked it because it reduced overtime pay.[19]

Managers in the public sector do not have the same flexibility to provide incentives as managers in the private sector, for four basic reasons: First, wage and salary differences in public employment are less sharp than in the private sector. This "equality" would be undermined if incentives were used extensively. Second, incentives require competition among employees, but there is not a long tradition of encouraging competition in the public sector. Third, civil service rules concerning pay, promotions, and the character of work often are at odds with incentive schemes. Fourth, collective-bargaining agreements often restrict a manager's ability to use incentives to stimulate improved performance.

Many of these limitations are changing, as we will see when we discuss public personnel practices. Indeed, many new innovations in personnel policy are precisely attempts to instill more incentives in existing personnel systems at all levels of government. Public employees, like everyone else, may not live by bread alone, but they also like to know that if they work harder, longer, and better, there may be a little more bread when their toil is over.

POSTSCRIPT

Management for What Ends? A Note on the Administrative Brilliance of Albert Speer

Some people might say that Albert Speer was a "nice" Nazi. Speer was Adolph Hitler's favorite architect, and he also became Hitler's minister of armaments and war. How did someone trained as an architect rise to such a prominent place in the Nazi hierarchy and become an important figure in the Third Reich's war machine? Speer was a superb manager.

The armaments industry of the Third Reich was overly bureaucratized, according to Speer.[20] He wanted to improve the performance of the industry by shifting the base of decisions from authority to results. He did this by initiating four major changes:[21]

1. Collegial decision making. Instead of rigid hierarchical decision making, Speer introduced group decision making in the Ministry of Armaments and War. Managers participated in committees and planning bodies to initiate innovations that would filter down through the armaments industry. Speer created an "open" atmosphere so that managers would feel comfortable making suggestions and criticisms—an atmosphere that was apparently not very common in Hitler's Germany.
2. Fluidity in the organization. Speer thought that most bureaucracies in the Third Reich were too rigid. He wanted his ministry to be dynamic—which meant that problems determined who would be responsible for

decisions. This policy was in sharp contrast to the more common situation in which a clear demarcation of organizational boundaries dictated what part of an organization would handle a problem. Speer did not want empire building in his ministry to stifle "creative" decision making.

3. Temporary systems. Organizations often live on even when their mission is over. Speer knew this and realized that organizational survival instincts would produce rigid bureaucracies. To counter this tendency, Speer tried to organize his ministry around tasks. When problems were solved, the organizational structures were dismantled.

4. Industrial self-responsibility. Speer recognized that to get things done subordinates must be given responsibility. Furthermore, they must feel that their self-interests are tied to the effectiveness of the organization. Using this simple proposition, Speer structured incentives and motivated his managers. The testimony that this approach worked was the fact that armaments production more than tripled from 1941 to the middle of 1944.

[handwritten margin note: Project Management]

Speer almost seems like the type of person you might want to work for. In the context of today's managerial language he was "innovative," "results oriented," and even "humanistic." He encouraged participative decision making and was concerned about the relationship between the organization and its members.

There were some problems, however. In addition to using slave labor from conquered territory in German factories, Speer directed a war machine for a nation that embarked on unprecedented aggression and human destruction. The objectives of Nazi Germany have been universally condemned. The Nuremberg trials found that individuals in the Third Reich could be held accountable for crimes against humanity. With hindsight, Speer accepted this responsibility. He was personally guilty of crimes committed by his ministry and, ultimately, the regime he served.

Management eventually leads to outcomes that have moral implications. Sometimes we like to think that we can separate operations from ultimate ends. There is a song by Tom Lehrer, a satirist popular in the 1960s, about the German scientist Werner von Braun, who after World War II came to the United States and assisted the U.S. military in the development of nuclear weapons. The song's lyrics say that von Braun helps the missiles "go up." But where do they come down? " 'That's not my department,' says Werner von Braun."

Speer eventually came to the conclusion that, unlike von Braun, he was responsible for the actions of the organization he managed and the regime he served.

SUMMARY

It is not always easy to identify public managers. They do not wear special clothes; they do not wear identification tags; and you can't always tell who they are by looking at their title or place in the organization. Managers are the people who have responsibility for using organizational resources to achieve programmatic objectives. There are basically four resources: organizational structure, people, technologies and information, and finances. Since resources are inevitably scarce, the effective manager is obviously the one who is able to select judiciously, from among these four resources, the right mix of ingredients that will get the job done.

The essence of public management is decision making. In this chapter two broad types of managerial decisions are emphasized. Deciding when to manage is a crucial first step to effective public management. You can't try to manage everything. There's a well-known saying in government: "When you're up to your ass in alligators, you forget that the objective was to drain the swamp." Deciding when to manage requires perspective—keeping the swamp in mind even while you are fighting off the alligators. Public managers must try to avoid managerial decisions that can be routinized (and therefore controlled). Rather, managers should concentrate on issues that are likely to include surprises, issues that are unpredictable. When uncertainty is the rule, the job of the manager is to manage.

Deciding how to manage is the second cluster of problems that confronts the typical public administrator. Giving orders alone will rarely be effective. Managers must exercise leadership, which means knowing when to delegate decision to subordinates, how to motivate personnel, and how to use incentives to reward (and punish).

Management, to repeat, is the use of organizational resources to achieve programmatic objectives. Sometimes the objectives are ethically suspect. They may be morally wrong, or they may be evil. In the postscript on the ex-Nazi, Albert Speer, it becomes apparent that the activities of public managers cannot be divorced from the ends they serve. When public managers decide how and when to manage, they may also be making moral choices.

You can now try your hand at public management. In the following case, "Regional Health Planning: A Response to Declining Resources," a manager is faced with a shrinking budget. The agency is going through a very difficult and painful period. Put yourself in the position of the executive director. Would you have done the same things? What would you have done differently? What actions should be taken in the next two years?

Regional Health Planning: A Response to Declining Resources*

INTRODUCTION

In early 1981, after several years of rather consistent federal support, the Centralia Health Systems Agency (CHSA) found itself facing a substantial reduction in the size of its basic federal grant from the U.S. Department of Health and Human Services' Bureau of Health Planning. Changes in the political and economic climate had contributed to a deemphasis on health planning, and the initial statements of the Reagan administration suggested a phase-out of the National Health Planning Program by 1983. Without federal support, which constituted about 80 percent of the agency's total budget, it was unlikely the CHSA could survive. Realizing that there could be as much as a 45 percent decrease in federal support for fiscal year (FY) 1981 (beginning July 1, 1981, for the agency), the CHSA had to reconsider its organizational structure, the allocation of resources, and the effectiveness of agency activities.

THE CHSA

The Centralia Health Systems Agency was established in 1976 under the guidelines of the National Health Planning and Resource Development Act. This law initiated the creation of two hundred Health Systems Agencies (HSA) across the nation that are designed to enable local citizens to participate in the progress and development of their community's health-care system. This is accomplished by a volunteer board of directors composed of consumers and providers of health-care services. The agency serves an eleven-county region in the central part of a large northeastern state. The Centralia Health Systems Agency is further divided into Sub-area Advisory Councils (SAC), single or multicounty, which have their own governing body and staff. The SACs gather information from their counties and serve as a link between the community and the regional planning body. Many policy actions begin here.

The major source of funds for the CHSA is a federal grant based on the Centralia Health Service area population. Also, local contributions, primarily from county governments, are matched by additional federal dollars. (See appendix for budget details.)

An HSA brings together residents of an area to evaluate their health system, identify problems, and work toward viable solutions. These objectives are realized through several activities required by federal law. One important function of the HSA, for example, is to review and comment upon proposed use of state and federal health funds in the region. If an area human services organization applies for a state or federal grant to add an alcohol counseling program, for instance, the CHSA would review and comment on the application. Comments on the need or appropriateness of the program would be forwarded to the funding agency for consideration in the decision-making process. The CHSA also takes part in reviewing licensing applications from health-care organizations or facilities. If an area hospital wants to add a pediatric intensive-care unit, the licensing application would be reviewed.

A second important activity is the collection and analysis of information concerning the health status of area residents, local health services, and health facilities. As part of this activity the HSA may provide technical assistance to organizations needing the expertise of health planners. If a community group is concerned about child abuse, for example, the CHSA might help in the preparation of an application for state funds to start an educational program.

Third, the CHSA is required to carry out an ongoing planning process, which involves studying the data collected from the area and proposing long- and short-range actions to improve segments of the health system. The product of this process is a five-year health-systems plan and a series of annual implementation plans. These plans are developed by a Plan Development and Implementation Committee with the assistance of agency staff. They are revised annually to reflect the changes that have occurred during the year and to set goals for the coming year. (See appendix for an outline of the CHSA organization and structure.)

THE FEDERAL CUTBACK

Health-planning budget troubles began during the last year of the Carter administration. Local health planning was targeted for a 30 percent cut in the March 1980 version of the 1981 budget. The Office of Management and Budget cited a lack of performance in cost containment as the program's principal failing. The final FY 1981 Carter budget cut the total national budget for Health Systems Agencies approximately 18.5 percent from $124.7 million to $101.7 million. For the CHSA this meant a reduction in the basic grant formula from 51 cents per capita to 40 cents for the area's 1.4 million people.

The Reagan administration was even more ambitious in efforts to reduce the National Health Planning Program. Upon entering office the administration proposed a phase-out of the program by 1983, beginning with deep cuts in federal appropriations in 1981 and no funds for local health planning in 1982. The administration cited three basic reasons for its action: (1) the program will not be needed when competitive market forces are unleashed in the health-care industry, (2) there was insufficient evidence of the program's effectiveness, and (3) health planning was more appropriately a state and local responsibility. Because of this the administration requested that Congress rescind $24 million of the FY 1981 appropriation for Health Systems Agencies. Added to the Carter cuts, this represented a 38 percent cut in the FY 1980 appropriation. Congress finally approved a recision of $18 million, which cut the basic grant formula to 32 cents per capita for Health Systems Agencies and cut CHSA revenue by 43 percent for its FY 1981 budget (July 1, 1981–June 30, 1982). (See appendix.)

In the absence of this federal support, the long-term prospects for the CHSA are not promising. Fortunately, the CHSA could delay the full, immediate impact. The agency generally operated below budget to maintain a contingency fund for just such occasions. At the time the cuts became known, the agency was spending at a level that would allow about 10 percent of the budget to be carried over into FY 1981. It also was just starting the third quarter of FY 1980, and some minor adjustments might further soften the impact. In the long run, however, if the agency was to survive, substantial change had to be considered.

AGENCY OPTIONS

Faced with the realities of impending budget cuts, the CHSA management had to determine the best way to reduce the level of operation without sacrificing functions it considered indispensable to the planning process. Doing this would likely involve reorganizing agency activities to minimize the impact of cuts and maximize efforts in areas determined to be high priorities. There were at least four major options available to the agency for responding to the budget cuts: (1) raise funds from alternative sources, (2) limit agency activities, (3) reduce personnel costs, and (4) reduce nonpersonnel costs such as rent and travel.

Some HSAs around the country had already been involved in fund raising and have been successful in raising funds from private businesses and foundations. Alternative funding sources, however, are limited by statutory restrictions that prohibit the HSAs from accepting contributions from any "individual or private entity which has a financial, judiciary, or other direct interest in the development, expansion, or support of health resources." This, for instance, includes health insurers who have a stake in health planning because of its potential for controlling medial costs. In any event, consideration of this option would have to include an examination of the costs of fund raising. Even if the agency has been successful in raising funds in the past, the return might not warrant the additional effort. The high costs might easily offset the additional gain.

A reduction of agency activities was also a viable option. In addition to developing an annual plan for the region's health-care systems, reviewing applications for changes in institutional health services, collecting data, and maintaining an extensive network of community advisory boards (SACs), the agency also conducts numerous special studies, participates in statewide planning activities, and provides technical assistance. Reductions in some of these areas could produce substantial savings by cutting personnel and nonpersonnel costs. Again, as with fund raising, there are statutory restrictions constraining the agency's actions. Plan development, data collection, and technical assistance, for example, are all mandated functions and could not be eliminated. Any agency decisions to reduce activities in functional areas would have to be made with careful consideration given to legislative restrictions.

Personnel reductions is another way to achieve budget cuts. Although there is no agency policy or legislative mandate that limits managerial decisions in this area, some staff positions may need to be retained to fulfill mandated agency functions. Since personnel costs comprise a large proportion of the agency budget, this seemed like an obvious option, given the size of the federal cuts.

Cost-cutting measures to reduce nonpersonnel costs was a final option. Office space, telephone, travel, and supplies all fall into this category. In light of the massive cuts, however, it would be difficult to limit budget reductions only to this area. As will be seen in the following section, the agency adopted a combination of these options.

AGENCY RESPONSE

By October 1981, nine months after the Reagan administration made its intentions known, and three months after the first round of budget cuts had taken effect, it was possible to begin to assess the agency's response to declining resources.

NEW SOURCES OF REVENUE

"New Sources of revenue are generally undeveloped," is how one informed planner put it. "The management believes we are at the vanguard of most HSAs in terms of local contributions per capita. The agency currently gets about 10 to 11 cents per capita from local county governments. Bill [the executive director] doesn't feel we can realistically expect more. The counties are feeling the same fiscal pressures we are. The management doesn't see how we can ask for more money and at the same time tell them we'll be cutting back commitments to local problems. They feel we will be doing well to maintain our current levels of local support next year."

While acknowledging that the agency is not rigorously pursuing local support, other staff members point to the agency's effort to gain state support to replace federal funds. "Bill, with other HSA directors in the state, successfully lobbied for a bill that provides $50,000 to each of the state's eight HSAs in 1981. They're hoping that this can be increased next year. They also hope that the state may assume completely the funding of HSAs if Reagan eliminates funding entirely. They feel there's enough legislative support."

Glen, a senior planner with the agency, disagrees. "Bill's putting too many eggs in one basket. He's being too short-sighted. The governor has no intentions of a long term bail-out of programs that are reduced by federal cutbacks. We can't rely heavily on the state. The $50,000 offered this year is about 5 percent of our total precutback budget. The agency's not doing enough to raise funds from private business. There has been a very minimal effort in this area. We need to contact more businesses and private foundations. We should also lobby to remove statutory restrictions that limit our sources. Private health insurers have a stake in health planning and would be willing to support it financially if it weren't for existing laws."

LIMITING AGENCY ACTIVITIES

One of the obvious areas for a cutback in activity was in the agency's highly decentralized board and committee structure. Maintaining it required a considerable amount of staff time and agency resources. Besides the seventy-three-member board of directors, the CHSA, since its creation, has maintained a network of eight Subarea Health Councils to enable residents of the region to voice local concerns and otherwise participate in the health planning process. These SACs usually meet on a monthly basis and frequently maintain their own committee structure to address local health concerns. Each SAC has assigned at least one agency planner to coordinate meetings and other activities.

In addition to having a general role in the CHSA plan development and review functions, these local bodies (which are chartered by the CHSA) also perform functions primarily related to the local health systems. These groups might organize health fairs, for instance, to familiarize citizens with available health services; they might assist the county in recruiting physicians; or they might try to improve the linkage between the local acute care hospital and the long-term case facility. Historically, the local SACs have had available to them 75 percent of one agency planner's time.

With an eye toward centralizing agency activity as a means of achieving savings, the agency management considered a number of alternative SAC structures. One proposal involved consolidating the existing eight SACs into three. It was estimated that with such a configuration the agency could eliminate six associate planners and one and one-half typists at a cost savings of $117,598. The consolidation would also cut costs by reducing the number of SAC meetings, the number of SAC activities requiring staff support, and the amount of technical assistance requested while still providing opportunities for community participation and agency visibility.

Such proposals to consolidate the SACs, however, proved to be unpopular among agency volunteers. There was a strong belief among volunteers that individual county SACs were crucial if there was to be local commitment to, and participation in, health planning. Bob Edwards, one SAC president, noted, "We have a strong SAC in our county and we're proud of the things we've accomplished. Our county legislature has backed us up by annually appropriating funds for the HSA. If our SAC is eliminated or consolidated we'll lose our voice. You can bet that if that is done, the legislature will have second thoughts about funding the HSA." Given that local governments were an important source of revenue for the agency, this opposition could not be overlooked. The agency decided that, at least for the next year, consolidation of the SACs was an unacceptable option. But they did not rule out a reconsideration of this issue in the future.

In lieu of a cutback in the number of SACs the agency management took other actions designed to cut back agency activities. They included:

1. Staff Role—Staff were no longer to be assigned to a single county SAC. Staff would be used for specific high-priority activities requiring special expertise or knowledge. The staff relationship to the SACs would be more on the order of technical assistance. Staffing assignments would be made only rarely to SAC committees.

2. SAC Maintenance—The mechanics of SAC maintenance (for example, meeting notices, agendas, minutes) would be shifted from being a staff responsibility to being a volunteer responsibility based on a Memorandum of Understanding between the SAC and the CHSA regarding responsibilities and expectations of volunteers and staff.

3. SAC Project Review—The agency management recommended that each SAC adopt a single-step project-review process with comments passing directly to the Regional Review Committee. Before this recommendation some SACs had multicommittee processes for the review of project applications.

All three of these measures were designed to free up agency staff from low-priority, time-consuming activities. With fewer planners tied up in a single county SAC and free of many of the routine community organization activities, it was expected that agency resources would be focused on high-priority, mandated activities. Local SAC volunteers, however, didn't take these cutbacks lying down either. Some expressed vigorous opposition to this agency decision to reduce staff support to local activities and increase emphasis on regional concerns. As one volunteer wrote, "We strongly disagree with the agency's unilateral decision to terminate the health planner assigned to our county and we request prompt replacement of that staff position! Our county government appropriates county funds to support the CHSA on the condition that the agency provide strong staff support for local initiatives." Another volunteer wrote, "It is deplorable to dismantle a successfully operating partnership which has provided a very generous financial 'county match' to the CHSA" and concluded that "the county will only provide continued support for the type of partnership that will provide strong support staff for local volunteer activities." The agency stuck with its general policy to reduce staff support to SACs but made some compromises with particularly determined SACs.

Also under the heading of limiting activities, the agency management considered reducing the size of the board of directors and the frequency of board meetings. The board was composed of seventy-five members representing all areas of the region. The agency was required, by law, to reimburse directors for all reasonable costs incurred in attending meetings or otherwise performing duties associated with the Health Systems Agency (for example, travel and child care). The full board met on a bimonthly basis and preparation material was mailed in advance to all directors. There were also periodic functions that members were encouraged to attend (for example, annual meeting and hearings). It was suggested that some savings could be achieved through a reduction in travel and expenses for governing body members. Eventually, though, the management decided that the board size should be maintained to provide breadth for participation, representation, and expertise. The proposal to reduce the frequency of board meetings was also rejected on the grounds that it would not produce substantial enough savings.

A final action of the agency to limit activity was to adopt new procedures for the regional review of health project applications. Each week the agency received dozens of applications from state and federal authorities that required HSA review and comment. The subject of these applications included everything from major hospital renovations to fixing a leak in the roof of a nursing home. Before the cutbacks the agency had conducted a full review of all but the most insignificant applications. To reduce the amount of staff time and resources that went to project review, a policy was adopted to limit review to only applications having a substantial impact on the health system.

PERSONNEL CUTBACK

At the same time the agency was deliberating and implementing these review and activity-level options, the executive director was taking other steps to prepare the agency for the impending cuts. Early in 1981 he decided it was not possible for the agency to carry the existing staffing arrangement into the new fiscal year. Personnel cuts would have to be made. As he observed, "personnel is the single largest item in our budget, there's no way we could have avoided making cuts in this area and still balance the budget." It was decided that to soften the impact of the overall cutback, it would be best to make the personnel cuts in the last quarter of FY 1980 (April–June 1981) and roll the savings over into FY 1981. It was projected that selective layoffs would allow the agency to achieve a savings of approximately $60,000 to $80,000 in the last quarter of FY 1980. This savings would be carried over into FY 1981 as unobligated nonfederal funds.

Based on this, the executive director terminated eight of twenty-six professional positions and three of eleven clerical positions. The specific breakdown is as follows:

Five associate health planners
One director of hospital planning
One coordinator of project review
One research associate
Three clerk typists

The executive director also eliminated six unfilled and unfunded positions from the agency organizational chart. (See appendix.)

The personnel cuts were based on a number of criteria, including:

1. The long-term functional priorities of the agency (for example, plan development, project review, data management) and the skills required to maintain such functions: The management prioritized those activities of the agency they considered most im-

portant to carrying out the agency mission and retained staff whose skills most closely matched the agency's needs.

2. Experience: Staff with the best experience to carry out the priorities of the agency were retained. Experience in a broad sense was considered (not simply seniority or experience in health planning).

3. Geographic assignment: The agency had three regional offices. The need to maintain some continuity required that this criteria be considered.

4. Flexibility: With declining resources it was necessary for the staff to be able to perform a number of different functions. A priority was placed on generalists.

5. Quantitative skills.

Exercising this option had some damaging effects on the agency. There was a consensus among the remaining staff that following the personnel cuts, there was a dramatic decline in the morale. Many of those not laid off felt betrayed by the management and unsure of their future. As one planner recalls, "We were kept in the dark. One day they were telling us everything would be all right. The next day they were handing out walking papers. We thought we were all safe through June at least. And, it wasn't just the timing of the cuts; it was who was cut. The management said they used criteria, and they did, but the criteria were so general that they were useless. It looked to many like they used retrenchment to move nonconformists out of the agency." Another planner observes, "People were confused and insecure after the first cuts. People spent a lot of office time talking about what had happened and speculating what was going to happen. People were generally not motivated to work, and many didn't seem to care anymore. There were many who started coming in later and leaving earlier. Almost all the nonmanagement staff began revising their resumes."

The personnel cuts also contributed to a decrease in productivity for remaining staff. "Staff started coming in late and leaving early" noted one staff member. Another commented that "people began to disinvest." The emotional shock of the cuts and the bleak funding outlook provided little incentive to work. People did what they had to do, to get by, and little else. One way or another most people expected to be gone before too long. In fact, six months after the layoff seven of the remaining eighteen professional staff had resigned to accept new positions elsewhere.

NONPERSONNEL COSTS

The final option available to the agency management was to reduce costs in nonpersonnel areas. Since this category comprised approximately 45 percent of the FY 1980 budget, there were significant possibilities for savings. Consideration must, however, be given to the impact that cuts in this area can have on staff performance.

The executive director made a number of decisions to reduce nonpersonnel costs.

1. Office space: The size of the central office was reduced by 50 percent. This cut the rental cost by $30,000 annually. In addition, one of the branch offices was relocated in donated space. This saved another $40,000 annually.
2. Staff travel was restricted. Whereas in the past the staff were able to travel about the region relatively unrestricted, now the written permission of the deputy director was required.
3. Efforts were made to schedule committee meetings carefully so as to reduce volunteer travel (for example, several meetings might be scheduled consecutively on one day in one location).
4. Efforts were made to reduce the amount of outside printing (for example, fewer agency brochures and public information pamphlets were printed).
5. Agency reliance on outside consultants was reduced.
6. Efforts were undertaken to reduce telephone usage.

SUMMARY

The CHSA may have successfully made the transition to a lower funding level. In response to the cuts the agency has chosen not to pursue vigorously a variety of new funding sources. Instead the management appears to be counting on assistance from the state. Meanwhile, they have opted for a limited reduction in areawide activities, personnel cutbacks, and a reduction in nonessential expenditures. Each of these actions had some costs. Was this the best way to respond to declining resources? Put yourself in the place of the CHSA executive director. How would you have done things differently?

The federal funding picture is bleak for the HSAs. The Reagan administration reduced further the support for national health planning. Can the CHSA withstand additional cuts and still carry out mandated functions? What is the likelihood that the state will pick up some, or all, of the costs of regional health planning? Again, put yourself in the place of the CHSA executive director. How would you go about preparing for the future?

□ * This case was prepared by Michael Mullane, under the supervision of Professor Jeffrey Straussman, as a basis for class discussion rather than as an illustration of either effective or ineffective handling of an administrative situation.

Appendix

	FY 1978	FY 1979	FY 1980	FY 1981#
Revenue				
Federal grant	868,864	897,125	978,343	555,527
Nonfederal	201,728	205,317	211,061	348,417*
(County government)	(150,807)	(172,854)	(175,649)	—
(Private)	(24,582)	(5,000)	(13,000)	—
(Use of capital)	(26,339)	(27,463)	(22,412)	—
Total Revenue	1,070,592	1,102,442	1,189,404	903,944

Appendix (*Continued*)

	FY 1978	FY 1979	FY 1980	FY 1981#
Expenditures				
Salaries	634,765	645,267	647,041	497,577
Employee benefits	133,300	147,754	141,532	119,418
Consultant costs	4,925	2,925	21,500	2,000
Computer services	12,030	12,550	5,900	3,550
Purchased services	7,960	4,000	4,500	6,000
Legal and auditing	3,300	3,700	6,000	5,000
Supplies	24,000	20,000	20,000	18,000
Postage and handling	17,571	20,396	24,100	27,000
Equipt. rental and				
maintenance	8,135	4,213	4,165	5,400
Photocopying	26,303	26,446	29,227	31,008
Telephone	29,754	26,864	33,000	26,000
Building occupancy	68,650	71,715	75,815	41,260
Travel	42,520	53,531	71,940	77,038
Outside printing	19,777	12,515	21,000	13,300
Air travel	6,786	7,224	16,825	—
Educational conferences	3,940	2,840	4,500	5,970
Public access and information	200	100	1,584	1,473
Recruitment	3,000	9,860	10,000	7,000
Reference material	2,500	3,000	3,000	2,000
Organizational memberships	9,450	7,950	5,734	1,100
Promotional media	1,000	1,000	500	1,500
Equipment purchased	10,726	1,600	31,900	0
Insurance	—	3,186	2,254	2,910
Interest expense	—	2,959	2,221	1,440
Appreciation and amortization	—	10,847	5,166	8,000
Total Expenditures	1,070,592	1,102,442	1,189,404	903,944

#Projected.
*Includes $50,000 grant from state and $133,000 nonfederal carry-over from FY 1980.

NOTES

1. Graham Allison, "Public and Private Management: Are They Fundamentally Alike in All Unimportant Respects?" in *Public Management*, ed. James L. Perry and Kenneth L. Kraemer (Palo Alto, Calif.: Mayfield Publishing Co., 1983), pp. 72–92.
2. Ibid.
3. Peter H. Schuck, *Suing Government* (New Haven: Yale University Press, 1983).
4. See Barry Bozeman and Jeffrey D. Straussman, "'Publicness' and Resource Management Strategies," in *Organizational Theory and Public Policy*, ed. Richard H. Hall and Robert E. Quinn (Beverly Hills, Calif.: Sage Publications, 1983), pp. 75–91.
5. Theodore R. Marmor, "Entrepreneurship in Public Management: Wilbur Cohen and Robert Ball," in *Leadership and Innovation*, ed. Jameson W. Doig and Erwin C. Hargrove (Baltimore: Johns Hopkins Press, 1987), pp. 248–251.
6. Stephen R. Rosenthal, *Managing Government Operations* (Glenview, Ill.: Scott, Foresman, 1982).
7. Martin Landau and Russell Stout, Jr., "To Manage Is Not to Control: Or the Folly of Type II Errors," *Public Administration Review* 39 (March/April 1979): 149.
8. Ibid.

9. Hugh Heclo, "Political Executives and the Washington Bureaucracy," *Political Science Quarterly* 92 (Fall 1977): 397.
10. Ibid.
11. Ibid., p. 398.
12. Ibid.
13. Joseph A. Califano, Jr., *Governing America*. New York: Simon and Schuster, 1981, p. 405.
14. Heclo, "Political Executives," p. 419.
15. Herbert Kaufman, *The Administrative Behavior of Federal Bureau Chiefs* (Washington, D.C.: Brookings Institution, 1981), p. 87.
16. Ibid., pp. 78–81.
17. Donald P. Warwick, *A Theory of Public Bureaucracy* (Cambridge, Mass.: Harvard University Press, 1975).
18. John M. Greiner et al., *Monetary Incentives and Work Standards in Five Cities: Impacts and Implications for Management and Labor* (Washington, D.C.: Urban Institute Press, 1977), pp. 61–72.
19. Ibid., pp. 47–57.
20. Albert Speer's memoirs are found in *Inside the Third Reich* (New York: Avon Books, 1971).
21. The following section on Albert Speer is drawn from Ethan A. Singer and Leland M. Wooton, "The Triumph and Failure of Albert Speer's Administrative Genius: Implications for Current Management Theory and Practice," *The Journal of Applied Behavioral Science* 12 (January/February/March, 1976): 79–103.

FOR FURTHER READING

Anderson, Wayne F., Chester A. Newland, and Richard J. Stillman III. *The Effective Local Government Manager*. Washington, D.C.: International City Management Association, 1983.

A practitioner-oriented guide for the local government manager.

Bower, Joseph L., and Charles J. Christenson. *Public Management Text and Cases*. Homewood, Ill.: Richard D. Irwin, 1978.

A collection of cases developed at the JFK School of Government, Harvard University, that emphasize the various dimensions of public management.

Kaufman, Herbert. *The Administrative Behavior of Federal Bureau Chiefs*. Washington, D.C.: Brookings Institution, 1981.

Kaufman observed six bureau chiefs for a year to draw a profile of public management in the federal government.

Lynn, Laurence E., Jr. *Managing The Public's Business*. New York: Basic Books, 1981.

Focusing on the federal govenment, Lynn emphasizes the many problems of public management.

Perry, James L., and Kenneth L. Kraemer, eds. *Public Management: Public and Private Perspectives*. Palo Alto, Calif.: Mayfield Publishing Co., 1983.

A good collection of articles, several from people who were top managers in business and government.

CHAPTER 6

Taxing and Spending in an Intergovernmental Context

Like individuals, governments need money (called revenue). The federal government can coin and print it. Other governments get the money needed to provide the large number of goods and services found in the public sector by taxing things, selling things, or receiving revenues from other governments. Without money governments cannot do very much (which is why advocates of less government often focus on reducing taxes). So the first question is, where do governments get their revenues?

SOURCES OF REVENUE

Essentially, governments have three ways to raise revenue: (1) They can impose taxes on individuals, corporations, activities, and property. (2) They can charge for use of government property, or they can impose a fee for the privilege of doing something. (3) They can receive funds from other governments.

Taxes

Surely you have heard the old saying, "There are two things you can't avoid, death and taxes." Taxes are really so pervasive in our daily lives that we sometimes don't even realize we are paying them. To illustrate, think about some of your activities today that were connected to taxes. First, you may have awakened in a house or an apartment. The owner probably has to pay property taxes on the structure. (If you woke up in a college dormitory it is probably tax exempt.) You may have turned on the lights, the heat, and the radio as well. The utility bills for this energy use are likely to include sales tax or a gross utilities tax. Did you receive a paycheck recently? If so, you certainly felt the impact of federal, state,

122

and maybe even local income taxes, and don't forget social security. Is all this talk about taxes getting you depressed? If you try to drink your sorrows away, you will have to pay one of the more famous "nuisance" taxes—the tax on alcoholic beverages.

Governments impose many different types of taxes. They may be placed on individual and corporate income, property, the sale of goods and services, and the inheritance of money and other assets. Exactly what is taxed depends on the level of government and the specific government under consideration. Table 6.1

TABLE 6.1. Revenue of All Governments by Source and Level of Government, Fiscal Year 1985 ($Millions)

Source	Total	Federal	State	Local
Total revenue	$1,418,369	$806,808	$438,954	$402,544
Intergovernmental	[a]	1,931	89,922	138,083
From federal government	[a]	—	84,469	21,724
From state government	[a]	1,931	—	116,359
From local government	[a]	—	5,453	[b]
Revenue from own sources	1,418,369	804,877	349,031	264,461
General	1,050,043	558,518	275,422	216,103
Taxes	803,830	454,037	215,320	134,473
Property	103,757	—	3,984	99,772
Individual income	401,015	330,918	63,644	6,453
Corporation income	80,489	61,331	17,637	1,521
Sales and gross receipts	175,440	49,159	105,325	20,956
Customs duties	12,176	12,176	—	—
General sales and gross receipts	84,292	—	69,629	14,663
Motor fuel	25,252	11,614	13,352	286
Alcoholic beverages	8,662	5,376	3,031	255
Tobacco products	8,926	4,483	4,247	195
Public utilities	14,945	4,898	6,203	3,845
Other	21,187	10,612[c]	8,863	1,712
Motor vehicle and operators' licenses	8,178	—	7,659	518
Death and gift	8,750	6,422	2,328	—
All other	26,201	6,207	14,743	5,253
Charges and miscellaneous	246,213	104,481	60,102	81,630
Utility and liquor stores	44,814	—	5,702	39,112
Insurance trust	323,512	246,359	67,907	9,246
Employee retirement	57,787	4,592	43,993	9,202
Unemployment compensation[d]	17,861	221	17,596	44[e]
Old-age, survivors, disability and health insurance	241,550	236,565	4,985	—
Railroad retirement	4,330	4,330	—	—
Other	1,984	651	1,333	—

[a]To avoid duplication, transactions between levels of government are eliminated in the combined total.
[b]Transactions among local units of government are excluded.
[c]Includes windfall profit tax.
[d]Relates to cooperative state–federal programs administered by state employment security agencies, including regular and extended or supplemental programs.
[e]Washington, D.C., only.
Source: Department of Commerce, Bureau of the Census.

illustrates different taxes and their contribution to total revenue for federal, state, and local governments. A careful examination of Table 6.1 will reveal some basic differences among governments concerning their sources of revenues and the proportion of revenues from various sources.

Federal government.   The largest amount of federal revenue comes from income taxes. Note that 41 percent comes from individuals and about 8 percent from corporations. The second largest tax at the federal level is the payroll tax. If you received a paycheck recently, look at the stub carefully. In addition to withholding for federal and state income taxes there is also a deduction for social security. Your employer will also pay the same amount that was withheld from you. Together, your contribution and the employer's contribution are part of the payroll tax collected by the federal government to finance the social security system in the United States. The payroll tax became an increasing percentage of the federal tax revenue between 1950 and 1970 because, quite simply, social security benefits have become increasingly more expensive—and (as of now) the payroll tax is the only source of revenue for the social security trust fund.

Other federal taxes are minor in terms of their contribution to federal revenue. If Aunt Bertha dies and leaves you her small fortune you will have to pay a tax on your unexpected financial windfall. If you take a trip to India, Nepal, and the People's Republic of China and bring back a bunch of oriental carpets valued at $8,000, you will have to pay a stiff custom duty tax for the privilege of placing the rugs under your feet. If you weren't aware of the tax you may be chagrined to learn that your "bargains" have been destroyed by Uncle Sam's tax bite. Look again at Table 6.1, however, and you will see that both types of taxes comprise small amounts of total federal revenue.

State government.   Sources of revenue for state governments vary greatly, depending on what types of taxes are imposed by each state. Like the federal government, many states impose income taxes on individuals and corporations. Table 6.1 shows that income taxes have gradually become more important at the state level (reaching about 18 percent of total state revenues). More important, however, is the heavy reliance on sales tax revenues—taxes on the sale of goods and services. Exactly what is taxed depends on the particular state. If you buy a pair of jeans in New York City, for example, you will pay an $8\frac{1}{4}$ percent sales tax. If you go across the George Washington Bridge to New Jersey to buy the same pair of jeans you won't pay any sales tax. If you get your car fixed in Michigan you'll pay a sales tax on the repair (it is a service that is taxed), but if you drive your car to New York and it breaks down you will not have to pay a sales tax on the labor portion of the bill.

State governments also collect special taxes, such as a gasoline tax. Sometimes this type of tax is put in a special fund that is restricted for a particular use—such as highway construction and repair. Restricted revenues are called dedicated or earmarked funds.

State governments also collect revenues by giving people the privilege of earning a living in the state, through licensing fees. Again this revenue will vary from state to state, but it is common to impose license fees on professions such as medicine, dentistry, social work, the practice of law, and teaching, to name a few. License fees can be imposed on recreational activities; fishing and hunting are widespread examples. State governments also collect revenues for the use of state property, for example, the admission charge to a state park.

Local governments.   Local governments receive about 25 percent of their revenues from property taxes. This percentage has been dropping over the years, however, especially as funds from other governments—state and federal aid in particular—have increased. Local governments, like states, also impose user fees and charges for services like zoos, parks, and parking meters. Local governments may also charge license fees. Your dog probably cost you a few dollars, for example, which you paid to a local government. If she was picked up by the dogcatcher for running off her leash, you may have contributed to the local government's coffers in another way, by paying a fine—yet another source of local government revenue. Some local governments are granted the authority (by the state) to impose sales taxes. Finally, a small number of local governments impose an income and commuter tax.

(Provides — Simon)

Principles of Taxation

Suppose you were appointed the finance director of a new local government.[1] Let's suppose, furthermore, that you did not care about the "history" of taxation. That is, you were unconcerned about what was done in the past. Rather, you wanted to set up a "good" tax structure. No one likes taxes, of course; we would rather not pay them. But we recognize that our local government will provide residents with services like police and fire protection, refuse collection, sewers, and parks. The government needs money, and taxes are the way to get it. What criteria should you, the new finance director, use to produce a good tax system?

Revenue productivity.   A tax structure is supposed to produce revenue. Clearly, one way to evaluate the effectiveness of a tax is to determine how much revenue will actually be collected from it. The amount of revenue that is produced by a given tax is related to the specific features of the tax such as the tax rate and the specification of what is actually taxable—the tax base.

When taxes are responsive to changes in income, they are said to be income elastic. The advantage of such a tax is that the government does not have to make decisions about the tax rate or base each time it wants more (or less) taxes. Taxes will tend to move in the same direction as income. In contrast, inelastic taxes tend not to be responsive to changes in income or economic activity. Liquor excise tax receipts (primarily state level), for example, do not change much when economic activity changes. Tax elasticity, then, will determine the amount of revenue produced.

Neutrality.   This principle, which means that the taxes achieve their intended results but do not interfere with other private economic activities, is not always easy to achieve in practice. A good illustration is the use of a tax on gasoline to discourage consumption. If the tax is large enough, consumption will—in the aggregate—decline. But since people at the lower end of the income distribution will still have to drive their cars for certain purposes, such as the trip to work, an increase in the gasoline tax will affect lower-income people more adversely than higher-income people.

Equity.   The principle of equity in taxation is multidimensional. One aspect is the equal tax treatment of individuals in the same situation. If a government wants to collect income taxes, for instance, all of those earning the same amount with the same set of circumstances (such as family size) should pay the same tax. This is called *horizontal equity.*   *equal treatment of equals*

Equity also involves the fairness of the tax burden among people who are not in similar situations. This is called *vertical equity.* If a tax rate increases as income increases, for example, the tax would be considered progressive and would have the effect of distributing income across individuals.   *unequal treatment of unequal*

A major problem for public administrators when evaluating alternative taxes is to determine what is a fair distribution of the tax burden. Ultimately, this must be a political choice; nevertheless, there are two additional equity principles that aid in taxation decisions—the benefits principle or the ability to pay. We could arrive at our equity arrangement by looking at who benefits from public expenditures and tax those beneficiaries accordingly. If a municipal swimming pool, for example, is used by lower-income people primarily, whereas a golf course is used, for the most part, by upper-income people, we could tax each group for the municipal services that they use. The problem, however, is that for some local government services, like police protection, neither the amount of benefits nor the actual number of beneficiaries is known with any degree of accuracy. Moreover, we could not successfully prevent people from "consuming" a service like police protection (these conditions apply to what economists call a "public good").   *(proportionally)*

Another principle from which to assess tax burdens is the "ability to pay," which means that people should pay taxes for services based on their income or wealth, regardless of the amount of benefits received. Naturally, this principle is a political issue that is addressed, if at all, in substantive tax legislation.

Tax exporting.   When benefits of government are enjoyed by nonresidents of a jurisdiction, there may be a case for taxing those nonresidents. Economists call this *tax exporting.* A simple widespread illustration comes from selected cities like Detroit and Buffalo. Suburbanites who commute to these cities to work pay a nonresident income tax. The justification for the tax is that these nonresidents enjoy public services, such as fire and police, sanitation, city streets, lighting, and parks, while they are in the city's limits. Since they are receiving benefits, they should pay for them. Tax exporting also occurs when corporations pay a local property tax because stockholders in the company pay the tax but receive very few government benefits since they do not live in the jurisdiction.

Administrative feasibility.   When choosing among alternative taxes, one important criterion is the relative ease of administration—especially collection. It does little good to design a tax that is efficient, neutral, equitable, but difficult to collect. A tax on illegal wagering may produce a great deal of revenue, but the difficulty in administering it is likely to be great.

These criteria, commonly used to evaluate tax alternatives, are by no means exhaustive. Alternatives, by definition, imply revenue policy trade-offs. There are no perfect taxes. Rather, some taxes are preferable to others, given an agreed-on set of criteria as well as political decisions that must inevitably accompany their selection.

INTERGOVERNMENTAL FISCAL RELATIONS

You will recall that governments also get money from other governments. The federal government provides funds to states and local governments, and states provide money to local governments like cities, counties, and school districts. These funds are called *intergovernmental revenue*. We will see, later, that some local governments, particularly financially hard-pressed cities, have come to depend on intergovernmental revenues.

Justification for Intergovernmental Aid

Why do higher-level governments give aid—money—to lower-level governments? In other words, why would a state government give funds to cities, counties, or independent school districts? Why should the federal government provide funds to states and local governments? There are a few basic reasons.

Separation between beneficiaries and optimal service delivery. Some services are best provided at the local level. A good example is primary and secondary school education, which, for both political and financial reasons, is a government activity that is highly decentralized. The idea of neighborhood, or community, schools is deeply ingrained in our country's political heritage. Still, we could say that the benefits of education extend beyond the walls of the schoolhouse. Not only is the child better off from having had a good education but also most of us would agree that, in some general ways, we are all somehow better off when a child is properly educated, even if we cannot clearly measure the precise benefit to ourselves from a more educated society. In a situation like this, it makes sense to provide some funds for education from higher levels of government while still funding a large share of the service from local monies.

Fiscal equalization. Some governments may be in a good position to raise funds but have a low need for services. Other governments may be in exactly the opposite situation. If we go back to education, for example, we can see that local governments—usually school districts—are limited in their ability to raise funds, much of which comes from the (inelastic) property tax. On the other hand, state governments can more effectively raise revenues from several tax sources—as was described earlier. A state may wish to equalize revenues for education across the state through intergovernmental aid to school districts. Indeed, in a few states (California, New York, Texas, and New Jersey, to name a few) there were court challenges to the financing of public education.[2] Most of the cases were based on the premise that unequal levels of spending for education, which were caused by the differences of "wealth" among school districts, violated the due process clause of the Fourteenth Amendment. In New Jersey, for example, the court found unconstitutional the reliance on the property tax for financing education. The state legislature eventually passed legislation for additional state taxes to provide the necessary revenues to "equalize" the fiscal resources of school districts throughout the state. Predictably, the decision to impose new state taxes was not popular with the legislature.

Income distribution.   When higher-level governments collect taxes and then provide funds to lower-level governments as intergovernmental aid, income redistribution is usually taking place. A simple illustration is in the area of public assistance. The aid to families with dependent children (AFDC) program provides income to eligible families—usually a female-headed household with young children. In many states the program is administered at the local level, usually by county departments of social services. Funds for the program come from all three levels: federal, state, and local. Since the federal funds are raised, to some extent, from a highly elastic tax—the income tax—we can say that the public assistance program redistributes income (from higher-income taxpayers to those who by definition of their eligibility are lower-income) through the intergovernmental aid system.

Administrative efficiency in tax collection.   A fourth justification for intergovernmental aid is that some governments are more efficient in collecting taxes than others. The federal income tax system, for example, is said to be very effective as a so-called voluntary tax. That is, the vast majority of taxpaying Americans (and residents who are citizens of other countries but are working in the United States) do pay what they are supposed to in terms of their tax liability. Similarly, many counties in the United States impose sales taxes on goods and services sold in their respective jurisdictions, but the tax is actually collected by the state government and then distributed to the counties as sales tax receipts.

Types of Grants

When higher-level governments provide funds for lower-level governments through intergovernmental aid, they do so in the form of grants. It is important to realize that there are a few basic types of grants, the differences depending on what they are expected to accomplish.

Categorical grants.   As the name implies, categorical grants are given for specific programmatic purposes. In theory, a government receiving a categorical grant from a higher-level government can use funds only for the purposes specified in the legislation establishing the grant. Categorical grants can be of two basic types: formula or project.

Formula grants tie the amount of funds a government receives to characteristics of the recipients. A formula, for example, may be based on the income of the residents of the state or its population. Alternatively, the grant may be based on the number of beneficiaries of the program, for example, the federal boat-safety program. This grant formula includes the number of registered boats, which will then determine the amount of federal aid for boat safety.[3]

In a project grant, applicants are usually asked to justify the use they will make of the funds. Many federal agencies, for example, have project grant programs that are supposed to benefit local governments. Local governments apply to the federal agencies for funding. These applications are reviewed by agency staff, who then determine which applications to fund and which to reject.

Between 1965 and 1974, for example, the U.S. Department of Housing and Urban Development had a program of water and sewer grants that provided federal funds, on a competitive basis, to local governments. Receiving a water and sewer grant was, in effect, a federal subsidy for local governments and, ultimately, local taxpayers. Since program administrators had discretion in awarding these project grants, they also faced some lobbying pressures—especially from members of Congress—when they made their allocations.[4]

Categorical grants require state and/or local matching—which means that the federal government requires lower-level governments to contribute some portion of the total grant if it is to receive any federal funds. In the public assistance example described earlier, the AFDC is really a formula-based categorical grant with a 50 percent matching requirement. The amount of money that goes to the eligible recipient is determined by the state. As an illustration, assume that the state decides that a family of four will receive $500 a month in public assistance. The federal government will pay $250 as part of its share, so the distribution will be federal, $250; state, $125; county, $125. One notable dimension of categorical grants highlighted by this example is the importance of the state's role. Notice that the state, not the federal government, establishes the amount of money that will go to the eligible recipient. This also means that there is a great deal of variation in the amount of public assistance recipients in the United States receive.

Block grants. Block grants began in 1966 and were expanded under President Nixon's notion of the ''New Federalism.'' A few basic justifications are offered for block grants. First, contrary to categorical grants, they can be used for many different purposes (as opposed to categoricals that require specific uses of the funds). Second, block grants, by consolidating existing categoricals, are supposed to be more efficient. Third, block grants decentralize programmatic decision making by giving local officials more influence on how funds will eventually be spent. In other words, block grants are supposed to give local governments money with very few strings attached.

From 1973 to 1981 (when the program was dropped), local governments received funds under the Comprehensive Employment and Training Act (CETA) to train and hire unemployed persons who met the eligibility standards of the act. Many fiscally hard-pressed cities depended on CETA funds to pay for part of their personnel costs. In Los Angeles, for example, 11 percent of the city's work force was funded by the CETA in 1978. In Rochester, New York, 13 percent was funded by the CETA in the same year.

County governments have also received block grants for social services. Known as Title XX funds, they pay for programs like child and adult foster care and placement, day care for children, counseling, adoptions, homemaker and chore services, and spouse abuse programs. The range of services funded by Title XX varies from state to state and even among county governments within a state. Again, this has been one of the justifications of block grants—local government flexibility.

A third program that is also important for fiscally troubled cities is the Community Development Block Grant program (CDBG), whose funds are supposed to be used for the following purposes: redevelopment of cities, code enforcement of buildings, water and sewer facilities, public works, housing rehabilitation, open space and neighborhood facilities, public services, and service-related facilities and equipment. Although these categories are broad, funds are supposed to benefit low- and moderate-income families.[5]

Despite the initial intent to loosen the intergovernmental strings between Washington and local governments, many grants have been guilty of "creeping recategorization," which happens when the federal government stipulates requirements along with the grant.[6] The Safe Streets Act, for example, a block grant program of the 1970s, required that 15 to 20 percent of the grant had to be used for correctional facilities.[7] Creeping recategorization has been criticized by the recipients of block grants because they feel that it violates the spirit of the grant—local autonomy.

Evolving Dependency on Intergovernmental Aid

Intergovernmental aid has come at a price—a price that has fiscal and political ramifications for the present and future of local governments. This is best seen by looking at the experiences of a single city, El Paso, Texas.[8]

El Paso is certainly not a declining city. On the contrary, it is clearly in the Sunbelt. Yet like most cities in the United States, by the beginning of the 1980s, it had learned to rely on intergovernmental aid—despite its best intentions to do otherwise.

The basic pattern is typical of many cities. In 1970, 6.6 percent of El Paso's revenues came from intergovernmental aid. More than half of this money came from the federal government. By 1976, 24.3 percent of revenues came from intergovernmental aid, and 90 percent of this aid came from the federal government. What is probably most important about federal funds is the way El Paso officials used the money.

Avoiding tax increases. When services expand but local taxes stay the same, federal funds allow local officials to avoid a tax increase. Naturally, local officials are reticent to admit this, but it is a most plausible assumption. After all, the elected official is in a very favorable situation. He or she can say that services expanded but taxes didn't—which is the local government's equivalent of having your cake and eating it too.

Expanding basic services. In a study of El Paso's spending habits, William Hudson found that federal funds were used for police salaries, fire hoses, street repairs, and traffic lights. Funding for these services came from the CETA, revenue sharing, and countercyclical revenue sharing.[9] Would El Paso have spent its own money for these services? It probably would have gotten by with fewer service additions.

Creating new political demands. A real problem in using federal funds for local programs is that the funds stimulate new programs but not necessarily those that local officials consider to have the highest priorities. Meanwhile, citizens become accustomed to an improved level of service, like seeing their streets repaired, for example. But local residents may not realize that funds for street repair come from federal funds like community development. When the federal funds wither away, the citizens still want the same level of services. This naturally creates pressures on local officials, and when it does, subtly alters local priorities.

Do all cities resemble El Paso when it comes to the reliance on federal aid? Not exactly. In 1982 an eleven-city study of the budgetary impact of federal aid, conducted by researchers associated with the Brookings Institution in Washington, D.C., concluded that cities that were financially hard pressed used federal aid to support basic services such as fire and police whereas cities that were relatively better off tended to use the aid for nonrecurring expenses, or expenses that were nonessential.[10] The lesson? When it comes to reductions in federal aid, the poor get poorer.

IMPACT OF HIGHER-LEVEL GOVERNMENT FISCAL DECISIONS ON LOWER-LEVEL GOVERNMENTS

It should already be clear that taxing and spending decisions do not occur in a political vacuum. In a federal system fiscal decisions of one level of government usually have some impact, either direct or indirect, on other levels and units of government. In particular, higher-level government fiscal decisions invariably influence the fiscal status of lower level governments. This is illustrated by summarizing the impact of the federal tax reforms of 1986 and the example of programmatic mandates.

Tax Reform Act of 1986

Reform of the federal tax system was an idea that had been percolating since the mid 1970s. The intentions of the Tax Reform Act of 1986 included the reduction of tax rates, the elimination or restriction of tax "breaks" that were inefficient and inequitable, and the overall "simplification" of the tax code. In the aggregate the changes were supposed to be "revenue neutral." That is, the overall swap of lower rates for a restriction in deductions, exclusions, credits, and exemptions was supposed to keep federal taxes at roughly the same prereform level.

Although the Tax Reform Act of 1986 focused on changes to the federal tax code, state and local governments were hardly immune from the changes. First, since most states that have state income taxes use federal tax returns to determine the tax liability of state taxpayers, state governments were expected to reap large tax windfalls. The reason is that the elimination or restriction of several federal tax deductions broadened the tax base. Although state government officials obviously wanted to take the politically astute decision to return the windfalls, they still had to estimate the size of the windfall, decide who to return it to, and the mechanism for returning the windfall.

A second consequence of federal tax reform is less obvious. Since federal income tax rates have dropped, the value of property tax deductions for homeowners who itemize deductions is less. This means that a local government, typically a suburban community, can no longer assume that high property taxes will be partially offset by deductability. Therefore, some economists estimate that there will be more competition among local governments because after-tax differences will narrow. Similarly, state governments are forced into greater competition because of the elimination of the deductibility of the state sales tax and lower marginal tax rates making states more alike than before the 1986 reform.

Government "Overload": The Case of Mandates

David B. Walker, a former assistant director of the Advisory Commission on Intergovernmental Relations, has called our system of federalism "overloaded."[11] That is, to a great extent the ability to implement broad objectives at the local level is out of sync with federal policy initiatives. What compounds the problem is that the sheer magnitude of intergovernmental responsibilities can overwhelm a typical local government. No better illustration can be found than the subject of mandates.

Mandates

Mandates are conditions imposed on a government, from a higher-level government, to do something or refrain from doing something.[12] They can be a direct order or a condition of aid; they may come from the executive, legislative, or judicial branches; and they can be procedural or programmatic. Following are some examples of different types of mandates:

Procedural

Financial reporting practices required of local governments by the federal government as a condition of aid

Personnel requirements, such as the necessity of a social worker in nursing homes, as a condition of Medicaid reimbursement

Revenue constraints, such as the prohibition against taxing certain types of properties like religious facilities or schools

Programmatic

Providing the handicapped with accessibility to public buildings and mass transit

Providing information on nutrition in school lunch programs

Criticisms of Mandates

Ask any local government officials what they don't like about intergovernmental relations and they'll point to red tape and the strings that are attached to so many federal and state programs. They especially don't like mandates.

Cost. This is probably the biggest complaint of local government officials. Although there is no precise estimate of the cost of mandates, a study done by Thomas Muller and Michael Fix, both of the Urban Institute, Washington, D.C., estimated that for the six local governments studied, five federal mandates produced an average per capita cost of $20 in 1978.[13]

Inappropriate application. It may make sense to require toilet facilities to be available every forty acres in farm areas where there are a lot of farm workers, but in some midwestern states like Montana it is clearly absurd—there are few people for miles around. Mandates can sometimes be inflexible, and critics often point to such examples to show that mandates are often applied inappropriately.

Lack of local discretion. Improving accessibility to public buildings and mass transit is a laudable federal objective. Indeed, few local government officials would object to improving the mobility of the handicapped. But listen to the former mayor of New York City, Ed Koch, on this subject with reference to Section 504 of the Rehabilitation Act of 1973: "It would be cheaper for us [the city of New York] to provide every severely disabled person with taxi service than make 255 of our subway stations accessible."[14]

There are counterarguments. Mandates, in principle, are supposed to fulfill national objectives. Indeed, their defenders point out that local governments, left to their own devices, would not reach the objectives that are behind many mandates. Programmatic mandates, in particular, are designed to benefit specific populations and to promote greater equality.

Mandates, then, represent just one important aspect of intergovernmental relations that cause friction between levels of government. Can this friction be reduced?

Reducing Intergovernmental Overload

Since 1978 there have been some countertrends. These trends have tried to reduce overload and the bias of centralization in the intergovernmental system.

Tax and expenditure limitation. In 1978 California voters passed the, by now, famous "Proposition 13." This proposition rolled back local property taxes and controlled the future growth of property taxation. Since 1978 many other states passed tax and expenditure limitations.

Such efforts varied quite a bit. Some rolled back property taxes; others limited state spending; still others tried to control future taxes or spending by pegging increases to some economic indicator, like the growth of personal income in the state. Although the various limitation devices were aimed at the state level, local public finances (cities, counties, townships, and villages) were directly affected for two reasons: (1) tax limitation efforts usually tried to limit or reduce property taxation, and (2) state aid to local governments was generally reduced because states were constrained in either their tax efforts or their spending.

Why was there a tax revolt at the state and local levels? First, in rapidly growing places like California, property values had increased dramatically, resulting in constantly higher property assessments. Although the tax rate remained relatively stable, the total amount of property taxes paid by the typical property owner in California (and other growing areas) increased sharply before the passage of Proposition 13. So there was some basis for the feeling among Californians that they were being taxed out of their homes. Second, the tax revolt represented a more basic feeling among taxpayers that they were not getting much for their money. The percentage of the public responding that government wastes a lot of money, for example, rose from 46 percent in 1958 to 80 percent in 1980. So the tax revolt was also an expression of dissatisfaction with government. Third, allied with a general dissatisfaction was the belief that government was simply too omnipresent. What better evidence of the Orwellian specter than the realization of the government's presence at tax time? With a dozen years of hindsight then, we can say that Proposition 13 and its friends was a cry to "get government off our backs." As it turned out, the tax revolt mania of the late 1970s was brought under control during the decade of the 1980s.

Reaganomics.   Extreme? Well, maybe. Yet at the national level efforts to curb governmental growth were a central feature of the initial months of Reagan's first year in office. He began by cutting the FY 1982 budget (first prepared by outgoing President Carter) by more than $30 billion. The administration pointed out that this cut would merely slow down the growth of federal spending; it would not really reverse it. The president seemed, at first, to enjoy popular support for his budget-cutting policies. Discretionary domestic spending programs were especially hard hit in 1981 and 1982. In addition, under the banner of streamlining the intergovernmental grants, nine block grants replaced fifty-seven categorical grants. On the tax side, he initiated a three-year tax cut to stimulate production by encouraging private investment. This was the centerpiece of the president's experiment with "supply-side" economics. The experiment was rapidly engulfed by a prolonged economic recession and a budget deficit that, at one point, topped $200 billion. Although "Reaganomics" may, initially, have represented a bold attempt to limit government spending while cutting taxes, it eventually produced a budgetary shift in resources from social services to defense—financed, in part, by increased indebtedness. Meanwhile, the looming deficit stimulated congressional action in the form of the Balanced Budget and Emergency Deficit Control Act of 1985 (known more popularly as Gramm–Rudman–Hollings). This act (see next chapter for a description) mandated deficit reduction targets and specified how and where the cuts should occur. State and local governments, via the grants system, were destined to lose federal apropriations.

Lowering the intergovernmental presence.   Intergovernmental fiscal relations are in rapid flux. When former Governor Carey of New York tried to summarize the transition from the 1970s to the 1980s, he remarked, "The days of wine and roses are over." With the election of President Reagan the roses wilted and the remaining wine began to turn. Federal aid, which had begun to slow down under President Carter, was no longer guaranteed. Several intergovernmental programs were earmarked for sharp budget reductions or early deaths. The Comprehensive Employment and Training Act, which subsidized a great deal of local government employment, was terminated. President Reagan, following his "less-is-better" philosophy, proposed a major overhaul of the intergovernmental grants system. Ostensibly, the administration wanted to give more autonomy to state and local governments; however, the streamlining was more than simply administrative. Consolidating certain social services grants into a block grant to provide a "safety net" for the "truly needy" also produced less federal spending for certain federal programs.

FISCAL OPTIONS

State and local governments cannot "go it alone" in the contemporary intergovernmental fiscal system of the United States. Nevertheless, changes in Washington require adaptations in the state houses and city halls around the country. What options do state and local governments have?

Taxing and Encouraging Sin

Many states have resorted to legalized gambling as a way to raise revenues, and its justification is very straightforward: People do it anyway, so why not make it legal and get some revenue from it? Also, the money from illegal gambling, which is run by organized crime, is used to support other types of criminal activity, like drug dealing and prostitution. By making gambling legal, these other activities will be reduced—or so goes the argument.

By 1988 twenty-six states were using some form of lottery to raise revenue, and some allowed casino gambling (Nevada and New Jersey). Some states have race tracks. Florida has dog tracks where betting takes place. In some states you can bet on horse races in "off-track" betting parlors (New York and Pennsylvania).

Legalized gambling provides hundreds of millions of dollars of revenues to state governments.[15] Yet there is a limit to the amount of legalized gambling that can produce revenue. Most analyses of gambling revenues show that they produce modest amounts compared to other major sources of revenue such as sales and income taxes. Pennsylvania, for example, received less than 5 percent of general revenues from the state lottery in 1984. No state received a larger percentage. Therefore, on the criterion of revenue yield, lotteries do not do well. How would you assess state lotteries, and legalized gambling in general, on the other taxation criteria described at the beginning of the chapter?

"Raising Revenue or Encouraging Sin?"

New Jersey, the brunt of many jokes and the home of Atlantic City, an old seaside town that was "rejuvenated" with legalized gambling several years ago, has had a successful state lottery for about nineteen years. Begun in 1970, the lottery was expected to raise about $480 million in 1988. Eleven gambling casinos brought in $2.5 billion in 1987. While this was not the take for the state, it represented brisk business. Legalized gambling receipts are usually earmarked for a special purpose—often education. In New Jersey some of the revenues raised from legalized gambling are earmarked for urban redevelopment projects. Nevertheless, not everyone was pleased with the growth of legalized gambling. In New Jersey the Council on Compulsive Gambling estimated that there are about 400,000 gambling addicts in the state. A representative from the Council claimed that 19 percent of the crisis calls received in 1987 by the Council came from people who habitually played the state lottery. This was up 5 percent from the previous year. One critic called for the resignation of the lottery's executive director with the charge that the director "apparently is too busy scheming how to squeeze more money out of the working men and women of this state to worry about social responsibility."

□ *Source: Joseph F. Sullivan, "Jersey's Gambling: Too Much of a Bad Thing," New York Times, January 28, 1988, p. E7.*

Creative Marketing: Sell Your Troubles Away

You have heard the saying, "Sometimes you just can't give it away." The little town of Falls City, Oregon (population 752), however, takes one of its headaches and sells it to willing buyers for a modest price. What does it sell? Potholes.

> To fill and repair a pothole, the purchaser pays the city $10 and receives a certificate describing the pothole site and the date it was filled. For $20, a super deluxe pothole can be purchased with the recipient's name swirled in fluorescent orange paint on top of the patch. A city spokesman reports that almost all potholes have been sold and filled.[16]

Can you imagine how much money big cities like Cleveland, Detroit, Los Angeles, and New York could make if they followed Falls City's example?

Make Crime Pay

There was a time when no local government official who wanted to stay in office would advocate that a prison should be located in the official's jurisdiction. According to an article in the *New York Times*, attitudes toward prisons are changing in Illinois towns that are short of cash.

The last time state officials looked for a site for a new corrections facility was five years ago. They found that few towns wanted a prison in their backyard.

Now, however, they are being welcomed with open arms by officials who believe that having a medium-security prison in town may be just the thing to make crime pay in a harsh economic climate.

Some towns are using pep bands, poetry and politicking to woo Governor James R. Thompson and Michael Lane, the State Corrections Director, over to their side.[17]

What is so wonderful, all of a sudden, about a prison in your back yard? Basically, a prison means jobs, and jobs mean retail business from prison employees with money in their pockets.

Start Charging for It

A few years ago I gave a talk to local government clerks in Michigan about the principle of user fees. One clerk happened to comment that her village provides a cemetery plot for the departed from the village. "How much does the village charge for the plot?" I asked. The clerk was aghast. She said that the idea of charging for one's eternal resting place was out of the question. Providing a cemetery plot was the least the village could do for a lifelong resident.

Naturally, the village wouldn't solve any financial problems by charging for cemetery plots. But it is possible, at least in principle, to produce revenue through such a user fee. Local governments are indeed recognizing that there are many services that they can, or should, charge for. They include various recreational services, adult education programs, refuse collection, and even nonessential fire and police services. Some oceanside communities like Sea Girt, New Jersey, found out that they could not only produce revenue by charging seven dollars a person for a weekend beach badge; they could also regulate the crowds by charging a price that discouraged some people coming to the beaches.[18]

Get Someone Else to Pay for It

One option for local governments afflicted with fiscal problems is to try to shift the burden of providing a service to another government. A city, for example, may try to get an overlying county government to "pick up" some of its services—which makes sense when services have regional characteristics. Planning, for example, is a prime candidate for this shift, as are social services and health care. Some burden shifting can be unusual, however, as in the case of Exeter, Rhode Island (population 4,500). According to a newspaper story, "Police officers are a waste of money, say the residents of this rural town of 4,500 people, where the only law officer is a part-time elected sergeant who carries no gun and has nothing to do with criminals."[19]

How does Exeter manage without police protection? It doesn't have to. Exeter receives police protection from the state police. Residents find this adequate; they do not feel that they must provide their own protection. Critics of Exeter argue that the state police are not supposed to provide towns with the level of service Exeter now receives. Exeter, in essence, is shifting its police burden to state taxpayers by having the state police provide the town with this essential service. So far it seems to be working for little Exeter; that is, the citizens are getting protection and someone else is paying for it.

Some local governments in Maine took the principle one step further by threatening jurisdictional suicide. Residents of Sherman, Maine, thought that the only way to stem the rising tide of property taxes was to give up their town name and revert to state jurisdiction. The state would take over education; county government or private contractors would provide other local services. What did Sherman and other small Maine towns have to lose? Town pride mainly.[20]

Public managers are challenged to be fiscally prudent. Some responses, like Falls City's pothole sales, are ingenious. Others are time-honored ones, such as shifting burdens to other jurisdictions. The fiscal climate for local governments is rarely rosy. Public managers will have to search for revenue alternatives while avoiding severe spending cuts whenever possible. The manager will have to make effective use of one of the most important resources—the budget. This is the topic of the next chapter.

SUMMARY

If money was truly the root of all evil, governments would be dens of iniquity. Recall the various ways governments get money from you. They tax your income, your purchases, your property, and your business. They charge you for the privilege of trying to earn a living, and they tax your heirs once your earthly remains are disposed of.

Sources of revenue differ according to levels of government. The federal government relies most heavily on individual and corporate income taxes. States, in contrast, receive the largest portion of their revenues from sales taxes. The property tax is still the largest single source of revenue for local governments.

What is a "good" tax? Economists have developed a list of general criteria to evaluate taxes. Taxes obviously should be efficient, for example—they should yield revenue. They should also be fair and collectable. It does little good to design a fair and efficient tax that is easily avoided. Public officials who have responsibility for revenues must frequently juggle these criteria when proposing new taxes or making changes in existing ones. It is not an easy job.

Governments receive money from other governments. Most commonly, lower-level governments receive grants from higher-level governments so that a policy objective may be accomplished. Lower-level governments—cities and counties, for example—receive grants from public assistance, community development, employment and training, and housing assistance (to name just a few). The most general observation that can be made is that intergovernmental revenue has become an increasingly larger percentage of the total revenues of local governments. One practical consequence of this trend is a tendency for local governments, especially fiscally hard-pressed cities, to become dependent on intergovernmental funds. But when federal policy changes, and the same amount of funds are not forthcoming, many cities must go through a painful withdrawal as they learn to live within their (reduced) financial means. When the intergovernmental fiscal trough begins to run dry, local governments are then forced to search for other revenue-producing alternatives. Selling potholes at ten dollars a crack is one of the more ingenious ones.

NOTES

1. This section is based on *Financing an Urban Government—1978* (final report of the District of Columbia Tax Commission, 1978), pp. 11–14.
2. The school finance fiscal equalization cases are discussed in Daniel L. Rubinfeld, "Judicial Approaches to Local Public Sector Equity: An Economic Analysis," in *Current Issues in Urban Economics*, ed. Peter Mieszkowski and Mahlon Straszheim (Baltimore: Johns Hopkins University Press, 1979), pp. 542–576.
3. See Richard A. Musgrave and Peggy B. Musgrave, *Public Finance in Theory and Practice*, 3d ed. (New York: McGraw-Hill, 1980), p. 55.
4. R. Douglas Arnold, *Congress and the Bureaucracy* (New Haven: Yale University Press, 1979).
5. Harold L. Bunce and Norman J. Glickman, "The Spatial Dimensions of the Community Development Block Grant Program: Targeting and Urban Impacts," in *The Urban Impacts of Federal Policies*, ed. Norman J. Glickman (Baltimore: Johns Hopkins University Press, 1980), pp. 515–541.
6. This view is expressed in David B. Walker, *Toward a Functioning Federalism* (Cambridge, Mass.: Winthrop Publishers, 1981).
7. George E. Hale and Marian Lief Palley, *The Politics of Federal Grants* (Washington, D.C.: Congressional Quarterly Press, 1981), p. 108.
8. The discussion of El Paso is drawn from William E. Hudson, "The Federal Aid Crutch: How a Sunbelt City Comes to Depend on Federal Revenue," *The Urban Interest* 2 (Spring 1980): 34–44.
9. Ibid., p. 39.
10. James W. Fossett, *Federal Aid to Big Cities* (Washington, D.C.: Brookings Institution, 1983), pp. 52–53.
11. Walker, *Toward a Functioning Federalism*, pp. 192–261.
12. A classification of different kinds of mandates is found in Max Neiman and Catherine Lovell, "Federal and State Requirements: Impacts on Local Government," *The Urban Interest* 2 (Spring 1980): 45–51.
13. Thomas Muller and Michael Fix, "Federal Rules, Local Costs," *Policy and Research Report* 11 (Spring 1981): 1–7.
14. Edward I. Koch, "The Mandate Millstone," *The Public Interest* 61 (Fall 1980): 45. (Italics in the original.)
15. For an excellent discussion of legalized gambling, see Jess Marcum and Henry Rowen, "How Many Games in Town?—The Pros and Cons of Legalized Gambling," *The Public Interest* 36 (Summer 1974): 25–52.
16. *Minnesota Cities* 66 (January 1981): 27.
17. "Cash-Shy Illinois Towns See Prison as Answer to Problem," *New York Times*, May 2, 1982, p. 58.
18. Iver Peterson, "On Jersey's Shore, Access Has Its Price," *New York Times*, August 9, 1987, p. E26.

19. "Town without a Police Force Rejects Proposal for 4th Year," *New York Times*, May 2, 1982, p. 59.
20. "The Maine Town That Wants to Die," *New York Times*, December 20, 1987, p. 54.

FOR FURTHER READING

Advisory Commission on Intergovernmental Relations. *Significant Features of Fiscal Federalism*. Washington, D.C.: U.S. Government Printing Office, most current year.

    An indispensable source book on federal, state, and local fiscal patterns. Published yearly.

Bahl, Roy. *Financing State and Local Government in the 1980s*. New York: Oxford University Press, 1984.

    This brief book covers several important issues that affected state and local governments during the past decade including government growth, fiscal stress, and the impact of regional shifts on economic activity.

Fisher, Ronald C. *State and Local Public Finance*. Glenview, IL: Scott, Foresman, 1987.

    A straightforward advanced undergraduate text that covers the basic principles of public finance.

Levine, Charles H., Irene S. Rubin, and George G. Wolohojian. *The Politics of Retrenchment*. Beverly Hills, Calif.: Sage Publications, 1981.

    Four local governments are described at length to show how they cope with fiscal stress.

Musgrave, Richard A., and Peggy B. Musgrave. *Public Finance in Theory And Practice*, 4th ed. New York: McGraw-Hill, 1984.

    A comprehensive text that is probably the best overview of public finance.

CHAPTER 7

Governmental Budgeting

When we say that so and so does not know how to budget, what do we mean? We mean that the person either spends too much money or spends it unwisely. That is, the person does not properly allocate his or her budget for the "right" things, in the "right" proportions.

When we say that a person does know how to budget, we usually mean that the person does not spend more than he or she can really pay for and that the amounts spent for various things seem reasonable. The person who knows how to budget is able to do two things: coordinate resources (income) and needs (spending desires) and allocate spending among different, and often competing, purposes. The person who knows how to budget makes comparisons and trade-offs: If I buy a record, then I will not go to the movies.

Personal budgeting is easy, even though so many of us would admit that we do it poorly. Imagine if you had to budget a few billion dollars, give or take a couple of hundred million, but it was not your money. This is what many federal government managers have to do. State and local government managers also spend other people's money, the money that we pay in taxes. Where does the money come from? How does the manager know how much to ask for? Who determines how much to give the manager? How does the manager spend the money? These are some of the questions of public budgeting that will be answered in this chapter.

THREE LEVELS OF ALLOCATION

Although we can say that budgets allocate resources, the way in which we interpret the budget is based on the level of aggregation that we use to analyze the allocation decision. Budgets, in other words, provide information on choices.

They serve as political documents that reveal information about past, present, and future preferences. How?

Budgets as a Reflection of Policy Priorities

Just like an individual who has a "wish list" of needs and desires, and not enough money to make all the wishes come true, governments also have wish lists of worthwhile projects and programs. Defending the country, protecting the environment, building roads, providing assistance to the poor, and educating the young all seem to be worthwhile endeavors. We express our choices about what the government should spend money on by electing representatives who, in turn, formulate public policy. We can think of public policy as an outline of budget priorities. Although every president has claimed that national defense is of the highest importance, for example, the relative importance can be determined only

TABLE 7.1. Outlays for Major Spending Categories, Fiscal Years 1962–1988 (In Billions of Dollars)

Fiscal Year	National Defense	Entitlements and Other Mandatory Spending	Nondefense Discretionary Spending	Net Interest	Offsetting Receipts	Total Outlays
1962	52.3	30.5	24.1	6.9	−7.0	106.8
1963	53.4	33.0	25.3	7.7	−8.1	111.3
1964	54.8	34.3	29.1	8.2	−7.8	118.5
1965	50.6	34.5	32.5	8.6	−8.0	118.2
1966	58.1	37.2	38.4	9.4	−8.5	134.5
1967	71.4	45.0	41.1	10.3	−10.3	157.5
1968	81.9	52.1	43.8	11.1	−10.8	178.1
1969	82.5	58.4	41.2	12.7	−11.1	183.6
1970	81.7	66.2	45.1	14.4	−11.6	195.6
1971	78.9	80.6	50.1	14.8	−14.2	210.2
1972	79.2	94.2	56.0	15.5	−14.2	230.7
1973	76.7	110.3	59.5	17.3	−18.1	245.7
1974	79.3	124.0	65.9	21.4	−21.3	269.4
1975	86.5	155.8	85.3	23.2	−18.5	332.3
1976	89.6	182.2	93.0	26.7	−19.7	371.8
1977	97.2	197.2	106.5	29.9	−21.6	409.2
1978	104.5	217.5	124.3	35.4	−23.0	458.7
1979	116.3	235.7	134.8	42.6	−26.1	503.5
1980	134.0	278.2	156.6	52.5	−30.3	590.9
1981	157.5	321.0	170.3	68.7	−39.3	678.2
1982	185.3	357.5	155.1	85.0	−37.2	745.7
1983	209.9	399.0	157.5	89.8	−47.8	808.3
1984	227.4	394.8	165.7	111.1	−47.2	851.8
1985	252.7	437.8	175.8	129.4	−49.5	946.3
1986	273.4	455.4	174.1	136.0	−48.6	990.3
1987	282.0	473.4	163.9	138.6	−54.1	1,003.8
1988	290.3	501.2	175.7	151.7	−54.9	1,064.1

Source: Congressional Budget Office.

when one policy area is compared with others. This trade-off is often captured in the popular phrase "guns versus butter." What this means is that more funds for defense spending must be accompanied by less funds for domestic programs. Can you do both? President Lyndon Johnson tried at the end of 1966 and 1967 when he rapidly expanded American involvement in the Vietnam War. Fearing a political backlash, he kept his Great Society domestic programs going with no budget cuts. The result? The economy experienced rapid inflation because government spending was "heating up" the economy.

Spending for national defense declined as a percentage of total spending from the 1960s to 1980. (see Table 7.1.) By 1980 this decline had become a major political issue in the presidential election. President Reagan vigorously pursued a policy of strengthening the defense establishment by increasing spending considerably in the first term of his administration. At the same time the percentage of the budget that went for health and income security was reduced after a dozen years of steady increases. The change represented a change in policy priorities. It was based, in part, on the belief that the federal government was fueling inflation by steadily increasing spending on health and income security. Policy-makers in the Reagan administration believed that the marketplace should be the primary place where the welfare of individuals is protected. One need not agree with such an assessment. The main point is that the budget is one good way to gauge major shifts in public policies.

Programs

Beneath policy priorities we can speak about program priorities. Budgets allow public managers to allocate resources among alternative programs within the organization. This is easily understood by thinking of a local fire department in the Village of Dullsville. Table 7.2 is the budget for the fire department.

Like most fire departments, the Dullsville department (1) puts out fires, (2) prevents fires, (3) acts as a rescue and ambulance service, and (4) trains fire-

TABLE 7.2. The Dullsville Fire Department Budget

	1988 Expenditures	1989 Appropriations	1990 Request
Expenditures			
Personnel	$250,000	$275,000	$291,000
Fuel	10,000	13,000	15,000
Equipment maintenance	15,000	15,500	16,000
Supplies	2,500	2,700	3,000
Travel	4,000	4,800	5,000
Total	$281,500	$311,000	$330,000
Revenue Sources			
Local taxes	$250,000	$260,000	$280,000
Fees	3,000	3,500	4,300
Bake sales	1,500	1,500	1,700
State and federal fees	27,000	46,000	44,000
Total	$281,500	$311,000	$330,000

TABLE 7.3. The Dullsville Fire Department Budget

Program	1989	1990	% Change
Suppression	$100,000	$115,000	15
Prevention	100,000	110,000	10
Rescue	50,000	50,000	0
Training	60,000	55,000	8
Total	$310,000	$330,000	6

fighting personnel. We can consider these four functions as programs, as described in Table 7.3.

Notice that program changes took place between FY 1989 and FY 1990. By treating the percentage change as an indicator of program priorities we can say that fire suppression was considered the highest priority and training the lowest (since it had an 8 percent reduction). A budget, then, can also tell us about the program priorities of a manager. We can infer that the fire chief in Dullsville wants to allocate more money to suppression to improve the performance of the fire department. Notice that the budget is a good reflection of this change in the manager's priorities because it is an important managerial resource.

Objects of Expenditure

Notice the categories of spending (personnel, supplies, and so forth). They are often called line items, or objects of expenditure, which are simply the things the fire department spends money for. In Dullsville the fire department records its spending plan in this way. An object-of-expenditure budget is one of the oldest and simplest ways to classify a budget. Notice that we can easily see what the fire department is spending money for. We can determine if labor costs are increasing; we can analyze the components of nonpersonnel expenditures. An object-of-expenditure budget format, however, does not easily tell us what the program priorities of the fire department are, nor can we tell, from the budget document, how these program priorities are changing. In practice, many governments use a combination of budget formats that include programmatic and line-item detail so that budgetary decision makers have adequate information to make different types of choices.

A TYPICAL BUDGET PROCESS

Most of you have heard the famous routine by the comedians Abbott and Costello called "Who's on First?" The point of the routine was that the baseball team was made up of players with names like Who, What, and Why—names that kept Costello confused.

Similar confusion exists in budgeting. There are agencies, budget analysts, legislative budget staff, appropriations committees, and auditors, to name just a few. Also there are several stages of a budget process—preparation, submission, review, appropriations, execution, and audit—several of which can be occurring at the same time. In addition, a government agency may be involved in several fiscal years at one time. The agency may be forecasting trends for the fiscal year 1993 budget while it is preparing the fiscal year 1992 budget just when the fiscal year 1991 started. Meanwhile, it is completing the execution of the fiscal year 1990 budget while the fiscal year 1988 budget is being audited. Confusing? It should be! Yet, even though budgeting can seem puzzling to the uninitiated, it usually follows a fairly uniform pattern:

1. Agencies request funds to perform activities aimed at achieving some objectives.
2. Another agency, typically a budget office, reviews the requests and recommends a budget for the agency to a chief executive, who may either accept the recommendation or change it.
3. The chief executive assembles the agency's various budgets into a single executive budget, which is submitted to a legislative body for review and approval.
4. The legislative body reviews the executive budget and either approves it as is or changes it through an appropriations process.
5. The budget, as approved by the legislature, then becomes the budget for the upcoming fiscal year and is executed by the executive agencies.
6. At some point after the end of the fiscal year the budget is audited to insure compliance with legislative intent.

Let's go through the budget process more slowly now and point out both the common steps taken by the major participants and the strategies used by each.

The Agency's Request

It is time to return to Dullsville. The fire chief has to prepare a budget for next year, and the basic problem is to decide how much to ask for. Consider the logical connections between the fire department's resources and its basic purposes. Essentially, a fire department tries to obtain some level of fire safety. But although we would all like Dullsville to be completely free of fires, we know this is unrealistic. Surely some fires are caused by factors beyond the control of the fire chief. What, then, is an acceptable level of fire protection? Suppose Dullsville had thirty fires in 1989, and the village trustees said that they wanted this figure cut by two-thirds. Now suppose further that this cut would require a much larger fire-fighting force, improved equipment, more extensive training, and a citizen education program. Would the village trustees be willing to double or even triple the budget for the fire department? Probably not, as there are other things to spend money on.

You can quickly see that it is difficult to gain all of the information needed for estimating the fire department's budget. The reasons are not difficult to find. First, there is likely to be some disagreement about what constitutes an acceptable level of fire safety. Second, even if this first question can be resolved, it is unlikely that the fire chief will know exactly how much larger a budget (and how to allocate the increase) is needed to achieve the level of fire safety desired. Instead, the fire chief is likely to adopt some of the following rules of thumb when deciding how much to ask for.

Avoid answering the unanswerable.   The connection between the fire department's budget and its public mission is not known with any degree of accuracy. If the fire chief claimed that he would be able to suppress 20 percent more fires if the budget were increased by 10 percent, we would be skeptical about his claim. We would not believe that he can make such a prediction with any reasonable amount of accuracy. So when asking for a budget for his department, the chief would be wiser to stick to more defensible claims. He might argue, for example, that he needs more money to hire additional fire fighters to "improve our fire-fighting efforts" or that more funds are needed "to expand our citizen education program so that our prevention program continues to be successful." In other words, the chief will try to stress the need for more funds to improve the performance of the Dullsville Fire Department.

Ask for more than you received last year.   Suppose the fire chief prepared a budget for the coming fiscal year that did not include a dime's increase over the previous year's budget. He was asking for the same number of personnel, paper, and rubberbands. A real efficient manager, you might say. A guardian of the public purse! More likely, you will think that the chief is trying to hide something, that maybe the village trustees gave him too much last year.

Why do public managers usually request more funds each year? They do so for several reasons. First, a budget is a major managerial resource. Usually, bigger is better. Second, public managers tend to hedge their abilities to support current operations by seeking slack resources. These extra funds give managers a cushion against unanticipated expenditures. Third, managers ask for more because they can sometimes use additional funds to expand operations and programs. Fourth, managers tend to see the budget's size as a sign of power and prestige. On balance, then, we can expect managers to ask for more when they prepare their budget requests for the upcoming year. If every manager's "wish list" were granted, however, there would not be adequate revenues to finance all government programs. Moreover, some items or programs on one or more wish lists would probably be out of favor with the elected chief executive or the majority of the legislature. The budget process provides such a check on these possibilities at the very next stage—the review of the manager's request, which is the job of the central budget office.

The Central Budget Office

The central budget office, in most governments, is a staff agency directly responsible to the chief executive. At the federal level it is the Office of Management and Budget (OMB). Several states also have an office of management and budget. Some states and many local governments call it a budget bureau, budget office, or finance office. At the federal level and in several large states the central budget office is divided into sections and staffed by budget examiners. Examiners have responsibility for specific departments and program areas (such as education, labor, and defense).

Common budget-review steps.   Budget examiners scrutinize budget requests with a skeptical eye. After all, they are familiar with the common budgetary expansion strategies. Budget review concerns four broad themes:

1. Are the chief executive's fiscal concerns adhered to by the various departments when they submit their budget request? The chief executive, whether the president, a governor, or a mayor, will probably have some view about the relationship between the budget and the economy. In recent years chief executives have tried to control spending as much as possible. When the budget examiners in the central budget office scrutinize the requests from the various departments, they often will look for requested increases that violate the chief executive's fiscal concerns.

2. Are policy priorities reflected in the department's requests? Chief executives usually get elected with some promise to do "something." This "something" often pertains to a new policy initiative in, say, the environment, employment, highway construction, or health. If chief executives want to make their policy dreams a reality they must translate them into concrete budgetary initiatives. But sometimes the budgetary priorities of departmental managers differ from those of the chief executive. It is the responsibility of the examiners in the budget office to insure that the chief executive's policy priorities are indeed found in the budget submissions of the various departments.

3. Are budget procedures followed? There is a routine to budgeting, which is repetitive. The basic budget cycle occurs over and over and is generally the same from one government to another and from one year to the next. But the particulars, the details, change frequently. The details pertain to the information that must be included in budget requests, the way the information must be displayed, and the precise time frame for submitting the required information. It is the responsibility of the examiners in the budget office to make sure that department managers follow the most current procedures.

4. Are budget requests adequately justified? When managers ask for more funds than they received last year, they are frequently required to justify the need for additional resources. They may show, for example, that costs have increased or that the demand for the services of their program has expanded. If they want to increase the scope of programs they may have to prove that the programs are efficiently managed. Managers may be asked to demonstrate that their programs achieve results. Again, the task of reviewing justifications falls on the shoulders of budget examiners. If justifications are inadequate the examiners may require additional information or recommend that increases not be granted; they can recommend program decreases as well.

There are natural tensions between the agencies and the central budget office. As a staff agency the budget office helps the chief executive balance and decide competing policy claims as they are reflected in budget submissions. In addition, the budget office holds a fiscal orientation toward the budget by keeping the budget within some predetermined target.[1] At the federal level this target is roughly equal to expected revenues plus an estimated deficit. At the state and local levels, where deficit spending is almost always prohibited by law, the budget must be accommodated to anticipated revenues. Since individual agencies are likely to try to expand their budgets, the sum total of all the agencies' requests will almost certainly be greater than anticipated revenues, a major reason why the budget office is forced to play a negative role. But agencies are not completely powerless in the face of a negative budget bureau. They sometimes appeal to the chief executive or, as we will see later, "end run" to the legislature.

The dynamics of agency and budget bureau interaction are illustrated rather well in the following Internal Revenue Service (IRS) budget request. The memorandum needs some clarification. The IRS wanted additional funds to increase its compliance efforts. That is, the IRS wanted to hire additional personnel so that it could increase the number of audits of tax returns. Notice the justification offered by the IRS. The agency claimed that it would more than offset the cost of hiring additional personnel by bringing in more money through the additional audits. In other words, the IRS was making a very old claim: "It takes money to make money."

1979 Presidential Budget Appeal, Department of the Treasury, Issue #1: Revenue-Producing Programs

1979, Issue #1: Revenue-Producing Programs

	1977 Act.	1978	1979 Agency Request	1979 Revised Allowance	1979 Agency Appeal	1979 OMB Rec.
Budget authority ($M)	1,808	1,875	2,043	1,946	+97	-0-
Outlays ($M)	1,795	1,874	2,035	1,938	+97	-0-
FTP employment	70,571	71,432	78,051	73,517	+4,534	-0-

DESCRIPTION OF APPEAL:

Treasury asks for reconsideration of its request for an additional $97 million and 4,534 positions to expand revenue producing programs in the Internal Revenue Service (IRS). Since the issue was presented to you on November 11, the estimates of revenues from increased audit effort have been revised downward to reflect the delay between the time of assessment and actual collection. Treasury has also revised the future years costs of the revenue package upward to include the costs of all IRS programs. These actions have lowered the net additional revenue to $1 B in 1981 and $1.7 B in 1983 (from previous estimates of $2 B in 1981 and $3 B in 1983) and increased the five-year Federal employment increase to 33,000 employees, including 14,000 to maintain the current program. The Treasury benefit/cost ratio has decreased to 4 to 1.

	1979	1980	1981	1982	1983
Increased revenue ($M)	$ 660	$1,027	$1,375	$1,726	$2,174
Increased costs ($M)	97	277	376	440	518
Net revenues ($M)	563	750	999	1,286	1,657
Yield/Cost Ratio	7:1	4:1	4:1	4:1	4:1
Additional positions to produce increased revenues	4,534	9,575	12,680	15,364	18,436
Total new positions	4,534	13,757	20,054	25,963	32,567

AGENCY POSITION:

Sizeable revenues have been and are being lost by continuing inadequate levels of tax administration. Compliance measurement studies show a projected underreporting of $80.3 billion in recommended individual income tax for the FY 1977–83 period. In contrast, the cumulative additional tax recommended through the IRS audit program will total approximately $11 billion at current resource levels. This amounts to a windfall for those not paying their fair share of about $70 billion over the 1977–83 period. Our self-assessment system depends on taxpayers' perceptions that all are paying their fair share of taxes.

The IRS operates proven cost-effective programs accounting for about 90 percent of all Federal receipts. It is in a unique position to help accomplish the President's goal of balancing the budget by seeing to it that a greater proportion of taxes owed, but not collected, are produced. IRS proposes greater equity for all taxpayers by collecting additional taxes from those underreporting their incomes. The FY 1979 budget request is a first step in a five-year plan to increase the flow of direct tax revenue, achieve more voluntary compliance, and obtain greater tax system equity.

Treasury believes the employment increases should be considered in light of the additional revenue of $1 B in 1981 and almost $2 B in 1983 which will come from taxpayers who had underreported, miscalculated, or failed to pay their legitimate tax liability. The net increase in revenue may well be higher by an unquantifiable amount because further additional revenue may accrue from the "ripple effect" of audits-improved voluntary compliance in response to more vigorous tax enforcement.

Concern has also been expressed about the substantial increase in audit coverage to high-income taxpayers, even though voluntary compliance in these classes was high. While compliance is indeed high in percentage terms (reported tax divided by tax actually owed), amounts owed but not correctly assessed are very substantial in actual dollar terms. The opportunities for high-income taxpayers to understate their tax liability are much greater than for the average person. One key to the success of the self-assessment system is the perception on the part of most taxpayers that all taxpayers, including the wealthy, are being fairly examined.

The probability of a taxpayer backlash from a rise in audit coverage from 2.4% to 3.8% is extremely remote because audit rates were in excess of 5% in 1963 and exceeded 3% from 1963 to 1969. During that time, there was no perceptible taxpayer backlash. More realistically, the risk of taxpayer backlash derives from the perception founded in fact, that for lack of adequate enforcement, many taxpayers are not paying their fair share of the tax burden.

In summary, Treasury recommends approval in order to bring in added resources and to improve the equity of the system.

OMB POSITION:

OMB believes that substantial expansion of IRS audit and collection efforts are not necessary to maintain a viable, voluntary tax collection system. The issue then is whether you wish to add 18,000 new IRS employees to generate an additional $1 billion in receipts in 1981 and $2 billion in 1983. Given your overall Federal employment goals and your desire to reduce the burden of the Federal Government on individuals, OMB does not believe the additional expenditure is worth the relatively small increase (0.3%) in tax revenues. OMB is also concerned about the public reaction to such a massive increase in tax enforcement effort (49% in staff by 1983 over 1978), and possible adverse impact on the very successful voluntary compliance system.

OMB believes that the possibility of a taxpayer backlash is real, given the magnitude of the proposed increases. Although the early 1960's audit rates were high, IRS would be "entering into uncharted waters" with the expansion since over half of the peak 1963 audits were lower cost and less intrusive correspondence audits. Such audits have dropped to 15% of total audits today as IRS has developed sophisticated computerized processing, ranking, and checking of returns. In addition, the public attitudes toward the government and willingness to accept further intrusion into their lives have changed.

The IRS equity argument is a matter of perception. While many taxpayers may perceive vigorous enforcement at higher income rates as fair, others may believe an audit rate of once every four years is excessive. At some point, the difference in audit rates between low- and high-income taxpayers may be perceived as unfair to the high-income taxpayer group which has the highest level of voluntary compliance. The 7,000 corporations with over $50 million in assets may also wonder about the self-assessment system since all will be audited every year after 1982.

OMB believes that there would be little "ripple effect" of these audits because of the heavy emphasis on those groups with higher compliance rates.

Finally, the marginal yield of 4 to 1 in the out years would slip to around 2 to 1 if taxpayer costs are included. We believe these real costs—as well as the hard to quantify costs of increased mental aggravation and anxiety—should be considered in making a decision on this issue.

OMB and Treasury agree that the increase is unneeded for a healthy tax system. We believe that the additional $1 B in revenues in 1980 is not worth the costs in terms of new employees and possible adverse effects.

THE WHITE HOUSE
Washington

November 10, 1977

MEMORANDUM FOR: BO CUTTER

FROM: STU EIZENSTAT
        BOB GINSBURG

SUBJECT: Treasury Request for Additional Funding for IRS Audit Enforcement

Treasury has requested an additional $135 million in FY 1979 to expand IRS's revenue producing programs (principally audit enforcement). OMB staff recommends that an additional $31 million be allocated for these purposes. We hope that OMB will move much closer to the Treasury request, for the following reasons:

1. As you know, we are talking about spending an additional $100 million (growing to approximately $400 million in FY 1983) in order to collect an additional $3–$4 billion in FY 1983, with additional revenue collections in the intermediate years in the billions (and these estimates are without taking into account the additional revenues which may accrue from the "ripple effect" of audits by improving voluntary compliance of other taxpayers). This kind of revenue can make a significant contribution toward balancing the budget or toward the funding of other worthwhile programs. For an administration operating on the budget goals and within the budget constraints that we are, we don't think we should forego this additional revenue unless there are very compelling reasons to do so.
2. We are really not persuaded by the OMB staff objections to the Treasury requests:
    a. The principal objection seems to be that "increased resources are not necessary to maintain a viable voluntary tax system." But

we don't think that increasing audit coverage from 2.5% to 3.9% of all tax returns by 1983 would endanger the voluntary nature of our tax system. And voluntariness is only one of the goals of our tax system—actual collection of taxes should be at least a coequal goal.

The real danger in increasing audit enforcement is possible negative public reaction. But again we don't think that the requested increase in audit enforcement would provoke that kind of reaction. Specifically, the tables do not support the assertion that under the Treasury request, an audit would be "either certain or very, very likely" for some individual (25% is the highest audit rate for individuals and that applies only to those with over $50,000 in income).

b. We don't think that the average taxpayer will have any problem with greater audit efforts going into the returns of upper-income taxpayers and large corporations (even if their compliance rates are higher than those for low-income individuals and businesses).

c. We don't think any of us could give serious weight (except maybe to support the Treasury position) to the staff argument that additional revenues from IRS compliance activities should be compared with the option of raising such revenue through higher taxes. In addition, unlike most spending programs, IRS audit enforcement really does not conflict with the objectives of other priority programs.

d. The request for additional personnel should be considered in the light of IRS's unique situation and the additional Federal revenues the personnel will produce.

3. Treasury really does make a fair point in arguing that this request should not be analyzed and treated as if it were just another request for some spending program which we think probably doesn't work but which we need to continue for political purposes. This is a proven, cost-effective program.

But the Office of Management and Budget did not agree. Notice that the OMB brought up issues beyond the anticipated additional revenues that the IRS claimed it would recover if it could hire the extra personnel. The OMB, for example, feared that more audits would endanger our "voluntary" tax system. Also, it was reluctant to add additional federal employees while the focus was on retrenchment.

When there is a substantial disagreement between an agency and the budget office that is not easily resolved by the parties, it is sometimes "appealed" to the chief executive for a decision. In this case the appeal went to the White House.

Notice that a memorandum was sent from two of President Carter's assistants—Stu Eizenstat and Bob Ginsburg—to Bo Cutter, who at the time was the deputy director of the OMB. Eizenstat and Ginsburg reviewed the opposing arguments of the OMB and IRS. Essentially, the White House assistants sided with the IRS; they wanted the OMB to increase the IRS's budget because they agreed that it was a cost-effective request. Also, they were not persuaded by the OMB's argument that additional audits would imperil the voluntary tax system in the United States.

Only a small number of budget requests require the active intervention of the chief executive. But when the chief executive does get involved, the political stakes are high, the bureaucratic conflicts inside the administration are intense, or the policy significance of the budget issue is important. Eventually, decisions are made. The chief executive will come down on one side or another in these appeals, after which the budget office will assemble the various agencies' budgets together into one executive budget. This document is now ready to begin the next phase of the budget cycle. It must run through the legislative gauntlet.

The Legislative Phase

This phase of budgeting is usually known as the appropriations process. Although the specifics of appropriations will vary from government to government, the general pattern is similar. First, the chief executive submits the executive budget to the legislature. Next, the budget is reviewed in parts by subcommittees of the appropriations committees in the upper and lower houses of the legislature. (At the federal level Congress performs a two-stage process. First, it must *authorize* programs. After authorizations Congress then *appropriates* funds.) These subcommittees hold hearings on the budget requests of the agencies under their domain. The hearings provide legislators with the opportunity to scrutinize the activities of the executive agencies. Agency heads, in turn, can use the hearings to bolster support for their programs. Following these hearings the subcommittees make appropriations recommendations to the full appropriations committee. The appropriations committee then combines departmental budgets into appropriations bills, which are voted on by the entire house. (If the legislature has a lower and an upper house, the process occurs in both.) When all of the appropriations bills are passed, we have the budget.

If you just got exhausted or confused by the description of legislative appropriations, put yourself in the position of a freshman legislator whose only experience with budgets extends to his checkbook. The intricacies of government budgeting are baffling. How do legislators cope with the complexities and time constraints?

The use of staff. Legislative budget work is more manageable when there is adequate staff to assist elected representatives. In Washington all members of Congress have their own staff. In addition, committees have staffs; therefore, a member of Congress on the appropriations committee, for example, can turn to the committee's staff for needed assistance during the appropriations phase of the budget process. Members of Congress may also receive budgetary information and analysis from the Congressional Budget Office, the Congressional Research Service in the Library of Congress, and the General Accounting Office.

Legislative staffs serve many functions. Most important, they assist legislators with their budgetary responsibilities; that is, they filter information and help legislators focus on the "important" parts of a particular appropriation. What is important will be determined by several factors: the chief executive's priorities, the legislator's views, the views of the key staff members, his or her constituency, public opinion, and interest-group pressure. The typical legislator cannot examine everything in the budget. On the contrary, only a small amount will be carefully reviewed, and the legislative staff help the legislators consider what parts of the budget fall into that portion.

The purpose of budget hearings.   Appropriations hearings can be funny. Aaron Wildavsky recorded the following exchange between former Representative Rooney and a foreign service officer, which took place many years ago over an item in the Department of State's budget request:

> REPRESENTATIVE ROONEY: I find a gentleman here, an FSO-6. He got an A in Chinese and you assigned him to London.
>
> MR. X: Yes, sir. That officer will have opportunities in London—not as many as he would have in Hong Kong, for example—
>
> REPRESENTATIVE ROONEY: What will he do? Spend his time in Chinatown?
>
> MR. X: No, sir. There will be opportunities in dealing with officers in the British Foreign Office who are concerned with Far Eastern affairs . . .
>
> REPRESENTATIVE ROONEY: So instead of speaking English to one another, they will sit in the London office and talk Chinese?
>
> MR. X: Yes, sir.
>
> REPRESENTATIVE ROONEY: Is that not fantastic?
>
> MR. X: No, sir. They are anxious to keep up their practice . . .
>
> REPRESENTATIVE ROONEY: They go out to Chinese restaurants and have chop suey together?
>
> MR. X: Yes, sir.
>
> REPRESENTATIVE ROONEY: And that is all at the expense of the American taxpayer?[2]

What does this anecdote tell us about legislative appropriations? First, the legislative budget process provides one of the best opportunities for legislative oversight. Notice how Representative Rooney was able to question some of the practices of the foreign service through the appropriations process. Second, it points out what is not a particularly effective bureaucratic tactic. Making claims that lack credibility are not likely to be successful. After all, would you believe anything else the foreign service officer, Mr. X, said after the chop suey episode?

Legislative hearings also provide representatives with the opportunity to alter executive priorities. Sometimes legislators will even restore funds from an agency's budget request that were cut by the budget bureau or the chief executive. In the FY 1983 budget, for example, President Reagan wanted to cut drastically the student loan program. It did not take long for criticism to mount. Student leaders from campuses around the country testified at congressional hearings against the president's proposed cuts. College and university presidents also complained, pointing out the dire effects that cuts in the program would have on their respective institutions: "It would cause financial hardships." "Graduate education would suffer enormously." Parents wrote to their representatives, criticizing the president's stance—and Congress restored much of the proposed cuts. Pressure can work.

The use of decision rules.   Legislators find ways to reduce the burdens of budgeting. Although staff resources help and hearings structure the appropriations process, what seems to be most important are rules of thumb for making decisions.

Wildavsky, one of the foremost authorities on budgeting, has identified "aids to calculation" that reduce the enormous complexity of governmental budgeting.[3] First, legislators let history be their guide. They usually resort to what happened in the past and focus on departures from it. They will scrutinize particularly new items in the budget and large increases in existing items. Second, legislators will usually judge the value of a budget by concentrating on what they know best; they specialize. Third, legislators will often go with the first satisfactory option when making decisions rather than trying to evaluate all conceivable options before them. In Herbert Simon's term, legislators *satisfice* when they make budget decisions.

Budget Execution

After the legislature appropriates funds, it is time to spend the budget, which is known as *budget execution*.[4] Suppose you were an unsavory bureaucrat and you said to yourself, "As soon as those dumb legislators give me my annual budget, I'll just hop on the next plane to Tahiti. They'll never know the difference because these politicians are too busy trying to get reelected." Is this possible?

It is not completely impossible, but it is unlikely. The phase of budget execution provides a few basic mechanisms to prevent budgetary abuse. Some of the most common are the following:

> *Apportionment*—amounts of funds that can be spent by an agency in a specified time. An agency's appropriation, for example, might be divided (apportioned) into quarterly amounts. This technique prevents overspending during the fiscal year.
>
> *Allotment*—amounts of funds that the agency head provides for subunits within the agency. Allotments are also apportioned to prevent overspending by units.
>
> *Preaudit*—a procedure whereby a proposed expenditure is checked to insure that (1) the purpose of the expenditure is approved and (2) there are enough funds for the expenditure.
>
> *Transfer of funds*—sometimes funds are moved from one account to another during the execution of the budget. Transfer controls usually limit the

amount of money that can be transferred. Transfer controls may also require some type of prior approval from the legislature.

The execution phase of budgeting sounds routine. Nevertheless, many a Tahiti
vacation has been subsidized in the past when controls were lax or nonexistent.
Even when outright abuse is absent, the execution phase of the budget can illustrate the classic problem of the separation of powers. The argument for transfer
controls maintains that executive-branch managers must have budgetary discretion to take care of unforeseen problems—natural disasters, war, and violence.
Budgetary transfers allow managers to shift money quickly to fund these pressing
emergencies.

But at what point does the administrator go beyond managerial flexibility and
usurp legislative prerogatives or alter legislative intent? Louis Fisher, perhaps the
leading expert on the spending powers of the president, has documented that "the
financing of the Cambodian War in 1972–1973 was facilitated by the existence of
large transfer authority made available to the Pentagon, amounting to $750 million
for fiscal 1973. The exercise of that authority was supposedly subject to congressional approval."[5] Fisher suggests that it was not.

Auditing

The last phase of the budget cycle is known as auditing, which occurs after the
fiscal year has ended.[6] Since spending from one fiscal year may not be completed
until the next fiscal year is well under way, auditing will usually take place at least
one year after the close of a fiscal year. Auditing of FY 1989, for example, may
first begin in FY 1991.

Audits are usually performed by an individual or institution separate from
the executive agencies. Whereas internal audits in the federal government are
done by the executive-branch departments, external audits are conducted by the
General Accounting Office (GAO). States often have a comptroller who is an
elected official. Large cities frequently have comptrollers as well. Smaller local
governments may hire outside public accounting firms to perform financial audits
of their spending practices. Rules governing audits vary across the states. Nevertheless, these purposes can be summarized in the following definition.

An audit is the examination of records conducted by an independent authority to support an evaluation, recommendation, or opinion concerning the

1.   Adequacy and reliability of information
2.   Efficiency and effectiveness of an agency's programs
3.   Faithfulness of the agency's adherence to rules and procedures
4.   Accuracy of financial statements and performance reports that are sup-
     posed to say something about the present condition, or past operation,
     of an organization

Notice that these four dimensions suggest different aspects of government operations. Number 4, for example, concerns financial information whereas number 2

is similar to program evaluation. The reason for these distinctions is that there are four major types of audits, ranging from relatively narrow (financial) audits to inclusive (program) audits.

Financial audit—This type of audit is restricted to financial records. The purpose is to determine that funds were legally and honestly spent and that documentation is reliable.

Compliance audit—This type of audit also examines the adherence to administrative rules and procedures (such as requirements for competitive bidding or enforcement of civil service hiring rules).

Operational audit—This audit focuses on the efficiency of an agency's operations. It may, for example, look into personnel turnover rates and productivity of employees to determine why an agency is not operating as efficiently as possible.

Program audit—This type of audit tries to determine whether an agency's programs have met their intended objectives.

CONGRESS AND THE BUDGET PROCESS

Criticism of the federal budget process in the United States by the end of the 1960s became increasingly harsh as budgetary life became more difficult for elected representatives. Appropriations were not completed on schedule. Something had to be done to coordinate the "parts" and the "whole" of the federal budget. Meanwhile, every year the budget grew larger. Members of Congress looked only at their pet programs and the agencies under their responsibility. No one in Congress looked at the relationship between the budget and the state of the economy, the size of the deficit, or the major functional categories of spending, such as defense, environment, health, agriculture, and income maintenance. No one questioned the accuracy and adequacy of the President's budgetary information.

Congress wanted to restore the balance of budgetary power it felt was lost to the executive branch. Liberals in Congress wanted to clip the budgetary wings of the president. They believed that Presidents Johnson and Nixon usurped their budgetary powers, in the former case because of military spending for the Vietnam War and in the latter case because of his refusals to release some funds for congressionally supported programs he disagreed with. These impoundments by President Nixon produced a great deal of wrath from many members of Congress. Although presidents have always used impoundments as a way to manage federal spending, Nixon's use of impoundments was qualitatively different because they reached so many different policy areas. Funds for agricultural programs were halted, as were funds for water and sewer grants, housing programs, and pollution control. Several impoundments ended up in court as local governments charged the president with a violation of the separation of powers doctrine. Conservatives, for their part, wanted a change in congressional budgeting. They thought that if they had the ability to look at the budget as a whole, to coordinate budgetary decisions with economic policy, deficit spending would be reduced and "runaway government spending" would be brought under control.

In 1974 Congress passed the Congressional Budget and Impoundment Control Act, which made the following major changes in congressional budgeting:[7]

> The fiscal year runs from October 1 through September 30—instead of from July 1 to June 30—to give Congress more time to make its budgetary decisions.
>
> The president reports a "current services budget," which estimates the cost of last year's budget adjusted for inflation and mandatory increases but with no policy changes.
>
> The Congressional Budget Office provides analysis and five-year projections and reports them to the House and Senate Budget Committees (new committees created as part of the act).
>
> Spending priorities are established by the budget committees and voted on in a first concurrent spending resolution.
>
> Appropriations take place in light of the spending priorities.
>
> A second budget resolution is passed to establish spending, revenue, deficit, and debate totals. These resolutions are supposed to be binding on the Congress and the president.

Did the Budget Control and Impoundment Act of 1974 work? By the early 1980s it became clear that congressional budgeting had not been fully repaired. Budgetary growth continued largely unabated. Second, after an initial period of punctuality, Congress returned to its preact tendency of passing some appropriations well after the beginning of the fiscal year (except for FY 1989). But most importantly, the deficit climbed to more than $200 billion at one point with pessimistic projections from the CBO pointing out that, with no change in policy, the deficit would remain high. By 1984 enough dissatisfaction in Congress percolated to provide a coalition for change in the form of the Emergency Deficit Control Act of 1985, better known as Gramm–Rudman–Hollings (G–R–H), after its three principal sponsors in the Senate.

The Essence of G–R–H

The principle behind G–R–H is simple. Members of Congress believed that the only way to reduce the federal budget deficit was to establish, *by law*, deficit-reduction targets and create a mechanism *requiring* automatic budget cuts if the projected deficit is above the statutorily established amount. The act created deficit reduction targets as indicated in the first column of Table 7.4 that were subsequently revised.

The act called for an elaborate mechanism for computing the estimated deficit. Shortly after the passage of the act the statutory responsibility given to the comptroller general of the United States, the head of the General Accounting Office, was the target of a lawsuit. Upon appeal from a special three-member federal court comprised of appellate judges, the Supreme Court in *Bowsher v.*

TABLE 7.4. Original and Revised Deficit Targets in the 1985 Balanced Budget Act, as Amended (Amounts in $ Billions)

Fiscal year	Original Target	Year-to-Year Decrease	Revised Target	Year-to-Year Decrease
1986	171.9	—		
1987	144	27.9		
1988	108	36	144	—
1989	72	36	136	8
1990	36	36	100	36
1991	0	36	64	36
1992			28	36
1993			0	28

Synar (1986) affirmed the lower court's decision that the responsibilities granted the comptroller general to order executive-branch agencies to implement budget cuts violated the separation of powers principle of the U.S. Constitution. Part of G–R–H was declared unconstitutional; nevertheless, the act contained "fallback" provisions to allow the main features of the law—deficit-reduction targets and mandatory budget cuts—to go forward. Cuts (called "sequestrations" in the language of G–R–H), would be shared equally by defense and nondefense programs. Certain programs, however, mainly entitlement programs such as social security, medicaid, food stamps, aid to dependent children, veterans' pensions, and a few others, were exempted from the sequestration process.

Has G–R–H worked?   What Congress can do, Congress can undo. In the aftermath of the *Bowsher* case and the subsequent difficulties in implementing G–R–H, Congress revised the timetable for reaching a balanced budget (as illustrated in Table 7.4). In retrospect, this was probably sound since the wrenching experience with sequestrations is something that members of Congress would prefer to avoid. After all, few members of Congress really want to defend budget cuts that adversely affect their legislative districts. Also, the "meat axe" method of cutting the budget is an approach that one can get very enthusiastic about.

BUDGETING AND FISCAL SCARCITY

The federal government has no monopoly on fiscal scarcity. Indeed, lack of resources to finance all worthwhile government programs is a basic fact of budgetary life. How does fiscal scarcity influence budgeting? If you had less money to spend, or if you were uncertain about how much you were likely to have in the near future, what should be the wise thing to do? You would try to control your spending impulses. You might even try to "trick" yourself by giving up charge cards, setting up a "rainy-day" fund, or giving up some expensive habit.

Governments have it a bit harder. Consider a single local government. Unlike you, the local government's funds are, to a great extent, affected by factors outside its control. If the economy worsens it is likely to receive less money while expenses go up. In addition, decisions made at the state and federal levels about intergovernmental grants will also affect the local government's financial condition. Mandates imposed by higher-level governments, or the courts, are also likely to increase spending. Also, let's not forget unforeseen developments: floods, hurricanes, volcanos, lawsuits, or a plant closing, to name a few. All of them are likely to make budget balancing more difficult.

Governments, particularly state and local governments, try to cope with fiscal scarcity and uncertainty in a few common ways. First, unlike the federal government, state and local governments (with the exception of only a few) have constitutional prohibitions against deficit spending. This is done in a few ways. A state constitution may require the governor to submit a balanced budget to the legislature. Alternatively, the law may require the legislature to appropriate a balanced budget. Some states require the executive branch to implement the budget so that the fiscal year ends in balance. In a few states any end-of-the-year deficit must be eliminated by a tax increase in the next fiscal year. This is surely a strong sanction against deficit spending.

Some states and local governments use a "rainy-day" fund to smooth out budgetary shortfalls caused by economic fluctuations. The idea is straightforward. Funds are set aside in the budget to be used only in the event of an unexpected downturn. A few states appropriate a set amount for the fund. Others establish a percentage of the total budget as the rainy-day fund. A third way to cope with budgetary uncertainly is to adopt a fiscally conservative decision-making guideline. This is done by overestimating expenditures and underestimating revenues.[8] This creates a built-in conservative bias that helps control spending. The problem, like the one of the boy who cried wolf, is that agencies soon begin to ignore the estimates when they realize the bias.

Budget managers anticipate the inclination of the spending departments to ignore estimates. One way to prevent the natural impulse to spend is to create additional hurdles for agencies to leap over during the execution phase of the budget cycle. Assume, for example, that a budget includes funds for travel to professional meetings. When the financial condition deteriorates, travel might be controlled by requiring agencies to justify each request to obligate funds for travel during the fiscal year. This tactic would probably slow down the rate of spending for travel, and if things worsen, a total freeze on travel might be initiated. Perhaps the most common way to halt spending is to impose a hiring freeze—a tactic that is used frequently at all levels of government—or to eliminate a position altogether. One thing is clear: The budget must take center stage whenever a government is forced to wrestle with fiscal adversity.

SUMMARY

It has been said that the budget is the "world series" of politics. This is perhaps an overstatement. But most public managers will tell you that the budget is a large part of their administrative world. They are either preparing it, justifying it, spending it, or evaluating it. The budget, one learns quickly, is a major managerial resource—and a big headache as well.

The enormous complexity of budgeting is moderated by its repetitive character. Managers know that every year they will prepare, justify, and spend their budgets. The rules of the game in budgeting—the strategies and the negotiations around them—are predictable because they are repetitive. Managers ask for larger budgets to support their programs; budget examiners in the central budget office anticipate that managers will do exactly this. Predictability, at least in the past, has made budgeting manageable.

But budgeting in recent years has become less predictable. At the federal level the constant battle between the "parts and the whole" encouraged the reform of the congressional budget process. The preoccupation mainly with department budget requests, along with the fragmentation of the budget, meant that no one looked at the budget as part of overall economic policy. With the passage of the Budget Control and Impoundment Act of 1974, procedures have been established to evaluate the budget as a whole—especially its impact on the economy.

At the state and local levels the budget has also come center stage because of the fiscal adversity that has afflicted so many governments in the 1970s and the 1980s. Faced with deteriorating tax bases, population losses, high unemployment, and inflation, many state and local governments have been forced to cut spending. Naturally, in an atmosphere of poor fiscal health, the budget becomes the political battleground as managers try to defend their bureaucratic turf and cope with the inevitable cuts.

In the case that follows, the budgetary battlefield is moved to the arena of higher education—Mid-American University to be exact. After reading and role playing "A Kick in the Seat of Higher Learning," do you think that the term *Ivory Tower* is still appropriate for universities? Or are professors capable of becoming battle-scarred budgetary warriors when they are forced to defend their organizational turf?

A Kick in the Seat of Higher Learning: Budget Cutting at Mid-American University

Mid-American University, the flagship institution of a widely respected state university system, is faced with problems that are all too familiar to beleaguered education administrators. The university is suffering from the one–two punch of postbaby-boom-enrollment decline (reducing tuition-based revenues) and pressures faced by every state agency in the face of a shrinking base of state government revenues. Indeed, the state is experiencing an unprecedented revenue shortfall (even after raising taxes for the third straight year).

Higher education is a prime target for cuts. The rationale is straightforward: there are fewer students than in the past, the university system has been lavishly supported in past years even as other state services were being cut back, and political sentiment indicates that cuts in higher education would be met with less opposition than cuts in other major programmatic areas (many of which have already been cut to the bone). The governor and the leadership of the state legislature's budget and higher education committees had little difficulty striking a deal whereby the appropriations for every institution in the state university system would be cut by 10 percent. The chancellors of the respective campuses would decide how to deliver the cut.

The chancellor of Mid-American University (MU), Lamar Knebbish, followed the course of least resistance and passed along the problem to the academic deans (of the Colleges of Engineering, Business Administration, Arts and Sciences, and Education). Each dean was instructed to deliver a cutback plan to Chancellor Knebbish. The plans would detail cuts in 10 percent of the faculty positions in each of the respective colleges (operating budgets and support personnel budgets were not subject to cuts since it was generally believed that they were already thin). In the absence of a miracle (e.g., an unexpected influx of new students, a great upsurge in the economy, the discovery of oil on the MU intramural fields), the plans would be implemented during the next fiscal year.

INSTRUCTIONS

You are part of a committee formed by the dean of the College of Arts and Sciences. The charge of the committee is to come up with a plan for cutting back 10 percent of the faculty positions in the college. Tenured faculty cannot be dismissed, however, unless their entire academic department is abolished. Examine the data given in the accompanying documents and tables to be better informed in your decisions. Your task is to detail the cuts and articulate your reasons for proceeding as you did. Expect that you will have to defend your decisions not only to the dean but also to your faculty colleagues (including perhaps some of those who will soon be ex-colleagues). You are not, however, concerned with making cuts targeted for individuals but with cuts in departments' faculty lines. The departments will decide who gets axed. Finally, specify information you would like to have (if any) that is not given in the data and documents and tables.

DOCUMENT A: OVERVIEW OF THE COLLEGE OF ARTS AND SCIENCES

The College of Arts and Sciences is the oldest and largest of the four colleges of Mid-American University. Almost half of Mid-American's undergraduate students have elected majors in one of the Arts and Sciences academic departments, and 43 percent of MU's graduate students are pursuing degrees (usually doctoral degrees rather than master's degrees) in the college. Nevertheless, Arts and Sciences has suffered the greatest attrition during the past five years of any of the colleges. Students are increasingly turning to fields such as business or engineering, which seem to offer more promising job prospects.

There are three major divisions in the College of Arts and Sciences: the Division of Physical and Life Sciences, the Division of Social Sciences, and the Division of Humanities. Most observers agree that the strongest departments (in terms of academic quality) are in the Division of Humanities—but it is these departments that are suffering the greatest declines in enrollment. The Division of Social Sciences includes some highly reputable departments and others generally assessed as mediocre. The Division of Physical and Life Sciences has actually been enjoying a modest upswing in enrollments—clearly bucking the college trend—but includes no highly respected programs and has been unable to attract prominent professors and researchers.

Each year the Undergraduate Student Association gathers teaching evaluations from students. The evaluations are generated for nearly every class taught at MU. Although there are substantial differences in teaching effectiveness, the differences are much more pronounced at the individual level than at the departmental level. There is a modest tendency for professors in the Department of History, English, and Psychology to receive somewhat higher ratings in aggregate.

The Division of Physical and Life Sciences has been the leader in bringing in resources through government and private grants and contracts. Social Sciences has had some success in generating external funds, but Humanities has had little success or, for that matter, little interest in bringing in big money for research.

DOCUMENT B: MEMORANDUM FROM DEAN TO DEPARTMENT CHAIRS

To: Department Chairs in Arts and Sciences

From: Dean I. M. Draconian

As you are no doubt aware, we have been asked by Chancellor Knebbish to come up with a plan to cut our faculty lines by 10 percent. Before we meet to hammer out a plan, I would like each of you to give me a brief response to the question "Why shouldn't my department be submitted to a cut of (at least) 10 percent of existing faculty positions?" This should not imply that each of you will necessarily be cut by 10 percent. You may be cut more; you may be cut less. At the extremes, it is possible that you won't be cut at all or (and I hesitate to even raise this spectre) that your entire department could go down the tubes.

I look forward to receiving your response within one week. Shortly thereafter we will meet and make our decisions.

DOCUMENT C: CHAIRS' RESPONSES (ABRIDGED) TO DEAN'S MEMO

V. J. Quark, Physics:

Need I point out that we have the largest enrollment in our division, the highest growth rate of any department in the college, and a smaller faculty than our two sister departments, Biology and Chemistry. We have also made substantial contributions to the fiscal health of MU by bringing in much more than our share of grants and contracts. . . . Moreover, consider the contributions of physics to our knowledge and mastery of the world and then consider the contribution of any (or all) of the social sciences. All the cuts should come from these charlatans in the Social Sciences Division.

Fred Beaker, Chemistry:

(no response to Dean's memo)

Jean Splicer, Biology:

As I'm sure you remember from your days as a professor in this department, we have always pulled our weight and received very little credit. We keep turning out good students and get them jobs and we will continue to do so if the department is not gutted (as it would be if I lost even one faculty member). . . . Quite frankly, our reputation is not all that I would hope it would be. That drop in the AUE ranks stung us a bit. But the new people we've hired here are beginning to make up for the dead wood in the tenured faculty. You can't possibly expect me to lose one of these good, energetic young faculty members when we have so many who have taken "early retirement."

Rock Kozel, Geology:

Look Drac, we've only got eight faculty. We just barely have a critical mass. If you cut us back we're dead. How are we going to compete if we can't even cover all the major specialty areas of geology?

Terrence Totem, Anthropology:

I think it is positively barbaric asking us to go through this kind of exercise. It is also stupid. How can we possibly make comparisons between, say, Physics and Anthropology? We might as well draw lots as to proceed as you suggest.

Niccolo Pluaralti, Political Science:

The state constitution requires that every kid who attends this hallowed institution has to pass through P.S. 101, American Government and Citizenship. This means that we are hard pressed even during the best of times. Even if our majors are somewhat fewer than in the past, there has been little or no reduction in P.S. 101. If you cut us we will not be able to deliver that course with class sizes under 500.

Bull Marquet, Economics:

Enrollments are up, faculty quality ratings are up (see latest AUE rank), average class size is up, sponsored research is up. 'Nuff said.

Philo Mindbender, Psychology:

Our enrollments are up. Take it out of the hide of those departments losing students.

Clio R. Cane, History:

Our enrollments are down but we actually have an increase in nonmajors taking history courses. Our courses in history of rock and roll and history of cinema have been filled each term. I think this shows a commitment to innovation. Also, I don't think there's any disagreement that we have one of the most prominent faculties at MU. As soon as this current obsession with vocational training goes away we will be back to normal. You don't want to be thought of as the person who destroyed a nationally recognized history department, do you?

Gerund Claus, English:

Everyone takes freshman English. Thus our average class size is the highest in the division and the second highest in the college. When you consider this, together with our high quality (see recent AUE rank), we don't seem a reasonable candidate for cuts.

Contem Platenavel, Philosophy:

Sure our enrollments are down, but since when does the market determine the importance of academic enterprise? The Accountancy Department in the Business School has four times as many faculty as we. Does this mean that debits and credits are more important than the nature of justice, aesthetics, clarity of argument, and ethics? Anyway, our enrollments are down only because they were artificially inflated during the 1960s and early 1970s when it was "in" to be a philosopher. We have fewer students but they are better.

Virgil Aeneid, Classics:

We have the smallest but the best department in the entire university. Each of our five faculty members has a national reputation in his or her

TABLE 1. Data for Arts and Sciences Departments of Mid-American University

	Tenured Faculty	Untenured Faculty	Undergrad. Majors	% Change (Five-Yr. Period)	Grad. Majors	% Change	Sponsored Research Dollars	Aver. Class Size*	AUE Rank†
Physics	5	7	99	+10	8	+5	$1,400,000	28	35
Chemistry	10	3	84	+3	10	—	1,850,000	27	38
Biology	3	11	81	+6	14	+10	960,000	33	35
Geology	2	6	32	-8	3	-50	40,000	6	27
Anthropology	1	6	18	-17	1	—	40,000	5	85
Political Sci.	12	8	110	-4	18	+8	57,000	38	50
Economics	10	10	115	+9	21	+12	820,000	44	65
Psychology	8	6	65	+1	6	+33	250,000	23	40
Sociology	14	10	49	-20	5	-20	15,000	12	48
History	10	14	61	-37	10	+10	25,000	37	85
English	15	17	52	-41	9	-50	0	41	80
Philosophy	4	6	31	-61	2	-80	0	5	62
Classics	4	1	18	-14	9	—	0	14	90

*Includes majors and nonmajors.
†High score indicates high-quality rank.

specialty. Many of your larger departments have not a single noteworthy scholar. We place our doctoral students in the very finest departments, and we expect to continue to function at this high level if you'll only leave us alone.

NOTES

1. See, for example, Barry Bozeman and Jeffrey D. Straussman, "Shrinking Budgets and the Shrinkage of Budget Theory," *Public Administration Review* 42 (November/December 1982): 509–515.
2. Aaron Wildavsky, *The Politics of the Budgetary Process,* 4th ed. (Boston: Little, Brown, 1984), pp. 96–97.
3. Ibid., pp. 8–16.
4. For a brief review of budget execution procedures, see George E. Hale and Scott R. Douglass, "The Politics of Budget Execution: Financial Manipulation in State and Local Government," *Administration and Society* 9 (November 1977): 367–378.
5. Louis Fisher, *Presidential Spending Power* (Princeton, N.J.: Princeton University Press, 1975), pp. 111–112.
6. On audits see Richard E. Brown, Meredith C. Williams, and Thomas P. Gallaher, *Auditing Performance in Government* (New York: Wiley, 1982).
7. See Allen Schick, *Congress and Money* (Washington, D.C.: Urban Institute Press, 1980).
8. Scarcity in developing countries is described in Naomi Caiden and Aaron Wildavsky, *Planning and Budgeting in Poor Countries* (New York: Wiley, 1974). For a case study of a single small county government in the United States, see Jane Massey and Jeffrey D. Straussman, "Budget Control Is Alive and Well: Case Study of a County Government," *Public Budgeting and Finance* 1 (Winter 1981): 3–11.

FOR FURTHER READING

Axelrod, Donald. *Budgeting for Modern Government.* New York: St. Martin's Press, 1988.
    A text that covers all levels of government budgeting in a comprehensive manner.
The Budget of the United States Government. Washington, D.C.: U.S. Government Printing Office, yearly.
    Those who really want to examine the budget should look at its appendix—much bigger, more detailed, and more comprehensive.
Rubin, Irene S., ed. *New Directions in Budget Theory,* Albany: State University of New York Press, 1988.
    A collection of essays by academicians who have followed the budgetary process for several years.
Schick, Allen. *Congress and Money.* Washington, D.C.: Urban Institute Press, 1980.
    A comprehensive work on the congressional budget process (until 1980) by one of its most perceptive observers.
Wildavsky, Aaron. *The New Politics of the Budgetary Process.* Glenview, Ill.: Scott, Foresman, 1988.
    A thoroughly revised version of his classic work that interprets the importance of major changes that have taken place in the federal budget process.

CHAPTER 8

Public Personnel

A friend of mine, a former professor of political science at the University of Rochester, told me about the following incident that occurred several years ago. An undergraduate student came to him one day asking for some guidance. The student wanted to know if it was possible to have a dual major in both music and political science. My friend replied that it was unusual but not impossible. The inquiry naturally sparked some curiosity on the part of the professor, so he asked the student why he wanted to major in both music and political science. The student said that he thought it would be best way to get the job he was seeking—a cultural attaché in one of the embassies of the U.S. government.

My friend, a patient man, asked the inquiring student to sit down. The professor proceeded to tell the student how one goes about getting a job in the U.S. Foreign Service. First, it is extremely competitive, my friend told the student. You have to take a very difficult written examination, which most people fail. If you happen to pass the examination, you then have to take an equally difficult oral examination before a committee. If you are one of the few select individuals to make it past this hurdle, you may be fortunate enough to get a position in Burkina Faso (you will probably have to consult a world map to find it) stamping passports for three years in 100-degree weather.

At this point my friend remembered that the student mentioned the specific position of cultural attaché. My friend commented that a cultural attaché could even be tone deaf. Some cultural attachés may not know the difference between Monet and Manet. Many factors that have nothing to do with artistic ability will determine the selection of cultural attachés. My friend was confident that the inquiring student, now properly informed, would be able to make a realistic appraisal about his chances of becoming a cultural attaché. After listening politely, the student asked the professor the following question: "Can I become a cultural attaché in Canada if I have a dual major in music and political science?"

Somehow this student could not understand that getting a government job involves complex procedures that sometimes defy elementary logic. The process is called public personnel management. It includes everything from hiring, paying, promoting, and evaluating to firing government employees. Personnel management is a very important part of the work of public administrators. It is inundated with numerous rules and regulations that have developed over many years. To understand how we arrived at the current state of public personnel management, it is useful to glance at the past.

HISTORY OF PUBLIC PERSONNEL *— Parallel to PA as a field —*

Phase 1: The Postrevolutionary Period *— or Aristocratic Period*

Two features characterized government service in the federal government of the Federalist era. First, government, as defined by the number of full-time employees, was small. By 1800 there were only about three thousand federal civilian employees in the United States; fewer than three hundred positions were in the nation's capital. Second, and perhaps even more significant, these positions were held by persons of "semiaristocratic" social backgrounds.[1] The Federalists, after all, were wary of excessive democracy and protective of their social and economic positions. In short, they were conservative.

Were our early bureaucrats incompetent, selected mainly because of their social position rather than any "objective" standard? Frederick Mosher, writing about this period, pointed out that in the first phase in the evolution of government employment the objective standard was "fitness of character."[2] This "could best be measured by family background, educational attainment, honor and esteem."[3] Yet there is general agreement among historians that these upper-class bureaucrats were competent. Summarizing the early administrative history Paul Van Riper wrote: *" The best should rule"*

> That the personal and partisan interests of political realists of the caliber of the Founding Fathers and their associates should be accompanied by administrative expertise, intelligence, and a high sense of responsibility to the country at large was indeed fortunate. Not only was a new nation placed on firm political foundations, but also its early civil service was established with a reputation for integrity and capacity that is remembered to this day.[4]

Phase 2: The Emergence of the Common Man

The very idea of a government administered by competent men of higher social status sounds alien today after more than two hundred years of American history during which we have been indoctrinated with the egalitarian idea. The notion that one's social position should be a primary consideration for government employment is downright undemocratic. But in 1800 it was perfectly reasonable.

By 1829, though, it was a little less reasonable. The election of Andrew Jackson to the presidency is often associated with the so-called spoils system. Spoils, later called patronage, meant providing jobs for people who loyally supported, and worked for, the candidate who was triumphant at the polls. It was not who you were but what you did that became important.

If Jacksonian democracy tried to broaden the social base of public employment, it did not exactly fill the government with a bunch of rogues. At least at the top level of government, the social position of bureaucrats under Jackson was not much different from the presidents who came before him.[5] Perhaps more important than social status was President Jackson's definition of government work: "The duties of all public offices are, or at least admit of being made, so plain and simple that men of intelligence may readily qualify themselves for their performance; and I can not believe that more is lost by the long continuance of men in office than is generally to be gained by their experience."[6] For Jackson, any regular person could perform government work.

The idea that government jobs were the spoils that went to the victors in elections was put into practice by the emerging political party machines in big cities such as Boston, New York, and Pittsburgh. These political party machines grew in influence after the Civil War and some, like the political machine of the Democratic party in Chicago, remained powerful until the 1960s. One of the more colorful political bosses, George Washington Plunkitt, Tammany Hall leader in New York around the turn of the century, said about patronage:

> When the people elected Tammany, they knew just what they were doin'! We didn't put up any false pretenses. We didn't go in for humbug civil service and all that rot. We stood as we have always stood, for rewardin' the man that won the victory. They call that the spoils system. All right, Tammany is for the spoils system, and when we go in we fire every anti-Tammany man from office that can be fired under the law.[7]

But by the time Plunkitt made this pronouncement, bosses were fighting a rearguard action. Charged with corruption and incompetence, political bosses were challenged by reformers who wanted to oust these political opportunists and their scruffy immigrant followers. Machines like Tammany Hall had to contend with civil service reforms. The "reign" of the common man gave way to professional administration.

Phase 3: The Birth of Civil Service

The year 1883 is significant in administrative history. In that year the Pendleton Act was passed, establishing the modern federal civil service system. Until 1881 reform of the civil service was limping along, but in 1881 an event occurred that speeded up the process. The president, James A. Garfield, was assassinated by a fellow named Charles Guiteau. It seems that Guiteau, a strong supporter of Garfield during the presidential election, expected to receive an appointment to a government job for his labors. When the job was not forthcoming, he was more than a little upset. Meanwhile, reformers were able to show the rather sorry end that the spoils system can bring.[8] Reform of civil service was not merely in the political wings but was brought to center stage.

The Pendleton Act established the U.S. Civil Service Commission. The act
established the following civil service procedures.

Open competitive examinations for government jobs
Probationary periods for new appointees
Legal protection from outside political pressures
Commission oversight of departmental personnel decisions
Presidential power to expand or contract the merit system in federal employment[9]

The purpose of these procedures was to eliminate corruption, political favoritism,
and incompetence from federal employment.

The three main features of the Pendleton Act—competitive examinations, job
security, and political neutrality—features that were modeled after the higher civil
service in Great Britain, remain very much intact to this day. Similar civil service
reforms were enacted in Massachusetts and New York. By 1900 sixty-five cities
had civil service commissions. Slowly, throughout the twentieth century, the basic ingredients of civil service reform found in the Pendleton Act spread across
state and local governments. But the reforms were not popular with everyone.
George Washington Plunkitt, for one, thought that they ushered in the "death"
of democracy, Tammany Hall style.

In 1887 an essay entitled "The Study of Administration" was published by
the young Woodrow Wilson.[10] In this famous essay Wilson advanced the thesis
that a professionally competent, and politically neutral, administrative cadre
could, and should, form the basis of the civil service. Wilson thought that civil
servants could achieve the first objective—professional competence—through
formal education. Perhaps naively, he believed that there were general administrative practices that cut across different types of governments and political cul-
tures. He believed that these practices can be learned and then replicated by aspiring professional administrators.

The second thesis—the political neutrality of professional administrators—
produced an ongoing debate in the field of public administration. Wilson made a
distinction between politics and administration. Following the reformers before
him, he argued, "administration lies outside the proper sphere of politics. Administrative questions are not political questions. Although politics sets the task for
administration, it should not be suffered to manipulate its offices."[11] From the
vantage point of the last decade of the twentieth century Wilson's famous politics–administration dichotomy seems simplistic. Few would deny that administrators are involved in making policy, not merely executing it, and the very term
bureaucratic politics belies the separation of politics from administration envisioned by Wilson. But his dream of professional administration went forward and
became part of the efforts to build of it a "science."

Phase 4: The "Science" of Administration

Reform took on a new twist in the first half of the twentieth century. When the
reformers railed against political bosses like Plunkitt, it was not only about their
corrupt practices and overall moral laxness. Reformers also criticized their over-

all incompetence. Good administration was supposed to be not only politically neutral but also efficient. This concept, the mainstay of many municipal reforms during the progressive era, became an overriding concern in the practice of public administration for a large part of this century.

Mosher has pointed out how the general idea of efficiency entered into personnel administration.[12]

> Jobs should be analyzed to determine how they should best be performed.
> Qualifications for government jobs should be spelled out. Jobs should be classified so that similar jobs have similar specifications and qualifications.
> Examinations should be designed to identify and measure the qualifications for jobs and predict performance of the candidates.
> Training should be undertaken to improve the performance of government personnel.

These features of personnel administration have their intellectual foundations in both Wilson's idea of a professional administration and the "scientific management" of Frederick Taylor who, as described in Chapter 4, believed that one could uncover, through study, the "one best way" of performing tasks. Many of our current features of personnel management, as we will see later, are based on these basic ideas that originated more than eighty years ago in the United States.

It is a logical progression to assume that if there is one best (and efficient) way to administer tasks—or jobs—there is one best way to manage people. Indeed, this was a major theme of administrative thinking and practice from the 1920s through the 1950s. With the development of the New Deal, President Roosevelt brought to his administration some of the leading academic theorists of public administration to help manage many of the new programs. What emerged from this period (1933–1945) and continues to this day is the belief that personnel management, whether thought of as a science or an art, is supposed to serve top political leadership. But how this should be done is the subject of ongoing debate in the field of public personnel.

A LEGACY OF CONTINUING CONFLICTS

These four phases of public personnel have left ongoing themes and continuing controversies in the field of personnel administration. We can summarize some of the most important features of the historical legacy by noting three of them.

The Chosen versus the Common Man

We noted that administrators in the first phase came from our country's aristocracy. It made sense that men of wealth and property held the top positions in the new government. These people were, by the standards of the day, well educated and most "fit" to govern. Yet the elitism of the first phase was challenged, in part, in the second phase. The egalitarian spirit that began during the Jacksonian period raised two basic arguments that are very much alive today. First, government work is not so specialized that it cannot be performed by a larger segment of the population. Second, government employment should reflect our basic philosophical commitment to egalitarianism—which means that government employees should mirror the socioeconomic characteristics of the population. In today's language this is called "representative bureaucracy."[13] Some of the ongoing conflicts in contemporary personnel administration focus on the extent that government employment is, or should be, "representative."

Merit versus Patronage   *Merit vs. Control by elected official* —

Reformers criticized the spoils system of the nineteenth century because it allowed corruption and incompetence to flourish. No one would deny that excesses occurred, and even today we occasionally hear about "no-show" political jobs. These jobs are given by elected officials, like governors or big-city mayors, to their political cronies and are called "no-show" jobs because they pay well but require little or no work.

The merit system, initiated with the Pendleton Act, was supposed to change government employment from whom you know to what you know. Competence rather than connections is supposed to be the hallmark of merit. We will see later, however, that the merit principle does not always work so well in practice.

Political Neutrality

The idea of a politically neutral civil service was advanced by Woodrow Wilson. Later, some scholars and practitioners claimed that politics and administration could be kept separate. Elected officials, in keeping with their constitutional responsibilities, would make public policies. Civil servants would implement them. The epitome of this idea could be found (until 1970) in the Budget Bureau, where career civil servants could practice what one political scientist called "neutral competence" in discharging the president's policies.[14]

The politics–administration distinction was not accepted by all. Paul Appleby, a former dean of the Maxwell School, Syracuse University, and a former director of the Division of the Budget in New York, pointed out that the varied tasks of administration require civil servants to engage themselves in public policy and, therefore, in politics.[15] None other than President Nixon recognized this fact of political life too well. Believing that many top civil servants opposed his political views and policy inclinations, Nixon sought to limit their involvement, as much as possible, in direct policy-making.[16] Similarly, Anne Gorsuch Burford, the controversial director of the Environmental Protection Agency in President Reagan's first term, "froze out" top career civil servants from policymaking in the agency. From her vantage point, these civil servants were unsympathetic to her initiatives. She knew that politics and administration were intertwined and tried—ultimately unsuccessfully—to limit administrative influence in political decisions.

With this important historical legacy as framework, we can now turn to the essentials of personnel management. The major features that follow will pertain to most governments throughout the United States that have civil service merit systems and will cover job classification, hiring procedures, promotions, disciplinary actions, and termination.

ESSENTIALS OF PERSONNEL MANAGEMENT

Classification

Is there any difference between driving a truck for the Department of Defense and driving one for the Department of Interior? Can the job of accountant be sufficiently described independent of individuals who hold the job so that the description is unambiguous about what constitutes the position itself? Can the duties of social worker II be distinguished from the responsibilities of social worker I so that the two positions are distinct? Should individuals holding the same kind of job, such as secretary or word processing operator, receive the same pay? These are some of the basic questions of classification in public personnel management.

Position classification "involves identifying the duties and responsibilities of each position in an organization and then grouping the positions according to their similarities for personnel administration activities."[17] That is, jobs (positions) must be analyzed to determine what type of work is performed; the positions must then be grouped together (or into classes) based on the similarity of the tasks performed; each class of positions must have standards that are written down so that they will be "objective"; positions will be distributed to the various classes in the personnel system.[18] These four steps form the rudiments of position classification, an idea that goes back to the reform period of the latter part of the nineteenth century. It was a major attempt to introduce merit and impartiality into the civil service system.

Let's see how position classification might work in a typical state government's civil service system. Suppose there is a need for a job we will call word processing operator. There are many positions for word processing operator throughout state government. The governor's office, for example needs word processing operators; the departments of labors, corrections, agriculture, and social services all have needs for word processing operators, who perform very similar duties in all these positions. They must type letters, memoranda, reports; they must file and retrieve documents; they must answer questions concerning the details of the respective government agencies. Obviously, many of the details of the duties are unique to the individual departments. Nevertheless, the basic responsibilities and duties of all word processing operator positions are similar enough to create a job classification with the title "word processing operator." Once the classification is determined, the next step is to establish the pay scale, criteria for hiring, and criteria for promotion.

Classification of positions in state and local governments is usually performed by a central personnel agency, often called the "department of civil service." This agency will establish classifications with the assistance of the various operating departments), list vacant positions, administer examinations for the positions, and monitor the agency's compliance with civil service regulations. At the federal level classification is performed by the department, but even in Washington, D.C., the Office of Personnel Management examines the practices of the various departments to check for abuse.

Although position classification was intended to fulfill the reformers' dream of a civil service based on merit, it is not without fault. One specific criticism is noteworthy as we approach the twenty-first century. As our society has grown more and more complex, so has government. Many of the very specialized positions found in the private sector are also present in the public sector. When a government needs to hire a person with a new specialization but at the same time tries to maintain the standard procedures of civil service, a problem arises. If the new specialization receives a civil service classification, for instance, it would clearly restrict people who lack the appropriate credentials from applying. Notice that when this occurs, classification does what it was designed to prevent. It bars entry into government employment except for a select few.[19]

Hiring

Suppose Sally Slick, a manager in a state social services department, has five vacancies for the position of caseworker, a position with the following responsibilities: (1) determining eligibility for various federal and state government programs such as aid to families with dependent children, day care, foster care, and food stamps; (2) determining whether clients are capable of working or receiving employment training; (3) providing assistance in home management; and (4) making referrals to various social services programs. Now let's suppose that Sally Slick just happens to have three friends and two second cousins who need jobs. Can she hire them? Probably not.

Why not? Most state and local civil service systems have rules and procedures concerning hiring. Once again, these rules evolved over the past one hundred years to prevent hiring that is not based on merit. Let's go through some of the basic steps that Sally Slick will have to follow.

First, the department of civil service in the state probably has already created a classification for caseworker—which means that the duties and responsibilities of the position of caseworker have been identified and listed. Second, to determine who is eligible for the position, education and/or experience criteria have been established. The educational requirement for caseworker, for example, may be an undergraduate college degree in one of the following: sociology, psychology, or human ecology. The position may require one year of experience in related employment (such as a hospital, nonprofit social service agency like Catholic Charities, or a nursing home). Often, civil service rules allow some substitution of employment experience for education or vice versa. The department of civil service, for example, may allow individuals with a master of social work (MSW) to substitute the advanced degree for one year of work experience.

Suppose Sally Slick's three friends and two second cousins all have appropriate education and/or experience requirements for the caseworker position. Can she now hire them without violating the civil service merit system? The answer is still probably not.

The next stage in hiring is the examination. Most civil service systems require eligible candidates to take a competitive examination, the purpose of which is to provide an objective method to rate candidates on their ability to perform the job. That is, the examination will try to predict future job performance. (Examinations that do, indeed, measure future job performance are said to be valid.) There are different types of examinations: Some are written; some are oral; some are written and oral. Occasionally, examinations are really ratings, by the department of civil service, of the education and experience of the applicants. Sometimes examinations test performance. A simple illustration is a typing test, measuring speed and accuracy, for applicants for a word processing operator position.

It is safe to assume that the examination for a caseworker will be at least a written test and perhaps an oral one as well. (Oral examinations are given when there are relatively few applications and when there is a prior screening device to narrow the number of candidates, such as a written examination.) The examination may test basic knowledge of government and social services policy; it may try to assess the applicants' judgments in situations they are likely to confront on the job. If there is an oral examination, its purpose may be to determine how well candidates can communicate and even whether they have some empathy for the types of people they would have to serve.

Suppose Sally Slick's three friends and two second cousins passed the examination. Could she hire them now? Probably not.

The next stage in hiring is crucial for Sally Slick. After the examination is given and scored, a list is drawn up that ranks the eligible candidates by their respective scores. When a position becomes vacant, the list of eligibles is sent to the department that wants to fill the vacancy. Under normal civil service procedures the manager who wants to hire someone to fill the vacancy must select candidates from this list but not from anywhere on the list. Rather, the manager must first interview candidates at the top of the list—those people with the highest score. Here is where the famous "rule of three" comes into play. As the principle was originally applied, when a position became vacant, the manager interviewed the top three individuals on the list. If all three were interested in the position (they were often referred to as "accepters"), the manager would have to hire one of the three. The manager could not, for example, say, "I didn't like number two's answers to my questions so I'll interview number four on the list." As long as number two wanted the job, the manager would have to choose among candidates one, two, or three. The rule of three is rarely used so literally anymore; nevertheless, the basic concept still applies. Managers must fill a vacant position from a personnel list that restricts the manager's total freedom of choice.

Now we can answer the question about Sally Slick, her three friends, and two second cousins. It is possible, though not probable, that she can hire them. If there are five vacancies for caseworkers, she must interview at least fifteen candidates. (She may have to interview more than fifteen if some of the people with high scores are uninterested in the position after learning about it in the interview.) If her three friends and two second cousins scored well on the case-worker examination and are among the top fifteen on the list, Sally Slick may be able to hire them without violating civil service rules and procedures.

This description of the rule of three (and obvious variations of it) does not include some of the adjustments that have been made to it throughout the years. In some states, for example, the rule of three has been modified to numerical ranks.[20] This means that everyone with the same score on the examination is in the same rank. Therefore, the rule of three will apply to the top three ranks. Assume that the top three ranks resemble the following:

Score	Number of Eligibles
97%	3
95	8
92	10

This means that the manager who wants to fill a position may consider twenty-one candidates rather than only the top three eligibles who received the score of 97 percent. Which approach seems more fair, the rule of three or numerical rank? What are the advantages and disadvantages of each?

Veterans' Preference

One common complication to the merit system just described is the principle of veterans' preference. This concept is based on the idea that since veterans risked their lives for our country, they are entitled to some extra consideration when they apply for government jobs. Veterans must still be eligible for the positions they apply for; they must also take competitive examinations. But they are awarded extra points for their veteran status. (Disabled veterans receive additional points beyond the number received by other veterans who are not disabled.) It is easy to see the effect of veterans' preference on hiring with the following hypothetical example. Suppose a state has a competitive examination for the position of "management analyst." The examination is scored zero to 100 percent. Moreover, the rule of three applies. Let us assume that ten people passed the examination, three of whom are veterans. Here is the rank order of the scores:

Rank	Score	Veteran's Preference
1	98%	102%
2	97	
3	95	
4	91	96
5	90	
6	87	97
7	86	
8	85	
9	80	
10	79	

Numbers two, four, and six are veterans. Let's assume that in this state a veteran receives five extra points and a disabled veteran receives ten extra points. Notice the adjusted scores. Persons in rank one, two, and three would ordinarily be the candidates for the position. But now the top scores are number two, a veteran with an adjusted score of 102 percent; number one, with a score of 98 percent; and number six, a disabled veteran with an adjusted score of 97 percent. Obviously, the person in rank three is most affected because the rule of the three now excludes this person from consideration for the position. Is veterans' preference fair? We will return to it in a different context later.

Getting Around the Merit System

Hiring practices in the public sector can be cumbersome. Recall that the reason is that the civil service is supposed to reflect competence and impartiality. The merit system places contraints on the public manager. The manager simply cannot hire the person he or she necessarily wants to hire. More often than not the criteria for hiring are determined by people other than the manager. The manager also cannot decide when to do the hiring. Public managers have invented three main ways to get around these constraints.

Creating a new classification.   Sometimes a manager wants to hire someone who lacks some of the job requirements. Perhaps the job seeker's educational background does not fit the classification; perhaps the job seeker's work experience is different from the experience outlined. Managers will sometimes appeal to the department of civil service to create a new classification. The manager will have to show how a new type of job is needed and, in addition, why existing classifications are inappropriate. In reality the manager may simply be trying to avoid existing classifications that have lists of eligible candidates. In other words, the manager does not want to hire "off a list" and be constrained by the rule of three. If a new classification is created, it is possible to tailor the job requirements to specific people and thereby hire the person(s) one really wants.

"Provisional" employees.   Sometimes a public manager needs to hire someone and there is no civil service list to use. This would happen if the job is new and, therefore, no classification exists. Provisional employees may also be hired if a civil service list has been exhausted (there is no one left on the list) and a new examination to create a list of eligibles has not been administered by the department of civil service. During this interim period managers may hire provisional employees. The advantage of doing so is that the restrictive rules and regulations pertaining to hiring do not apply. Although provisional employees do not enjoy all of the benefits of government employment (they may also be "bumped" if a new list appears for the classification), some of them can remain in their position for some time. During the heyday of Mayor Daley's reign in Chicago, some temporary employees who were not supposed to remain on the job for more than 180 days lasted for twenty years.[21] Hiring provisional employees, in other words, is one way to maintain political patronage.

"Breaking the list."   What happens if a manager has provisional employees whom he or she wants to retain but who do not have job security because of their temporary status? Remember, once an examination is given and scored and a list is established, managers must fill all positions occupied by provisional employees with eligibles from the list. In other words, people on the list can "bump" provisional employees who are in the jobs.

Often, managers would like to retain provisional employees. They may like their performance; they know what they have and they also know that civil service rules may force them to hire someone they do not really want to hire. These managers may try to "break the list."

The objective of breaking the list, from the point of view of the manager, is to get people at the top of the list to decline the position. Remember, people at the top of the list under the rule of three (and even modifications of the rule) must be interviewed for the job. If three people want the position after being interviewed, one of the three must be hired. To break the list, then, the manager must get enough people to decline the position so that there are not enough "acceptors." The manager may use different tactics, for example, describing the position in a very unappealing way, requiring interviews at inconvenient times, and even intimidating candidates in the following manner: "I realize that I may have to hire you if you accept this position because of civil service rules, but you are not really suitable for it. You don't have the appropriate experience, so if I have to hire you, I'll watch you very closely for the first six months." Is this approach reasonable and fair?

Compensation

Now that you know how hiring practices are supposed to work in government, and how they often do work in reality, it is time to determine how much to pay public employees. Are there any rules of thumb to follow?

Imagine that you have just been appointed city manager of a new city in the Sunbelt. The city has a population of five thousand people. You have to hire a police force, people for the public works department, a clerk, three secretaries, and a few additional employees. How much should you pay them? Here are some guidelines.

Ability to pay.   You may be a very generous person. You may think that people who work for your city should get paid handsomely. Perhaps you feel that if they get paid well, they will do good work. But you are not paying your employees; the taxpayers are. Consequently, the amount of money available for wages is going to be determined by the amount of taxes collected. If residents are unwilling or unable to tax themselves, it doesn't matter how generous you, the new manager, want to be. The amount of money you will be able to offer potential public employees will depend on your ability to pay.

Comparable wages in the private sector.   You now have to figure out how much to pay your public employees. How much should you pay the secretaries, for example?

The answer to this question will depend on the supply and demand of labor. Basically, if there is a shortage of secretaries in the city, you will have to pay more than you would like to pay. On the other hand, if there are plenty of people who want the job, you may be able to pay less than you initially estimated. A good rule of thumb is that wages in the private sector will determine how much you, the city manager, will have to pay. If you try to pay secretaries much less than the wages they can earn in the private sector, you will have trouble finding competent secretaries or you will have high turnover.

Comparable wages in neighboring jurisdictions.   Let's consider the police now. You, the city manager, cannot use private sector wages to determine how much to pay, for a simple reason. There aren't any policy personnel in the private sector analogous to city police. Still, the supply and demand factor applies. When people decide that they want to become police officers, their decision is based, in part, on overall job possibilities available to them and the compensation paid to police in the general area. This means that you should consider two basic aspects of wages. First, what is the average wage for workers with similar characteristics as police officers? You may, for example, use the average skilled blue-collar wage as an indication of how much to pay, based on the principle that someone who wants to become a police officer may have skilled blue-collar employment opportunities. Second, you should see how much neighboring jurisdictions—other cities, towns, counties—are paying their law-enforcement personnel, which will give you a good idea of the "prevailing wage" for police officers. It is unlikely that you will be able to pay much less than the prevailing wage, and there is no reason to pay more unless there is a shortage of available labor.

Grade and schedules.   Setting pay scales in a small city of five thousand is a relatively easy task because the number of government employees and the number of different types of employees are both limited. It is more difficult in larger jurisdictions—big cities, state government, and the federal government.

When there are many different types of employees governments will often combine similar jobs and create a grade as the basis for pay. Skilled blue-collar workers, for example, may comprise a single grade even though there are different types of skilled blue-collar jobs in several departments. Similarly, a common grade may be assigned to a secretarial classification. Grade levels identify entry-level salaries and the maximum salary in the grade. Grades are subdivided into salary steps, which are used to grant wage increases to employees. A salary schedule is a list of grades and steps for a civil service system. Table 8.1 illustrates a salary schedule from the federal government. As a rule of thumb, it is a good idea to have several steps in a grade if there are few chances of promotion to a different job (and therefore a higher-paying grade). This rule would apply to blue-collar workers and the secretarial staff. When promotions are possible, especially in professional occupations, fewer steps are needed.

Additional compensation issues.   So far we have considered only wages. In practice, governments provide employees with many types of nonwage compensation,

TABLE 8.1. Federal Government General Salary Schedule (as of April, 1989)

GS	1	2	3	4	5	6	7	8	9	10
GS-1	10,213	10,555	10,894	11,233	11,573	11,773	12,108	12,445	12,461	12,780
GS-2	11,484	11,757	12,137	12,461	12,531	12,972	13,343	13,714	14,085	14,456
GS-3	12,531	12,949	13,367	13,785	14,203	14,621	15,039	15,457	15,875	16,293
GS-4	14,067	14,536	15,005	15,474	15,943	16,412	16,881	17,350	17,819	18,288
GS-5	15,738	16,263	16,788	17,313	17,836	18,363	18,888	19,413	19,938	20,463
GS-6	17,542	18,127	18,712	19,297	19,882	20,467	21,052	21,637	22,222	22,807
GS-7	19,493	20,143	20,793	21,443	22,093	22,743	23,393	24,043	24,693	25,343
GS-8	21,590	22,310	23,090	23,750	24,470	25,190	25,910	26,630	27,350	28,070
GS-9	23,846	24,641	25,436	26,231	27,026	27,821	28,616	29,411	30,206	31,001
GS-10	26,261	27,136	28,011	28,886	29,761	30,636	31,511	32,386	33,261	34,136
GS-11	28,852	29,814	30,776	31,738	32,700	33,662	34,624	35,586	36,548	37,510
GS-12	34,580	35,733	36,886	38,039	39,192	40,345	41,498	42,651	43,804	44,957
GS-13	41,121	42,492	43,863	45,234	46,605	47,976	49,347	50,718	52,089	53,460
GS-14	48,592	50,212	51,832	53,452	55,072	55,072	56,692	58,312	61,552	63,172
GS-15	57,158	59,063	60,968	62,873	64,778	66,683	68,588	70,493	72,398	74,303
GS-16	67,038	69,273	71,508	74,743	75,473	75,500	75,500	75,500	75,500	75,500
GS-17	75,500	75,500	75,500	75,500	75,500					
GS-18	75,500									

181

including pensions, health insurance, educational benefits, and paid leave time. These "fringe benefits," as they are often called, can amount to between 20 and 35 percent of an employee's wages. They comprise a major expense for governments at all levels. Governments often adjust their wages to the amount of fringe benefits they provide. A local government, for example, may pay less for secretaries than the prevailing private sector wage if it offers fringe benefits that are better (such as an attractive pension plan). This decision is based on the principle that workers will evaluate total compensation—wages and fringe benefits—when choosing a job.

Another compensation issue is pay for special consideration. The most common is overtime pay (which usually does not apply to professional employees). Extra pay may be granted for hazardous duty, and employees of the federal government receive cost-of-living allowances (if a job is in an area where expenses are higher than the average location). Employees may receive clothing allowances or "in-kind" benefits such as free or subsidized meals. All of these additional types of compensation should be considered when the cost of personnel is evaluated by public managers. Although some may appear to be nickel and dime issues, many financial officers will tell you that they add up to a lot of money rather quickly.

PERFORMANCE EVALUATION AND REMOVAL

There is an old joke that goes something like this:

> MAN: "What are you doing?"
> SOLDIER WITH RIFLE: "Protecting us from wild dinosaurs."
> MAN: "There haven't been any dinosaurs around here for years."
> SOLDIER: "See what a good job I'm doing."

Evaluating the performance of personnel in the public sector is often not much different from evaluating the performance of the soldier. Still, evaluating performance is necessary if (1) incompetents are to be discovered and fired, (2) satisfactory performance is to be rewarded, (3) personnel practices are to be altered to improve the productivity of the program or agency.

Some types of personnel are easier to evaluate than others. Consider, first, an easy one. Most governments employ janitors, whose jobs are fairly well circumscribed. It is not too difficult to evaluate the quality of the work performed by custodial staff and individual janitors. Most likely it would be done by direct observation of the work done. A supervisor would, for example, note the performance on some scale, which would determine whether performance was satisfactory or unsatisfactory. (There would probably be four or five gradations.)

Consider a much more difficult job. What constitutes a "good cop?" One of the basic problems in assessing performance is that a police officer does many different things, some of which are difficult to measure. How do you know, for example, how many crimes a police officer prevents? If a police officer gives out a lot of parking tickets, is that good performance? Would the number of arrests made in a month be a good indicator of performance?

In a study of personnel practices in Oakland, California, Frank Thompson found that jobs related directly to life and property (police and fire) had the most complicated types of assessment. Ratings were made on multiple factors in an attempt to capture the various dimensions of the job. Police officers, for instance, were evaluated on one hundred different factors, which were then scored.[22] Although such an evaluation procedure may seem unnecessarily cumbersome, it acknowledges that the job is complex and that no single indicator would adequately, or fairly, assess a person's performance.

Getting rid of someone in government is not very easy, as a political appointee in the Carter administration learned. It seems that an economist in the Department of Housing and Urban Development (HUD), earning $25,000 a year in 1978, when confronted by the political appointee with the charge that he did nothing and even used his time to write free-lance articles, replied that he was protected by civil service rules. "I'll spend whatever time it takes," the HUD official recalls saying. "You'll see," the economist confidently replied, "I'll wait you out just like I did all the others."[23] Why is it so hard to fire people who work for government?

One reason involves performance evaluation. For many jobs, it is difficult to assess a person's performance because of the nature of the job. Moreover, for many jobs, factors beyond the control of the worker may affect performance. Is it only the teacher's fault if Johnny can't read? Should we blame Officer Joe if the crime rate goes up? Supervisors will often err on the side of leniency in such a situation. Only in glaring cases of gross incompetence will they be willing to press for dismissal.

Suppose a supervisor does feel that a person is incompetent. The next stage usually involves formal charges, followed by a hearing to determine their veracity. Often a civil service commission will hear appeals from public employees threatened with dismissal.

As a practical matter, outright dismissal is not very common. Rather, managers may try one of the following tactics if a worker's performance is considered unsatisfactory:

Encourage the worker to resign
Transfer the worker to another job
Encourage the worker to transfer to another department
Change the worker's job and responsibilities
Demote the worker

In reality, these tactics are difficult to implement because they may violate the employee's constitutional right of due process.

The process of removal is lengthy and complex. Frank Thompson's analysis of the politics of removal in Oakland summarizes the difficulty in firing someone by pointing out the steps involved. The first step is to determine if the employee's job performance is poor enough to warrant dismissal. Since many government jobs do not have clearly established job standards, even this first step may be difficult to achieve. If the employee's performance has been very poor, the next step is to encourage the person to resign. If the employee refuses, the next stage is to tell the chief executive officer (like the city manager) that you, the department manager, want to discharge the employee. Now the chief executive officer may not agree with you. Even if he or she does accept your arguments for dismissal, it is still possible that the department may receive some "bad press" because of the personnel action. If this doesn't happen, you are still not in the clear. The employee may appeal the dismissal to the civil service commission. Even if the commission does not reinstate the employee, he or she may still have legal recourse in the state courts. Finally, if the employee either does not turn to the courts or is unsuccessful in the effort, he or she may be dismissed.[24]

SELECTED TOPICS

Public personnel has been changing rapidly in the United States, although we can think of everything in this chapter, up to this point, as the "staples" of public personnel management. What follows are some topics that have been in a state of flux during the past twenty years.

Improving Public Management: Civil Service Reform Act of 1978

There is a common perception of bureaucrats—they don't do anything, they are overpaid, and you can't get rid of them. Naturally, these charges are extreme. Still, presidents and their political appointees have often been frustrated by high-level bureaucrats, well entrenched, who subverted policy initiatives they did not agree with. The main response by modern presidents has been to build up a centralized policy cadre of political appointees in the executive office of the president who would be more responsive to the president's initiatives.[25] High-level bureaucrats possess a great deal of knowledge about their agency's programs, however, and they have an extensive "institutional memory," both of which can be valuable to newly appointed political executives. An alternative approach is to provide incentives to high-level bureaucrats in the form of money and responsibility. By trading some security for selected incentives, it is hoped that high-level bureaucrats will be both more responsive to political executives and more productive.

In 1978 Congress passed the Civil Service Reform Act, which included features of the second approach. Here are some of the major parts of the act:

1. The U.S. Civil Service Commission was divided into two parts. The personnel functions of the commission are now performed by the Office of Personnel Management. The quasi-judicial functions of the commission—hearing grievances, complaints, and dismissals—are now handled by the Merit System Protection Board.

2. Merit pay for middle-level managers (GS 13–15) was initiated. These pay increases, and cash bonuses, are based on performance evaluations.
3. Terminating incompetent employees was made easier.
4. Whistle-blowers were given additional protection.
5. A Senior Executive Service (SES) was created. The SES is composed of approximately seven thousand top managers in the federal government (GS 16–18) who are assigned throughout the government as needed. They are also given merit pay increases based on performance evaluations.

The SES, the most well-known and controversial aspect of the Civil Service Reform Act, is based on the idea that top civil servants should be more accountable to political executives—departmental secretaries and assistant secretaries who are appointed by the president. To achieve this end, civil servants who enter the SES give up some of their traditional security and, in turn, receive greater decision-making responsibilities. In addition, salary increases are linked to performance. Proponents of the SES thought that it would greatly improve the management of the federal government. Alan Campbell, one of the architects of the SES and the first director of the Office of Personnel Management under President Carter said, ''We believe the executive management service would give top management substantial freedom in assigning talented people to critical new program needs, and in forming new units to help achieve the goals of that organization. It would be a new kind of flexibility for top managers in the federal government.''[26]

Not everyone initially found the concept of the SES so wonderful. Bernard Rosen, director of the Civil Service Commission from 1971 to 1975, feared that political executives would reassign (and often demote) SES managers they judged to be undesirable.[27] His concern was not completely unfounded. Many SES managers were given virtually no responsibilities during the initial period of the Reagan administration because their loyalty to the administration's objectives was suspect. An academic critic of the Civil Service Reform claimed that it was ''theory X triumphant'' because it elevated the principle of administrative efficiency to the central task of management by fostering competition among members of the SES.[28] Rufus Miles, Jr., who spent many years in Washington, questioned the assumption behind the SES that the federal government needs a top level of generalist managers. This idea, which dates from Woodrow Wilson's famous essay in 1887, is, in Miles's view, simply unrealistic. He says, ''Let us face frankly the fact that in the executive branch as much as in complex business enterprises the demonstrated command of essential program knowledge is of at least as great importance in the development and selection of top-level career program managers as managerial skills.''[29]

These criticisms might be dismissed as the initial observations of disgruntled former high-level civil servants who simply liked it better the old way and ivory tower academic sniping that, in any case, has no practical significance. With the passage of more than a decade of experience with the SES, can we say anything more definitive?

The initial evidence was mixed. In less than two years after the passage of the act, dismissals of federal employees increased sharply. By June 1980 dismissals of federal civilian employees had reached 10,700, an increase of 10 percent over 1977. Removals for poor performance, a central objective of the act, increased fifteenfold from 115 in 1977 to 1,738 between July 1979 and June 1980. Meanwhile, the bonus plan in the SES got off to a peculiar start. According to a report in the *Washington Post,* in 1980 sixteen SES managers in the National Labor Relations Board (NLRB) were eligible for bonuses that made them higher paid than the top six NLRB officials. Said one bonus winner, "This doesn't make good sense for the top policy people of an agency to make less than their subordinates. . . . It's just not the way to run a government."[30]

More systematic appraisals have followed. One criticism, for instance, is that the SES has been "politicized." Although this is an ambiguous concept, some evidence bears on the allegation. The Civil Service Reform Act tried to guard against politicization of the SES by establishing a 10 percent limit for noncareer political appointees to all SES positions governmentwide and a 25 percent limit for any single executive-branch agency. A 1987 study done by the General Accounting Office (GAO) compared career and noncareer SES positions in fiscal year 1980 and fiscal year 1986. Career SES positions declined by 5.3 percent whereas noncareer SES positions increased by 13.1 percent.[31] Although this does not prove politicization of the higher civil service, it does indicate that the administration was filling more positions with political appointees.

Anecdotal evidence also suggests that the original intentions of the SES may have been circumvented. A 1983 article in the *National Journal* featured the acrimony that surrounded several controversial political appointees—Office of Personnel Management Director Donald Devine, Secretary of the Interior James Watt, and Environmental Protection Agency head Anne Gorsuch Burford—and high-level civil servants under them. Two SES civil servants in the EPA, the regional administrator in Chicago and the deputy administrator in the EPA's Dallas office, both took their cases to Congress when they felt that the political leadership of the EPA made decisions that were antithetical to sound professional judgment.[32] Although President Reagan changed the top leadership of the EPA to get the agency off the front page of the newspapers, the underlying tension between high-level civil servants and political executives continued.

Another indication that the SES is less than a complete success is reflected in the number of SES individuals who left the service. By the end of 1985, 52 percent of the original SES group had left.[33] Although the reasons are varied, a 1985 GAO survey found that 47.3 percent listed dissatisfaction with top management, and 43.1 percent listed dissatisfaction with political appointees as among the ten most important reasons for leaving the SES.[34]

Can the trend be reversed? Paul Volcker, a former powerful head of the Federal Reserve, chaired a temporary National Commission on the Public Service to look into the matter. Volcker cited salaries that were not competitive with the private sector, low morale, and political interference as chief factors causing the malaise in the civil service.[35] Aaron Wildavsky, professor of political science, University California at Berkeley, was more pessimistic. In his view, lack of agreement among political party leaders about the appropriate role of government as we approach the twenty-first century has heightened ideological dissensus. Civil servants, in this ideological environment, are ripe for attack from all sides.[36] Perhaps. But any changes to the Senior Executive Service will not be able to dodge the inherent tension, noted by many practitioners and scholars, between the policy-making and policy-implementation responsibilities of political appointees and career civil servants.

Rights and Duties of Public Employees

Do public employees have the same rights (and responsibilities) as other citizens of the United States? Not exactly. Consider the most well-known restriction placed on civil servants—restriction of the right to engage in political activity. The Hatch Act, passed in 1939, specifically prohibits civil servants from serving as delegates to a political party convention, having anything to do with campaign contributions, and engaging in partisan political activity (including running for a partisan political office). The justification of the Hatch Act has always been the argument that nonpartisan public employees should not be placed in a position in which they can be intimidated by elected officials. Nor should they be able to use public funds to further their own political ambitions. Opponents of the Hatch Act contend that it restricts the First Amendment rights of public employees—freedom of speech, assembly, and petition.[37] Yet although Hatch Act restrictions on state and local public employees have loosened, the act is substantially intact at the federal level.

During the past twenty years the rights of public employees have been gradually enlarged. In 1972 two Supreme Court cases, *Roth v. Board of Regents* and *Perry v. Sindermann,* extended procedural due process rights to public employees who were dismissed from their jobs. Basically, the Court said that in individual situations, the dismissed employee may be entitled to a statement explaining the basis for the dismissal or to a hearing. Substantive due process rights, particularly First Amendment rights of expression, association, and thought, have also been extended to public employees by the Supreme Court in *Pickering v. Board of Education,* 1968.

Although the courts have protected the rights of public employees, they have also extended the rights of ordinary citizens who have been wronged by the actions of public employees. Until 1960 public officials enjoyed immunity from civil suits initiated by citizens. But a series of Supreme Court decisions during the past fifteen years has eroded this immunity. As a result, individual public employees may be personally liable for damages caused by infringements on the constitutional rights of ordinary citizens.[38]

Discrimination, Equal Opportunity, and Affirmative Action

Can a woman be a cop? Can a woman drag a person from a burning building? Do some civil service examinations discriminate against black applicants? Is it necessary to have blacks and Hispanics in urban police departments when there are large black and Hispanic populations? How many minorities and women should there be in top positions in the bureaucracy?

Public employers obviously discriminate when they hire people. They discriminate by demanding specialized skills, knowledge, or experience. They also discriminate by selecting candidates who possess skills, knowledge, and experience and by rejecting candidates who do not appear to have these characteristics. Public employers discriminate by selecting people with potential. In other words, the very process of hiring requires discrimination.

But personnel practices may discriminate (often unintentionally) by excluding a class of individuals from employment. Beginning in 1964 a series of legislative actions and executive orders sought to ban such discrimination. Title VII of the Civil Rights Act of 1964 made it unlawful to discriminate in hiring, firing, compensation, and other conditions of employment based on race, color, religion, sex, or national origin. In an important Supreme Court case, *Griggs, et al. v. Duke Power Company* (1971), the court held that employment examinations that have the effect of excluding minorities, where the exclusion cannot be shown to be related to job performance, are discriminatory and must be halted. In 1972 the *Griggs* decision was extended to the public sector by the Equal Employment Opportunity Act.

What might be a discriminatory examination? Consider physical tests for fire fighters. In Los Angeles applicants must, among other physical tests, lift a 14-foot ladder weighing 80 pounds and put the ladder in brackets that are 5 feet above the ground. The applicant must then take the ladder down. The time allowed for this part of the test is 90 seconds. In New York the candidate is required to drag a 50-foot hose 75 feet. After carrying another hose up a three-floor building the 50-foot hose must be pulled through a window. Time allowed—3 minutes. Are these tests job related and thereby not in violation of the *Griggs* decision? More generally, can a woman perform the duties of a fire fighter? Here is a story of Jacqueline Jones, Newark, New Jersey's first female fire fighter.

Woman Accepted as a Firefighter
David W. Dunlap

Newark—The name on the Fire Department's roster is "Jones" and the firefighter works the hose line for an engine company here.

That Jacqueline Jones is the only woman among 647 Newark firefighters seems beside the point to her colleagues, her bosses and the men who trained her to take up her duties.

"If I had to accept 45 female firefighters—based on my experience with Jackie—I would," said Fire Chief Stanley J. Kossup.

He referred to a recent court ruling in which New York City was ordered to hire up to 45 women who had failed a physical test that was found by a Federal judge to have been inappropriate and discriminatory.

The Fire Commissioner of New York intends to appeal the ruling. New

York firefighters, speaking for themselves, have expressed wariness and skepticism about the prospect of women on the firefighting lines.

COMPANY 13 SEEMS CONTENT:

But the men of Engine Company 13 on Mount Prospect Avenue in Newark seem content with the arrangement. And so does Mrs. Jones, who was appointed last May and now works on the hose line.

"The climate in the firehouse didn't change," said James Imposimato, who has been in the company for eight years and is now its acting captain, "that's what surprised me."

"I've been here 10 years," said another firefighter, Richard Doherty, "and, as far as in the house, I don't see any difference. You look around here and all you see are blue uniforms."

"People have a tendency to imagine problems where there are none," Mrs. Jones said. "In an emergency situation, I'll get the job done."

"It's not a big dramatic story," she said. "I needed a job. I never saw a female firefighter before, but it never registered to me that there were none."

Mrs. Jones attended high school, worked as a nursing aide and also counseled drug abusers before turning to the Fire Department. Her husband, Theodore, is an X-ray technician and the couple have a 12-year-old daughter, Tia.

"Nothing surprises Ted about anything I do," she said. "He had no doubt I'd get through training, even if I came home and cried."

Speaking of the six-week course, Deputy Chief Alfred Freda said: "We made a commitment to treat her the same as everybody else. She did it quite well. She was always in the front. She didn't balk at anything."

Another training officer, Battalion Chief Fred Boehringer, said Mrs. Jones not only passed the standard battery of training exercises but also acquitted herself very well when she and the other 30 members of her class met their first real fire—one that had been deliberately set by the Fire Department in an abandoned three-story frame building.

"Why the hell am I here?" was how Mrs. Jones recalled her first thought when confronting the blaze, the last training exercise before graduation. "After that, I was comfortable with it."

FIREHOUSE "FAIRLY BUSY":

The company to which she is assigned in the North Ward of the city was described by Deputy Chief John Griggs as a "fairly busy house." It responds to calls at high-rise housing projects, industrial buildings and single-family homes. Engine 13 shares quarters in a modern, one-story structure with Ladder Company 6.

The only physical change that has been made to accommodate Mrs. Jones was the placing of sliding locks on the bathroom doors. Her bunk is in the same dormitory room as those of the men.

"She goes to bed early," said Mr. Doherty. "Most of the time we don't even see her."

Mrs. Jones said she had been detailed to other houses and "they were not all favorable when I arrived." However, she said, "nine out ten times we had better rapport before I left."

The only difficulties Mrs. Jones said she faced were personality problems but she said she was not alone. "The men who are nasty and bad in the firehouse, even the men don't get along with," she said.

CHIEF PRAISES "JONESY":

"When a training group comes through, you always have filtration," said Chief Griggs. "They filter out in the field. But I've observed Jonesy when conditions aren't so good and she shapes up."

Chief Kossup, who has also been on the scene to watch Mrs. Jones's performance while fighting fires, said: "I've found that the experience has been a good one. There has been absolutely no critical comment from company personnel or from commanding officers."

"Once she puts on her helmet and mask and coat, she is no different than anyone else," he said.

The single departure from standard procedure that the Fire Chief noticed since Mrs. Jones's appointment 11 months go occurred at the ceremony marking the end of training.

"It was the only time," Chief Kossup said, "that the director was kissed by a graduate."

□ *Source:* "Woman Accepted as a Fire fighter," by David W. Dunlop, April 12, 1982. © *1982 by The New York Times Company. Reprinted by permission.*

But Jacqueline Jones's story has not been easily replicated elsewhere. According to a story in The *New York Times*, as of late 1987 only 1,500 of the 218,000 paid fire fighters in the United States were women.[39] Although some cities have taken steps to increase the number of female fire fighters, one major obstacle remains for women in several cities—proving in the courts that specific parts of physical tests that emphasize speed and strength are not job related and discriminate on the basis of sex.

Equal employment opportunity (EEO) has been public policy for more than a quarter of a century. In 1964 the Civil Rights Act established the Equal Employment Opportunity Commission (EEOC) and gave the commission the right to initiate litigation against private employers who discriminate in employment practices. A year later President Johnson issued Executive Order 11246, which banned discrimination in federal employment and activities that included federal government contracts. In 1972 the Equal Opportunity Act made the antidiscrimi-

TABLE 8.2. Minority Group Employment in Federal Government

Pay Grade	Percentage of Total		
	1972	1978	1985
GS 1–4	28.4	30.2	37.3
GS 5–8	19.8	24.0	29.2
GS 9–12	8.7	12.8	18.3
GS 13–15	5.0	7.0	10.6
GS 16–18	3.7	4.5	6.5

nation features of Title VII of the 1964 Civil Rights Act applicable to state and local governments.[40]

Why is it a good policy? Some have argued that bureaucracies should be "representative," which means that their composition should reflect the ethnic, racial, gender, and economic characteristics of the population as a whole.[41] The argument for a representative bureaucracy rests on the belief that public employment is one way to promote equality in the United States and that social background influences attitudes and behavior, which in turn affect the treatment citizens receive from civil servants. Consequently, it is desirable to have a diversified bureaucracy to serve the citizenry in an equitable fashion.

Has EEO policy achieved these objectives? Look at Tables 8.2 and 8.3. Whereas minorities and women are broadly representative of the population as a whole in total federal government employment, they are clearly underrepresented at the higher levels (GS 13–15 and GS 16–18). How can we summarize the trends? It depends on whether you say the glass of water is half empty or half full.

Affirmative action can be thought of as an active approach to the objective of equal employment opportunity. That is, affirmative action requires public employers to take steps to increase representation of minorities and women among the work force. Often, agency heads will design and implement an affirmative-action plan. Efforts will be made to eliminate any personnel procedures that discriminate against minorities and women in hiring, pay, or promotions. The plan will usually establish affirmative action targets or goals. Suppose an agency

TABLE 8.3. Female White-Collar Employment in the Federal Government

Pay Grade	Percentage of Total		
	1970	1978	1985
GS 1–6	72.2	72.8	74.5
GS 7–10	33.4	42.9	50.3
GS 11–12	9.5	16.6	29.5
GS 13–15	3.0	6.2	12.6
GS 16–18	1.4	4.2	6.1

has five hundred employees. Only 5 percent of the managers are women and minorities. An affirmative-action plan may set, say, a goal of 12 percent to be reached at the end of five years. The plan will also say how this goal will be reached. The agency may recruit minority and female candidates from the private sector, perhaps at selected universities; or it may initiate a special training program internally to promote minority and female employees to managerial positions.

Not everyone likes affirmative action. Some claim that goals are, in reality, quotas that discriminate against qualified white males. Here are some pro and con positions:

Pro

Years of employment discrimination can be reversed only if employers are forced to act affirmatively.
Affirmative action is the only way to reach a representative bureaucracy.
The so-called merit system has excluded certain groups.
Affirmative action will bring people to public service who can better relate to clients of public agencies.

Con

Qualified white males are not responsible for past discrimination practices.
Since affirmative action is really "reverse discrimination," it replaces one wrong with another.
Affirmative action has allowed less qualified people to be hired.
Public employees identify with their job, agency, or profession more strongly than the people they serve.

Since affirmative-action programs necessarily affect existing civil service procedures, it is not surprising that the issue reached the federal courts. Important decisions were reached in 1986 and 1987. In *Firefighters v. Cleveland* (1986) the Supreme Court found that a consent decree between a group representing black and Hispanic fire fighters and the city of Cleveland establishing promotional opportunities for minorities was consistent with Title VII even though the recipients of the promotions may not have actually suffered from past discrimination. In the same year the Court held, in *Sheet Metal Workers v. EEOC* (1986) that lower-court judges may order preferential treatment when the prior discrimination was particularly "egregious." In 1987 the Supreme Court, in *Johnson v. Transportation Agency* held that a public employer's affirmative-action plan that gave hiring preference to women over men to obtain a more balanced work force was permissible under Title VII of the Civil Rights Act.[42]

The legal victories are unlikely to end controversies surrounding affirmative action because the policy pits groups against one another over a valuable resource—public employment. When government must retrench, the controversies are likely to become more intense. In fact, the Supreme Court has distinguished between affirmative-action hiring goals and rules for determining layoffs. When the city of Jackson, Michigan, implemented a layoff plan that required white teachers to be laid off before minority teachers, the Court held, in *Wygant v. Jackson Board of Education* (1986) that the plan violated seniority rights.[43]

Comparable Worth — Next step beyond Affirmative Actin

Should a woman be paid the same as a man for the same job? Actually, it no longer matters what your personal view is on this subject; it is the law. Should a woman be paid the same as a man for *comparable* work? Now this sounds different from the previous question.

Let's think about certain jobs that are common in the public sector. Should nurses earn the same as sanitation workers? Who should earn more, day-care workers or custodians who clean public buildings? Should psychiatric social workers earn the same as clinical psychologists? Are clerk typists just as valuable to government as public works employees who dig ditches?

These rhetorical questions form the basis of "comparable worth," the idea that certain jobs, traditionally considered female-dominated positions, should be valued equally with other positions that are male dominated. By the early 1980s the issue was ripe for political debate because of some incontrovertible facts:

—A significant pay gap exists between men and women in public employment.
—Female employees tend to be in sex-segregated jobs.
—Female-dominated jobs tend to be lower paid than male-dominated jobs;
—A relatively small percentage of women are in higher-paying managerial positions in public service.

Taking steps to correct pay inequities.   The first flurry of activity in the 1980s surrounding comparable worth occurred when several states, led by Washington, undertook comprehensive analyses of their civil service systems. The objective was to identify job titles that were female dominated and determine the extent of pay inequity that existed. Through sampling and other statistical procedures the various studies tried to locate the job titles that were female dominated and then estimate the amount of pay disparity with comparable job titles that were not female dominated. Naturally, matching job titles—the heart of the comparable worth debate—is controversial since it requires a method for demonstrating that different job titles have comparable importance in public sector activities. The various state studies tried to develop various job *tasks* that are performed across several job titles. By analyzing and weighting the incidence of the tasks (such as physical activities, communications, decision making, knowledge requirements), the studies attempted to come up with measures of comparability.

"Comparable Worth Comes to Minnesota"

The State of Minnesota, like many other states, contracted with a private consulting firm to conduct a pay equity study. The firm, Hay Associates, found that female-dominated jobs had lower pay than jobs of equal value that were male-dominated. Many of the jobs were in health care and clerical positions—about one third of the state's public workforce. This amounted to 8,225 employees. These employees received pay hikes averaging $1,600 over two years to eliminate the pay inequity. The cost, covering the years 1983 to 1987 was estimated to be about $44 million; 151 job titles were included in the pay equity determination. Comparable worth pay raises were 4 percent of the state's salary budget. In Minnesota comparable worth did not bust the bank.

▫ *Source: Marilyn Marks, "State Legislators, Judges and Now Congress Examining 'Comparable Worth,' " National Journal 16 (September 8, 1984): 1668.*

By the mid-1980s more than half of the states conducted studies that examined gender-based wage disparities. Several have followed Minnesota and have implemented pay-equity policies to reduce past gender-based wage discrimination. Nevertheless, the future of comparable worth is cloudy. First, litigation, initially supportive of the concept, was reversed. The initial optimism of *AFSCME v. State of Washington* (1983) in which federal district court judge Jack Tanner ruled that the state must award back pay to 15,500 employees in female-dominated state jobs who were victims of sex discrimination was reversed on appeal in 1985 by Judge Anthony Kennedy (appointed to the Supreme Court in 1988 by President Reagan). Second, critics of comparable worth have continued to voice a series of objections:

The so-called objectivity of comparable worth studies is false. Glaring inconsistencies appear in job evaluations from one state to another. In addition, what constitutes a female-dominated job title is not consistently applied.[44]
The marketplace rather than legislation should determine jobs and pay.
Comparable worth programs will be prohibitively expensive and therefore affect adversely the state and local government budgets.
If the costs of hiring women increase, employers will hire fewer women.
If wages in female-dominated job titles increase, women will be discouraged from seeking employment in male-dominated jobs.[45]

With strong advocates on both sides of the issue, comparable worth will remain on the political agenda throughout the 1990s.

Retrenchment

The world of public personnel management would be pleasant if the most difficult problem was deciding how to reward civil servants who perform their jobs well. Unfortunately, public managers also must fire people—even people who are doing good work. Governments at all levels cannot afford to retain all their employees. Since personnel costs are the largest single expense, managers who are forced to cut their budgets must trim their personnel. How do they do it?

Hiring freezes.   One approach frequently used by the federal government, many state governments, and several large cities is to institute a hiring freeze; that is, managers may not fill vacancies for the duration of the freeze. A job freeze has a few basic advantages. First, it can take place immediately. Second, it does not threaten existing personnel. Third, it prevents increases in personnel cost, which, as we said, is the largest single expense. Fourth, it can be imposed selectively across classifications and departments, and fifth, it can be lifted immediately if and when the financial picture brightens.

But hiring freezes have some shortcomings. Some departments may develop critical shortages in selected positions, which may adversely affect the performance of the department. President Reagan encountered the following additional problems when he entered office:[46]

> Early freezes by President Carter already had trimmed the growth of federal employment. An additional freeze would have only a modest impact.
> Several agencies had to be exempt from the freeze.
> A freeze slows down the rate of attrition because federal employees are increasingly reluctant to leave their jobs.
> A freeze makes agencies top-heavy because most of the turnover is at the lower levels.

Yet even with these shortcomings, Reagan officials boasted that five hundred federal government jobs were eliminated every day in fiscal year 1981. The freeze, in their view, was successful. In reality, the freeze lasted a short time, and contrary to the image that was presented, the freeze had no significant permanent impact on the size of the federal work force.

Reduction in force.   Sometimes attrition is not sufficient. If government employees are not retiring or quitting fast enough, managers may have to adopt an active approach to personnel reductions. This is called reductions in force (RIF), or "riffing," in bureaucratese.

The most common rule that applies when riffing takes place is seniority, often known as "last hired, first fired." Obviously, older workers, those who have been on the job the longest, are most protected from a reduction in force, whereas new workers are the first to go. Younger workers are often better educated, and they may have skills that older workers lack. Organizations sometimes give up innovations when they are forced to lay off "new blood."

Reductions in force can cause dislocations in an agency. In Washington, D.C., and in many state governments this is illustrated by the "bumping" rights that go with seniority. A government employee who loses his or her job may bump an employee in a lower-level job who has less seniority. For every "riffed" position there may be two to three personnel changes in a government agency. One former civil servant, Marlene Moody, a power-rate specialist with the U.S. Department of Energy, was bumped from a GS-14 grade to a lower-level budget-analyst grade of GS-11. Moody had more than twenty years of government experience, but she had no experience with the type of budget job she was forced to accept if she wanted to stay in the Department of Energy. She left instead. Her comments about the impact of the reduction in force on her departure included the following observation: "[T]he best people aren't being retained and the people who are being retained are being shuffled off to jobs where they aren't being productive anymore. There has to be a better way to reduce the federal work force than this kind of chaos."[47]

Sometimes a reduction in force can lead to unexpected results. Personnel losses may undermine the effectiveness of the agency and even sabotage the basic mission. The Coast Guard and the Bureau of Alcohol, Tobacco, and Firearms in the U.S. Department of Treasury are both charged with apprehending drug smugglers. Managers in both agencies, in the early phase of President Reagan's personnel reductions, complained that they could not fulfill the mission of their agencies. Similarly, personnel cuts in revenue-producing agencies, such as the Internal Revenue Service, may lead to revenue losses that exceed the savings brought about by the reductions.

Finally, personnel cuts may adversely affect specific employment objectives such as affirmative action. Since women and minorities tend to have less seniority than white males, they bear a disproportionate impact of reductions in force. Although the principle of seniority has tended to prevail over affirmative action, as long as layoffs did not have a discriminatory intent, this may slowly change. On May 7, 1982, a federal appeals court held that an agreement between the city of Memphis and its minority employees (which was part of a court-supervised consent decree) took precedence over a collective-bargaining agreement that held seniority as the basis for layoffs. The decision was subsequently reversed, however, in June, 1984, by the U.S. Supreme Court, thereby reaffirming seniority protections when layoffs become necessary. In Boston, the school system fired one thousand tenured white teachers because the Boston School Committee believed that a 1974 desegregation order did not allow the number of black teachers to fall below 20 percent of all teachers in the system. The federal courts are likely to be busy for the rest of the decade with disputes generated by conflicting interests in personnel that are exacerbated by reductions in force.

SUMMARY

Personnel is a staple of public management. Every aspiring administrator needs to know the essentials of public personnel management, many of which were established almost a hundred years with the passage of the Pendleton Act of 1883.

The establishment of open and competitive examinations, probationary periods for new employees, legal protection from political pressure, and a civil service commission to oversee the personnel process have become part of the merit system of public employment throughout the United States at all levels of government.

There are five broad essentials of personnel management: job classification, hiring, compensation, evaluation of employees' performance, and the removal of employees. Simple on first blush, each essential ingredient is filled with exceptions, caveats, and "ways around" the official procedures. Public personnel can be frustrating until the managers become familiar with all of the subtleties of the process—the normal routines and the myriad exceptions.

The field of public personnel is constantly in flux; it takes a great deal of time and attention to stay abreast of the rapid changes in personnel management. Among some of the most important developments that have emerged in the past twenty years, the legal dimensions of public personnel has become more and more complicated. Public managers need to know the developing case law, for example, which affects the procedural and substantive due process rights of government employees. Administrators must also be familiar with federal and state equal-employment-opportunity legislation and affirmative-action policies to insure that their personnel practices are not discriminatory in intent or effect. Often public managers are required to develop procedures that will enhance the employment opportunities of women and minorities. Moreover, personnel management is more difficult in an era of retrenchment. When government must cut back, it takes only a short time before personnel are adversely affected. Managing personnel in an era of less is a difficult way to be popular, as the following case, "Vacancy Review in Tight Belt County," illustrates.

Vacancy Review in Tight Belt County

As administrative assistant to Tight Belt County's Board of Supervisors, you have been asked to prepare an analysis of a new expenditure-control policy currently under consideration. The new policy was proposed to control personnel expenditures by requiring a more careful review of vacancies. Because the county is facing a difficult financial future, the supervisors' primary goal in considering this policy is to limit spending. As usual, the next board meeting is coming up quickly and you must prepare your analysis based on the following limited information.

THE SETTING

Tight Belt County is a rural county with a population of approximately sixty-five thousand. The county's economy is based principally on agriculture, although a few of its towns and villages are within commuting distance of a large city in a neighboring county. The county has only one sizable municipality, that of Silver, which has just over ten thousand people.

The county has no chief executive officer. Instead, it is governed by a board of fifteen elected town supervisors and four legislators from Silver. The town supervisors are part-time executives of their townships. County policy and administrative decisions are made by the predominately Republican board, led by a chairman, through a weighted voting system based on the population of the towns in the county. The board has a committee structure of twenty-one committees overseeing various policy areas (for example, veterans affairs, insurance, and apportionment) and county departments (for example, sheriff and highway).

The county's finances are presided over by the county treasurer, an elected official who also acts as budget officer. The county treasurer is a fiscal conservative who tries to watch expenditures closely but finds himself facing a worsening financial picture. Although the treasurer and other county officials are quick to describe the county's current financial condition as excellent and can point to the county's respectable bond rating (Aa), they nevertheless have cause for concern.

The county's financial problems are threefold. First, the county faces a reduction in state and federal aid. This is particularly onerous because over 50 percent of the county's budget comes from those sources (see Table 1). More than $2 million in CETA funds will be lost in 1982, and although the county has prudently used CETA funds for only thirty county jobs, the loss of these funds will hurt. In addition, federal revenue-sharing funds have been reduced. Long-term prospects for aid from both federal and state government look grim as those governments engage in their own financial austerity programs. Second, county officials do not believe that they can raise significant additional revenues by increasing property taxes. The county's property tax base is relatively static—from 1970 to 1980 the county gained only 3,432 housing units, a 16.8 percent increase. The number of delinquent property taxes seems to be increasing, perhaps as a result of deteriorating economic conditions nationwide. In addition, county officials are still smarting from the citizens' outrage after a 32 percent tax increase in 1976. Although revenue requirements forced the eventual acceptance of that tax increase, the public hearings were bitter and the press reports were scathing. That response has left supervisors unwilling to face so much wrath again. The third problem impacting on county finances is the rising cost of labor, energy, and many other goods and services the county must buy.

That the county finds itself in a financial bind is disconcerting to county officials who pride themselves on being conservative and financially responsible. The unwritten operating rule in the county might easily be described as "watch your pennies and the dollars will take care of themselves." It is fair to say that the county's financial worries came about through very little fault of its own.

County officials have sought to be responsive to these financial problems by minimizing budget increases (and accompanying tax increases) during the past four years. Some changes have been made in service delivery, such as altering maintenance schedules for county roads to delay resurfacing work. The county has also relied heavily on traditional expenditure control devices to check spending during the execution phase of its budget cycle.

EXPENDITURE CONTROLS

Expenditure-control devices are used by governments to insure that budgets are followed, to prevent waste and fraud, to account for funds properly, and to adjust spending levels as the fiscal year progresses. Tight Belt County, for example, has transfer controls that require department heads to obtain permission from the treasurer for all fund transfers between accounts. The county also requires prior approval by the Board of Supervisors for all out-of-state trips. Even though funds have been approved for travel during the budget process, this requirement gives the board a second opportunity to control spending. In addition, the county requires employees to share a portion of the cost of attending a conference by paying for their own transportation. This saves the county some money, probably discourages travel, and is in keeping with the philosophy among supervisors that the employee receives as much, or more, of the benefits from travel as does the county.

The county also used another common expenditure-control device, the vacancy-review policy. The county's policy for filling vacant positions requires that a department head check with his department's committee and, with their approval, submit a request to the county's version of a Ways and Means Committee. The Ways and Means Committee then makes its recommendation to the board, which must pass a resolution authorizing the vacancy to be filled.

Personnel costs, however, are the county's single largest line-item expenditure. During the past ten years, the county's budget and number of personnel have doubled, even though the county's population grew only 3.6 percent during the same period. Consequently, the county has of late been concentrating on ways to further control costs in this area. County supervisors accepted the recommendation of a blue-ribbon citizens' advisory committee to hire a director of personnel. The county received a one-year grant from the federal Office of Personnel Management for the new personnel director's salary, and they were able to hire Mr. Flowers, a professional from a nearby city, to fill the position.

THE NEW VACANCY-REVIEW PROPOSAL

In a natural outgrowth of the county's concern over personnel costs and its emphasis on expenditure control, and soon after Flowers joined the county, Supervisor Grant suggested that personnel vacancies be reviewed more closely. His original suggestion was for the board to create a vacancy-review committee. There was resistance to his idea, mainly because of misgivings about how the move would affect the existing committee structure. In particular, there was opposition to the vacancy-review committee's taking an important power away from the Ways and Means Committee. Grant dropped his recommendation for a new committee but suggested that Flowers and the Personnel Committee review vacancies.

The proposed new vacancy-review policy, as drafted by Flowers, requires department heads to go through a four-step process before a vacancy can be filled (see Attachment A). First, the department head will have to obtain approval from the committee that oversees the department. Approval from the operating committee would allow the department head to submit a request with accompanying justification to the director of personnel. After studying the request and consulting with the board's Personnel Committee, Flowers would make a recommendation to the Ways and Means Committee. The Ways and Means Committee would make a recommendation to the full board. The Board of Supervisors would then consider passage of a resolution authorizing the department head to fill the vacancy. The entire process could be completed in two to four weeks.

The proposed vacancy-review policy has met with some controversy among supervisors and department heads. Some question whether the plan will accomplish its cost-cutting objective or if it is the best way to accomplish the objective. Others are reluctant to increase the work load and limit the flexibility of county managers by further complicating the bureaucratic routine. Supervisor McNeil protests that departments have already been cut back and will continue to be during the budget adoption process. Other board opponents oppose the plan on the grounds that it will not be effective and will serve to hold positions open for as much as a month longer than necessary.

Flowers understands why some supervisors and department heads might be averse to the vacancy review policy. He realizes that it is seen by some department heads as an infringement on their managerial prerogatives. He also knows that the Board of Supervisors is still split on the question of whether of not there is a real need for a personnel director. He attributes that split to the board's not yet having enough experience with a professional personnel director to be familiar with the position's functions. For Flowers, the vacancy-review plan is part of the process of selling county supervisors and staff on the concept of professional personnel administration. Although he hopes to implement such personnel activities as a comprehensive compensation study and incentives to reduce absenteeism, Flowers is realistic about his current status with the county. He knows that the county does not have the funds for the kinds of studies and personnel programs that he thinks are needed. He also knows that right now the Board of Supervisors is more concerned with costs than with the human development aspects of the personnel function. The new vacancy-review policy, if successful, could be an important step toward consolidating his role in the county government.

Flowers is viewed with suspicion by some of the department heads. Many are not completely sure where he fits into the county organization. The vacancy-review plan has deepened that suspicion. In particular, department heads who might legitimately fear personnel cuts tend to see Flowers as the supervisors' hit man and oppose the new plan. The Mental Health and Social Services departments fall into this category. These two departments symbolize everything that is wrong with government to many of the Republican supervisors. As one supervisor put it, "My kids were never on drugs or had a problem with alcohol. People should take responsibility for themselves and their families." Another supervisor says that these services are not needed in rural counties like Tight Belt. If it were not for the fact that much of what those departments do is state mandated and at least partially state funded, the county would probably provide only limited social services.

But the objections that Dr. Heap, head of the Mental Health Department, and Mr. Spies, head of the Social Services Department, have against the vacancy review plan do originate from more than fear of its effects. Heap views many of the county's expenditure control policies with disdain. He sees the kind of redundant approval required by the travel policy as "mickey mouse" and views the vacancy-review proposal in the same way. If they wish to review the county's personnel positions, he reasons, they should do a comprehensive review of all the positions. He believes that the policy as currently formulated is cumbersome and probably not worth the effort. As far as Heap is concerned, this is just one more way in which the county seeks to hamper his ability to manage his department.

Spies would agree with Heap's recommendation that positions should be reviewed comprehensively or not at all. Spies's department would be seriously affected by the new policy because of its high turnover rate and current understaffing. Social service caseworkers, who should have a normal load of 75 to 80 cases, are now carrying about 105 cases each. Although Spies is a retired army colonel who considers himself a tough-minded budgetary conservative, he feels that this attempt at expenditure control is wrongheaded. He believes that department staffing should be set by work load. Such a system would allow him to automatically add caseworkers during heavy work periods, such as the current one, and require him to cut staff during slack periods. Spies views the whole vacancy-review proposal as one that will interfere with necessary managerial discretion. He emphatically claims that he has no intention of following such a policy to the letter.

Of course, a difference in perspective and goals is bound to result in some antagonism between the board and department heads. Department heads are rightly concerned with providing services in the best way they know how. The supervisors must balance this optimum service perspective with their financial responsibilities. That Heap and Spies oppose the proposed vacancy-review policy would probably be taken as a good sign by its proponents on the board. Their opposition might confirm the supervisor's belief that many requests to fill vacancies should be denied. Supervisor Carter says that approval of the plan would be one of the best steps the board has ever taken. Grant, who proposed the more thorough review of vacancies, is, of course, enthusiastic about the new policy. Both Grant and Carter believe that the policy will result in positions being eliminated and real savings for the county. The board chairman hopes that the policy can be used to achieve zero personnel growth for the county. These and other proponents of the plan believe that this is the only way the board can closely review personnel positions. They say that a comprehensive review is out of the question because it is too expensive. The budget-adoption process is much too complex and broad in scope to allow supervisors to evaluate many specific positions. In addition, the vacancy-review proposal will force department heads to reevaluate their operations and will give the personnel director a chance to make recommendations for better use of personnel. It will also allow the board to reconsider service-delivery levels in light of financial conditions as the year progresses. They dismiss any increase in vacancy time as insignificant.

Not all department heads object to the vacancy-review plan. Some departments are so small or so effectively protected by interest groups as to be shielded from expenditure-reduction efforts. Sheriff Homes, for example, is not concerned about institution of the policy and has found Flowers to be helpful. Staffing levels at the county jail are mandated by the state. His small staff of six deputies to patrol county roads is already low and probably not in danger of cuts. In addition, Homes is an elected official with his own political base and with state-mandated powers. That circumstance, coupled with the essential nature of his department's services, allows him to see vacancy review rather benignly.

Another example of a secure department is that of Fire Control headed by Tom Cassidy. Cassidy's department has only six positions and a very low turnover rate. Its function is to serve as dispatch center for every fire department and ambulance service in the county, with the exception of the Silver Fire Department. All twenty-five fire companies whose calls are handled by Cassidy's department are manned by volunteers. The volunteer fire departments provide a powerful lobbying group for the Fire Control Department. Again, the department's services are of a rather basic nature. Cassidy has not given either Flowers or the proposed policy much thought one way or the other—neither one is important to his ability to operate Fire Control.

THE ANALYSIS

The Board of Supervisors has asked you to prepare an analysis of the vacancy-review proposal to be distributed to all members before the next board meeting, when the proposal is to be considered. In your analysis, you have been asked to discuss the strengths and weaknesses of the proposal. The supervisors would like to know if this policy is likely to save the county any money and if so where the savings will come from and what the likely magnitude of those savings will be. You may also wish to comment on the use of expenditure-control devices in general to produce budget savings. What are the benefits and limitations of relying on expenditure control to deal with financial constraint?

The supervisors would also like to have an analysis of the policy's probable effects on department operations. If the policy appears to have significant flaws, what are some alternative ways to achieve the county's goal of minimizing budget increases, especially in personnel expenditures? Should the county consider the alternatives suggested by Heap and Spies? Is the proposed policy an improvement over the current vacancy-review procedure?

TABLE 1. County Financial Review

	1979	1980	1981
Total Budget	22822691	24927190	26763266
Revenues			
Property Taxes	5224771	5556225	6351055
(% of Total Budget)	22.89	22.29	23.73
State Aid	3442022	4577019	4464196
(% of Total Budget)	15.08	18.36	16.68
Federal Aid	7557162	7652804	7844905
(% of Total Budget)	33.11	30.7	29.31
Other	6598736	7141142	8103110
(% of Total Budget)	28.91	28.65	30.28
Property Tax Increases (%)			
	1976	32	
	1977	8	
	1978	4	
	1979	1	
	1980	6	
	1981	5	
Inflation Rate for State and Local Government Purchases of Goods and Services*			
	1976	6.56	
	1977	7.99	
	1978	10.35	
	1979	13.45	
	1980	14.9	

*Source: U.S. Department of Commerce, Bureau of Economic Analysis, *Survey of Current Business*, January 1980, Vol. 60, No. 1, Table C, p. 40; *Survey of Current Business*, June 1981, Vol. 61, No. 6, Table 7.14B, p. 17. (Derived from implicit price deflators for state and local government purchases of goods and services.)

ATTACHMENT A: VACANCY REVIEW

If a department head wants to fill a vacant position or create a new position he or she should first advise the departmental committee chairman. If authorized to proceed, the department head should submit the request to the director of personnel. The request and accompanying information package should contain the following information:

1. A new position duties statement for this position that completely and accurately describes the current or proposed duties for the position. In the case of certain positions that have a high turnover rate or that require the immediate filling of a vacancy, the department head should submit the request and the accompanying information package to the director of personnel for processing before an actual vacancy.

2. A current organization chart showing the position being vacated or created, the titles of positions from whom the subject position receives supervision, the titles of positions who receive supervision from this position, and the titles of positions doing substantially the same kind and level of work as the subject position. The organization chart does not need to accompany requests to fill vacancies after an initial submission, unless there are adjustments to the organizational framework.

3. A narrative description of the function of the vacant or created position and specific reasons in support of filling or creating the position, information relative to any reimbursement factors, and the specific impact to the department if the position is not filled. Information should be as quantifiable as possible. If the impact of not filling a position is an increase in overtime expenditures, for example, the anticipated dollar expenditures for such increased overtime should be determined as best possible.

The Department of Personnel will process the request from the department and submit an analysis to the county Officers and Affairs Committee as well as consulting with the Civil Service and Personnel Committee. Vacant positions should not be filled by any means until the utilization review is completed and the department is so notified. The review process cannot begin until the department submits the complete information package as outlined above. In the case of proposed new positions the county Civil Service Commission must formally classify the position before the position is authorized to be filled.

The Department of Personnel may conduct field audits in certain instances. Because of staffing limitations, however, it must rely on the department head to supply all relevant information in sufficient detail and clarity to minimize the need for further information or field audits where at all possible.

□ *This case was prepared by Jane Massey under the supervision of Professor Jeffrey D. Straussman as a basis for class discussion rather than to illustrate either effective or ineffective handling of an administrative situation.*

NOTES

1. This historical section is based largely on Frederick C. Mosher, *Democracy and the Public Service* (New York: Oxford University Press, 1968), pp. 58–59. See also Paul P. Van Riper, *History of the United States Civil Service* (Evanston, Ill.: Row, Peterson and Company, 1958).
2. Mosher, *Democracy,* p. 57.
3. Ibid.
4. Van Riper, *History,* p. 27.
5. Ibid., p. 57.
6. Ibid.
7. William L. Riordan, *Plunkitt of Tammany Hall* (New York: E. P. Dutton, 1963), p. 12.
8. Jay Shafritz, *Public Personnel Management: The Heritage of Civil Service Reform* (New York: Praeger, 1975), pp. 21–23.
9. Ibid., pp. 23–24.
10. Woodrow Wilson, "The Study of Administration," in *Classics of Public Administration,* ed. Jay M. Shafritz and Albert C, Hyde (Oak Park, Ill.: Moore Publishing Co., 1978), pp. 3–17.
11. Ibid.
12. Mosher, *Democracy,* p. 73.
13. See, for example, Samuel Krislov, *Representative Bureaucracy* (Englewood Cliffs, N.J.: Prentice-Hall, 1974).
14. Hugh Heclo, "OMB and the Presidency—The Problem of 'Neutral Competence,' " *The Public Interest* 38 (Winter 1975): 80–98.
15. Paul Appleby, *Policy and Administration* (University: University of Alabama Press, 1949).
16. Joel D. Aberbach and Bert A. Rockman, "Clashing Beliefs within the Executive Branch: The Nixon Administration Bureaucracy," *American Political Science Review* 70 (June 1975): 456–468.
17. N. Joseph Cayer, *Public Personnel Administration in the United States* (New York: St. Martin's Press, 1975), p. 57.
18. O. Glenn Stahl, *Public Personnel Administration,* 7th ed. (New York: Harper & Row, 1976), p. 79.
19. For a criticism of position classification, see Jay Shafritz, *Position Classification: A Behavioral Analysis for the Public Service* (New York: Praeger, 1973).
20. Stahl, *Public Personnel Administration,* pp. 151–152.
21. Cited in Shafritz, *Public Personnel Management,* p. 1.
22. Frank J. Thompson, *Public Personnel Policy in the City* (Berkeley: University of California Press, 1975), pp. 145–146.
23. Quoted in Karen Elliot House, "Civil Service Rule Book May Bury Carter's Bid to Achieve Efficiency," *Wall Street Journal,* September 26, 1977, p. 1.
24. Thompson, *Public Personnel Policy,* pp. 149–150.
25. For an excellent analysis of this development, see Terry M. Moe, "The Politicized Presidency," in *The New Direction in American Politics,* ed. John E. Chubb and Paul E. Peterson (Washington, D.C.: Brookings Institution, 1985), pp. 235–271.
26. Alan K. Campbell, "Revitalizing the Civil Service," in *Public Employees and Policymaking,* ed. Alan Saltzstein (Pacific Palisades, Calif.: Palisades Publishers, 1979), pp. 247–253.
27. Bernard Rosen, "Merit and the President's Plan for Changing the Civil Service System," *Public Administration Review* 38 (July/August 1978): 301–304.

206 PUBLIC PERSONNEL

28. Frederick Thayer, "The President's Management 'Reforms': Theory X Triumphant," *Public Administration Review* 38 (July/August 1978): 309–314.
29. Rufus E. Miles, Jr., "Rethinking Some Premises of the Senior Executive Service," in *Improving the Accountability and Performance of Government,* ed. Bruce L. R. Smith and James D. Carroll (Washington, D.C.: Brookings Institution, 1982), pp. 35–52.
30. Warren Brown, "Where Are Aides Paid More than Bosses?" *Washington Post,* November 25, 1980, p. 4.
31. General Accounting Office, *Trends in Career and Noncareer Employee Appointments in the Executive Branch* (GAO/GGD-87-96FS, July 1987), p. 9.
32. Dick Kirschten, "Administration Using Carter-Era Reform to Manipulate the Levers of Government," *National Journal* 15 (April 9, 1983): 732–736.
33. Cited in Patricia W. Ingraham, "Building Bridges or Burning Them? The President, the Appointees, and the Bureaucracy," *Public Administration Review* 47 (September/October 1987): 431.
34. General Accounting Office, *Senior Executive Service Reasons Why Career Members Left in Fiscal Year 1985* (GAO/GGD-87-106FS, August 1987), p. 8.
35. Martin Tolchin, "Is Quality of Federal Work Force Deteriorating?" *New York Times,* January 15, 1988, p. B6.
36. Aaron Wildavsky, "Ubiquitous Anomie: Public Service in an Era of Ideological Dissensus," *Public Administration Review* 48 (July/August 1988): 753–755.
37. Cayer, *Public Personnel Administration,* pp. 115–116.
38. For an extended analysis of this trend, see Peter H. Schuck, *Suing Government* (New Haven: Yale University Press, 1983).
39. Anne Zusy, "For Women Who Fight Fires, Acceptance and Frustrations," *New York Times,* October 12, 1987, p. 1.
40. For a study that focuses on equal apportunity and affirmative actiion at the state and local levels, see Frances Gottfried, *The Merit System and Municipal Civil Service* (Westport, Conn.: Greenwood Press, 1988).
41. Harry Kranz, *The Participatory Bureaucracy* (Lexington, Mass.: Lexington Books, 1976).
42. Gottfried, *Merit System,* pp. 78–79; see also Herman Schwartz, "The 1986 and 1987 Affirmative Action Cases: It's All Over but the Shouting," *Michigan Law Review* 86 (December 1987): 524–576.
43. Gottfried, *Merit System,* p. 81.
44. See, for example, Richard E. Burr, "Are Comparable Worth Systems Truly Comparable?" (Center for the Study of American Business, Washington University), no. 75 (July 1986).
45. Rita Mae Kelly and Jane Bayes, "Comparable Worth and Pay Equity: Issues and Trends," in *Comparable Worth, Pay Equity, and Public Policy,* ed. Rita Mae Kelly and Jane Bayes (Westport, Conn.: Greenwood Press, 1988), pp. 5–8.
46. T. R. Reid, "Reagan Advisers Encountered Problems with Job Freeze," *Washington Post,* November 25, 1980, p. 4.
47. "One Unhappy Departure," *New York Times,* November 8, 1981, p. 18.

FOR FURTHER READING

Hartman, Robert W. *Pay and Pensions for Federal Workers.* Washington, D.C.: Brookings Institution, 1983.
    The title is self-explanatory.

Mosher, Frederick C. *Democracy and the Public Service*. 2d ed. New York: Oxford University Press, 1982.

    The history of civil service in the United States is analyzed against the background of American political values.

Rabin, Jack, Thomas Vocino, W. Bartley Hildreth, and Gerald J. Miller, eds. *Handbook of Public Personnel Administration and Labor Relations*. New York: Marcel Dekker, 1983.

    Comprehensive essays that try to explain the "state of the field" in several areas of public personnel administration.

Sylvia, Ronald D. *Critical Issues in Public Personnel Policy*. Pacific Grove, Calif.: Brooks/Cole, 1989.

    This brief book does a good job discussing current personnel issues such as equal opportunity, job rights, affirmative action, and off-duty rights of public employees.

Thompson, Frank J., *Personnel Policy in the City*. Berkeley: University of California Press, 1975.

    Although this study of Oakland, California, is now fifteen years old, it is still one of the few case studies of local government personnel practices.

CHAPTER 9

Unions and Collective Bargaining

As a child I used to notice a sign in the New York City subways. It said, "If you don't come in Sunday, don't come in Monday." It was an advertisement by the International Ladies' Garment Workers' Union (ILGWU), a union organized to represent workers in the garment industry. The message was clear. Before unionization, management was free to push workers around and fire them at will, and an unpleasant job was always better than no job at all.

Can you imagine such a sign on the front door of city hall? Somehow the history of unionization in the public sector does not seem very dramatic. Yet it has its own history of labor–management conflict, fraught with success, failure, and accommodation.

ARE PUBLIC UNIONS DIFFERENT?

Public unions came of age in the 1960s. Table 9.1 provides data illustrating the growth of unionization in the public sector for selected employee organizations. Now, approximately one-third of government workers are associated with bargaining units. Unionization affects employment practices, public services, and the financial condition of state and local governments. One overriding question, encompassing almost all of these issues, is, are public unions different from unions in the private sector? There is no clear consensus on the answer. The following are four pro and con issues (the pro view argues that public unions are different from their private sector counterparts, and the con view holds that there are no substantial differences).

1. The legal position of government affects unionization.
    Pro: Public sector labor relations is different because elected officials are supposed to represent the public interest rather than special groups

208

TABLE 9.1. Membership in Selected Government Employee Organizations (In 1,000s): 1975, 1987

Union	1975	1987
American Federation of State, County and Municipal Employees (AFSCME)	647	1032
American Federation of Teachers (AFT)	396	499
American Postal Workers Union	249	230
International Association of Firefighters	123	142
Transport Workers	95	85

Source: U.S. Bureau of the Census, *Statistical Abstract of the United States,* 1988 (Washington, D.C.: U.S. Government Printing Office, 1988), p. 401.

such as unionized public employees. This responsibility should not be eroded by giving some of it up through collective bargaining.

Con: Elected and appointed officials already listen to, and are sometimes influenced by, many kinds of interest groups. Moreover, the notion of a public interest is vague and hard to identify in practice. Public employees should have the same right and opportunity as other groups to press their own demands through the political process.

2. Government services are like monopolies; therefore, public employees are in a very strong bargaining position.

Pro: Services such as police, fire, and education are provided by local government employees only. Taxpayers have little or no choice in deciding how much of the service they are willing to pay for. Taxpayers cannot really "shop around" for the services of local government.

Con: Taxpayers have more choices than we usually consider. Some services are partly financed through user fees, which do allow local residents to say how much of a service they really want. Citizens can choose jurisdictions (or move from jurisdictions) based on their perceptions of the cost and quality of local services like schools, police, libraries, and fire protection. Besides, there are also monopolies in the private sector (telephone companies and private utilities) that are unionized. It makes no difference whether a monopoly is private or public.

3. Public employees receive job protection through elaborate personnel systems that are unavailable in the private sector.

Pro: Civil service personnel systems are said to establish rules for merit and impartial procedures for hiring, promotion, and firing. Therefore, there is no need for unions and collective bargaining in the public sector.

Con: Although it is true that personnel procedures in the public sector are much more extensive than in the private sector, this does not negate the need for unions. Unions are still necessary to negotiate wages and fringe benefits and negotiate conditions for advancement, job protection, and removal.

4.   Since pay differentials in the public sector are more ''egalitarian'' than in the private sector, there is less need for unions to protect the economic position of public employees.

Pro: Wage differences across jobs in the public sector are smaller than in the private sector. Total compensation for nonprofessional public sector jobs tend to be on a par with private sector counterparts.

Con: Public sector compensation is on a par with private sector compensation because of successful union pressure. Besides, public employees are victims of inflation, the whims of the electorate, and government budget cutting. Therefore, they need public unions to halt the erosion of their hard-won economic position.

You can see from these positions that there is a good deal of controversy over the similarities and differences between unions in the private sector and unions in the public sector. In the following pages some of the obvious differences between private and public sector collective bargaining will become apparent. But these differences should not be overdrawn, since there are also many similarities.[1]

The Militancy of Public Unions

Public unions flexed their political muscles during the 1960s and the 1970s through the collective-bargaining process. Sometimes their expression took the form of work stoppages. Interns and residents in the municipal hospitals of New York City struck in 1980. Both police officers and fire fighters went on strike in San Francisco in the summer of 1975. Sanitation workers were on strike in Detroit just before the 1980 Republican party presidential convention. President Reagan almost received his party's nomination amidst a mound of garbage. Teachers' strikes at the beginning of the school year are commonplace.

A glance at Table 9.2 shows the trend in public employee strikes from 1958 to 1981. (Comprehensive strike data are unavailable after 1981 because budget cuts at the U.S. Department of Labor halted the gathering of such information.) Notice that the strike activity of state and local government employees is mea-

TABLE 9.2. Work Stoppages by State and Local Government Employees, Selected Years

Year	Number of Work Stoppages	Number of Employees (in thousands)	Days of Idleness (in thousands)
1966	142	105	455
1970	409	178	1,375
1975	490	316	2,421
1978	488	178	3,542
1980	553	233	2,135

Sources: Bureau of Labor Statistics, *Work Stoppages in Government,* Report no. 348; *Government Work Stoppages,* 1960, 1969, and 1970. Summary Report; Bureau of the Census, *Statistical Abstract of the United States,* 1982–1983, p. 412.

sured along three dimensions. The frequency is measured by the number of work stoppages by employee groups in a given year. Notice the large increase between 1966 (133 work stoppages at the local level) and 1980 (493 work stoppages). The intensity is measured by the number of workers that took part in work stoppages. Although this dimension of militancy peaked in 1975, strike intensity increased substantially during the fourteen-year period. The duration of public employee strikes is measured by the number of days workers are idle in a year. Here again, strike duration peaked in the latter part of the 1970s. Although there is no reason to expect government employees to return to the relative docility of earlier decades, strike activity is influenced by the political atmosphere at the time that can be either sympathetic or, on the contrary, hostile to, public unions and the fiscal condition of state and local governments.

Until recently most federal, state, and local government employees were prohibited from striking, and penalties were often imposed for illegal work stoppages. In Nevada, for example, the public employer may "dismiss, suspend, or demote" public employees engaged in an illegal strike. In 1981 air traffic controllers, represented by the seventeen thousand-member Professional Air Traffic Controllers Organization (PATCO) engaged in an illegal strike. President Reagan issued a back-to-work order that was largely ignored. He fired all air traffic controllers who refused to abide by his order. Twelve thousand PATCO members lost their jobs; the bargaining unit was decertified, thereby ending its existence. Unions may also lose their "check-off" privileges (whereby public employees have their union dues taken out of their paycheck by the employer and turned over to the union).

Reasons for strikes.   Obviously, strike prohibitions have not prevented strikes, as Table 9.2 makes clear. Public employees break the law and engage in illegal strikes for several reasons:

  Union recognition—Strikes have occurred because government employers have refused to recognize organized employee groups.
  Wage and benefit increases—Public unions, like private unions, sometimes resort to strikes as a way to exert pressure for improved wage and benefit packages.
  Job security—Unions sometimes strike when jobs are in jeopardy.
  Administrative matters—Public unions occasionally resort to strikes as an attempt to influence personnel decisions such as hiring procedures, grievance machinery, and employee evaluations.

Prohibitions against strikes by public employees are based on the belief that these employees provide "essential" services that should not be interrupted.[2] This argument has not always been persuasive even to those employees that are clearly essential, such as fire fighters and police officers. In some cities police personnel have, on occasion, come down with a bad case of "blue flu" and called in "sick," thereby producing a de facto work stoppage (instead of an illegal strike). Fire fighters discovered another ingenious tactic, following rules and regulations to the letter. The result is a de facto slowdown of service. But work stoppages by any other name are still work stoppages.

In the past few years there has been some relaxation of the strike issue. Eleven states now give public employees the limited right to strike: Alaska, California, Hawaii, Illinois, Minnesota, Montana, Ohio, Oregon, Pennsylvania, Vermont, and Wisconsin. The statutes vary greatly; nevertheless, one common thread runs through them all. Essential employees—police and fire—are prohibited from striking. Nonessential employees, on the other hand, are granted some right to strike after other dispute remedies have been exhausted.[3] The most common case of legal public sector strike activity is teacher work stoppages. Although relatively common, the risks associated with teacher strikes are low. Mandated days of instruction are usually made up by rescheduling; consequently, the school district does not risk the loss of instruction or the loss of state aid. Similarly, teachers are able to make up lost income from striking by overtime pay via rescheduling. Still, thirty-eight states have no-strike statutes, and penalties for striking are identified in twenty-two of the state laws.

COLLECTIVE BARGAINING AND DISPUTE SETTLEMENT

Let's suppose that the fire fighters of the city of Breth want a 10 percent increase in wages so that they will be "equal" to police officers. The police say they will not sit idly by if fire fighters get a wage settlement in their new contract making the two groups equal. Meanwhile, the mayor certainly does not want a police slowdown or any other job action that would be a protest against a new fire fighters' contract. He also knows that a 10 percent increase for fire fighters—even an 8 percent increase—would encourage other city unions to demand more when their contracts come up for negotiation. If there is one thing the mayor wants to do, it is to avoid a tax increase this year; otherwise his political life will end in the next election. He thinks taxpayers are fed up with high taxes, but even a modest wage increase for public employees will probably require some new revenues. He'll have to deal with the fire fighters first and then take it from there.

Political Context

Who has it worse, the mayor of Breth or, say, an owner of a company that employs three hundred employees who are represented by a single union? The answer should be obvious. Politics complicates public sector collective bargaining. Consider just four political dimensions of the collective-bargaining environment.

Intergovernmental factors.   The legal context of state and local government collective bargaining is established by state statutes. That is, managers have only limited flexibility to change the contours of the bargaining environment. Collective-bargaining legislation varies from state to state; nevertheless, statutes usually include the extent that governments must bargain with organized employee groups, the criteria for determining and recognizing bargaining units, the ways in which bargaining impasses will be resolved, the types of employees covered under the state legislation, grievance procedures, and strike prohibitions and penalties.

Public employees as voters.   Public employees are also voters. At the local level they include teachers, police officers, fire fighters, health and hospital workers, and sanitation employees. They may try to influence the collective-bargaining environment by voting for public officials who are supportive of their interests and defeating propositions that are against their interests. Public employees, for instance, were quite vocal in their opposition to proposals to limit taxes and expenditures in California, Massachusetts, and Michigan.[4]

Divided management.   Unlike the small company in the private sector, public management is often divided. Consider a small- to medium-sized city. Who is management? This depends on the specific place; nevertheless, management tends to include the city council, the mayor, the city manager, the personnel director, and perhaps the finance officer. (If the city has a professional labor relations specialist, this person is likely to take the lead in bargaining with the organized employees in the city.) It should be clear from simply looking at the list of who could be included in the management "team" that they will not have a clearly defined position at the outset of collective bargaining. In fact, there is likely to be some internal conflict among them.[5] In addition, public unions have sometimes gone outside the formal collective-bargaining structure to gain benefits from the city council, the courts, and the mayor. Peter Feuille, in a study of police labor relations, found that police unions often made "end runs" in such cities as Hartford, Boston, Detroit, and Buffalo, when it was advantageous to do so.[6]

Electoral-tax interaction.   When public employees' wages go up, the state or local budget goes up accordingly—which usually means higher taxes. No better illustration can be found than local public school financing and collective bargaining. A large portion of a typical school district's funds comes from property taxation. Teacher salaries, in turn, are the largest single expense of school districts. So the relationship is reasonably straightforward: if the teachers' union negotiates a sizeable salary increase, property taxes will go up.

When taxpayers are particularly upset about their tax burden, or when elected officials think they are upset, it may subtly affect the collective-bargaining environment. In particular, a taxpayer "backlash" may constrain the options available to public unions when the financial climate is poor—a theme we will return to later in the chapter.

Impasse Procedures

Let's return to the city of Breth. The fire fighters' contract is about to expire, and they have said that it will not be "business as usual" if a new contract has not been negotiated. Not only are they asking for a 10 percent wage increase, they also want two extra personal leave days a year, a two-hour reduction in the work week, a no-layoff clause in the event of technological innovations like the mini-pumper, and an improved fire-prevention education program for the elementary schools.

The city's labor relations specialist, Bill Beaseley, has had several meetings with the union officials. Despite the union's public pronouncements, Beaseley convinced the union leaders to reduce some of their demands. They were willing to take one additional personal leave day rather than two; the two-hour reduction in the work week was dropped; and the layoff clause was softened to say that the city would "make all reasonable efforts" to retain existing personnel affected by technological innovations. But beyond these changes, the unions would not budge. The city, in turn, was unwilling to accept the other demands in their present form. A stalemate has been reached.

Because this situation is common in the public sector, many states have included mechanisms in their collective-bargaining legislation to aid the parties in resolving disputes. These are known as *impasse procedures*. There are three basic impasse procedures: mediation, fact finding, and arbitration.

Mediation. Mediation involves a third party—the mediator—who is both outside the dispute and neutral. The central role of the mediator is to bring the two parties to the dispute closer together so that an agreement can be reached. Mediation has a few basic characteristics. The mediator is usually selected from a list of mediators drawn up by the state government's administrative agency responsible for public sector labor relations. Typically, the mediator tries to clarify the issues in the dispute; the mediator may also bring the offers and responses back and forth from one party to the other. Nevertheless, mediation is nonbinding; that is, either management or labor is free to ignore the mediator if it so chooses. Moreover, not all employee groups are necessarily covered by mediation, although "essential" employees generally are.

The timing of mediation to resolve disputes also varies from state to state. In Florida, for example, mediation may begin after a reasonable period of negotiation or if no agreement is reached within 60 days after the beginning of collective bargaining. Parties may jointly appoint a mediator or request that one be appointed by the Public Employees Relations Commission. In Iowa, impasse procedures begin if an agreement is not reached within 170 days of the budget submission date. Either party can ask the Public Employment Relations Board to appoint a mediator.[7]

Fact finding. This is a more formalized version of third-party mediation. The third-party neutral—the fact finder—tries to discover what a "real" compromise settlement would include. In doing this the fact finder is generally asked to provide a written report detailing the substance of the fact-finding opinion. Like mediation, fact finding is nonbinding on the parties to a dispute.

Suppose the basis for the fire fighters' wage demand included the argument that the fire fighters in Breth were paid less than those in neighboring cities. Suppose the city claimed that a 10 percent wage increase would require an average property tax increase of $200, which was too much for taxpayers to bear. A fact finder might do two things in this dispute: first, actually examine wage scales for fire fighters in the neighboring jurisdictions to see if there is any basis for the union's claim; and second, examine the "ability-to-pay" argument by the city, namely, that it could not realistically raise taxes to support a wage increase. When was the last increase? How much was it? What has happened in neighboring cities?

Like mediation, fact-finding provisions vary greatly across the states, but it is common for fact finding to be used after mediation has failed to resolve a dispute. In Kansas, for example, a fact-finding board is appointed by the state's Public Employment Relations Board if an impasse continues seven days after the appointment of a mediator. In New Hampshire fact finding is initiated either by agreement of the parties or if mediation does not produce an agreement forty-five days before the date for budget submission. There are, of course, variations on these illustrations, depending on the specific states in question.

Arbitration. Now let's suppose that fact finders render an opinion that the fire fighters of Breth are actually incorrect when they claim that a 10 percent wage increase would give them the wages of fire fighters in neighboring cities. Rather, the fact finders found that an 8 percent wage increase would make Breth wages comparable. It is important to remember that the fact finders are not recommending that the city grant no more than an 8 percent wage increase; they are merely clarifying some "facts" in the dispute. The fire fighters' union is unhappy with these "facts" and is unwilling to accept the city's wage offer from Beaseley. Beaseley, in turn, said that there is no way that the city will meet the union's demands—and he now is pointing to the fact finders' report to support the city's contention that the union's wages demand is "excessive." Although the fire fighters are prohibited from striking according to state labor relations law, they are hinting again that they will "do something" if a settlement is not reached.

Arbitration, another method to resolve an impasse between parties in a collective-bargaining dispute, is often used when mediation and fact finding have been unsuccessful. Like the other two procedures, arbitration is performed by an outside, neutral third-party. But unlike the other two, the arbitrator produces a recommendation for the resolution of the dispute.

Arbitration is sometimes viewed as an alternative to the strike and is most commonly applied to essential services—police and fire. In fact, some states make arbitration compulsory and binding if a dispute is not resolved in a given time. That is, the decision of the arbitrators (usually a three-person panel) must be accepted by the parties. But there are exceptions to the general rule. In Oklahoma arbitration is final and binding if the public employer—the government jurisdiction—accepts the majority decision of the arbitration panel. (Obviously, the law favors management in the arbitration provision.) "Final offer" arbitration, a variation on compulsory, binding arbitration, requires both sides to provide the arbitration panel with its "last, best" offer. The panel then makes a decision on the outstanding issues in the dispute.

Assessment of Impasse Procedures

Impasse procedures have been praised as an important alternative to strikes, and they do go a long way in helping the parties to a collective-bargaining dispute—public unions and management—negotiate a settlement. Compulsory arbitration, adopted by only a handful of states in the 1960s is now used in twenty-three states. But impasse procedures are not without their critics, especially in the case of binding arbitration.

One criticism of binding arbitration is that it has a "chilling effect."[8] To understand this notion we will return to the city of Breth one more time. Should the fire fighters' union (or, for that matter, the city) have voluntarily reached a settlement before the arbitration stage was reached? To what extent could the union be worse off after binding arbitration than at any state before it? Only if the arbitration panel awards a settlement that is less than Beaseley's last offer before binding arbitration. The union's negotiators can feel reasonably confident that this outcome is unlikely; consequently, the union has very little to lose by not settling before the onset of binding arbitration. There is indeed evidence to support the idea that compulsory arbitration causes a chilling effect on collective bargaining in the public sector.[9]

An additional criticism of impasse procedures is that they produce a "narcotic effect," an alleged dependence on them as a way to resolve collective-bargaining disputes. Once a city, county, or state government uses, say, arbitration to settle a dispute, it is more likely to resort to arbitration in the future—especially in a dispute with the same public union. Once again, there is some evidence to support this argument.[10]

Perhaps the strongest criticism of compulsory arbitration has come from management. The argument is straightforward: When a city is required to give up its negotiating responsibility to an outside third party, it is abrogating its duty to protect the public interest. Political sovereignty is undermined, and elected officials are less accountable to the electorate. If an arbitration panel awards a wage increase to the union that necessitates a tax increase, the city officials can say that it was not their decision, that it was out of their hands.

IMPACTS OF COLLECTIVE BARGAINING

Hundreds of cities like Breth have never been the same since collective bargaining has become part of the established political landscape. But exactly how state and local governments have been affected by unions and collective bargaining is not always clear. More heat than light has been shed on this subject.

Unions, Collective Bargaining, and Compensation Costs

If there is one issue of general misunderstanding it is the supposed impact of unions and collective bargaining on the wages of state and local government employees. Basically, conventional wisdom has it that public unions have been extracting very large wage concessions from public employers. The taxpayer, of course, has been footing the bill. The actual evidence suggests otherwise.[11]

> Fire fighters have done best with collective bargaining. About 2 to 28 percent of their increases are attributable to the impact of union power.
> Transit workers have also done reasonably well. Between 9 and 12 percent of their wage increases are related to unionization.
> Police unionization has not, in the aggregate, had much impact on wages.
> Other municipal employees—parks and recreation, sanitation, highways— have not benefited greatly from unionization.

The first half of the 1980s was a favorable period for public employee compensation when compared with the private sector. Private sector pay suffered as result of several factors including foreign competition, a rising dollar against other currencies (thereby increasing the costs of U.S. exports), and recession. The result was a series of wage concessions between 1980 and 1986. Public employees were largely protected from these trends. In addition, teacher salaries increased substantially after many years of lagging behind pay hikes for other public employees and employees in the private sector. It would be incorrect, however, to attribute the favorable wage posture for public employees in the first half of the 1980s to public unions. The increase in teacher salaries may have been caused by supply and demand factors, for example, rather than union pressure. Many school districts were experiencing a return to teacher shortages—something that they had not faced since the middle 1960s.

If there is little evidence to show that public unions have had a dramatic impact on wages, there is only fragmentary evidence on the effects of nonwage compensation (fringe benefits). Here, the limited number of studies tend to show that public unions have improved the fringe benefits of their membership.[12] From the standpoint of economic theory, benefits paid in the form of wages or, say, vacation days should be the same for the public employer. Yet since some benefits may not require a direct, current cash payment, some public employers may be willing to give public employees future benefits that do not have the same political visibility as wages.

The careful reader will have noticed a tentative tone in the preceding paragraphs. So far our understanding of the impact of unions and collective bargaining is limited. One reason is that good data on wages and fringe benefits are hard to find and difficult to collect. In addition, there are many problems in making judgments about the comparability across jurisdictions of wages and, in particular, fringe benefits. Take a simple example. What value should be put on an educational benefit that allows a public employee to take courses at the college level? Should we use the actual tuition cost? Some average cost across the country? The subjective value of the benefit to the employee? Such problems of data and interpretation abound when we seek to determine what influence unions have on wage and nonwage compensation.

Impact of Unions and Collective Bargaining on Personnel Issues

When public employees and organized employee groups bargain, it is inevitable that personnel practices will be affected. David Lewin and Raymond Horton explained why this is so: "Organized public workers seek to limit managerial discretion over the terms and conditions of employment; generally speaking, managers seek to maintain or extend their discretion in these spheres."[13] Labor–management conflicts on the terms and conditions of employment can be settled in two ways. They can be resolved in traditional personnel departments through established personnel procedures, or they can be resolved through collective bargaining. When personnel issues are brought to collective bargaining, they may constrict the traditional personnel process. Some local governments have tried to avoid this problem by including "management rights" clauses in contracts that state that traditional management prerogatives involving supervision, hiring, discharge, discipline, work assignment, and layoffs are reserved for management. These managements rights, while traditional, are sometimes included in contracts so that third-party mediators and arbitrators realize that it is not the intention of management to bargain over them during a contract negotiation with organized public employees.[14]

Consider the alternative—a situation where management rights become the subject of labor–management negotiation. Criteria for promotions, for example, have traditionally been established by personnel departments, but some unions have pressured management to include seniority in personnel decisions.[15] When seniority as a criterion for promotions is included as a legitimate issue in collective bargaining, it becomes an encroachment on the traditional personnel function.

Public managers may feel that this exemplifies union "interference" with the merit principle. O. Glenn Stahl, for example, a former head of the old U.S. Civil Service Commission and the author of a widely read book on public personnel management, has argued that union attempts to obtain a closed shop, to insist on seniority as the main basis for promotions or rehiring, to establish preferences for employees from special bargaining units for promotion, all represent efforts to circumvent the merit system.[16]

It would be naive to ignore the fact that some public unions have tried to influence the personnel process and thereby bypass the merit principle. Yet posing the issue in such a fashion really misses the crucial point, namely, that both collective bargaining and personnel are inherently political. The merit principle is not above the reach of politics. It is instructive to return to the illustration of merit, seniority, and the rule of three:

> Managers may use the rhetoric of merit when opposing seniority . . . unions may cite the merit principle as justification for the rule-of-one. In short, management advocates merit when a merit rule suits management's perceptions of self-interest, usually seen in terms of enhanced discretion in personnel decision-making. . . . Public employee unions, of course, have no cleaner hands than management when it comes to the contravention of merit rules in the pursuit of self-interest.[17]

So here again we have Rufus Miles's famed "law" of public administration: "Where you stand, depends on where you sit." Merit is suddenly not such a lofty principle when it enters the political fray.

THE FUTURE OF COLLECTIVE BARGAINING

If state and local managers were asked if they would prefer a simpler government of an earlier day, with unorganized public employees, they would probably answer in the affirmative. Unions and collective bargaining, after all, have not made public management any easier. Yet both are here to stay. How will unions and collective bargaining continue to affect public management?

Local Government Services

Public unions influence the way local services are provided. The following is a brief list of issues frequently negotiated through collective bargaining.

The size of the work crew in sanitation and highways
The maximum number of students in classes in public schools
The number of cases in a worker's caseload
The allocation of police personnel in a twenty-four-hour day

Management is usually required to adhere to these work rules, which obviously will affect the provision of services to residents and taxpayers.

Some contracts may also prevent management from unilaterally altering the way services are provided if a change could adversely affect employment. A good example comes from Monroe County, New York (which includes the city of Rochester). A past contract between the county and the Monroe County Federation of Social Workers stipulated that "The County agrees to meet and confer with the past Federation prior to any County decision to subcontract, consolidate, merge, transfer, or terminate work regularly performed by members of the bargaining unit."[18] From the vantage point of the union this clause provides some job security. It restricts management's options in reorganizing service delivery arrangements. In an era when "privatization" has been bandied about as a way to reduce the presence of government at all levels, many collective bargaining conflicts at the state and local level will involve the perennial issue of job security.

Productivity Bargaining

Public management is not completely helpless when it comes to bargaining with employee groups over the quality and quantity of public services. Some local governments have demanded that organized employee groups improve performance through productivity gains in exchange for increased benefits. A city may demand, for example, that sanitation personnel lower labor costs by reducing the amount of overtime while maintaining quality service—clean streets—in exchange for a compensation settlement. Productivity bargaining of this type has been tried in a few places like Detroit, Michigan; Flint, Michigan; and New York City.[19] Although sound in theory, productivity bargaining has had limited success for two basic reasons. First, there are tremendous obstacles in determining how to measure and evaluate public sector productivity.[20] Second, the receptivity to productivity bargaining by both management and organized labor in the public sector is largely based on their respective political power. If labor is very strong, for example, as it has been in New York City, the city is unlikely to be better off after a productivity bargain is negotiated because the city will have to pay the full costs for any real improvements in productivity.[21] When labor is politically weak, the objectives of productivity bargaining can probably be reached without negotiating a formal productivity agreement.[22]

Unions and Fiscal Austerity

Productivity bargaining is part of a larger effort to reverse the political tide of public unions, according to those who feel that state and local officials virtually "gave away the store" in the 1960s and 1970s. Fiscal austerity of the late 1970s and first half of the 1980s altered the political position of unions. Some elected officials, looking for scapegoats, pointed accusing fingers at "greedy" unions who, in their view, exacerbated the fiscal problems of local governments. In reality, unions have often acted responsibly by sharing with local officials the job of bringing government back to fiscal health. In New York City public unions used their pension funds to purchase municipal bonds in an effort to reverse the financial crisis in 1975. In 1981 Detroit was on the verge of bankruptcy. Mayor Coleman Young, himself a strong advocate of organized labor, was nevertheless forced to "get tough" with the city's unions. He offered them a choice: either agree to a two-year wage freeze or he would initiate large layoffs of municipal employees. The unions reluctantly agreed to the freeze—the lesser of the two evils.[23] Cooperation was smarter politics than confrontation.

The future of public unions and collective bargaining is uncertain. From the unions' standpoint the period of "catch-up" is long gone. Unions are most concerned about losing their hard-fought gains—gains that include wages, fringe benefits, and political power. In Syracuse, New York, the union representing public school teachers agreed to accept management's demand for a wage freeze in 1983–1984 in exchange for no layoffs. In some states where tax and expenditure limitations placed fiscal handcuffs on local governments, public employees were not as lucky as the Syracuse teachers. In June 1983 trustees of the school system in San Jose, California, filed for bankruptcy. They were faced with a "catch-22' situation in which the court ordered the collectively bargained teachers' salaries to be paid, but Proposition 13 did not permit local taxes to be raised to pay for the increase.[24] In Massachusetts, about twelve thousand teachers were laid off in the aftermath of Proposition 2-1/2. Overall, public sector employment in the state was reduced by more than thirty-six thousand positions between November 1980 and November 1981.[25]

Concession bargaining.   An alternative to layoffs is "concession bargaining." Common in the private sector, the logic of concession bargaining is simple. Unions negotiate some job security by giving back a benefit won in a previous collective-bargaining round. Concessions include wage freezes, wage increase rollbacks, elimination of inflation escalator clauses (that tie wage increases over the life of the contract to changes in an inflation index), tying wages more directly to future government revenues, and the reduction of selected nonwage compensation benefits. Although concession bargaining is not as common in the public sector as the private sector, it has been used by governments that have experienced fiscal austerity.[26]

Contracting for services.   Besides the "get-tough" approach of many big-city mayors and the effects of tax and expenditure limitations, there is a more important threat to the survival of public unions. Forced to search for cost savings by taxpayers' resistance, many local governments have been adopting private sector alternatives for providing government services. "Contracting out"—hiring private companies to do the work that was once performed by local government employees—is considered a viable option for financially strapped localities. Contracting out is used to provide refuse collection, tree trimming, animal control, snow removal, and many other local services. Advocates of contracting claim that private firms invariably are more efficient than public employees.[27] Public unions charge that contracting is "government for sale."[28] Although both positions are overstated, two facts are incontrovertible: First, contracting represents just one illustration of a search by public managers to reduce labor costs; and second, contracting highlights the fact that public sector unions are on the political defensive.

Technological Change

Sometimes technological change can have an adverse impact on public sector unions. A good illustration comes from local government sanitation. Although 40 percent of local government sanitation workers were members of employee organizations in 1980, this represented a decline from the early 1970s. What caused the drop in local government sanitation workers?

There are two basic explanations. First, in the mid-1970s studies were done that compared the costs of public versus contract provision of refuse collection. The studies concluded that contracting for sanitation was less costly than providing refuse collection through direction provision. The reasons? Contractors used fewer workers and provided bonus systems to stimulate productivity. Second, newer side-loading sanitation trucks allowed contract firms and municipal departments to reduce the number of workers needed. Other innovations involving containers and the technology of curbside pickup in refuse collection have led to the substitution of capital for labor. Several cities that adopted technological innovations initially experienced employee militancy since jobs were on the line. In some cities unions recognized that it would be in their interest to negotiate the ramifications of technological change. Phased reductions in force through attrition (rather than immediate layoffs), incentive schemes to raise productivity, alternative financing of refuse collection, and skills upgrade have all been used to soften the blow of job losses caused by technological change.[29]

SUMMARY

Since the 1970s public personnel management has included collective bargaining with unionized government employees. The period of the 1960s through the first half of the 1970s has often been called the time of "catch-up" for public unions. Public unions caught up to their private sector counterparts in several respects. First, an increasing percentage of public employees became members of unions. By 1980 almost half of the state and local government employees were represented by organized groups. Second, during the 1960s and 1970s more and more states passed collective-bargaining legislation to govern labor-management relations at both the state and local levels. Third, public unions negotiated compensation packages for their memberships that put many government jobs on a par with comparable jobs in the private sector. Fourth, public unions also caught up with their private sector counterparts in militancy. Despite the fact that strikes by public employees were (and still are), for the most part, illegal, public unions increasingly resorted to work stoppages during collective-bargaining impasses.

By the end of the 1970s collective bargaining became an acknowledged fact of political life for public administrators. The public manager must now be familiar with the legal environment of collective bargaining to determine the rights and duties of the unions representing the government's employees and the rights and responsibilities of the public employer. The manager must also grapple with the tension between the demands of public unions and the taxpayers' ability and willingness to pay for government services. Collective bargaining is inherently filled with conflict. But behind the rhetoric there is a good deal of hard negotiations on how best to achieve one important shared objective—the continued economic and fiscal health of state and local governments. Public unions are very much a part of the political and administrative challenges that this objective demands.

NOTES

1. See James L. Perry, "Private Sector Model," in *Handbook on Public Personnel Administration and Labor Relations,* ed. Jack Rabin et al. (New York: Marcel Dekker, 1983), pp. 319–339.
2. This view is forcefully expressed in Harry Wellington and Ralph D. Winter, Jr., *The Unions and the Cities* (Washington, D.C.: Brookings Institution, 1971).
3. Details on each state are found in Helene S. Tanimoto and Joyce M. Najita, *Guide to Statutory Provisions in Public Sector Collective Bargaining Strike Rights and Prohibitions* (Honolulu: University of Hawaii, Industrial Relations Center, January 1981).
4. See Winston C. Bush and Arthur T. Denzau, "The Voting Behavior of Bureaucrats and Public Sector Growth," in *Budgets and Bureaucrats,* ed. Thomas E. Borcherding (Durham N.C.: Duke University Press, 1977), pp. 90–99.

5. Peter Feuille, "Police Labor Relations and Multilateralism" (Proceedings of the Twenty-Sixth Annual Winter Meeting of the Industrial Relations Research Association, 1973, Madison, Wisconsin).

6. Ibid.

7. Specific details for the impasse procedures for each state are found in Helene S. Tanimoto, *Guide to Statutory Provisions in Public Sector Collective Bargaining Impasse Resolution Procedures* (Honolulu: University of Hawaii, Industrial Relations Center, 1977).

8. For a study of this aspect, see Peter Feuille, "Final Offer Arbitration and the Chilling Effect," *Industrial Relations* 14 (October 1975): 302–310.

9. See Thomas A. Kochan and Jean Baderschneider, "Dependence on Impasse Procedures: Police and Firefighters in New York State," *Industrial and Labor Relations Review* 31 (July 1978): 431–449.

10. Ibid.

11. These findings are summarized in David T. Methe and James L. Perry, "The Impacts of Collective Bargaining on Local Government Services: A Review of Research," *Public Administration Review* 40 (July/August 1980): 359–371.

12. See, for example, Elizabeth Dickson, Harold A. Hovey, and George E. Peterson, *Public Employee Compensation: A Twelve City Comparison.* 2d ed. (Washington, D.C.: Urban Institute, 1981).

13. David Lewin and Raymond D. Horton, "The Impact of Collective Bargaining on the Merit System in Government," in *Public Sector Labor Relations*, ed. David Lewin, Peter Feuille, and Thomas A. Kochan (Glen Ridge, N.J.: Thomas Horton and Daughters, 1977), p. 417.

14. Craig E. Overton and Max S. Worthman, Jr., "Significant Management Rights Clauses in Municipal Police Contracts," in *Collective Bargaining by Government Workers: The Public Employee,* ed. Harry Kershen (Farmingdale, N.Y.: Baywood Publishing Company, 1983), pp. 26–33.

15. Ibid., pp. 417–418.

16. O. Glenn Stahl, *Public Personnel Administration*, 7th ed. (New York: Harper & Row, 1976), p. 362.

17. David Lewin, Raymond D. Horton, and James W. Kuhn, *Collective Bargaining and Manpower Utilization in Big City Government* (New York: Universe Books, 1979), pp. 133–134.

18. From Agreement between County of Monroe and Monroe County Federation of Social Workers Local 381, I.U.E., A.F.L.C.I.O.-C.L.C., January 1, 1980, to December 31, 1982, p. 30.

19. Case studies of productivity efforts are in John Greiner et al., *Monetary Incentives and Work Standards in Five Cities: Impacts and Implications for Management and Labor* (Washington, D.C.: Urban Institute, 1977).

20. See John Ross and Jesse Burkhead, *Productivity in the Local Public Sector* (Lexington, Mass.: Lexington Books, 1974).

21. Ronald Smothers, "Productivity-Gain Talks with Sanitationmen Fail," *New York Times,* November 19, 1980, p. B1.

22. Raymond D. Horton, "Productivity and Productivity in Government: A Critical Analysis," *Public Administration Review* 36 (July/August 1976): 407–414.

23. John Holusha, "Detroit Rescue Plan Seems to Clear Union Hurdle," *New York Times,* July 30, 1981, p. A14.

24. Robert Lindsey, "5 Years after Property Tax Slash: Power Shifts to California Capital," *New York Times,* June 5, 1983, p. 26.

25. Gary D. Altman, "Proposition 2-1/2: The Massachusetts Tax Revolt and Its Impact on Public Sector Labor Relations," *Journal of Collective Negotiations in the Public Sector* 12 (1983): 1–19.
26. Daniel J. B. Mitchell, "Collective Bargaining and Compensation in the Public Sector," in *Public Sector Bargaining,* 2d ed., ed. Benjamin Aaron, Joyce M. Najita, and James L. Stern (Washington, D.C.: Bureau of National Affairs, 1988), pp. 128–136.
27. Robert W. Poole, Jr., *Cutting Back City Hall* (New York: Universe Books, 1980).
28. John D. Hanrahan, *Government for Sale: Contracting Out, the New Patronage* (Washington, D.C.: American Federation of State, County and Municipal Employees, 1977).
29. This last section is based on David Lewin, "Technological Change in the Public Sector: The Case of Sanitation Service," in *Public Sector Labor Relations,* ed. David Lewin et al. (Lexington, Mass.: Lexington Books, 1988), pp. 297–319.

FOR FURTHER READING

Aaron, Benjamin, Joyce M. Najita, and James L. Stern, eds. *Public-Sector Bargaining,* 2d. ed. Washington, D.C.: Bureau of National Affairs, 1988.

   A valuable collection of essays that review the trends and research on major topics including: compensation, the legal environment, dispute resolution, judicial actions, and management organization.

Kochan, Thomas, *Collective Bargaining and Industrial Relations.* Homewood, Ill.: Richard D. Irwin, 1980.

   A comprehensive text that covers both the private and public sectors.

Lewin, David, Peter Feuille, Thomas Kochan, and John Thomas Delaney. *Public Sector Labor Relations: Analysis and Readings.* Lexington, Mass.: Lexington Books, 1988.

   A collection of articles on topics such as public employee strikes, impasses, compensation, and labor–management relations.

Lewin, David, Raymond D. Horton, and James W. Kuhn. *Collective Bargaining and Manpower Utilization in Big City Governments.* Montclair, N.J.: Allanheld Osmun and Co., 1979.

   A comparative study of public sector labor relations in Chicago, Los Angeles, and New York City.

Wellington, H. H., and R. K. Winter. *The Unions and the Cities.* Washington, D.C.: Brookings Institution, 1971.

   An early study that claimed that public unions should be considered differently from private unions.

CHAPTER **10**

Information, Communication, and Decision Making

"If I knew then what I know now, I would have done it differently"—a common phrase, an indication of distress or sometimes the simple realization that an outcome is less than ideal. "If I only knew how boring it would be to fill out people's tax returns I would not have become an accountant; I would be a brain surgeon or a disk jockey." Or "If I only realized how sloppy Bill really was, I would have married Jim when he asked me."

What do we mean when we sigh with resignation and mumble something about the past? We are saying that some time in the past, we made a decision, perhaps a major decision—whom to marry, which university to go to, where to live, what profession to select. But things did not turn out as anticipated: Fame and fortune eluded us, or happiness did not come our way. Whatever the gap between a former image and a present reality, we are perhaps sadder now, though most assuredly wiser.

The phrase "If I only knew then what I know now" suggests that obtaining wisdom is partly a function of time. We can substitute, "With the passage of time I now know so many more things that should enter into the decision I made hastily (foolishly?) so many years ago."

Notice how an extremely important assumption has crept into our reasoning. "What I know now" implies that with the passage of time, we have acquired additional information crucial to a decision—and the additional information is so important that it would actually lead to a different decision, assuming that we could go back in time and correct our mistakes.

When we retrace our steps in such a way we have two basic objectives in mind. First, we want to make ourselves feel better. That is, we want to convince ourselves that our original decision was not really so dumb given the information we had at the time. A person needs time to put decisions into a wider perspective to discover how wise or foolish they really were. Time also allows a person to reflect on the full range of alternatives that were available when the choice was made. Jim may not have been serious, for example, when he asked you to marry him. Or could you really have been a brain surgeon—given that you can't stand the sight of blood?

Second, we also retrace our steps to use the information we have now learned so that future decisions will be informed by our retrospection. We say to ourselves, "I want to learn from my mistakes"—presumably because such learning will help us to minimize future ones. Going over the past, then, is an important technique in error reduction.

Error reduction is certainly a goal of public managers who try to acquire information to improve the bases of their decisions. But if information is a necessary step in decision making, it is certainly not a sufficient one. Information must be processed. In other words, it must be recorded, analyzed, and transformed into data that are usable and useful for managers. But for information to be useful it must also be communicated to those who need it. Finally, information, effectively communicated, becomes part of a decision process. These four stages—the acquisition of information, the processing of information, the communication of information, and the use of information in decision making—comprise the subjects of this chapter.

DATA ACQUISITION

Let's consider a common setting in a typical county government, say an office of a department of social services. Mrs. Jones, mother of three, lost her job and, having no other sources of income, applies for public assistance (often somewhat incorrectly called "welfare").

Jones will be greeted by a county employee, often called an "intake" worker. The intake worker will have to acquire information from Jones before a decision can be made concerning her application for public assistance. The worker, for instance, may ask her questions about her employment history. Next, she will probably have to provide information about her assets—cash in savings accounts, house, car, and so on. Child support payments for Jones's three children will also have to be documented, and she may be required to provide evidence of her monthly expenses. Basically, the purpose of this intake process is to gather data to help county social services personnel to make a decision—on whether Jones is, or is not, eligible for public assistance.

Notice that the gathering of data is an integral part of the decision process. The data do not make the decision on eligibility; people do. More accurately, county social services personnel will have to evaluate the data acquired in the intake. We can say, then, that data acquisition is one important ingredient of the intake decision process—indeed, an extremely important first step.

Data are needed for other areas of social services management as well. At another level of organization, public assistance "cases" will have to be assigned to caseworkers, who have primary responsibility for "monitoring" public assistance recipients. That is, they insure that recipients remain eligible for benefits.

Should a client find employment, for example, caseworkers would remove the individual from the public assistance rolls. Caseworkers also provide clients with services such as home management, referrals for job training, health care, and legal assistance.

In the process of overseeing cases, workers acquire valuable information for higher-level managers. It would be useful, for instance, to know the relationship between the rate of new cases and the rate at which cases are closed. Information of this type allows a manager to assign cases so that workers have roughly the same caseload. It also provides basic information that is needed for planning. Managers can tell whether the caseload is declining, increasing, or remaining stable—important for determining the number of personnel needed in the agency and the appropriate size of the budget. Moreover, information gathered by caseworkers concerning the characteristics of clients—age, family size, work experience— can be valuable in assessing and reassessing the provision of social services to public assistance recipients.

Governments collect data on all sorts of things; consider the following list:

Rainfall
Soviet military troop movements in Eastern Europe
The condition of plumbing in cities
Unemployment insurance
Teenage pregnancies
The price of consumer goods

Data by themselves, in their raw form, are rarely useful. If you were told, for instance, that in 1989 there were fifteen unwanted teenage pregnancies per one thousand population, what would you make of this datum? Having absolutely no additional data you would not be able to interpret it satisfactorily. Is it good or bad? High or low? Can it be altered? Should it be changed? How might the number be affected? None of these questions can be answered with one datum only.

When data are transformed from their raw form to something usable, we can say that they have become information. Information has the potential of being usable. A change in the rate of unwanted pregnancies, for example, might be an interpretable piece of information for, say, a state health planner or a sex-education specialist in a state department of education. For a second illustration we can move from sex to the military—the Soviet military to be precise. If we learned through intelligence data-gathering techniques that the Soviet Union decreased the numbers of its troops on the eastern side of the Carpathian Mountains after diplomatic negotiations to improve relations between the superpowers, we would have some information that we did not have before. What the information might mean, how it could or should be interpreted, is a more complicated matter—one we will return to later in the chapter. For now, it is enough to say that we have gathered some new information in an area of some concern to us.

The acquisition of data and their transformation into information is a major task for public managers, one fundamental to their organizational existence. Recall some of the previous chapters. Managers, after all, need information about financial resources. They need to know whether they can expect a financial wind-fall or, more likely, a situation dominated by financial penny-pinching. If the latter is the rule, managers will need to know how, when, where, and why funds are spent. We also learned that personnel practices are filled with information-gathering episodes. Information is needed in all areas: hiring, compensating, promoting, rewarding, punishing, and firing personnel. It is needed, as we will learn in the following chapters, to make both ethical and wise choices and to evaluate perfor-mance. Gathering data and producing information, then, are indispensable to pub-lic management.

PROCESSING INFORMATION

Information must be processed in ways that are useful to us. Recall that the intake worker asked Mrs. Jones, the applicant for public assistance, a series of questions that had some bearing on her eligibility. The intake worker presumably recorded Jones's answers and, in addition, verified the documentation that she was re-quired to submit along with her application. The intake worker may have recorded the information on forms created for the process. These forms may have been developed by the county social services department or, perhaps, by the state de-partment of social services. The intake worker may have made a decision about the adequacy of Jones's documentation or even the proper place to record some of the data provided.

What happens after Jones completes the intake process? The information col-lected will probably be entered into a computer file and then analyzed so that a decision can be made on her request for public assistance. We can say that from the time the application is completed until a final determination is made, the infor-mation is processed. That is, the data collected by the intake worker concerning Jones's situation will be evaluated against specific criteria. In this example the information-processing stage is reasonably simple and straightforward. The intake worker, or perhaps a first-line manager, will compare the information gleaned from the intake interview with public assistance eligibility criteria. If Jones meets the requirements as outlined in department rules and regulations, she will most likely receive public assistance.

Sometimes errors are made during the information-processing stage. Data provided by an applicant, for instance, may be inadequate, inaccurate, or simply false; they may be recorded incorrectly by the intake worker; and they may be interpreted erroneously. The results of all of these mistakes produce what social services personnel call error rates, which refer to the percentage of people receiv-ing public assistance benefits who are not really entitled to them. Naturally, error rates bother public managers. They bother taxpayers even more when public at-tention focuses on "welfare cheats." (Mistakes also occur in the other direction. Some applicants who are eligible for public assistance may incorrectly be denied benefits. This type of error, as you may expect, does not receive the same public outcry.)

Error rates are lowered when the processing of information is improved. Sometimes the problem may be the poor training of intake workers. If, for instance, they do not understand the social services rules and regulations that pertain to public assistance eligibility, they will obviously make mistakes when collecting, recording, and transmitting information. If this is the problem, employee training may help. The work flow, however, may be such that intake workers, operating under pressure, may be prone to error. This would happen if the number of applications increases dramatically with no change in the number of intake workers or in the method of processing applications. When the economic climate deteriorates and unemployment increases, the number of applications for public assistance in a typical county social services department will go up. The work load will obviously intensify.

Governments at all levels have adapted to problems of data management and information processing by installing management information systems (MIS). The rudiments of MIS for our hypothetical social services department will resemble the following sequence.

Raw data collected from intake interviews are recorded on forms and "stored." Years ago the storage was quite primitive. It was the intake worker's file cabinet. At this stage the data were not very useful. The worker had to review the data, present them in some meaningful way—perhaps as a series of checkoffs on a standardized form—and then make a recommendation concerning the eligibility of applicants to someone else in the social services department. Applicants who were deemed eligible became cases (or "clients"), and public assistance payments were then arranged.

Notice that the various steps may have required nothing more than written or oral communication. Taken together, the steps in the transformation of data into information became part of a management information system—a process to assist managers in making decisions. In reality, an MIS is more complicated but also more efficient. Computers have altered the way we gather and store data and transform them into information that is useful to public managers. Let us consider, then, the place of computers in our hypothetical social services department.

The data provided by Jones will be put in machine-readable form so that they can be stored and accessed on the county's computer. It is even possible that the intake worker will put the data directly into the computer if there is a computer terminal at his or her desk. If not, the handwritten data will be typed into the computer at a later time. Jones's application has now become a "case record." With a few simple commands to the computer through the on-line terminal, her record can be retrieved for inspection on the monitor facing the worker. Once this stage is completed, Jones's record can be evaluated in light of a "public assistance eligibility program." In other words, the computer may store a program—a series of prearranged decision steps—that will allow the intake worker to evaluate Jones's application.

Notice that in this illustration some immediate improvements can be made in information-processing capabilities. A manager may request information, for example, on the number of applications for public assistance in a given period. Perhaps the manager wants to know the rate of new applications. If a manager wants to plan budget priorities based on the services that will have to be provided to clients, he or she may want some information on the profiles of new recipients. How many have employment histories? What are the ages of the children of new applicants? Computer-generated information processing can answer such questions quickly and accurately.

Computers in Government

Computers are now commonplace in government. They are used for three main purposes. First, governments store a great deal of information. The information often requires updating and retrieval to answer questions concerning subsets of the data that is stored. Data-base management systems are commonly used for this purpose. The systems are used on both large main frame computers and personal computers. (Several commercial products are available. Alternatively, a government may have a custom designed data-base management system prepared for one or more of its major functions such as personnel or budgeting.)

Our hypothetical social services agency may include the following data on individual case records:

> Name of recipient
> Age of recipient
> Sex of recipient
> Marital status
> Children
> Work history
> Other government benefits

Suppose the head of the social services agency wants to know how many recipients receive benefits from two or more government programs. A data-base management program will allow the manager to sort the data according to this criterion. Using the list above, what other possibilities do you see for data-base management?

A second common use of computers in government is for forecasting and financial management. Spreadsheets such as the popular Lotus 1-2-3 program or SuperCalc are most suitable for these tasks. A spreadsheet consists of cells that are created by columns and rows. Cells may contain data, text such as the names of budgetary objects of expenditures or mathematical formulas. The spreadsheet programs allow the user to perform many procedures to the data. Most useful is the ability to do "what if" scenarios. Suppose, for example, the user entered the budget for the agency and wants to see what next year's budget will look like under different assumptions. The user may try different inflation scenarios, say 3, 5, or 6 percent. The spreadsheet will recalculate the budget for each scenario. It is a lot faster than a calculator.

The third common use of computers in government is word processing. Word processing has practically replaced typewriter preparation as the way to produce printed materials. As most readers of this text already know, word processing provides a great deal of flexibility for changing and updating information, storing and retrieving information, and performing repetitive clerical tasks such as reproducing form letters and mailing labels. Moreover, since so many word processing software packages now offer "desktop publishing," reports can be prepared and printed with quality that matches highly sophisticated and expensive commercial publication. Have computers "revolutionized" government? Hardly. The initial fear (or hope, depending on one's point of view) by some that computers would be labor-saving and therefore reduce the work force of governments at all levels has clearly not happened. Nor can it be claimed that computers have generated cost savings. On the contrary, rapid advancements in computer hardware and software technologies have created some dilemmas for governments, especially smaller governments, concerning what products to purchase, the necessary personnel that specialize in computers, and appropriate applications for public management. Despite some initial reluctance governments have increasingly invested in computers and computer applications of essential public management tasks. Every aspiring public manager must now be minimally computer literate. Nevertheless, even the most elaborate computer hardware and software cannot substitute for "communication skills."

COMMUNICATION

Prospective employers usually inquire about the "communication skills" of job applicants. What do they really want to know? Basically, employers are trying to determine if an applicant can speak and write clearly. *Communication skills* is a fancy term that tries to capture a person's ability to transmit information efficiently and effectively through the written and spoken word.

Government officials are often accused of speaking and writing "bureaucratese," that special language spoken by people in the employ of the taxpayer, that seems designed to frustrate or, at the very least, obfuscate meaning.

Alexander Haig, President Reagan's first secretary of state, was a notoriously poor communicator. Reporters quickly dubbed his linguistic skills as Haigspeak—a reference to his unique style of grammar and word usage, which often obscured his real meaning. When he was given an award by an educational organization for advancing the English language (all in good fun to be sure), Haig, a former general and head of NATO, said that it would only be "proper" to acknowledge the real source of his communications prowess—the U.S. Army—where he spent so much of his professional life.

When bureaucrats speak and write poorly, is it because they simply lack basic communication skills? To put it another way, are our government organizations filled with people who flunked first-year English? The answer to both questions is no. Obfuscation can be deliberate—intended to achieve a political objective.

Take the case of Lawrence A. Kudlow, formerly the chief economist of the U.S. Office of Management and Budget in the Reagan administration. President Reagan, an early devotee of supply-side economics, found that economic necessities were making it increasingly difficult to "stay the course"—a reference to his 1982 congressional election slogan. Supply-side economics dictated tax cuts, something the president had pushed through Congress. Unfortunately, the continuing economic recession during 1981 and 1982 expanded the federal budget deficit, clearly a political liability for a conservative president. The president wanted to stay his supply-side course, but he also wanted to reduce the deficit. He chose a decidedly nonsupply-side route, tax increases, to be specific. But since no one likes to admit to the need for tax increases, and since they were clearly antithetical to the president's economic program, they had to be called something else. Lawrence A. Kudlow to the rescue! He dubbed the idea of a tax increase "revenue enhancement." When quizzed by reporters about the dubiousness of this term, which, after all, sounds an awful lot like taxes, Kudlow said he came up with another one to disguise a tax increase proposal. He called it "receipts strengthening." Why not call tax increases tax increases? Kudlow replied, "There's no better way to sell economic theory than by the euphemistic route."[1]

Kudlow recognized a basic fact of political and bureaucratic life. Conscious obscurantism, or "weasel words" if you want to sound nasty about it, have real value. They allow a person to provide a deliberately vague response to an inquiry, an ambiguous statement of intent or preference, when clarity would foreclose options—or at least make some options more difficult to pursue. Since no one likes taxes, there would be little served, from the standpoint of achieving an objective (closing the budget deficit), by stating absolutely clearly that a tax increase was in the offing. Opposition to the idea would simply surface more quickly. It does take some time to figure out what "revenue enhancement" and "receipts strengthening" mean. For Kudlow, euphemisms are effective communication. The tactic did not exactly begin with him, as the following excerpt from an interview with John Lofton, editor of the *Conservative Digest*, and President Reagan's White House press secretary, Larry Speakes, shows. Should the good press secretary have changed his name to Larry Doublespeaks?

Notable & Quotable: From a White House Press briefing May 7 [1982] with press secretary Larry Speakes. The questions were initiated by John Lofton, editor of *Conservative Digest*.

Q: *Larry, do you think the administration's economic policy is coherent?*

Mr. Speakes: *Yes.*

Q: *Let me ask you for openers about The Wall Street Journal's lead editorial this morning that the President has bought a "pig in a poke" with this Domenici compromise. Which are the taxes that are to be raised to produce the $95 billion over the next three years?*

Speakes: *We haven't decided.*

Q: *But the $40 billion in so-called Social Security savings, will this come from more taxes or spending cuts?*

Speakes: *The commission will decide that.*

Q: *The President said yesterday, I believe, that none of the new taxes that are being considered of the $95 billion will be the kinds of things that will impinge on the incentive features of his business and individual tax cuts.*

Speakes: *That's true.*

> **Q:** *What are the kinds of taxes that might not impinge on business or individual incentives?*
>
> **Speakes:** *Loophole closings and base-broadening.*
>
> **Q:** *Where? Taxes on what?*
>
> **Speakes:** *We'll find some places for people who haven't been paying taxes that ought to be paying taxes and we'll put the pinch on them.*
>
> **Q:** *Finally, the President says that the compromise—the Domenici compromise—will bring down the growth in federal spending. Do you have those figures as to what the growth rates will be?*
>
> **Speakes:** *Yes. What we have is a $416 deficit reduction package.*
>
> **Q:** *No. $416 billion.*
>
> **Speakes:** *$416 billion deficit reduction over three years.*
>
> **Q:** *In other words, the Domenici compromise would bring the rate down from what to what? What would it—what are the figures?*
>
> **Speakes:** *I just had those figures—but we can surely figure what, if we do nothing, what it will do. We figure if you do nothing, it would be $416 billion versus about—what is it—$42 billion that we figure to reduce it to? That—*
>
> □ *Source: Reprinted with permission of the Wall Street Journal, May 17, 1982. Copyright 1982 Dow Jones and Company, Inc. All rights reserved.*

The year 1987 was also a good one for political doublespeak. During the congressional investigation of the Iran–Contra affair the two main protagonists, Lieutenant Colonel Oliver North and Rear Admiral John Poindexter, came up with some ingenious euphemisms to try to shade their true actions. Poindexter, for example, did not admit to lying. Rather, he engaged in "plausible deniability." Nor did he authorize weapons shipments that may have violated legislative intent. Instead, he "acquiesced" when the issue arose. Nor did North lie or accept the lying of others. On the contrary, he "was provided with additional input that was radically different from the truth." In any event, was there a cover-up of the Iran–Contra affair? Not according to Fawn Hall, North's secretary at the time. In her words, "I don't use the word cover-up. I would use the word protect." Perhaps we are just splitting linguistic hairs anyway!

Obfuscation comes in forms other than the spoken word. Consider the work of the artist who prepared charts for one of President Reagan's television speeches on the economy. A few years ago there were two different tax proposals, one from the president and a rival one from the Democratic-controlled House Ways and Means Committee. Naturally, the president wanted to show that his proposal was better than the proposal from the committee. The way to do it was to portray a much stiffer tax bill for the average family under the Democratic plan. By removing the actual numbers, changing the scale of the chart, and using bright colors, the artist created a chart that was most favorable to the administration—implying a sizeable difference between the two proposals. During the president's nationally televised speech he said, "On the one hand you see a genuine and lasting commitment to the future of working Americans [his plan]. On the other just another implied promise [the committee's proposal]." In truth, the maximum difference between the two proposals was $217. Clearly, the president's language was a bit strong for $217. But according to Gerald Rafshoon, President Carter's media adviser, the entire episode proved again that President Reagan was a "great communicator."[2]

You should not get the impression that all effective communication in government must be laden with bureaucratese and be made consciously vague. For most situations clarity and economy are the preferred routes to good communication. President Carter tried to promote both. First, he insisted that whenever possible the language of government emanating from bureaucracy should be as clear and as simple as possible. A nonlawyer and proud of it, President Carter waged war on unnecessary legalese in government. Why does government material sound like it was written by lawyers rather than "normal" people? To a great extent, government legislation and regulations are written by lawyers, the most common profession of elected officials, and most departments at the state level (and certainly the federal level) have legal staffs.

President Carter's second effort to implement clarity and economy came with the passage of the Paperwork Reduction Act of 1980. Here is what government bureaucrats who investigated the problem in 1981 found:[3]

> Americans would spend (in 1981) 1.276 billion hours on government forms—about five thousand different kinds to be exact.
> If filling out forms paid $10 an hour, it would produce a payroll of $12,276 billion.
> The amount of work in filling out government forms comes to an average of over five hours per person in the United States.
> The main paperwork "producers" are the Internal Revenue Service (50 percent of the work), Department of Transportation (20 percent), and Department of Agriculture.

The Paperwork Reduction Act, which sought to reverse the growing deluge of government paper, established an Office of Information and Regulatory Affairs (OIRA) in the Office of Management and Budget (OMB) to reduce the production of information. The office requires agencies to submit a "paperwork budget." Specifically, government agencies must estimate the time it would take to fill out government forms and justify the need for the information. If the OIRA disagrees with an agency's estimates and justification, it may reduce the paperwork requirements requested. The paperwork budget is much like the normal budget-review process; however, instead of reviewing financial requests, the office reviews paperwork requests.

In the first year, FY 1981, agencies sought 1.284 billion work-hours of paperwork; the office reduced this amount to 1.228 billion.[4] If the trend continues, the rate of increase (rather than the absolute level) of government paperwork may indeed decline. More important than the aggregate change in paperwork, however, is the effect of the act on the federal government's information policy. During the Reagan administration efforts were made to restrict the amount of information available to the public. Budget cuts at the National Archives, for instance, where all sorts of government information is stored, were made in the interest of economy. The federal government also stopped collecting some routine statistical series. Both of these efforts by the Reagan administration were criticized by researchers and scholars, who naturally rely on government data for their work. The Reagan administration pressed ahead. Many government publications available from the Government Printing Office were discontinued, again in the interest of economy and the implementation of the Paperwork Reduction Act. No longer can you get a federal government report instructing you in how to purchase a Christmas tree or how to clean a kitchen sink.[5]

Perhaps an even more important role of the OIRA, and the major unintended consequence of the Paperwork Reduction Act, is central clearance of agency regulations. What appears to be a mere effort to reduce red tape and streamline communications has turned into a political powerhouse: The OIRA can control regulations emanating from the executive-branch agencies—and this type of control reinforces presidential power over policy and administration.

Changes in the availability of information, brought about by economizing efforts, can have even more ramifications. The Reagan administration reduced the opportunities of citizens to gain access to information through the Freedom of Information Act. Assistant Attorney General Jonathan Rose, who was responsible for restricting such access, claimed, "I believe . . . that there is an effort to balance the value of collecting and disseminating information against other values we think are important. Freedom of Information is not cost free; it is not an absolute good."[6] The Reagan administration extended this view of information by trying to censor scientific papers by researchers if, in the opinion of administration officials, the information had national security implications. According to Admiral Bobby Inman, deputy director of the Central Intelligence Agency (CIA) in the Reagan administration, a great deal of security-related material was reaching the Soviet Union via scientific research.[7]

Critics of efforts like this are fearful that limitations on the access or availability of information seriously undermine individual rights. Besides, efforts to curb fraud, waste, and abuse in government, the critics contend, require access to government information. But the administration had its favorite rebuttal. According to President Reagan's director of the Federal Bureau of Investigation (FBI), organized crime has obtained information through the Freedom of Information Act to learn what the FBI knew about meetings of such groups. In this way the groups could possibly uncover FBI informants.[8] Defenders of the act would counter that even if the organized crime argument were true, it would be a necessary price that would have to be paid for open, accountable government.

DECISION MAKING

Information is communicated for a simple reason—to make decisions. Recall that Jones applied for public assistance, and a decision had to be made concerning her eligibility. With modern information processing, it would be possible for a decision to be made almost instantaneously. The intake worker types in the data provided by Jones on a remote terminal and calls up an eligibility program stored in the computer that will analyze Jones's data. The intake worker could then make a simple either/or decision. "I have bad news for you, Mrs. Jones. You are not eligible for public assistance." Or "I have good new for you, Mrs. Jones; you are eligible for public assistance. You should receive your first check in one week."

This action is not much different from buying a ticket at an airport. The airline employee will perform the simple procedures in front of you; the information will be called up on the terminal, and you will be told immediately whether there is room on the flight you wish to go on. If the flight is completely booked the employee will tell you so.

This comparison tells us something about the limits of routine decision making in government. Would you want to tell Jones that she was ineligible to receive public assistance? How much easier it would be to take the more "official" and less personal route—a (form) letter from the director of the department notifying Jones that she is ineligible and the reasons why this decision was reached. In other words, even though computer-based information processing can greatly increase the speed of routine decisions, there may be other reasons (in this case, interpersonal relations) to bypass the opportunity.

Many decisions in organizations are routine. By definition, they require little in the way of judgment. Jones either is or is not eligible for public assistance. Once the eligibility criteria have been established, the application of the criteria to a new case becomes a routine decision.

Suppose the rate of new applications for public assistance has increased dramatically. Maybe a national recession has produced more unemployment or a major plant in the county closed. Intake workers were having trouble processing the increased work load. What type of decision may be required?

The director of the department has a few basic options. One is to hire additional intake workers. Another is to reassign some caseworkers to the intake unit. The director may try to manage the intake process by restricting the hours of intake, thereby lengthening the waiting time of new applicants. (This option would not necessarily reduce the number of applicants. Rather, it would merely allow workers to "plan" for the numbers of cases they would have to process in a given day.) The director may also search for ways to reduce the time spent with each new applicant, thereby allowing intake workers to process more cases. We can say that all of these alternatives represent operational decisions.

Sometimes routine decisions can be routine—and funny. Government agencies, for example, routinely notify beneficiaries of government programs about changes in the status of their benefit. This may include a change in services provided, a change in the amount of the benefit, or a change in the recpient's status. On p. 236 is an illustration of the latter—the decision to determine a person's medical assistance benefit. Why? The benefit was terminated because his status changed to "deceased." A good reason to be sure, but did the notice have to be sent to the beneficiary who was no longer of this world?

NOTICE OF INTENT TO DISCONTINUE/CHANGE MEDICAL ASSISTANCE

NOTICE DATE: 11/20/87	EFFECTIVE DATE: 11/18/87	NAME AND ADDRESS OF AGENCY/CENTER OR DISTRICT OFFICE
CASE NUMBER MA15448S	CIN / RID NUMBER	Madison County Department of Social Services P.O. Box 637 Wampsville, N.Y. 13163

CASE NAME (And C/O Name if Present) AND ADDRESS	
John Doe 1 Main Street Oneida, NY 13421	

GENERAL TELEPHONE NO. FOR QUESTIONS OR HELP _____

OR Agency Conference _____

Fair Hearing information and assistance _____

Record Access _____

Legal Assistance information _____

OFFICE NO.	UNIT NO.	WORKER NO.	UNIT OR WORKER NAME	TELEPHONE NO.
			Jane Smith	400-1000

This is to advise you that this Department intends to take the action(s) indicated on your Medical Assistance case:

☐ CHANGE

    ☐ We will ☐ Increase ☐ Decrease the amount the Medical Assistance household must spend or incur on medical expenses each month in order to receive Medical Assistance coverage, based on the following calculations:

Gross Monthly Income	$ _____
Total Deductions	$ _____
Balance	$ _____
Allowable Income Standard	$ _____
New Monthly Excess Income	$ _____
New Excess Income (six months)	$ _____

The former monthly excess income amount was $ _____

The former excess income amount for six months was $ _____

    ☐ We will change the manner in which we compute the Medical Assistance spenddown as follows:

Gross Monthly Income	$ _____
Total Deductions	$ _____
Balance	$ _____
Allowable Income Standard	$ _____
Excess Income (monthly)	$ _____
Excess Income (six months)	$ _____

These calculations **do not** result in any change in the amount you must spend or incur on medical expenses each month in order to receive Medical Assistance coverage for the eligible individuals.

This change is effective _____ and is being made as a result of:

    ☐ Change in income as follows: _____

    ☐ Other (non-financial) change in circumstances: _____

Please read the enclosed explanation of the EXCESS INCOME PROGRAM.

☒ DISCONTINUE the Medical Assistance coverage for (name(s)) __John Doe_____

_____ effective ___11/18/87_____ because:

    deceased _____

_____

The LAW(S) AND/OR REGULATION(S) which allows us to do this is _____ .

If any of these actions were taken because of financial circumstances, we have enclosed a budget worksheet(s) so that you can see how we determined eligibility for benefits.

The essence of an operational decision is a trade-off between alternative uses of "inputs" to achieve a stated objective.[9] Consider the option of reassigning caseworkers to the intake unit. This option, like all operational decisions, is not cost-free. If caseworkers are indeed reassigned, it means that some activities (or services) that they would have performed will be given up. The director must decide if improved capacity in the intake process is worth more than the activities or services that must be given up if the caseworkers are reassigned. Naturally, to answer this question the director will draw on all pertinent information that is available. How many additional applications would be processed if, say, two caseworkers were reassigned? How much "output" will be lost through such reassignment? The quality of existing information will obviously affect the decision. But ultimately the director must decide if caseworkers should be reassigned or another option should be selected.

Operational decision making occupies much of the time and energy of public managers because these decisions comprise their day-to-day work; they must see to it that the garbage is collected, the children are educated, the taxes are collected, crimes are investigated, and so on. In other words, operational decisions must be made to insure that the functions of governments are performed.

Sometimes decisions of a different type must be made. Suppose the rate of new applications for public assistance is increasing not only in our hypothetical county but also throughout the state. This development has state officials worried. Because public assistance must be paid by the state, if the number of new applicants is very large, it will put a strain on the state's budget. Besides, welfare is never popular with the voters, and the occasional scandal of welfare "cheats," always picked up by the news media, doesn't help. Something must be done.

Before something is done, alternatives must be assessed. We are now faced with a decision that is qualitatively different from an operational one. Consider some of the options:

1. Eligibility requirements can be changed (stiffened) to reduce the number of new cases.
2. An earnings "disregard" could be initiated to allow public assistance recipients to keep part of their benefits when they find a job (subject to an income maximum) in order to provide an incentive to work.
3. Recipients may be required to "work off" their benefits by performing local government jobs. If they refuse, their benefits will be terminated. (Indeed, mandatory "workfare" is now official federal government policy that is being phased in at the state and local levels.)
4. Benefit levels can be lowered.
5. Employment training programs can be initiated to get "employables" back to work.

These five options would probably have different chances of success. Some are easily implemented (lower benefit levels); others would take some time to be put into place. The payoffs would vary among the alternatives, but one thing is common to all of them: They are all aimed at making a large dent in the so-called welfare problem. What factors would influence the choice? Here are just a few: political feasibility, administrative ease of monitoring, cost of implementation, budgetary savings, and impact on recipients. Each one of these factors would deserve careful analysis and would have to be weighed against one another. Then each option would have to be compared with the others (based on some assessment of the "value" of the factors used for comparison). Finally, a choice of the best option among those evaluated would be made.

Decisions that follow the route just outlined can be called strategic decisions. Strategic decision making requires a great deal of information so that available options can be carefully evaluated and compared. Notice that the term *available options* rather than *all possible alternatives* was used. Theorists of decision making have pointed out over and over again that a comprehensive evaluation of all conceivable choices is an impossible goal.[10] Even strategic decision making is difficult in practice. Time is short and information is frequently missing, inaccurate, or incomplete.

TWO DYSFUNCTIONAL ASPECTS OF DECISION MAKING

Inappropriate Models

"If we can land a man on the moon, why can't we solve the problems of the ghetto?"[11] This sentence begins one of the most perceptive books on public policy analysis, *The Moon and the Ghetto*. Economist Richard Nelson pointed out that many failures of public decision making arise from an inappropriate image of how decisions should be made. Think about the first sentence again. A metaphor, it implies that some "steering mechanism" allowed public decision makers to harness the energies of the country, the resources of the country, so that a mission could be achieved. The mission was the landing of a man on the moon. "Implicit in this basic characterization of problems and solutions is the image of some person or mechanism that is actively involved in steering, in making the policy decisions that guide the ship of state. The image involves both a steersman and a steering wheel well connected to the rudder."[12] This image is inappropriate because, Nelson said, "In many instances no such steersman cum steering wheel may exist."[13]

That is, the "steersman" image of decision making is inappropriate because it implies that there is someone—president, governor, or even general—who weighs the pertinent information, harnesses the available resources, and makes a decision. Didn't President Kennedy say that before the end of the decade (the 1960s) the United States would land a man on the moon? The problem with this image is that it assumes, naively, that public sector problems are easily identified and that their solutions are similarly apparent to the decision maker in charge. In reality, problems, especially the intractable social problems of poverty, unemployment, crime, and discrimination, are not so easily identified—and their solutions seem as elusive as ever. Meanwhile, politics always intrudes on the decision to make it much more complicated than a simple cost–benefit calculation. Politics stymies presidents, governors, generals, prime ministers, and even dictators.

Another belief is that knowledge improves decisions. Surely knowledge must be superior to ignorance, and if it will not exactly set us free, it will at least improve our decisions.

This model of decision making assumes that if we place a great deal of time and money in research and development, we will produce new knowledge and new technologies that will improve our bases for making decisions. To put it another way, this perspective assumes that failures of public policy lie in ignorance rather than, say, political complexities that stymie national decisions.

Technological advances can, of course, aid decision makers. But to aid decisions is not to solve problems. Drug addiction is a good illustration. Methadone is a synthetic drug used to treat heroin users. Basically, it substitutes one type of physiological dependence with another—methadone for heroin. But unlike heroin, methadone usage is not accompanied by a ''high''; consequently, the user can function in a relatively normal fashion. In particular, it is hoped that the user, once off heroin, will no longer commit crimes or perform acts harmful to oneself or others.

Notice that methadone is a technological ''fix.'' It does not solve the heroin problem. That is, it does not deal with the causes of heroin use but merely alleviates some of the more harmful symptoms. In the absence of knowledge, then, a technological fix can aid decisions.[14]

The problem with this approach to public decisions is that often the source of ''poor'' decisions is neither ignorance nor technological backwardness. Rather, a so-called rational decision may be too costly or injurious to political power. Knowledge is only one criterion among several that affect decisions. If you believe that the obtainment of ''truth'' will improve public decisions, you may be disappointed.

Managing by the Numbers

A friend told me about a custom concerning child rearing that was common many years ago in his native South Africa. Many years ago physicians gave parents very strict instructions about how to treat their infants—how much sleep they should be allowed at any one time and exactly how much formula the infant should consume. Parents dutifully recorded the ''data'' for the physician's inspection. The physician would make a house call, look at the data, and say, ''The baby is doing fine,'' without even checking the baby at all. Similarly, it is common to hear mothers complain that when they were in labor and about to give birth, physicians seemed more interested in the data from the fetal monitor than in the patient. The familiar complaint is that the preoccupation with technology is ''dehumanizing.''

Sometimes public decisions can err because of undue faith in ''the numbers.'' This will happen when a quantitative indicator is used as a measure of performance. Errors occur when a manager decides to maximize the quantitative indicator to obtain good results. Here are three illustrations of managing by the numbers:

1. "Body counts" of Viet Cong insurgents killed in battles during the Vietnam War were used by military and civilian planners to evaluate the success of the U.S. pacification effort. This led to more U.S. involvement in Indochina—a series of decisions that was most unfortunate.
2. Between 1968 and 1973 a nationwide crackdown on crime was evaluated by an index of seven crimes: murder, forcible rape, robbery, aggravated assault, burglary, larceny over $50, and auto theft. Because the index was a simple sum of these seven crimes, murder was worth no more than a $50 larceny. In Washington, D.C., pressure was put on district commanders to reduce crime in their respective districts. Suddenly, the crime rate, as measured by the index, declined. Upon investigation, reporters from the *Washington Daily News* discovered that goods stolen in a single larceny were often valued at $49, even though insurance companies paid much more in compensation.
3. In mental health, mandated lengths of stay are often determined by a psychiatric diagnosis. When bureaucratic pressure to alleviate the population of state psychiatric hospitals is the rule of the day, diagnoses are altered (correspondingly) to "match" population estimates. Similarly, shifts in the meaning of various psychiatric diagnoses occur to accommodate changes in what is the acceptable hospital population.[15]

In each case excessive preoccupation with the numbers led to faulty decisions, something that happens when the manager relies only on the quantitative indicator to make a decision. Managing only by the numbers is bad management. Donald Campbell, a distinguished social psychologist, identified two "laws" inherent in excessive preoccupation with numbers: (1) "The more any quantitative social indicator is used for decision making, the more subject it will be to corruption pressures" (2) "and the more apt it will be to distort and corrupt the social processes it is intended to monitor."[16]

SUMMARY

Decisions begin with the collection of data. But data in their raw form are rarely useful. Managers need information to guide decisions; therefore, a second step in the decision-making sequence is to transform data into usable information. Information must then be processed—organized in a way that will be useful to the manager.

So far we have identified three elementary features of a rudimentary management information system (MIS). In reality, an MIS is much more elaborate. Data storage, retrieval, transformation of data into information, and information processing are now all done with the help of computers. Computers are particularly valuable because they simplify operational decisions and thereby make them easier to manage. Consider once again the example of gasoline inventory in the garages of a hypothetical city's Department of Public Works. The manager needs to know if there is enough gasoline available for the vehicles should there be an unexpected storm. The manager should be able to determine the gasoline capacity of the vehicles, the number of vehicles that will be needed, and the number of miles they will have to travel. A computer-based information system that includes data for these factors would enable the manager to determine the most appropriate inventory for gasoline. In short, the availability of computers has changed the way many operational decisions are made at all levels of government. They have become indispensable to public managers.

Not all decisions are that simple. When decisions concern changes in policy, when they are strategic, a great deal of communication takes place before the actual decision. Sometimes the president is planning to propose a change in tax policy. Or a governor may be contemplating the alternatives available to deal with the state's welfare problem. In most instances clear and concise communication of the options is the preferred mode before the actual decision, but not always. Often a decision will help some and hurt others; there are almost always winners and losers. Policy-makers may wish to defer the inevitable flack they are likely to get from a decision that will be unpopular with a sizeable segment of the population. Fuzzy communication is the most common approach to this situation. Policy-makers may profit (in a political sense) when the information used to guide decisions is kept consciously vague.

You should not get the impression that government is filled with extraneous information and poor communication. Governments have tried to streamline information, facilitate its flow, and reduce red tape, for example, with the Paperwork Reduction Act of 1980 and President Carter's "plain English" campaign (a campaign that some state and local officials joined as well).

One last word—information does not make decisions. People do. Sometimes decision makers are lulled into a false sense of security. They erroneously believe that the information is so telling, is so straightforward, that the decision is obvious. This mistake is called "managing by the numbers." When managers put excessive faith in the numbers, they invariably make faulty decisions. Information, no matter how much and how good, should not substitute for human judgment.

NOTES

1. "A Euphemist Takes a Bow," *New York Times*, October 21, 1981, p. A28.
2. "That Numberless Presidential Chart," *New York Times*, August 2, 1981, p. F17.
3. Clyde H. Farnsworth, "Bureau of Federal Paperwork: A Billion Citizen Hours a Year," *New York Times*, January 18, 1981, p. 1.
4. Ibid., p. 27.
5. David Burnham, "Government Restricting Flow of Information to the Public," *New York Times*, November 15, 1982, p. B5.
6. Ibid., p. 1.
7. Ibid.
8. Ibid., p. B5
9. See Stephen R. Rosenthal, *Managing Government Operations* (Glenview, Ill.: Scott, Foresman, 1982).

10. See Herbert Simon's classic description of "satisficing" in *Administrative Behavior*, 3d ed. (New York: Free Press, 1976).
11. Richard Nelson, *The Moon and the Ghetto* (New York: W. W. Norton, 1977).
12. Ibid., p. 24.
13. Ibid.
14. Amitai Etzioni and Richard Remp, "Technological 'Shortcuts' to Social Change," *Science* 175 (January 7, 1972): 31–37.
15. The dysfunctional aspects of "managing by the numbers" is the subject of Pauline Ginsberg, "Predicting the Institutional Impact of Regulatory Efforts: Some General Principles and their Relationship to Mental Health Services" (Ph.D. diss., Syracuse University, 1982).
16. Donald Campbell, "Assessing Impact of Planned Social Change," *Evaluation and Program Planning* 2 (1972): 67–97.

FOR FURTHER READING

Arnold, David S., Christine S. Becker, and Elizabeth K. Kellar. *Effective Communication: Getting the Message Across*. Washington, D.C.: International City Management Association, 1983.
  A guide designed to improve the local government practitioner's communication skills.
Danziger, James N., Kenneth L. Kraemer, and William H. Dutton. *Computers and Politics*. New York: Columbia University Press, 1982.
  An empirical study of the effects of computerization in local governments.
Lindblom, Charles, "The Science of Muddling Through." *Public Administration Review* 19 (Spring 1959): 79–88.
  The classic statement on incremental decision making.
Public Administration Review 46 (November 1986).
  This special issue, edited by Barry Bozeman and Stuart Bretschneider, includes fifteen articles on various aspects of public management information systems.
Relyea, Harold C., ed. "The Freedom of Information Act a Decade Later," *Public Administration Review* 39 (July/August 1979): 310–332.
  Four articles that appraise the first ten years of the Freedom of Information Act.
Simon, Herbert A. *Administrative Behavior*, 3d ed. New York: Free Press, 1976.
  How decisions are made in organizations is Simon's major contribution to "administrative science."

CHAPTER 11

Implementation and Intergovernmental Management

A SERIES OF EPISODES

Episode 1

In the very distant past I was once a caseworker for the Department of Social Services in New York City. By the second week on the job I had to make my very first home visit to one of my newly inherited "cases." As I approached the steps of the building, a boy about ten years old asked if I was the new welfare worker. When I said yes, he continued, "My mother ain't home." I asked where she was, and he replied, "She's at work." On the job for two weeks and I had my first ethical dilemma. The boy's mother should have notified the department that she was working. I had a decision to make.

Episode 2

When I was in basic training in the U.S. Army I witnessed the following incident: After my basic training company returned from a weekend pass on a Sunday afternoon, the drill sergeant made us all change into fatigues. He then ordered us to run around a lake near our barracks to "get the weekend out of us." A young recruit protested. He said it was "illegal" to make us do that on a Sunday and he further claimed that he would tell his father, who knew congressman so and so, who, in turn, would inform the secretary of the army about this alleged infraction. The drill sergeant put on as mean a face as he could, looked at the recruit, and said, "I run this basic training company, not the secretary of the army." So much for formal lines of hierarchy and chains of command.

Episode 3

Several years ago I taught at a college in western New York State. It was next to a small city called Dunkirk. Dunkirk, like many cities, received federal funds under the Model Cities Program, the broad objective of which was to aid the redevelopment of deteriorating central cities.[1] Dunkirk officials wanted to halt the growing decay of the city—particularly the erosion of business activity—by building a shopping center of some kind. The first stage was completed, and an area was cleared for the site. But a problem arose. The city exhausted its model city funds and no additional funds for development were available. Essentially, then, the federal government funded what amounted to a big parking lot in the middle of the city. Dunkirk is not a unique case.

Episode 4

Mainstreaming is a policy that requires children with special needs—physical, mental, or emotional—to be put in regular classrooms in public schools to the extent that it is practical. The objective is to reduce the tendency to treat children with special needs as "different." I asked two teachers about mainstreaming. One of them said that a certain child in her class who was hyperactive was often "bananas," "climbing up the walls," and required an excessive amount of attention. "It's not fair to the rest of the kids" was the summary judgment. "It sound good in theory," they said, "but it doesn't work in practice."

Episode 5

This last episode comes from the annals of international brinksmanship. In 1961 a serious conflict arose between President Kennedy and Premier Khrushchev of the Soviet Union concerning the placement of Soviet missiles in Cuba.[2] During thirteen very nervous days of conflict and negotiation, the following "minor" incident occurred. It seems that Khrushchev needed something in return if he agreed to take the Soviet missiles out of Cuba so he demanded that U.S. missiles, aimed at the Soviet Union, be removed from Turkey. President Kennedy was unwilling to negotiate, but accounts of the thirteen days say that he was upset, to say the least, about the missiles in Turkey. It seems that he had ordered their removal well before the onset of the crisis, but for reasons not fully understood, they were not removed as ordered. It was a hell of a time to find out.

THE ESSENCE OF THE IMPLEMENTATION PROBLEM

There are several principles hidden in these five episodes:

1. Decisions are not self-executing. The fact that President Kennedy ordered the missiles removed from Turkey did not automatically mean that they would be removed.

2. Formal hierarchy in organizations does not necessarily correspond to the way "routine" decisions are made and carried out. Not only was the drill sergeant literally correct in saying that he, not the secretary of the army, ran the basic training company, but also, the secretary probably wouldn't know how to run a basic training company. It was not part of the secretary's decision-making arena.

3. Program objectives designed in Washington do not necessarily receive the same importance (or even interpretation) at the local level. If the meaning of urban development was not well defined in Washington's Model Cities Program, it was probably even less defined in places like Dunkirk, New York. Also, urban development most likely meant different things in different places.

4. Unintended consequences of programs are frequently overlooked when programs are designed with a given objective in mind. Mainstreaming of children with special needs may be a fine objective. But its effects on the whole classroom are important to its success as well as to other educational objectives. Second-order consequences should be anticipated before a program is actually begun.

5. Individuals at the local level with primary responsibility for providing services will greatly affect the success or failure of programs depending on how their (inevitable) discretion is actually used. The caseworker can choose to enforce regulations concerning work or "overlook" unrecorded employment. This is the discretion that is built into the job. Police personnel, teachers, caseworkers—all have this kind of discretion in their capacity as primary service providers.

Put all of these principles together and we have what is called implementation—what happens after a policy decision has been made, or the carrying out of a policy decision.[3] We might also think of it as a series of actions taken to make plans a reality. The concept of implementation is fuzzy; it is hard to define because it includes so many things: strategy, bargaining and negotiation, incentives, and decisions. It is also hard to say when the implementation process starts and when it ends. Implementation is continuous. When actions put policy plans into reality, implementation tells how those plans must be altered to reach objectives. It is therefore a crucial link in the policy process.[4]

WHEN IMPLEMENTATION PROBLEMS SURFACE

Implementation problems surface when program goals are fuzzy or, on occasion, contradictory. Consider welfare policy and the objectives of public assistance. Recipients of public assistance would probably say that welfare is supposed to make sure that people like themselves have some minimum income to live decently (if not as well as they would like). Now if we switch the focus to the secretary of the U.S. Department of Health and Human Resources, he or she would say something similar—provide minimum income for a target population—

and may perhaps add a comment about income distribution. But what about the intake workers in the local social services agency? Would they say the same thing? Perhaps. In an operational sense, however, they have a "subgoal"—processing applications.[5] They are unlikely to think about abstract objectives like income distribution. Similarly, the director of the welfare center is unlikely to think about income distribution either. On the contrary, things like "processing time," "error rates," and staff turnover are more important. Two points are important here: (1) Program objectives are not always clear and (2) participants in implementation often have different perspectives on just what the objective of a program is supposed to be. Consider the following illustrations:

Multiple Objectives: The Case of Food Stamps

Programs often have multiple objectives. Implementation problems may surface when multiple objectives are not considered together at the time program decisions are being made. For instance, the success of a program will often depend on the participation of many different organizations or groups. Often groups have overlapping, though not identical, interests. The key to success is to emphasize shared interests to insure that the program receives sufficient attention by public officials. Obviously, what keeps interested parties interested is the program objective that each organization or group identifies with. Meanwhile, the coalition of political support helps keep the implementation process moving forward.

A good example is the federal government's Food Stamp Program.[6] Just what is its objective?

Income support. Persons eligible for food stamps can purchase the stamps and then use them to buy food. The recipient pays less for the stamps than their face value (that is, the purchasing power of the stamps). Suppose you paid $20 for $30 worth of stamps, for example, Assume, furthermore, that you would ordinarily buy $30 worth of food for one week. With the stamps the food only costs $20. You can now spend $10 on something else. What the Food Stamp Program has done, then, is to provide you with an income support. But this isn't its only objective.

Food supplement. One of the original ideas for the program was that every household would be able to have "an opportunity to obtain a nutritionally adequate diet." That is, the program would allow recipients to purchase food that is healthier. It was assumed that this objective could be achieved because, with food stamps, people would consume more food. Yet it should be obvious, particularly to the "junk food junkies" reading this passage, that food consumption and nutrition are not synonymous.

An indirect benefit to farmers. The Food Stamp Program replaced an older food-commodity distribution program whereby food surpluses were distributed to the needy. With stamps the individual can decide when to buy food and just what to buy (within program restrictions). But there is one carry-over from the older program. To use the economic language that is appropriate here, the Food Stamp Program stimulates the demand for food and thereby provides some benefit to farmers. Although this may no longer be the primary objective, the fact that the Food Stamp program is located in the Department of Agriculture indicates that stimulating market demand for food is also an objective.

These multiple objectives bring together three diverse groups. (1) Farmers obviously benefit from the subsidy effect of the program. (2) Local governments, which provide benefits to the poor, have a stake in the program because it gives people in need an income supplement. (3) Organizations that promote the rights of the poor have the same interest, as do groups concerned with children's nutrition. Multiple objectives allow the program's managers to cultivate enough support to insure that its political life will not be brought to an untimely end.

When Objectives Conflict: Law Enforcement

When objectives are in conflict, success is difficult to achieve. Consider the broad objective of local law enforcement.[7] Law-enforcement agencies (local police departments) want to be efficient. For a certain budget, for example, they would like to maximize their "output"—here defined as the number of arrests. But this is only one objective. Law-enforcement agencies also want to promote equity. In law enforcement the concept of equity is fairly precise:

The probability that you will be victimized
The amount of compensation (if any) you will receive if you are victimized
The probability that you, as the perpetrator of crime, will get caught
The severity of the punishment that you, the convicted criminal, will receive
  on sentencing

Notice that the implementation of law-enforcement policy at the local level depends on the weight placed on efficiency versus equity.

Suppose there is political pressure on the police to make more arrests as a sign that they are making a greater effort to fight crime. Suppose, furthermore, that crimes such as prostitution and loitering are easier to apprehend than, say, murder and rape. If police are ordered to concentrate on " cleaning up the streets," it is likely that there will be more arrests for loitering and prostitution. In the meantime, the probability of being murdered or raped is likely to increase. (This argument assumes that a police presence deters some potential murders and rapists.) Also, the probability of being caught for committing murder or rape is likely to decline.

This discussion highlights an important aspect of the implementation problem. When objectives are in conflict with one another at the outset, it is difficult to implement programs so that they will, on balance, be successful. Managers are faced with constant trade-offs, which is the essence of decision making. In law enforcement, for example, trade-offs are not only ever-present but, also, perhaps, never ending. Implementation necessarily must adjust, and readjust, to trade-off decisions. As a result, implementation as an integral part of the policy process is filled with many fits and starts as programs go from ideas to reality.

Economic versus Political Criteria:
The Case of Peak-Load Pricing

Did you ever try to drive from Long Island, New York, to the island of Manhattan on, say, a Monday morning at 7:30? How about from Disneyland to downtown Los Angeles? Or from Skokie, Illinois, to the loop in Chicago? If you are a seven-minute-a-mile (or better) jogger, you might be able to do the trip faster on your feet than in your car.

Traffic congestion into and out of big cities is a common problem, although its solution is fairly straightforward. Given the options available, many people drive into the cities (and thereby cause congestion, pollution, and the waste of valuable energy) instead of using mass transit or car pools. If, however, we alter the costs of the various options, we could shift the "preferences" of drivers to some other alternative and thereby relieve congestion and the other harmful effects of too many cars in the city. That is, if we increase the "price" of driving into the city, we could alter the choices of many drivers. This is called *peak-load pricing*.[8] When drivers go over the toll roads and bridges to the city, for example, we could charge more, perhaps double, between 7 and 9 A.M. and between 4 and 6 P.M. (in the other direction). Or we could charge more for cars with only a driver and no passengers, give a discount to cars with four or more persons, and also increase parking fees in the city. The basic point is simple: The price mechanism will do the job.

There is just one problem: Politics tends to get in the way. Elected officials think that voters won't like the idea—and they are probably right. So although elected officials may wish to reduce congestion, they also want to stay in office. This does not mean that some peak-load pricing efforts are not used. But a thorough application of the price mechanism, unfettered by political considerations, is unrealistic. Thus even though the mechanisms for effective implementation are fairly straightforward and uncomplicated, their application is constrained by political feasibility.[9] Political feasibility often requires policy-makers to search for second-best implementation strategies because the obvious one—peak-load pricing in this case—has a low probability of success.

Analytical Complexity and Uncertainty: The "War on Drugs"

Sometimes the state of knowledge about a policy issue in need of a solution is incomplete. Actually, this is the normal state of affairs. Consider the problem of drugs in the United States.

The year 1988 heralded a "war on drugs." The issue made front page news, in part, because of the attention given to it by Reverend Jesse Jackson, a candidate for the Democratic party's nomination for president. In the same year allegations of major international drug dealing by Central American and South American politicians surfaced. The "war on drugs" was an issue in the presidential election. After he took office, President Bush picked William Bennett, secretary of education in the Reagan administration, to be his "drug czar"—a symbol that the war on drugs was not merely campaign rhetoric.

What were some of the options available for policy-makers? They can be divided, roughly, into supply options and demand options. That is, the first set of alternatives concerns controlling the availability of drugs. The latter set focuses on the users and the potential users. For example, the Reagan administration's campaign "Say No to Drugs," spearheaded by the first lady, Nancy Reagan, was a demand-side approach. Interdicting drug smugglers before they enter the country is a supply-side approach. The state of Illinois adopted a unique approach:

"If It's Illegal, Why Not Tax It Out of Existence?"

Illinois initiated its own "war on drugs." The state legislature passed a law requiring dealers of illegal drugs such as cocaine and marijuana to purchase tax stamps. Drug packages are supposed to have a stamp affixed to them. A marijuana leaf stamp with a slash through the leaf costs $5. Another stamp has a skull and crossbones on it. A stamp for a gram of cocaine costs $250. Drugs not sold by weight require a stamp in the amount of $2,000.

A drug dealer who is caught without the stamps can receive fines totalling four times the tax, a $10,000 fine, and a prison term of three years. Skeptics claim that no one would really buy the stamps if they are dealing in illegal drugs. However, advocates of the idea in Illinois say that the dealers cannot incriminate themselves merely by purchasing the stamps. Rather, supporters of the new law say that it gives the state additional legal ammunition in the war on drugs. And as Bob Fletcher, spokesman for the State Police mused, "People can say the taxes and the law are ridiculous, but they should think back a little bit and remember how Al Capone was convicted." It was not for murder; it was for tax evasion.

□ *Source: "Illinois Imposes a Tax on Illegal Drug Dealers,"* New York Times, *January 7, 1988, p. A19.*

Which approach is likely to be more effective? Supply-side advocates would beef up Coast Guard efforts, border patrol activities, and security at ports of entry into the country. Similarly, stiffer penalties including the death penalty for convicted drug smugglers is a supply-side approach. In addition, foreign policy is included in the supply-side arsenal. The range includes subsidies for peasants and farmers who currently grow poppy seeds so that the economic incentive to grow alternative crops is improved, to limited military action directed at political leaders who refuse to end their country's drug trade. Demand-side advocates point out that many of the supply-side options have been tried and have failed. They point to the huge cost of supply-side options. Their alternatives include education programs aimed at young drug users and potential users and selected enforcement of criminal sanctions that are intended to have deterrent effects. Neither side has adequate information to show that one approach is superior to the other. Yet an analytical breakthrough would lead policy-makers to some implementation alternatives and a rejection of others.

INTERGOVERNMENTAL MANAGEMENT AND IMPLEMENTATION   *Federalism*

Remember the famous quote by Harry Truman concerning Dwight Eisenhower? "Poor Ike. He'll sit here and he'll say 'Do this! Do that!' and nothing will happen." President Truman was referring to the fact that managing a government is not the same as commanding an army. Implementation is like this also. The federal government also says do this, do that, and often state and local governments don't listen. When officials in Washington, D.C., originated the Model Cities Program, no one thought that cities like Dunkirk would produce parking lots in their centers.

It's a Long Way from Washington to Peoria

Federal managers in Washington, D.C., need policy professionals to guide local governments through the implementation of federal programs. These policy professionals are often found in regional offices, which are supposed to monitor local compliance with federal program objectives. The relationship among the federal agency in Washington, the policy professionals in the regional offices, and the local governments can be tumultuous.

Consider the now defunct federal employment program established in 1973 under the Comprehensive Employment and Training Act (CETA). Its basic purpose was to change the structure of federal employment programs so that local governments would have more discretion concerning the use of federal funds to promote employment opportunities for low-income individuals. The mechanism for this program was the block grant. Federal funds went to "prime sponsors" (about four hundred local government units) who either provided employment and training services directly or contracted to community agencies.[10] The amount of funds a prime sponsor received was based on a formula that included (1) the area's unemployment rate, (2) the number of poor families, and (3) the amount of federal funds received under previous categorical manpower programs. Local prime sponsors were accountable to a regional Department of Labor (DOL) office—the federal department responsible for the program. There were ten regional offices around the country.

The regional office of the DOL was supposed to assist prime sponsors in implementing the CETA through two basic functions: first, providing local prime sponsors with "technical assistance" on how to achieve the program's objectives and, second, monitoring the activities and performance of prime sponsors to insure compliance with the intent of the CETA. These two functions were performed by regional DOL personnel through "field assessments"—on-site inspections—and the review of reports prepared by prime sponsors that supposedly detailed the steps taken to implement CETA objectives.

On the surface this intergovernmental structure seems hierarchical. That is, it may appear that the steps of implementation go from Washington, D.C., through the regional offices and then to the prime sponsors. But intergovernmental management is not so simple. One way to appreciate the complexity is to view the implementation of programs as conflict and bargaining among the intergovernmental participants.[11]

Mutually reinforcing interests.   What did the U.S. Department of Labor want to achieve through the CETA program? This question does not have a simple answer; nevertheless, for our purposes we can say that the DOL wanted to stimulate employment through the effective use of the CETA. The specific agency in the DOL responsible for the national administration of the CETA had many objectives, including the continued health (and perhaps expansion) of the program: A bigger program is better than a smaller program. Regional DOL offices wanted satisfactory compliance from prime sponsors so that the regional offices were looked upon favorably from Washington, and the prime sponsors wanted a continuing funding source. Notice that these various objectives are not inherently in conflict with one another, but they are also not automatically compatible. Thus intergovernmental implementation includes both bargaining and conflict. Often the focal point for bargaining is the regional office because it tries to accommodate the interests of Washington, D.C., and the local governments at the same time—which could sometimes be difficult.

Carl Van Horn tells the story of how the Chicago regional office of the DOL tried unsuccessfully to accommodate the interests of Washington, D.C., and the prime sponsors. A staff member in the Chicago office, for example, approved a plan that would use CETA funds to hire regular city employees who had been laid off. But the DOL in Washington, which had previously allowed such a practice, had reversed its position; this use of CETA funds could be made only if the city had a severe fiscal crisis. So the application from the prime sponsor, though approved in Chicago, was reversed in Washington. A regional DOL staff person summarized the whole incident by saying, "I zigged when I should have zagged."[12]

This illustration shows that conflict is built into the implementation process, as is bargaining. When personnel from regional offices make site visits to local governments, they are trying to determine the level of program compliance. This is rarely a simple task. The assessment of compliance requires some reasonable performance standards, and performance standards, in turn, make sense only if there are clear program goals. Remember that program goals are often fuzzy, multiple, or contradictory. Compliance levels, then, are usually fairly broad. For the CETA, for example, they were as follows:[13]

Satisfactory
Marginal
Significant underperformance
Unsatisfactory

Actual compliance levels for other intergovernmental programs may be somewhat different. The ultimate sanction is the loss of federal funds for unsatisfactory performance, but although in theory this sanction exists, it is rarely exercised. Consequently, bargaining—often tacit—occurs between regional offices and local government grant recipients. Just what the local officials have to do to improve implementation is often the subject of intense negotiations, as indicated by the following case of Buffalo's problems with the regional office of the Department of Housing and Urban Development over its Housing Assistance Plan—a requirement of all recipients of Community Development Block Grant funds.

Buffalo's Housing Assistance Plan
Donald Rosenthal

When Congress passed the Housing and Community Development Act of 1974, it made the receipt of Community Development Block Grant (CDBG) funds contingent upon the submission of applications which were to include Housing Assistance Plans (HAPs). The latter would identify the housing needs of low- and moderate-income persons and outline efforts that were planned by the locality to meet those needs using HUD resources. In the case of Buffalo the $11.7 million in CDBG funds promised for the first year came at a time when the city was particularly deep in financial difficulty. It was regarded as essential to maintaining even a minimal level of existing services.

At the outset of the CDBG Program, the HAP was understood by many local governments to be little more than a symbolic activity.[1] This was in keeping both with the spirit of non-intervention associated with the New Federalism and the need to develop formal procedures for reviewing local applications. Thus, inadequacies in Buffalo's HAP might have gone uncriticized, as was the case elsewhere, had the area office of the Department of Housing and Urban Development (HUD) lacked an aggressive director. However, Frank Cerabone had been in charge of the Buffalo office since 1970 and had become very concerned with the failure of the city to develop what he regarded as a balanced housing program, providing sufficient opportunities for assisted housing for low- and moderate-income persons, particularly large families. In keeping with HUD mandates, that housing was expected to be located outside areas of minority and low-income concentration and away from those neighborhoods where public housing had been traditionally concentrated. These principles were unacceptable to many white citizens of Buffalo and to some of the members of the Buffalo Common Council who represented them.

As with the previous case, the conflict that arose around Buffalo's HAP reflected a history of difficulties between municipal leadership and a federal agency. In this case, Cerabone and the mayor of Buffalo had signed a "memorandum of understanding" in 1972, under which HUD promised to fund two senior citizens projects desired by the city in return for an agreement by the city to develop a plan for assisted family housing. The city was very slow to deliver on that commitment. One site discussed as early as 1971 involved an essentially white neighborhood in which thirty units of family housing were to be constructed. Announcement of selection of that site had stirred considerable opposition among residents. That earlier conflict had died down when a designated developer failed to move forward expeditiously. It was only in late 1974 that attention was drawn to that project, once again, when Cerabone wrote to the city's Public Housing Authority and the developer about their plans on the project. Both indicated continued interest. This set off a new uproar among neighborhood residents, who demanded a meeting with Cerabone in February 1975, at which they complained about plans for the project. At the meeting, the newly seated member of the Common Council from the district played a prominent role in opposition to the project. A temporary halt on the project was agreed to by Cerabone while the matter was reviewed by HUD, but on April 7, Cerabone announced that HUD still planned to proceed with funding.

It was against this background of conflict that work began on the city's application for CDBG funds. That document, including the city's HAP, was submitted to HUD on April 14. It contained a list of sites which might be developed using HUD housing assistance programs, but it did not indicate specifically which sites would be used to meet the needs of low- and moderate-income families, especially those of minority backgrounds. Furthermore, many of the sites were in areas which had been designated earlier for urban renewal or pubic housing construction (areas surrounded by blight). They were neighborhoods regarded by HUD as inappropriate for housing programs since they already were characterized by considerable "impaction." What turned out to be equally controversial was the inclusion on the list of the disputed site mentioned earlier.

It was because of the controversy surrounding selection of that particular site that Cerabone was invited to a meeting of a committee of the Common Council on April 18, at which time he was closely questioned about the selected site and about block grant and HAP processes. For three hours, members of the council assaulted him verbally for the sins of commission and omission by HUD over the years. After this direct confrontation, on April 29, the council moved to rescind the city's commitment to the proposed neighborhood project. This clearly angered the area director, who wrote to the mayor on May 5 warning that this action "must be taken into account" in HUD's review of the city's HAP. He asked the city to revise the HAP that had already been submitted and to submit alternative proposals by May 28, outlining "how it would provide a reasonable choice of housing for low- and moderate-income households."[2]

Unfortunately, no one in city hall moved immediately to do so. Therefore, on May 23, Cerabone met with the mayor and warned him that he would recommend the rejection of the city's block grant application if no action was taken. Indeed, Cerabone proceeded to prepare materials in support of a rejection and to consult with the central office of HUD in Washington about doing so. Nevertheless, city hall still seemed to be relying on the belief that HUD would not really come to a showdown on the issue given first-year uncertainties surrounding the requirements of the program. It was also clear that the mayor was incapable of achieving an agreement among members of the Common Council about making non-impacted sites available in their districts.

Originally, the area office provided no directions about what would be necessary to satisfy its demands. In the course of discussion, however, Cerabone indicated that he would accept a commitment by the city to undertake the construction of ninety units of assisted housing for families. HUD staff and city housing officials met on June 3 to discuss the implication of this admittedly arbitrary figure. At that time, the city proposed four specific sites. After review, HUD rejected all four, three on the grounds of being in "impacted" areas and one as "environmentally unacceptable." Despite this rejection, the Common Council went ahead and affirmed its backing for a list which included two of the four rejected locations, both of which were long-vacant urban renewal sites. However, some room for maneuver remained since there was ambiguity built into HUD's position on whether all of the sites had to meet the "non-impaction" criteria or only a certain proportion.

On June 12, Cerabone met with the mayor, who argued that he was unable to come up with a commitment from the council that would be acceptable to HUD. Cerabone indicate that he was working against a deadline of June 27 for review of CDBG applications. This point was reinforced, on June 17, by a telegram in which he called upon the mayor to secure passage of a resolution by the council no later than June 24 in which it committed the city to putting sixty of the ninety units in "areas not having an undue concentration of assisted persons or low-income persons." This was the first time that HUD specifically had stated a willingness to accept a sixty-thirty division. The telegram was brought to the council at its next meeting on June 24. At this eleventh hour, the council passed a resolution of the kind requested by Cerabone. Even that resolution involved only a commitment "in principle" to a list of sites, not a definite commitment to the use of those sites for specific types of units.

On the same day, Cerabone was in Washington discussing the situation both with officials at HUD and with the three area congressional representatives. Interestingly, none of the three indicated any desire to play an active role in defense of the city's position. Indeed, one Washington-based HUD official later noted that "unlike other cities, what Buffalo did not do was come to Washington. No effort was really made by the city to go over the head of Cerabone."

Equally important, senior officials at HUD counseled Cerabone against pushing the city over the brink, for internal review of the legal position of the department had indicated that an action cutting off CDBG funds might have been untenable if the city brought a suit. At the time of the

controversy, the act was not yet backed by regulations detailing procedures for implementing the HAP requirements. As one official remarked,
"That is why we told [Cerabone] that he should work out the best deal
he could. He had gotten into the crisis in the first place and he had to
work himself out of it."

The result was a climb-down disguised as a compromise in which the
area office director chose to accept the council's resolution of June 24 as
an adequate sign of good faith on the city's part. However, he insisted
that the city continue to refine the list of sites and to go forward with
commitments on the ninety units.

Unable to exercise political leverage over the members of the Common
Council, the mayor retreated from the bargaining process and turned the
matter over to the Majority Leader of the council for direct negotiations
with HUD. One of the first things the latter did was to arrange a private
meeting among Cerabone and his HUD staff and several members of the
council. That meeting lasted six and one-half hours and turned out sur-
prisingly well. As one HUD participant recalled, "For the first time we
had someone in city hall who was willing to act responsibly. As a result,
we worked closely with [the majority leader] over the next three or four
months to come up with an acceptable set of sites."

One of the steps taken involved a further retreat by HUD from a strict
definition of impaction in the case of one of the urban renewal sites that
had been proposed earlier and had been rejected on impaction grounds.
It is now to be counted as a location satisfying nonimpaction criteria and
would house thirty families. Negotiations continued in order to identify
sites for thirty additional units. A compromise was finally ratified on September 30, 1975, when the Common Council voted ten to four to accept
a list moved by the Majority Leader.

■ 1. On this point, see U.S. Department of Housing and Urban Development,
Block Grants for Community Development, by Richard P. Nathan et al., Washington, D.C. Department of Housing and Urban Development, January 1977, p. 68,
where they state, "Assistant Secretary Meeker adopted as a slogan, 'No second-
guessing of local officials and a minimum of red-tape.' " However, former senior
officials of HUD insist it was not their intention to give any locality a first-year
"free ride." A more recent study of CDBG by Nathan and his associates indicates,
however, the numerous occasions on which HUD raised objections to aspects of
local plans during the first two years of the program and the way those intergovernmental issues were resolved. See Richard P. Nathan and Paul R. Dommel,
"Federal-Local Relations Under Block Grants," Political Science Quarterly 93 (Fall
1978): 421–442. Nathan and Dommel suggest that local jurisdictions "tended to
prevail on substantive issues, whereas on procedural issues HUD tended to prevail." (p. 430)

■ 2. This quote and others used in this section come from materials in the Buffalo area office and central office files of HUD.

□ Source: Publius: The Journal of Federalism 10 (Summer 1980); 28–32. Reprinted
with permission.

Role of incentives.   When it comes to program implementation, money isn't everything. Although local governments generally want to accept federal funds, the use of money as a lever of influence is rarely effective. The reason, quite simply, is that federal agencies seldom actually halt the flow of federal money because of noncompliance with program requirements. Incentives for implementation, therefore, must be more subtle.

A perennial problem in democratic politics is that elected officials have a relatively short time horizon. Taking political credit for new program initiatives has higher value than overseeing effective implementation. There are few incentives to focus on implementation, whereas there are definite political incentives to focus on initiation.

Government employees responsible for implementing programs also lack strong incentives, for two basic reasons: First, the inherent nature of many public programs makes them difficult to evaluate in terms of effectiveness. Second, if we cannot easily measure progress in the program, it is even more difficult to evaluate the role of the civil servant in promoting (or retarding) progress. Bureaucrats have dealt with this problem by substituting private goals (such as budget growth of the agency as a sign of power and prestige) for public goals. The problem, according to Charles Wolf, is that the achievement of private goals not only may be unrelated to the achievement of public goals but also may actually hinder the attainment of public objectives. Wolf calls this development "nonmarket failure."[14]

CONDITIONS OF EFFECTIVE IMPLEMENTATION

There are no guarantees in politics. There are no guarantees in implementation either. Indeed, it is sometimes a wonder that any government programs get much beyond the legislators' drawing boards. When are programs more likely to be implemented successfully? Two keen observers of the process of implementation, Daniel Mazmanian and Paul Sabatier, have identified six important "conditions of effective implementation."[15]

First, they believe that the policy objectives in the legislation should be "clear and consistent." Now this may seem elementary, but you have to remember that during the legislative process policy objectives are frequently altered as bargaining and accommodation take place to create the legislative coalition needed to pass the bill. During the legislative process objectives can become rather vague. What seems like vagueness, however, may really be a tactic to forge a legislative coalition broad enough to pass a bill. A good illustration is the Employment Act of 1946 in which the government was committed to the promotion of "maximum" employment. Early advocates of a government "guarantee" of jobs sought to have the legislation promote "full" employment. But a problem soon surfaced. The definition of full employment was the subject of intense debate. In addition, some sympathetic allies believed that a commitment to full employment must be tempered with a realization that other economic goals may sometimes conflict with the employment objective. The compromise? The concept of "maximum" employment allows a sufficient amount of flexibility for policy-makers who want to balance the objectives of the Employment Act of 1946 with other economic priorities.

Second, the legislation that establishes the policy objective should have a "theory" of the major factors likely to influence its attainment. In their well-known study, *Implementation*, for example, Jeffrey Pressman and Aaron Wildavsky described a program, funded by the Economic Development Administration (EDA) in Washington, D.C., that was supposed to create jobs in the city of Oakland, California. Grants and loans were given to businesses and the port of Oakland to stimulate economic activity, which, in turn, would create jobs for the unemployed. But few permanent jobs were actually created. Pressman and Wildavsky concluded the following:

> Behind the seemingly endless number of roadblocks in the path of the EDA employment program in Oakland lay deficiencies in concept. The economic theory was faulty because it aimed at the wrong target—subsidizing the capital of business enterprises rather than their wage bill. Instead of taking the direct path of paying the employers a subsidy on wages after they had hired minority personnel, the EDA program expanded their capital on the promise that they would later hire the right people. Theoretical defects exacerbated bureaucratic problems.[16]

Implementation was not successful in this situation because the method chosen to achieve the policy objective was conceptually faulty. The result was that few new jobs were created in the city. The lesson? Choosing the right "theory" could have a large impact on the successful implementation of public programs. Consider this lesson in the context of reducing teenage drinking. Which theory seems more plausible to you?

"Will the Correct Theory Please Stand Up?"

Alcohol consumption among teenagers is considered to be a pressing social issue. It is harmful to one's health. It interferes with other more important endeavors such as school, work, friends and family. Few people would deny that reducing teenage drinking is good idea. But how?

The federal government adopted a none-too-subtle approach. The federal government urged states to raise the legal age to twenty-one and threatened the cutoff of federal highway funds if a state failed to raise the legal drinking age. By 1988 all of the states complied. The theory behind the decision to raise the drinking age is elementary. By making what was once legal illegal, and imposing sanctions for breaking the law—sanctions for the underage drinker and, more important, the bar owner or liquor store owner who served or sold the underage individual the alcohol—teenage drinking would go down.

There is an alternative approach. Will teenagers reduce their consumption of alcoholic beverages if the price goes up? Economists call this the "elasticity of demand"—the relationship between the change in the price of a good and the corresponding change in demand. If the demand for alcoholic beverages is "inelastic," increases in the price of beer, wine, and liquor would have little or no impact on consumption. If, on the other hand, demand is "price elastic," a substantial increase in the cost of alcohol will reduce consumption. The implication of this approach is straightforward. Impose a stiff tax (which increases the cost) and consumption should decline. Implementation takes care of itself!

The third condition of successful implementation is that the agencies chosen to implement the programs should be "sympathetic" to them. They should also be given adequate resources to carry out their mission. The EDA program is instructive here too. In the early 1960s, the EDA was not an agency that dealt with urban problems. In 1966, however, Eugene Foley, head of the EDA, wanted to shift the agency's attention from its rural emphasis to urban redevelopment—which was fine as long as Foley was the chief administrator. But Foley left the EDA in 1966, and no sooner did he leave than the project in Oakland was downgraded in Washington.[17] The success of the jobs program in Oakland was adversely affected by the weak institutional support it had in the implementing agency.

The fourth condition of successful implementation seems obvious. Agencies responsible for implementing public programs should be led by administrators who are good managers. In October 1969 the governor of the commonwealth of Massachusetts, Francis Sargent, hired Jerome Miller to head the state's new Department of Youth Services.[18] Miller's objective was to change a juvenile justice system that only punished and housed delinquents to one that treated and rehabilitated them. Miller closed the repressive state institutions and put the juveniles in group homes. He hired new staff sympathetic to his reformist philosophy. A major overhaul of the juvenile justice system took place in three years. There was a little "wrinkle" in Miller's massive reforms, however. Bills weren't paid, people were hired and not paid for months, and some of the group homes (the service providers) were about to go under financially. Federal funds to the Department of Youth Services were suspended. Miller, in the meantime, resigned to take a job in Illinois, leaving an administrative nightmare in his wake.

Programs need continual "stroking." That is, if a program is to be implemented successfully, supporters must work for the program during its formative period; otherwise, it is likely to fade away. Daniel Mazmanian and Paul Sabatier showed the importance of this fifth condition of effective implementation by analyzing the "new communities" program of the Department of Housing and Urban Development. The idea of creating new towns as part of an urban policy started in 1965 under President Johnson. The president was interested in the idea, although it seemed that few other people were. By 1968 only two housing subdivisions—but no entire new communities—were completed. President Nixon, it turned out, was opposed to the idea. The Office of Management and Budget

(OMB) was opposed as well. Congress went ahead anyway and passed the Urban Growth and New Community Development Act of 1970. We already learned that legislation alone does not a program make. By 1975 HUD stopped accepting applications for new communities. Fourteen were approved at that time, well short of the ambitious estimate of one hundred new towns. Mazmanian and Sabatier concluded that the deck was stacked against the program: The president was opposed to it; the agency in charge of it, HUD, was not overly enthusiastic; outside supporters like the National League of Cities and the U.S. Conference of Mayors did not sustain their support. The fifth condition was simply not there.[19]

Finally, successful implementation is affected by changes in the broader socioeconomic climate. Sometimes changes may take place that weaken the rationale behind a statute's objectives. The new communities program, for example, required active participation by real estate investors, developers, and home buyers. But the recession of 1973–1974 seriously hurt the financial position of these important groups. A change in the economic climate, then, had a severe and negative impact on the success of the new communities program. Although the change in the economic climate could not be anticipated during the formative years of the program, it was significant enough to cause a good deal of permanent harm.

The five conditions of effective implementation may lead one to conclude that the prospects for success for intergovernmental programs is low. Indeed, a good deal of political rhetoric over the past decade drew this conclusion. In reality, intergovernmental programs can rarely be judged as complete successes or complete failures. It takes several years to go from program design to program implementation and, finally, program assessment. In addition, a program may be successful in some local governments but not in others. Some programs turn out to have questionable "theoretical" underpinnings—but this may not be clear for several years after the initiation of the program.

In a sober analysis of intergovernmental programs, *When Federalism Works*, Paul Peterson, Barry Rabe, and Kenneth Wong drew some useful lessons about the implementation of intergovernmental programs from case studies of health maintenance, special education, and rent-subsidy programs in four local governments. Some programs are *developmental*—they are designed to improve the competitive position of an area. They may include funds for vocational education or funds to subsidize hospital construction. *Redistributive* federal programs are intended to help low-income people or people designated as needing some type of asistance. Funds to provide educational services to the handicapped or funds to subsidize the rents of low-income individuals fall into this second category. The authors found that developmental programs were relatively easy to manage, and most importantly, local political needs (such as enhancing the popularity of a mayor) and fiscal requirements could be accommodated within federal objectives that were loosely specified. Federal redistributive programs are more controversial and require greater managerial dexterity. But competent policy professionals can serve as buffers between the federal government and local governments. *When Federalism Works* shows when they were more successful and when (and where) they were less successful. Sometimes policy professionals' knowledge, for example, is more persuasive in one setting than another. What is a compelling claim in education, for instance, may be more controversial in housing. When the claims of expertise of policy professionals are debatable other issues may be more important than simply knowledge. Peterson, Rabe, and Wong noted that cost factors will often dominate expertise. Finally, old-style local government politics will rarely take a back seat to implementation based on knowledge of the policy area alone. Yet even though redistributive intergovernmental programs are more complicated than developmental ones, *When Federalism Works* shows that there are solid reasons to put an optimistic interpretation on the history of intergovernmental implementation of many of the federal programs of the past twenty or more years.[20]

IMPLEMENTATION AND THE STREET-LEVEL BUREAUCRAT

Citizens draw conclusions about the effective or ineffective implementation of public programs by observing things that occur around them—or to them. They appraise the conditions of effective implementation by evaluating "street-level bureaucrats."[21]

These are the government employees who ticket our cars, fight crime, pick up the garbage, teach children, and make decisions about whether you are entitled to public assistance, food stamps, or social security disability benefits. Street-level bureaucrats are the workers who actually provide public service. As primary service providers they have a good deal of discretion, and their actions will have a great impact on the implementation of public programs. Let's think about mainstreaming again. What ultimately affects the quality of education that a hearing-impaired child in elementary school receives? Does Public Law 94-142, the Education for All Handicapped Children Act, guarantee that a hearing-impaired child receives a quality education? Of course not. Legislators don't teach the children; teachers do. State bureaucrats in the department of education are too far removed from the real action—which is not in the superintendent's office or the principal's office or the office of the administrator for special education. It is in the classroom: The teacher who is responsible for teaching the hearing-impaired child largely determines whether or not the child learns. Thus mainstreaming as a program rises or falls on the actions of teachers. Street-level bureaucrats have a great deal of power, but another group of actors has entered the stage of public administration. In the next chapter, law and the courts take the leading role.

SUMMARY

Programs are not self-executing; they must be implemented. Implementation is what happens after a program decision is made. It is the process of carrying out a decision, of transforming policy into action. Implementation can involve intergovernmental management. Policy objectives initiated in Washington, D.C., are carried out (or not carried out) in Oshkosh, Salem, San Diego, Laramie, Peoria, or Poughkeepsie.

Since so many programs involve intergovernmental cooperation, implementation is fraught with difficulties. Often national policy objectives are not equally shared by local government officials. Then the essence of implementation is a game of bargaining and conflict. Often the federal government's desire is to achieve a national policy objective, such as "fair housing" or education in the "least restrictive environment." Local governments may appreciate, or even desperately need, the federal funds that accompany this objective, but they rarely appreciate the red tape and strings attached to program requirements. So in the process of implementing the programs, local governments negotiate—they bargain over—just which strings and red tape they must take seriously. Federal bureaucrats, meanwhile, cajole and occasionally threaten local administrators into compliance. We call all of this implementation.

Why do some programs actually succeed? We identified six conditions of effective implementation: statutory clarity, a "theory" of implementation success implicit in the legislation, sympathetic agencies responsible for carrying out the program, managerial competence, continual support during the formative period of the program, and no harmful environmental factors. However, the people responsible for providing services—police personnel, parole officers, teachers, public welfare workers—will often determine whether programs live or die. Street-level bureaucrats, as they have been called, are the crucial link in the policy chain from initiation of a program through its implementation.

You are now in a position to watch the drama of implementation unfold in the following case: "The Siting of a Public Housing Project." Let me warn you in advance: The trials of implementation of which you are about to read are not unique—only the facts are. You may also be interested in the postscript. The housing project you will read about was eventually built; people live in it; there is no longer any controversy surrounding it. After reading the case, answer the following question: Did federalism work?

The Siting of a Public Housing Project

INTRODUCTION

In September 1978 the Fobia Housing Authority (FHA) received a funding commitment from the U.S. Department of Housing and Urban Development (HUD) to construct sixty units (apartments) of low-income public housing for families. This was the first step in a process that should have taken two-and-a-half years from application to project completion and occupancy. The project is now into its fifth year and ground has not yet been broken.

The project has met with every form of opposition, including bureaucratic red tape, neighborhood opposition, local government interference, an angry congressman, an inspector general's audit, and numerous lawsuits. The project's unending difficulties all stem from one issue—where to build it.

This case will describe the course of events that have delayed construction and examine the interrelations of various forms and levels of government as they worked for, and against, the project.

THE SETTING

The city of Fobia has a population of 170,000. It is generally viewed as a conservative, overgrown small town. Fobia has a strong mayoral form of government and a weak, but ambitious, Common Council.

The Democratic mayor is a three-term veteran of the office. Republicans control the council with a five to four majority. The registered Republican voters outnumber the Democrats on a citywide basis.

The Fobia Housing Authority is a separate, quasi-public agency, state mandated and federally funded. The FHA owns and manages the city's twenty-five hundred units of public housing but has not built any new family housing in more than fifteen years. Aside from its own tenant constituency, the FHA has maintained a low profile in city government and in the community as a whole.

The Authority's Board of Commissioners and the director are appointed by the major. The present director was appointed when the major was first elected in 1970. The authority is one of the largest in the state and is the third oldest in the country. Its reputation among its peers is solid and well respected.

THE FEDERAL PERSPECTIVE

The U.S. Housing Act of 1937 enabled the federal government to make monies available to locally established Public Housing Authorities (PHAs) for the provision of "decent, safe, and sanitary housing." The PHAs are state-mandated authorities. A public housing project is built with tax-exempt bonds issued by the PHA. The debt service and operating expenses are paid for by the federal government through an Annual Contributions Contract, which supplements the rental income. The PHAs pay the locality a payment in lieu of taxes (PILOT). The structure of a PHA and its relation to the locality varies from city to city and state to state.

Projects are built to provide adequate housing for low- and moderate-income people at a rent they can afford. During the first twenty-five years of the program it was considered very successful. Projects tended to be filled with upwardly mobile families who needed temporary assistance while they were getting started. But by the 1960s, as the middle class left for the suburbs, the projects became the permanent homes of a "new welfare class."

Public housing went through many changes including the enactment of the first set of federal regulations governing their operations, federally established maximum and minimum rents, and a performance-based funding system. Overall, the federal government tried to exert more control over public housing projects. The federal government also wanted to professionalize the management of the projects as a way to protect the taxpayers' investment in low-cost public housing.

In 1977 new federal regulations stipulated that new public housing could no longer be built in census tracts where the minority concentration was more than in the Standard Metropolitan Statistical Area (SMSA). The new regulation was a major factor in the site-selection process and in the eventual selection of the Josiah Avenue project site. High concentration areas are called "minority impacted." New projects, like the Josiah Avenue project, were expected to attract an income mix of tenants who would provide greater rental income, stabilize the PHAs, and reduce the federal operating subsidy needed to maintain the projects. It was also an attempt to desegregate public housing and provide "equal housing opportunities."

Another of the new regulation directives requires increased private sector involvement in the development of new public housing. Until 1977, for instance, the PHAs could opt to use either the conventional or the "turnkey" development method. Under the conventional method, the PHA acts as the developer. The 1977 regulations set a "preference" for the turnkey method. (The conventional method could only be used if the PHA could demonstrate a cost savings.) Under the turnkey method, the PHA advertises for developers to submit proposals. The developer does the architectural work and bids the project. In addition, the developer, not the PHA, selects the site. The developer who submits the best proposal enters into a contract of sale with the PHA and HUD to build the project. Upon completion the developer will then "turn over the keys" to the PHA. The developer receives payment upon completion and acceptance of the project from both the PHA and HUD.

THE PROCESS

In March 1978 the regional area office of the HUD Area Office sent out a Notice of Funding Availability (NOFA) to PHAs requesting applications. The NOFA specified the funding for new construction, family public housing, and the turnkey method. The Fobia Housing Authority applied for and received a funding reservation for sixty units in September 1978.

In the spring of 1979, the FHA began to put together a developer's packet. A developer's packet sets forth the proposal guidelines that the prospective bidders should follow. Some of the guidelines are HUD regulations and others are local preferences. The packet is approved by HUD before it is advertised.

The FHA's packet stated a local preference for townhouse-style construction in small clusters of buildings (no more than six units per build-ing). Preference would be given to proposals using city-owned vacant land.

When responding to the request for proposals, the developer is re-quired to submit a preliminary site report, preliminary drawings and specifications, evidence of site control, cost estimates, and references. The FHA then rates the proposals using a HUD guide form and ranks them by score. The score is selected, and then all of the packets, rating sheets, and the FHA recommendation are sent to HUD for review and approval.

Some of the criteria for evaluation include:

1. Availability of utilities.
2. Site characteristics such as proper zoning, minority concentra-tion, and environmental impact
3. Access to services such as public transportation
4. Overall design and functional objectives
5. Safety and security
6. Quality of proposed construction
7. Energy efficiency
8. Comparative price

All of the responding developers used a city-owned site. The FHA rated and ranked the responses, selected the Greene Homes proposal, and sent them off to HUD for review in November 1979.

In April 1980 HUD rejected every proposal for being in minority-im-pacted areas. The FHA and the city requested and received a compromise between the HUD regulations and the city's housing goals. HUD allowed the FHA to readvertise for proposals in which "at least thirty of the sixty units are located outside areas of minority concentration."

In July 1980 the FHA readvertised for two-site proposals. All of the same developers responded to the second request for proposals. One of the developers had requested permission to submit a single-site proposal, with all of the units outside the impacted areas. All other responses were for two sites.

The FHA again rated and ranked the proposals and came up with a tie. The smaller sites were thought to be crowded and less optimally located. The FHA requested that HUD allow the FHA to make a split award be-tween the two developers, taking the best of the sites. In January 1981 HUD denied the request and urged the FHA to reevaluate the proposals. The FHA did so and tentatively selected the single-site Goniff proposal. This selection meant not using city-owned land, which had previously been a heavily weighted factor in the evaluations.

In April 1981 a HUD representative from the regional office went to Fobia and reviewed all of the proposals and toured the sites. He con-firmed the choice of the Goniff proposal and urged the FHA to proceed.

The routine development process would then follow a series of steps. The following is a summary of the milestones in that process.

1. The FHA announces the award of the project to Goniff.
2. Goniff prepares construction documents and submits them to the FHA for review and approval.
3. The FHA sends the documents as approved to HUD for review and approval.
4. A development conference is held with all parties at the regional HUD office. The various HUD departments present their comments and revisions. This essentially is a negotiating session.
5. Goniff then goes through the city departments for their review and approval. This is strictly a construction review conducted by the fire and engineering departments and others.
6. HUD then issues Final Site Approval and conducts a final review of the construction documents and land acquisition and closing documents.
7. The FHA, HUD, and Goniff sign a contract of sale, and construction begins.

This summary represents what should have occurred. The next section describes what actually occurred and why.

THE EVENTS

The Goniff proposal consists of a single seven-acre site that is hilly and wooded and located at the end of a dead-end street on land owned by a large university in the city. The plans included finished basements, family rooms, individual patios, a community building, and other "suburban-like" amenities. These factors, its location outside the impacted areas, and Goniff's competitive price were the deciding factors in the selection.

Before submitting the proposals to HUD, informal protocol was followed when the Common Council member who represented the area that included the site was briefed on the project. The newly elected Ms. Miller (liberal Democrat) expressed extreme dissatisfaction with the Goniff site because of its location in a predominantly middle-class white neighborhood. Miller was told about the HUD constraints and the history of the selection of the site. She flatly rejected any explanation and stormed out of the meeting without further discussion.

Although the FHA was not a participant in this meeting it was advised of the outcome. The FHA decided that any opposition would be minor and short lived. Besides, there simply wasn't another site to choose. The FHA officials planned to proceed with the project.

During the summer and fall the FHA and Goniff went to the HUD regional office for no fewer than three development conferences. Each time HUD would cite additional restrictions on the design and request more changes. The regional office was receiving instructions from HUD Washington to take cost-reduction measures with all new projects. The FHA and Goniff resisted measures that would mean a reduction in the value of the tenants' living conditions (for example, smaller bedrooms) and cutbacks in quality that would result in more maintenance (for example, cheaper kitchen cabinets). The working relations among HUD, the FHA, and Goniff were becoming strained and slow moving. Despite the problems, Final Site Approval was granted on August 9, 1981.

One of the local actions necessary to proceed with the project was an application to the Planning Commission for a resubdivision. This action would consolidate the seventy small parcels that made up the existing site into a single large parcel. The resubdivision application was the only step in the whole development process that required notification of the proposed project to area residents and a public hearing.

Goniff applied for the resubdivision shortly after the site approval was granted. The hearing was scheduled for October, one month before the mayor was up for reelection. Fearing adverse reaction, the application was rescheduled for late November. The mayor was narrowly reelected.

On November 13 (a Friday), the FHA, Goniff, and HUD met and came to a final agreement on the construction documents. The date for signing the contract of sale was set for December 21, 1981. The process to date had taken three years. It should have taken one and a half years.

THE OPPOSITION BEGINS

The same weekend of November 13, the notices were published in the papers concerning the resubdivision and public hearing. Postcards were sent to area residents announcing the upcoming hearing. On Tuesday the papers carried articles about the proposed project, quoting angry neighbors and an angrier Miller. The headlines shouted eleventh-hour, dead-of-the-night trickery. Miller claimed never to have been informed of the project or the site and led the residents to battle.

Josiah Avenue residents went on record as saying, "This project will make our quiet neighborhood into a hotbed of crime." The media quickly picked up on the discrimination issue. Miller quickly regrouped and organized the neighborhood, instructing them to voice more acceptable complaints such as noise, traffic congestion, drainage, and sewer problems.

On November 18 the Planning Commission held its public hearing in front of three television stations, the newspapers, and a standing-room-only crowd. The Planning Commission (all of whom are mayor appointed) had the difficult job of making it clear to the angry residents that they were not there to review the proposed use for the land since the land was properly zoned for multifamily housing. They only had the power and right to review the grounds for resubdivision. The application was approved on December 9.

Miller and the newly formed Josiah Avenue Residents Association appealed to their congressman, William McNutt. Congressman McNutt was a first-term Republican who had never before held public office. He was also a member of the House Subcommittee for Housing and Community Development. His area was being redistricted, and he was slated to run against a two-term, lifelong politician, in a tough primary.

McNutt requested that the main office, HUD Washington, review the project for irregularities just days before the scheduled signing of the contract of sale. Under routine processing, HUD Washington would not ordinarily become involved in the review and approval of a project. (This authority is vested with the regional office manager.) This highly unusual review lasted until June 1982 when McNutt announced that the project was dead. HUD Washington had determined that the mayor's letter of endorsement of the project had been sent prematurely—before the selection of the Goniff site. Washington publicly proclaimed that it was an Area Office procedural error; the FHA would have to readvertise and start all over again.

The regional office manager's reaction was anger at Washington's interference in the process. In fact, the regional HUD office informally urged the FHA to take legal action.

The FHA, Goniff, and the Public Housing Tenants Association filed suit against HUD, pointing out that the mayor had sent three letters in support of the project at various stages of the process. They contended that the so-called error of sending the first letter too soon was not grounds for rejection of the project.

In late July the HUD regional area manager called the director of the FHA and requested that the FHA seek a waiver of the requirement for the mayor's letter. The FHA promptly complied and requested the waiver; the regional office granted it, and the lawsuit was dropped. (The Washington HUD office involvement in this was low keyed but approving.) The project was reinstated on August 3, 1982.

The resulting newspaper coverage quoted Miller as saying, "I think William McNutt should be called to task for this. Obviously, his word doesn't count for much in Washington."

The FHA and Goniff blew the dust off the plans and began where they had left off. In addition, they held a meeting of the major social service agencies to make a presentation of the project to point out how the plans differed from traditional public housing. (The meeting was a failure because of the controversy surrounding the project.)

The local papers were printing at least one letter to the editor a week against the project. Area residents were portrayed as victims of arbitrary government action.

The Josiah Avenue Residents Association hired an attorney in August. Miller lobbied to gather the support of the other members of the Common Council. She won over all of the Republican councillors and all but two of the Democrats. During the following two months there was a flurry of attempts to halt the project before the November elections.

PAPER STREETS

In August the city auditor, Rick Victor, announced that he had found a way for the Common Council to stop the project. He had discovered the presence of two "paper streets" through the project on several of the city engineering maps.

Paper streets are unbuilt streets that are shown in the official city map and represent an easement on the property's title. Sidewalks and a sewer had been installed by the city in 1908 along a section of one of the "streets." The Common Council has jurisdiction over city-owned land and thus over the paper streets. The corporation counsel, Jeff Smith, immediately countered that the streets did not appear on the official city maps and did not appear as an easement on the property. Rick Victor was quoted as saying, "If it quacks like a duck and walks like a duck, it's a duck. If it's got sidewalks and a sewer, it's a street."

The Common Council passed legislation in late August denying the city's abandonment of paper streets. Smith flatly refused to enforce the legislation.

The controversy caused the title insurance company to balk and rescind its insurance binder to Goniff. Title insurance was essential to the purchase of the property and to HUD approval of the contract of sale between the FHA and Goniff. In addition, the option on the land would expire at the end of the month, and the university was hinting that it would not give an extension.

REZONING

At this same time the Josiah Avenue Residents Association and Miller sponsored a request to the council to rezone the area from the multifamily designation to a single-family designation. Jeff Smith made it clear to the council that it did not have the jurisdiction to make a zoning change. It would have to take its request to the Planning Commission. He also advised that to rezone the area would be a poorly timed and possibly illegal action.

If the Planning Commission approved the request, the zoning would be changed. If it denied the request, the council could step in and override its decision. The mayor could then veto the council action, and the council could override the mayor with a three-fourths majority vote.

Goniff threatened to hold the individual councillors personally liable, claiming that the rezoning would be "confiscatory and exclusionary." The FHA threatened a civil rights suit.

The air was thick with hostility. The local papers' editorial headlines ran, "Common Council Needs a Civics Teacher, Not a Lawyer," and "The Josiah Avenue Project Shows Where the Power Lies."

The council members asked Smith if he would represent them if Goniff sued them. Smith told them that he represented the city as a whole, not some neighborhood or interest group. The editorials, meanwhile, went on to say, "What is really getting under their [councillors] skins is that whole issue of whether anything built on Josiah Avenue proves that the Common Council has no power. The power lies with the Mayor."

The Planning Commission reviewed the rezoning request, held another well-attended public hearing, and denied the zoning change. The Common Council overrode the denial by one vote. The ball was in the mayor's court.

The mayor stated, "I'm trying to be pragmatic. There is no sense in trying to make a gesture when it's only a gesture." It seemed clear that the council would have just enough votes to override a veto. The whole thing was bound to end up in the courts.

Jeff Smith informed the councillors that rezoning the area would be an illegal action and that they could be held personally liable. This hit home hard because the councillors had just been found personally liable on a separate issue by the courts.

The mayor vetoed the Common Council's action. The Common Council debated. The paper ran the headline "Josiah Zoning Veto Override Unlikely." On October 21, 1982, the Common Council vetoed and overrode the mayor's veto. The zoning was changed to single family. The Josiah Avenue Residents Association's lawyer was credited for the coup.

MEANWHILE . . .

While all of this was occurring, the FHA and Goniff proceeded. Goniff secured another extension to the option to the property by sending the university a legal notice reminding it that it was under contract to provide "clear and insurable title." The university assisted Goniff in securing a new title insurance company that would issue a policy.

Goniff also secured a building permit on August 13 (another Friday), long before the zone was changed. He hoped to protect the project against a zone change under the "grandfather clause," a reference to the immunity of preexisting conditions to changes in the zoning ordinances. The FHA, Goniff, and HUD scheduled a final review conference for the second week in September.

INSPECTOR GENERAL'S AUDIT

Shortly before the primaries, Congressman McNutt requested a review of the project by the Office of the Inspector General. An inspector was sent to Fobia immediately. The regional office of HUD unofficially called it a formality, a move to appease the congressman before the elections. The inspector gave the regional office a verbal go-ahead to sign the final contract of sale.

MEANWHILE . . .

On September 29 the contract of sale was signed, the funds were secured, and Goniff had HUD approval to begin construction. Goniff chose not to close on the purchase of the land and begin construction until the zoning issue was resolved. The lawyers did not feel that starting construction would protect them against a subsequent zone change under the grandfather clause. They advised against the financial risk, which proved to be good cautious advice given the eventual rezoning.

Congressman McNutt defeated his opponent in the primaries.

LAWSUITS

The Josiah Avenue Residents Association, the Common Council, and Congressman McNutt filed an enjoining suite against Goniff, claiming that the project would endanger their neighborhood.

Goniff and the FHA filed suit against the city on the zoning and paper streets issues. They did not sue the individual councillors.

The FHA and the Public Housing Tenants Association filed a civil rights suit against the city.

The project appeared to be destined for lengthy court battles, and the 1982 building season would be lost.

HUD RESCINDS THE CONTRACT OF SALE

On October 25, only four days after the Common Council changed the zoning, Congressman McNutt announced, for the second time, that the project was dead. Headlines read, "HUD Yanks Developer to Josiah Avenue Project." Again this came as a complete surprise to the HUD area office, the FHA, Goniff, and local officials. Again HUD Washington cited a minor technicality as grounds for rejecting the project even after HUD had signed the contract. The inspector general's office was publicly credited with the determination. McNutt had quietly met with HUD Secretary Pierce just two days earlier.

The inspector general's report noted that the second round of advertising had called for proposals using two sites. Goniff's proposal was for a single site. The advertising did not clearly state that a single site in a nonimpacted area was acceptable. HUD used this as grounds for rescinding the contract of sale and advised the FHA to begin readvertising all over again.

Goniff was quoted, "Here we are a week before elections, and unusual things happen." The paper also quoted the HUD regional area manager: "The regional office felt that they had processed the application correctly, the Inspector General's office is basically saying it was not processed correctly."

Again the regional office was publicly embarrassed and angered as a result of Congressman McNutt's influence in Washington. They again informally advised the FHA to seek legal recourse.

THE COMEBACK

The mayor, the director of the FHA, the director of Community Development, and Jeff Smith petitioned for and received a meeting with Secretary Pierce in Washington. The papers reported, "Fobia Housing Authority said Pierce seemed pleased both with the sketches of the project as well as the city officials' presentation on the need for the housing." The FHA director said, "Pierce said he would look into it and get back to us." McNutt was quoted as saying, "The Mayor is just being a real SOB on this thing."

On November 26 the paper street and zoning issues came before the state supreme court. The judge reserved decision. On December 7 the judge issued a summary judgment dismissing the paper streets issue as having no legal merit. The zoning issue would have to go to trial.

In May 1983 the zoning issue was tried before the state supreme court and the judge ruled that the council had "acted in excess of the power granted them and therefore illegally." He further stated that the council's zoning ordinance was not "in accordance with well considered plan but was an isolated, unfounded, unsupported, and arbitrary change in the permissible land use of the tract."

A councillor was quoted as saying, "I'm bitterly disappointed. Even the City Council can't fight City Hall."

The paper's editorial section printed the following opinion:

> We would be shocked if the Board of Estimate, which the mayor dominates, would commit the city's financial backing to unlimited legal action since (1) there's little likelihood of success and (2) this week's court decision was in support of the mayor's original position.
>
> We're not inclined to assign motives to the actions of our elected leaders beyond those they tell us about, so we'll assume neither side of this dispute was entered into on anything less than the loftiest of moral grounds. We are disturbed, though, when members of the Council continue to give hope to the residents of the Josiah area where, in fact, the courts have left little room to be hopeful. The chance of a successful appeal appears negligible.

On July 11 the council voted to file an appeal. The mayor allowed them to continue to retain the special attorney—paid for by the city.

On September 22, a U.S. District Court judge issued a summary judgment against HUD for rescinding the contract of sale, stating, "HUD knew months in advance exactly where these units were to be built. HUD's contention that it has the unfettered discretion to terminate an otherwise binding contract is equally without merit." The contract of sale was reinstated.

CONCLUSION

To date HUD has not decided whether or not to appeal the court's decision to reinstate the contract of sale. The council's appeal of the zoning issue is pending. The area residents and councillors have publicly stated that they will find new ways to block the project. A resident was quoted: "We're really pleased that we've held them off for two years, and we're not going to quit now."

POSTSCRIPT

HUD did not appeal. The zoning appeal was rejected. The developer eventually built the housing. Opposition withered. Tenants moved in. Case closed.

QUESTIONS FOR DISCUSSION

1. Think about the local political situation. How did it affect the implementation process?
2. The Fobia Housing Authority was relatively autonomous from local government. Did this make any significant difference?
3. Think about the actions that were taken by the regional HUD office and Washington HUD. How did the actions of the two HUD offices seem to affect the implementation of the housing project?
4. What could the FHA have done differently in its relations with HUD, the Common Council, and the Josiah area residents?
5. Assume that you are a staff member at the FHA. The director has asked you to prepare a memorandum entitled "Implementation Lessons Learned from the Josiah Avenue Public Housing Controversy." What would you include in this memo?

CHRONOLOGY

The Process

1.	Fund reservation	9/19/78
2.	Initial advertisement	7/26/79
3.	Initial proposals rejected by HUD; FHA instructed to readvertise for two site proposals	4/16/80
4.	Readvertised project, specifying two sites	7/28/80
5.	Proposal deadline extended to	9/17/80
6.	Goniff asks if one site would be responsive to advertisement	9/10/80
7.	FHA recommends split award	12/15/80
8.	HUD rejects split award	1/31/81
9.	FHA/HUD make a tentative selection; Goniff proposal	4/81
10.	Final Site Approval awarded	8/9/81

The Events

11.	Resubdivision request	11/4/81
12.	Planning Commission approval	12/9/81
13.	Congressman McNutt requests HUD review	12/81
14.	HUD rejects project; timing of the mayor's letter	6/28/82
15.	HUD reinstates project; waiver of letter	8/3/82

Paper Streets

16.	Victor/Council raise paper street issue	8/2/82
17.	Council votes not to abandon streets	8/82

Rezoning

18.	Council requests rezoning to single family	8/23/82
19.	City Planning Commission denies request	9/22/82
20.	County Planning Commission denies request	9/28/82
21.	Council overrides Planning Commission	10/4/82
22.	Mayoral veto	10/14/82
23.	Council override	10/21/82
24.	HUD, FHA, Goniff execute Contract for Sale	9/21/82

Inspector General's Audit

25.	Inspector comes to Fobia	9/13/82

HUD Rescinds Contract for Sale

26.	HUD rescinds Contract; two-site issue	10/25/82

Lawsuits

27.	Goniff files with State Supreme Court to overturn zoning and paper street legislation	10/29/82
28.	Goniff and FHA file suit against HUD for contract rescission	11/29/82

The Comeback

29.	State Supreme Court dismisses paper streets issue	12/7/82
30.	State Supreme Court hears zoning trial and reinstates multifamily zoning	5/83
31.	Common Council appeals zoning decision	7/11/83
32.	U.S. District Court reinstates HUD Contract for Sale	9/22/83

□ *This case was written by Katherine L. Potter under the supervision of Jeffrey Straussman. Although the events reported are true, the names have been changed.*

NOTES

1. See Bernard J. Frieden and Marshall Kaplan, *The Politics of Neglect: Urban Aid from Model Cities to Revenue Sharing* (Cambridge, Mass.: MIT Press, 1975).
2. For an insider's account, see Robert F. Kennedy, *Thirteen Days: A Memoir of the Cuban Missile Crisis* (New York: W. W. Norton, 1971).
3. The topic of implementation is widely discussed in public policy analysis. The classic is Jeffrey Pressman and Aaron Wildavsky, *Implementation,* 2d ed. (Berkeley: University of California Press, 1979); Eugene Bardach, *The Implementation Game: What Happens after a Bill Becomes a Law* (Cambridge, Mass.: MIT Press, 1977); Richard Elmore, "Organizational Models of Social Program Implementation," *Public Policy* 26 (Spring 1978); 185–228.
4. Erwin C. Hargrove, The Missing Link (Washington, D.C.: Urban Institute, 1975).
5. See, for example, Tana Pesso, "Local Welfare Offices: Managing the Intake Process," *Public Policy* 26 (Spring 1978): 305–330.
6. This section is based, in part, on the study by the Congressional Budget Office, *The Food Stamp Program: Income or Food Supplementation?* (Washington, D.C.: U.S. Government Printing Office, 1977).
7. See Lester Thurow, "Equity versus Efficiency in Law Enforcement," *Public Policy* 18 (Spring 1970): 321–354.
8. William S. Vickery, "Economic Efficiency and Pricing," *Public Prices for Public Products,* Selma Mushkin, ed. (Washington, D.C.: Urban Institute, 1972), pp. 53–72.
9. For a very good discussion of how political feasibility constrains local revenue decisions, see Arnold Meltsner, *The Politics of City Revenue* (Berkeley: University of California Press, 1971).
10. This discussion of the CETA program is based on Carl E. Van Horn, "Implementing CETA: The Federal Role," *Policy Analysis* 4 (Spring 1978): 159–183.
11. This concept is discussed in Helen Ingram, "Policy Implementation through Bargaining: The Case of Federal Grants-in-Aid," *Public Policy* 25 (Fall 1977): 499–526.
12. Van Horn, "Implementing CETA," p. 176.
13. Ibid., p. 170.
14. Charles Wolf, Jr., "A Theory of Non-Market Failures," *The Public Interest,* no. 55 (Spring 1979): 114–133.
15. Daniel A. Mazmanian and Paul A. Sabatier, *Implementation and Public Policy* (Glenview, Ill.: Scott, Foresman, 1983), p. 41.
16. Pressman and Wildavsky, *Implementation,* p. 147.
17. Ibid., p. 48.
18. The description of Dr. Jerome Miller and his experience as commissioner of the Department of Youth Services comes from "Department of Youth Services" (HBS Case Services, Harvard Business School, 9-378-940).
19. Mazmanian and Sabatier, *Implementation,* pp. 76–84.
20. Paul E. Peterson, Barry G. Rabe, and Kenneth K. Wong, *When Federalism Works* (Washington, D.C.: Brookings Institution, 1986).
21. For an analysis of street-level bureaucrats, see Michael Lipsky, *Street-Level Bureaucracy* (New York: Russell Sage Foundation, 1980).

FOR FURTHER READING

Bardach, Eugene. *The Implementation Game: What Happens after a Bill Becomes a Law.* Cambridge, Mass.: MIT Press, 1977.

    Based on mental-health legislation in California, Bardach argues that implementation is a series of "games."

Lipsky, Michael. *Street-Level Bureaucracy.* New York: Russell Sage Foundation, 1980.

    The most complete statement about the role of local government service providers in the implementation process.

Mazmanian, Daniel A., and Paul A. Sabatier. *Implementation and Public Policy.* Glenview, Ill.: Scott, Foresman, 1983.

    Five public policy cases are developed and interpreted in light of the authors' perspective on effective implementation.

Peterson, Paul E., Barry G. Rabe, and Kenneth K. Wong. *When Federalism Works.* Washington, D.C.: Brookings Institution, 1986.

    Coming when it was fashionable to criticize the ineffectiveness of many intergovernmental programs, this solid study evaluates the implementation of nine federal grant-in-aid programs in four local governments.

Pressman, Jeffrey L., and Aaron Wildavsky. *Implementation.* 2d ed. Berkeley: University of California Press, 1979.

    This study of the EDA's employment programs in Oakland, California, stimulated the subject of "implementation analysis."

Williams, Walter, et al. *Studying Implementation.* Chatham, N.J.: Chatham House Publishers, 1982.

    A collection of essays that focus on research problems in implementation analysis.

CHAPTER 12

Law, the Courts, and Public Administration

A caseworker in a local government social services department overheard a neighbor of one of her case recipients comment, "Mrs. Smith is ripping off the welfare department again. She's working and collecting her welfare check at the same time." Now suppose the caseworker said to herself, "Mrs. Smith failed to inform me that she is working. Her public assistance benefits will have to be terminated since she is clearly breaking the law." Let's suppose, furthermore, that Mrs. Smith's benefits were terminated. Would she have any recourse?

Consider a much different situation. A citizens' survey in Frugle City showed that a majority of the respondents thought that the city was "too dirty." The city manager received approval from the city council to begin an "area beautification" program as long as its cost were kept "within bounds." The manager calculated wage costs at the federal minimum wage and informed the council that the program would cost $150,000. Council members balked; it was too expensive, they claimed. When the city manager tried to assure the council that the minimum wage was all that he planned to pay, one council member retorted, "Why pay minimum wage? Offer less than the minimum wage. There are a lot of people around here who would be more than happy to take the area beautification jobs." Can a city pay less than the federal minimum wage?

Now consider a completely different set of circumstances. Podunk High was having its Winter Fling. A group of boys, believing that the party should "liven up" a bit, spiked the punch by slipping a bottle of vodka into it when the chaperones weren't looking. When one of the teachers took a drink and noticed the distinct change that had taken place in the punch bowl, she notified Podunk High's principal, Mrs. Boarring. "A violation of state law and school board policy," exclaimed the shocked Mrs. Boarring. She found the culprits and identified them to the school board. They were suspended from school for two weeks for their little prank. Was the school board legally justified in taking the action?

One more situation: Iggy "the Blade" McNasty was found guilty of first-degree murder after stabbing someone to death in a barroom brawl. McNasty said the victim "looked at him funny" so he wanted to "teach him a lesson." McNasty's defense lawyer said that the victim taunted poor Iggy, knowing that "the Blade" wouldn't want to jeopardize his parole from a previous criminal sentence. The jury didn't buy it. McNasty was sentenced to life imprisonment. After serving a couple of years in the state prison, McNasty noticed that more and more inmates were being brought to the prison. "The place is going to burst soon," thought McNasty. "Even a prisoner has some rights. I barely have room to lie down in this cell." Was McNasty correct? Did he have any "rights," as he claimed?

These four situations—fictitious but based on real events—share one broad theme in common. Each of them highlights a place where law, the courts, and public administration meet. McNasty's complaint, for instance, focuses on alleged constitutional rights violations. Podunk High's punch bowl episode concerns the legal liabilities that public officials might incur when they make decisions. Frugle's area-beautification program is (ultimately) a question about the meaning of federalism. The first episode—the termination of public assistance benefits—puts us squarely in the middle of the administrative law process. As even these brief vignettes point out, no public administrator can function effectively without at least a rudimentary knowledge of the legal foundations of administrative practice—which is the purpose of this chapter.

It is wise to begin by examining the Constitution of the United States. Although the legal foundations of public administration in the Constitution are not described in detail, they nevertheless form the bedrock of contemporary issues and controversies.

SEPARATION OF POWERS

Article I of the Constitution of the United States of America establishes the legislative powers in Congress. Nevertheless, the ten sections of Article I will reveal few explicit constitutional guidelines about the legal underpinnings of legislative and administrative relationships. Section 8, for instance, lists the various powers held by Congress (power to tax, regulate commerce, declare war, and so on). To carry out these powers, Congress may "make all laws which shall be necessary and proper for carrying into Execution the foregoing Powers." Congress does not literally carry out, or execute, its laws. This function is given to the executive branch. The Constitution vests executive power in the president and grants specific responsibilities such as the appointment of subordinates and the management of executive agencies. The delicate relations among the branches is manifested in the famed "checks and balances" that at once preserve the separation of powers and insure that no one branch becomes too powerful. Appointment of selected presidential appointees, for example, requires the "advice and consent" of the Senate—a constitutional principle that preserves checks and balances. Similarly, the ability of the judiciary to find legislative and executive acts unconstitutional allows the federal courts to check and balance the legislative and executive branches.

Modern constitutional scholarship has shown that powers are shared rather than literally separated.[1] This is best illustrated by the *delegation* of legislative authority. Simply stated, delegation refers to the legislative authority granted to administrative agencies in the executive branch to carry out the law passed by Congress. Just what is delegated and, more generally, the breadth of delegation makes up one important component of the legal foundations of public administration.[2] Second, although agencies are charged with executing legislative intent, Congress has the power to review the way executive agencies go about implementing legislation through *oversight* of agency activities. An important constitutional dimension of the legal context of public administration, then, is the balance between delegation and oversight. Let's consider delegation first.

Delegation of Powers

Phillip Cooper, in *Public Law and Public Administration*, identified four sources of discretionary authority.[3] First, agencies are given delegated authority because legislatures pass statutes that contain language susceptible to various interpretation. Vague statutory language gives agencies much discretion to interpret the intent of the statute. After interpreting intent, agencies may have a great deal of latitude in deciding how a policy objective will be implemented.

This basic distinction between the formulation of policy through law and its implementation was observed by Woodrow Wilson in his famous essay "The Study of Administration" almost a hundred years ago. Wilson wrote, "Public administration is detailed and systematic execution of public law. Every particular application of general law is an act of administration."[4] This distinction between public law and administration is still useful today because it highlights the constitutional issue of the separation of powers between the legislative and executive branches of government.

A second source of delegational authority is expertise. Administrators often have served in their positions for longer periods than elected representatives and have acquired a great deal of knowledge about their specialized areas of expertise. In contrast, legislators are often generalists. They must deal with many different policy domains, rarely having the time or interest in truly mastering one area. Naturally, legislators who have been in office a long time are exceptions; they may have a great deal of substantive expertise in a policy domain. But even these legislators do not have the same type of direct access to scientific and technical staffs that high-level administrators have to help them make decisions.

A third source of delegation is what Cooper calls the "experience factor."[5] When an administrator has served for a number of years in the same agency, the administrator is the repository of the agency's "institutional memory"—which means that the administrator will often know what is workable and what is not. When it is necessary to acknowledge the importance of experience in carrying out legislative intent, the administrator is given discretion. Discretion is accompanied by delegated authority.

Fourth, agencies are often able to muster political support from public opinion and interest groups. In budgeting, for example, agencies bring these resources to bear before the legislature during the appropriations process. When agencies can successfully generate outside political support for their policy positions, legislators will defer to their judgment. Political support, then, is a fourth source of delegated authority.

Judicial Interpretations of the Delegation of Authority

How much delegation of legislative power is defensible? The Constitution, obviously, gives no guidance on this score. Rather, it has been left to the courts to answer this difficult, though important, question. Kenneth Culp Davis, one of the foremost experts on administrative law, noted that the Supreme Court has almost always upheld the right of Congress to delegate power to executive branch agencies. He wrote, "If Congress were to go to the ball game and authorize the page boys to legislate, the delegation would be unconstitutional. But no responsible delegation is likely to be held unconstitutional."[6]

During President Franklin D. Roosevelt's New Deal, efforts were made to expand the federal government's intervention in the economy. During his first term in office legal challenges to some of his programs reached the Supreme Court. In 1935 the Supreme Court heard two cases concerning the constitutionality of the delegation of legislative power to administrative agencies. Both cases centered on the National Industrial Recovery Act—the legislative centerpiece of his administration's efforts to combat the depression that was afflicting the nation. In *Panama Refining Co. v. Ryan* (1935), the court held that the exercise of presidential power, granted in a section of the act (power to regulate the transportation of illegally produced oil), was an unconstitutional delegation of legislative power." In *Schecter Poultry Corp. v. United States* (1935), the Supreme Court held that the section of the act that gave the president the authority to establish "codes of fair competition" was "an unconstitutional delegation of legislative power."[7] What is important to remember about the *Panama* and *Schecter* cases is that they are anomalies. They are rare instances when delegation of legislative power has been successfully challenged before the court.

Although direct (and successful) constitutional challenges have been rare, two types of judicial narrowing of delegated power have taken place.[8] Donald Barry and Howard Whitcomb, in *The Legal Foundations of Public Administration*, cited *Kent v. Dulles* (1958) as one type of the judicial narrowing of congressional delegation. In this case the defendants were not granted U.S. passports because of a regulation initiated by the secretary of state denying passports to people who would "further communism." The secretary's regulation was based on his interpretation of a congressional statute that gave him power to "grant and issue passports." The Supreme Court held: "Since we start with an exercise by an American citizen of an activity included in constitutional protection, we will not readily infer that Congress gave the Secretary of State unbridled discretion to grant or withhold it."[9] In other words, the Court believed that Congress could not have delegated to the secretary of state the power to restrict travel. The Supreme Court interpreted travel to be included in the meaning of liberty embodied in the Fifth Amendment to the Constitution.

In *Environmental Defense Fund Inc. v. Ruckelshaus* (1971), the U.S. Court of Appeals, District of Columbia Circuit, adopted a second type of judicial narrowing of delegated power. In this case the court decided that when Congress fails to specify how a statute should be implemented, it is the responsibility of the agency to do so. *Environmental Defense Fund* is an important case because, in his opinion, Chief Judge David Bazelon articulated the position that the courts have a responsibility to scrutinize administrative actions that are based on delegated power. Judge Bazelon wrote, "Courts should require administrative officers to articulate the standards and principles that govern their discretionary decisions in as much detail as possible."[10] This view of the proper scope of judicial review places the courts on equal footing with the legislative and the executive branches in the administration of the public's business.

Legislative Oversight of Administration

There is no specific statement in Article I of the Constitution concerning the power of Congress to scrutinize the activities of executive-branch agencies. Nevertheless, it is only a small leap of logic to see that if Congress is given the authority to enact law, it must be able to see to it that the law is carried out. This process is known as legislative oversight of administration.

You have already encountered an illustration of legislative oversight in the budgeting chapter in the discussion of appropriations. Look again at the interchange between Representative Rooney and the foreign service officer over the infamous "chop suey" episode. This episode, actually, is about legislative oversight. Rooney was concerned with more than the activities of the Chinese-speaking foreign service officer in London. He was really probing into some of the practices and procedures of the State Department—and he didn't like what he found.

The budget process, especially the appropriations phase, provides perhaps the most extensive opportunities for legislative oversight. When agencies ask for money, appear before legislative committees in budget hearings, and attempt to justify their activities and programs, elected representatives are in a good position to ask administrators about what they did or didn't do, and why. But budgeting is not the only time that the legislature takes on its oversight responsibilities. Research by political scientists has uncovered a few basic patterns: (1) Oversight of executive agencies is performed when the majority party believes that it can gain partisan political advantage from the publicity produced from committee hearings. (2) Oversight is likely to take place when policy changes are being considered. (3) Oversight is likely to be performed by committees that are prestigious and have a great deal of legislative work to do.[11]

Legislative Veto

The legislative veto was a rather unusual mechanism designed to provide Congress with the power to review executive-branch decisions. The veto began in 1932 and was incorporated into more than two hundred statutes. Basically, it allowed Congress (usually either the House or the Senate) to review decisions taken in accord with legislative intent. If Congress disapproved of the executive-branch agency's actions, it could overrule the decision with the use of the legislative veto. In 1983 the Supreme Court ruled that the legislative veto was unconstitutional.

To clarify how the veto worked and the basis of the 1983 Supreme Court decision, let's consider the case before the court in that year. *Chadha v. Immigration and Naturalization Service* (1983) revolved around Section 244(c)(2) of the Immigration and Nationality Act. The section gave either the Senate or the House of Representatives the power to pass a resolution stating that it did not favor the decision to suspend the deportation of an alien that had been made by the attorney general. Notice that this legislative veto gave Congress the power to overturn administrative decisions that it disagreed with—in this case, decisions by the Justice Department.

The facts of the case were simple. An East Indian from Kenya, Chadha, came to the United States on a student visa, which expired in 1972. In 1973 the Immigration and Naturalization Service asked Chadha to show cause why he should not be deported. In 1974 his deportation was suspended by an immigration judge, and the attorney general supported the suspension before Congress. In 1975 a resolution opposing the granting of permanent residence to six aliens was passed by the House of Representatives. Chadha was one of the six. The House action invoked the legislative veto in Section 244(c)(2) of the Immigration and Nationality Act. Chadha brought the decision to the Court of Appeals, Ninth Circuit, where Section 244(c)(2) was found to be unconstitutional. The case was appealed to the Supreme Court, which upheld the decision of the Court of Appeals.

What was the Supreme Court's rationale in declaring the legislative veto unconstitutional? Here is the heart of the majority opinion, written by Chief Justice Warren E. Burger:

> Congress made a deliberate choice to delegate to the Executive Branch and specifically to the Attorney General, the authority to allow deportable aliens to remain in this country in certain specified circumstances. It is not disputed that this choice to delegate authority is precisely the kind of decision that can be implemented only in accordance with the procedures set out in Art. I.
>
> Disagreement with the Attorney General's decision to deport Chadha—no less than Congress' original choice to delegate to the Attorney General the authority to make that decision, involves determinations of policy that Congress can implement in only one way: bicameral passage followed by presentment to the President. Congress must abide by its delegation of authority until that delegation is legislatively altered or revoked.
>
> Since it is clear that the action by the House under Section 244(c)(2) was not within any of the express constitutional exceptions authorizing one house to act alone, and equally clear that it was an exercise of legislative power, that action was subject to the standards prescribed in Article I. The bicameral requirement, the presentment clauses, the President's veto, and Congress' power to override a veto were intended to erect enduring checks on each branch and to protect the people from the improvident exercise of power by mandating certain prescribed steps.
>
> To preserve those checks, and maintain the separation of powers, the carefully

defined limits on the power of each branch must not be eroded. To accomplish what has been attempted by one house of Congress in this case requires action in conformity with the express procedures of the Constitution's prescription for legislative action: passage by a majority of both Houses and presentment of the President.[12]

What is the essence of Chief Justice Burger's decision? The majority of the court concluded that the legislative veto was an unconstitutional shortcut around the carefully constructed separation of powers designed by the Founding Fathers. Thus the Supreme Court was called on to resolve a major constitutional question concerning the meaning of the separation of powers—all within the context of agency decision making.

Bowsher v. Synar (1986) was a challenge to the constitutionality of the power granted to the comptroller general of the United States in the Emergency Deficit Control Act of 1985. The act was passed in an effort to bring down the large federal budget deficits that had accumulated by the mid-1980s. In essence, the act established yearly deficit-reduction targets and set up an elaborate method to reach the statutory budget deficit limits. The legislation gave the comptroller general of the United States the power to order the president to implement the deficit-reduction procedures it specified in the act. Since the comptroller general could be removed by Congress, the Supreme Court held that the executive powers granted to the comptroller general violated the separation-of-powers principle. Critics of the Bowsher decision charged that Chief Justice Warren Burger's opinion in the case applied a wooden and "formalist" interpretation of the separation of powers principle. The president, for example, is actively involved in the legislative process through the supervision of legislation and promulgates executive orders that have the force of law. Similarly, although Congress does not execute, functions such as oversight of administrative agencies clearly involve the congressional branch in executive-branch responsibilities.[13]

LEGAL BASIS FOR AGENCY DECISIONS: ADMINISTRATIVE PROCEDURE ACT

In the United States, agencies of the executive branch are invariably at the center of the administrative process—which does not simply entail carrying out legislative intent. When public managers manage, they not only carry out decisions made by others but also initiate decisions; that is, they frequently make policy.

A major piece of legislation governing the administrative behavior of federal executive-branch agencies is the Administrative Procedure Act of 1946. The act is long and complicated, but the major portions may be outlined as follows:[14]

A fair information-practices section includes policy concerning the availability of government information to the public, the protection of individuals concerning information collected by government agencies, and participation of interested parties in the activities of agencies.

A rule-making section details the procedures that agencies must follow when they enact quasi-legislative rules.

An adjudication section describes the procedures to be followed in quasi-judicial hearings to insure that individuals receive ''due process'' rights.

A section outlines the authority of administrative law judges who conduct adjudication hearings.

A section describes the rationale for judicial review of administrative actions.

Agency Rule Making and Regulation

You will recall that executive-branch agencies enjoy delegated authority. In reality, when an agency acts on its delegated authority it is acting in a quasi-legislative manner. The authority to act on behalf of the legislature stems from the statute that established the agency in the first place. The mechanism to perform quasi-legislative functions is known as agency rule making.

Rule making is supposed to be of general applicability. That is, when an agency invokes a rule, it is supposed to affect a large number of individuals, firms, and organizations—usually for an intermittent time. There are three basic types:[15]

1. Procedural rules—These rules are made by agencies to inform interested parties how the agency conducts its business. Agencies may issue rules of evidence, for example, that must be followed during administrative hearings.

2. Substantive rules—These rules are enacted by agencies to allow them to implement the intent of policy as promulgated in legislative statute. The pizza rule below is an example of a substantive rule.

3. Interpretive rules—These rules are enacted by agencies to identify the current interpretation that they give to the legislative statutes they must administer. Suppose, in the illustration of the pizza rule described below, the agency said, ''For the purposes of this rule cheese will be defined as a substance that is primarily a dairy product.'' This would be an interpretive rule.

Agency rules are published in the *Federal Register* so that affected parties will be notified and given the opportunity to respond. No subject is too large or too small for agency rule making, as the following demonstrates.

Food Safety and Inspection Service

9 CFR Parts 317, 319, and 381

[Docket No. 78-733P]

Labeling for Meat and Poultry Products with Cheese Substitutes; Revised Pizza Standard

Agency: Food Safety and Inspection Service, USDA.

Action: Proposes rule.

Summary: This document proposes to establish more informative labeling requirements by amending the Federal meat and poultry products inspection regulations on the labeling of cheese substitutes in meat and poultry products to more prominently identify the use of these substances. This document also proposes to amend the Federal meat inspection regulations on the standard of pizza to specify both a minimum cheese content of 6 percent of the total product and a minimum of 12 percent cheese and cheese substitute content in order to assure the marketing of these products in accordance with established consumer expectations. In addition, the pizza standard as it relates to the use of meat would be revised to clarify that only cooked meat or meat food products can be used. The revision would make the standard consistent with the requirement for sausage pizza.

Date: Comments must be received on or before October 3, 1983.

Address: Written comments should be sent in duplicate to: Regulations Office, Attn: Annie Johnson, FSIS Hearing Clerk, Food Safety and Inspection Service, U.S. Department of Agriculture, Room 2637, South Agriculture Building, Washington, DC 20250. Oral comments provided under the Poultry Products Inspection Act should be directed to: Mr. Robert G. Hibbert, (202) 447-6042. (See also "Comments" under Supplementary Information.)

For further information contact: Mr. Robert F. Hibbert, Director, Standards and Labeling Division, Meat and Poultry Inspection Technical Services, Food Safety and Inspection Service, U.S. Department of Agriculture, Washington, DC 20250, (202) 447-6042.

□ *Source: Federal Register 48, no. 152 (August 5, 1983): 35,654.*

Extent of Agency Rule Making

How extensive is agency rule making? In 1960 the *Federal Register* had 9,562 pages; in 1981 it was 63,553 pages long. There are about 76,500 federal employees located in fifty-seven agencies that make and enforce rules supposed to regulate the economy, environment, health and safety, and business practices. The budgets of these agencies totalled $6.3 billion in the 1983 fiscal year.[16]

The growth of agency rule making was part of the overall increase in federal regulation. Recall from Chapter 1 that the development of industrial capitalism from the 1880s to the outbreak of World War I in 1914 was accompanied by federal involvement in the regulation of the economy. In 1887 the Interstate Commerce Commission (ICC) was founded; the Federal Reserve system was created in 1913; in 1914 the Federal Trade Commission (FTC) was born. During the New Deal several new regulatory agencies were established: Federal Home Loan Bank Board (1932), Federal Deposit Insurance Corporation (1933), Farm Credit Administration (1933), Securities and Exchange Commission (1934), and National Labor Relations Board (1935). All of the agencies mentioned so far have one thing in common: Their regulatory emphasis is economic; that is, their main concerns include the regulation of economic markets, setting rates, and licensing.

Social Regulation

From the New Deal to the present a second large category of regulation, social regulation, has developed. Social regulation "affects the conditions under which goods and services are produced and the physical characteristics of products that are manufactured," for example, pollution standards set by the Environmental Protection Agency on a manufacturer's operations.[17] Or the Consumer Product Safety Commission may establish regulations on a product to insure some minimum level of safety.[18] The difference between the older economic regulation and social regulation is striking. Whereas the latter focuses on specific markets and economic sectors, social regulation is much broader in its impact. It applies to many more industries and many more consumers and also affects all stages of the production process of goods and services.

Social regulation has been part of the expanding scope of government activity that was described in Chapter 1. Regulatory agencies make rules governing air and water quality, consumer protection, energy, and safety at the workplace. Sometimes more than one agency will become involved in the regulation of a substance, activity, or problem. Consider asbestos.

Asbestos has been used for many years as an insulator. In the mid-1970s it was learned that asbestos was a cancer-causing agent. Three federal agencies—Occupational Safety and Health Administration (OSHA), Consumer Product Safety Commission (CPSC), and the Environmental Protection Agency (EPA)—turned their attention to asbestos. But why three agencies? It turns out that the OSHA can set exposure limit standards for about 2.5 million workers who may be exposed to asbestos on the job but is not concerned directly with products that contain asbestos. That is the province of the CPSC. What is the long-range environmental impact of asbestos? Neither the OSHA nor the CPSC addresses this broad question, but the EPA does.[19] It is really not so unusual for more than one agency to regulate a single product.

The Attack on Regulation

The tremendous growth of government regulation eventually produced a backlash, which began under Presidents Ford and Carter and has continued to the present. Although deregulation has been part of a more general effort to reduce the dominance of government, it includes three basic assumptions. First, regulation is said to be costly. Murray Weidenbaum, former chairman of the Council of Economic Advisors and director of the Center for the Study of American Business at Washington University, estimated that total regulatory costs in 1979 amounted to $102.7 billion.[20] Second, many regulations are not efficient. Cost–benefit analyses often claim to show that the benefits of regulation do not exceed the costs. Third, it is argued that the public interest can often be served more effectively by devising incentives through the price mechanism rather than by resorting to the more cumbersome regulatory process.[21]

President Carter started deregulation by issuing Executive Order 12044, which required agencies to consider cost–benefit analyses and regulatory alternatives in an effort to curb the continuing increase in rules. President Reagan issued Executive Order 12291, which went even further since it required agencies to perform a "regulatory impact analysis" for new regulations. Remember the proposed rule concerning the pizza standard? Here is the agency's response to Executive Order 12291 as it applies to pizza ingredients.

Supplementary Information: Executive Order 12291

This action has been reviewed in conformance with Executive Order 12291 and has been classified as not a "major rule." It will not result in an annual effect on the economy of $100 million or more; a major increase in costs or prices for consumers, individual industries, Federal, State, or local government agencies, or geographic regions; or significant adverse effects on competition, employment, investment, productivity, innovation, or on the ability of the United States-based enterprises to compete with foreign-based enterprises in domestic or export markets.

□ *Source:* Federal Register *48, no. 152 (August 5, 1983): 35,654.*

Meanwhile, the pizza regulatory analysis has to go to the Office of Information and Regulatory Affairs in the Office of Management and Budget for review. The objective, you have probably reasoned by now, is to eliminate unnecessary regulations and rules.

Rules, Deregulations, and the Courts

Attempts to deregulate by changing or eliminating agency rules sometimes end up in the courts. Some people are likely to be better off from deregulation; others are likely to be worse off. Between 1981 and 1983 several suits were brought by public interest groups challenging changes in administrative rules that would, in their opinion, have adverse effects on some segment of the population. Here are three illustrative cases:

Save Our Cumberland Mountains Inc. et al. v. Watt (1982). In this case the U.S. District Court for the District of Columbia held that the U.S. Department of the

Interior did not enforce certain regulations of the Surface Mining Act by failing to impose penalties against coal-mine operators.[22]

Center for Science in the Public Interest v. Treasury Department (1983). The same court found that the department's elimination of a rule requiring the labeling of the contents of alcoholic beverages was "ill-considered and superficially explained."[23]

NAACP v. FCC (1982). In this case the U.S. Court of Appeals for the District of Columbia Circuit had to decide whether the FCC could revoke a rule that had limited the number of television stations that could be owned in the top fifty television markets. The circuit court upheld the actions of the FCC.[24]

"There Ought to Be a Rule. And Then Again, Maybe There Oughtn't. Or Should There?"

Sometimes an agency rule can travel a rocky political road before it ends up in the courts. Consider the history of automobile air bags—which are supposed to inflate automatically upon impact so that injuries and deaths from automobile accidents are dramatically reduced.[25] Simple in principle but very difficult to put into practice.

Although seat belts have been required since 1968, it is widely acknowledged that a large percentage of drivers simply don't use them. Seat belts save lives but not if they aren't fastened. Air bags would be a "passive" restraint: The driver wouldn't have to do anything, but the bags would be activated automatically upon impact.

President Ford's secretary of transportation, William Coleman, Jr., decided in 1976 that a rule would not be designed to force automobile companies to install air bags in their cars. His successor, Brock Adams, reversed the decision and required a three-year phase-in period beginning with the 1982 model automobiles. The Department of Transportation (DOT) figured that air bags could save nine thousand lives a year and prevent one hundred thousand injuries.

In 1981 the Reagan administration reversed Brock's rule, claiming that it would cost the automobile industry about $1 billion a year when the companies were having a good deal of financial trouble. The debate on air bags focused on different cost–benefit estimates concerning the administrative rule requiring them.

In *State Farm Mutual Automobile Insurance Co. v. Department of Transportation* (1982), the D.C. Circuit Court reversed the recision of the air-bag rule, saying that it mattered "not whether evidence shows that usage rates will increase . . . but whether there is evidence showing they will not."[26] The case was appealed to the Supreme Court. In June 1983 the court, in *Motor Vehicle Manufacturers Association of the United States, Inc., et al., v. State Farm Mutual Automobile Insurance Co., et al.,* upheld the decision of the Court of Appeals, which found that the DOT's decision to rescind the passive restraint rule was "arbitrary and capricious." On July 17, 1984, DOT issued a final rule. It announced that full passive protection would be required in all automobiles marketed after the 1989 model year. Manufacturers would be allowed to choose from a variety of passive restraint technologies. A court challenge to this final rule was turned aside by the D.C. Circuit Court of Appeals in 1986.

FEDERALISM   *Intergovernmental Relations*

Courts are sometimes described as a place where disputes between parties are resolved. Often, the parties to a dispute are two or more governmental jurisdictions: state governments, county governments, cities, towns and villages, and, naturally, the federal government. As government activity expanded, especially from the last part of the nineteenth century to the present, so did the activity of the courts. It became increasingly necessary to interpret the constitutional and statutory dimensions of the relationship between the states and the federal government.

Supremacy Clause and Preemption

The Constitution refers directly to the economic relations among levels of government. In particular, states are prohibited from coining and printing money. Most important, the power to regulate commerce with foreign nations, and among the states, resides with Congress.

In general, the federal courts have prohibited states from encroaching on congressional authority. The constitutional basis is the supremacy clause of Article VI of the U.S. Constitution, which has been interpreted to mean that federal law supercedes (and overrides) state law. Although the supremacy clause seems straightforward, federal domination over states in the area of economic regulation is certainly not complete. On the contrary, the push and pull of intergovernmental economic relations is reflected in judicial decisions, which must, of course, balance state and federal interests. An evolving legal doctrine that illustrates the judicial balancing act is *preemption*. In a nutshell, preemption refers to a situation in which Congress has "staked out" its statutory turf in a particular regulatory arena. When Congress chooses to act, say in the case of nuclear regulation, it preempts the field and thereby limits state legislative options. What if a state government initiates and passes its own legislation in the area that has been preempted by Congress? The Supreme Court must decide if the state action is constitutional. Here are four interesting cases to illustrate the constitutional foundations of federalism.

In *Askew v. American Waterways Operators, Inc.* (1973), the Supreme Court had to decide if a Florida statute aimed at correcting pollution caused by oil spills was in conflict with federal law. Basically, the Florida statute was more stringent than the federal statute. The importance of Askew is that the court upheld the right of a state to exercise the "police" power inferred in the Tenth Amendment, in this case, to protect its environment. More generally, the case was a victory for states that wanted to pursue a vigorous environmental policy.[27] The outcome could also be interpreted as a triumph for the view that federalism is a system of shared powers among levels of government in the United States.

For the next illustration of federalism we must return to the city of Frugle. The issue is whether the city manager could pay area-beautification workers less than the federal minimum-wage rate. This hypothetical situation is loosely based on *National League of Cities v. Usery* (1976).

In 1974 the Congress passed amendments to the Fair Labor Standards Act that required that almost all state and local government employees must be covered by federal minimum-wage provisions. In *National League of Cities* the Supreme Court invalidated these 1974 amendments; local governments were not obligated to pay minimum wages.

In applying the Tenth Amendment to the facts of the case, the Court argued that there was a distinction between private individuals and businesses and states (and their political subdivisions). The determination of which services to provide citizens and how much to pay for them is a decision that resides with the states. The Supreme Court held that the 1974 amendments to the Fair Labor Standards Act represented an unwarranted intrusion on the sovereignty of the states, thereby violating the Tenth Amendment.[28]

In 1985 the Supreme Court did something it does only rarely; it changed its mind. In a landmark decision, *Garcia v. San Antonio Metropolitan Transit Authority*, the Court once again was asked to rule on the constitutional basis for national government regulation of state governments. The Court held that the minimum-wage laws and the overtime provisions of the Fair Labor Standards Act applied to state and local governments. Contrary to the opinion in *National League of Cities*, the Court said that state and local governments enjoyed no immunity from the commerce clause of the constitution, which gave Congress the sole power to regulate interstate commerce. Cities, like our hypothethical Frugle, would be forced to alter certain wage and overtime practices that were protected by the now defunct *League of Cities* case.

Consider a fourth case that deals with federalism in an interesting way: *Community Communications Co., Inc. v. Boulder, Colorado* (1982). Community Communications had a franchise from Boulder for the city's cable television. The city wanted to impose a moratorium on new cable until it decided whether to grant the additional work to Community Communications or to entertain bids from other companies that might want some of Boulder's cable television business. The question that the court had to decide was whether a city can be sued by a company for violation of the Sherman Antitrust Act. In other words, if a city (Boulder in this case) grants a franchise to only one firm, can other firms excluded from doing business with the city bring suit against it? In *Community Communications Co.* the Supreme Court reasoned that states are not required to comply with the antitrust laws because of their sovereignty, as protected by the system of federalism in the Constitution. But the political subdivisions of the state—cities, counties, townships, and villages—enjoy no such constitutional protection. The Court concluded that since there are so many local governments, if they were all immune from the antitrust laws, the economic system of free enterprise would be adversely affected.[29]

The city of Boulder settled out of court to avoid stiff legal fees. Nevertheless, *Community Communications Co.* may have far-reaching consequences for local governments. If local governments are not immune from antitrust laws, as states are, it means that they can be sued by trash haulers, taxi companies, ambulances, and other types of businesses that may claim they are being excluded from competing for a city's business. *Community Communications Co.* has not made it any easier for local government managers to manage.

INDIVIDUAL RIGHTS

Procedural Due Process

The right to procedural process is granted to individuals in the Fifth Amendment of the Constitution. The amendment states that the federal government may not deprive a person of "life, liberty, or property, without due process of law." The Fourteenth Amendment extends the right by making the sanction applicable to state governments as well. Although procedural due process provides no guarantee that the outcome of an action will be favorable for an individual—persons have been executed in state prisons after all due process appeals have been exhausted—the right is supposed to guarantee "fair" administrative procedures. Exactly which process is due an individual depends on which right is at stake. A person who is charged with murder, for example, is entitled to a jury trial as a procedural due process right. But what about a high school student who has violated a school rule and is about to be suspended? What fair administrative process is due her? The federal courts have been called upon to resolve controversies surrounding the constitutionality of administrative procedures that pertain to precedural due process.

Agency adjudication. Agencies also make quasi-judicial decisions when they carry out legislative intent. These decisions form the bases of fair administrative procedures and may sometimes be challenged if they allegedly violate procedural due process guarantees. In the incident that began this chapter—the public assistance recipient whose benefits were terminated—the agency's actions taken on this case, and the subsequent judicial intervention into the agency's actions, comprise the power and limits of quasi-judicial decisions. The essentials of administrative adjudication should become clear as I proceed to merge the hypothetical situation of the public assistance recipient—let's call her Mrs. Jones now—with real events that have taken place in administrative law.

In 1967 when Jones's benefits were terminated, she had the right to request a fair hearing before an independent hearings officer. At this hearing Jones would be able to show cause why the termination of her benefits was in error. If the hearings officer agreed with her arguments, her benefits would be restored. Do you believe that Jones was receiving due process protection? Let's consider a real situation.

The Supreme Court was asked to answer this question in a case that came to it on appeal. In *Goldberg v. Kelly* (1970) the court had to decide whether due process requires a hearing before benefits are terminated. The Court held that the recipient was indeed entitled to a hearing before benefits are terminated as a matter of due process. In so deciding the Court made the following points: (1) public assistance benefits are a statutory entitlement for persons eligible to receive the funds; (2) public assistance benefits, as entitlements, are like property; (3) receiving public assistance is therefore not a privilege but a right for those who qualify; and (4) a person whose benefits are cut off will probably be in dire financial straits. It would be extremely difficult for such a person to try to exercise due process rights against the welfare bureaucracy under these conditions.[30]

Goldberg v. Kelly was an important decision. The right to a hearing before negative action could be taken was extended to the revocation of parole, the revocation of probation, suspension of drivers' licenses, suspension from high school, and removal from public housing.[31] The administrative fallout of the *Goldberg* decision caused Judge Henry J. Friendly to refer to the early 1970s as the "due process explosion."[32] But by 1976, perhaps echoing the mood in the country, the Supreme Court moderated its landmark decision. In *Matthews v. Eldridge* (1976) the Court evaluated the argument that a hearing must be provided before social security disability benefits can be terminated. Writing for the majority, Justice Powell devised a "balancing" principle. The due process rights of the individual have to be balanced against "the administrative burden and other societal costs that would be associated with requiring, as a matter of constitutional right, an evidentiary hearing upon demand in all cases prior to the termination of disability benefits."[33] But although Powell's balancing principle was a step back from the decision in *Goldberg,* it certainly did not reverse it. Due process fair hearings are a permanent part of the administrative landscape.

Politics behind administrative hearings.   Administrative hearings have not been free from criticism. Hearing officers, known as administrative law judges, for instance, have come under attack for being too zealous in their support of individuals who have been denied benefits. Critics have charged that these adjudicative decisions have cost the government billions of dollars in settlements. Lawyers who have appeared before administrative law judges have sometimes voiced different concerns. The judges are not impartial because they have worked in the same agency for years, it is charged. In response, Judge Blair, an administrative law judge at the Securities and Exchange Commission, countered, "We zealously guard our independence."[34]

Another form of administrative-law politics is perhaps more serious than that just described. In 1983 administrative-law judges for the Social Security Administration charged that the Reagan administration was exerting pressure on them to be harder on benefit claims in their hearings. The administrative law judges claimed that quotas were set on judges to dispose of a certain number of claims per month in an effort to root out ineligibles and save about $2 million a year.

Social security officials denied the charges of pressure but confirmed that a "minimally acceptable level of decisional output" would be required (by the Social Security Administration) of the 780 administrative law judges.[35] Does this sound like political pressure to you?

Equal Protection

Can governments discriminate? Of course! Recall from the public personnel chapter that one function of civil service examinations is to discriminate on the basis of expected job performance. This, after all, is a major purpose of the examinations—to identify those most likely to succeed in a job title and then use the scoring procedure to fill positions in government. Can governments discriminate in other ways? For example, can local governments refuse to hire females as law enforcement officers by claiming that females are not fearless and "macho" enough? Returning to the public personnel chapter again, can fire departments discriminate based on strengths and thereby refuse to hire females claiming that they are not strong enough? Can a local government social services agency refuse to hire a person because he has a heavy Spanish accent arguing that clients will have difficulty understanding him? These illustrations come under the heading of equal protection.

The Fourteenth Amendment of the U.S. Constitution includes the phrase "nor deny to any person within its jurisdiction the equal protection of the law." (Recall that the Thirteenth, Fourteen, and Fifteenth amendments, passed after the Civil War, pertain to the states.) The concept of equal protection, although not actually mentioned in the first ten amendments to the Constitution, has been inferred by the Supreme Court to apply to the federal government through the due process clause of the Fifth Amendment.

Not all governmental classifications, however, are unconstitutional. The Supreme Court has devised a three-tiered test to determine whether a classification violates the equal protection clause. First, a classification that discriminates on the basis of race is subject to the most exacting scrutiny by the Court and is rarely upheld. Second, a classification that discriminates on the basis of gender, for example, is subject to an intermediate level of scrutiny and will be upheld if it serves an important governmental objective and is substantially related to the achievement of the objective. Third, most classifications are subject to a "rational basis" test and will be upheld if they are rationally related to some conceivable governmental purpose.

One illustration of the rational basis test is government-imposed mandatory retirement laws. In *Massachusetts Board of Retirement v. Murgia* (1976) the court upheld a mandatory retirement law that required state police officers to retire at age fifty. Clearly, the federal courts are less willing to intervene in a governmental classification under the rational basis test than under the strict scrutiny standard.

Equal protection and fundamental rights. Sometimes state governments enact statutes to discourage individuals from taking some action. In the 1960s some states tried to control their burgeoning welfare case rolls that were causing a drain on their budgets by imposing a residency requirement (for example, one year residence in the state) before the person would be eligible for public assistance. States that imposed these residency requirements wanted to discourage poor people from moving from one state to another to receive more welfare benefits. In a landmark decision, *Shapiro v. Thompson* (1969) the Supreme Court held that the right to travel was a fundamental right. Actually, no such right is stated in the U.S. Constitution; however, the Court interpreted the right as included in the equal protection clause of the Fourteenth Amendment as well as other locations in the Constitution. Essentially, the Court held that the fundamental right dominated the states' interest—the attempt to discourage poor people from migrating for the purposes of collecting welfare payments.

Are fundamental rights absolute? When a person enters into government service, he or she does not give up fundamental constitutional rights—First Amendment rights of speech, religion, and assembly and Fifth and Fourteenth Amendment due process guarantees. But these rights are not absolute. Although government employees enjoy constitutional protection against unwarranted interference with the exercise of fundamental rights, a government may abridge a fundamental right if it can show a "compelling state interest" in restricting the right.

THE JUDGE AS MANAGER

The practicing public administrator cannot avoid the legal ramifications of public management. The Constitution frames the broad outlines of legal constraints that affect the administrator's day-to-day concerns, and the courts continually redefine the constraints. Judges have become increasingly involved in the world of administration. In this section you will learn just where courts have intervened in the management of the public's business.

Liability of Public Administrators

At one time public administrators did not have to worry much about being liable for wrongs they may have inflicted on the citizenry—wrongs caused by actions taken in their capacity as civil servants. But this was long ago—1788 to be exact. In *Russell v. Men of Devon County* the English court found that a person who suffered personal damages to his horse-drawn wagon, damages caused by actions taken by individuals in the employ of Devon County, could not sue for damages against the county. Basically, you couldn't sue the monarch, who could do no wrong in a legal sense. The principle was known as sovereign immunity, which meant that the monarch could not be held liable (unless the monarch would consent to being held liable) for his or her actions or actions taken on his or her behalf. This principle from English common law became part of the U.S. Constitution with the passage of the Eleventh Amendment in 1795. The amendment reads, in part, "The Judicial Power of the United States shall not be construed to extend to any suit in law or equity, commenced or prosecuted against one of the United States by citizens of another state, or by citizens or subjects of any foreign state." But if there is one single trend in the evolution of administrative law it is the following: The official immunity of public administrators has slowly but continuously eroded. During the past fifteen years the pace of this erosion has quickened.

In 1946 Congress passed the Federal Tort Claims Act, a key part of which is the following passage: "The United States shall be liable, respecting the provisions of this title relating to tort claims, in the same manner and to the same extent as private individuals under like circumstances." The meaning of this phrase must be interpreted by the courts; moreover, there are several exceptions stipulated to it. Most important, the act does not apply to claims "based upon the exercise or performance or the failure to exercise or perform a discretionary function or duty on the part of a federal agency or an employee of the Government, whether or not the discretion involved be abused."[36]

A major job of the federal courts since 1946 has been how to interpret the meaning of discretionary action, a prerequisite for establishing governmental liability under the act. Commenting on this aspect of the Federal Tort Claims Act, Kenneth Davis, a nationally recognized legal scholar and expert in administrative law observed, "The discretionary function exception is necessary, but the courts have tended, in many cases, to expand it beyond the reasons behind it."[37] He added, "Probably immunity should be retained for discretionary determinations at high levels involving basic policies but not for abuse of discretion or other fault at the operating level by officers who are not making basic policies."[38] Although Davis's criticisms may have been justified for acts committed by federal officials, the same observation would not hold for state and local governments and their public officials.

Section 1983.   Suppose police officers illegally search a person's house. Are they personally liable for their actions? How about those students who spiked the punch bowl in the episode at the beginning of the chapter? Were any of their rights violated when the Board of Education suspended them from school? A city has an unconstitutional pregnancy rule that forces female employees to take time off without pay. Do the women have any recourse? A city fires a police chief; the chief claims that he was not afforded due process rights. What is the outcome? An individual wins a suit to restore terminated government benefits. The defendant is a state government employee. Does the state have to pay the individual's attorney's fees?

What do all of these situations have in common? They all depend on the interpretation of Section 1983 of Title 42 of the U.S. Code—originally part of the Civil Rights Act of 1871. The critical passage reads as follows:

> Every person who, under color of any statute, ordinance, regulation, custom or usage of any state or territory, subjects or causes to be subjected any citizen of the United States or other person within the jurisdiction there of to the deprivation of any rights, privileges, or immunities procured by the Constitution and laws shall be liable to the party injured in any action at law, suit in equity, or other proper proceeding for redress.

This passage brings judges into the public administrative process for it requires them to determine whether actions taken by state and local officials are violations

of a person's constitutional and statutory rights. To appreciate the importance of
the judicial decisions for public administration, it would be useful now to answer
the previous questions. The answers all come from Supreme Court decisions that
were based on interpretations of Section 1983.

The incident concerning the illegal search by police officers in Chicago produced *Monroe v. Pape* (1961). The court ruled that the city of Chicago could not
be held liable for the unconstitutional actions [illegal search and seizure] of its
police officers because the city was not a "person" under Section 1983. In the
spiked-punch episode, *Wood v. Strickland* (1975), the school board suspended the
guilty students without providing them with a hearing, thereby denying their due
process rights. The question facing the Court was whether the public officials
were liable for the infringement of constitutional rights if they were unaware that
their actions would cause this outcome. The Court established the following logic:
A public official must be sincere in his or her actions; yet a violation of a person's
constitutional rights cannot be justified solely on the basis of the official's sincer-
ity. If the official knew that his or her actions violated a person's constitutional
rights, the official would not be immune from liability for damages.

The *Wood* case is important not for its cumbersome logic but, rather, for
opening the door to citizens who believe their rights have been violated by government officials. But before public entities could be sued, the *Monroe* case
would have to be reversed.

In the pregnancy case *Monell v. Department of Social Services* (1978), the
Supreme Court reversed the *Monroe* decision and ruled that local governments
were persons under Section 1983 and could therefore be held liable for rights
violations. Sovereign immunity did not extend to local governments.

The case of the police chief who was fired without due process led to *Owen
v. City of Independence* (1980). *Owen* went even further than both *Monell* and
Wood. Like the *Monell* case, the Supreme Court affirmed the right of individuals
to sue local governments for rights violations; local governments enjoyed no immunity under Section 1983. Unlike *Wood*, in this case the Court held that local
government entities must enforce Fourteenth Amendment due process rights.
Owen held that the city of Independence—as a public entity—could not use the
good-faith defense that previously protected local officials from civil rights suits
brought under Section 1983. In other words, the Court held in *Owen* that the city
managers of Independence, Missouri, should have anticipated that the way in
which the police chief was terminated violated Fourteenth Amendment due process rights.[39] Obviously, *Owen* makes it just a little harder to manage.

So far the discussion of Section 1983 has been restricted to constitutional
issues. If you recall, there is one last question that I posed at the beginning of this
section: whether a person's legal fees would be paid by the defendant—a state
government—if the person was victorious in court. This issue was decided in
Maine v. Thiboutot (1980). *Maine* is not the kind of case that makes a good television movie. On the surface it is rather dull. Lionel Thiboutot's benefits through
the AFDC were reduced by Maine's Department of Human Resources. Thiboutot
claimed that Section 1983 was applicable; the department's action violated the
Social Security Act (which includes the AFDC program). In addition, Thiboutot

wanted his legal fees paid under the Civil Rights Attorney's Fees Act of 1976, which was included in his Section 1983 suit. The majority of the Supreme Court held in favor of Thiboutot for both issues.

Maine v. Thiboutot is important because it went far in extending the scope of Section 1983. Before Maine, Section 1983 cases were based only on constitutional violations. Now plaintiffs may bring suit against governments and their public officials for alleged violations of all sorts of federal statutes. Obviously, the liability of governments and their officials has been greatly expanded; immunity, in turn, has been further eroded.

Some ramifications of Section 1983 decisions.   The cumulative effect of Section 1983 decisions is to extend the right of individuals to sue for damages against state and local governments and their public officials. But these decisions are not without their costs. What would you do now, if you were the city manager of Independence, Missouri, in the aftermath of the *Owen* decision? Wouldn't you at least be much more cautious and deliberate in your dealings with city personnel?

Peter Schuck, in a provocative book entitled *Suing Government,* identified some ramifications of Section 1983 suits. Inaction is the first possibility. Schuck wrote, "If officials perceive that performing their legal duty may generate personal costs that exceed their duty thresholds, they may refrain from acting."[40] A police officer who looks the other way when a crime is unfolding is an illustration of just such inaction. A second possibility is delay, which will occur when subordinates, fearful of legal action against them, require clearance from a superior before making a decision.[41] Third, officials may engage in what Schuck called formalism, building a case to avert a potential lawsuit. Schuck's illustration is easily appreciated—the public health physician who orders many tests to protect against charges of medical malpractice.[42] Fourth, public employees may even alter the nature of their decisions. Again, Schuck's illustration is instructive—the parole officer who does not recommend release for an individual because the officer fears that the parolee may commit further crimes.[43] Finally, Section 1983 suits impose financial costs on state and local governments and their public officials. Some government employees protect themselves against the risk of lawsuits by purchasing liability insurance from private carriers. Some local governments do the same thing, though premiums are expensive and many local governments simply cannot afford them. In the end, the cost of official liability will be distributed to the taxpayer. Again, judicial involvement in the administrative process makes the task of management more complex.

Institutional Litigation: The Case of Prisons

Recall Iggy "the Blade" McNasty's complaint that the prison he was serving time in was overcrowded. This hypothetical illustration was based on a series of federal district court cases that began in 1969 and continue to the present. All are concerned with the constitutionality of state prison conditions.

Arkansas was the first state in which confinement in its penitentiary system was ruled to be cruel and unusual punishment under the Eighth Amendment of the U.S. Constitution. *Holt v. Sarver*, known as *Holt I*, was the first in a series of litigations in Arkansas that began in 1969.[44] Besides critically overcrowded facilities, orders from the court covered the elimination of the trustee guard system, inmate safety, brutality and reprisals, racial segregation, medical services, and general sanitation levels. In 1978 the Supreme Court upheld lower court orders establishing a maximum inmate population for the prison facilities and a deadline of thirty days for relieving unconstitutional conditions. All prison suits in Arkansas were later consolidated in 1978 under a consent decree in which the Arkansas Department of Corrections, and all other parties, settled the issues raised by the suits. A compliance coordinator was appointed as a monitor to observe compliance with the court orders.

Unlike the situation in Arkansas, where litigation applied to the entire state prison system, Ohio's court-ordered reform focused on specific prisons.[45] A consent decree in 1972 settled a case brought by the prisoners at the Marion Correctional Institution challenging several aspects of the conditions of confinement. In December 1975 the court appointed a special master to monitor compliance with the court order; in 1976 a final court decree was issued stipulating that when substantial compliance was achieved, the special master would be dismissed. During the litigation, a ceiling was placed on the prison population at Marion. Two other Ohio correctional facilities now face litigation. Southern Ohio Correctional Facility was under court order for monthly population reduction. The Columbus Correctional Facility was under court order by consent decree to close in 1983 and now operates with a ceiling on its total population.

Mississippi's pattern of litigation combined features of those in both Arkansas and Ohio.[46] Like Ohio's, Mississippi's first case focused on the conditions at the state penitentiary. Like that in Arkansas, the whole prison system eventually came under court order regarding overcrowding and total conditions. Unlike the situation in Arkansas and Ohio, however, the Mississippi U.S. district court retained jurisdiction over the earliest case. This allowed the court to maintain direct control over the implementation of the court order. In August 1973 a federal monitor was appointed to check all phases of prison administration, management, and operations. A district court decision in 1975 ordered the prison administration to submit a plan to the court to reduce the prison population so that there would be not less than fifty square feet of living space per inmate. To achieve this goal, the court in 1976 reduced the inmate population by closing several facilities and prohibited the defendants from accepting any prisoners until the requirement was met. In 1978, the court found that some of the prison facilities still could not be effectively maintained, and it ordered that they be closed.

In Oklahoma, the first U.S. district court decision occurred in 1974, soon after a prison riot that resulted in $20 million in damages.[47] The court found violations in almost every aspect of prison life and ordered immediate relief. Compliance hearings were held every six months to monitor the implementation of the court order. After three years of hearings, the court ruled that the Department of Corrections was not complying with the court orders and required the inmate population at the two most crowded facilities to be reduced by fifty to one hundred prisoners per month. After a lengthy appeals process the case was sent back to the district court. The court accepted the Department of Correction's plan, which included an implementation timetable. After a compliance hearing in September 1978, the court found that substantial compliance still had not occurred. Thus it issued a new set of all-inclusive specific remedies with the mandate that if the deadlines were not met, there would be severe penalties, including the closing of offending facilities or fines of up to $250,000 per day.

The cases in Arkansas, Ohio, Mississippi, and Oklahoma had far-reaching effects on their respective state prison systems. Although in each state some aspect of the prison system was ruled unconstitutional, there were important differences among them. The litigation histories show that the courts have adopted varying notions of what constitutes minimally acceptable conditions, alternative mechanisms to enforce state compliance, and different degrees of judicial interference in the implementation process. In Mississippi, for example, the U.S. district court ruled that fifty square feet of living space was the minimally acceptable level per prisoner. In Oklahoma the court established a level of sixty square feet for inmates in dormitories as the constitutional minimum. In both instances, a cumbersome mechanism was established to monitor the implementation of the decisions, including a reliance on court hearings, lengthy written reports, or special masters. Thirty-five states have now had prison reform litigation. Yet in many states alleviation of the unconstitutional conditions has not been reached (to the satisfaction of the courts) even after years of litigation and further direct court involvement in the actual implementation of the judicial decisions.

The courts' influence in the actual implementation of their judicial decisions has varied from low involvement to high involvement. At the low end are simple court orders for vaguely worded prison reforms. A stronger level includes court-ordered compliance deadlines, timetables for reports, and compliance hearings. Ceilings placed on and specified reductions in the prison population represent even further direct court involvement, as does the establishment of a human rights committee or the appointment of a special master (who reports directly to the judge) to oversee compliance. Further involvement includes a voluntary "consent decree" that is agreed to by all parties in the litigation. Finally, a condition of receivership, the most extensive level of court involvement, means that the court takes on the administrative responsibilities and prison managers become directly accountable to the court.

Other areas of institutional reform litigation.   Judges have not restricted their involvement to prisons. States manage other types of institutions as well, in particular, facilities for people who are mentally ill or mentally disabled. During the past fifteen years many states have been brought into federal court by plaintiffs who have charged that the conditions in these institutions violate the constitutional rights of their inhabitants. As in the prison cases, judges have frequently outlined detailed remedial actions that must be taken to alleviate unconstitutional conditions. Alabama was the site of the earliest and most famous case in the area of mental health, *Wyatt v. Stickney.*

Bryce Hospital is located in Tuscaloosa. By 1970 conditions in the mental health hospital were extremely poor. The food allowance per patient was about fifty cents per day; there were few doctors, and there were charges of physical abuse committed by some of the hospital staff. In 1971 *Wyatt v. Stickney* came before federal Judge M. Johnson, Jr.—the same judge who ruled on the constitutionality of Alabama's prison system in the *Holt* cases. In his landmark decision in *Wyatt*, Judge Johnson ruled that patients who were involuntarily committed to state institutions must receive adequate treatment, which, he reasoned, was part of a patient's due process rights. He said that adequate treatment consisted of three dimensions: (1) a proper physical and psychological hospital environment, (2) a suitable amount of qualified staff, and (3) treatment plans tailored to each patient in the hospital.[48] Concrete specifications of what each of these three dimensions meant in practice were appended to the *Wyatt* decision. Judge Johnson appointed a human rights committee, which gathered information on the operations of Bryce Hospital (and two other state institutions included in the *Wyatt* decision) in the aftermath of the court ruling. The committee was responsible for monitoring compliance with Judge Johnson's order and reporting rights violations to him.

Since the pathbreaking *Wyatt* case, many states have had to grapple with the problems involved in implementing reforms in their state institutions. In the wake of successful court challenges to unconstitutional conditions, judges have become intimately involved in the details of the administrative process. They have had to determine how many square feet of prison cell fulfills the Eighth Amendment guarantee; they have had to determine what types of psychiatric treatment are appropriate for different kinds of diagnoses; they have had to determine what types of education tools and methods conform to a "least restrictive environment" for the handicapped student. Should judges make these decisions? Are they capable of making these kinds of decisions?

Should Judges Make Policy?

We have now returned to the first theme in this chapter—the constitutional requisites of public administration. When a judge declares that a patient is entitled to a certain type of treatment as a condition of the patient's involuntary commitment to a state psychiatric institution, the judge is interpreting the meaning of the due process clause. The constitutional issue in the case is not too difficult to comprehend. But there are two other, more complicated and more troublesome, dimensions. First, when the court dictates a judicial remedy to, say, prison overcrowding or conditions in state hospitals, it is taking on quasi-legislative and quasi-executive functions. After all, public policy is most commonly formulated by the legislative branch when it enacts laws, and policy is implemented when executive-branch agencies carry out the laws. Second, when federal courts evaluate the constitutionality of conditions in state facilities, the courts are encroaching on the sovereignty of the states—obviously, an important facet of the constitutional principle of federalism. Should judges be so active? Do they have the capacity to enforce their decisions? There has been a great deal of debate on both questions since the beginning of institutional reform litigation more than fifteen years ago. Some of

the issues can be summarized in a few pro and con positions. Those who believe that the courts should (and could) take an active place in the formulation and implementation of policy are associated with the pro side. In contrast, those who believe that the courts should be passive and, furthermore, do not have the capacity to enforce their decisions comprise the con side of the argument. Here are some contrasting views:

Pro

It is the responsibility of the courts to uphold the constitutional rights of individuals. Besides, persons in state institutions have no political leverage with the other two branches of government. The courts are their only refuge.

Con

Whereas the courts are, indeed, supposed to uphold the constitutional rights of individuals, it is up to the legislative and executive branches to fashion remedies and implement them.

Pro

The courts are forced to fashion and implement remedies precisely because the executive and legislative branches of government have failed to discharge their responsibilities.

Con

Judges do not understand the complex political ramifications of institutional reform litigation, which must be taken into account when remedies are being designed.

Pro

Judicial use of expert opinion in designing remedies in institutional litigation cases is not much different from the design of legislation and agency implementation plans.

Con

Judges do not really comprehend the often subtle debates that lie behind expert opinion in institutional litigation cases.

Pro

Knowing that the courts will not defer to the other two branches when rights are consistently violated has led to more "progressive" treatment of individuals who are potential plaintiffs in institutional reform litigation.

Con

Experience with institutional reform litigation has shown that judicially mandated changes take years to implement and are frequently thwarted anyway. Meanwhile, a political backlash against an activist judiciary has been created, threatening the independence of the judiciary.

Legal scholars, judges, administrators, and politicians have taken positions on both sides of these issues, which are, ultimately, about what a "system of shared powers" really means in practice. But one thing is clear: The courts are unlikely to retreat from their involvement in matters that were once thought to be the sole province of the legislative and executive branches. Public managers must become accustomed to the presence of judges as full partners in the administrative process.

SUMMARY

Much ground has been covered in this chapter—some of it rather difficult terrain. Let's review some of the key points. First, the relationship between the courts and public administration is framed by the Constitution. The Constitution says almost nothing about public administration per se. The president is given appointment powers in Article II, from which we may infer authority to establish executive-branch agencies. Similarly, Article I gives the Congress the authority to "make all laws which shall be necessary and proper for carrying into Execution the foregoing Powers." From this phase has grown one of the most important constitutional links between the legislative and executive branches of government—the delegation of powers. A most important chapter in the constitutional history of administrative agencies is the way the courts have interpreted the meaning of delegation. When agencies make quasi-legislative decisions—when they make rules, for instance—it often falls on the courts to interpret the constitutional appropriateness of the agencies' actions. To repeat: The Constitution frames a good deal of the relationships between courts and public administration.

Second, what are the essential components of the administrative-law process? That is, what guides the conduct of administrative agencies? Agencies at the federal level are governed by the Administrative Procedure Act of 1946. Although a long and complicated piece of legislation, the act essentially gives agencies the authority to make rules and regulations and to make quasi-judicial determinations in the form of adjudications. Recall that rules and regulations are quasi legislative. That is, when an agency makes a rule it is implementing the intent of a statute. Since statutes are often vague, rules and regulations are supposed to provide a modicum of precision to the legislation by interpreting legislative intent with, for example, standards of performance or guidelines for behavior.

Unlike rule making, which is intended to be general and affect large numbers of people, adjudication is done on a case-by-case basis. In this sense, agency adjudication is quasi judicial. For example, before a person's benefits for, say, public assistance are terminated, the person is entitled to a fair hearing before a hearings officer in the agency. The purpose of this procedure is to insure that the person receives due process protection. This constitutional right became a major part of the administrative landscape in the aftermath of the Supreme Court decision in *Goldberg v. Kelly* (1970).

Third, the legal foundations of public administration are really quite extensive. Even more important, judges have become increasingly involved in the details of public administration in two ways: (1) in the liability of state and local governments and their public officials; (2) by taking a strong hand in the administration of state institutions like prisons and hospitals for the mentally ill and the mentally disabled. The purpose is to protect the constitutional rights of those committed to state facilities. Both these developments—judicial interpretations of the liability of state and local governments and institutional reform litigation—highlight perhaps the most important conclusion of this chapter. In the past, public administrators may have paid only modest attention to the activities of the courts. This is no longer possible. The courts are now full partners in the management of the public's business. The judicial dimension of public management is illustrated in the following case, "The Basic County Jail."

Judicial Intervention in Public Management: The Basic County Jail

The Basic County Jail is located in the downtown section of Benton, a city of one hundred thousand, located in the Midwest. Benton is a "typical" midwestern city with population decline, gradual loss of manufacturing employment that has only partially been replaced by jobs in the service sector, and a fiscal climate that is precarious. The city and the county have fairly high tax burdens and pressures for public spending that must somehow be checked. Like other local governments in the region, the crime rate has been growing.

Basic County Jail is used to house pretrial detainees. It is rated by the state corrections board to have a capacity of 200. From 1985 to 1987, however, the jail population increased substantially. The average daily population during this period was 239. Although the reasons for the increase were not entirely clear, explanations included the following:

1. Tougher enforcement of Driving While Intoxicated (DWI) laws
2. Housing state prisoners because the state prison system was at 106 percent of capacity
3. Accepting out-of-county prisoners from other counties in the state as well as federal prisoners because Basic County earns $50 a day, which, in 1987, was about $800,000 in revenues.

Ben Vane, a deputy sheriff, was also the chief of jail administration. His job was getting frustrating. Each year he would request additional funds for the jail. During the past few years he had told the budget office and the county legislators that the overcrowding situation should be alleviated. Vane was no "bleeding heart." He strongly believed that everyone in the jail really belonged there. Nevertheless, he also believed that sound professional correctional management required adequate space for inmates. For instance, it was important to properly classify prisoners and avoid inappropriate double celling. The political problem, as he saw it, was that there was no constituency for jail expansion. After all, no one campaigns for the inmate vote, and with other pressing issues, the county legislators are not about to spend additional funds for something with little or no political payoff. Chief Vane knows this. Still, he also argues that the jail population can double in less than ten years. He dismisses "knee-jerk" responses such as "alternatives to incarceration" by claiming that all of these alternatives are already used in Basic County. There is no way around it, he says. The county has to build more jail space.

In November 1987 a lawyer from the American Civil Liberties Union (ACLU) brought suit against the county claiming that the overcrowding violated the Fifth, Eighth, and Fourteenth amendments of the U.S. Constitution. The lawyer's objectives were to alleviate the gross overcrowding by "getting some of the inmates off the floor"—the catwalk between the cells. Second, she wanted to enjoin the county from putting additional prisoners in the jail. Third, she wanted the county to submit a plan to the court showing how the jail would be brought into compliance with constitutional safeguards.

Chief Vane, though nominally one of the defendants, welcomed the suit. Although no great supporter of the ACLU, he nonetheless thought that this was one way to prod the county legislature into providing additional funds for the jail. If it takes a lawsuit, so be it!

The ACLU won the suit. By late 1988 the state had removed its prisoners and the judge ordered the county not to accept out-of-county inmates. This action resulted in a loss of about $800,000 in revenues. The judge also ordered the county to bring down the inmate count to 230 by March 10, 1989. When the date arrived, the inmate population was 238. The judge ordered the county to bring down the count to 230 in four days or risk a fine of $4,000 a day per prisoner for every prisoner above the 230 limit. When the date arrived, the count was 235. No penalties were imposed. The judge ordered the parties to appear in court in August 15, 1989. At that time he wanted to see some progress in resolving the overcrowding problem.

When August 15, 1989, arrived, the county attorney told the judge that "good-faith" efforts were being made to comply with his order. The county legislature commissioned an architectural study to survey jail-renovation and jail-expansion options. Also, $150,000 was appropriated to convert gymnasium space into temporary cells. The judge set a new time-table for the alleviation of overcrowding. He said that, beginning January 1, 1990, he would impose a fine of up to $8,000 a day for every inmate above the rated capacity of 200 if the actual jail population exceeded 200 for four consecutive days.

Meanwhile, Chief Vane was preparing his budget request for the forth-coming fiscal year. In his request he was requesting capital construction funds to build an additional one hundred cells. He justified the request by saying that the additional cells were necessary to respond adequately to the court order. Second, he projected substantial inmate increases during the next decade. Third, he argued that the jail expansion could be financed in part by, once again, taking in out-of-county prisoners.

Questions for Discussion

1. How did the intervention of the court affect the management of Basic County Jail?
2. Do you think that Vane was "helped" or "harmed" by the litigation?
3. Why didn't the judge follow through on his threat to impose the fines? Should the judge impose the fines after January 1, 1990, if the jail population exceeds his order?
4. Suppose you are a budget analyst in the budget office of the county. Would you go along with Chief Vane's request for capital expansion funds?

NOTES

1. Louis Fisher, *The Politics of Shared Powers: Congress and the Executive*, 2d ed. (Washington, D.C.: Congressional Quarterly Press, 1987).
2. Donald D. Barry and Howard R. Whitcomb, *The Legal Foundations of Public Administration* (St. Paul: West Publishing Co., 1981).
3. This section is based on Phillip J. Cooper, *Public Law and Administration* (Palo Alto, Calif.: Mayfield Publishing Co., 1983), pp. 220–223.
4. Woodrow Wilson, "The Study of Administration," in *Classics of Public Administration*, ed. Jay M. Shafritz and Albert C. Hyde (Oak Park Ill.: Moore Publishing Co., 1978), p. 11.
5. Cooper, *Public Law*, p. 222.
6. Kenneth Culp Davis, *Administrative Law Text*, 3d ed. (St. Paul: West Publishing Co., 1972), p. 27.
7. See Barry and Whitcomb, *Legal Foundations*, pp. 54–55.
8. This paragraph relies on ibid., pp. 57–66.
9. Ibid., p. 58.
10. Ibid., p. 65.
11. Randall R. Ripley, *Congress Process and Policy*, 2d ed. (New York: W. W. Norton, 1978), p. 338.

12. Quoted in "Excerpts from Supreme Court Decision on Legislative Vetoes," *New York Times,* June 24, 1983, p. B5.
13. William C. Banks and Jeffrey D. Straussman, *"Bowsher v. Synar:* The Emerging Judicialization of the Fisc," *Boston College Law Review* 28 (July 1987): 659–688.
14. See Cooper, *Public Law,* pp. 103–107.
15. Ibid., pp. 111–113.
16. These data are cited in *Regulation Process and Politics* (Washington, D.C.: Congressional Quarterly, 1982), p. 1.
17. William Lilley III and James C. Miller III, "The New Social Regulation,' " *The Public Interest,* no. 47 (Spring 1977): 53.
18. Ibid.
19. Walter Pincus, "Asbestos Coming under Massive Attack by 3 Regulatory Agencies," *Washington Post,* December 8, 1980, p. A3.
20. Cited in *Regulation Process and Politics,* p. 27.
21. For example, see Charles L. Schultze, *The Public Use of Private Interest* (Washington, D.C.: Brookings Institution, 1977).
22. Michael Wines, "Administration Critics Play Legal Cat and Mouse Game on Agency Rules," *National Journal* 14 (December 12, 1982): 2159.
23. Quoted in James L. DeLong, "Repealing Rules," *Regulation* 7 (May/June 1983): 29.
24. Ibid.
25. The airbag controversy is summarized in *Regulation Process and Politics,* pp. 131–132.
26. Quoted in DeLong, "Repealing Rules," p. 29.
27. Lee S. Weinberg, "Askew v. American Waterway Operators, Inc.: The Emerging New Federalism," *Publius* 8 (Fall 1978): 37–53.
28. For a somewhat unusual though intriguing interpretation of League of Cities, see Laurence H. Tribe, *American Constitutional Law* (Mineola, N.Y.: Foundation Press, 1978), pp. 308–318.
29. A very good discussion of this case is found in Rochelle L. Stanfield, "Cities and Counties Ask Congress: 'Save Us from the Antitrust Laws,' " *National Journal* 15 (March 12, 1983): 558–561.
30. Cooper, *Public Law,* p. 143.
31. Ibid., p. 364.
32. Henry J. Friendly, "Some Kind of Hearing," *Pennsylvania Law Review* 123 (June 1975): 1273.
33. Quoted in Barry and Whitcomb, *Legal Foundations,* p. 191.
34. Robert Pear, "Administrative Law Judges Are Washington's Potent Hybrids," *New York Times,* November 23, 1980, p. E3.
35. Robert Pear, "Pressure to Cut Off Benefits Reported by Disability Judges," *New York Times,* June 9, 1983, p. B9.
36. This paragraph is based on Barry and Whitcomb, *Legal Foundations,* pp. 264–266.
37. Davis, *Administrative Law Text,* p. 483.
38. Ibid.
39. See Walter S. Groszyk and Thomas J. Madden, "Managing without Immunity: The Challenge for State and Local Government Officials in the 1980s," *Public Administration Review* 41 (March/April 1981): 270–271.
40. Peter H. Schuck, *Suing Government* (New Haven: Yale University Press, 1983), p. 71.
41. Ibid., p. 73.
42. Ibid., p. 74.

43. Ibid., p. 75.
44. Arkansas' overcrowding litigation includes Holt v. Sarver 300 F. Supp 825 (1969), 309 F. Supp 362 (1970) affd 442F.2d. 304 (1971); Finney v. Arkansas Board of Corrections 505 F.2d. 194 (1974); Finney v. Hutto 309 F. Supp 362 (1972), 410 F.Supp 251 (E.D. Ark 1976), affd 548 F.2d 740 (1976), affd 437 U.S. 678 (1978), 442 F.2d 304, 363 F.Supp 194, 505 F.2d 194; Finney v. Mabry, 458 F.Supp 720 (1978).
45. Ohio's overcrowding litigation includes Taylor v. Perini, 413 F.Supp 189 (N.D. Ohio 1976), 413 F.Supp 198 (1976), 421 F.Supp 740 (1976), 431 F.Supp 566 (1977), 446 F.Supp 1184 (1977), 455 F.Supp 1241 (1978); Chapman v. Rhodes, 434 F.Supp 1007; Steward v. Rhodes, C.A. No. C-2-78-220 [S.D. Ohio (12/79)]; Boyd v. Denton, C.A. 78-1054A (N.D. Ohio).
46. Mississippi's overcrowding litigation includes Gates v. Collier, 390 F.Supp 482 (1975), affd 535 F.2d 965 (1976), 394 F.Supp 881 (1972), affd 501 F.2d 1291 (1974), 371 F.Supp 1368, vacated 522 F.2d 81, 390 F.Supp 482, affd 525 F.2d 665, 407 F.Supp 1117, 423 F.Supp 732, affd in part 548 F.2d 1241, 70 F.R.D. 341, affd in part, rev'd and rem'd in part, 559 F.2d 241, 500 F.2d 1382, 501 F.2d 1291, 522 F.2d 81, 454 F.Supp 567 (1978).
47. Oklahoma's overcrowding litigation includes Battle v. Anderson, 376 F.Supp 402 (1974), 595 F.2d 792 (10th cir 1979), 477 F.Supp 516 (1977), affd in part, rem'd in part, 564 F.2d 388 (1977), opinion on remand 457 F.Supp 719 (1978).
48. Judge Johnson's rulings in Holt and Wyatt are described in Tinsley E. Yarbrough, "The Judge as Manager: The Case of Judge Frank Johnson," *Journal of Policy Analysis and Management* 1 (Spring 1982): 386–400.

FOR FURTHER READING

Cooper, Phillip J. *Hard Judicial Choices*. New York: Oxford University Press, 1988.
    Applying a "decree-litigation model," Cooper examines five federal court decisions that cover housing, school desegregation, right to treatment in mental health facilities, prison overcrowding, and police practices. His cases are carefully constructed and his analysis is persuasive.
Cooper, Phillip J. *Public Law and Public Administration*, 2d ed. Englewood Cliffs, N.J.: Prentice-Hall, 1988.
    This second edition of a fine book on public law provides a great deal of material that is relevant to the student and practitioner of public administration.
Horowitz, Donald L. *The Courts and Social Policy*. Washington, D.C.: Brookings Institution, 1977.
    Based on four major cases, this book presents an excellent analysis of the potentials and limits of judicial capacity in making public policy.
Mashaw, Jerry L. *Bureaucratic Justice*. New Haven: Yale University Press, 1983.
    A Yale Law School professor takes you through the labyrinth of the social security disability claims adjudicative process. An excellent study.
Schuck, Peter H. *Suing Government*. New Haven: Yale University Press, 1983.
    Another first-rate study by a Yale Law School professor who describes and then criticizes the existing system of tort liabilities that now apply to government officials.

CHAPTER 13

Evaluation

The controversial mayor of New York City during the decade of the 1980s, Edward Koch, began his tenure in office by asking the average person on the street, "How am I doing?" Some said, "Great, keep it up." Some said, "So-so." And some said, "You stink, you bum." Now it doesn't take much to figure out that "great" is better than "so-so," not to mention the third assessment.

One wonders what Mayor Koch did with these "citizen surveys." If he *really* wanted to improve his performance as mayor, he probably tried to do things to minimize the most negative evaluation. Of course, it is possible that he only wanted to give the *appearance* of caring what the average person thought about his performance. Mayor Koch probably wanted to be a good mayor; he probably wanted to find out how well he was doing; and he wanted to create an image that he truly cared. For Mayor Koch there was a bottom line: He wanted to get reelected.

THE NEED FOR EVALUATION

How do organizations evaluate their performance? For a small manufacturing company, the answer is simple. The owners of the company will look at the amount of profit, or lack of profit, at the end of the year. Other things are also important—inventories, availability and quality of labor, consumer demand—but ultimately *profits* determine the survival of the company.[1] If the company makes a profit, it is doing well; if it loses money it must do better if it expects to stay in business.

Lack of Self-Evident Criteria

Suppose Mayor Koch actually recorded the responses to his question. Leaving aside for the moment all of the things that make his "evaluation instrument" suspect (that is, his question to whomever he felt like asking it, whenever the spirit moved him, and wherever he happened to be), he surely knew that if the responses tended to be predominantly "You stink, you bum," he was probably not doing so well. If the responses shifted so that a plurality said "Great, keep it up," Koch could have felt reasonably confident that his performance had improved, or at least that people thought it had. The manufacturer has it even easier. The owners know that a $500,000 profit is better than a $400,000 profit, and $600,000 would be better yet.

Deciding on the determinant of success for many public organizations can sometimes be quite vexing. Consider a simple illustration. Suppose you are the chief librarian for a municipal library with several neighborhood branches. To evaluate your performance, would you examine the number of books circulated? The number of new books? Complaints? The number of participants in library-sponsored activities? How about the entertainment and/or educational "value" of the books that have been circulated? Maybe you think some of these criteria are too abstract. Would you look at the cost per circulated book?

Some of these criteria of performance may seem more reasonable than others. In any event, the point should be clear: Determining the criteria of success in the public sector is much more problematical than in the private sector. Nor is the library illustration unique. Thousands of government programs, from support for the arts to the National Science Foundation's grants for zoological research, have objectives that are hard to define and to measure, and even harder to evaluate.

Evaluation as Error Reduction

If evaluation is so hard in the public sector, why bother with it at all? One reason is that administrators would like to make fewer mistakes. Civil servants in public organizations make many decisions, usually with less information than they would really like. *Evaluation can improve the information bases of public decision making.*[2]

Suppose you were the manager of a supervised job program for inmates in a state prison. More specifically, suppose a group of carefully selected (minimum-risk) convicts were given jobs in the community with some amount of supervision by prison employees. Let us further assume that the program has a few basic objectives. First, the program tries to provide the convicts with "marketable" skills so that when they are eventually released they can find employment. The underlying premise is that the convicts are less likely to engage in criminal activities after they are released if they are employed. Second, some of the wages earned by the convicts go to a state Crime Victimization Fund that is used to compensate victims of crime. The idea here is that convicts not only have to pay their debt to society by "serving time" but also have to pay a monetary debt to their victims. Third, public officials want to show that they are taking creative and effective steps to rehabilitate convicted criminals.

Let us further assume that the program has been in effect on an experimental basis for three years, with three hundred participants during that period. The governor has asked the superintendent of prisons for a "recommendation" on the program. There are basically five options: (1) terminate the experiment, (2) expand the project in its present form, (3) continue the program as a limited experiment for an additional period, (4) alter the program and keep it limited in size, and (5) alter the program and expand it.

We will go through the evaluation procedures later in the chapter. But right now we could envisage evaluation as serving one major purpose: It will provide the governor with some information concerning the three-year experimental program. *Evaluation may affect but will not determine the governor's decision.* There is a good chance that the governor and the relevant policy-makers in this area already have a viewpoint on the experiment. Additionally, there are probably several pressures on the governor that will affect his or her decision: budgetary issues, the political climate toward crime, his or her own views on punishment and rehabilitation, and the views of key members in the state legislature.

How might an evaluation of the program reduce error? The governor, who plans to run for reelection in about fourteen months, wants to draw up a list of successful programs initiated under his or her administration. Prison reform is one of them. He or she is ready to expand the supervised job program to about four thousand convicts; nevertheless, "proof" is wanted that it is a successful program. The evaluation unit in the office of the superintendent of prisons did a study of the experiment to date. Here are the basic results:

Inmates still participating	125
Inmates dropped out	50
Inmates released	125
Employed	70
Unemployed, worked briefly	20
Unemployed, never worked	35
TOTAL	300

We should add a couple of additional pieces of information. During the three years of the experiment the inmates in the program produced $500,000 for the state's Crime Victimization Fund, or 20 percent of the fund's total. The cost of the experiment for the three years was $1.2 million. Based on the information just given, what would you do if you were the superintendent? Could the governor claim that the program was a success?

Evaluation and Accountability

Even if the governor is not up for reelection, there is a good chance that the program will be evaluated. Evaluation is one way to promote accountability. But who would require evaluation to make sure that bureaucrats are doing their jobs?

It is an established fact that legislators, especially at the federal and state levels, have not valued oversight of administrative agencies as highly as other legislative activities.[3] Making speeches to the Rotary Club seemed more important than asking a bureaucrat how much money was really spent for office supplies or whether a certain amount of travel funds was really necessary. With a changed mood of the citizenry—more skepticism about the worth of government—has come increased attention to the oversight function. Legislators now want to know if government programs are needed and, more important, whether they are cost effective.

At the federal level Congress has required agencies to evaluate new programs as part of the implementation process. In fact, authorizing legislation establishing new programs like public employment, community development, and so on has *required* agencies to evaluate the cost effectiveness of these programs. Often 1 percent of a program's appropriations is set aside precisely for this purpose. These funds have spurred two major developments. First, most federal departments have evaluation units headed by an assistant secretary. These evaluation units can be large—often organized according to the major functional policy areas of the department. Evaluation units evaluate government programs as mandated by Congress or as required by policy-makers (the department head or the president) or they contract with profit or nonprofit firms to evaluate government programs.

When government agencies contract for evaluation work they generally issue a "request for proposal" (RFP), which describes the work that is needed and the time frame for completion. The RFP is supposed to generate competition ("bids") for the evaluation contract. The federal agency is supposed to select a contractor from the group of respondents. Clearly, the second major development created by congressional requirements for evaluation has been the proliferation of consulting firms—both large and small—that want to get a piece of the federal evaluation market. These firms, sometimes called "beltway bandits"—because they literally have rented space next to the Washington, D.C., beltway and have received millions of dollars of federal evaluation funds—represent yet another extension of government. Evaluation has become big business, but this would have been impossible without Congress' interest in it as a method of oversight.

MULTIPLE SOURCES OF INFORMATION

Congress

The major users of evaluation in Congress are committees and subcommittees. In addition to committee staff, which occasionally do evaluation studies, there are four major sources of evaluation information for Congress.[4]

1. *Office of Technology Assessment* (OTA). This office, established in 1972, has a small staff (approximately fifty) with a modest budget—by federal standards. As its title suggests, the OTA provides Congress with techni-

cal analyses of the potential effects of technological changes. Much of the analytical work is contracted out.

2. *General Accounting Office* (GAO). This is the auditing arm of Congress. The GAO is a large agency with more than five thousand employees. *Most* of its work is program evaluation.

3. *Congressional Research Service* (CRS). A research agency in the Library of Congress, the CRS responds to information requests from members of Congress on almost any conceivable issue. They may vary from brief, short-term projects to longer, detailed analyses of proposed legislation or the impact of existing legislation. The CRS staff frequently organize existing research in some area into a form that is usable by members of Congress.

4. *Congressional Budget Office* (CBO). This office is largely responsible for providing budgetary information to the House and Senate budget committees, appropriations committees, and tax committees. It was established as part of the Budget and Impoundment Control Act of 1974. In addition, the CBO does "in-house" program analyses of specific programs of the federal government as requested.

State and Local Governments

The demand for evaluation has increased at the state and local level as well. Like many other facets of intergovernmental management, this demand is partly attributable to the complexity of intergovernmental programs. Furthermore, this complexity has forced state and local legislators to professionalize the legislative process. To a great extent this means an expansion of analytical staff, and with such expansion comes program evaluation.

Program evaluation at the state and local levels is also a stepchild of program retrenchment. Public officials, forced to trim programs, and even terminate them, will sometimes require evaluation as a source of information to help their decision-making responsibilities. Performance criteria and evidence of success may also be required from agencies as part of their annual budget request. A few states have initiated a "sunset review" process, which requires agencies to demonstrate that their programs are effective; otherwise, the legislature ceases future funding. The burden of proof, at least in theory, shifts to the agency, which clearly links evaluation to legislative oversight.

EVALUATION: STAGES OF RESEARCH

Identifying the Problem

Before trying to evaluate something, it is nice to know what the problem is. Consider a "simple" illustration like heroin use.[5] Some will say that the problem is crime. That is, heroin users commit a disproportionate amount of serious crimes. Others say that the problem is the illicitness of heroin itself. If heroin were legalized, organized crime would not be involved in its distribution (because it would be available legally at a "reasonable" price), and heroin users would not have to commit crimes to get money to support their habits. Others say the heroin problem is really about the quality of life of the users—their health and individual welfare. Still others say the problem is more complex and broader than everything mentioned so far. Heroin use, some say, is really about the conditions in society—unemployment, poor housing, poverty—that predispose a segment of the population to become addicted.

Some policy-makers have adopted one view of the heroin problem; some have adopted other views. Indeed, these problems are not mutually exclusive; therefore, there is no "correct" answer. But the specification of the problem is an important beginning in program evaluation because it leads directly to the next stage—*identifying program objectives.*

Identifying Program Objectives

Program objectives are not easily identified because most programs are the product of a lengthy political process that terminates in legislation authorizing the program. The political process produces legislative language that specifies multiple, vague, and frequently contradictory objectives. Other times multiple objectives reflect the push and pull of interest groups on a particular program. Sometimes multiple program objectives exist simply because they make good, sound political and economic sense.

Consider the illustration of the food-stamp program. What is it supposed to achieve? Food stamps are available to individuals who have income below a level established by the federal government. A person eligible for the program buys the stamps (most commonly at banks) and then uses stamps to purchase food. Since the price of a one dollar stamp is less than one dollar, we can say that the program provides *income support* to the individual. In addition, since the individual now has increased purchasing power for food, program advocates assumed that the food stamp program would improve the *nutritional quality* of beneficiaries' food consumption.

Who else is served by the food stamp program? Farmers, of course! After all, if the purchasing power for food of a particular population is increased, this should similarly increase the *demand for agricultural products.* As such, we can think of the food-stamp program as an indirect subsidy for farmers since it expands aggregate demand. Presto, we have three different, though mutually reinforcing, objectives for the food-stamp program.

More often than not, legislative intent is translated into program objectives by the agencies charged with carrying out the legislation. Thus objectives become more easily discernible during the *implementation stage* of programs. One way to think of this process is to imagine legislation as a plan, sometimes only a hope or a wish, and implementation as the series of steps taken to make the plan a reality. The first step in making programs a reality is deciding what they are supposed to achieve.

Evaluators must go further. If a police-deployment program in a city is supposed to "reduce crime," the evaluator must determine, first, what the objective "to reduce crime" means and, second, how to measure it. Among law-enforcement officials and specialists in law-enforcement evaluation, there is a good deal of criticism of published crime data as well as the proper interpretation of the information. Still, crime tends to be measured as a *rate* (number of violent crimes like murder, rape, or armed robbery per one hundred thousand population), arrests, or clearance of suspects. We can think of these measures as attempts to *operationalize* the concept "to reduce crime." Thus we can at least conclude that things are improving if the rate goes down, and things are getting worse if the rate goes up. Operationalizing an objective, then, is specifying the objective in a way that is both observable and measurable. Try to operationalize some of the following program objectives:

> Revitalization of the central business districts of old cities
> Adequate housing for all those with family incomes below $9,000 a year
> Health insurance to protect against catastrophic illness
> Project READ, a program to end illiteracy for all Americans of high school age.

CHOOSING THE EVALUATION DESIGN

Once you have figured out what the program objectives are and you think you know how to measure them, the next step is, at the same time, difficult and simple. It is choosing an evaluation design. This step is simple because the nature of some public programs, the quality of information available, the time frame surrounding the program, the availability of funds, and the needs of policy-makers all combine to favor some types of designs and make others unacceptable. At the same time, choosing an evaluation design is difficult because not all designs are equally sound. Often there is a mismatch between the type of design used to evaluate a program and the type of design that *should* be used if no obstacles are present. Some of these problems are illustrated in the following research designs.[6]

Single-Group Design

Let's evaluate the inmate employment program described in the beginning of the chapter. Remember that the program was started as a pilot project with three hundred inmates, for a three-year period.

If we simply selected the three hundred inmates based on their willingness to participate in the program, we are essentially limited to a "posttest" design. What we want to know is whether the program achieved the following objectives: Did it provide job skills for inmates? Did it reduce recidivism? Did released inmates find jobs and keep them? We can look at the "numbers" at some time after the program, say, two years, and ask some basic questions: How many inmates completed the program? How many found jobs after they were released? How many are employed two years after the program ended? How many ended up back in prison? Let's change the numbers from the earlier table. Suppose the results look like this:

Started program	300
Completed program	210
Found jobs	125
Working after two years	90
Back in prison	30
(those who completed the program)	

Was the program successful? This is very hard to say. Imagine just some of the problems of interpretation. Fourteen percent of those who completed the program were recidivists; but then, 70 percent finished the program, and 59 percent of those completing the program found jobs after being released from prison. But only 43 percent of those who completed the program were working two years after the program ended.

Why is it difficult to interpret these results? For one thing, they are ambiguous. We are not really sure what constitutes satisfactory performance for the inmate employment program. Only if program objectives were explicitly determined at the outset would we have quantitative benchmarks to evaluate the actual outcomes. For the sake of argument, let us assume that the superintendent of prisons thought that a 50 percent job-placement rate for inmates who completed the program and a 40 percent employment rate after two years were both realistic objectives. Can we now make the claim that the program was successful?

There are some basic reasons why the superintendent of prisons would be wise *not* to make dramatic claims based on these results. It is possible, for example, that those who completed the program and found jobs were highly motivated, whereas those who did not find jobs were poorly motivated. Maybe those who retained jobs two years after being released had more work experience *before* entering prison. Maybe they had more skills. There is no way of knowing whether these factors are at all important, that is, whether they, rather than the program, are responsible for the results. Sometimes even a single group, one set of observations, can tell us something about the effectiveness of a program, especially when the "results" are dramatically positive or extremely negative. But the inherent limitations of this design mean that we should try, whenever possible, to overcome them by using a design that is more robust.

Pretest, Posttest Design

Suppose some of the limitations of the previous design were anticipated at the outset. The director of the program, for example, may have asked the participating inmates to fill out a form listing things such as their level of education, employment histories, and specific job skills. For purposes of illustration let us break down the 210 inmates who finished the program as follows:[7]

	Employed Two Years After	Unemployed Two Years After	Total
Employed before prison	75	65	140
Unemployed before prison	15	55	70
Total	90	120	210

Was the program successful? Clearly, we want inmates who were unemployed before prison to be employed after the program, and we certainly want those who were employed before prison to hold jobs after prison. Notice that we have some additional information in this pretest, posttest design; nevertheless, we still must be extremely careful when attributing success or failure to the program. There are a number of threats to the validity of this type of design.[8] For our purpose, let us consider one "internal" threat and one "external" threat. Suppose during the program some inmates became motivated and eager to get out of prison, whereas others became apathetic. These traits may be unrelated to the program; yet they may affect the outcome. We can incorrectly attribute success and failure to the program even though some of the reasons lie in the motivations of the inmates. This example is an internal threat to validity. If there are characteristics of these particular inmates that make them unique (they are somehow different from all other inmates), the results of the evaluation could not be generalized. This is sometimes called external validity, and it clearly limits the usefulness of the evaluation.

Time-Series Design

Sometimes programs are initiated as a response to a perceived problem. A national speed limit of fifty-five miles per hour was initiated as a way to conserve gasoline. The death penalty might be brought back because policy-makers think that it will deter crime. The federal government promotes an inoculation program to eradicate measles. A governor decides that a crackdown on speeders will reduce traffic fatalities.

All of these examples have something in common: The evaluation design question is whether the program has had the desired effect. To visualize this we have to think of a *trend* in the behavior or activity we wish to alter. In the case of measles, for example, we might graphically portray the rate of measles per one hundred thousand for a period before the eradication program.[9] We continue to collect data after the program is initiated and compare the two periods.[10]

Figure 13.1 shows a (hypothetical) time-series trend for the rate of measles.

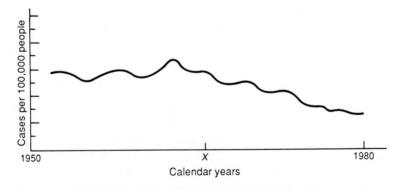

Figure 13.1. Reported Cases of Measles, 1950–1980

The X represents the year the eradication program began. Did the program have a positive effect?

Program evaluators will tend to favor a time-series design over less rigorous ones, but three basic problems inhibit its usefulness in the real world of public policy. First, the design requires accurate, uniform data over an extended period. Many programs fail this first test. Second, the time-series design can be done only by evaluators with sophisticated statistical competence, which usually requires exposure to statistics and research methods in graduate programs such as economics, education, public administration, political science, and sociology. Third, and most important, public officials often want to know whether a program is working soon after it is implemented, perhaps after three years. This may be too short a period to use a time-series design. Still, if policy-makers want to alter a program that has been in place for several years and if they want to increase funding, decrease funding, or even terminate the program, a time-series may be appropriate.

Experimental Design

If you have taken an introductory course in psychology you probably have heard about experimental evaluation designs. Experiments concerning pleasure, pain, fear, sexual arousal—you name it—have been done with this type of design, often on laboratory animals.

The basic procedure is straightforward. Suppose we wanted to find out if a new drug-counseling approach would reduce drug use among users who are attending a drug-treatment program. Assume that the program has two hundred clients. We divide the clients into an "experimental" group and a "control" group by randomly assigning them to one or the other. Next, we provide the new counseling approach to the experimental group only. At the end of the experiment, say one year, we compare the two groups with respect to the program objective—in this case a reduction in drug abuse. If the incidence of drug abuse is significantly different between the two groups (lower for the experimental group), we can say that the new counseling approach is successful in reducing drug abuse.

Here are actual experimental designs:

Phoenix, Arizona, used a controlled experiment to help evaluate its Alcohol Safety Action Program (ASAP). Problem drinkers referred to the program by the courts for driving while intoxicated were randomly assigned (by a court employee) to one of three types of treatment. The three types differed in terms of educational and therapeutic effort. Follow-up, in-person interviews were conducted with about 190 clients of the program in the sixth, twelfth, and eighteenth months after entry. Data on a number of criteria were obtained, including amount of drinking, employment status, physical health, and extent of drinking-related problems.

The courts opposed the use of a no-treatment control group, so the minimum-treatment group was used as the control group. The interviews were conducted by several part-time ASAP employees who received approximately ten hours of training. Federal funds supported the evaluation effort.

The District of Columbia Bail Agency conducted an experiment to determine the effects of the degree of supervision of persons charged with felonies who had been given conditional releases prior to trial. For two months in 1975, 300 defendants were randomly assigned to one of three levels of supervision (100 to each level). At the lowest level of supervision, the defendants themselves initiated contacts with supervisors. The second level of supervision involved biweekly telephone calls or letters to defendants. The highest level of supervision involved monthly visits by the supervisor to the defendant's residence or place of employment.

Data on the outcome of the experiment were collected two years later, after all the cases had been disposed of by the court. The outcomes assessed were pretrial crime as indicated by rearrest rates, failure-to-appear rates, and compliance with conditions of release (such as maintaining regular contact with bail agency and refraining from contact with complaining witnesses). The rearrest rates showed no significant difference (overall, about 26 percent of the defendants were rearrested, but a slightly higher percentage of those under intensive supervision were rearrested, that is, 28 percent). The group under intensive supervision did somewhat better than the other two groups on the other two measures. The agency reported that the experiment was conducted with relatively little difficulty. It felt that the major reasons for the success of the experiment were the availability of sufficient resources to design, implement, and evaluate the experiment and staff continuity over the two-year period.

To assess its employment and training program, the Michigan Department of Social Services randomly assigned 231 clients not served by existing employment programs to one of two groups. Those in the experimental group were given employment, educational, and training opportunities. Those in the control group were left to pursue employment opportunities on their own. Each client was interviewed by phone between six and ten months later about their experiences in finding employment. The experimental group was found to be more successful in finding jobs as compared to the control group for those persons who had the fewest barriers to employment (e.g., who had transportation or who were not handicapped).

□ Source: Harry P. Hatry, Richard E. Winnie, and Donald M. Fisk, Practical Program Evaluation for State and Local Governments, 2d ed. (Washington, D.C.: The Urban Institute Press, 1981), pp. 41–42. Copyright 1981, reprinted with permission.

Experimental evaluation designs seem straightforward in theory. They are less so in practice. In the mid-1960s the Office of Economic Opportunity wanted to test the hypothesis that a guaranteed income for low-income families would have no adverse effect on the principal wage earner's desire to work. A study was designed by researchers at the Institute for Research on Poverty at the University of Wisconsin. The researchers prepared an almost textbook-perfect experimental design. First, a site for the experiment was selected. The site included four communities in New Jersey and one in Pennsylvania. New Jersey *seemed* an ideal location because the state did not give welfare assistance to male-headed families. Second, a randomized sample of thirteen hundred families was selected for the experiment. Third, a "negative income tax" was designed to insure that families would fall below the officially defined poverty level.

Soon the almost perfect case began to fall apart. After the experiment was under way, the state of New Jersey changed its welfare policy, and families with unemployed males became eligible for public assistance. Some families in the experiment accepted *both* the income payments and their newly acquired welfare benefits—clearly antithetical to the experiment and illegal besides. Finally, many families either dropped out of the negative income experiment or participated only sporadically. The original group of thirteen hundred was reduced to only seven hundred for analysis.[11]

This experiment highlights several practical problems: intergovernmental complications, cooperation from the recipients or clients, "missing" data, and political pressures to produce results. What makes experimental designs difficult is that these problems cannot all be anticipated in advance. In addition, experiments are limited because of one basic fact: Program benefits often cannot be denied to eligible recipients. In other words, target populations are usually "entitled" to benefits, or they have a "right" to treatment or service. These rights or entitlements effectively rule out an experimental design for many government programs because the evaluator is prohibited from creating a control group. Even when the right to a treatment or benefit is not strictly required, there is often an implicit moral obligation to provide it. Rehabilitation programs in prisons, for example, may not necessarily be mandated by state law. But denying some inmates rehabilitation programs to see if they work—that is, using an experimental design—may be an unacceptable approach to evaluation.

Let's try to assess the various strengths and limitations of evaluation research designs in a hypothetical situation. Your task is to uncover as many problems with the evaluation as possible. The program is Controlling Recidivism among Parolees—better known as Project CRAP.

Case Exercise Project CRAP

Project CRAP (Controlling Recidivism among Parolees) is a state-funded effort to reduce the probability that parolees will be going back to jail. The formal statement of objectives is that "Project CRAP participants should be less likely to return to prison over a period of time than parolees not participating in CRAP."

After receiving a $400,000 grant from the state (acting as a funding distributor for the new Federal Office of Crime Control), the Public Safety Department of the City of Fernwood set about translating the objective into a real program. The department's Division of Probation and Parole assigned eight employees to Project CRAP. Most of them agreed that one of the greatest obstacles to "making it on the outside" is the frequent failure of parolees to obtain a meaningful job. It was determined that one of the best ways to reduce recidivism would be to provide occupational training.

Given that they were understaffed and overworked, they decided to train the parolees to be paraprofessional probation officers. That is, the parolees enrolled in the program would work closely with the project staff and do many of the same kinds of things that a professional probation officer would do (though their authority would be more limited). They decided that a six-week training program would be set up, and parolees who completed the program would be offered jobs as paraprofessional probation officers.

It was not possible to force parolees to participate in the project. Thus the staff solicited volunteers, stipulating only that a high school diploma was required and parolees convicted of violent crimes were ineligible. After a mailing to all of Fernwood's six hundred parolees, the project administrators obtained twenty-two volunteers who met program requirements. Three of these volunteers *had* committed violent crimes but were retained in the program nonetheless (it seemed desirable to have more than twenty in the program).

A week after the program had begun, an additional $75,000 was sent by the state for an evaluation. After deliberation the project officials reasoned that they were the most qualified to do the evaluation since they were most intimately familiar with the program. They quickly decided on a quasi-experimental approach as the most rigorous and, thus, most desirable. Given that the objective was to reduce recidivism, they decided on a combination of behavioral and attitudinal indicators.

A control group was set up composed of 22 of the 578 parolees who had *not* volunteered. The sample was drawn by telephoning parolees (at least those who had telephones) on an alphabetical list of the 600. By the time the officials had gotten to the D's, 22 parolees had agreed to participate in the control group ($50 was offered for participation). The research design was set up to see if the project objective (see first paragraph) had been reached.

Three indicators were used, each of which was to be given equal weight in assessing program accomplishments: (1) whether after six weeks more members of the control group or the treatment group had gone back to prison; (2) whether morality (experimental morality, that is) was greater among the control group or the treatment group; (3) whether the control group or the treatment group showed more attitudinal change based on scales constructed to measure "criminal behavior predispositions" (the scales were constructed during a brainstorming session among program administrators). The last indicator served as the pretest.

The findings indicated that one person dropped out of the treatment group but three dropped out of the control group (5 percent attrition versus 15 percent attrition). Also, two people in the control group, but no one in the treatment group, were convicted during the six-week period. Most interesting to the program administrators was the fact that the treatment group showed a 20 percent mean shift in the "criminal predisposition scale" (and in the "right" direction), whereas there was no difference at all in the mean for the control group. They concluded that the program was a smashing success and mailed their evaluation report to the state and federal Office of Crime Control.

Work and Welfare: Analysis of AFDC Employment Programs in Four States

In 1988 Congress passed a law that changes the administration of public assistance in the United States. One part of the law attempts to achieve one of the long-standing objectives of welfare policy—motivate individuals who are able to work to get off the welfare rolls and onto the payrolls. Several states have tried different ways of encouraging recipients of the Aid to Families with Dependent Children (AFDC) program to obtain employment. How sucessful have the efforts been?

In January 1988 the General Accounting Office prepared a report summarizing the experiences of the Work Incentive (WIN) Demonstrations in four states: Massachusetts, Michigan, Oregon, and Texas. Assume that you are a policy analyst in the U.S. Department of Health and Human Services. After reviewing the data provided below, prepare a memorandum to the secretary of health and human services summarizing your interpretation of the findings. In other words, based on the results from the four states, should we expect the mandatory work incentive programs for the AFDC recipients that is now part of the 1988 law to succeed?

TABLE 13.1. Program Models and Goals

	Massachusetts	Michigan	Texas	Oregon
Program name	Employment and Training Choices (ET).	Michigan Opportunity and Skills Training (MOST) program.	Employment Services Program.	JOBS
Model	Multiple services provided by multiple nonwelfare agencies. Program acts as broker to obtain services for participants.	Multiple services provided by both program and nonwelfare agencies. However, program varies by local office.	One basic service provided primarily by program staff and Texas Employment Commission (TEC) under contract.	One basic service provided primarily by program staff.
Goals	Place welfare recipients in meaningful jobs; reduce welfare dependency; save tax dollars. Local offices cited helping participants achieve self-sufficiency.	Help people get off public assistance and become self-sufficient by overcoming barriers to employment and helping them find a job.	Achieve maximum number of employment entries. Individual regions may aim for higher quality placements.	Assist JOBS participants to become self-supporting.
Jobs sought for participants	"Priority" or "meaningful" jobs: those that pay $5 or more per hour, last thirty days or more, and are full time.	At least minimum wage and thirty hours a week. Jobs must be retained for ninety days for placement credit. Caseworkers divided between participants taking any job and those taking only jobs leading to self-sufficiency.	Many caseworkers aim for the best jobs available to match interest and skills. In reality, hope for full-time job paying at least minimum wage.	Participants must accept any bona fide job offer, including temporary, permanent, full time, part time, or seasonal. Must pay wage equal to federal or state minimum wage. (In practice, caseworkers are more flexible.)

TABLE 13.1. *(cont.)*

	Massachusetts	Michigan	Texas	Oregon
Administrative structure	Central office sets policy. Local offices administer, generally following central office guidance although some variations do occur.	Local offices have significant discretion over program content. Variation among sites in terms of policies and services offered.	State provides general guidance. Administered through regions, which have discretion over program shape. Local offices within the regions, some of which cover huge areas, deliver the program services.	State office sets broad policy and local offices flexible within those bounds. Administered through regional and local offices.
Intake procedures	Income-eligibility case-workers, who function as overall case managers, refer recipients needing education or training to ET caseworkers. Other participants may be referred directly to Employment Security for placement. Voucher day care workers arrange child care.	Income-eligibility caseworkers refer mandatory and voluntary participants to MOST caseworkers, who assign them to activities and arrange support services.	Depending on local offices, income-eligibility case-workers refer mandatory and voluntary participants either to employment program caseworkers or TEC for employment-related services. Support services arranged by same unit that administers employment program.	Varies by local offices. In some, income-eligibility workers refer mandatory participants to JOBS caseworkers, who arrange terms of job search and any support services provided. In others, JOBS caseworkers are responsible for intake.

TABLE 13.2. AFDC Employment Program Expenditures by Sources of Funds, Fiscal Year 1986 (Dollars in Thousands).

Funding Source	Massachusetts		Michigan		Texas		Oregon	
	Amount	Percent	Amount	Percent	Amount	Percent	Amount	Percent
Federal:								
IV-A	$6,800	16	$2,429	7	$2,178	24	$ 2,893	24
WIN (fiscal year 1986)	5,100	12	14,765	44	4,093	46	5,641	47
WIN carried forward[a]	3,100	7	000	0	000	0	000	0
Special project	000	0	000	0	146	2	000	0
Subtotal	15,000	35	17,194	51	6,417	72	8,534	71
State:								
Match for federal	7,600	18	4,070	12	2,497	28	3,520	29
Additional state	20,300	47	12,474	37	000	0	000	0
Subtotal	27,900	65	16,544	49	2,497	28	3,520	29
Local	000	0	000	0	000	0	000	0
Total budget	$42,900	100	$33,738	100	$8,914	100	$12,054	100
Average expenditures per participant (actual)	$1,257[b]		$410		$170		c	
Average expenditures per placement (actual)	$3,333		d		$457		$810	

[a]WIN funds not expended in one year can be carried forward for use in the next.

[b]Massachusetts' average child-care expenditure per participant was $510 (41 percent of average expenditures per participant). These figures represent total expenditures averaged over all participants and do not reflect an actual amount per participant who received child care.

[c]Cannot be calculated because total participants unavailable.

[d]Cannot be calculated because total placements unavailable.

TABLE 13.3. Economic and Demographic Factors

	Massachusetts	Michigan	Texas	Oregon
Population (1985)	5,822,000	9,088,000	16,370,000	2,687,000
Poverty rate (1985)	9%	15%	16%	12%
Number of AFDC recipients (1985)	236,100	672,600	398,900	78,300
AFDC recipients as percentage of population (1985)	4	7	2	3
AFDC payment standard[a] for family of three (1987)	$510	$512/$548[b]	$184	$412
AFDC recipients:				
Black	17%	46%	43%	9%
Hispanic	21%	2%	38%	4%
Unemployed parent	2%	14%	c	3%
Unemployment rate (1986)	4%	9%	9%	9%
Average annual pay (1986)[d]	$20,737	$22,869	$19,976	17,857
Per capita income (1985)	$16,380	$13,608	$13,483	$12,622
Employed (1986):[e]				
Manufacturing	21%	27%	15%	19%
Wholesale/retail	24%	22%	26%	25%
Services	28%	22%	21%	22%
Government	13%	16%	17%	19%
Other	15%	12%	22%	15%

Source: Bureau of the Census, *Statistical Abstract of the United States, 1987*, for total population, welfare receipt, and per capita income; Congressional Research Service, *Aid to Families with Dependent Children (AFDC): Need Standards, Payment Standards, and Maximum Benefits for Families with no Countable Income* (September 28, 1987), for AFDC payment standards; U.S. Bureau of Labor Statistics, *Employment and Earnings*, May 1987, for unemployment and job structure; and U.S. Bureau of Labor Statistics, *Average Annual Pay by State and Industry* (Press release, September 1, 1987), for average annual pay.

TABLE 13.4. Participation Rates (Fiscal Year 1986)

	Massachusetts	Michigan	Texas	Oregon
Adult AFDC recipients:				
Monthly	84,427	220,050	119,032	28,198
Annual	120,000	312,171	173,508	a
Employment program registrants:				
Monthly	a	215,844	42,679	a
Annual	a	a	85,562	a
Employment program participants:[b]				
Monthly	16,513	53,140	15,077	13,060
Annual	34,128	82,333	52,540	a

TABLE 13.4. Participation Rates (Fiscal Year 1986) (*cont.*)

	Massachusetts	Michigan	Texas	Oregon
Participants as percentage of registrants:				
Monthly	a	25	35	a
Annual	a	a	61	a
Participants as percentage of AFDC recipients:				
Monthly	20	24	13	46
Annual	28	26	30	a

a. Not available.
b. Massachusetts counted as participants those people who received a service such as education or training, not those receiving only orientation or assessment. Michigan included all registrants who participated in any component of the MOST program, including orientation or assessment. Texas counted people who were involved in any program activity, including assessment and self-placement. Oregon included anyone required to participate or volunteering to participate in the JOBS program.

TABLE 13.5. Job Placements and Wage Rates, 1986

	Massachusetts	Michigan	Texas	Oregon
Number placed in jobs	12,870	a	19,509	18,324
Placement rate (percent)[b]	38	a	37	a
Percentage full time	68	a	71	65
Average wage	$5.45[c]	$4.70[d]	$3.76[e]	$4.09
Percentage earning hourly wage of:				
Under $3.35	0	1[d]	4[e]	0
$3.35–$4.00	32	a	70[e]	34
$4.01–$5.00	30	a	16[e]	65
$5.01–$6.00	18	a	7[e]	1
$6.01 or more	20	17[d]	4[e]	0
Percentage retaining jobs:				
30 days	85[f]	a	81	a
90 days	a	76[d]	a	a
180 days	82[f]	69[d]	a	a
270 days	a	64[d]	a	a
360 days	a	61[d]	a	a
Percentage of AFDC grant closures lasting:				
90 days	a	76	84[g]	a
180 days	a	69	68[g]	a
270 days	a	64	a	a
360 days	86	61	56[g]	a
Cost per placement	$3,333	a	$457	$658

a. Not available.
b. Number of participants finding jobs during the year as a percentage of annual participants.
c. Data are only for full-time jobs.
d. Data are only for placements made by contractors, which serve about half of MOST participants.
e. Based on placements made by TEC, which were 31 percent of all placements.
f. Based on all DES placements, representing 50 percent of all ET placements. Program staff believe they are representative of all placements.
g. Fiscal year 1985 data.

TABLE 13.6. Job Placements by Occupation, Fiscal Year 1986 (Percentages)

Occupational Category	Placements in Category			
	Massachusetts[a]	Michigan[b]	Texas[c]	Oregon[d]
Professional, technical, managerial	10	3	3	5
Clerical	34	11	20	19
Sales	4	5	6	e
Service/domestic	18	27	54	48
Farming, forestry, fishing	2	3	1	10
Processing	4	f	3	6
Machine trades	6	22[g]	1	2
Bench work	7	f	6	4
Structural/construction	7	7	2	2
Transportation	2	3	1[h]	f
Packing/handling	6	f	f	f
Helpers and laborers	f	18	f	f
Other	f	1	5	4

a. Based on all DES placements, representing 50 percent of all ET placements. Program staff believe they are representative of all placements.
b. Based on placements by MOST contractors, who served about half of program participants in 1986.
c. Information is for participants finding jobs through TEC, representing 31 percent of total placements.
d. Information is for all placements.
e. This category is included in clerical occupations.
f. Not applicable (the program does not use this category).
g. Includes occupations described as "Mechanical/repair" and "Production," some of which may belong in categories other than "Machine trades."
h. Described as "Motor freight transportation."

SUMMARY

In the public sector many government programs lack self-evident criteria of success. That is, it is not always obvious whether programs are succeeding or failing. Since managers are often faced with competing purposes *and* limited resources, it is wise to try to determine what works and what doesn't. This, in a nutshell, is the task of program evaluation.

Program evaluation is also important because it provides managers with additional information to help them make decisions. At the federal level several agencies perform program evaluation: Office of Technology Assessment, General Accounting Office, Congressional Research Service, and Congressional Budget Office. State and local governments also employ program evaluation staff in both the executive and legislative branches. Evaluation has now become common at all levels of government because it fosters accountability of government. In short, program evaluation is a tool that helps public administrators improve performance in the public sector.

Evaluation in government proceeds in three broad stages. First, program objectives must be *operationalized*—put in quantitative terms whenever possible—so that the evaluator can determine whether or not there has been some improvement in the program. Second, the evaluator chooses an *evaluation design*. Although evaluation designs vary in their internal and external validity, the choice often depends on one or more of the following: the time frame of the evaluation, the adequacy of program data, legal constraints, and the sophistication of the evaluator. Third, evaluation results must be seen to have an effect. At this stage, research and politics mix. Program evaluating may be threatening to managers who learn that some of their programs are not very effective. If the evaluation results are positive, you are in a position to justify program development or, at least, maintenance. But remember: evaluation is only one dimension in the complex world of bureaucratic politics.

NOTES

1. See, for example, W. Michael Blumenthal, "Candid Reflections of a Businessman in Washington," in *Public Management*, ed. James L. Perry and Kenneth Kraemer (Palo Alto, Calif.: Mayfield Publishing Co., 1983), pp. 22–23.
2. Aaron Wildavsky, *Speaking Truth to Power* (Boston: Little, Brown, 1979), pp. 212–237.
3. A standard work on legislative oversight is Joseph P. Harris, *Congressional Control of Administration* (Washington, D.C.: Brookings Institution, 1964).
4. The four examples are based on Allen Schick, "The Supply and Demand for Analysis on Capitol Hill," *Policy Analysis* 2 (Spring 1979): 230–232.
5. See Mark H. Moore, "Anatomy of the Heroin Problem: An Exercise in Program Definition," *Policy Analysis* 2 (Fall 1976): 639–662.
6. Donald T. Campbell and Julian C. Stanley, *Experimental and Quasi-Experimental Designs for Research* (Chicago: Rand McNally, 1963).
7. The table is based on Emil J. Posavac and Raymond G. Carey, *Program Evaluations: Methods and Case Studies* (Englewood Cliffs, N.J.: Prentice-Hall, 1980), p. 166.
8. Campbell and Stanley, *Experimental and Quasi-Experimental Designs*.
9. Robert Albritton, "Cost-Benefits of Measles Eradication: Effects of a Federal Intervention," *Policy Analysis* 4 (Winter 1978): 1–22.
10. For those interested in learning statistical tests, see Jan Kmenta, *Elements of Econometrics* (New York: Macmillan, 1971).
11. See Peter H. Rossi, Howard Freeman, and Sonia R. Wright, *Evaluation: A Systematic Approach* (Beverly Hills, Calif.: Sage Publications, 1979), pp. 56–57, 190–191.

FOR FURTHER READING

Bingham, Richard D., and Claire L. Felbinger. *Evaluation In Practice*. White Plains, N.Y.: Longman, 1989.
    A clear presentation, filled with many examples and cases, of the major evaluation designs. This book can be read with little difficulty by undergraduates.

Campbell, Donald T., and Julian C. Stanley. *Experimental and Quasi-Experimental Designs for Research.* Chicago: Rand McNally, 1963.
　　The "bible" for evaluators who want to review alternative research designs.

Hatry, Harry P., Richard E. Winnie, and Donald M. Fisk. *Practical Program Evaluation for State and Local Governments.* 2d ed. Washington, D.C.: Urban Institute, 1981.
　　A how-to approach designed for state and local administrators.

Meltsner, Arnold. *Policy Analysts in the Bureaucracy.* Berkeley: University of California Press, 1976.
　　Still one of the few studies documenting the political precariousness of the research enterprise in bureaucracies.

Wholey, Joseph S. *Evaluation and Effective Public Management.* Boston: Little, Brown, 1983.
　　Shows how evaluation is an integral part of public management.

CHAPTER 14

Ethics and Accountability

FOUR ETHICAL DILEMMAS

Ethical Dilemma 1

Psychiatrists who were in charge of various units in the psychiatric division of a large municipal hospital were employed "three-quarters time." That is, they worked thirty hours a week. The psychiatrists worked less than a full week because they supplemented their income from the municipal hospital with income from private psychiatric practices.

As it turned out, the psychiatrists actually worked somewhat less than thirty hours. It was common for them to work about twenty-two to twenty-five hours a week, because they wanted to get a "head start" on their private practices. About $90 an hour, five to eight hours a week, was not exactly small change.

The chief psychiatrist, the head of the psychiatric division, knew about this discrepancy between official and unofficial working hours, but she chose to ignore it. Her reasoning was as follows: Any good psychiatrist will have a private practice. It is not that easy to get top-notch psychiatrists to take the positions in this division. The pay isn't bad, but it is not exactly wonderful either. Psychiatrists who would accept the job and really put in thirty hours would be mediocre, so it was better, in the long run, to look the other way. That is, she was better off, the hospital was better off, and even the patients were better off.

Ethical Dilemma 2

A private hospital started a clinic for "sex disorders." So far there was no public sector involvement and no ethical dilemmas. Every patient who went to the clinic had a complete physical examination, and the laboratory work was performed at a nearby municipal hospital (the same hospital mentioned in ethical dilemma 1, as it turned out). There was an "informal" arrangement between the director of the sex clinic and the director of the lab. The lab did the sex clinic work, which was really not very extensive, along with the other lab work it received from the private hospital. There was one "minor" wrinkle in this arrangement: The municipal hospital received no payment (or reimbursement) for the lab work it did for the clinic. That is, the taxpayers of the municipality, who supported the municipal hospital, were subsidizing the sex clinic and its patients.

Ethical Dilemma 3

Police Officer Joe was a neighborhood friend. When he walked his beat, residents felt safe. Kids looked up to him. Criminals feared him. Officer Joe had a reputation as a tough cop. He could be mean, especially if you tried committing a crime against the defenseless people in his neighborhood.

Officer Joe had been walking the same beat for eighteen years. Once a day, occasionally twice, he would stop in at Johnny's Luncheonette. He usually had a cup of coffee and occasionally a donut or a sandwich. Several years ago, after Officer Joe had prevented a holdup, Johnny refused to accept any money from Officer Joe—and he has refused to accept money ever since. Officer Joe protested; he said he was just doing his job. But Johnny wouldn't hear of it. Eventually, Officer Joe stopped offering payment, and Johnny stopped refusing. Neither of them thought anything of it.

Last year a full-scale corruption probe took place in the police department. Any type of irregularity, large or small, was ripe for investigation. Officer Joe's superior, Sergeant Dogood, who knew about the informal arrangement between Officer Joe and Johnny, told him that he would have to "write up" this irregularity and report it to the precinct captain. At first, Officer Joe thought that Sergeant Dogood was kidding, but he soon realized that he wasn't. "I have to put it down on my report, Joe. But you know the captain. He'll ignore Mickey Mouse stuff like this. It's the big fish they're after." Officer Joe seemed worried. Suddenly, he was not able to forget about all those coffees, donuts, and sandwiches, and he began to think about his eighteen years on the force, his pension, and his future. "But maybe there really is no reason to worry," he thought. "After all, coffee, donuts, and sandwiches are Mickey Mouse, aren't they?"

Ethical Dilemma 4

It is common for civil servants to be asked to talk to various groups and organizations. College professors in political science and public administration, for example, often invite civil servants to talk to their classes. Similarly, professional organizations will frequently have luncheon meetings that include speakers who discuss some timely topic that concerns the organization.

Should civil servants be paid for these speaking engagements? Most governments make it easy to answer this question. A common rule is as follows: Civil servants are prohibited from accepting money for a speaking engagement if the engagement takes place during working hours.

Several years ago I taught a graduate-level course entitled "Public Budgeting." The class met once a week in the evening. During one semester I invited four state government employees to talk to my class. Not knowing the specific regulations concerning payment for speaking arrangements, I offered each a modest honorarium for the talks. Three declined, saying either that it simply "wasn't necessary" or that they weren't supposed to accept payment if they were giving a talk related to their job. One person accepted the honorarium.

WHY ETHICS IS AN ISSUE

Most of you have heard the phrase "Let your conscience be your guide." Obviously, it implies that your own sense of "right" behavior, perhaps guided by some ethical standard, will help you make "moral" choices. Surely, we do not mean by this statement that everyone, left to his and her own devices, will choose the morally superior alternatives whenever decisions are necessary. Rather, we assume that "something" will "guide" people toward the correct choices.

What might guide bureaucrats toward ethical decisions? We can think about the sources of obligation that impinge on their behavior. Dwight Waldo offers a list of twelve.[1]

1. Obligation to the Constitution
2. Obligation to law
3. Obligation to the nation
4. Obligation to democracy
5. Obligation to organizational norms
6. Obligation to the profession
7. Obligation to family and friends
8. Obligation to self
9. Obligation to "middle-range collectivities" (like social class, race, or political party)
10. Obligation to the public interest
11. Obligation to humanity
12. Obligation to religion or God

Even a quick glance at this list will reveal that all of these obligations cannot guide ethical choices at any one time. Some will clearly conflict with others. Surely, an obligation to nation will sometimes conflict with an obligation to self or religion or humanity, perhaps when the moral rightness of a nation's action (such as unprovoked military aggression) violates another obligation. On an operational level, the bureaucrat is in an ethical quagmire precisely because there are so many different sources of ethical constraints that affect the bureaucrat at any one time.

This discussion gives rise to the problem of "moral ambiguity," which occurs when there are several alternative sources of ethical guidance that could influence the bureaucrat.[2] Moreover, ethical standards change over time. Consider Tammany Hall boss George Washington Plunkitt's comments on the "subtle" distinction between "honest" and "dishonest" graft:

> Everybody is talkin' these days about Tammany men growin' rich on graft, but nobody thinks of drawin' the distinction between honest graft, and dishonest graft. . . . There's an honest graft, and I'm an example of how it works. I might sum up the whole thing by sayin': "I seen my opportunities and I took 'em."
>
> Just let me explain by examples. My party's in power in the city, and it's goin' to undertake a lot of public improvements. Well, I'm tipped off, say, that they're going to lay out a new park at a certain place.
>
> I see my opportunity and I take it. I go to that place and I buy up all the land I can in the neighborhood. Then the board of this or that makes its plan public, and there is a rush to get my land, which nobody cared particular for before.
>
> Ain't it perfectly honest to charge a good price and make a profit on my investment and foresight? Of course, it is. Well, that's honest graft.[3]

With such "opportunities," Plunkitt said, there was no reason to turn to dishonest graft, like blackmailing people who broke the law. Would you make the same distinction today that Plunkitt made more than eighty years ago? Probably not. We would treat Plunkitt's "opportunities" as, at least, ethical lapses. More likely, they would be against the law. Indeed, when a person breaks the law there is no "moral ambiguity," no mere "ethical lapse." Whereas ethics surely involve dilemmas and decisions that are susceptible to alternative interpretations, breaking the law offers no such opportunity.

Let's return to the third ethical dilemma. Did Officer Joe wrestle with moral ambiguity? Yes, he did. You will recall that he initially did not want to receive free coffee, donuts, and sandwiches from Johnny, but Johnny made it hard for him to say no, and Officer Joe probably thought there was "no harm" done by accepting Johnny's food.

Was any harm done? Suppose Officer Joe actually violated a police department regulation about accepting payment or bribes. We know that he was not being bribed by Johnny, though the free food was like a payment. To determine if harm had been done, we should think about the purposes of the regulation. Most likely, it was designed to insure that police officers would be impartial in the enforcement of the law. Yet police officers are not merely supposed to be impartial; they are also supposed to be effective. Officer Joe was clearly an effective cop. There was no reason, moreover, to think that he was not impartial. Indeed, refusing Johnny's offers, and thereby the tacit acknowledgment of Officer Joe's importance to the neighborhood (by not charging for the food), could have been counterproductive. Johnny and the law-abiding residents may have interpreted Officer Joe's refusal as a sign of aloofness. So Officer Joe really had a moral dilemma: He did violate a regulation; there is no doubt about that. But there is some doubt about whether any harm occurred, and there is also some question about whether the neighborhood was better off, or worse off, because of Officer Joe's indiscretion. This is the essence of moral ambiguity.

Sometimes moral ambiguity can be lessened. Consider ethical dilemma 4. Why did three civil servants refuse an honorarium and one accept? After all, all four of them spoke in the evening. Perhaps the three who refused reasoned as follows: Their jobs are not neatly circumscribed between the hours of nine and five. They often work in the evenings during peak periods in the state's budget process. They frequently take work home. Consequently, that the class met in the evening did not alter the fact that they were not supposed to accept payment. Moreover, since they were talking to the class about budgeting, the talk was really just an extension of their work. Also, anything they would say would be based on information and knowledge received from their tenure as a civil servant. (Obviously, the fourth civil servant did not accept these caveats or chose to ignore them.) Is there an operating rule of thumb in this ethical dilemma? When there is even an appearance of irregularity it is best to err on the side of a stringent ethical stance. Even if the fourth civil servant was technically correct, the other three opted for a strict interpretation of the regulation so that there would be no appearance of impropriety. The problem of moral ambiguity would therefore be reduced.

"The End of Free Lunches in Washington?"

An advisory decision by the Office of Government Ethics called for an end to "free" breakfasts, lunches and dinners for executive branch employees paid for by everyone from journalists to lobbyists. The decision threatened a widespread Washington tradition where information was exchanged over "working lunches." The reason for the action was straightforward. In the words of the chief counsel of the Office of Government Ethics at the time, the memorandum was designed to "heighten the sensitivity within the Federal work force of the standards of conduct that are expected." One top level executive employee had an alternative interpretation of the ruling. In his words, "It's going to mean I'll starve."

□ Source: David Johnson, "New Reasons to Fight for the Bill at Lunch," New York Times, October 29, 1987, p. A28.

ETHICAL DILEMMAS ARISING OUT OF ORGANIZATIONAL BEHAVIOR

Organizations do things that people would prefer not to do. Organizations kill people; they look into the private lives of people; they besmirch the honor and reputation of people; they tell lies; they cheat.

These things are done in the name of national defense or internal security. Sometimes they are done in the name of competition, and sometimes they are done because a manager assumed that such actions would further the organization's mission.

When would an individual face an ethical dilemma brought about by an action (or inaction) in the organization taken without the individual's knowledge? Let's go back to ethical dilemma 2—the sex clinic. Consider the problem of the lab technician in the municipal hospital who is responsible for performing the various chemical tests in the laboratory. The financial arrangements and accounting procedures are not his responsibility. Of course, after a while, he had learned about many of the arrangements, and he assumed that the financial and accounting procedures were taken care of by the appropriate officer.

One evening a friend told the lab technician about the new sex clinic. "You are probably doing the lab workups on these sex clinic patients," his friend mentioned matter of factly. "I doubt it," said the lab technician. "We only have a contract to do their hematology work, nothing else."

The lab technician thought about his friend's comment. The more he thought about it, the more plausible it seemed. First, he had noticed an increase in the lab work in hematology that had come from the private hospital, and as he thought of it, he recalled work he had done in addition to blood analysis. "Well, even if my friend is right, I'm sure that the accounting department knows about it," he thought. But the more he thought about it, the less confident he was that accounting did know. Something didn't seem "normal" about this whole thing.

Now put yourself in the lab technician's place. What should he do? One option is to verify the "information arrangement" between the sex clinic and someone in the municipal hospital. The next step is to turn the situation to one's own advantage. The lab technician could inform the parties to the arrangement that he knows about it, for example, and wants "part of the action"; otherwise he will expose the deal. This option obviously assumes that the lab technician is, himself, less than ethical.

At the other extreme, he could do nothing. This option is straightforward, and it could be the best post hoc choice. If there were no irregularities, he would seem rather foolish implying that something was wrong. The next two options require action by the lab technician. He could "leak" the rumor to a third party, who in turn would investigate further. A local newspaper, for example, may find the rumor important enough to assign a reporter to follow up on the story. Alternatively, the technician can investigate the rumor himself. He can discuss it with his supervisor or with the accounting officer. The problem with this fourth option is that he may risk his reputation or job by "poking around" in the hospital.

The ethical dilemma faced by the lab technician is very common. It occurs when organizational behavior conflicts with the ethical standards of the individual, as well as the individual's attempt to uphold the public interest. Those who have chosen not to "look the other way" are called whistle-blowers.[4] That is, they "blow the whistle" on—bring to public attention—wrongdoing of their organizations. Here is the testimony of Jake Lapin, a government auditor, who blew the whistle on the Department of the Navy and paid a heavy price for his actions:

Statement of Jake Lapin, Department of the Navy

Mr. Lapin. Good morning, Madam Chairman. My name is Jake Lapin, and I have been employed by the U.S. Government as an auditor for 25 years. But even as I appear here today before your subcommittee, my job is in severe jeopardy because I am a whistleblower who refused to look the other way when I uncovered improprieties.

I would like to respectfully submit that notwithstanding your subcommittee's hard work and determination to legislate protection for whistleblowers within the Civil Service Reform Act of 1978, the protection mechanism does not work in practice, as a brief recounting of my personal experience will show.

I was forced to resign by the Naval Audit Service in March 1976, when my supervisors became aware that I was going to call certain improprieties on their part to the attention of higher authority. I appealed my case, and in December 1977, the Federal Employee Appeals Authority ordered the Naval Audit Service to restore me to my former position. Instead, the Service filed a petition to reopen my case. In August 1979, I was again ordered restored to my former position, this time by the Merit Systems Protection Board, which was created by the Civil Service Reform Act.

So far, so good. However, the Naval Audit Service still refuses to properly restore me, has no intention of doing so, and in fact has attempted to transfer me involuntarily in reprisal. That transfer has been preliminarily enjoined, but the Service is marshaling its considerable legal forces against me as never before. Removal action was initiated against me as never before. Removal action was initiated against me within the past 2 weeks in an attempt, in my opinion, to prevent me from appearing before this subcommittee.

As you are aware, the Code of Ethics for Civil Servants has been incorporated into law. This code, among other things, requires that Federal employees place their first loyalty to the highest moral principle, and to country. I have endeavored to comply with this mandate as an internal auditor concerned with the best interests of the United States Treasury. However, I have continually met severe opposition by the Federal agencies I worked for, and my superiors who did not comply with the Code of Ethics.

For example, I have found that Federal agencies would rather overlook the statutory requirement to pursue restitution and fines from those known to have defrauded our Government than be subjected to the publicity of having allowed themselves to be defrauded. Also, Federal agencies employing internal auditors expect them to assist in circumventing certain laws regarding the administrative control over appropriated funds in order that unobligated funds at the end of a fiscal year, which should be returned to the Treasury, are illegally retained, and used after the expiration date for obligation.

□ *Source: U.S. House of Representatives, Hearings, Subcommittee on Civil Service of the Committee on Post Office and Civil Service Reform Oversight—1980, 96th Cong. 2nd Sess., 1980, p. 81.*

How widespread is whistle-blowing? Not very. In a survey done in 1980 by the U.S. Merit Systems Protection Board, 45 percent of the eighty-five hundred respondents said that they had personally seen waste, fraud, or gross mismanagement. Yet almost three-quarters of them admitted that they said nothing and did nothing about it. Some respondents said that fear of reprisal deterred them, but most simply said that they thought nothing would be done to correct the situation.[5]

Why isn't there more whistle-blowing if, indeed, there are waste, fraud, and abuse in government? One reason was graphically depicted in the 1970s movie *Serpico*. Frank Serpico, a New York City police officer, charged that graft and corruption were widespread in the police department. The charge led to a probe of corruption by a body called the Knapp Commission. Several incidents of corruption were exposed, but Serpico was ostracized by his fellow officers, and in fact, his life was threatened. He ultimately left the police force and moved to Switzerland.

Few whistle-blowers are threatened with murder. Rather, their institutional loyalty is questioned by colleagues. To be effective, whistle-blowers must rise above institutional loyalty and appeal to a broader audience. The public interest, often difficult to define in practice, usually serves as the focal point for the whistle-blower's dissent. Saving the taxpayers' money is a nice, concrete way to highlight this concept.

Even when an appeal to higher values has credibility (or at least some logic), civil servants may still be reluctant to blow the whistle on their organization's irregularities. There is simply little to be gained, from a personal standpoint—and much to lose. The Civil Service Reform Act of 1978 tried to provide protection for whistle-blowers. A Special Counsel's Office, linked to the Merit System Protection Board (MSPB), is supposed to receive and investigate charges against agencies and particular employees. Moreover, charges can be brought anonymously, thereby protecting whistle-blowers from reprisals. The special counsel may also start an action before the MSPB on behalf of government employees who become whistle-blowers and, as a result, suffer from negative personnel procedures by their agencies. Hearings held in 1980 by the House Subcommittee on Civil Service heard testimony from several whistle-blowers who claimed that they were harassed by their agencies despite the MSPB protection. The whistle-blowers offered little encouragement to future government employees who were planning to come forward with charges of waste, fraud, and abuse.[6] Here is how Jake Lapin described his experiences with the procedures:

The Civil Service Reform Act is sometimes called the whistleblowers act, but my experience shows that it is anything but that. An Office of Special Counsel has been established to receive reports from whistleblowers regarding a gross waste of funds, violations of public laws, and mismanagement. Accordingly, I have reported several instances of a gross waste of funds and violations of public laws. The Special Counsel concurred in my reports, and used its authority to initiate an inquiry into the matter. However, the agencies responsible for getting restitution from those known to have defrauded the Government, or overpaid by it, either will not, or cannot take the action required to make the Treasury whole again.

Furthermore, in my case, the Merit Systems Protection Board has clearly demonstrated that it cannot either prevent, discourage, or stop reprisals and abuses to which whistleblowers are automatically heir. Unfortunately, the whistleblower normally will not have access to the courts to protect himself because the law requires that he first exhaust his administrative remedies. It is during this administrative process that whistleblowers incur reprisal actions frequently resulting in dismissal. Then, when the whistleblower seeks remedial action in the Federal court, those persons who harassed and abused him are protected by the U.S. Government attorneys with unlimited funds available to them. Under such a scenario, potential whistleblowers are reluctant to make disclosures. This is especially true after the Merit Systems Protection Board has issued so many decisions supporting management at the expense of the whistleblower. In my case, I received a favorable final decision by the Board, but the pressures put on the Board by top Navy management induced it to reverse itself in a very irregular manner.

In view of the proven record of the Merit Systems Protection Board as being unable to adequately protect the whistleblower, I have taken unilateral action to arrange for some semblance of protection for whistleblowers in the Federal courts for the ninth circuit. Specifically, in my lawsuit, Lapin v. Taylor, volume 475 of the Federal supplement, page 446, tried in the Federal Court for the District of Hawaii in 1979, I managed to get the court to recognize that whistleblowers constitute a class entitled to the protection of the Civil Rights Act, and can bring actions directly to Federal court against those who conspire to interfere with their legally protected rights because of the whistleblowing activities.

I have also noted that the special counsel for the Merit Systems Protection Board admits it does not have authority to issue injunctions to prevent reprisal transfers of whistleblowers. Thus, in another of my lawsuits, Lapin v. Claytor, et al., Civil No. 77-0412, District Court for the District of Hawaii, I managed to get the court to recognize that there is no adequate administrative remedy available to a whistleblower for enjoining a reprisal transfer, and thus my reprisal transfer has been preliminarily enjoined. Such injunctive relief should be available through the administrative law process, as well.

Even though a whistleblower can bring a civil action against those in supervision who interfere with the exercise of his legal rights, the supervisors being sued are given full protection by the Government. This practice affords no deterrent to reprisals and abuses. What is needed is legislation to allow whistleblowers immediate access to the Federal courts to sue those who abuse, harass, or bring reprisal actions against them in their personal capacity, with the burden of proof being put on the wrong-

doer to rebut a prima facie case. Without the availability of Government legal services, a supervisor will think twice about harassing or abusing whistleblowers. Also, such a deterrent will encourage potential whistle-blowers, heretofore silent because of the fear of reprisal, to make disclosures of a gross waste of funds, violations of public laws, and mismanagement.

Madam Chairman, by protecting whistleblowers, who really are only men and women simply trying to do their job, you will set into motion the means to save literally billions of dollars now being lost to mismanagement and waste in Government. Speaking only as one auditor, I can personally identify in one case alone more than $100 million that is owed to the Federal Government. I have initiated legal action as a private citizen in this case since the Government has made no attempt to collect this money. Multiply my experience by scores of other auditors who also have uncovered waste, fraud, and mismanagement, but who are unprotected from reprisals, and you can project the far-reaching consequences of the work of your committee.

There are many good people in Government who want to do the right thing and save money and prevent waste. Our perilous economic condition dictates that we redouble our efforts to make every dollar go as far as possible in Government. Protection for the whistleblower will strike a blow against waste and inefficiency, and will make our Government stronger.

□ *Source: U.S. House of Representatives, Hearings, Subcommittee on Civil Service of the Committee on Post Office and Civil Service, Civil Service Reform Oversight—1980, 96th Cong. 2nd Sess., 1980, p. 81.*

Basically, if dissent is not tolerated, if public employees believe they have something to lose by blowing the whistle, administrative safeguards will not be sufficient to encourage them to subordinate institutional loyalty to either their individual morality or the public interest.

Since Jake Lapin's experiences, some efforts have been made to improve the plight of whistle-blowers. In the wake of Department of Defense procurement scandals in 1988 Congress is more encouraging to civil servants who are willing to come forward with charges of illegality or impropriety. In addition, in 1985 Donald R. Soeken, a psychotherapist and himself a former whistle-blower, started the Whistle-blower Assistance Fund, an organization that helps individuals who suffer economic loss and psychological harm as a result of their actions. Soeken lists the following "tips" for potential whistle-blowers:

Make a decision whether you want to go public with your charges or act anonymously. If you choose the latter route, find an appropriate group or investigative reporter to hear your story.

Make sure to tell your family what you plan to do since they will most likely
be affected by your decision.

Gather supporting documentation for your charges.

Maintain a good professional relationship with superiors and colleagues at
work.[7]

DISCRETION AS THE SOURCE OF ETHICAL DILEMMAS

Consider a situation like the following. You are driving a car, but daydreaming,
and you suddenly realize that you committed a traffic violation. You went through
a red light or did not stop completely at a STOP sign, or perhaps you were speed-
ing without knowing it. Suddenly, you realized you had just committed the infraction and at the same time noticed a police car in your rearview mirror. However,
the patrol car drove right past you without stopping. Why were you so lucky?

The police officer surely noted your infraction but, for some reason, chose
to ignore it. Maybe the officer had just received a call on the dispatch radio or
had to stay in place because of a "stakeout." You were lucky because the police
officer was using discretion. That is, the officer was in a position to choose between stopping you or doing something else—something more important at the
precise moment. If we want things to happen, if we want services to be provided,
we must give civil servants discretion to make operational decisions in situations
like this. Street-level bureaucrats—police officers, teachers, caseworkers, parole
officers, fire fighters—constantly make decisions that affect the people they are
supposed to serve. Not only does discretion affect the services provided, but also
it forces ethical choices.

Let's return to ethical dilemma 1 to examine how discretion forces ethical
choices. On one level, we can say that all of the psychiatrists in the story were
guilty of an ethical lapse. They were cheating the municipal hospital and, therefore, the taxpayers of the city. But let's focus on the chief psychiatrist. Although
she did not participate in short-changing the hospital (in terms of working hours),
we can say that since she knew about the practice and did nothing to stop it, she
was culpable. On this level, we are concluding that her inaction is an obvious
ethical lapse. We are also denying discretion by reaching this conclusion. That is,
we are saying that in such a situation a morally correct decision requires the chief
psychiatrist to take action against the offending psychiatrists. Ethical discretion
does not apply.

Consider a different formulation of the problem. Suppose the chief psychiatrist's main concern is to provide high-level services to psychiatric patients, a
primary consideration when she hired the psychiatrists to begin with. In her judgment, the psychiatrists are first-rate. It would be difficult to find better psychiatrists willing to take the jobs. The chief psychiatrist reasoned that although she
could "lean" on them a bit, too much pressure would be counterproductive. They
might resent the pressure and work less hard, or they might quit.

This ethical dilemma is common in the public sector. In general, rules and procedures should be followed.[8] Obviously, however, they should not be followed when more harm would result from doing so than from circumventing them. Public administrators, who make these decisions, are responsible for them and, indeed, cannot avoid them, because of the discretion that is inherent in their jobs.

THIRD-PARTY GOVERNMENT AS A SOURCE OF ETHICAL PROBLEMS

Did you ever notice that it is easier to spend someone else's money than your own? It is especially easy to spend someone else's money if you think that by doing so you are benefitting a third party. In other words, it is easy to be charitable when you don't have to bear the cost of your generosity. Or put another way, you are less accountable for your actions because of this third-party arrangement.

Big government is third-party government. That is, funds to achieve a public purpose often go from the federal government to local government and then to the beneficiaries (in the form of services). Providers of services may be less than frugal in the way they spend the federal government's money. Some doctors who treat Medicaid and Medicare patients, for instance, sometimes require unnecessary tests and treatments: The patient is not paying for it; the government is. Some public employees make personal phone calls while at the office; some take home office supplies; others use the public mail for personal correspondence.

All of these illustrations involve ethical lapses, and legal sanctions may be imposed for them. Even though they fall under the rubric of waste, fraud, and abuse, however, it is rare to hear of a public employee who suffered because a Christmas card was mailed from the office, thereby passing on a private cost to the taxpayers.

What causes such ethical lapses? The very characteristics of third-party government breaks downs accountability. A patient goes to a physician who accepts Medicare reimbursement as payment for services. The patient is given a full set of x-rays, a blood test, an electrocardiogram, and perhaps a few other tests. The patient is dubious about the need for all of these tests but doesn't complain. The patient is not paying for most of the bill. Is the doctor performing services and tests that are not needed? We do not know for sure. We may ask, however, would the physician require the same tests for a patient with a similar medical problem who has no insurance (the bill was $250)? The physician's bill is sent to the regional office responsible for processing Medicare claims. No one questions the bill or the services provided.

Who is at fault in this situation? To put it another way, who may be guilty of an ethical lapse? Or who is responsible? To answer these questions we must determine who is accountable for the decision. The problem is that we cannot easily attach accountability to one party, and since we cannot, we provide an environment where ethical shortcomings may flourish. This is a dilemma of big, complex government.

INDIVIDUAL AND
ORGANIZATIONAL ACCOUNTABILITY

I once taught at a state college that employed a philosopher I affectionately called "Crazy Marvin." Crazy Marvin was good for about one funny stunt a year. One year he dressed up in a "philosopher's robe" and, with cane and lantern in hand, went around the campus looking for an "honest man." He made it all the way to the president's office, but dejected, he admitted defeat—not an honest man to be found.

Crazy Marvin was really making a simple point. At one time, the *institution* of higher learning produced honest people. One learned ethical standards, *not* by taking ethics courses but by having standards that permeated *everything*. It all changed when higher education became more complex, bureaucratized, and open to more. Crazy Marvin was searching for a lost era.

There is also a lost era in the *ethos* of government service. From the late nineteenth century to, perhaps, the 1930s, there was no clear separation between theorists of and practitioners of public administration. For these early practitioner–theorists, "good" administration was "efficient" administration. On the practical side of this equation were the various managerial reforms that were implemented at the municipal level in the first two decades of this century. Budget control, auditing, the merit system, and position classification were all part of "good" administration. Their moral dimension can be appreciated if you recall that they were supposed to counteract the corruption that was so widespread in many cities. The moral administrator was above "dirty" politics. The public could count on these professional administrators to preserve, through their administrative actions, the moral foundations of democratic government.

Notice that there is a certain fuzziness in this description of a moral standard from a time that has since past. There were no exact principles, no codes, no formal classes in ethics. But somehow you knew a moral administrator when you saw one, and the ethos—the basic characteristics of "good administration" and "good government"—was understood by the professionals of the day. Words like *duty* and *responsibility* meant something. Crazy Marvin would have been comfortable then; he would have had no trouble finding an honest man.

From Ethos to Professional Codes

The breakdown of an older ethos of professional administration had to come; it was merely a question of time. The growing complexity of modern society resulted in an expansion of government activity. The corresponding complexity of government meant that public employment grew and became increasingly diverse. The norms of a professional administration would no longer be adequate to insure ethical standards. Moreover, the breakdown of the belief that politics and administration are separate meant that the ethos of an earlier era would not be able to provide moral guidance for the administrator in the last third of this century. Ethical standards would have to be clarified—and codified.

One way to encourage ethical behavior is to specify what is, and is not, acceptable. Many professional organizations—for physicians, lawyers, dentists, social workers, and others—have adopted codes of ethics that do precisely this.

These professions have national organizations—American Bar Association, National Association of Social Workers, American Medical Association—with codes of ethics to guide the behavior of their members. They also have internal procedures to review wrongdoings and to impose sanctions whenever necessary. Government employees who are members of a professional group are also bound by professional codes of ethics.

Governments and professional organizations such as the International City Management Association (ICMA) have codes of ethics for three basic reasons:

1. They help foster sound ethical standards in government.
2. They help foster confidence between government employees and the general public.
3. They help public officials make decisions when they are involved in ethically uncertain situations.[9]

City managers who are members of the ICMA subscribe to a detailed code of ethics with accompanying procedures for implementation. They include guidelines for seeking employment, relationships with the elected governing body, responsibilities for personnel, relationship with the community, and personal conduct. A Committee on Professional Conduct hears allegations of misconduct of member managers. Here is one illustration of the committee's activities.

Omission in a Resume

A consultant hired to review applicants for a position knew one of the individuals applying for the job. After reviewing this person's resume, the consultant realized that the applicant had omitted any reference to two cities where he had previously been employed as manager. The consultant then wrote ICMA to see whether Article 3 of the ICMA Code of Ethics had been violated. The person in question was then notified by the Committee on Professional Conduct that a statement of information and belief had been registered against him and that he should respond according to the rules of procedure.

The manager explained that the reason this employment was omitted was because he did not include in his resume short-term employment that occurred more than seven years ago. He also said that if he had listed his entire employment record, his resume would have been too long, but that he had made every effort to correct this mistake.

The state association's investigation concluded that the individual had extended his employment dates in one city in which he had served and had omitted employment in cities to shorten the length of his resume and to reduce the appearance of high employment turnover. Subsequently, the dates had been corrected, and the person's present resume reflected all periods of employment.

At this time the Committee on Professional Conduct and the state association gave the accused an opportunity to answer the charges. He could
do so in person, in writing, or by using a tape. In this particular case, the
board felt that it had set a precedent since it had considered a number of
cases involving falsifying a resume and voted public censure. The board
considered falsification of an application (intentional or not) a serious
violation of the ICMA Code of Ethics. The manager involved was publicly
censured in the ICMA Newsletter.

□   *Source: Reprinted with special permission from* PM (Public Management) *mag-
azine,* © *1981, by the International City Management Association, Washington,
D.C.*

Sometimes local governments will enact their own codes to govern the behavior of their public employees. Often, these codes adopt the views that (1) the
mere appearance of unethical behavior constitutes a violation of the code, and (2)
public trust requires an ethical standard for public employees higher than one
would find in the private sector. The village of Glen Ellyn, Illinois, for example,
has a code that includes this statement: "What is acceptable in private business
may not be proper conduct by elected and appointed officials."[10] To avoid any
ambiguity about the implications of working less than the required time, the city
of New Orleans mentions the topic directly in its Code of Ethics: "Full-time employees shall perform a full day's work each and every working day."[11]

Institutionalizing Accountability

The 1970s saw a great amount of activity in the area of ethics and accountability,
following the infamous Watergate affair during President Nixon's second term.
Political operatives were found to have "bugged" Democratic party headquarters
during the 1972 presidential election campaign. Top White House aides were
linked to the illegal break-in at the Watergate apartment complex. After lengthy
congressional hearings that looked into the charges and then investigated wrongdoings of top administration officials, impeachment proceedings were started
against President Nixon. Ultimately, he resigned from office.

The Watergate scandal naturally caused a great deal of public distrust of
elected officials. Perhaps to counter this cynicism, reforms were initiated to instill
more confidence in government officials. An important piece of legislation was
the federal Ethics in Government Act of 1978—which created an Office of Government Ethics in the new Office of Personnel Management. The Office of Government Ethics has a staff of approximately twenty-five and a modest annual budget of $1.25 million. A major feature of the act is the requirement that officials of
the executive branch submit written financial statements to insure no conflict of
interest upon assuming public office. This fear arises because many of these officials come from large corporations and industries that the officials regulate once
they assume public office and that they return to upon leaving office.

About one hundred individuals in the Reagan administration were accused of violating ethics rules. Some top officials, for instance, including Secretary of Defense Caspar Weinberger and Secretary of State George Schultz, were officers in the Bechtel Corporation, an engineering company that has had a considerable amount of business with Arab countries in the Middle East. Some members of Congress were concerned that this association could influence their policies toward the Middle East and tilt American support for Israel to a more pro-Arab stance. Secretary of Labor Raymond Donovan was accused of having connections with organized crime in New Jersey and New York. The director of the Central Intelligence Agency, William Casey, was criticized for some private stock transactions; Attorney General William French Smith was similarly criticized for questionable tax deductions taken to reduce his liability.[12] Although some people may have questioned a lack of sensitivity to personal financial issues among President Reagan's appointees, his was the first administration to be significantly affected by the Ethics in Government Act.

Financial disclosure requirements are also used by many state and local governments to reduce the risks of conflict of interest among their public officials. Yet despite their obvious appeal, these statements have been criticized for two reasons. First, they are thought to be intrusions into the privacy of public officials, who are subjected to considerable scrutiny because of their financial disclosures. But this is exactly the purpose. The requirement is supposed to instill a higher ethical standard than that required in the private sector. The second complaint may have more credence. Some critics point out that financial disclosure requirements have discouraged some excellent candidates from accepting executive positions. E. Pendelton James, President Reagan's personnel director, had charged that it has become difficult to recruit some business executives to Washington.[13] Former governor of New York, Hugh Carey, found that after a 1975 executive order that required financial disclosures, he had more trouble finding qualified candidates for appointed positions who were willing to take them. Yet even if this becomes an increasingly common problem, it is unlikely that legislative efforts to mandate accountability of government officials will be weakened.

Let the Sunshine In

Another way to encourage ethical behavior among public employees is to insure that citizens can observe them in action or obtain information concerning what they have done. Visible government is accountable government.

A well-known illustration of this principle is the federal Freedom of Information Act (FOIA), which allows public access to government documents and files. Individuals must make a request for information to the appropriate federal agency. The agency determines, first, if the information requested is exempt from the act (that is, can be withheld for security reasons); if not, the information is supposed to be released to the individual upon payment of a fee for the cost of reproduction. If a request for information is not granted, the individual may file suit against the agency to provide the information that was denied.

Not everyone is satisfied with the FOIA. Many individuals who have sought information from executive agencies have been critical of the way they have responded. Delay was common (although 1974 amendments to the act corrected this problem to a great extent); the costs of reproduction to be paid by the person making the request have sometimes been excessive; information has been deleted for reasons of security or privacy. The American Civil Liberties Union (ACLU) charged that the Reagan administration allowed agencies to classify more and more information as being exempt from the act. Other critics claimed that the act is costly to administer. Some critics believe that some information that is not given exempt status should be kept from the public, and some skeptics think that "open government" has allowed unscrupulous people to obtain information that is then used for personal financial gain.[14] The act will surely continue to be a source of tension in the future.

State governments also make information available to the public. Almost all states have passed "sunshine" laws, which make most government meetings open to the general public. Only a few specific subjects are restricted—those for which unfair advantage can be gained from information that may be presented at the meeting. Collective bargaining negotiations and discussions concerning the sale of government properties, for example, are both usually exempt from sunshine legislation. In general, sunshine laws are based on a simple premise: When government officials know that their words and actions will be recorded, they will tend to act in a responsible manner. Sunshine laws encourage accountability. Of course, bureaucrats will be bureaucrats. Here is how one former government official said he, and his fellow commission members, "got around" the federal sunshine requirements. Instead of having a meeting on some subjects, one official would speak to another one on the telephone—even if they occupied adjoining offices. The second would speak to the third official, who would than get back to the first. By using this method the government officials did not hold a "public" meeting and were therefore not subject to sunshine regulations. Naturally, the substance of their information "nonmeeting" was not available as a public record either.

The ethical problems public administrators face are complex. They are also fuzzy. Sometimes it is not easy to choose right from wrong. But public officials must choose. How ethical are you?

Personal Values Quiz

1. A fellow employee who is a friend of yours has been taking petty cash. You have some knowledge of your friend's actions. What would you do?
   __ You tell the appropriate authority what you know.
   __ You keep quiet because you don't want your friend to get into trouble over such a small matter.
2. You have worked with a supplier for many years and enjoy the sales representative personally. He mentions that he has some season tickets to a professional basketball game that he cannot use. He suggests that you and your wife accept them as a gift.

— You accept the tickets because the sales representative is your friend. You list the tickets on your financial disclosure form.
— You turn down the offer for tickets because you are concerned that the gift might compromise your objectivity when you are evaluating bids in the future.

3. You are very impressed with one of the candidates for the governing body. You have worked with her in the League of Women Voters and believe she would be an excellent council member. She has asked you to circulate a petition for her.
— You agree to circulate the petition because you believe she would be a good council member. What is most important is that the community have good leadership.
— You explain that it would be awkward for you to circulate the petition because of your position on the council. Your professionalism might be questioned if it became known that you were involved in the campaign.

4. Your department is converting to a new computer system. Although the new system is very good, it will take some time to learn how to use it. Only a small amount of money is available for training.
— You sign up for a two-week management training program on Hilton Head Island. You feel that improving your own skills is the highest priority, especially since you have been working so hard lately.
— You arrange for in-house training for your entire staff. You feel that all of your employees need to become comfortable with the new system as quickly as possible.

5. The local government's policy allows for a per diem for hotel and meals when employees travel on business. You have a friend in the town where you are going and decide to stay with him.
— Since you consider yourself underpaid, you use the per diem to treat your friend to elegant dinners.
— You claim only those expenses you incurred and pay for dinner for your friend out of your own pocket.

6. A new house has come on the market that you and your husband want to buy. The problem is, you're having trouble selling your current home. You casually mention this to a developer whom you know well from your work in the planning department. He offers to lend you the money at an interest rate below the prime.
— You thank the developer, but turn down the offer for a loan.
— You accept the loan since you do not anticipate any issues involving the developer will come before the council in the next year.

7. The county has just approved your recommendation to refurbish the playgrounds in the county parks with the latest equipment. The manufacturer of this equipment offers to pay for you and your husband to visit another city to see how the playgrounds were set up.
   — You accept since the council has already approved the purchase. Besides, you feel it is good business to let the private sector pay for something that is in the county's interest.
   — You decide to go on the trip, but pay for your expenses with county funds. Although you anticipate no further decisions with the manufacturer, you are concerned about the appearance of accepting a free trip.

8. One of your employees has had many personal problems this year. The employee is frequently late and has had trouble meeting deadlines.
   — You document the problems carefully and tell the employee that her performance is not acceptable. You give her a timetable to improve.
   — You are sympathetic about the employee's problems and look the other way when she's late and misses deadlines. You don't want to add to her problems.

9. You just found out that many building inspections were not completed last year, even though they were so reported. The supervisor who falsified the inspection report has since left city employment.
   — You keep the problem to yourself because the person responsible is gone and you do not want to damage the reputation of the other employees.
   — You immediately inform the city manager and propose budget shifts to catch up on the inspections. You know the story will probably find its way into the local newspaper.

10. You recently married a lawyer who often has represented clients in presentations to city council. Since you are often on opposite sides of an issue, you anticipate problems.
   — You disclose your wife's employment to the council, but otherwise make no changes. After all, both of you are entitled to careers.
   — Because of the potential for conflicts of interest, you and your wife discuss how you can change your respective careers. This is likely to cause at least temporary financial setbacks for you.

FINDING ETHICAL SOLUTIONS

The situations above illustrate the kind of ethical and moral issues that local government employees face every day. As the following comments on each situation suggest, these ethical dilemmas do not necessarily have a right or a wrong answer. What is important is ability to exercise sound judgment and make decisions consistently.

1. This situation pits personal and organizational loyalties against each other. It could be argued that if you say nothing, your friend might try more serious embezzlement in the future.

2. Most public servants find their lives are less complicated if they make it a practice not to accept gifts of any kind from those who do business with the local government. Others follow the guidelines prescribed by state financial disclosure laws; they simply list small gifts on their financial disclosure forms.

3. One of the most important qualities for a public servant is professional credibility. Supporting a candidate for the governing body can raise questions about an employee's objectivity. (If an ICMA member circulated a petition, it would be a violation of the ICMA Code of Ethics.)

4. The moral authority of a leader commands more respect from subordinates than any other type of authority. If you spend all your department's training budget on yourself, you may convince yourself it was the right thing to do, but you probably won't be able to convince your employees.

5. One of the easiest ways to set yourself up for problems is to misuse travel funds in any way. Even if you don't spend more than the per diem, the appearance of impropriety may be created if you spend the money in ways other than those for which it was intended.

6. You can never be sure that you will not have to make a recommendation on an issue involving that developer. Even if you disclose the loan and remove yourself from the issue, the objectivity of your subordinates may be questioned.

7. This situation poses a conflict between the value of saving money for the county and accepting a gift from someone who does business with the county. If you believe it is in the county's interest to go on the trip, the county should pay. The manufacturer could more appropriately donate some equipment to the county.

8. By ignoring the problem of the employee's performance, you not only would be doing a disservice to the organization, you could also be tacitly supporting destructive behavior. You may not know why the employee's performance is slipping, but you do need to let the person know there are problems. It is possible the employee needs professional help to cope with her problems.

9. Although there could be short-term embarrassment to your department if you flag the problem of the false report, it pales by comparison with the outcry that would result if you were later

accused of a cover-up. Imagine the outrage if there were a fire due to faulty wiring in a building that never was inspected.

10. Most two-career marriages are less complicated than this one. It is usually enough to disclose your spouse's employment to the governing body. These circumstances might require one or the other to change jobs, or the lawyer might change her practice somewhat to avoid presentations before the council.

□ *Reprinted with permission from* The Ethics Factor *(Washington, D.C.: International City Management Association, 1988).*

ETHICS AND PUBLIC POLICY

Surely you have heard the phrase "You can't legislate morality." Not only is it repeated over and over again, but also it is dead wrong. Think about the subject of sex. Here are just a few legislated restrictions as identified by Professor Stephen Wasby.

You can't do it with your mother, father, son, daughter, and maybe even with some cousins. You can't do it with animals, and certainly not with dead humans. If you're a man, you're not supposed to do it with a man, or if you're a woman, with a woman, although in some states you can do it in private. You aren't supposed to do it at all in public. You aren't supposed to do it with more than one other person at the same time. And you aren't supposed to look at other people doing it, at least not through someone's window. You can't expose what you do it with. The law even tells us what parts we can use and can't use. You can't do it with force, perhaps, even to your spouse. You can't whip, chain, or hurt someone in doing it even if they want it. You can't do it for pay. With or without pay, you can't do it with someone not your spouse, and if you aren't married, you'd better not do it with someone who is married. Even if both of you aren't married, you still can't do it in most places.[15]

For something that is ostensibly private and not amenable to legislation, there is a great deal of regulation.

When governments enact laws, when they make public policies, they do so partly on the basis of ethical considerations. Often, political conflict surrounding the policy focuses on disagreements over its ethical underpinnings. A good illustration is the highly controversial subject of abortion.

Let's consider different dimensions of this issue. Some people believe that life begins at conception; therefore, abortion is tantamount to murder. Those who feel this way would argue that abortions should be illegal; those who perform abortions, and undergo abortions, would then be subject to criminal sanctions. Notice that this moral perspective leads to a simple policy stance: Since abortions would be illegal, policy-makers would have to do very little once the legal prohibitions are enacted. Presumably, the implementation of the sanction would be a police responsibility.

One could hold a negative view of abortion and yet take a different view toward public policy. One might argue, for example, that abortion is morally wrong; nevertheless the decision to have an abortion is an individual decision, protected by the right to privacy. This perspective does not require any government intervention. That is, the decision to have an abortion is an individual one, and the arrangements are between the woman and her physician—similar to any other "market" exchange. There is, of course, a middle ground between the two positions. One could argue that the decision to have an abortion is protected by the right to privacy for a specified number of weeks. Once a given number of weeks have passed, government can regulate abortions and, in fact, prohibit them (unless the mother's life is in danger).

So far public policy is limited to a regulatory function. Abortion is not condoned by government; indeed, the scope of government activity as outlined is compatible with an ethical position that holds abortion to be a morally wrong act. Nevertheless, the right to privacy supercedes, thereby restricting government intervention.

We have set the stage for an additional ethical consideration. Is it just to permit a situation in which those women who want and can afford an abortion can have one, whereas those women who want but cannot afford one are, in effect, denied the opportunity? If we restrict a person's choice because the choice is dependent on income, are we not thereby restricting (and thus intruding) on the person's right to privacy? To put it another way, to insure this right, must the government provide the means for the individual to exercise the right?

Those who believe that a woman's right to have an abortion should not be affected by income support the public financing of abortion through Medicaid. Notice that this position holds not only that the right to privacy and individual choice are paramount values when it comes to abortion but also that equality among persons requires the government to provide the opportunity for poor women to exercise their freedom of choice and privacy.

At this point opponents step in once again: Abortion, to repeat, is morally wrong. Some opponents reluctantly concede that some women will have abortions anyway. There is no way to prevent abortions if people want to have them. But government should do nothing to encourage abortions. Medicaid funding of abortions, in this view, legitimizes a morally wrong act. Consequently, public funding of abortions should be halted for ethical reasons. Equity is irrelevant. One need not be concerned about making a morally wrong action available to a subset of the population.

These various positions illustrate the fact that public policies have ethical roots. Sometimes, as in the case of abortion, the ethical positions are easy to determine, and sometimes it is not difficult to draw the logical connection between a value stance and the appropriate policy that should be enacted. Our definitions of ''problems'' are often based on ethical perspectives, which, in turn, suggest some policy options and eliminate others.

Let us imagine a series of hypothetical conversations between a philosopher and a public official who is concerned about the heroin problem.

Conversation 1

PUBLIC OFFICIAL: I am worried. Too many people in my city are using heroin.
PHILOSOPHER: So what is the problem?
PUBLIC OFFICIAL: Heroin is bad for people.
PHILOSOPHER: So is too much food, too much drink, not to mention diet soft drinks.
PUBLIC OFFICIAL: What should I do about all this heroin use?
PHILOSOPHER: What do you do about overeating?
PUBLIC OFFICIAL: Nothing, of course!
PHILOSOPHER: Then use the same approach for heroin.

The philosopher is really making a deceptively simple argument. People do many things that aren't good for them. But they choose to do them. No one forces a person to overeat, to spend money foolishly, to drink to excess. It is not the responsibility of government to force people to behave in ways that are good for them and refrain from behavior that harms them. People are responsible for what they do, or don't do, to and for themselves.

Conversation 2

PUBLIC OFFICIAL: I am worried. Too many people in my city are using heroin.
PHILOSOPHER: So what is the problem?
PUBLIC OFFICIAL: These heroin users are committing crimes to support their habit. What should I do?
PHILOSOPHER: If they commit crimes, lock them up.
PUBLIC OFFICIAL: But they are heroin users.
PHILOSOPHER: You did say that they committed crimes, didn't you?

Here the philosopher is also making a simple argument. People who commit crimes should be punished, pure and simple. Why a person engages in criminal activity is unimportant. No one forced the heroin user to use heroin; no one forced the user to commit a crime. Both were individual choices. Heroin users are responsible for their actions; therefore, punishment is an appropriate response for all criminals whether they use heroin or do not use heroin.

Conversation 3

PUBLIC OFFICIAL: I am worried. Too many people in my city are using heroin.
PHILOSOPHER: So what is the problem?
PUBLIC OFFICIAL: These heroin users are committing crimes to support their habit. What should I do?

> PHILOSOPHER: Legalize heroin. This will make it cheaper and easier to get. Heroin users will stop committing crimes.

Here the philosopher advises the public official to eliminate the cause of crime that is committed by users: the high price of illegal heroin. If it were legalized, heroin would be plentiful, and users would not have to commit crimes to support their habits. The philosopher assumes that the cost of legalized heroin would be modest.

Conversation 4

> PUBLIC OFFICIAL: I am worried. Too many people in my city are using heroin.
>
> PHILOSOPHER: So what is the problem?
>
> PUBLIC OFFICIAL: Heroin is ruining the lives of these people and destroying their families. What should I do?
>
> PHILOSOPHER: First, remove their physiological dependence on heroin. Next, give the users and their families the necessary counseling so that they will not become heroin users again.

Notice that the approach to heroin use has now shifted. The philosopher suggests that the "quality of life" of the user should be improved. Once the user is "cured" of physical and psychological dependence on heroin, the problem will be solved.

Conversation 5

> PUBLIC OFFICIAL: I am worried. Too many people in my city are using heroin.
>
> PHILOSOPHER: So what is the problem?
>
> PUBLIC OFFICIAL: These users see no hope, no future. They are poor, usually unemployed, and not adequately educated. Their environment is unsafe and unhealthy. They have no opportunities so they "escape" by using heroin. What should I do?
>
> PHILOSOPHER: Give them jobs and adequate housing and send them to night school. Clean up their neighborhoods. Tell them tomorrow will be better than today. They will have hope and opportunities. Then they will stop using heroin.

We have now shifted to an "opportunity-structure" analysis. The philosopher says that if the broad environment changes so that people who are prone to use heroin are given alternatives, they will seek these alternatives rather than "retreating" into heroin use.

We can now assess the ethical roots behind the philosopher's alternative specifications of the heroin problem. In conversation 1 the philosopher assumes that people are essentially responsible for what they do to, and for, themselves. As long as a person's actions cause no harm to others, there is no reason, indeed no justification, for government to intervene in a person's "private" activities. People are free to do what they like, even if what they like may be foolish or even harmful (to themselves).

The second conversation assumes the same operating principle as the first. The only difference here is that the user has harmed another person. Notice that this perspective does not require us to ask why a person may have committed a crime. Since a person is responsible for his or her actions, regardless of the reasons for the actions, a heroin user who commits a crime must be punished for the crime. This reasoning follows from the principle that allows us freedom to do as we wish as long as our actions cause no harm to others.

Conversation 3 has the same ethical root as the previous two. Once again, the philosopher wants to maximize individual freedom, and again, it obviously allows people to do things to themselves that are foolish and even harmful. Government has no responsibility, in fact no right, to intervene in private decisions. In conversation 3 the philosopher is merely willing to entertain the hypothesis that the criminal activity of heroin users is caused by the cost of illegal heroin. By making heroin legal (and thereby cheaper), the philosopher does not want to save money for the user; nor does the philosopher want to encourage or discourage heroin use. The philosopher believes that these are not appropriate concerns of government. Rather, the philosopher merely wants to protect innocent third parties—nothing more.

With conversations 4 and 5 our ethical underpinnings of the heroin problem change. No longer does the philosopher hold the position that individuals are solely responsible for their actions, and government has no responsibility to interfere with private activity. Notice in conversation 4 that the philosopher takes a much different approach. Government must do something to help the heroin user. Exactly what government should do depends on the state of our current knowledge about heroin usage. Nevertheless, government has an obligation—we can even call it a moral imperative—to help heroin users. The same principle underlines conversation 5, only in this case the obligation does not end once current heroin users are helped. Government has an obligation to alter the environmental conditions that encourage some people to use heroin in the first place.

There is no "correct" ethical stance, nor is there a "best " policy option. Yet you can now see that there are essentially two different ethical roots that lead to different definitions of what constitutes the heroin problem. One root places a great deal of value on individual freedom and responsibility. This root leads to a definition of the heroin problem found in conversations 1, 2, and 3. The second root shifts the locus of responsibility. Government has an obligation to help some people who are unable to help themselves (even when the causes of their problems are of their own making, as in conversation 4). When this ethical stance is held, policy options 4 and 5 are most appropriate, and by definition, options 1, 2, and 3 are not.[16]

You can now try the same type of analysis with a different issue—legalized gambling through state run lotteries. Here are the essential facts:

> Twenty-eight states use lotteries to raise state revenues. Many states earmark the revenues for selected programs such as public education. In 1987 $12.4 billion was bet on state lotteries.
> Many lotteries have large monetary prizes and games of chance that tell players immediately if they have won.

Lottery tickets can usually be purchased in grocery stores or other places where consumers shop.

States use sophisticated marketing ploys to increase the number of players.

Here is the rub. Some researchers who have looked into state lotteries claim that they are really a form of regressive taxation. The argument rests on the point of view that when lower-income individuals play the lottery, the payment is like other "sin" taxes such as the taxes on cigarettes and alcohol. More seriously, evidence is growing that a small, though perhaps increasing, percentage of lottery bettors have become addicted to the games of chance. Indeed, New Jersey puts the telephone number of the Council of Compulsive Gambling on state lottery machines. Question: Do you think other states should follow New Jersey's lead?[17]

SUMMARY

Public administration is filled with ethical challenges, which come from two basic sources. First, the typical civil servant will have some discretion in his or her daily organizational life. Discretion implies choices, and choices usually contain within them ethical challenges. Why can't there be a straightforward ethical "guide" for the civil servant? The problem here is not that there is no guide; on the contrary, as I pointed out early in the chapter, the typical civil servant has many ethical guides. But this is exactly the problem—and the second source of ethical challenges. How does the bureaucrat choose among, say, obligation to country, obligation to self, obligation to profession, and obligation to law when selecting the appropriate guide for an ethical choice? This dilemma is what Stephen Bailey called "moral ambiguity." Since standards of right and wrong behavior change over time (recall Plunkitt's distinction between "honest" and "dishonest" graft), moral ambiguity will always confront the public administrator.

Governments, however, have passed laws that identify ethical requirements of public administration. The Civil Service Reform Act of 1978 includes a section on ethics. State and local governments have statutes that establish ethical standards for their public employees. In addition to legislation, professional organizations often have codes of ethics to guide their members. By now you should have taken the "ethical test" designed by the International City Management Association—a test that is supposed to help the ICMA members identify right from wrong.

Ethics surrounds the subject of public policy. The idea that "you can't legislate morality" is certainly inaccurate when you think about the ethical controversies that surround current policy disputes: abortion, legalized gambling, capital punishment, and regulation of sexual conduct. Can you identify the ethical positions for contrasting positions on each of these issues? It would certainly be useful for many public administrators to undertake such an ethical analysis if and when they become entangled in a controversial policy dispute while managing their programs. Put yourself in the position of an administrator of a county hospital who must explain to antiabortion groups why the hospital continues to perform abortions. Or put yourself in the position of a warden of a state maximum-security prison with inmates on "death row" while the state legislature is debating whether or not to reinstitute capital punishment. What will you tell the inquiring reporter who wants to know "your personal opinion" on the subject?

FOUR ETHICAL EXERCISES

You are now ready to put yourself in the position of a public manager who must wrestle with ethical underpinnings of administrative decisions. Let's return to the four ethical dilemmas that were described at the beginning of the chapter. Following are a few additional details. Each dilemma will now put you in a situation that will require a decision. In each case you should specify the bases for your choices.

Ethical Dilemma 1

Auditors from the city's Comptroller's Office performed a compliance audit in the municipal hospital. While conducting the audit the auditors uncovered the discrepancies between the job requirements of staff psychiatrists and the hours that were actually worked. In the audit report the auditors noted that "the discrepancies were known to the chief psychiatrist."

You are the assistant director for administration of the hospital. The hospital's director, Dr. Timothy Delegation, wants to know how you plan to deal with the situation, which has now hit the newspapers because of the disclosures in the auditors' report. Prepare a memorandum to Dr. Delegation outlining the steps you plan to take.

Ethical Dilemma 2

The lab technician, it turns out, wrote an anonymous letter to the director of the municipal hospital describing the alleged "informal" arrangement between the director of the sex clinic and the director of the lab. The hospital director, Dr. Hardnoze, was anything but pleased to receive the information. Dr. Hardnoze was proud of his reputation for running a "tight ship." As director of Medical Services you received instructions from Dr. Hardnoze to (1) investigate the allegations and (2) if it is true, to inform him how you will resolve it. You discover that the allegations are mainly true. Prepare your memorandum to Dr. Hardnoze.

Ethical Dilemma 3

You are the police captain. Sergeant Dogood gave you some reports of police wrongdoing—sleeping on the job, accepting payoffs from numbers runners, illegal gambling, and drug dealing. Corruption seemed to be getting out of hand in the precinct. "At least there are some good cops left, like Joe," you say to yourself. No sooner does this thought go through your head than you come across Sergeant Dogood's report on Joe. "I have a real mess on my hands," you say to yourself, "and now I even have to worry about donuts." Meanwhile, division headquarters wants a memorandum in a week from every captain about alleged corruption in their precincts. What do you do about Officer Joe?

Ethical Dilemma 4

The state legislature recently passed a statute requiring all civil servants above a certain grade level to file an annual statement itemizing outside sources of earned income. The purpose of the statute is to prevent "public managers from using their positions in state government or their specialized knowledge of state government for the purpose of substantial private gain."

You are the commissioner of the department that includes the civil servant who accepted the honorarium. The civil servant listed the payment on the statement of outside sources of earned income. It is your responsibility to interpret the intent of the new statute. How will you interpret the payment received by the civil servant?

NOTES

1. Dwight Waldo, *The Enterprise of Public Administration: A Summary View* (Novato, Calif.: Chandler & Sharp Publishers, 1980), pp. 103–106.
2. See Stephen Bailey, "Ethics and the Public Service," *Public Administration Review* 23 (December 1964): 234–243.
3. William Riordan, *Plunkitt of Tammany Hall* (New York: E. P. Dutton, 1963), p. 3.
4. For a discussion of whistle-blowing, see Sissela Bok, "Blowing the Whistle," in *Public Duties: The Moral Obligations of Government Officials,* ed. Joel L. Fleishman, Lance Liebman, and Mark H. Moore (Cambridge, Mass.: Harvard University Press, 1981), pp. 204–220.
5. O. Sulzberger, Jr., "Study Finds Apathy among Federal 'Whistle Blowers,' " *New York Times,* April 16, 1981, p. A22.
6. Phillip J. Cooper, Public Law and Public Administration (Palo Alto, Calif.: Mayfield Publishing Co., 1983), p, 339.
7. Clyde H. Farnsworth, "In Defense of the Government's Whistle Blowers," *New York Times,* July 26, 1988, p. B6.
8. Donald P. Warwick, "The Ethics of Administration Discretion," in Joel L. Fleishman, Lance Liebman, and Mark H. Moore, eds., *Public Duties: The Moral Obligations of Government Officials* (Cambridge, Mass.: Harvard University Press, 1981), pp. 93–127.
9. Joseph F. Zimmerman, "Ethics in the Public Service" (Paper presented at the Maxwell School, Syracuse University, July 9, 1980), p. 5.
10. Ibid., p. 6.
11. Ibid., p. 8.
12. Jeff Gorth, "Private Wealth and Public Service," *New York Times,* June 8, 1982, p. A24.
13. Ibid.
14. The largest number of FOIA requests comes from businesses and foreign governments. I am indebted to Robert Gilmour for bringing this point to my attention.
15. Stephen L. Wasby, "The Impotency of Sex Policy: It's Not All in the Family (or: A Non-Voyeuristic Look at a Coupling of Sex and Policy)," *Policy Studies Journal* 9 (Autumn 1980): 117–118.
16. Mark H. Moore, "Anatomy of the Heroin Problem: An Exercise in Problem Definition," *Policy Analysis* 2 (Fall 1976): 639–662.
17. Lena Williams, "For Some Bettors, Lotteries Create a Chance for Disaster," *New York Times,* July 24, 1988, p. 17.

FOR FURTHER READING

Bowman, James S., symposium ed. "Ethics in Government." *Public Personnel Management* 10, no. 1 (1981): 1–199.

> The entire issue of the journal is devoted to ethics, with articles covering historical overviews, legal issues, and ethical dimensions of public management.

Burke, John P. *Bureaucratic Responsibility.* Baltimore: Johns Hopkins University Press, 1986.

> When do bureaucrats in the course of their jobs come up against situations in which responsibility cannot be avoided? Burke provides the reader with multiple illustrations.

Fleishman, Joel L., Lance Liebman, and Mark H. Moore, eds. *Public Duties: The Moral Obligations of Government Officials.* Cambridge, Mass.: Harvard University Press, 1981.

> A collection of essays focusing on current ethical dilemmas that confront public officials.

Rohr, John A. *Ethics for Bureaucrats: An Essay on Law and Values.* New York: Marcel Dekker, 1978.

> An attempt to link ethics to the "regime values" as embodied in law.

Schelling, Thomas C., "Economic Reasoning and the Ethics of Policy." *The Public Interest,* no. 63 (Spring 1981): 37–61.

> A thought-provoking essay arguing that the ethical dimensions of policy issues can be clarified by economic analysis.

Thompson, Dennis F. *Political Ethics and Public Office.* Cambridge, Mass.: Harvard University Press, 1987.

> Ethics as viewed from the vantage point of political action and the corresponding impact on democracy is the organizing theme of this book.

CHAPTER 15

Evolving Public Administration

There was a time when what you studied was related to what you eventually would do. If you got a degree in accounting you didn't become a brain surgeon, and animal husbandry majors didn't become elementary school music teachers. I am not so sure anymore. I teach public administration at the Maxwell School of Syracuse University. Actually, the full title is the Maxwell School of Citizenship and Public Affairs. That tells you something about the original mission of the place. Graduates of our program are found throughout the public sector at all levels of government in the United States—indeed, around the world. Distinguished public service is what we expected from our students.

More recently, however, students here have also found employment with major commercial banks, investment firms, bond-rating companies, hospitals, and consulting firms. In the past, students of public administration would not have considered these types of employers to be appropriate; the feeling would have been mutual. Why would a commercial bank be at all interested in hiring a person who has learned only about public administration?

Students taking graduate courses in public administration are a diverse group. Here are just some of the students I have encountered in my public budgeting course in the past ten years.

A clinical psychologist with a Ph.D. who was a director of a community health center and wanted to get some basic understanding of government budgeting

A registered nurse who was getting a dual degree in social work and public administration

Practicing administrators of higher education who were about to get budgetary responsibility

Military officers in a master of business administration program who had
some financial responsibilities in the U.S. Army

Students of a graduate social work program who planned to work for nonprofit agencies (such as Catholic Charities and United Way)

Midcareer students from federal government agencies who expected to be
promoted after their educational leave was completed

The list continues, and the message is clear: No longer are students on a single
employment track, and no longer is it only governments that want job applicants
who know something about government.

Not that this is a new development. Throughout our history there has been
a great deal of interaction between the public and private sectors, and a clear line
could not be drawn between public and private management. Nevertheless, the
symptoms I have observed in my own graduate program are part of an ongoing
transformation of organizational life. In particular, what is private and what is
public is by no means obvious. In the first part of this chapter I describe the
similarities of resource management strategies in both business and government
organizations. By focusing on only one theme I will illustrate my basic point:
Public organizational life has indeed become more complicated, and will continue
in this fashion in the future. The public administrators of tomorrow will face a
different type of organization than the public administrators of yesterday.

Future public administrators will have to face more than the new. They will
also have to grapple with the old—those ongoing problems of public administration that have troubled the profession for more than a hundred years. I end this
book by restating what they are and the challenges they present for the public
managers of tomorrow.

RESOURCES IN BUSINESS AND GOVERNMENT
ORGANIZATIONS: MOTIVATIONS AND OBJECTIVES

All large organizations have the same underlying motivations and assumptions
in their resource acquisition process. Whether they are business organizations,
government organizations, public enterprises, or nonprofit organizations, they all
seek stable growth, decision-making autonomy, and control. These three motivations can explain what organizations do, and why they do what they do, more
than any attempt to understand the central "mission" of an organization. Let's
look at each one in turn.

Stable Growth

Organizations defend their "turf." We saw this type of organization behavior in
the budgeting chapter, where strategies to preserve and enhance government
agencies were revealed. Similarly, in Chapter 2 we discovered that one way for
organizations to persevere in the world of bureaucratic politics is to adopt strategies of maintenance and growth.

One obvious explanation is that jobs and careers are at stake. If organizations do not grow and prosper, people's futures will turn sour. But members are committed to the programs of their organizations; they believe in them, and they want their organizations to do well—to grow and prosper.

Also, when programs expand, when responsibilities are increased, when the number of people to be supervised goes up, and the budget becomes bigger, a person's career is typically enhanced. Indeed, in the federal government these components of growth are often used to determine promotions. So resource acquisition not only enhances organizational growth but stimulates career growth as well. The two are intertwined.

What about managers in business organizations? Conventional wisdom has it that they are more prudent. Specifically, resource and growth strategies should be tailored to profit maximization, not to self-aggrandizement, because since profits can be measured, private managers will eventually be held accountable to the "bottom line."

The problem with this argument is that it takes a very simplistic view of the so-called bottom line. In fact, it is often difficult to determine an individual manager's contribution to profit. It is even harder to attribute a manager's contribution to potential profits. So the place of a manager in a firm's performance is really a matter of perception: Managers who are lucky enough to be part of profitable businesses will be rewarded because it is perceived that they contributed to profit. When times are hard, in contrast, the manager may become a scapegoat.

Public organizations may pursue growth by trying to expand their budgets. Private organizations may seek to enlarge profits. But stable growth complicates both these interpretations of organizational behavior. Stability imposes a constraint on either profit or budget objectives because almost all organizational members are likely to achieve benefits from stable growth, whereas only a minority will truly benefit from rapid growth. Besides, rapid growth is risky. In business it can lead to overextension and failure. Stable growth, then, is a conservative, organization-conserving strategy.

Autonomy and Control

The conventional wisdom is that government organizations, unlike business organizations, have limited autonomy and a sharply constrained ability to control their environment. Not only are agencies answerable to superiors in the executive branch, but they are also subject to congressional oversight and, most important, dependent on the congressional largesse in the budgetary process. For years political scientists have shown that this image of government organizations is incorrect. Government agencies are not passive actors mechanistically responding to the will of executive and legislative superiors.[1] Moreover, managers in government agencies surely try to influence public policy.

In the private sector, autonomy allows organizations to adjust to the market, as conditions require, by expanding production, limiting production, initiating new products or services, stockpiling resources, and creating slack resources. Business organizations that are autonomous can sometimes manipulate the market and in many instances create demand through advertising, aggressive marketing, expansion of sales resources, or development of new clients. Just think of the instant success, several years ago, of Jordache "designer" jeans—a French-sounding company started by three Israeli-born brothers who lived in Brooklyn! Often government organizations are more constrained than business organizations. Still, the motivations for resource acquisition, or even the processes for resource acquisition, are not invariably different in government and business organizations. Both seek to enhance autonomy and organizational control, and they do so with varying levels of success. The difference is not one of basic motivation; the objectives in resource acquisition are much the same, but the means to those ends sometimes differ.

A major difference is that government organizations can rarely act independently and often resort to indirect measures in seeking to enhance autonomy. Yet there are similarities in resource acquisition strategies. Although most government organizations cannot directly influence the market for their goods and services and cannot expand or contract "production" on their own authority, they can and do mobilize support for activities in much the same way that business firms create consumer demand. Government organizations cultivate constituencies and can occasionally be aggressive in their "marketing" activities. A good example is the traditional "games of chance," more commonly known as the state lottery:

A Dollar and a Dream!

What would you do if you won the New York State lottery? "I would buy my company, hire my boss, and then fire him." "I would go fishing." "I would . . ." This simple question, and the answers to it, was a very successful marketing ploy used by the state of New York to increase the number of players in the lottery in the past few years. Was it successful? You bet! After all, most people have a dream, and what's a dollar these days anyway?

Some dreams are funny; some are downright ridiculous. But the dreamers are real people. Camera people representing the lottery film people in their communities and then select the most "marketable" responses. The objective? That's obvious. It is to increase the number of dreamers with a buck to spare.

Nor does the limited ability of government organizations to control resource acquisition directly necessarily bear great importance. When it comes to budgeting and appropriations, government organizations are not exactly passive. Even when economic times are hard, they are able to influence legislators, cultivate budget examiners, and mobilize constituency support.

By the same token, it is easy enough to overemphasize the autonomy of business organizations. Not only are mergers and takeovers a threat to their autonomy and control, but also they are subject to governmental constraints. Outcries against government regulation have become so routine that some people have become immune to the message, but in other ways the dependencies of business organizations are similar to those of government organizations. The government is not only a constraint on resource acquisition and autonomy but also a provider of resources. Business organizations depend in many instances on government contracts, subsidies, loans, loan guarantees, and even appropriations (not to mention tax incentives). The model of the autonomous business organization controlling its destiny as it competes in the free, competitive market (a view that was not even entirely accurate in Adam Smith's day) is as antiquated as the model of the apolitical government agency.

This does not mean that there are not important differences in the resource-acquisition processes of government and business organizations. Important differences are insured because government agencies are often tied to a yearly budget cycle, they have limited ability to manage the flow of resources (and to carry resources over from one year to the next), and large-scale program initiatives require legislative authorization. The key point is that there are nearly as many similarities as differences in the resources-acquisition processes of government and business organizations. The underlying motivations are similar; both seek to enhance their resources and extend autonomy and control. The significance of the profit motive is easily exaggerated.

CONVERGENCE OF RESOURCE PROCESSES AND STRATEGIES

Recent trends indicate that business and government organizations can be expected to become more and more alike in their resource-acquisition processes and strategies. Indeed, we may find that some government organizations will more closely resemble business organizations than most other government organizations; by the same token, some business organizations may have as much in common with government organizations as with other business organizations.

Increasing "Publicness" of Business

Even in this day of blurring sectors, some firms operate in a marketplace largely unfettered by government regulation and largely independent of government largesse. But with only a few exceptions, the largest and most important corporations are nearly as closely tied to government as government agencies themselves. The interdependence of business and government is sufficiently pervasive and familiar. In the 1970s, for instance, the federal government took an active hand in preventing the financial collapse of both the Chrysler and Lockheed Corporations. To make these examples even more compelling, let us consider the following question: In what essential way is the federal government's loan guarantee for New York City in 1975 different from that for the Chrysler Corporation? Consider the rationales for each. It was argued that the failure of Chrysler (and New York) must be prevented in order to allay unemployment and economic hardship for a city and region; it was argued that New York (and Chrysler) is a national asset and that its bankruptcy would be counter to the public interest; it was argued that a transfusion of capital would make Chrysler (and New York) self-sufficient; it was argued that a bankrupt New York would ultimately present an even greater drain on the federal treasury (it was argued that a bankrupt Chrysler would ultimately yield a net reduction in federal revenues through the loss of corporate taxes).

This is only one illustration—though a rather extreme one—of private sector dependence on the government. Crop subsidies and licensing agreements in agriculture, for example, are crucial to agricultural firms. Entire industries have grown up around government contracting for products and services, including everything from vendors who receive the majority of their receipts from the General Services Administration to metropolitan Washington-based "beltway bandits" who exist almost solely as providers of government-sponsored research and development.

Probably more important than direct government payments, government contracts, loans, and subsidies is government regulation. Some people have even attributed much of the decline in the national rate of productivity growth to regulatory costs.[2] The stakes in deregulation are enormous, as the turmoil in the airlines, bus, and trucking industries suggests. Government regulation of consumer products, and especially food and drugs, has significant impact on firms' resource acquisition strategies as well as their very survival. The more intense (some would say careful) regulation of pharmaceuticals in the United States has had great consequence for the structure and even the geographic distribution of the drug industry.

Business firms are also greatly influenced by government tax policy. Modest changes in depreciation allowances, corporate income taxes, investment tax credits, and various tax incentives can have marked influence on business planning and policy. The Reagan administration's initiatives aimed at "freeing" businesses to compete in the marketplace can be viewed as yet another government-centered equation in the firm's investment calculus. Special tax reductions and forgone revenues are no less a government influence (albeit a generally preferred one) than direct expenditures. The study of finance must include the study of public finance; otherwise it is incomplete.

Increasing Privateness of Government

For many years there have been "mixed-type" government organizations that acquire resources in ways similar to so-called private organizations. With increasing fiscal austerity the privateness of public sector organizations will grow.

The most common type of resource acquisition in the public sector occurs through the budget process. The agency's budget—its resources—is obviously dependent on actions of the legislature through appropriations. Although the agency is not helpless in influencing the outcome of the appropriations process, resource acquisition is determined mainly by outside factors.

But this description, although roughly correct in general, does not accurately describe a number of specific types of government organizations. One common exception is public enterprises, which abound in developing and industrialized countries around the world. They produce electricity, air and rail transport, bridges, and tunnels, and they manufacture products. In the United States public enterprises are less predominant; nevertheless, hundreds of municipally owned power companies are public enterprises. The Tennessee Valley Authority (TVA), founded in 1933, and the Port of New York and New Jersey have assets in the hundreds of millions of dollars. Other public enterprises include Energy Security Corporation, AMTRAK, Corporation for Public Broadcasting, COMSAT, the Postal Service, and Synthetic Fuels Corporation. The distinguishing features of public enterprise that highlight privateness are the following:

They can raise capital by selling securities to private investors.
They produce revenues by selling goods and services.
They charge fees or rents.

Public enterprises, in other words, generate some portion of their resources through earnings. Like private organizations, public enterprises borrow money for the purposes of maintenance and growth.[3] Although public enterprises clearly have a more varied resource mix than most government organizations, their resources are less predictable since they are affected by market forces. Some public enterprises have been successful in achieving stable growth by expanding their activities far beyond their original purposes. A conspicuous example is the New York Port Authority, which entered the lower Manhattan real estate market by building the World Trade Center.

Another example of the privateness of the public sector comes from intergovernmental contracting arrangements. Every government has several "make or buy" decisions. It can provide a service like police protection to its residents directly, for example, or it can purchase the service from a neighboring government. In the latter case, the two governments negotiate the level and quality of service and the price (that is, the cost of the contract). A well-known example is the Lakewood Plan in Los Angeles County. About twenty-five cities that have incorporated between 1954 and 1961 have contracted with the county for basic services. The justification for the idea is straightforward. By contracting, cities can avoid large initial capital outlays and, at least in theory, purchase the amount of services appropriate for the local government. The market operates because the local government can choose to provide services directly if and when local officials become dissatisfied with the contract arrangement. This threat imposes some (imperfect) market discipline in the exchange between the service provider and the local government that receives the service.

There are two ways to view the contracting option. From the standpoint of the organization (or local government) providing the service, contracting is one way to expand the resource mix. The contract, either between government or even an intragovernmental contract (between two government agencies in the same government), reduces the agency's reliance on the legislature at budget time. From the vantage point of the other party, the contract allows for program growth even if other resources, such as personnel, are frozen because of fiscal belt tightening.

The privateness of government resource acquisition can be seen in another way. State and local governments have traditionally adopted fees and charges for many goods and services. The reasons for charging for fishing licenses, library books, greens fees for golf players, rental of building space, and parking places are quite simple. The government has something to sell, and there is a demand for the good or service. Furthermore, the beneficiaries are easily identified. Like all other consumption decisions, individuals who enjoy the benefits of the services should be expected to pay for them. Those who do not use the services should not have to pay for them, and government organizations that depend on user fees for their resources should be responsive to market demand.[4]

IMPLICATIONS FOR TOMORROW'S PUBLIC ADMINISTRATORS

This blurring of sectors has ramifications for the public administrators of tomorrow. For one thing, no longer can we assume that it is possible, or even wise, to distinguish completely managerial education based on government organizations or business organizations. The differences between public and private management will not fade away, however. Nor is "generic" management a solution. We can accept the insider accounts of top managers from the private sector who, having served in Washington and survived to write about it, report that public management is more difficult than private management.[5] Yet even with these caveats in mind, it is important to identify a few of the basic trends in the education of tomorrow's public managers.

Greater Sensitivity to Marketing

Some activities, once thought to be solely the preserve of business, are becoming almost routine in government. Perhaps the best example is marketing. Even a superficial glance at television commercials will show you how some government organizations are trying to "market" their products. "Be all the things you can be in the Army," you are told—"Not just a job but a future." "What would you do if you won the lottery?" is a lead-in question in one state's Madison Avenue marketing approach that is unabashedly designed to encourage more players. Of course, traditional "social marketing" aimed at discouraging bad behavior and encouraging good behavior fills television and radio. Remember the egg, cracked and quickly fried? The actor says, "This is your brain; this is your brain on drugs. Any questions?" Quick, slick, and graphic.

Sell It if You Can!

In Great Britain the government under Prime Minister Margaret Thatcher has been "privatizing" at a furious pace. The public telecommunications system, the national airlines, petroleum, and utilities have all been sold to willing investors. The reasons for these assets sales are varied and complicated, but they surely include the following two themes:

> The private sector is presumably more sensitive to market signals; therefore, privatization will stimulate efficiency.
> Privatization allows the government to raise revenues while lessening the scope of government activities.[6]

The United States has not gone as far as Great Britain (or France); nevertheless, privatization is attractive to some political officials because it brings into sharp focus the fundamental question for government—what is the proper scope of government activity? Once we raise this question in the context of privatization there is almost no limit about what we can put up for sale. Yellowstone National Park? The Coast Guard? The Washington Monument? The White House?

O.K, these examples sound farfetched! But selling things less grandiose than my short list above still requires the manager of tomorrow to grapple with the tension between what seems like a "public good" versus what is more like a private good that could be sold like any commodity. Some government agencies have learned that they can no longer give away things for free. The Department of Housing and Urban Development, long a distributor of free published materials on all sorts of topics concerning urban life, now charges for its publications. In the FY 1983 executive budget, President Reagan proposed new (and increased) user fees for federal recreation areas; for water traffic to pay for locks, dams, and channels; and for transaction charges on commodity futures. But lest you believe that it is only the federal government's managers of tomorrow that will adopt marketlike mechanisms, recall our sample of tiny Falls City, Oregon (population 752), which did a booming business selling its potholes at $10 a shot.

Ability to Innovate

One criticism of public officials is that, unlike their private sector counterparts, they are unwilling to take risks. There is some grain of truth in this. After all, public officials have a "fiduciary" responsibility; they manage the taxpayers' money, and they pass legislation on behalf of the citizenry. We wouldn't want our government officials to be speculating in "junk bonds" or pork belly futures with our tax dollars! But the charge of pervasive risk aversion among public officials belies the truth that, in fact, government officials have been willing to take risks and innovate to improve the performance of the public sector. They have ranged from the use of rubber bullets in riot control to "slippery water" in fire fighting to "flexitime" in personnel management. Naturally, not all innovations panned out as the saga of Gale Wilson reveals:

"Government Windmills for Sale—Cheap"

In 1981 the price of oil was $37 a barrel. It was time to think about alternative sources of energy, in the view of Gale Wilson who was city manager of Fairfield, California. He envisioned 35 giant windmills with blades 300 feet long. His plan was intriguing. The windmills would produce enough energy for the city and the excess would be sold to Pacific Gas and Electric. The estimated cost of the project was almost $500 million, but the windmills would produce about $5,000 of worth of power a day. Investors were quickly lined up. In 1983 Wison won the International City Management Association's (ICMA) Outstanding Management Innovator award.

Don't go to Fairfield to look at the famous windmills. There aren't any. As it turned out, the price of oil did *not* climb as predicted; the windmill manufacturer experienced "technical difficulties"; and people for some reason balked at buying houses near a field of giant windmills—so property values were affected by the idea. But not all was lost. In 1985 Wilson's windmills won first prize in ICMA's Fabulous Flops contest!

□   Source: "Fabulous Flops, 1985" Public Management, *February 1988, pp. 17–20.*

Innovation can be less dramatic than Gale Wilson's windmill fiasco. Recall that computers were first used in private industry in the 1950s. Their use was soon adapted to selected government purposes even in the 1950s and extensively in the 1960s, and computer applications spread rapidly during the 1970s and into the 1980s. Soon most middle-level managers at all levels of government had some exposure to computers. At one time a minimum requirement my have been the ability to read a computer printout. Now, a basic understanding of computers is indispensable for public managers if they are to have the ability to manage effectively. Information management now includes everything from hardware and software interfacing, the identification of information needs and data retrieval, and the appropriate linkages between information systems and other management resources (such as personnel, budget, and organizational structure).

Remaining Cognizant of Evolving Societal Complexity

The novelist Kurt Vonnegut, Jr., includes the following passage in *Cat's Cradle:*

> Beware of the man who works hard to learn something, learns it, and finds himself no wiser than before. . . . He is full of murderous resentment of people who are ignorant without having come by their ignorance the hard way.[7]

The bureaucrats of tomorrow will have to fight the urge to retreat into complacency. To serve us well, they will have to struggle to overcome ignorance.

But why is ignorance likely to be their reward for hard work? Simply, societal complexity will make it difficult to arrive at solutions for public problems. Indeed, it will not even be simple to distinguish between a private and a public problem. Consider some ostensibly "easy" questions: When does life begin? Are decisions concerning your own body only yours to make? Can you decide when to die? These three questions all have complex dimensions—dimensions that include moral, legal, and technological components. What's more, they all show that public and private are not very sharply delineated. On the contrary, the blurring of what is public and what is private creates an ambiguity that causes confusion and frustration. The public lives of tomorrow's bureaucrats will be engulfed by such ambiguity.

There is a tendency, when complexity is so predominant, to seek refuge in simplicity. When Jimmy Carter became president, he was going to be the "outsider," the person who would fight and ultimately conquer Washington's intransigence. Things moved too slowly, too inefficiently, and too ineffectively for Jimmy Carter. This outsider status, he thought, would be an asset. It would allow him to move and shake the Washington establishment. How much moving and shaking actually occurred between 1976 and 1980 is a subject for future historians, who will most likely discover that it was less than President Carter's optimistic estimates. By the time he ran for reelection, Carter was emphasizing the complexity of problems and their resistance to change. Ronald Reagan did the same.

President Reagan argued throughout his tenure that the "spirit of voluntarism" (or the private sector) could better serve the needs of millions of Americans than a clumsy federal bureaucracy. Private donations to the arts, self-help approaches to poverty and unemployment, even voluntary action to fight natural disasters like floods fit the president's image of a simpler era—when people did not depend on government to solve their problems. At one point President Reagan urged employers to "hire just one unemployed person." By so doing, he reasoned, the unemployment problem would be licked. It was as though recessions could be ended with just a little old-fashioned "pull yourself up by your own bootstraps" encouragement. No need to ponder the intricacies of modern economics.

One way to remain cognizant of evolving complexity is to ponder tomorrow's dilemmas today. In his "valedictory lecture" the Albert Schweitzer Distinguished Service Professor Dwight Waldo did some pondering for us. Here is a list of just some of the issues he raised for tomorrow's public administrators.[8]

Coping with scarcity.   Scarcity in resources, especially budgetary scarcity, is likely to be a permanent feature of government in the future. Throughout this book we have observed scarce conditions in budgeting, personnel management, and intergovernmental relations. The permanence of scarcity provides many challenges for future administrators. In particular, they will have to be deeply involved in restructuring the country's economic system. Tomorrow's managers will need to have the skills necessary to manage economic incentives. Obviously, this requires knowledge of economics—a subject that has become an integral part of the graduate public administration curriculum.

Coping with scarcity also means that program growth gives way to struggles for organizational survival. Furthermore, motivating subordinates and providing incentives for performance are more difficult in an environment of less. Naturally, this calls for creative management.

Evolving interpretations of efficiency and effectiveness.   Efficiency and effectiveness are old public administration values. Indeed, if there is one theme that has permeated the thinking and practice of public administration during the past one hundred years, it is the search for ways to improve the performance of public organizations. The search continues.

Delivering services more efficiently and effectively is one area of constant concern, an area where sector "blurring" has particular relevance. In the past few years, for instance, many local governments have become more "businesslike" in the way they provide services. They charge fees for many services; they negotiate productivity bargains with their unions to insure that they receive a "fair day's work for a fair day's pay." Technological improvements, from new garbage trucks to word processing, help civil servants to do their jobs more efficiently.

Effectiveness, however, is always problematical. How do we know when we are doing better? Social scientists have devised elaborate ways to study public programs, but people don't stand still long enough to be measured and evaluated. Recall the chapter on evaluation. Have you found a solution to project CRAP?

Public administration will have to search for the continually elusive criterion of program and policy effectiveness. For one thing, the search is dictated simply by the preoccupation with financial shortfalls. If we constantly have less than we really need, something must be eliminated. Although it would be politically naive to say that evaluation results determine such matters, they do help political decision makers decide what should be terminated. Also, public administrators both do and manage evaluations.

Future managers will also have to be cognizant of shifting standards of efficiency and effectiveness. What was acceptable yesterday may not be so tomorrow. If there is any crystal ball to look at in this connection, it will tell us that standards are becoming more, not less, stringent. The old saw of accountability now includes the performance of bureaucrats as well as the performance of programs and policies.

The specialist versus the generalist.   Organizational life is increasingly specialized. In this sense the originator of the concept of bureaucracy, Max Weber, was right. Expertise has become a distinguishing feature of complex organizations, a prediction Weber made about eighty years ago. As he saw it, the role of the expert and the specialist's inevitable rise to political influence were unavoidable features of industrial society.

The rise of the expert in organizational life was seen as a salvation. A group of engineers founded an organization called Technocracy in the 1930s and advanced the belief that the problems of the world would be solved if only experts could reign. This was not an original idea. From Plato's philosopher king to Henri

Saint-Simon's government by savants to Technocracy—the idea of government by experts has been advanced as a way of achieving progress.

Rule by experts has not come to pass. It is time to repeat Machiavelli's sage advice on this subject from his famous treatise, *The Prince:*

> A prince . . . ought always to take counsel, but only when he wishes, not when others wish; on the contrary he ought to discourage absolute attempts to advise him unless he asks it, but he ought to be a great asker, and a patient hearer of the truth about those things of which he has inquired.[9]

Machiavelli's advice about holding experts in check has been practiced, by and large, by public officials throughout the centuries. Still, even a perceptive observer of bureaucracy such as Weber feared that politicians would be reduced to mere "dilettantes" in the onslaught of organizational society. Although Weber may have exaggerated the problem, we do hear similar concerns about the influence of congressional staffs, law clerks, and the higher civil service, who so greatly influence public decisions.[10]

The same topic manifests itself in public management. We now ask the question, "What place is there for the generalist manager in large government organizations?" To put it another way, what is the proper balance between specialization and generalization? We can end this introduction to the problems of tomorrow's public administrators by considering the view of two distinguished former managers who later became equally distinguished educators—Harland Cleveland and Rufus Miles, Jr.

> The leader as manager, indeed, is very likely to be unsuccessful unless he or she has once been an expert, unless he or she is good at judging whether the experts who stream through the office and create the information entropy on his or her desk are getting to the bottom of their subjects[11]

But Cleveland then added the following caveat: "Integrators" are needed to make sense of what experts are saying and doing. Integrators, in Cleveland's view, are those people who show a "can-do spirit of generalist leadership."[12] He added, "They all learned enough about enough subjects to use expertise without being mesmerized by the experts."[13] Integrators, in short, heed Machiavelli's scripture about the proper balance between experts and generalists.

Now for Miles:

> Let us face frankly the fact that in the executive branch as in complex business enterprises the demonstrated command of essential program knowledge is of at least as great importance in the development and selection of top-level career program managers as managerial skills. . . . It is well not to fight this technology but to accept it, work with it, and improve upon it.[14]

What do both comments mean? At the federal level and probably the state level as well, the days of the generalist public manager are over. Organizational life requires substantive expertise—just as Weber predicted. Does this mean that tomorrow's public managers will not have to know about the traditional subjects of personnel, budgeting, information processing, and intergovernmental management? On the contrary, the managers of tomorrow will have to know more about these traditional administrative concerns, not less. But they will have to know also a great deal about substantive areas of expertise—what Miles referred to as program knowledge. What Cleveland called "integrative all-stars" (those people who are able to combine substantive and generalist knowledge) must know what they are integrating.

Ethical complexity.   Ethics is a timeless subject. Yet as a subject for public administration education, it has had a curious cyclical history. From the 1930s through the 1960s it was a subject that was routinely taught in public administration programs. It even initially withstood the analytical philosophers' criticism that it was entirely subjective, totally lacking in any scientific rigor. Eventually, however, in the education of future public managers, "hard" matters drove out "soft" ones. We want our students—the public administrators of tomorrow—to learn quantitative skills, economic analysis, budgeting and financial management, and computer applications. Ethics can't be quantified; you can't do it on a spreadsheet or apply a data base system to it. Mainly you have to read, reflect, think, and question— almost old-fashioned methods of inquiry compared with the "harder" subjects of public administration.

Perhaps paradoxically, ethics as a subject of public administration is back in full force. Actually, it is not so surprising. For one thing, there has been no shortage of ethical lapses in the past several years. A juicy public scandal of major proportions is a boon for ethics courses! But more seriously, moral ambiguity is becoming even more pronounced for the typical civil servant. In the past, some bureaucrats were guilty of "moral myopia." While concentrating on the efficient means to achieve a task, some bureaucrats failed to consider the moral questions that inevitably surface over the ends of bureaucratic action.

In a study of the behavior of Nazi officials during the Holocaust in World War II, Fred Katz argued persuasively that Nazi bureaucrats actually possessed a great deal of discretion and autonomy in the fulfillment of their jobs. The defense "I was only carrying out orders" as a justification for participation in mass killings of innocent civilians was a symptom of moral myopia. It was also inaccurate. Nazi officials were responsible for their moral failing because they exercised discretion while carrying out their jobs.[15] Similarly, during the Vietnam War, a second lieutenant named William Calley was found guilty of leading a massacre of civilians in the village of My Lai. Calley's defense about "following orders" was not accepted because, as an infantry officer, he was in a position to exercise discretion, and with discretion comes moral responsibility.

Ethical complexity for tomorrow's public managers is made more complicated by some incontrovertible trends. Organizations are bigger now, and with more people comes the opportunity for more ethical lapses. But more important, the blurring of sectors creates large "gray areas," to use Waldo's phrase.[16] The gray areas arise because legal arrangements are murky, and what is "private" and what is "public" are no longer so straightforward. Waldo suggested that the gray area, the blurring of sectors, makes organizations more complex while reducing the importance of hierarchy. As he put it, it gets pretty hard to answer the question, "Who's in charge here?"[17]

Finally, the public policy issues confronting tomorrow's managers are imbued with moral dilemmas. Let's end by listing a few:

> How much of the resources of working men and women should be used to finance the care of the chronically ill elderly?
>
> What responsibility does society have for providing care and shelter to individuals who *choose* to live on the streets?
>
> Should governments have the right to require drug testing as a condition of employment?
>
> Should legislatures pass laws requiring doctors to reveal the names of their patients who have diseases that are transmitted through sexual activity?

These questions are not rhetorical. They illustrate some of the very difficult issues of public policy that our elected and appointed officials are currently struggling with. They are difficult either because the knowledge needed to solve a problem is missing or incomplete; the political conflicts surrounding alternative policy options is intense; or moral dilemmas are not easily accommodated to logical (if not politically acceptable) alternatives. But look at the bright side: seemingly intractable problems such as the brief list just supplied will guarantee that the professional life of tommorrow's managers will not be dull!

SUMMARY

As we head toward the twenty-first century it must be acknowledged that organizational life will become more and more complex. As a result, the tasks of tomorrow's public managers will be both difficult and more challenging.

The most important observation of this concluding chapter is that the separation between the private and public sectors—a separation that was never total anyway—has been eliminated. "Sector blurring" is now pervasive. Organizations in the private and public sectors have similar motivations and objectives; characteristics once thought to be the sole province of only one sector can easily be found in the other. Business resource-acquisition strategies, for example, have become more "public," and government organizations have adopted strategies once believed to be associated only with profit-seeking organizations.

Growing societal complexity has three important implications for the public managers of tomorrow. First, to manage effectively, tomorrow's administrators will need to be familiar with the ramifications of all facets of sector blurring, including the role of government in restructuring the national and international economic system, the applicability of marketlike mechanisms to standard public management tasks (such as service delivery and productivity), and the adaptability of private sector innovations to standard government operations.

Second, the public administrators of tomorrow will face ethical dilemmas.

Gray areas abound in government and will surely become an even larger part of the administrative terrain. The danger, however, is that with the ever-increasing attention to "hard" skills—economic analysis, statistics, financial management, and computer applications—we may lose sight of the ethical underpinnings of administrative behavior. Complexity makes the subject of ethics more important than ever.

Third, societal complexity, in a strange way, brings us back to a theme first enunciated by Max Weber. Weber was concerned that with the evolution of industrial society, the politician would became a mere dilettante, forced to give up real power to the professional administrator. This has not happened, but at the federal and state levels of government the truly generalist managers may be rapidly becoming extinct. To avoid falling into the category of obsolete organizational species, managers of tomorrow will have to couple traditional tools of administration with detailed substantive program knowledge. It is the only way to cope with the complexity that surrounds us.

Professional life for tomorrow's public managers will be both challenging and frustrating. When top managers leave government service—often for financially lucrative opportunities in the corporate world—they recount their own challenges and frustrations. More often than not, the latter receives more attention than the former.

The world of government awaits aspiring public managers who have the skills and knowledge to tackle tomorrow's frustrations and relish its challenges. If this book has stimulated a few to try, it will have served its purpose.

NOTES

1. See Francis E. Rourke, *Bureaucracy, Politics, and Public Policy,* 2d ed. (Boston: Little, Brown, 1976).
2. See Paul W. MacAvoy, *The Regulated Industries and the Economy* (New York: W. W. Norton, 1979).
3. Annmarie Walsh, *The Public's Business* (Cambridge, Mass.: MIT Press, 1979).
4. User fees along with other marketlike mechanisms are discussed in Jeffrey D. Straussman, "More Bank for Fewer Bucks? Or How Local Governments Can Rediscover the Potentials (and Pitfalls) of the Market," *Public Administration Review* 41 (January 1981): 150–159.
5. Laurence E. Lynn, Jr., *Managing the Public's Business* (New York: Basic Books, 1981).
6. For a good analysis of privatization, see Jeffrey R. Henig, Chris Hamnett, and Harvey B. Feigenbaum, "The Politics of Privatization: A Comparative Perspective," *Governance* 1 (October 1988): 442–489.
7. Kurt Vonnegut, Jr., *Cat's Cradle* (New York: Dell Publishing Co., 1963), p. 187.
8. Dwight Waldo, *The Enterprise of Public Administration* (Novato, Calif.: Chandler & Sharp Publishers, 1980).
9. Niccolo Machiavelli, *The Prince* (New York: Mentor Books, 1952), p. 117.
10. On staffs, see Michael J. Malbin, *Unelected Representatives: Congressional Staff and the Future of Representative Government* (New York: Basic Books, 1980). On law clerks, see Bob Woodward, *The Brethren* (New York: Simon and Schuster, 1979).

11. Harlan Cleveland, "The Future of Public Administration," *The Bureaucrat* 11 (Fall 1982): 7.
12. Ibid.
13. Ibid.
14. Rufus E. Miles, Jr., "Rethinking Some Premises of the Senior Executive Service," in *Improving the Accountability and Performance of Government,* ed. Bruce L. R. Smith and James D. Carroll (Washington, D.C.: Brookings Institution, 1982), pp. 41–42.
15. Fred E. Katz, "Implementation of the Holocaust: The Behavior of Nazi Officials," *Comparative Studies of Society and History* 24 (July 1982): 510–529.
16. Waldo, *Enterprise,* p. 114.
17. Ibid.

FOR FURTHER READING

Bozeman, Barry. *All Organizations Are Public.* San Francisco: Jossey-Bass, 1987.
   An unconventional approach to organization theory that takes a fresh look at the "blurring" of sectors.
Goodsell, Charles T. *The Case for Bureaucracy.* 2d ed. Chatham, N.J.: Chatham House Publishers, 1985.
   You may not agree with everything in this book, but it is a strong antidote to "bureaucrat bashing" and antigovernment rhetoric.
Hayek, Frederick Von. *The Road to Serfdom.* Chicago: University of Chicago Press, 1944.
   It is always worthwhile reading or rereading Hayek's fears about the consequence of "collectivism" as we approach the twenty-first century.
Smith Bruce L. R., and James D. Carroll, eds. *Improving the Accountability and Performance of Government.* Washington, D.C.: Brookings Institution, 1982.
   Noted practitioners and academics present their observations on topics ranging from the budget process and presidential management to accountability in government.
Wilson, Woodrow, "The Study of Administration." *Political Science Quarterly* 2 (June 1887): 197–222.
   When thinking about the future of public administration it is wise to go back to where the intellectual thrust began.

Selected Bibliography

CHAPTER 1

Bardach, Eugene, and Robert A. Kagan. *Going by the Book: The Problem of Regulatory Unreasonableness*. Philadelphia: Temple University Press, 1982.

Bell, Daniel. *The Coming of Post-Industrial Society*. New York: Basic Books, 1973.

Brittan, Samuel. "The Economic Contradictions of Democracy." *British Journal of Political Science* 5 (April 1975): 129–159.

Buchanan, James M., and Richard E. Wagner. *Democracy in Deficit*. New York: Academic Press, 1977.

Caro, Robert. *The Power Broker: Robert Moses and the Fall of New York*. New York: Knopf, 1974.

Chandler, Ralph Clark, ed. *A Centennial History of the American Administrative State*. New York: Free Press, 1987.

Danielson, Michael N., and Jameson W. Doig. *New York: The Politics of Urban and Regional Development*. Berkeley: University of California Press, 1982.

Downs, George W., and Patrick D. Larkey. *The Search for Government Efficiency*. New York: Random House, 1986.

Drucker, Peter. *The Age of Discontinuity*. New York: Harper & Row, 1969.

Friedman, Milton. *Capitalism and Freedom*. Chicago: University of Chicago Press, 1962.

Gartner, Alan, and Frank Riessman. *The Service Society and the Consumer Vanguard*. New York: Harper & Row, 1974.

Gross, Bertram M. *Friendly Fascism*. New York: M. Evans and Co., 1980.

———. "An Organized Society?" *Public Administration Review* 33 (July/August 1973): 323–327.

Heilbroner, Robert L. *An Inquiry into the Human Prospect*. New York: W. W. Norton, 1974.

Herzlinger, Regina, and Nancy M. Kane. *A Managerial Analysis of Federal Income Redistribution Mechanisms: The Government as Factory, Insurance Company, and Bank.* Cambridge, Mass.: Ballinger Publishing Co., 1979.

Hughes, Jonathan R. T. *The Governmental Habit.* New York: Basic Books, 1977.

Huntington, Samuel P. *American Politics: The Promise of Disharmony.* Cambridge, Mass.: Harvard University Press, 1981.

Kelman, Steven. *Making Public Policy: A Hopeful View of American Government.* New York: Basic Books, 1987.

King, Anthony. "Overload: Problems of Government in the 1970s." *Political Studies* 23 (June–September 1975): 290–295.

Knott. Jack, and Gary Miller. *Reforming Bureaucracy: The Politics of Institutional Choice.* Englewood Cliffs, N.J.: Prentice-Hall, 1987.

Lekachman, Robert. *The Age of Keynes.* New York: Vintage Books, 1966.

Levy, Frank S., Arnold J. Meltsner, and Aaron Wildavsky. *Urban Outcomes.* Berkeley: University of California Press, 1974.

Lindblom, Charles E. *Politics and Markets.* New York: Basic Books, 1977.

McCaffrey, David P. *OSHA and the Politics of Health Regulations.* New York: Plenum, 1982.

MacPherson, C. B. *Democratic Theory: Essays in Retrieval.* Oxford, Eng.: Clarendon Press, 1973.

McWilliams, Cary Wilson. *The Idea of Fraternity in America.* Berkeley: University of California Press, 1973.

Meadows, Donella H., et al. *The Limits to Growth.* New York: University Books, 1972.

Mitnick, Barry M. *The Political Economy of Regulation: Creating, Designing, and Removing Regulatory Forms.* New York: Columbia University Press, 1980.

Musgrave, Richard A. *The Theory of Public Finance.* New York: McGraw-Hill, 1959.

Mydal, Gunnar. *Beyond the Welfare State.* New Haven: Yale University Press, 1960.

O'Connor, James. *The Fiscal Crisis of the State.* New York: St. Martin's Press, 1972.

Olson, Mancur. *The Rise and Decline of Nations.* New Haven: Yale University Press, 1982.

Orwell, George. *Nineteen Eighty-Four:* New York: Harcourt Brace Jovanovich, 1949.

Palmer, John L., and Isabel V. Sawhill, eds. *The Reagan Experiment.* Washington, D.C.: Urban Institute Press, 1982.

Plotnick, Robert D., and Felicity Skidmore. *Progress against Poverty: A Review of the 1964–1974 Decade.* New York: Academic Press, 1975.

Rogers, David. *Can Business Management Save the Cities?* New York: Free Press, 1978.

Sharkansky, Ira. *Wither the State?* Chatham, N.J.: Chatham House Publishers, 1979.

Skowronek, Stephen. *Building a New American State: The Expansion of Administrative Capacities, 1877–1920.* Cambridge: Cambridge University Press, 1982.

Stein, Herbert. *The Fiscal Revolution in America.* Chicago: University of Chicago Press, 1969.

Stone, Alan. *Regulation and Its Alternatives.* Washington, D.C.: Congressional Quarterly Press, 1982.

Straussman, Jeffrey D. "What Did Tomorrow's Future Look Like Yesterday?" *Comparative Politics* 8 (October 1975): 166–181.

———. "Spending More and Enjoying It Less." *Comparative Politics* 13 (January 1981): 235–252.

Tufte, Edward R. *Political Control of the Economy*. Princeton, N.J.: Princeton University Press, 1978.

Weidenbaum, Murray. *The Modern Public Sector*. New York: Basic Books, 1969.

Wilson, James Q. "The Rise of the Bureaucratic State." *The Public Interest*, no. 41 (Fall 1975):77–103.

———, ed. *The Politics of Regulation*. New York: Basic Books, 1980.

Wolfe, Alan. *The Limits of Legitimacy*. New York: Free Press, 1977.

CHAPTER 2

Aldrich, Howard. *Organizations and Environments*. Englewood Cliffs, N.J.: Prentice-Hall, 1979.

Anderson, James E., David W. Brady, and Charles Bullock III. *Public Policy and Politics in America*. North Scituate, Mass.: Duxbury Press, 1978.

Arrow, Kenneth J. *The Limits of Organization*. New York: W. W. Norton, 1974.

Balutis, Alan P. "Death by Reorganization." *The Bureaucrat* 10 (Summer 1981):38–44.

Behn, Robert D. "Closing a Government Facility." *Public Administration Review* 38 (July/August 1978): 332–338.

Chubb, John E. *Interest Groups and the Bureaucracy*. Stanford, Calif.: Stanford University Press, 1983.

Corwin, Ronald. *Reform and Organizational Survival: The Teacher Corps as an Instrument of Educational Change*. New York: Wiley, 1973.

Crafton, Carl. "The Creation of Federal Agencies." *Administration and Society* 10 (November 1975): 328–365.

Davis, Louis. "Evolving Alternative Organization Designs: Their Sociotechnical Bases." *Human Relations* 30 (March 1977): 261–273.

Downs, Anthony. *Inside Bureaucracy*. Boston: Little, Brown, 1967.

Emery, F. E., and E. L. Trist. "The Causal Texture of Organizational Environments." *Human Relations* 18 (February 1965): 21–32.

Etzioni, Amitai. *Modern Organizations*. Englewood Cliffs, N.J.: Prentice-Hall, 1964.

Freeman, John H., and Michael T. Hannan. "Growth and Decline Processes in Organizations." *American Sociological Review* 40 (April 1975): 219–228.

Galbraith, Jay. *Organization Design*. Reading, Mass.: Addison-Wesley, 1977.

Galbraith, John Kenneth. *A Life in Our Times: Memoirs*. Boston: Houghton Mifflin, 1981.

Gawthrop, Louis C. *Bureaucratic Behavior in the Executive Branch*. New York: Free Press, 1969.

Glassberg, Andrew. "Organizational Responses to Municipal Budget Decreases." *Public Administration Review* 38 (July/August 1978), 325–332.

Goodsell, Charles F. *The Case for Bureaucracy*. 2d ed. Chatham, N.J.: Chatham House Publishers, 1985.

Hall, Richard. "Effectiveness Theory and Organizational Effectiveness." *Journal of Applied Behavioral Science* 16 (October–November–December 1980): 536–545.

————. *Organizations: Structure and Process.* 3d ed. Englewood Cliffs, N.J.: Prentice-Hall, 1982.

Head, John G. *Public Goods and Public Welfare.* Durham, N.C.: Duke University Press, 1974.

Hirschman, Albert O. *Exit, Voice, and Loyalty.* Cambridge, Mass.: Harvard University Press, 1970.

Kaufman, Herbert. *Are Government Organizations Immortal?* Washington, D.C.: Brookings Institution, 1976.

————. *The Limits of Organizational Change.* University: University of Alabama Press, 1971.

————. *Time, Chance, and Organizations.* Chatham, N.J.: Chatham House Publishers, 1985.

Kimberly, John, et al. *The Organizational Life Cycle.* San Francisco: Jossey-Bass, 1980.

Kolko, Gabriel. *The Triumph of Conservatism.* New York: Free Press, 1963.

Lowi, Theodore J. *The End of Liberalism.* 2d ed. New York: W. W. Norton, 1979.

McKelvey, Bill. *Organizational Systematics: Taxonomy, Evaluation, Classification.* Berkeley: University of California Press, 1982.

Mansfield, Harvey C. "Federal Executive Reorganization: Thirty Years of Experience." *Public Administration Review* 29 (July/August 1969): 332–345.

March, James G., and Herbert A. Simon. *Organizations.* New York: Wiley, 1958.

Meyer, Marshall W. *Change in Public Bureaucracies.* London: Cambridge University Press, 1979.

Meyer, Marshall W., and M. Craig Brown. "The Process of Bureaucratization." *American Journal of Sociology* 83 (September 1977): 364–385.

Mosher, Frederick C., ed. *American Public Administration: Past, Present, Future.* University: of Alabama Press, 1975.

Moynihan, Daniel P. *Maximum Feasible Misunderstanding.* New York: Free Press, 1969.

Nystrom, Paul C., and William H. Starbuck. *Handbook of Organizational Design: Vol. 1, Adapting Organizations to Their Environments.* New York: Oxford University Press, 1981.

————. *Handbook of Organizational Design: Vol. 2, Remodeling Organizations and Their Environments.* New York: Oxford University Press, 1981.

Olson, Mancur, Jr. *The Logic of Collective Action.* Cambridge, Mass.: Harvard University Press, 1965.

Pfeffer, Jeffrey. *Power in Organizations.* Marshfield, Mass.: Pitman, 1981.

Rainey, Hal G., Robert W. Backoff, and Charles A. Levine. "Comparing Public and Private Organizations." *Public Administration Review* 36 (March/April 1976): 233–244.

Rubin, Irene. *Shrinking the Federal Government: The Effects of Cutbacks on Five Federal Agencies.* White Plains, N.Y.: Longman, 1985.

Salamon, Lester M. "The Goals of Reorganization: A Framework for Analysis." *Administration and Society* 12 (February 1981): 471–500.

Steiner, Gilbert Y. *The State of Welfare.* Washington, D.C.: Brookings Institution. 1971.

Wamsley, Gary, and Mayer N. Zald. *The Political Economy of Public Organizations.* Bloomington: Indiana University Press, 1973.

CHAPTER 3

Aberbach, Joel D., and Bert A. Rockman. "The Overlapping Worlds of American Federal Executives and Congressmen." *British Journal of Political Science* 7 (January 1977): 23–31.

Arnold, R. Douglas. *Congress and the Bureaucracy*. New Haven: Yale University Press, 1979.

Bailey, Stephen K. *Congress Makes a Law*. New York: Random House, 1950.

Birnbaum, Jeffrey H., and Alan S. Murray. *Showdown at Gucci Gulch*. New York: Vintage Books, 1987.

Cain, Bruce, John Ferejohn, and Morris Fiorina. *The Personal Vote: Constituency Service and Electoral Independence*. Cambridge, Mass.: Harvard University Press, 1987.

Chubb, John. *Interest Groups and the Bureaucracy*. Stanford, Calif.: Stanford University Press, 1983.

Dodd, Lawrence, and Richard L. Schott. *Congress and the Administrative State*. New York: Wiley, 1979.

Dodd, Lawrence, Richard L. Schott, and Bruce I. Oppenheimer. *Congress Reconsidered*. 3d ed. Washington, D.C.: Congressional Quarterly Press, 1985.

Fenno, Richard F. *The Power of the Purse*. Boston: Little, Brown, 1966.

Fiorina, Morris. *Congress, Keystone of the Washington Establishment*. New Haven: Yale University Press, 1977.

Fisher, Louis. *The Politics of Shared Powers: Congress and the Executive*. 2d ed. Washington, D.C.: Congressional Quarterly Press, 1987.

Harris, Joseph P. *Congressional Control of Administration*. Garden City, N.Y.: Doubleday, 1964.

Lowi, Theodore J. *The End of Liberalism*. 2d ed. New York: W. W. Norton, 1977.

Moe, Terry. "An Assessment of the Positive Theory of Congressional Dominance." *Legislative Studies Quarterly* 12 (November 1987): 475–520,

Ogul, Morris. *Congress Oversees the Bureaucracy: Studies in Legislative Oversight*. Pittsburgh: University of Pittsburgh Press, 1976.

Ripley, Randall B., and Grace Franklin. *Congress, the Bureaucracy, and Public Policy*. 4th ed. Chicago: Dorsey Press, 1987.

Shepsle, Kenneth A. *The Giant Jigsaw Puzzle: Democratic Committee Assignments in the Modern House*. Chicago: University of Chicago Press, 1978.

Sundquist, James L. *The Decline and Resurgence of Congress*. Washington, D.C.: Brookings Institution, 1981.

Wilson, James Q. *Political organizations*. New York: Basic Books, 1973.

CHAPTER 4

Argyris, Chris. "Organizational Man: Rational *and* Self-Actualizing." *Public Administration Review* 33 (July/August 1973): 354–358.

Bacharach, Samuel B., and Edward J. Lawler. *Power and Politics in Organizations*. San Francisco: Jossey-Bass, 1980.

Barnard, Chester I. *The Functions of the Executive.* Cambridge, Mass.: Harvard University Press, 1938.

Blau, Peter M. *The Dynamics of Bureaucracy.* Chicago: University of Chicago Press, 1955.

Burke, W. Warner. "Organizational Development and Bureaucracies in the 1980's." *Journal of Applied Behavioral Science* 16 (July–August–September 1980): 423–437.

Carroll, Stephen J., and Henry L. Tosi. *Organizational Behavior.* Chicago: St. Clair Press, 1977.

Crozier, Michel. *The Bureaucratic Phenomenon.* Chicago: University of Chicago Press, 1964.

Daft, Richard L. *Organization Theory and Design.* St. Paul, Minn.: West Publishing Co., 1983.

Denhardt, Robert B. *Theories of Public Organization.* Monterey, Calif.: Brooks/Cole, 1984.

Downs, Anthony. *Inside Bureaucracy.* Boston: Little, Brown, 1967.

Eddy, William B. *Public Organization Behavior and Development.* Cambridge, Mass.: Winthrop Publishers, 1981.

Fiedler, Fred E. *A Theory of Leadership Effectiveness.* New York: McGraw-Hill, 1967.

Gerth, H. H., and C. Wright Mills, eds. *From Max Weber: Essays in Sociology.* New York: Oxford University Press, 1971.

Golembiewski, Robert T., and William B. Eddy, eds. *Organization Development in Public Administration.* Parts 1 and 2. New York: Marcel Dekker, 1978.

Goodsell, Charles T. *The Case for Bureaucracy.* 2d ed. Chatham, N.J.: Chatham House Publishers, 1985.

Gross, Bertram M. *Organizations and Their Managing.* New York: Free Press, 1968.

Gulick, Luther, and Lyndall Urwick, eds. *Papers on the Science of Administration.* New York: Institute of Public Administration, 1937.

Hall, Richard H., and Robert E. Quinn, eds. *Organizational Theory and Public Policy.* Beverly Hills, Calif.: Sage Publications, 1983.

Harmon, Michael, and Richard T. Mayer. *Organization Theory for Public Administration.* Boston: Little, Brown, 1986.

Landau, Martin. "On the Concept of a Self-Correcting Organization." *Public Administration Review* 33 (November/December 1973): 533–543.

Levine, Charles. "Organizational Decline and Cutback Management." *Public Administration Review* 38 (July/August, 1978): 316–325.

Likert, Rensis. *The Human Organization.* New York: McGraw-Hill, 1961.

———. *New Patterns of Management.* New York: McGraw-Hill, 1961.

March, James, ed. *Handbook of Organizations.* Chicago: Rand McNally, 1965.

Maslow, Abraham. *Motivation and Personality.* New York: Harper & Row, 1954.

McGregor, Douglas. *The Human Side of Enterprise.* New York: McGraw-Hill, 1960.

Milward, H. Brinton, and Hal G. Rainey. "Don't Blame the Bureaucracy!" *Journal of Public Policy* 3 (May 1983): 149–168.

Mohr, Lawrence B. *Explaining Organizational Behavior.* San Francisco: Jossey-Bass, 1982.

Niskanen, William A., Jr. *Bureaucracy and Representative Government.* Chicago: Aldine, 1971.

Odione, George S. *Management by Objectives*. New York: Pitman, 1965.

Parkinson, C. Northcote. *Parkinson's Law*. New York: Ballantine, 1975.

Perrow, Charles. *Complex Organizations*. 2d ed. Glenview, Ill.: Scott, Foresman, 1979.

Peters, B. Guy. *The Politics of Bureaucracy*. 3d ed. White Plains, N.Y.: Longman, 1989.

Pfeffer, Jeffrey. *Power in Organizations*. Marshfield, Mass: Pitman, 1981.

Rourke, Francis E. *Bureaucracy, Politics, and Public Policy*, 3d. ed. Boston: Little, Brown, 1978.

Sabrosky, Alan, James Thompson, and Karen McPherson. "Organized Anarchies: Military Bureaucracy in the 1980's." *Journal of Applied Behavioral Science* 18, no. 2 (1982): 137–153.

Savas, E. S. *Privatization*. Chatham, N.J.: Chatham House Publishers, 1987.

Shafritz, Jay M., and Philip H. Whitbeck, eds. *Classics of Organization Theory*. Oak Park, Ill.: Moore Publishing Co., 1978.

Simon, Herbert. *Administrative Behavior*. 3d ed. New York: Free Press, 1976.

Staw, Barry M., and Gerald R. Salancik, eds. *New Directions in Organizational Behavior*. Chicago: St. Clair Press, 1977.

Taylor, Frederick Winslow. *The Principles of Scientific Management*. New York: W. W. Norton, 1967.

Thompson, James D. *Organizations in Action*. New York: McGraw-Hill, 1967.

Vroom, Victor. *Work and Motivation*. New York: Wiley, 1964.

Warwick, Donald. *A Theory of Public Bureaucracy*. Cambridge, Mass.: Harvard University Press, 1975.

CHAPTER 5

Anderson, Wayne F., Chester A. Newland, and Richard J. Stillman III. *The Effective Local Government Manager*. Washington, D.C.: International City Management Association, 1983.

Argyris, Chris. *Personality and Organization*. New York: Harper & Row, 1957.

Barnard, Chester I. *The Functions of the Executive*. Cambridge, Mass.: Harvard University Press, 1938.

Bower, Joseph L. "Effective Public Management: It Isn't the Same as Effective Business Management." *Harvard Business Review* 55 (March/April 1977): 131–140.

———. *The Two Faces of Management*. Boston: Houghton Mifflin, 1983.

Bower, Joseph L., and Charles J. Christenson. *Public Management Text and Cases*. Homewood, Ill.: Richard D. Irwin, 1978.

Bozeman, Barry. *Public Management and Policy Analysis*. New York: St. Martin's Press, 1979.

Campbell, Colin, S. J. *Managing the Presidency*. Pittsburgh: University of Pittsburgh Press. 1986.

Chase, Gordon, and Elizabeth C. Reveal. *How to Manage in the Public Sector*. Reading, Mass.: Addison-Wesley, 1983.

Chase, Richard B., and Nicholas J. Aquilano. *Production and Operations Management*. Homewood, Ill.: Richard D. Irwin, 1981.

Cleveland, Harland. *The Future Executive*. New York: Harper & Row, 1972.

Cyert, Richard, and James March. *A Behavioral Theory of the Firm*. Englewood Cliffs, N.J.: Prentice-Hall, 1963.

Doig, Jameson W., and Erwin C. Hargrove, eds. *Leadership and Innovation*. Baltimore: Johns Hopkins University Press, 1987.

Downs, Anthony. *Inside Bureaucracy*. Boston: Little, Brown, 1967.

Drucker, Peter F. *The Effective Executive*. New York: Harper & Row, 1967.

———. "Managing the Public Service Institution." *The Public Interest,* no. 33 (Fall 1973): 43–60.

Fottler, Myron D. "Is Management Really Generic?" *Academy of Management Review* 16 (January 1981): 1–13.

Golembiewski, Robert T., and Michael White. *Cases in Public Management*. 4th ed. Boston: Houghton Mifflin, 1983.

Greer, Ann L. *The Mayor's Mandate*. Cambridge, Mass.: Schenkman, 1974.

Heclo, Hugh. *A Government of Strangers: Executive Politics in Washington*. Washington, D.C.: Brookings Institution, 1977.

Ink, Dwight A. "The President as Manager." *Public Administration Review* 36 (September/October 1976): 508–515.

Kaufman, Herbert. *The Administrative Behavior of Federal Bureau Chiefs*. Washington, D.C.: Brookings Institution, 1981.

Landau, Martin, and Russell Stout. "To Manage Is Not to Control: Or the Folly of Type II Errors." *Public Administration Review* 39 (March/April 1979): 148–156.

Levine, Charles H., Irene S. Rubin, and George G. Wolohojian. *The Politics of Retrenchment*. Beverly Hills, Calif: Sage Publications, 1981.

Likert, Rensis. "System 4: A Resource for Improving Public Administration." *Public Administration Review* 41 (November/December 1981): 674–687.

Lynn, Laurence E., Jr. *Managing Public Policy*. Boston: Little, Brown, 1987.

———. *Managing the Public's Business*. New York: Basic Books, 1981.

Lynn, Laurence E., Jr., and John M. Seidl. " 'Bottom-Line' Management for Public Agencies." *Harvard Business Review* 55 (January/February 1977): 144–153.

Malek, Frederick V. *Washington's Hidden Tragedy*. New York: Free Press, 1978.

Martin, David L. *Running City Hall*. University: University of Alabama Press, 1982.

Ouchi, William, *Theory Z*. Reading Mass.: Addison-Wesley, 1981.

Perry, James L., and Kenneth L. Kraemer, eds. *Public Management: Public and Private Perspectives*. Palo Alto, Calif: Mayfield Publishing Co., 1983.

Pinkus, Charles E., and Anne Dixson. *Solving Local Government Problems*. London: George Allen & Unwin, 1981.

Rosenthal, Stephen R. *Managing Government Operations*. Glenview, Ill.: Scott, Foresman, 1982.

Schuck, Peter H. *Suing Government*. New Haven: Yale University Press, 1983.

Selznick, Philip. *Leadership in Administration*. New York: Harper & Row, 1957.

Speer, Albert. *Inside the Third Reich*. New York: Macmillan, 1970.

Stewart, Debra W., and G. David Garson. *Organizational Behavior and Public Management*. New York: Marcel Dekker, 1983.

Straussman, Jeffrey D., and Glen E. Hahn. "Budget 'Reform' as a Technique of Managerial Assertiveness." *Public Administration Review* 38 (November/December 1978): 584–588.

Waldo, Dwight. "The Future of Management." *The Bureaucrat* 6 (Fall 1977): 101–113.

Warwick, Donald P. *A Theory of Public Bureaucracy*. Cambridge, Mass.: Harvard University Press, 1975.

Weinberg, Martha Wagner. *Managing the State*. Cambridge, Mass.: MIT Press, 1977.

Wholey, Joseph S. *Evaluation and Effective Public Management*. Boston: Little, Brown, 1983.

CHAPTER 6

Aaron, Henry J. *Who Pays the Property Tax?* Washington, D.C.: Brookings Institution, 1975.

Advisory Commission on Intergovernmental Relations. *Categorical Grants: Their Role and Design*. A-52. Washington, D.C.: U.S. Government Printing Office, 1978.

———. *City Financial Emergencies: The Intergovernmental Dimension*, A-42. Washington, D.C.: U.S. Government Printing Office, 1973.

———. *Significant Features of Fiscal Federalism, 1981–82 Edition*. Washington, D.C.: U.S. Government Printing Office, 1982.

Arnold, R. Douglas. *Congress and the Bureaucracy*. New Haven: Yale University Press, 1979.

Aronson, J. Richard, and Eli Schwartz, eds. *Management Policies in Local Government Finance*. Washington, D.C.: International City Management Association, 1981.

Bahl, Roy, ed. *Financing State and Local Government in the 1980s*. New York: Oxford University Press, 1984.

———. *The Fiscal Outlook for Cities*. Syracuse, N.Y.: Syracuse University Press, 1978.

Berne, Robert, and Richard Schramm. *The Financial Analysis of Governments*. Englewood Cliffs, NJ: Prentice-Hall, 1986.

Burchell, Robert W., and David Listokin, eds. *Cities under Stress: The Fiscal Crisis of Urban America*. Piscataway, N.J.: Center for Urban Policy Research, 1981.

Burkhead, Jesse, and Jerry Miner. *Public Expenditure*. Chicago: Aldine, 1971.

Caraley, Demetrios. "Congressional Politics and Urban Aid." *Political Science Quarterly* 91 (Spring 1976): 19–45.

Clark, Terry Nichols, and Lorna Crowley Ferguson. *City Money*. New York: Columbia University Press, 1983.

Derthick, Martha. *Uncontrollable Spending for Social Services Grants*. Washington, D.C.: Brookings Institution, 1975.

Dommel, Paul R. *The Politics of Revenue Sharing*. Bloomington: Indiana University Press, 1974.

Fisher, Ronald C. *State and Local Public Finance*. Glenview, Ill.: Scott, Foresman, 1988.

Glickman, Norman J., ed. *The Urban Impacts of Federal Policies*. Baltimore: Johns Hopkins University Press, 1980.

Hale, George E., and Marian Lief Palley. *The Politics of Federal Grants*. Washington, D.C.: Congressional Quarterly Press, 1981.

Hudson, William E. "The Federal Aid Crutch: How a Sunbelt City Comes to Depend on Federal Revenue." *The Urban Interest* 2 (Spring 1980): 34–44.

Kirlin, John J. *The Political Economy of Fiscal Limits*. Lexington, Mass.: Lexington Books, 1982.

Koch, Edward I. "The Mandate Millstone." *The Public Interest*, no. 61 (Fall 1980): 42–57.

Ladd, Helen F., and John Yinger. *America's Ailing Cities*. Baltimore: Johns Hopkins University Press, 1989.

Larkey, Patrick D. *Evaluating Public Programs: The Impact of General Revenue Sharing on Municipal Government*. Princeton, N.J.: Princeton University Press, 1979.

Levine, Charles H., and Irene Rubin, eds. *Fiscal Stress and Public Policy*. Beverly Hills, Calif.: Sage Publications, 1980.

Lovell, Catherine H. "Coordinating Federal Grants from Below." *Public Administration Review* 39 (September/October 1979): 432–439.

Marcum, Jess, and Henry Rowen. "How Many Games in Town? The Pros and Cons of Legalized Gambling." *The Public Interest*, no. 36 (Summer 1974): 25–52.

Maxwell, James A., and J. Richard Aronson. *Financing State and Local Governments*. 4th ed. Washington, D.C.: Brookings Institution, 1986.

Meltsner, Arnold J. *The Politics of City Revenue*. Berkeley: University of California Press, 1971.

Merget, Astrid E. "The Fiscal Dependency of American Cities." *Public Budgeting & Finance* 1 (Summer 1981): 20–30.

Mieszkowski, Peter, and Mahlon Straszheim, eds. *Current Issues in Urban Economics*. Baltimore: Johns Hopkins University Press, 1979.

Morris, Charles R. *The Cost of Good Intentions*. New York: W. W. Norton, 1980.

Musgrave, Richard A., and Peggy B. Musgrave. *Public Finance in Theory and Practice*. 4th ed. New York: McGraw-Hill, 1984.

Mushkin, Selma J., ed. *Public Prices for Public Products*. Washington, D.C.: Urban Institute, 1972.

Neiman, Max, and Catherine Lovell. "Federal and State Requirements: Impacts on Local Government." *The Urban Interest* 2 (Spring 1980): 45–51.

Oates, Wallace E. *Fiscal Federalism*. New York: Harcourt Brace Jovanovich, 1972.

————, ed. *The Political Economy of Fiscal Federalism*. Lexington, Mass.: Heath, 1977.

Pechman, Joseph A., and Benjamin A. Okner. *Who Bears the Tax Burden?* Washington, D.C.: Brookings Institution, 1974.

Phares, Donald. *Who Pays State and Local Taxes?* Cambridge, Mass.: Oelgeschlager, Gunn & Hain, 1980.

Poole, Robert W., Jr. *Cutting Back City Hall*. New York: Universe Books, 1980.

Sbragia, Alberta M., ed. *The Municipal Money Chase: The Politics of Local Government Finance*. Boulder, Col.: Westview Press, 1983.

Wagner, Richard E. *Public Finance*. Boston: Little, Brown, 1983.

Walker, David B. *Toward a Functioning Federalism*. Cambridge, Mass.: Winthrop Publishers, 1981.

Walzer, Norman, and David L. Chicone, eds. *Financing State and Local Governments in the 1980s*. Cambridge, Mass.: Oelgeschlager, Gunn & Hain, 1981.

Wright, Deil S. *Understanding Intergovernmental Relations*. 3d ed. Pacific Grove, Calif.: Brooks/Cole, 1988.

CHAPTER 7

Axelrod, Donald. *Budgeting for Modern Government*. New York: St. Martin's Press, 1988.

Banks, William C., and Jeffrey D. Straussman. "Bowsher v. Synar: The Emerging Judicialization of the Fisc." *Boston College Law Review* 28 (July 1987): 659–688.

Bennett, James T., and Thomas J. Dilorenzo. *Underground Government: The Off-Budget Public Sector*. Washington, D.C.: CATO Institute, 1983.

Berman, Larry. *The Office of Management and Budget and the Presidency, 1921–1979*. Princeton, N.J.: Princeton University Press, 1979.

Borcherding, Thomas, ed. *Budgets and Bureaucrats: The Source of Government Growth*. Durham, N.C.: Duke University Press, 1977.

Bozeman, Barry, and Jeffrey D. Straussman. "Shrinking Budgets and the Shrinkage of Budget Theory." *Public Administration Review* 42 (November/December 1982): 509–515.

Brown, Richard E., Meredith C. Williams, and Thomas P. Gallagher. *Auditing Performance in Government*. New York: Wiley, 1982.

Burkhead, Jesse. *Government Budgeting*. New York: Wiley, 1956.

Caiden, Naomi, and Aaron Wildavsky. *Planning and Budgeting in Poor Countries*. New York: Wiley, 1974.

Danziger, James N. *Making Budgets*. Beverly Hills, Calif: Sage Publications, 1978.

Davis, Otto A., M. A. H. Dempster, and Aaron Wildavsky. "Toward a Predictive Theory of Government Expenditure: U.S. Domestic Appropriations." *British Journal of Political Science* 4 (October 1974): 419–452.

Ellwood, John. "Making and Enforcing Federal Spending Limitations: Issues and Options." *Public Budgeting & Finance* 1 (Spring 1981): 28–42.

Fenno, Richard. *The Power of the Purse: Appropriations Politics in Congress*. Boston: Little, Brown, 1966.

Fisher, Louis. *Presidential Spending Power*. Princeton, N.J.: Princeton University Press, 1975.

Gansler, Jacques S. *Affording Defense*. Cambridge, Mass.: MIT Press, 1989.

Greider, William. "The Education of David Stockman." *The Atlantic Monthly* 248 (December 1981): 27–54.

Haider, Donald F. "Zero Base: Federal Style." *Public Administration Review* 37 (July/August 1977): 400–407.

Hale, George E., and Scott R. Douglass. "The Politics of Budget Execution: Financial Manipulation in State and Local Government." *Administration & Society* 9 (November 1977): 376–378.

Hammond, Thomas, and Jack Knott. *A Zero-Based Look at Zero-Base Budgeting*. New Brunswick, N.J.: Transaction Books, 1980.

Heilbroner, Robert, and Peter Bernstein. *The Debt and the Deficit*. New York: W. W. Norton, 1989.

Key, V. O., Jr. "The Lack of a Budgetary Theory." *American Political Science Review* 24 (December 1940): 1137–1144.

Lee, Robert D., and Ronald W. Johnson. *Public Budgeting Systems*. 3d ed. Baltimore: University Park Press, 1983.

Lehan, Edward A. *Simplified Governmental Budgeting*. Chicago: Municipal Finance Officers Association, 1981.

LeLoup, Lance. *The Fiscal Congress*. Westport, Conn.: Greenwood Press, 1980.

Lyden, Fremont J., and Marc Lindenberg. *Public Budgeting in Theory and Practice*. White Plains, N.Y.: Longman, 1983.

Massey, Jane, and Jeffrey D. Straussman. "Budget Control Is Alive and Well: Case Study of a County Government." *Public Budgeting & Finance* 1 (Winter 1981): 3–11.

Meltsner, Arnold J. *The Politics of City Revenue*. Berkeley: University of California Press, 1971.

Mikesell, John L. *Fiscal Administration*. 2d ed. Chicago: Dorsey Press, 1986.

Mosher, Frederick C. *A Tales of Two Agencies*. Baton Rouge: Louisiana State University Press, 1984.

Mosher, Frederick C., and Max O. Stephenson, Jr. "The Office of Management and Budget in a Changing Scene." *Public Budgeting & Finance* 2 (Winter 1982): 23–41.

Ott, David J., and Attiat F. Ott. *Federal Budget Policy*. 3d ed. Washington, D.C.: Brookings Institution, 1977.

Pechman, Joseph A., ed. *Setting National Priorities: The 1984 Budget*. Washington, D.C.: Brookings Institution, 1983.

Prenchand, A. *Government Budgeting and Expenditure Controls*. Washington, D.C.: International Monetary Fund, 1983.

Pyhrr, Peter A. *Zero-Base Budgeting*. New York: Wiley, 1973.

Rubin, Irene, ed. *New Directions in Budget Theory*. Albany: State University of New York, 1988.

Schick, Allen. *Congress and Money*. Washington, D.C.: Urban Institute, 1980.

———. "Contemporary Problems in Financial Control." *Public Administration Review* 38 (November/December 1978): 513–519.

Schultze, Charles L. *The Politics and Economics of Public Spending*. Washington, D.C.: Brookings Institution, 1968.

Sharkansky, Ira. "Agency Requests, Gubernatorial Support and Budget Success in State Legislatures." *American Political Science Review* 62 (December 1968): 1220–1231.

Stockman, David. *The Triumph of Politics*. New York: Harper & Row, 1986.

Straussman, Jeffrey D. "Government Overload Revisited: The Case of the Federal Budget Deficit. *International Journal of Public Administration* 8, no. 1 (1986): 79–102.

———. "A Typology of Budgetary Environments: Notes on the Prospects of Reform." *Administration & Society* 11 (August 1979): 216–226.

———. "V. O. Key's 'The Lack of a Budgetary Theory: Where Are We Now?' " *International Journal of Public Administration* 7, no. 4 (1985): 345–374.

Straussman, Jeffrey D., and Glen E. Hahn. "Budget 'Reform' as a Technique of Managerial Assertiveness." *Public Administration Review* 38 (November/December 1978): 584–588.

Thompson, Fred, and William Zumeta. "Control and Controls: A Reexamination of Control Patterns in Budget Execution." *Policy Sciences* 13 (February 1981): 25–50.

Wildavsky, Aaron. *Budgeting: A Comparative Theory of Budgetary Practice*. Boston: Little, Brown, 1975.

———. *How to Limit Government Spending*. Berkeley: University of California Press, 1980.

———. *The Politics of the Budgetary Process*. 4th ed. Boston: Little, Brown, 1984.

Worthley, John A., and William G. Ludwin, eds. *Zero-Base Budgeting in State and Local Government*. New York: Praeger, 1979.

CHAPTER 8

Aberbach, Joel D., and Bert A. Rockman. "Clashing Beliefs within the Executive Branch: The Nixon Administration Bureaucracy." *American Political Science Review* 70 (June 1976): 456–468.

Appleby, Paul. *Policy and Administration*. University: University of Alabama Press, 1949.

Balzer, Anthony J. "Quotas and the San Francisco Police: A Sergeant's Dilemma." *Public Administration Review* 37 (May/June 1977): 276–285.

Case, Harry L. *Personnel Policy in a Public Agency: The TVA Experience*. New York: Harper & Row, 1955.

Cayer, N. Joseph. *Public Personnel Administration in the United States*. New York: St. Martin's Press, 1975.

Clynch, Edward J., and Carol A. Gandin. "Sex in the Shipyards: An Assessment of Affirmative Action Policy." *Public Administration Review* 42 (March/April 1982): 114–121.

Gottfried, Frances. *The Merit System and Municipal Civil Service*. Westport, Conn.: Greenwood Press, 1988.

Hartman, Robert W., and Arnold R. Weber, eds. *The Rewards of Public Service: Compensating Top Federal Officials*. Washington, D.C.: Brookings Institution, 1980.

Harvey, Donald R. *The Civil Service Commission*. New York: Praeger, 1970.

Heclo, Hugh. *A Government of Strangers: Executive Politics in Washington*. Washington, D.C.: Brookings Institution, 1977.

———. "OMB and the Presidency—The Problem of 'Neutral Competence'." *The Public Interest*, no. 38 (Winter 1975): 80–98.

Kaufman, Herbert. *Administrative Feedback: Monitoring Subordinates' Behavior*. Washington, D.C.: Brookings Institution, 1973.

Kelly, Rita Mae, and Jane Jayes, eds. *Comparable Worth, Pay Equity, and Public Policy*. Westport, Conn.: Greenwood Press, 1988.

Klinger, Donald, E., ed. *Public Personnel Management*. Palo Alto, Calif.: Mayfield Publishing Company, 1981.

Kranz, Harry. *The Participatory Bureaucracy*. Lexington, Mass.: Lexington Books, 1976.

Krislov, Samuel. *Representative Bureaucracy*. Englewood Cliffs, N.J.: Prentice-Hall, 1974.

Lawler, Edward E. III. *Pay and Organizational Effectiveness*. New York: McGraw-Hill, 1971.

Lee, Robert D., Jr. *Public Personnel Systems*. Baltimore: University Park Press, 1979.

Martin, Philip L. "The Hatch Act in Court: Some Recent Developments." *Public Administration Review* 33 (September/October 1973): 443–447.

Milward, H. Brinton, and Cheryl Swanson. "Organizational Response to Environmental Pressures: The Politics of Affirmative Action." *Administration & Society* 11 (August 1979): 123–143.

Monroe, Michael L. "The Position Classifier's Dilemma." *The Bureaucrat* 4 (July 1975): 204–206.

Mosher, Frederick C. *Democracy and the Public Service.* 2d ed. New York: Oxford University Press, 1982.

Neuse, Steven M. "Professionalism and Authority: Women in Public Service." *Public Administration Review* 38 (September/October 1978): 436–441.

Nigro, Felix A., and Lloyd G. Nigro. *The New Public Personnel Administration.* 2d ed. Itasca, Ill.: Peacock, 1981.

Pearce, Jone L., and James L. Perry. "Federal Merit Pay: A Longitudinal Analysis." *Public Administration Review* 43 (July/August 1983): 315–325.

Rabin, Jack, et al., eds. *Handbook on Public Personnel Administration and Labor Relations.* New York: Marcel Dekker, 1983.

Rainey, Hal G. "Perceptions of Incentives in Business and Government: Implications for Civil Service Reform." *Public Administration Review* 39 (September/October 1979): 440–448.

Riordon, William L. *Plunkitt of Tammany Hall.* New York: E. P. Dutton, 1963.

Roberts, Robert. " 'Last Hired, First Fired' and Public Employee Layoffs: The Equal Opportunity Dilemma." *Review of Public Personnel Administration* 2 (Fall 1981): 29–48.

Rose, Winfield H., and Tiang Ping Chia. "The Impact of the Equal Employment Opportunity Act of 1972 on Black Employment in the Federal Service: A Preliminary Analysis." *Public Administration Review* 38 (May/June 1978): 245–251.

Rosen, Bernard. "Merit and the President's Plan for Changing the Civil Service System." *Public Administration Review* 38 (July/August 1978): 301–304.

Rosow, Jerome. "Public Sector Pay and Benefits." *Public Administration Review* 36 (September/October 1976): 538–543.

Shafritz, Jay. *Public Personnel Management: The Heritage of Civil Service Reform.* New York: Praeger, 1975.

———. *Position Classification: A Behavioral Analysis for the Public Service.* New York: Praeger, 1973.

Stahl, O. Glen. *Public Personnel Administration.* 8th ed. New York: Harper & Row, 1982.

Sylvia, Ronald D. *Critical Issues in Public Personnel Policy.* Pacific Grove, Calif.: Brooks/Cole, 1989.

Thayer, Frederick. "The President's Management 'Reforms': Theory X Triumphant." *Public Administration Review* 38 (July/August 1978): 309–314.

Thompson, Frank J. *Personnel Policy in the City.* Berkeley: University of California Press, 1975.

———, ed. *Classics of Public Personnel Policy.* Oak Park, Ill.: Moore Publishing Co., 1979.

Van Riper, Paul. *History of the United States Civil Service.* New York: Harper & Row, 1958.

Vroom, Victor. *Work and Motivation*. New York: Wiley, 1964.

Wood, Norman. "Equal Employment Opportunity and Seniority: Rights in Conflict." *Labor Law Journal* 26 (June 1975): 345–349.

CHAPTER 9

Aaron, Benjamin, Joseph P. Gordon, and James L. Stern, eds. *Public-Sector Bargaining*. 2d ed. Washington, D.C.: Bureau of National Affairs, 1988.

Altman, Gary D. "Proposition 2½: The Massachusetts Tax Revolt and Its Impact on Public Sector Labor Relations." *Journal of Collective Negotiations in the Public Sector* 12, no. 1 (1983): 1–19.

Benecki, Stanley. "Municipal Expenditure Levels and Collective Bargaining." *Industrial Relations* 17 (May 1978): 216–230.

Bent, Alan Edward, and T. Zane Reeves. *Collective Bargaining in the Public Sector*. Menlo Park, N.J.: Benjamin/Cummings, 1978.

Bretschneider, Stuart, Robert C. Rodgers, and Jeffrey D. Straussman. "Public Unions and Penalties for Striking across the States." *Review of Public Personnel Administration* 6 (Summer 1986): 19–36.

Chickering, A. Lawrence, ed. *Public Employee Unions*. San Francisco: Institute for Contemporary Studies, 1976.

Derber, Milton, and Martin Wagner. "Public Sector Bargaining and Budget Making under Fiscal Adversity." *Industrial and Labor Relations Review* 33 (October 1979): 18–23.

Dickson, Elizabeth, Harold A. Hovey, and George E. Peterson. *Public Employee Compensation: A Twelve City Comparison*. Washington, D.C.: Urban Institute. 1980.

Eberts, Randall. "How Unions Affect Management Decisions: Evidence from Public Schools." *Journal of Labor Research* 4 (Summer 1983): 239–247.

Feuille, Peter. "Final Offer Arbitration and the Chilling Effect." *Industrial Relations* 14 (October 1975): 302–310.

Gustely, Richard D. *Municipal Public Employment and Public Expenditure*. Lexington, Mass.: Heath, 1974.

Hamermesh, Daniel S., ed. *Labor in Public and Nonprofit Sectors*. Princeton, N.J.: Princeton University Press, 1975.

Hanrahan, John D. *Government for Sale: Contracting Out, the New Patronage*. Washington, D.C.: American Federation of State, County and Municipal Employees, 1977.

Horton, Raymond D. *Municipal Labor Relations in New York City*. New York: Praeger, 1973.

———. "Productivity and Productivity Bargaining in Government: A Critical Analysis." *Public Administration Review* 36 (July/August 1976): 407–414.

Juris, Harvey A., and Peter Feuille. *Police Unionism*. Lexington, Mass.: Heath, 1973.

Katz, Harry C. "Municipal Pay Determination: The Case of San Francisco." *Industrial Relations* 18 (Winter 1979): 44–58.

Kearney, Richard C. *Labor Relations in the Public Sector*. New York: Marcel Dekker, 1984.

———. "Municipal Budgeting and Collective Bargaining: The Case of Iowa." *Public Personnel Management* 9 (March/April 1980): 108–114.

Kochan, Thomas. *Collective Bargaining and Industrial Relations*. Homewood, Ill.: Richard D. Irwin, 1980.

Kochan, Thomas, and Jean Baderschneider. "Dependence on Impasse Procedures: Police and Firefighters in New York State." *Industrial and Labor Relations Review* 31 (July 1978): 431–449.

Kochan, Thomas, and Todd Jick. "The Public Sector Mediation Process." *Journal of Conflict Resolution* 22 (June 1978): 209–240.

Kochan, Thomas, and Hoyt Wheeler. "Municipal Collective Bargaining." *Industrial and Labor Relations Review* 27 (October 1975): 46–66.

Kolb, Deborah. *The Mediators*. Cambridge, Mass.: MIT Press, 1983.

Lewin, David. "Mayoral Power and Municipal Labor Relations: A Three City Study." *Employee Relations Law Journal* 6 (Spring 1981): 635–665.

Lewin, David, and Mary McCormick. "Coalition Bargaining in Municipal Government: The New York City Experience." *Industrial and Labor Relations Review* 34 (January 1981): 175–190.

Lewin, David, Peter Feuille, and Thomas Kochan, eds. *Public Sector Labor Relations: Analysis and Readings*. 2d ed. Glen Ridge, N.J.: Thomas Horton and Daughters, 1981.

Lewin, David, Raymond D. Horton, and James W. Kuhn. *Collective Bargaining and Manpower Utilization in Big City Government*. New York: Universe Books, 1979.

Methe, David T., and James L. Perry. "The Impacts of Collective Bargaining on Local Government Services: A Review of Research." *Public Administration Review* 40 (July/August 1980): 359–371.

Morris, Charles R. *The Cost of Good Intentions*. New York: W. W. Norton, 1980.

Olson, Craig A. "The Impact of Arbitration on the Wages of Firefighters." *Industrial Relations* 19 (Fall 1980): 325–339.

Poole, Robert W., Jr. *Cutting Back City Hall*. New York: Universe Books, 1980.

Rodgers, Robert C., and Jeffrey D. Straussman. "What Factors Contribute to the Duration of Strikes by Public Employees?" *International Journal of Public Administration* 6, no. 2 (1984): 183–199.

Ross, John, and Jesse Burkhead. *Productivity in the Local Public Sector*. Lexington, Mass.: Lexington Books, 1974.

Rubin, Irene S. *Running in the Red*. Albany: State University of New York Press, 1982.

Smith, Russell L., and William Lyons. "The Impact of Fire Fighter Unionization on Wages and Working Hours in American Cities." *Public Administration Review* 40 (November/December 1980): 568–574.

Stanley, David T. *Managing Local Government under Union Pressure*. Washington, D.C.: Brookings Institution, 1972.

Stieber, Jack. *Public Employee Unionism*. Washington, D.C.: Brookings Institution, 1973.

Straussman, Jeffrey D., and Robert Rodgers. "Public Sector Unionism and Tax Burdens: Are They Related?" *Policy Studies Journal* 8 (Winter 1979): 438–448.

Tanimoto, Helene S. *Guide to Statutory Provisions in Public Sector Collective Bargaining Impasse Resolutions Procedures*. 3d issue. Manoa, Hawaii: Industrial Relations Center, 1981.

Tanimoto, Helene S., and Joyce M. Najita. *Guide to Statutory Provisions in Public Sector Collective Bargaining Strike Rights and Prohibitions*. Manoa, Hawaii: Industrial Relations Center, 1981.

Washnis, George J., ed. *Productivity Improvement Handbook for State and Local Government*. New York: Wiley, 1980.

Wellington, Harry, and Ralph D. Winter, Jr. *The Unions and the Cities*. Washington, D.C.: Brookings Institution, 1971.

Zagoria, Sam, ed. *Public Workers and Public Unions*. Englewood Cliffs, N.J.: Prentice-Hall, 1972.

CHAPTER 10

Ackoff, Russell L. "Management Misinformation Systems." *Management Science* 14 (December 1967): 147–156.

Allison, Graham T. *Essence of Decision: Explaining the Cuban Missile Crisis*. Boston: Little, Brown, 1971.

Argyris, Chris. "Some Limits of Rational Man Organization Theory." *Public Administration Review* 33 (May/June 1973): 253–267.

Arnold, David S., Christine S. Becker, and Elizabeth K. Kellar. *Effective Communication: Getting the Message Across*. Washington, D.C.: International City Management Association, 1983.

Beer, Stafford. *Decision and Control*. London: Wiley, 1966.

Behn, Robert D., and James W. Vaupel. *Quick Analysis for Busy Decision Makers*. New York: Basic Books, 1982.

Bozeman, Barry, and Stuart Bretschneider. "Public Management Information Systems: Theory and Prescription." *Public Administration Review* 46 (November 1986): 475–487.

Braybrooke, David, and Charles E. Lindblom. *A Strategy of Decision*. London: Collier-Macmillan, 1963.

Brewer, Garry D. *Politicians, Bureaucrats, and the Consultant*. New York: Basic Books, 1973.

Campbell, Donald. "Assessing Impact of Planned Change." *Evaluation and Program Planning* 2 (1972): 67–97.

Danziger, James N., Kenneth L. Kraemer, and William H. Dutton. *Computers and Politics*. New York: Columbia University Press, 1982.

Deutsch, Karl W. *The Nerves of Government*. New York: Free Press, 1963.

Etzioni, Amitai. "Mixed Scanning: A 'Third' Approach to Decision Making." *Public Administration Review* 27 (December 1967): 385–392.

Etzioni, Amitai, and Richard Remp. "Technological 'Shortcuts' to Social Change." *Science* 175 (January 7, 1972): 31–37.

Garson, G. David. "Microcomputer Applications in Public Administration." *Public Administration Review* 43 (September/October 1983): 453–458.

General Accounting Office. *Data Base Management Systems: Without Careful Planning There Can Be Problems*. Washington, D.C.: U.S. Government Printing Office, 1979.

Helmer, Olaf. *Social Technology*. New York: Basic Books, 1966.

Hitch, Charles J. *Decision-Making for Defense*. Berkeley: University of California Press, 1965.

King, John, and Kenneth Kraemer. *The Dynamics of Computing*. New York: Columbia University Press, 1985.

Landau, Martin. "Redundancy, Rationality, and the Problem of Duplication and Overlap." *Public Administration Review* 29 (July/August 1969): 346–358.

Lindblom, Charles. *The Intelligence of Democracy*. New York: Macmillan, 1965.

——. "The Science of Muddling Through." *Public Administration Review* 19 (Spring 1959): 79–88.

——. "Still Muddling, Not Yet Through." *Public Administration Review* 39 (November/December 1979): 517–526.

March, James C., and Johan P. Olsen. *Ambiguity and Choice in Organizations*. Bergen, Norway: Universitetsforlaget, 1976.

Meyer, Marshall W. "Automation and Bureaucratic Structure." *American Journal of Sociology* 74 (November 1968): 256–264.

Nelson, Richard. *The Moon and the Ghetto*. New York: W. W. Norton, 1977.

Pesso, Tana. "Local Welfare Offices: Managing the Intake Process." *Public Policy* 26 (Spring 1978): 305–330.

Quinn, Robert E. "The Impacts of a Computerized Information System on the Integration and Coordination of Human Services." *Public Administration Review* 36 (March/April 1976): 166–174.

Raiffa, Howard. *Decision Analysis: Introductory Lectures on Making Choices under Uncertainty*. Reading, Mass.: Addison-Wesley, 1968.

Redfield, Charles. *Communication in Management*. Chicago: University of Chicago Press, 1953.

Rivlin, Alice M. *Systematic Thinking for Social Action*. Washington, D.C.: Brookings Institution, 1971.

Rosenthal, Stephen R. *Managing Government Operations*. Glenview, Ill.: Scott, Foresman, 1982.

Schelling, Thomas A. *Micromotives and Macrobehavior*. New York: W. W. Norton, 1978.

Simon, Herbert. *Administrative Behavior*. 3d ed. New York: Free Press, 1976.

——. *The New Science of Management Decision*. Englewood Cliffs, N.J.: Prentice-Hall, 1960.

——. *The Sciences of the Artificial*. Cambridge, Mass.: MIT Press, 1969.

Steinbruner, John D. *The Cybernetic Theory of Decision*. Princeton, N.J.: Princeton University Press, 1974.

Stokey, Edith, and Richard Zeckhauser. *A Primer for Policy Analysis*. New York: W. W. Norton, 1978.

Straussman, Jeffrey D. *The Limits of Technocratic Politics*. New Brunswick, N.J.: Transaction Books, 1978.

Whisler, Thomas L. *The Impact of Computers on Organizations*. New York: Praeger, 1973.

Wildavsky, Aaron. *Speaking Truth to Power: The Art and Craft of Policy Analysis*. Boston: Little, Brown, 1979.

Wilensky, Harold L. *Organizational Intelligence: Knowledge and Policy in Government and Industry*. New York: Basic Books, 1967.

CHAPTER 11

Bardach, Eugene. *The Implementation Game: What Happens after a Bill Becomes a Law.* Cambridge, Mass.: MIT Press, 1977.

Bardach, Eugene, and Robert Kagan. *Going by the Book.* Philadelphia: Temple University Press, 1982.

Baum, Lawrence. "The Influence of Legislatures and Appellate Courts over the Policy Implementation Process." *Policy Studies Journal* 8, no. 4 (1980): 560–574.

Berman, Paul. "The Study of Macro- and Micro-Implementation." *Public Policy* 26 (Spring 1978): 157–184.

Cohen, David, and Eleanor Farrar. "Power to the Parents?—The Story of Educational Vouchers." *The Public Interest,* no. 48 (Summer 1977): 72–97.

Congressional Budget Office. *The Food Stamp Program: Income or Food Supplementation?* Washington: D.C.: U.S. Government Printing Office, 1977.

Derthick, Martha. *New Towns in-Town.* Washington, D.C.: Urban Institute, 1972.

Elmore, Richard. "Organizational Models of Social Program Implementation." *Public Policy* 26 (Spring 1978): 185–228.

Frieden, Bernard J., and Marshall Kaplan. *The Politics of Neglect: Urban Aid from Model Cities to Revenue Sharing.* Cambridge, Mass.: MIT Press, 1975.

Goggin, Malcolm L. *Policy Design and the Politics of Implementation: The Case of Child Care in the American States.* Knoxville: University of Tennessee Press, 1987.

Harbert, Anita S. *Federal Grants-in-Aid: Maximizing Benefits to the States.* New York: Praeger, 1976.

Hargrove, Erwin C. *The Missing Link.* Washington, D.C.: Urban Institute, 1975.

Ingram, Helen. "Policy Implementation through Bargaining: The Case of Federal Grants-in-Aid." *Public Policy* 25 (Fall 1977): 499–526.

Ingram, Helen, and Dean Mann, eds. *Why Policies Succeed or Fail.* Beverly Hills, Calif.: Sage Publications, 1980.

Kennedy, Robert F. *Thirteen Days: A Memoir of the Cuban Missile Crisis.* New York: W. W. Norton, 1971.

Kettl, Donald F. *Managing Community Development in the New Federalism.* New York: Praeger, 1980.

Levy, Frank S., Arnold J. Meltsner, and Aaron Wildavsky. *Urban Outcomes.* Berkeley: University of California Press. 1974.

Lipsky, Michael. *Street-Level Bureaucracy.* New York: Russell Sage Foundation, 1980.

Luft, Harold. "Benefit Cost Analysis and Public Policy Implementation." *Public Policy* 24 (Fall 1976): 437–462.

Majone, Giandomenico. "Choice among Policy Instruments for Pollution Control." *Policy Analysis* 2 (Fall 1976): 589–614.

Massey, Jane, and Jeffrey D. Straussman. "Another Look at the Mandate Issue: Are Conditions-of-Aid Really So Burdensome?" *Public Administration Review* 45 (March/April 1985): 292–300.

Mazmanian, Daniel A., and Paul A. Sabatier. *Implementation and Public Policy.* Glenview, Ill.: Scott, Foresman, 1983.

———, eds. *Effective Policy Implementation.* Lexington, Mass.: Heath, 1981.

Meltsner, Arnold. *The Politics of City Revenue*. Berkeley: University of California Press, 1971.

Moore, Mark. "Anatomy of the Heroin Problem: An Exercise in Program Definition." *Policy Analysis* 2 (Fall 1976): 639–662.

Murphy, Jerome. "Title I of ESEA." *Harvard Educational Review* 41 (February 1971): 35–63.

Nakamura, Robert T., and Frank Smallwood. *The Politics of Policy Implementation*. New York: St. Martin's Press, 1980.

Nelson, Richard, and Douglas Yates, eds. *Innovation and Implementation in Public Organizations*. Lexington, Mass.: Heath, 1978.

Peterson, Paul E., Barry G. Rabe, and Kenneth K. Wong. *When Federalism Works*. Washington, D.C.: Brookings Institution, 1986.

Pressman, Jeffrey, and Aaron Wildavsky. *Implementation*. 3d ed. Berkeley: University of California Press, 1983.

Radin, Beryl. *Implementation, Change, and the Federal Bureaucracy: School Segregation Policy in HEW, 1964–1968*. New York: Teachers College Press, 1977.

Rodgers, Harrell, and Charles Bullock. *Coercion to Compliance*. Lexington, Mass.: Heath, 1976.

Schultze, Charles. *The Public Use of Private Interest*. Washington, D.C.: Brookings Institution, 1976.

Thomas, Robert D. "Implementing Federal Programs at the Local Level." *Political Science Quarterly* 94 (Fall 1979): 419–435.

Thompson, Frank. "Bureaucratic Discretion and the National Health Service Corps." *Political Science Quarterly* 97 (Fall 1982): 427–445.

Thurow, Lester. "Government Expenditures: Cash or In-Kind Aid?" *Philosophy and Public Affairs* 5 (Summer 1976): 361–381.

Van Horn, Carl E. "Implementing CETA: The Federal Role." *Policy Analysis* 4 (Spring 1978): 159–183.

———. *Policy Implementation in the Federal System*. Lexington, Mass.: Lexington Books, 1979.

Van Meter, Donald S., and Carl E. Van Horn. "The Policy Implementation Process: A Conceptual Framework." *Administration & Society* 6 (February 1975): 445–485.

Weathley, Richard A. *Reforming Special Education: Policy Implementation from State Level to Street Level*. Cambridge, Mass.: MIT Press, 1979.

Williams, Walter. *Government by Agency*. New York: Academic Press, 1980.

Williams, Walter, and Richard Elmore, eds. *Social Program Implementation*. New York: Academic Press, 1976.

Wolf, Charles, Jr. "Policy Implementation through Bargaining: The Case of Federal Grants-in-Aid." *Public Policy* 25 (Fall 1977): 499–526.

Wright, Deil S. *Understanding Intergovernmental Relations*. 3d ed. Pacific Grove, Calif: Brooks/Cole, 1988.

CHAPTER 12

Barry, Donald D., and Howard R. Whitcomb. *The Legal Foundations of Public Administration*. St. Paul: West Publishing Co., 1981.

Bazelon, David. "The Impact of the Courts on Public Opinion." *Indiana Law Journal* 52 (Fall 1976): 101–110.

Berger, Raoul. *Government by Judiciary*. Cambridge, Mass.: Harvard University Press, 1977.

Chayes, Abram. "The Role of the Judge in Public Law Litigation." *Harvard Law Review* 89 (May 1976): 1281–1316.

Cooper, Phillip J. *Hard Judicial Choices*. New York: Oxford University Press, 1988.

———. *Public Law and Public Administration*. 2d ed. Englewood Cliffs, N.J.: Prentice-Hall, 1988.

Cramton, Roger C. "Judicial Law Making and Administration." *Public Administration Review* 36 (September/October 1976): 551–555.

David, Kenneth Culp. *Administrative Law Text*. 3d ed. St. Paul: West Publishing Co., 1978.

———. *Discretionary Justice: A Preliminary Inquiry*. Baton Rouge: Louisiana State University Press, 1969.

Dimock, Marshall E. *Law and Dynamic Administration*. New York: Praeger, 1980.

Diver, Colin S. "The Judge as Political Powerbroker: Superintending Structural Change in Public Institutions." *Virginia Law Review* 65 (1979): 43–106.

Gilmour, Robert S. "Agency Administration by Judiciary." *Southern Review of Public Administration* 6 (Spring 1982): 26–42.

———. "The Congressional Veto: Shifting the Balance of Administrative Control." *Journal of Policy Analysis and Management* 2 (1982): 13–25.

Glazer, Nathan. "Should Judges Administer Social Services?" *The Public Interest*, no. 50 (Winter 1978): 64–80.

———. "Toward an Imperial Judiciary?" *The Public Interest*, no. 41 (Fall 1975): 104–123.

Groszyk, Walter S., and Thomas J. Madden. "Managing without Immunity: The Challenge for State and Local Government Officials in the 1980's." *Public Administration Review* 41 (March/April 1981): 268–278.

Grumet, Barbara R. "Who Is 'Due' Process." *Public Administration Review* 42 (July/August 1982): 321–326.

Harriman, Linda, and Jeffrey D. Straussman. "Do Judges Determine Budget Decisions? Federal Court Decisions in Prison Reform and State Spending for Corrections." *Public Administration Review* 43 (July/August 1983): 343–351.

Harris, M. Kay, and Dudley P. Spiller. *After the Decision: Implementation of Judicial Decrees in Correctional Settings*. Washington, D.C.: U.S. Government Printing Office, 1977.

Horowitz, Donald L. *The Courts and Social Policy*. Washington, D.C.: Brookings Institution, 1977.

Johnson, Frank M. "The Constitution and the Federal District Judge." *Texas Law Review* 54 (June 1976): 903–916.

Katzmann, Robert A. *Regulatory Bureaucracy: The Federal Trade Commission and Antitrust Policy*. Cambridge, Mass.: MIT Press, 1980.

Kirp, David L. "School Desegregation and the Limits of Legalism." *The Public Interest*, no. 47 (Spring 1977): 101–128.

Kirp, David L., and Donald N. Jensen. "What Does Due-Process Do?" *The Public Interest*, no. 73 (Fall 1983): 75–90.

Lehne, Richard. *The Quest for Justice*. White Plains, N.Y.: Longman, 1978.

Marfin, Gary C., and Jerome J. Hanus. "Supreme Court Restraints on State and Local Officials." *National Civic Review* 70 (February 1981): 83–89.

Mashaw, Jerry L. *Bureaucratic Justice*. New Haven: Yale University Press, 1983.

Melnick, R. Shep. *Regulation and the Courts*. Washington, D.C.: Brookings Institution, 1983.

Neely, Richard. *How Courts Govern America*. New Haven: Yale University Press, 1981.

Ogul, Morris S. *Congress Oversees the Bureaucracy: Studies in Legislative Supervision*. Pittsburgh: University of Pittsburgh Press, 1976.

Rebell, Michael A., and Arthur R. Block. *Educational Policy Making and the Courts*. Chicago: University of Chicago Press, 1982.

Regulation Process and Politics. Washington, D.C.: Congressional Quarterly, 1982.

Rice, Mitchell F. "Municipal Services and the Judiciary: The Immunity Doctrine in the Service Delivery Process." *International Journal of Public Administration* 5 (1983): 89–118.

Schuck, Peter H. *Suing Government*. New Haven: Yale University Press, 1983.

Straussman, Jeffrey D. "Courts and Public Purse Strings: Have Portraits of Budgeting Missed Something?" *Public Administration Review* 46 (July/August 1986): 345–351.

Tribe, Laurence H. *American Constitutional Law:* Mineola, N.Y.: Foundation Press, 1978.

Wasby, Stephen L. "Arrogation of Power or Accountability: 'Judicial Imperialism' Revisited." *Judicature* 65 (October 1981): 208–219.

Weinberg, Lee S. "Askew v. American Waterway Operators, Inc.: The Emerging New Federalism." *Publius* 8 (Fall 1978): 37–53.

West, William F. "Institutionalizing Rationality in Regulatory Administration." *Public Administration Review* 43 (July/August 1983): 326–334.

———. "The Politics of Administrative Rulemaking." *Public Administration Review* 42 (September/October 1982): 420–426.

West, William F., and Joseph Cooper. "The Congressional Veto and Administrative Rulemaking." *Political Science Quarterly* 98 (Summer 1983): 285–304.

Yarbrough, Tinsley E. "The Judge as Manager: The Case of Judge Frank Johnson." *Journal of Policy Analysis and Management* 1 (Spring 1982): 386–400.

CHAPTER 13

Aaron, Henry J. *Why Is Welfare So Hard to Reform?* Washington, D.C.: Brookings Institution, 1973.

Ackoff, Russell L. *The Art of Problem Solving*. New York: Wiley, 1978.

Akland, Henry. "Are Randomized Experiments the Cadillacs of Design?" *Policy Analysis* 5 (Spring 1979): 223–242.

Albritton, Robert B. "Cost-Benefits of Measles Eradication: Effects of a Federal Intervention." *Policy Analysis* 4 (Winter 1978): 1–22.

Bingham, Richard D., and Claire L. Felbinger. *Evaluation in Practice*. White Plains, N.Y.: Longman, 1989.

Blalock, Herbert M., Jr. *Causal Inferences in Nonexperimental Research*. Chapel Hill: University of North Carolina Press, 1964.

Campbell, Donald T., and Julian C. Stanley. *Experimental and Quasi-Experimental Designs for Research*. Chicago: Rand McNally, 1963.

Cook, Philip J. "Reducing Injury and Death Rates in Robbery." *Policy Analysis* 6 (Winter 1980): 21–45.

Dunn, William N. *Public Policy Analysis*. Englewood Cliffs, N.J.: Prentice-Hall, 1981.

Epstein, Paul D. *Using Performance Measurement in Local Government*. New York: Van Nostrand Reinhold, 1984.

Goldenberg, Edie N. "The Three Faces of Evaluation." *Journal of Policy Analysis and Management* 2 (Summer 1983): 515–525.

Guess, George M., and Paul G. Farnham. *Cases in Public Policy Analysis*. White Plains, N.Y.: Longman, 1989.

Hargrove, Erwin C. "The Bureaucratic Politics of Evaluation: A Case Study of the Department of Labor." *Public Administration Review* 40 (March/April 1980): 150–159.

Hatry, Harry P., Richard E. Winnie, and Donald M. Fish. *Practical Program Evaluation for State and Local Governments*. 2d ed. Washington, D.C.: Urban Institute, 1981.

Haveman, Robert H., and Julius Margolis, eds. *Public Expenditure and Policy Analysis*. 3d ed. Boston: Houghton Mifflin, 1983.

Huff, Darrell. *How to Lie with Statistics*. Middlesex, Eng.: Penguin Books, 1973.

Kmenta, Jan. *Elements of Econometrics*. New York: Macmillan, 1971.

Langbein, Laura Irwin. *Discovering Whether Programs Work: A Guide to Statistical Methods for Program Evaluation*. Santa Monica, Calif.: Goodyear, 1980.

Lindblom, Charles E., and David K. Cohen. *Usable Knowledge: Social Science and Social Problem Solving*. New Haven: Yale University Press, 1979.

MacRae, Duncan, Jr., and James A. Wilde. *Policy Analysis for Public Decision*. Belmont, Calif.: Duxbury Press, 1979.

May, Peter J. "Hints for Crafting Alternative Policies." *Policy Analysis* 7 (Spring 1981): 227–244.

Meltsner, Arnold. *Policy Analysts in the Bureaucracy*. Berkeley: University of California Press, 1976.

Mishan, E. J. *Cost-Benefit Analysis: An Informal Introduction*. 3d ed. New York: Praeger, 1976.

Mosher, Frederick C. *The GAO: The Quest for Accountability in American Government*. Boulder, Col.: Westview Press, 1979.

Murphy, Jerome T. *Getting the Facts*. Santa Monica, Calif.: Goodyear, 1980.

Okun, Arthur M. *Equality and Efficiency: The Big Trade-Off*. Washington, D.C.: Brookings Institution, 1975.

Palumbo, Dennis J. *Statistics in Political and Behavioral Research*. New York: Columbia University Press, 1977.

Poister, Theodore H. *Performance Monitoring*. Lexington, Mass.: Lexington Books, 1983.

Posavac, Emil J., and Raymond G. Carey. *Program Evaluations: Methods and Case Studies*. Englewood Cliffs, N.J.: Prentice-Hall, 1980.

Quade, E. S. *Analysis for Public Decisions,* 3d ed. New York: North Holland, 1989.

Rivlin, Alice. *Systematic Thinking for Social Action*. Washington, D.C.: Brookings Institution, 1970.

Rossi, Peter H., Howard Freeman, and Sonia R. Wright. *Evaluation: A Systematic Approach*. Beverly Hills, Calif: Sage Publications, 1979.

Rossi, Peter H., and Katherine C. Lyall. *Reforming Public Welfare: A Critique of the Negative Income Tax Experiment*. New York: Russell Sage Foundation, 1976.

Siegal, Sidney. *Nonparametric Statistics for the Behavioral Sciences*. New York: McGraw-Hill, 1956.

Stokey, Edith, and Richard Zeckhauser. *A Primer for Policy Analysis*. New York: W. W. Norton, 1978.

Tufte, Edward R. *Data Analysis for Politics and Policy*. Englewood Cliffs, N.J.: Prentice-Hall, 1974.

Weiss, Carol. *Evaluation Research: Methods of Assessing Program Effectiveness*. Englewood Cliffs, N.J.: Prentice-Hall, 1972.

————, ed. *Using Social Research in Public Policy Making*. Lexington, Mass.: Heath, 1977.

Wholey, Joseph S. *Evaluation: Promise and Performance*. Washington, D.C.: Urban Institute, 1979.

Wildavsky, Aaron. "The Self-Evaluating Organization." *Public Administration Review* 32 (September/October 1972): 509–520.

————. *Speaking Truth to Power*. Boston: Little, Brown, 1979.

Williams, Walter. *Social Policy Research and Analysis*. New York: Elsevier, North-Holland, 1971.

CHAPTER 14

Appleby, Paul. *Morality and Administration in Democratic Government*. Baton Rouge: Louisiana State University Press, 1952.

Bailey, Stephen. "Ethics and the Public Service." *Public Administration Review* 23 (December 1964): 234–243.

Banfield, Edward C. "Corruption as a Feature of Governmental Organization." *Journal of Law and Economics* 18 (December 1975): 587–605.

Bok, Derek C. "Can Ethics Be Taught?" *Change* 8 (October 1976): 26–30.

Bowman, James S., ed. "Special Symposia Issue: Ethics in Government." *Public Personnel Management* 10, no. 1 (1981).

Broadnax, Walter D. "The Tuskegee Health Experiment: A Question of Bureaucratic Morality?" *The Bureaucrat* 4 (April 1975): 45–56.

Brown, Peter G. "Ethics and Public Policy: A Preliminary Agenda." *Policy Studies Journal* 7 (Autumn 1978): 132–137.

Burke, John P. *Bureaucratic Responsibility*. Baltimore: Johns Hopkins University Press, 1986.

Caiden, Gerald E. "Ethics in the Public Service." *Public Personnel Management* 10 (1981): 146–152.

Douglas, Paul H. *Ethics in Government*. Cambridge, Mass.: Harvard University Press, 1957.

Fleishman, Joel L., Lance Liebman, and Mark H. Moore, eds. *Public Duties: The Moral Obligations of Government Officials*. Cambridge, Mass.: Harvard University Press, 1981.

Gawthrop, Louis C. *Public Sector Management, Systems, and Ethics*. Bloomington: Indiana University Press, 1984.

Hampshire, Stuart, ed. "Public Policy and the Nature of Administrative Responsibility."
Public Policy 1 (1940): 3–24.

———. *Public and Private Morality*. Cambridge, Mass.: Cambridge University Press,
1978.

Held, Virginia. *The Public Interest and Individual Interests*. New York: Basic Books,
1970.

Hirschman, Albert. *Exit, Voice and Loyalty*. Cambridge, Mass.: Harvard University Press,
1970.

Horwitz, Robert H., ed. *The Moral Foundations of American Democracy*. Charlottesville:
University of Virginia Press, 1977.

Kaplan, Abraham. *American Ethics and Public Policy*. New York: Oxford University
Press, 1963.

Martin, Roscoe C., ed. *Public Administration and Democracy*. Syracuse, N.Y.: Syracuse
University Press, 1965.

Marx, Fritz Morstein. "Administrative Ethics and the Rule of Law." *American Political
Science Review* 43 (December 1949): 1119–1144.

Moore, Mark H. "Anatomy of the Heroin Problem: An Exercise in Problem Definition."
Policy Analysis 2 (Fall 1976): 639–662.

Rae, Douglas, et al. *Equalities*. Cambridge, Mass.: Harvard University Press. 1981.

Rawls, John A. *A Theory of Justice*. Cambridge, Mass.: Harvard University Press. 1971.

Redford, Emmette S. *Democracy in the Administrative State*. New York: Oxford University Press, 1969.

Rescher, Nicholas. *Distributive Justice*. New York: Bobbs-Merrill, 1966.

Riordon, William. *Plunkitt of Tammany Hall*. New York: E. P. Dutton, 1963.

Rivlin. Alice M., and Michael P. Timpane, eds. *Ethical and Legal Issues of Social Experimentation*. Washington, D.C.: Brookings Institution, 1975.

Rohr, John. *Ethics for Bureaucrats*. New York: Marcel Dekker, 1978.

Rose-Ackerman, Susan. *Corruption: A Study in Political Economy*. New York: Academic
Press, 1978.

Schelling, Thomas C. "Economic Reasoning and the Ethics of Policy." *The Public Interest,* no. 63 (Spring 1981): 37–61.

Sundquist, James L. "The Crisis of Competence in Our National Government." *Political
Science Quarterly* 95 (Summer 1980): 193–208.

———. "Reflections on Watergate: Lessons for Public Administration." *Public Administration Review* 34 (September/October 1974): 453–461.

Szasz, Thomas. *Ceremonial Chemistry*. Garden City, N.Y.: Anchor Press, 1974.

Thompson, Dennis F. *Political Ethics and Public Office*. Cambridge, Mass.: Harvard University Press, 1987.

Vickers, Sir Geoffrey. *Value Systems and Social Process*. New York: Basic Books, 1968.

Wakefield, Susan. "Ethics and the Public Service: A Case for Individual Responsibility."
Public Administration Review 36 (November/December 1976): 661–666.

CHAPTER 15

Aldrich, Howard. *Organization and Environments*. Englewood Cliffs, N.J.: Prentice-Hall,
1979.

Arrow, Kenneth J. *The Limits of Organization.* New York: W. W. Norton, 1974.

Bozeman, Barry. *All Organizations Are Public.* San Francisco: Jossey-Bass, 1987.

Bozeman, Barry, and Jeffrey D. Straussman, eds. *New Directions in Public Administration.* Monterey, Calif.: Brooks/Cole, 1984.

Chubb, John, and Paul E. Peterson, eds. *The New Direction in American Politics.* Washington, D.C.: Brookings Institution, 1985.

Cleveland, Harlan. "The Future of Public Administration." *The Bureaucrat* 11 (Fall 1982): 3–8.

Dahl, Robert A. *Dilemmas of Pluralist Democracy: Autonomy vs. Control.* New Haven: Yale University Press, 1982.

Drucker, Peter F. "The Deadly Sins in Public Administration." *Public Administration Review* 40 (March/April 1980): 103–106.

Fitzgerald, Randall. *When Government Goes Private.* New York: Universe Books, 1988.

Fosler, R. Scott, and Renee A. Berger, eds. *Public-Private Partnership in American Cities: Seven Case Studies.* Lexington, Mass.: Heath, 1982.

Goodsell, Charles T. *The Case for Bureaucracy.* 2d ed. Chatham, N.J.: Chatham House Publishers, 1985.

———, ed. *The Public Encounter: Where State and Citizen Meet.* Bloomington: Indiana University Press, 1981.

Hall, Richard H., and Robert E. Quinn, eds. *Organizational Theory and Public Policy.* Beverly Hills, Calif.: Sage Publications, 1983.

Hayek, Frederick. *The Road to Serfdom.* Chicago: University of Chicago Press, 1944.

Hillman, Jordan Jay. *The Export-Import Bank at Work.* Westport, Conn.: Quorum Books, 1982.

Hood, Christopher C. *The Limits of Administration.* London: Wiley, 1976.

Katz, Fred E. "Implementation of the Holocaust: The Behavior of Nazi Officials." *Comparative Studies of Society and History* 24 (July 1982): 510–529.

Kaufman, Herbert. "Fear of Bureaucracy: A Raging Pandemic." *Public Administration Review* 41 (January/February 1981): 1–9.

Kettl, Donald F. *Government by Proxy.* Washington, D.C.: Congressional Quarterly Press, 1988.

LaPorte, Todd, ed. *Organized Social Complexity.* Princeton, N.J.: Princeton University Press, 1975.

Lewis, Eugene. *Public Entrepreneurship: Toward a Theory of Bureaucratic Political Power.* Bloomington: Indiana University Press, 1980.

Lindberg, Leon N., ed. *Politics and the Future of Industrial Society.* New York: David McKay, 1976.

Lindblom, Charles E. *Politics and Markets.* New York: Basic Books, 1977.

Lowi, Theodore. *The End of Liberalism.* 2d ed. New York: W. W. Norton, 1979.

Mead, Laurence. *Beyond Entitlement.* New York: Basic Books, 1986.

Mosher, Frederick C. "The Changing Responsibilities and Tactics of the Federal Government." *Public Administration Review* 40 (November/December 1980): 541–548.

———, ed. *American Public Administration: Past, Present, Future.* University: University of Alabama Press, 1975.

Musolf, Lloyd. *Uncle Sam's Private, Profitseeking Corporations.* Lexington, Mass.: Lexington Books, 1983.

Olson, Mancur. *The Rise and Decline of Nations*. New Haven: Yale University Press, 1982.

Ostrom, Vincent. *The Intellectual Crisis in American Public Administration*. Rev. ed. University of Alabama Press, 1974.

Peters, B. Guy. "The Problem of Bureaucratic Government." *Journal of Politics* 43 (February 1981): 56–82.

Riker, William H. *Liberalism against Populism: A Confrontation between the Theory of Democracy and the Theory of Social Choice*. San Francisco: W. H. Freeman, 1982.

Rose, Richard, and Guy Peters. *Can Government Go Bankrupt?* New York: Basic Books, 1979.

Rose-Ackerman, Susan. "Reforming Public Bureaucracy through Economic Incentives?" *Journal of Law, Economics, and Organization* 2 (Spring 1986): 131–161.

Rourke, Francis E. *Bureaucracy, Politics, and Public Policy*. 2d ed. Boston: Little, Brown, 1976.

Salamon, Lester M. "Rethinking Public Management: Third Party Government and the Changing Forms of Government Action." *Public Policy* 20 (Summer 1980): 255–275.

Savas, E. S. *Privatizing the Public Sector*. Chatham, N.J.: Chatham House Publishers, 1982.

Sharkansky, Ira. *Wither the State?* Chatham, N.J.: Chatham House Publishers, 1979.

Smith, Bruce L. R., and James D. Carroll, eds. *Improving the Accountability and Performance of Government*. Washington, D.C.: Brookings Institution, 1982.

Straussman, Jeffrey D. *The Limits of Technocratic Politics*. New Brunswick, N.J.: Transaction Books, 1978.

———. "More Bank for Fewer Bucks? Or How Local Government Can Rediscover the Potentials (and Pitfalls) of the Market." *Public Administration Review* 41 (January 1981): 150–158.

Tucker, Robert C. *Politics and Leadership*. Columbia: University of Missouri Press, 1981.

Waldo, Dwight. *The Enterprise of Public Administration*. Novato, Calif.: Chandler & Sharp, 1980.

Walsh, Annmarie. *The Public's Business*. Cambridge, Mass.: MIT Press, 1978.

Wilson, Woodrow. "The Study of Administration." *Political Science Quarterly* 2 (June 1887): 197–222.

Wriston, Michael J. "In Defense of Bureaucracy." *Public Administration Review* 40 (March/April 1980): 197–283.

Index

Wilson, Woodrow, 8–9, 15, 68, 171, 173, 185, 279
Windmills, 368
Wisconsin, 212
Wiseman, Jack, 10–11
Wolf, Charles, 257
Women. *See* Affirmative action; Gender
Wong, Kenneth, 260–261
Wood v. Strickland (1975), 296
Word processing, 230–231

Works Projects Administration (WPA), 24–25
Work stoppages, 210. *See also* Strikes
Wyatt v. Stickney, 299–300
Wygant v. Jackson Board of Education (1986), 192–193

Yale University, 90
Young, Coleman, 220